THE SEIDENFELD EDITION

Gems from the ספר נתיבות שלום
NESIVOS SHOLOM

פרקי אבות

The classic teachings of the late
Slonimer Rebbe, Reb Sholom Noach Berezovsky ztz"l,
expounded by a talmid

RABBI S. BINYOMIN GINSBERG

Copyright © 2015 by Rabbi S. Binyomin Ginsberg

ISBN 978-1-60091-368-6

All Rights Reserved

No part of this book may be reproduced in any form
without written permission from the copyright holder.
The Rights of the Copyright Holder Will Be Strictly Enforced

Book & cover design by:

SRULY PERL • 845.694.7186
mechelp@gmail.com

Proofreading by E.M. Sonenblick
esonenblick@gmail.com

Distributed by:

 **Israel Bookshop Publications**
501 Prospect Street
Lakewood, NJ 08701
Tel: (732) 901-3009
Fax: (732) 901-4012
www.israelbookshoppublications.com
info@israelbookshoppublications.com

Printed in the USA

Distributed in Israel by:
Shanky's
Petach Tikva 16
Jerusalem
972-2-538-6936

Distributed in Europe by:
Lehmanns
Unit E Viking Industrial Park
Rolling Mill Road,
Jarrow, Tyne & Wear NE32 3DP
44-191-406-0842

Distributed in Australia by:
Gold's Book and Gift Company
3-13 William Street
Balaclava 3183
613-9527-8775

Distributed in South Africa by:
Kollel Bookshop
Ivy Common
107 William Road, Norwood
Johannesburg 2192
27-11-728-1822

YESHIVAT BETH ABRAHAM SLONIM JERUSALEM

I am honored to present our dear, esteemed friend and *talmid*, Rav Sholom Binyomin Ginsberg *shlita* with a letter of approbation. This is a man who has successfully undertaken tremendous endeavors; a person of sufficient stature to stand before great scholars. He is an expert in the field of *chinuch* and has a special flair for touching the hearts of his audience. Having already published valuable works and contributed greatly to the Torah world, he will soon be releasing another written work comprising a new collection of his renowned essays – this time based on the Slonimer Rebbe's *Nesivos Sholom* on *Pirkei Avos*. *Chazal* say, "One who wants to become a chassid should fulfill the teachings of *Avos*"; as is explained in the *sefer*, "*Middos* are the *Avos* to the entire Torah, as is written, 'And you shall do what is upright and good in Hashem's eyes.'" This is the exclusive straightforward path that man should select; it is "a credit to himself and earns him the esteem of fellow men," and is the true success in life. Rav Sholom Binyomin Ginsberg has completed this *sefer* with much Heavenly assistance; may he merit to complete many more works. Hashem has already granted him the *zechus* to teach and contribute, and may he merit to continue and disseminate his wonderful material, as his *zikui harabim* is tremendous.

I write this letter on behalf of the Admor *shlita* whose *brachah* to him is that Hashem be with him in whatever he does.

His close friend who holds him in the highest esteem,

Shlomo Weinberg

Menahel ruchani of the Yeshivah

ישיבת בית אברהם סלונים ירושלים (ע"ר)
YESHIVAT BETH ABRAHAM SLONIM JERUSALEM
מיסודו של כ"ק אדמו"ר בעל "נתיבות שלום" זי"ע

בס"ד, לס' ועשית הישר והטוב בעיני ה' אלקיך, תשע"ג

ראיתי איש חזית מהיר במלאכתו, חכמה שהיא מלאכה, לפני מלכים יתייצב, מאן מלכי רבנן, ידידינו ותלמידינו הדגול הרה"ג רבי שלום בנימין גינסבערג שליט"א, ידיו רב לו בחינוך ומסילות ללב שומע, ההולך מחיל אל חיל, ועומד להוציא כעת יצירה נוספת משיעוריו המפורסמים לתהלה, והם משיעוריו בפרקי אבות המבוססים על הספה"ק "נתיבות שלום" ממו"ח אדמו"ר מסלונים זצוק"ל. וכבר אמרו חז"ל האי מאן דבעי למיהוי חסידא לקיים מילי דאבות, וכמבואר בספר שהמידות המה האבות לכל התורה ועשית הישר והטוב בעיני ה', והם הם הדרך הישרה שיבור לו האדם כל שהיא תפארת לעושיה ותפארת לו מן האדם, והמה אושר החיים האמיתי. וכשם שסיימתם ברוב סייעתא דשמיא ספר זה כן תזכו להתחיל ולסיים עוד ועוד, כאשר חנן אתכם ה', ללמד להועיל. וזכות הרבים תלויה בו.

והנני שלוחא דמרן כ"ק אדמו"ר שליט"א, המברככם כי יהי ה' עמך בכל אשר לך.

מוקירו מאד וידידו עוז

שלמה וינברג

מנהל רוחני דישיבתנו הק'

נוסדה בברנוביץ - פולין
בשנת תרע"ח
ונוסדה מחדש בא"י
בשנת תש"ב

Founded at
Baranowice Poland
In 1918
Founded in Israel 1942

נשיא וראשי המוסדות
כ"ק אדמו"ר מסלונים שליט"א
ראש הישיבה:
הג"ר משה ברזובסקי שליט"א
מנהל החשיבה
הרב שלמה וינברג שליט"א

ישיבה גדולה
ישיבה לצעירים
בית מדרש גבוה
לאברכים "צמח דוד"
מרכז תורני "יד ואהל"
תלמודי תורה
"ברכת אברהם"
סלונים
בתי מדרש
וכוללי אברכים
ברחבי הארץ

Salant St.
Cor. Rabbi Abraham
of Slonim St.
P.O.Box 5020 Jerusalem 91050
Tel. 972-2-6287756
Fax. 972-2-6288682
info@slonim.org.il

Address in USA:
Yeshiva Beth Abraham
of Jerusalem Inc.
73W. 47th St. NYC 10036

לתרומות בכרטיס
אשראי 24 שעות
1-800-50-20-50

Table of Contents

Introduction 13
Acknowledgments 21

הקדמה

הקדמה 27

הקדמת כל ישראל יש להם חלק לעולם הבא
Introductory Passage: All Yisroel Has a Portion in the World to Come 43

כל ישראל יש להם חלק לעולם הבא
All Yisroel Has a Portion in the World to Come 59

פרק א'

משה קבל תורה מסיני
Moshe Received the Torah from Sinai 71

על שלשה דברים העולם עומד
The World Stands on Three Things 83

הוו כעבדים המשמשין שלא על מנת לקבל פרס
Be Like Servants Who Serve Not for the Sake of Receiving a Reward 93

ג' המימרות דהלל
Hillel's Three Statements 103

הוי מתלמידיו של אהרן
Be of the Disciples of Aharon 113

אם אין אני לי מי לי
If I Am Not for Me – Who Is for Me? 123

על שלשה דברים העולם קיים
The World Endures on Three Things 135

פרק ב'

איזוהי דרך ישרה שיבור לו האדם
What Is the Upright Path That a Man Should Choose for Himself 147

שהיא תפארת לעושיה ותפארת לו מן האדם
(One) That Is Honorable to the One Who Does It, and Accords Him Honor from Man 167

הסתכל בג' דברים ואין אתה בא לידי עבירה
Look at Three Things and You Will Not Come to the Hands of Sin 179

עשה רצונו כרצונך
Make His Will as Your Will 189

אין בור ירא חטא ולא עם הארץ חסיד
A Boor Cannot Be Sin-Fearing, an Ignoramus Cannot Be Pious 205

איזוהי דרך טובה שידבק בה האדם
What Is the Good Path to Which a Person Should Attach Himself 225

יהי כבוד חברך חביב עליך כשלך
The Honor of Your Fellow Should Be as Precious to You as Your Own 235

עין הרע ויצר הרע ושנאת הבריות
The Evil Eye, Evil Inclination, and Hatred of People 251

הוי זהיר בקריאת שמע ובתפלה
Be Meticulous with the Reading of Shema and Prayer 265

פרק ג'

דע מאין באת וכו'
Know from Where You Came, etc. 279

שנים שיושבין ויש ביניהם דברי תורה
Two Who Sit Together and There Are Words of Torah Between Them 289

כל המקבל עליו עול תורה
Whoever Accepts the Yoke of Torah upon Himself 303

תן לו משלו שאתה ושלך שלו
Give Him What Is His, for You, and What Is Yours, Are His 319

השוכח דבר אחד ממשנתו
One Who Forgets a Single Item from His Studies 329

כל שיראת חטאו קודמת לחכמתו
Anyone Whose Fear of Sin Precedes His Wisdom 339

כל שמעשיו מרובין מחכמתו
Anyone Whose Deeds Exceed His Wisdom 347

כל שרוח הבריות נוחה הימנו
Anyone with Whom People Are Pleased 363

הוי קל לראש ונוח לתשחורת
Be Light in the Beginning and Easy in Old Age 375

חביבין ישראל
Beloved Are Yisroel 385

הכל צפוי והרשות נתונה
All Is Foreseen, yet Freedom of Choice Is Granted 403

פרק ד'

בן זומא אומר איזהו וכו'
Ben Zoma Says: Who Is… 413

איזהו גבור הכובש את יצרו
Who Is Mighty? One Who Conquers His Inclination 425

איזהו עשיר השמח בחלקו
Who Is Rich? One Who Is Happy with His Portion 437

ששכר מצוה מצוה
For the Reward of a Mitzvah Is a Mitzvah 451

מאד מאד הוי שפל רוח
Be Very, Very Humble of Spirit 465

ודאשתמש בתגא חלף
He Who Exploits the Crown Shall Perish 479

התקן עצמך בפרוזדור כדי שתכנס לטרקלין
Prepare Yourself in the Hallway so That You Enter the Banquet Hall 495

הקנאה התאוה והכבוד
Jealousy, Desire, and Honor 505

עד שבא אברהם אבינו וקבל שכר כולם
Until Our Forefather Avraham Arrived, and Received the Reward Due Them All 523

עשרה נסיונות נתנסה אברהם אבינו
With Ten Tests Was Our Forefather Avraham Tested 535

עשרה נסים נעשו לאבותינו בבית המקדש
Ten Miracles Were Performed for Our Forefathers in the Holy Temple 553

גלות באה לעולם וכו'
Exile Comes to the World... 563

ארבע מדות באדם
There Are Four Traits in a Person 575

כל אהבה שהיא תלויה בדבר
Any Love Which Is Conditional on Something 587

כל מחלוקת שהיא לשם שמים
Any Dispute Which Is for the Sake of Heaven 599

תלמידיו של אברהם אבינו
Disciples of our Forefather Avraham 613

הוי עז כנמר וכו'
Be as Bold as a Leopard... 635

עז פנים לגיהנום ובושת פנים לגן עדן
The Brazen-Faced to Gehinnom, and the Shamefaced to Gan Eden 649

הפך בה והפך בה דכלא בה
Delve into It Again and Again, for All Is in It 659

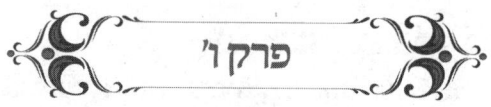
פרק ו׳

העוסק בתורה לשמה זוכה לדברים הרבה
One Who Engages in Torah Study for Its Own Sake Merits Many Things 673

זוכה לדברים הרבה
He Merits Many Things 699

ענין העוסק בתורה לשמה
(Discourse on) the Topic of Engaging in Torah Study for Its Own Sake 713

אוי להם לבריות מעלבונה של תורה
Woe Is to People for Their Insult to Torah 735

התורה נקנית בארבעים ושמונה דברים
The Torah Is Acquired Through Forty-Eight Items 751

גדולה תורה שהיא נותנת חיים לעושיה
Great Is Torah for It Grants Life to Those Who Adhere to It 771

Introduction

The *Sefarim Nesivos Sholom*

With a heart full of praise and thanks to the *Ribono Shel Olam* (Master of the Universe) for the success of the first volume of *Gems from the Nesivos Sholom*, we now present the second volume in what we hope will continue to be a source of inspiration to the English-speaking community.

While to the Slonimer Chassidim, Reb Sholom Noach was their Rebbe in every sense of the word, to the world at large he was known as the Nesivos Sholom, the title of the many *sefarim* (holy books) he authored. Few *chassidishe sefarim* (chassidic holy books) published in the latter half of the twentieth century have had the effect on Klal Yisroel that the *Nesivos Sholom* had, and has, on those who learn it. Its impact is felt far beyond the tight-knit chassidic enclave of the Slonimer *chassidus*; the *Nesivos Sholom* has become a standard text in *batei medrash* (study halls) and homes of Jews from one end of the spectrum to the other.

Many have referred to the *Nesivos Sholom* as "the *Mesillas Yesharim* (*Path of the Just*) of our generation" and many contemporary chassidic Rebbes suggest the *sefarim* to those wishing to taste *chassidus* for the first time. But even as the *sefarim* appear simple, profound thinkers and accomplished scholars of *chassidus* also find within its pages layers of depth.

While the Nesivos Sholom influenced many *talmidim* (disciples) and chassidim during his lifetime, his teachings and *sefarim* have had a very far-reaching influence. The connections he developed during his lifetime continued with growing momentum even after his death.

13

The Birth and Lineage of Slonim

The Slonim dynasty was founded by Reb Avraham Weinberg of Slonim *ztz"l* (1804-1883). Upon Reb Avraham's *petirah* (passing) in 1883, his grandson Reb Shmuel *ztz"l* (1850-1916) was designated the second Slonimer Rebbe.

After Reb Shmuel's *petirah* in 1916, his younger son, Reb Avraham Weinberg *ztz"l* (1884-1 Iyar 1933), was appointed as the Slonimer Rebbe in Baranovich. He is also known as the author of *Beis Avraham*.

After Reb Avraham's *petirah*, twenty-year-old Shlomo Dovid Yehoshua *Hy"d* was officially named the Slonimer Rebbe in 1935. He served as Rebbe during the German occupation, leading the *chassidus* as a model of *emunah peshutah* (unquestioning belief) in the midst of the Nazi onslaught, until he was murdered in 1944 in a labor camp just outside of Baranovich.

After his *petirah*, Reb Avraham Weinberg *ztz"l* of Teveriah and Yerushalayim (Rosh Chodesh Tammuz 1889-12 Sivan 1981) was chosen as the new Rebbe. He was also known by the name of one of his *sefarim*, the *Birkas Avraham*.

Reb Sholom Noach Berezovsky *ztz"l*, author of *Nesivos Sholom* and son-in-law of the Birkas Avraham, was appointed as his father-in-law's successor.

Reb Sholom Noach Berezovsky

Reb Sholom Noach was born on 24 Av 5671 (August 18, 1911) in Baranovich to Reb Moshe Avraham, a leader of the community, and Rebbetzin Tzivia (Weinstock), a granddaughter of Reb Hillel, a brother of the first Slonimer Rebbe.

In 1933 Reb Sholom Noach married Rebbetzin Chava Miriam, daughter of Rabbi Avraham Weinberg of Teveriah, the Birkas Avraham.

Reb Sholom Noach was a *talmid* in the Slonimer yeshivah, Toras Chessed in Baranovich. The *rosh yeshivah*, Rabbi Avraham Shmuel Hirshovich, was a grandson of Rabbi Eliezer Gordon of Telshe. The

INTRODUCTION

mashgiach (spiritual advisor), Rabbi Moshe Midner, was a grandson of the Yesod Ha'avodah and a student of Rabbi Chaim Soloveitchik.

One of the differences between Toras Chessed and other *chassidishe yeshivos* in other cities was that the Slonimer yeshivah combined the Lithuanian style of learning with the *chassidishe* approach. Reb Sholom Noach considered the *mashgiach*, Rav Moshe, as the *rebbi* who showed him the combination of unadulterated, joyful *chassidus* mixed with incisive and penetrating *lomdus* (academic depth).

In 1930, the Beis Avraham asked Reb Sholom Noach to listen carefully to every word of Torah shared during Shabbos and to transcribe the *ma'amarim* (discourses) he delivered every Shabbos. These *ma'amarim* were later published under the name *Beis Avraham*.

Reb Sholom Noach arrived in Eretz Yisroel in 1935, and was appointed *rosh yeshivah* of Achei Temimim, the Lubavitcher yeshivah in Tel Aviv. In 1941, he opened the Slonimer yeshivah in Yerushalayim with just five students. On Friday nights, Reb Sholom Noach would sit with the students for hours, teaching them the traditional Slonimer melodies and regaling them with the Torah he absorbed from his saintly *rabbeim*. In addition to his duties as teacher, he also recaptured the atmosphere of Slonim that had gone up in the black flames of the Holocaust. He collected those *divrei Torah* (Torah thoughts) that had been passed down through the generations and committed them to writing. He would sit with the *bachurim* (young students) and teach them forgotten *niggunim* (melodies), rebuilding the *chassidus* with his warmth and wisdom.

The Slonimer dynasty was virtually wiped out during the Holocaust; the yeshivah in Yerushalayim served as the focus for its revival. As part of his effort to rejuvenate the Slonimer *chassidus*, Reb Sholom Noach was responsible for collecting the oral traditions ascribed to previous Slonimer Rebbes (who did not commit their teachings to writing) in works such as *Divrei Shmuel* and *Toras Avos*.

Reb Sholom Noach also authored many volumes of his own teachings. These include his *magnum opus*, the seven-volume *Nesivos Sholom*, as well as numerous smaller works on education, marital harmony, and other prevalent community issues.

He led the *chassidus* until his *petirah* on 7 Av 5760 (August 8, 2000). He was succeeded by his son, Reb Shmuel *shlita*, who serves as the current Slonimer Rebbe.

Before You Begin

Before delving into the study of this *sefer*, there are several important points of clarification with which the reader should become acquainted.

- This volume on *Pirkei Avos* is the second in the *Gems of the Nesivos Sholom* series. The first volume, discussing the period from Rosh Hashanah to Yom Kippur, also included a somewhat detailed introduction about the birth of chassidism and the Slonim dynasty. In the listing of the different Rebbes of Slonim in the first volume, I inadvertently omitted one of the Rebbes, Reb Shlomo Dovid Yehoshua *Hy"d*. I have included him here in the lineage outlined above.

- **To reap maximum benefit from this volume, it is crucial** that the reader obtain as clear a picture as possible of its nature and purpose. Each *ma'amar* in this work is based on the original text of the corresponding *ma'amar* in the Hebrew-language *sefer*. **Nonetheless, as with the first volume, it is not intended to serve as a direct translation** of the *Nesivos Sholom*. In the planning stages of this series, the pros and cons of this genre were considered and weighed. While direct translations certainly have their place in Torah dissemination, the determination was made that, in this case, the readership would be better served by a different format.

- The primary goal of these volumes is to convey the content-rich and uplifting teachings of the Nesivos Sholom to the greater English-speaking public. It was strongly felt that the teachings would be much better absorbed and appreciated when conveyed in a way to which this audience could best relate. Merely converting the text verbatim into English may have removed a language barrier, but the product would have been far from a simple read.

INTRODUCTION

- And so, the decision was made to convey the elevated thoughts and profound ideas of the *Nesivos Sholom* in adaptation form; that is, to present each *ma'amar* in a manner most palatable to those for whom the English language is their "comfort zone." To be sure, this is no simple undertaking. It entails a delicate balance, one that may even appear paradoxical on the surface. On the one hand, this work aims to provide an accurate representation of the teachings of the original *Nesivos Sholom*. Yet, speaking at a *tisch* to his circle of chassidim and *talmidim*, the Nesivos Sholom would have refrained from employing a parable that draws on a cell-phone battery, for example; he may have felt it inappropriate for that particular audience, time, and setting. The current volume, however, *is a completely different forum*. Such an illustration may provide just the right flavor to bring out the point for the intended readership.

- In conveying the important teachings of the *Nesivos Sholom* in this volume, **the author has gone to great lengths** to provide an accurate representation of the profound thoughts and concepts in the "language" of the audience. I hope and pray that I have realized this desired goal.

- This *sefer* contains fifty-five *ma'amarim*, corresponding to the fifty-five *ma'amarim* of the *Nesivos Sholom* that discuss various mishnayos of *Pirkei Avos* (Ethics of the Fathers).

- To make it easier for the reader, each *ma'amar* is introduced with the complete mishnah on which the *ma'amar* is based, followed by a summary of the key *pesukim* (verses) and *ma'amarei Chazal* (statements of the Talmudic Sages) that are the focus of that individual *ma'amar*. This way, when the *passuk* (verse) or *ma'amar Chazal* is referred to in the *ma'amar*, the reader will be familiar with that source.

- In the study of *Pirkei Avos* there are various versions of where each mishnah begins and ends. For example, one version may have one mishnah broken up into three separate mishnayos and the second version may have all in one long mishnah. There is no special reason to choose one version over the other. As you

17

may want to reference a *ma'amar* with the actual mishnah in a Mishnayos or siddur, you may find that the numbering won't be the same as we have them numbered. Just look ahead or behind one or two mishnayos and you should find it.

- This *sefer* has several references to different teachings of Kabbalah. To really explain those concepts in detail and to make them totally understandable for someone without previous knowledge, I would need several volumes as a preface. An effort was made to write brief introductions and explanations of some concepts of Kabbalah when it would be helpful for understanding a *ma'amar*. These brief explanations cannot be considered a true lesson in kabbalistic teachings.

- Several themes and ideas flow through the *sefer*, some of which are repeated several times. The reason for this repetition is to reinforce these ideas, but each time with a different emphasis of the same idea, often based on a different source for that idea.

- There are seven main volumes of the *Nesivos Sholom*. The material on which this *sefer* is based is just one section of the third volume of the *Chamishah Chumshei Torah* (Five Books of the Torah).

- Throughout the process of writing, editing, and proofing, there were many questions as to which exact words to use in the *sefer*. For example, when referring to Hashem, should we use the word Hashem, God, G-d, the Almighty, *Hakadosh Baruch Hu*, or something else? The question always boiled down to a more general question: Who is the intended audience of this *sefer*? As we presume that the audience is broad, we used the terms we felt would be best for a broad audience of readers. While a specific word may not be what you use in your language, we hope that you will nevertheless understand the meaning of those words.

- To further facilitate a smoother read, we decided at times to transliterate the Hebrew when quoting from *pesukim* and the like and at times to keep the Hebrew in its original form. While obviously no substitute for its pristine, original form,

we felt that this method would be the most practicable for the reader. Given the English-language format, the need to revert too frequently between English and Hebrew characters could present somewhat of a challenge for the eyes.

- While the summary at the conclusion of each *ma'amar* is an excellent review of the *ma'amar*, it is just that — a summary. We strongly encourage you not to read the summary before first reading the entire *ma'amar*, as you will miss out on its main message.

Acknowledgments

First and foremost, I must express my humble appreciation to the *Ribono Shel Olam* for all the gifts and successes He has given me, among them to make some sort of contribution to the lives of others. In reality, if all the heavens were parchment, if all the trees of the forest were pens, if all the waters of the sea were ink, they would not suffice for me to describe my feelings of gratitude to my Master for all that I have. Any success I, *baruch Hashem*, have enjoyed is only because of Hashem's greatness. While I can't fully express all that Hashem has done for me, Hashem, the reader of all minds, knows how much gratitude I have for His countless gifts.

"Wow, who wrote these *ma'amarim*?" "The person who wrote these must have heard these *shmuessen* (discourses) directly from the Rebbe!" "The writer is a prolific writer in every sense of the word." These were some of the comments from the editors and proofreaders after reading the manuscript. However, this work is not the result of any individual's effort; rather, the skills and talents of many individuals went into what resulted in a masterful piece.

There is one individual to whom I would like to express my deep *hakaras hatov* (gratitude) for his contribution. Actually, contribution is the wrong word. He more than contributed to the *sefer*; he made it happen. His work with this *sefer* was just better than superb.

Rabbi Tzvi Hebel is the combination of a great *talmid chacham* (Torah scholar), a brilliant worldly scholar, a prolific writer, and a modest person full of *middos tovos* (positive character traits). In this *sefer*, he tried to convey the essence of the Nesivos Sholom's brilliance with clarity. I knew that I could always rely on him for a job well done. May Hashem grant him, together with his wife, continued *nachas* (gratification) from their children with *gezunt* (health), *simchah* (joy), and *arichus yamim* (many long years)!

GEMS FROM THE *SEFER NESIVOS SHOLOM*

Anyone who was ever involved with the publication of a book knows that it takes major assistance from others. The author and writers simply can't get it done alone. A *sefer* of this magnitude needed much more than one or two editors. If I were to write what each person contributed to the quality of this book, I would need a book in itself.

Special thanks are in order to Rabbi Yosef Chaim Danziger, Mrs. Malky Deutcher, Rabbi Avrohom Meir Gluck, Reb Chaim Dovid Greenberg, Ms. Farla Klaiman, Reb Reuven Mathieson, Mr. Zale Newman, Mrs. Shaindy Perl, Mrs. Esther Malky Sonenblick, Mrs. Brocha Speyer, Reb Boruch Twersky, Dr. Moshe Yosef Weissman, Mrs. Meira Zisovitch, and several others who requested to remain anonymous. I simply could not have done this without each and every one of you and there is no doubt that without you, there would be no book! *Der Eibishter* should give all of you *gezunt*, *simchah*, and *arichus yamim*!

What began with a simple worry developed into panic attacks. I wasn't sure if I could do justice to the great work of my Rebbe. Would I convey the message correctly? Would I understand a particular *ma'amar* or point in the *ma'amar*? Would I use the correct word to get across what I intended to share? I finally had the courage to call Reb Shlomo Weinberg, the *menahel* of the Slonimer yeshivah and a son-in-law of the Nesivos Sholom, and shared my concerns with him. As he was instrumental in making this work a reality, and had a keen understanding of all the issues and possible complexities, I knew he was the go-to person for such concerns.

In one question, summarizing all of my concerns, I asked if he could designate a representative to review the *sefer* for accuracy, and to make sure that it remained in line with the Slonimer *hashkafos* (philosophical perspective). It didn't take him too many seconds to respond. He said, "Reb Naftoli Reich is the man. He is an expert in the *Nesivos Sholom*, is a *talmid chacham*, and has an excellent command of the English language." Reb Shlomo, thank you for the direction. Reb Naftoli, thank you for accepting the task.

Anyone who has ever authored a book knows that after all is

22

ACKNOWLEDGMENTS

written, proofed, reviewed, and printed, there is one final task — get it into the hands of the reader. For that I called on the expertise of Israel Bookshop Publications.

If you need it to get done, just ask Rabbi Moshe Kaufman, Mrs. Malkie Gendelman, and Mrs. Liron Delmar; you can be sure that the book will be a success. They only accept the best work, and it is because of their selection process that their books are well received.

I would also like to express my *hakaras hatov* to Rabbi Gershon Eichorn and Rabbi Zalman Glick, partners in so many projects. Your input and advice is most valuable.

We are told never to judge a book by its cover, yet the visual appearance, the design, and the layout are essential to make the material easy to read and a pleasure to look at. Those requirements were met as we were fortunate to have the talents of Reb Sruly Perl. With such attention to detail and with such an understanding of the goals for the book, he has designed a masterpiece, from cover to cover. He didn't contribute only his time and expertise; his heart and soul were very much part of what he gave.

There is one great individual whom I must thank publicly, though he would wish that his contribution to the success of this *sefer* remain a *mattan b'seiser* (anonymous). Reb Hersh, you did it and you fulfilled *yo'atzunu tov* (granting us good advice) at the highest level.

I would be remiss if I didn't acknowledge the support and guidance I received from someone whom I am privileged to count as one of my dearest friends, Rav Moshe Tuvia Lieff. In him I have a unique combination of friend and guide.

I am fortunate to have spent the last fifteen years of my life in Minneapolis and to enjoy a deep friendship with the *rav* of the Bais Yisroel *kehillah*, Rabbi Yechezkel Greenberg. I am sure that as an avid *talmid* of the *Nesivos Sholom sefarim*, Rabbi Greenberg had a deeper appreciation for this work. May *Hakadosh Baruch Hu* reward him and his family with great *brachah* and *hatzlachah*.

What are we without family? That question doesn't need an answer. I feel so fortunate to have been born into my family. While we

can't choose family, if I had the opportunity to make the selection, I couldn't have chosen a more supportive and loving one. I don't think that a child can ever convey a true and complete thank you to his parents. I won't even attempt to go there. My only hope is that I am a source of *nachas* to my parents.

Much of my work is deeply influenced by my father, Rabbi Moshe Yosef Ginsberg *ztz"l* and, *tblc"t*, my mother, Mrs. Leah Ginsberg. Being a child of such parents created a high standard for me to follow. My *brachah* is that my mother should live and be well with health and happiness and be *zocheh* (merit) to continue seeing generations following in her footsteps.

I must acknowledge my father-in-law and mother-in-law, Rabbi Shlomo *ztz"l* and Rebbetzin Esther *a"h* Poupko. They were a great source of inspiration, encouragement, and motivation for all that I undertook in life.

One of the large holes in my life was the loss of my dear brother Eluzar Yonah *a"h* and my dear sister Perel *a"h*. I don't think a day has gone by since their passing that I don't miss them. May this book serve as a *zechus* for them, and let them please each continue serving as a *meilitz yosher* (celestial advocate) for our family.

During the years that I worked on this project, my children became all too familiar with the phrase "I can't now." They knew what that meant and they allowed me the peace of mind and luxury of time to get my tasks done. My heartfelt *brachah* is that they continue giving us *nachas* and continue our *mesorah* (tradition) with their own families. Eliezer and Tzvi Avigdor, I love you! We are grateful to *Hakadosh Baruch Hu* for sending us two daughters-in-law. Lesli and Tehilla, thank you for joining our family.

It was just a few weeks ago that we were blessed with our first grandchild, Esther, the daughter of Eliezer and Lesli. May *Hakadosh Baruch Hu* bring more and more *simchos*.

Acharonah acharonah chavivah (the last is the most cherished), my greatest debt of appreciation and my most special thanks is due to my true *eishes chayil* (woman of valor), Raffi. She knows more than anyone else that without her, this book and every other

ACKNOWLEDGMENTS

accomplishment would not have materialized. Without much help, she created a home that stands on Torah, *avodah* (Divine service), and *chessed* (kindness). Because of her self-sacrifice, she made it comfortable for me to work all hours of the day and night. May *Hakadosh Baruch Hu* grant us health, happiness, and loads of *nachas* with *arichus yamim*!

I am forever indebted to Dr. Avraham Seidenfeld and his *eishes chayil*, Susan, for partnering with me to make this a reality. It takes a wise person to immediately recognize an investment with great potential and we benefitted from this clarity. Knowing both sets of parents — all Holocaust survivors from Hungary — makes it easy to understand how Dr. and Mrs. Seidenfeld became who they are. They had exemplary role models for how to live with *bitachon* (trust in Hashem) and *simchas hachaim* (joy of life).

May *Hakadosh Baruch Hu bentch* (bless) them with much *nachas* from their dear children, Mordechai, Aaron, Dov, Yosef, Ahuva Libe and Eliezer, along with their spouses and their grandchildren. May they enjoy *arichus yamim* with health and happiness, *simchah* and *hatzlachah ad bli dai* (without end) in all matters of *ruchniyus* (spirituality) and *gashmiyus* (the mundane).

V'yiheyu na amarinu l'ratzon lifnei Adon kol... May the wisdom and depth of the Nesivos Sholom's writings enrich and enlighten the next generation of *Yidden* (Jews) who seek to strengthen their connection with *Hakadosh Baruch Hu* and live a more meaningful and spiritual life in This World and the hereafter.

Binyomin Ginsberg
Minneapolis, Minnesota
15 Shevat 5775

Gems from the ספר נתיבות שלום NESIVOS SHOLOM

הקדמה

הקדמה

האי מאן דבעי למהוי חסידא לקיים מילי דאבות

One Who Desires to Be Pious – Let Him Fulfill the Dictates of (*Maseches*) *Avos*

GEMS FROM THE *SEFER NESIVOS SHOLOM*

SOURCES:

הַאי מַאן דְּבָעֵי לְמֶהֱוֵי חֲסִידָא, לְקַיֵּים מִילֵּי דְאָבוֹת. (בבא קמא ל.)

One who desires to attain piety should fulfill the dictates of (*Maseches*) *Avos*. (*Bava Kamma* 30a)

מִימֵיהֶן שֶׁל אֲבוֹתֵינוּ לֹא פָּרְשָׁה יְשִׁיבָה מֵהֶם. (יומא כ"ח:)

Throughout all the days of our forefathers, there was always a yeshivah among them. (*Yuma* 28b)

יַעֲזֹב רָשָׁע דַּרְכּוֹ וְאִישׁ אָוֶן מַחְשְׁבֹתָיו. (ישעיה נ"ה ז')

Let the wicked abandon his ways, and the sinful one his thoughts. (*Yeshayah* 55:7)

מוּסַר ה' בְּנִי אַל־תִּמְאָס. (משלי ג' י"א)

My son, do not despise Hashem's admonishment. (*Mishlei* 3:11)

כָּל יִשְׂרָאֵל יֵשׁ לָהֶם חֵלֶק לָעוֹלָם הַבָּא. (סנהדרין י' א')

Every Jew has a portion in the World to Come. (*Sanhedrin* 10:1)

30

The Nature — and Meaning — of *Avos*

Maseches Avos — an entire *masechta* (tractate) devoted to the study of *middos* (character traits). An important area of focus, no doubt; but do we have a clear handle of what, exactly, this notion of *middos* is all about? The Torah does not issue explicit commands concerning the cultivation of *middos*; are they to be viewed as being on the same level as other mitzvos (commandments)? How are we even to understand the idea of a *masechta* about *middos*? Are *middos* something we can learn, like any other topic in *halachah* (ritual law)?

The title of this *masechta* is another noteworthy feature, one that bears closer examination. Mishnayos (written embodiments of the Oral Torah) are usually accorded titles that in some way describe the subject matter under discussion. The term *Avos* could be translated any number of ways — fathers, patriarchs, main categories, principles. How is *Avos* an appropriate title for a study of *middos*? Furthermore, when encountering such a term, the Gemara (work explaining Mishnah) usually makes the obvious inference: *Avos, michlal d'ika toldos* — "'Main categories' implies that there are 'subcategories'" (*cf. Bava Kamma* 2a). How does this apply to the study of *middos* — does our topic contain any such derivatives of the "parent" concept? If so, what are they?

The Nesivos Sholom opens his analysis of these issues by first establishing the monumental importance of this area of study, citing the Gemara in *Bava Kamma* (30a): הַאי מַאן דְּבָעֵי לְמֶהֱוֵי חֲסִידָא, לְקַיֵּים מִילֵי דְאָבוֹת — One who desires to attain piety should fulfill the dictates of (Maseches) Avos. In highlighting the significance of this statement of *Chazal*, the Rambam quotes the well-known *Bereisa* of Rabbi Pinchas ben Yair (*Avodah Zarah* 20b). In that teaching, Rabbi Pinchas ben Yair outlines the steps leading towards the acquisition of *ruach hakodesh* (Divine inspiration): Torah leads to caution, which leads to alacrity, which leads to cleanliness, etc. On that continuum, *chassidus* (piety) is one of the highest levels, one step away from *ruach hakodesh*, the ultimate human perfection. As we have seen, the prerequisite for acquiring the level of *chassidus* is compliance with the axioms of this

tractate. What emerges, the Rambam concludes, is that fulfillment of the precepts of *Avos* enables one to approach the spiritual zenith of prophecy.

Clearly, then, describing this work as a list of rules for good manners or proper etiquette would be a gross mischaracterization, and it is not merely a self-help book on becoming a nice person. The principles of character development contained herein are so vital and so personally elevating that one who successfully incorporates them will be well positioned for Divine inspiration.

In this light, the perplexities mentioned above become all the more glaring. What exactly is the role of *middos* in our personal *avodah*? Above all, how can it be that the Torah omits the mention of something so crucial and monumental in reaching Hashem?

The Nesivos Sholom explains that, in reality, one question is answered by the other. What are *middos*? Essentially, they are nothing more and nothing less than the definition of a Yid, forming our identity and very substance. Character development entails the fundamental reworking of our innermost drives and sensations to be entirely in tune with those of a Jew. It means rewiring our mind to *think* as a Jew should think; resetting our heart to *feel* as a Jew should feel; readjusting the emotions to *react* as a Jew would to any stimulus; and reprogramming our limbs to function with the instincts of a Jew. To be sure, this kind of deep-rooted change to our natural tendencies is the most difficult *avodah* we can perform. But it is also the most important, for it enables us to acquire the identity of a Jew. Only as a Jew will it be possible to learn and absorb Torah, to do mitzvos, and to enjoy a relationship with Hashem. As the *passuk* says (*Tehillim* 147:20), לֹא עָשָׂה כֵן לְכָל־גּוֹי וּמִשְׁפָּטִים בַּל־יְדָעוּם — *He has not done so with any other nation, nor has He made His statutes known to them*. Hashem's wisdom, in its fullest sense, is unattainable by anyone other than the Jewish Nation, membership in which requires certain basic changes in human nature.

Thus we can begin to understand why *middos* are not discussed in the Torah. Rav Chaim Vital tells us that *middos* are not included *in* the Torah because character refinement must take place even *before*

we consider fulfilling the Torah. A well-known aphorism states, *Derech eretz kadmah laTorah* — "Refined behavior precedes Torah and mitzvos." While certainly true, Rav Chaim's teaching imparts a deeper, more pointed message, which cuts to the very definition of a potential Torah scholar: to live, learn, and behave as a Jew, one must first *be* a Jew. And that is the subject matter of *Maseches Avos*.

Why the name *Avos*? What are the subcategories of this work? It may seem incredible, but the Torah *itself* is actually a *toldah* (subcategory) of *Maseches Avos*! Torah, mitzvos, attaining *ruach hakodesh* — all are predicated on the refinement of *middos*, and thus can follow a thorough restructuring of our psyches based on the teachings of this one small tractate. How fitting, then, is the title *Avos*, as this is indeed the parent discipline for *all* areas of *Yahadus* (Judaism).

Continuing with this theme, the Nesivos Sholom perceives yet another level of understanding to the title *Avos*. He cites a fascinating historical observation regarding the very early *yeshivos* (Torah academies). Regarding our Patriarchs, Avraham, Yitzchak, and Yaakov, *Chazal* tell us that, מִימֵיהֶן שֶׁל אֲבוֹתֵינוּ לֹא פָּרְשָׁה יְשִׁיבָה מֵהֶם — *Throughout all the days of our forefathers, there was always a yeshivah among them* (*Yuma* 28b). What was the curriculum? We may gain insight from what *Chazal* inform us further about the accomplishments of the *Avos*. We are told that Avraham Avinu was the individual who perfected the *middah* (attribute) of *chessed*. All our subsequent achievements in this area are based on the ideology promulgated by Avraham throughout his lifetime. Similarly, Yitzchak established and epitomized the doctrine of *gevurah* (might), the *middah* of serving Hashem through awe of His greatness. And Yaakov developed and excelled in the *middah* of *tiferes* (magnificence).

In light of our current discussion, it seems clear that these two statements of *Chazal* complement each other. The *Avos* spent their days and years toiling in Torah. In that pre-*Mattan Torah* (giving of the Torah) era, a crucial focus of study was this very foundational subject: analysis and dissemination of the *middos* that serve as the basis and vessel for Hashem's Torah. Only after this introductory

dogma was firmly entrenched was it possible for the Torah itself to exist on this earth.

This, then, is *Maseches Avos*, a title which can be understood as "The Patriarchs' Tractate." For the subject matter therein was their principal form of study. It formed the thrust of their lifetime *avodah*: preparing and refining the world to be a vessel worthy of receiving the Torah.

As it was on the macro level, so it is on the personal level. This is the first step for any of us who seek to absorb the Torah's lofty teachings. We must prepare ourselves to be worthy vessels by learning and practicing *Chazal's* lessons in the area of *middos*. That is, we must master the *sugyos* (study topics) of the *Avos*.

The Ultimate *Mussar Shmuess*

Every fast day, we hear once again, in the *Haftorah* (portion read from the Prophets), the powerful cry of Yeshayah Hanavi urging his people to repentance: יַעֲזֹב רָשָׁע דַּרְכּוֹ וְאִישׁ אָוֶן מַחְשְׁבֹתָיו — "Let the wicked abandon his ways, and the sinful one his thoughts" (*Yeshayah* 55:7). From these words of the *navi* (prophet), the Rambam (*Hilchos Teshuvah* 7:3) learns that the obligation to repent is not limited to violations of actual sins delineated in the Torah. Rather, *teshuvah* (repentance) is necessary even for exhibiting poor character traits, such as quickness to anger or a jealous nature. "Abandon your *ways*," not merely your actions, but your way of thinking, of feeling; your very way of being, of life!

Middos, as we've discussed, form the necessary introduction to Torah. However, now we see that the notion goes much further — they are actually an intrinsic part of Torah in their own right. Unchecked, bad *middos* not only stunt our growth in *avodas Hashem* (Divine service) but are grave sins that demand penitence. The issue raised before thus comes back into focus: Why, indeed, is there no explicit mitzvah in the Torah regarding proper *middos*? True, this question was addressed by Rav Chaim Vital, who explained that *middos* must precede and form the basis for the remainder of the Torah. It would still seem, however, that additional elucidation is in order, especially

in light of what we have garnered from the Rambam — that *middos* are intrinsically a part of the Torah framework, necessitating *teshuvah* like anything else. Why, then, aren't they spelled out like any other mitzvah?

An additional point which deserves clarification is that of the *middos*/mitzvah comparison. By all other categories of mitzvos and *aveiros* (sins), we are informed of the attendant *onesh* (punishment) for their violation. What is the punishment for bad *middos*? And why doesn't the Torah even warn us about them, at least providing a deterrent? The answer may lie, as we shall see, in a profound and poignant teaching of the Saba Kadisha of Slonim *zy"a*.

In one area, we do find a significant distinction between *middos* and the mitzvos of the Torah. The Torah contains hundreds of mitzvos, with various degrees of significance. The numerous prohibitions carry with them consequences of varying forms and gravity in the event of violation. For some the penalty is lashes, for others a monetary fine, and for still others death; either by human hand or by Hashem's. But regardless of how grievous the *aveirah* (transgression) is, Hashem reassures us that — despite our transgressions — He continues to be *Shochen itom b'soch tumosom* — "Dwelling among them in the midst of their impurity" (*Vayikra* 16:16). But defective *middos* are a different matter entirely. For example, *Chazal* tell us (*Sotah* 5a), כָּל אָדָם שֶׁיֵּשׁ בּוֹ גַּסּוּת הָרוּחַ, אָמַר הַקָּבָּ"ה: אֵין אֲנִי וָהוּא יְכוֹלִין לָדוּר בָּעוֹלָם — *Anyone in possession of a haughty spirit, Hashem says (regarding that person): "I and he cannot dwell in the world together."* This means, of course, that one of them has got to vacate — and it will absolutely not be Hashem. Hashem simply cannot bear, *kaviyachol* (if it may even be said), that a haughty person remain in His Presence. Serious deficiencies in the area of *middos*, which comprise one's *derech* (way of life), are simply too loathsome to Him.

מוּסַר ה' בְּנִי אַל־תִּמְאָס

מוּסַר ה' בְּנִי אַל־תִּמְאָס, says Shlomo Hamelech (*Mishlei* 3:11). This *passuk* is normally understood based on its literal translation, as an exhortation to accept instruction: "My son, do not be repelled by

Hashem's admonishment." The Saba Kadisha of Slonim *zy"a* renders this verse with a homiletic twist, seeing in it the very basis for the concept of *middos*. He understands the *passuk* as presenting the ultimate *mussar shmuess* (ethical discourse) delivered by Hashem to each and every Yid. *Mussar Hashem* — what is the admonition that Hashem gives us? *B'ni, al timas* — "You are My son; therefore, ensure that you do not become repulsive!" That is it; Hashem need not say more! As far as *middos* are concerned, there is no need for dire warnings, no need for threats of punishment. All Hashem has to do is remind us of what we are: "*B'ni*! You are *My son*, son of the King!" Far be it from the royal offspring to betray and degrade their elevated status. By straying along the crooked path of improper *middos*, that is exactly what will happen; and we would thus render ourselves despicable in the eyes of our very own Father.

There is a *chiyuv teshuvah* (obligation to repent) for lapses in *middos* because they are, after all, an intrinsic part of Torah. Yet, they are not specifically spelled out in the form of an injunction. This is because only one warning is necessary — only one warning is *possible* — to convey the importance of character improvement: *B'ni!* — "My son!" Is there an *onesh* for exhibiting bad *middos*? *Oy*, is there an *onesh*! The inner defilement itself serves as the direst of consequences; his essence has become so abhorrent as to cause even his Father to seek a safe distance. "*Al timas!*"

It is this aspect of *middos* that distinguishes a Jew from the rest of the nations. As stated previously, *middos* are what define a Jew as a Jew. To be sure, it is certainly possible for a gentile to be pleasant and polite; indeed, many are. But their refinement does not stem from the same source. As such, their gentility will never reach the same depth as *middos tovos* (positive character traits) properly cultivated by a Jew. The civility of the nations is but a product of social convention, whereas a Jew's *middos* result from the exhortation of "*B'ni!*" The refinement worthy of a child of Hashem is thus manifest in a Jew's personality.

And thus we have arrived at yet another understanding of the name chosen for this *masechta*. When we sit down to learn the *sugya*

of *middos*, we do so with the awareness that this is the blueprint for living up to our Almighty Father in Heaven. As we move from mishnah to mishnah, we continually encounter yet another facet to the great program of *middos* development. And all the while, we hear in the background the call of the one admonishment that sums it all up: "My son! *Al timas!*" Each detail and nuance is the loving instruction of a Father to His only son, in fact, to each of us, guiding us on the proper path in life. How appropriate, indeed, that this handbook of paternal counsel should bear the title *Maseches Avos*.

The End Game

אֲנִי מַאֲמִין בֶּאֱמוּנָה שְׁלֵמָה בְּבִיאַת הַמָּשִׁיחַ — *I believe, with complete faith, in the coming of Mashiach!* We say it. We sing it. We cling to it. And we draw from it the strength to continue our trek through this long, dark *golus* (exile).

The idea is a simple one. We are in *golus*, suffering and oppressed, if not so much physically, then even more so spiritually. Our Beis Hamikdash (Holy Temple) is no more, and a monument to a foreign faith stands on its site. Through the familiar declaration above, we constantly remind ourselves that this situation is not permanent. We have Hashem's reassurance that He will eventually return us to our land and rebuild His home — if not today, then someday soon.

Even basic concepts such as this, when scrutinized, can reveal deep inner meaning. The above *Ani Ma'amin* formulation is a paraphrase of one of the Rambam's thirteen principles, which together summarize the essentials of Jewish faith. The rejection of any of these principles, including belief in Mashiach's arrival, would constitute actual heresy, *Rachmana litzlan* (*R"l*, Heaven forbid).

Yet, this notion itself bears some elucidation. We can intuitively understand how such a severe appellation could be applied to a denier of basic notions of *Yahadus*. Someone, for example, who formulates his own ideas in the areas relating to Hashem's existence rather than accepting our *mesorah* (transmitted tenets) is challenging the essentials of Judaism. A person who doubts the coming of Mashiach, thinking that this *golus* will last forever, is certainly wrong, and an imbecile. But why a heretic? How is this on par with the heinous denial of the centrality of Judaism? The same query may be asked regarding belief in the revival of the dead, another of the thirteen principles. What is it about these two items that are in fact so foundational to *emunah* (faith)?

The answer, asserts the Nesivos Sholom, can be gleaned, to a large extent, by taking a simple look at the world around us. Viewing the state of the modern world, we behold an environment of levity, *tumah* (defilement), and absolute disregard for *kavod Shamayim* (the honor of Heaven). We cannot step out in the street or read a newspaper without encountering some new way that mankind has devised to pervert the world that Hashem created. Tragedy, strife, and despair abound. Is it possible that this is it?! Can this be the end result of Hashem's master plan in *ma'aseh bereishis* (the work of Creation)? A thousand times no! Anyone with an iota of appreciation of Hashem's power and greatness must instinctively realize that this picture is not the finished product or intended outcome. There simply must be an ultimate purpose and state of perfection in store for This World.

With this insight, we can better understand the gravity of denying the tenets of Mashiach or *techiyas hameisim* (revival of the dead). Someone who rejects these notions apparently accepts the world as it is. He basically assumes the world to have been fashioned without a higher purpose, devoid of a more meaningful, future existence. In so doing, he essentially fails to recognize the greatness of Hashem Himself. Thus, these two beliefs fit very comfortably into the list of fundamentals of faith.

Having established that there must be an ultimate state of perfection in the works, the natural next step would be to try to understand the nature and characteristics of such a utopian state. But let us digress for a moment, using our new-found depth of thought to examine the well-known mishnah from which the Rambam delineates his thirteen principles.

כָּל יִשְׂרָאֵל יֵשׁ לָהֶם חֵלֶק לְעוֹלָם הַבָּא — *Every Jew has a portion in the World to Come* (Sanhedrin 10:1). Traditionally, we recite this mishnah before learning *Pirkei Avos*. On careful reading, the wording of the mishnah seems strange. What can it mean that every Jew *has* a portion in *Olam Haba*? The World *to Come*, by definition, is not here yet. Wouldn't it have been more accurate to state that every Jew *will have* a portion in *Olam Haba*?

The truth, explains the Nesivos Sholom, is that of course the mishnah's intimation is the correct one. Every Jew *currently* has a dormant portion in the ultimate state of perfection. Being intimately connected with the *Ribono Shel Olam* — Who is the ultimate in perfection — our current, transient state of existence cannot be considered definitive of a Jew's being. This notion follows the very formulation stated previously. It is inconceivable that the world, in its present state, is the final product of creation; in the same fashion, each individual's life must be viewed merely as a passageway to something higher. As a Jew, you *have* a portion with your name on it. It is waiting for you, and it is the true definition of your existence. True, it is possible for someone to be temporarily denied access to it, pending purification from *aveiros*, *chas v'shalom*. But it is there nonetheless, and we must work on rectifying ourselves in This World in order to live up to it.

What, then, is this ultimate goal? What does perfection look like? While we cannot begin to grasp it, *Chazal* describe *Olam Haba* for us. It is a world where tzaddikim (the righteous) sit and bask in the radiance of Hashem's glory. *This* is the real purpose of the world. *This* is the purpose of a Jew's life. Simply to draw close and experience the nearness of Hashem's Presence.

And so we have come full circle. Why do we recite the mishnah of *Kol Yisroel* before learning *Pirkei Avos*? Because *Pirkei Avos* is the instruction manual of good *middos*. Good *middos* define a human being as *B'ni*, a child of *Hakadosh Baruch Hu*. Without proper *middos*, we cannot remain in Hashem's Presence. And so, before we begin, we remind ourselves of our real purpose and goal; of what our real *definition* is. To live up to that piece of real estate out there with our name on it. To come closer and closer to the Divine light. And for this we need the internal transformation that can only result from careful study and practice of *Pirkei Avos*.

We can learn from this *masechta* anytime and anywhere, but special focus is given to it during the summer *Shabbosim* (Sabbaths), most notably between Pesach and Shavuos. The true lead-up to *Kabbalas HaTorah* (receiving the Torah) is the purification of the self; reconstructing our personal identity as that of a Jew. Who can possibly approach such a daunting task? Through *Pirkei Avos*, we all can.

In Summary

What's in a name? Quite a lot, especially when it comes to the title by which a classic work of *Chazal* is known. Moreover, the title *Avos* — alternately meaning main categories, patriarchs, fathers — is very illuminating of the crucial content of this *masechta*.

The focus of this *masechta* is on the area of *middos*, refined character traits. The Sages wonder why this essential subject is not addressed in the Torah in the same manner as the mitzvos; why are there no specific commands regarding proper traits? Rav Chaim Vital famously explained that *middos* can't be relegated to the category of mitzvos because, essentially, they are the basis of the entire Torah. As the Nesivos Sholom elaborates, to learn and fulfill the Torah, one must — first and foremost — be a *Jew*. And it is *middos* that define what a Jew is.

This profound concept enables us to better understand the title of the *masechta*. In a *halachic* context, when encountering the term *Avos*, the Gemara is wont to react with an inference, *Avos, michlal d'ika toldos* — "'Main categories' implies that there are derivative subcategories." What, then, are the *toldos* of the axioms of this *masechta*? As we have seen, the entire Torah, in fact, is predicated and rests upon the foundation of *middos*; thus, it is the mitzvos of the Torah that are the *toldos* of the "principal axioms," the lessons of *middos* contained in this *masechta*.

The Nesivos Sholom notes further how our Patriarchs, Avraham, Yitzchak, and Yaakov, were constantly involved with *yeshivos* in their times. What subject did they study in this pre-*Mattan Torah* era? Our forefathers were known to have developed outstanding *middos*, with each one excelling in particular in a certain designated trait, which they cultivated and disseminated to their followers. Thus, the principal focus of their learning was in the area of *middos*. In this capacity, they fulfilled Rav Chaim Vital's dictum on a national scale, readying the world to eventually receive the Torah by first laying the framework of *middos*. And so the *masechta* of *middos* contains the central themes to which our *Avos* dedicated their lives. This, then, is yet another dimension to the content and title of *Maseches Avos* — the *Masechta* of the Patriarchs.

In yet another vein, the concept of *middos* in general, and the theme of *Pirkei Avos* in particular, can be summed up by a single *passuk*. The words of *Mishlei* contain a simple yet potent admonition, the ultimate *mussar shmuess* delivered to us by Hashem Himself. *Mussar Hashem*, Hashem's discourse to us, is, "*B'ni! Al timas!*" Hashem reminds each of us, "You are My child. As royal progeny, therefore, you must take care to preserve your dignity and self-respect." *Al timas* — don't allow yourself to become loathsome, the inevitable consequence for a person whose poor character remains unchecked. This, then, is the ultimate in parental advice; the loving Father exhorts us, His children, to protect and refine our *middos*, so that our Jewish essence remains unsullied. Otherwise, even our Father will not be able to abide our presence. This is yet another demonstration of the fact that the *masechta* of *middos* is aptly named. It is *Pirkei Avos*, the instruction of a Father to His children, to us.

The above informs our practice of reciting the mishnah from *Sanhedrin* before studying *Pirkei Avos*. That mishnah states that every Jew has a portion in *Olam Haba*. As such, it forms the perfect introduction to the study and mastery of the topic of *middos*. The mishnah of *Kol Yisroel* reminds us that, in This World, we have not yet arrived at our ultimate destination, for the final state of perfection and spiritual bliss awaits in the World to Come. That is the place where the righteous sit and bask in the Divine Presence, fulfilling the ultimate goal of existence: attaining closeness with the Almighty. And this itself revolves around the admonition that forms the core of

GEMS FROM THE *SEFER NESIVOS SHOLOM*

Pirkei Avos: *"B'ni! Al timas!"* For it is only through the cultivation of proper *middos*, the cornerstone and essence of being a Jew, that we can remain in Hashem's Presence. Thus, through study of *Pirkei Avos* and adherence to its precepts, we can transform our essence and become worthy of the ultimate goal of cleaving to Hashem in eternal closeness.

הקדמת כל ישראל יש להם חלק לעולם הבא
Introductory Passage: All Yisroel Has a Portion in the World to Come

כָּל יִשְׂרָאֵל יֵשׁ לָהֶם חֵלֶק לָעוֹלָם הַבָּא, שֶׁנֶּאֱמַר וְעַמֵּךְ כֻּלָּם צַדִּיקִים לְעוֹלָם יִירְשׁוּ אָרֶץ נֵצֶר מַטָּעַי מַעֲשֵׂה יָדַי לְהִתְפָּאֵר: (סנהדרין פרק י' משנה א')

All Yisroel has a portion in the World to Come, as it states (*Yeshayah* 60:21): "And your nation are all righteous, they shall inherit the land forever; they are a branch of My planting, the work of My hands in which to be glorified" (*Sanhedrin* 10:1).

הקדמה

GEMS FROM THE *SEFER NESIVOS SHOLOM*

SOURCES:

הִסְתַּכֵּל בִּשְׁלֹשָׁה דְבָרִים וְאֵין אַתָּה בָא לִידֵי עֲבֵרָה. דַּע, מֵאַיִן בָּאתָ, וּלְאָן אַתָּה הוֹלֵךְ, וְלִפְנֵי מִי אַתָּה עָתִיד לִתֵּן דִּין וְחֶשְׁבּוֹן. מֵאַיִן בָּאתָ, מִטִּפָּה סְרוּחָה, וּלְאָן אַתָּה הוֹלֵךְ, לִמְקוֹם עָפָר רִמָּה וְתוֹלֵעָה. וְלִפְנֵי מִי אַתָּה עָתִיד לִתֵּן דִּין וְחֶשְׁבּוֹן, לִפְנֵי מֶלֶךְ מַלְכֵי הַמְּלָכִים הַקָּדוֹשׁ בָּרוּךְ הוּא. (אבות ג׳)

Focus on three things, and this will prevent you from coming to the hands of sin. Know from where you came, to where you are going, and before Whom you are destined to give an account and reckoning. From where did you come? From a putrid drop. To where are you going? To a place of dust, worms, and maggots. And before Whom are you destined to give an account and reckoning? Before the Supreme King of kings, the Holy One Blessed is He. (*Avos* 3)

כְּמַעֲשֵׂה אֶרֶץ־מִצְרַיִם אֲשֶׁר יְשַׁבְתֶּם־בָּהּ לֹא תַעֲשׂוּ וּכְמַעֲשֵׂה אֶרֶץ־כְּנַעַן אֲשֶׁר אֲנִי מֵבִיא אֶתְכֶם שָׁמָּה לֹא תַעֲשׂוּ וּבְחֻקֹּתֵיהֶם לֹא תֵלֵכוּ. (ויקרא י״ח ג׳)

Do not perform the practice of the land of Egypt in which you dwelled, and do not perform the practice of the land of Canaan to which I will bring you, and do not walk in their statutes. (*Vayikra* 18:3)

וַתִּשָּׂא אֵשֶׁת־אֲדֹנָיו אֶת־עֵינֶיהָ אֶל־יוֹסֵף וַתֹּאמֶר שִׁכְבָה עִמִּי. וַיְמָאֵן וַיֹּאמֶר אֶל־אֵשֶׁת אֲדֹנָיו... אֵינֶנּוּ גָדוֹל בַּבַּיִת הַזֶּה מִמֶּנִּי וְלֹא־חָשַׂךְ מִמֶּנִּי מְאוּמָה כִּי אִם־אוֹתָךְ בַּאֲשֶׁר אַתְּ־אִשְׁתּוֹ וְאֵיךְ אֶעֱשֶׂה הָרָעָה הַגְּדֹלָה הַזֹּאת וְחָטָאתִי לֵאלֹקִים... וַתִּתְפְּשֵׂהוּ בְּבִגְדוֹ לֵאמֹר שִׁכְבָה עִמִּי וַיַּעֲזֹב בִּגְדוֹ בְּיָדָהּ וַיָּנָס וַיֵּצֵא הַחוּצָה. (בראשית ל״ט ז׳-י״ב)

And the wife of his master lifted her eyes to Yosef and she said, "Lie with me." And he refused, and he said to his master's wife, "...There is no one greater in this house than I, and (your husband) has not withheld anything from me save for you, in that you are his wife; and how could I do this great evil, thereby sinning to G-d?... And she grabbed his garment, saying, "Lie with me." And he left the garment in her hand, and fled and went outside. (*Bereishis* 39:7-12)

רַבִּי חֲנַנְיָא בֶּן עֲקַשְׁיָא אוֹמֵר, רָצָה הַקָּדוֹשׁ בָּרוּךְ הוּא לְזַכּוֹת אֶת יִשְׂרָאֵל, לְפִיכָךְ הִרְבָּה לָהֶם תּוֹרָה וּמִצְוֹת. (מכות ג' ט"ז)

Rabbi Chananya ben Akashya says: Hashem wished to bestow merit upon Yisroel; He therefore gave them Torah and mitzvos in abundance. (*Makkos* 3:16)

Who Are You?

What is the most difficult thing in the world to do? Some would say brain surgery. What could require more delicacy, precision, and skill than working with the intricate system of nerves that make up the human brain? The more sedentary inclined may suggest that mountain climbing ranks as the toughest task. Scaling the world's most challenging peaks requires infinite endurance to withstand the weeks of constant exertion — an almost unimaginable prospect for those of us who cherish the comforts of home. Of course, one who appreciates the labors of in-depth Torah study will maintain that the feat of finishing all of *Shas* (the six orders of the Talmud) is unparalleled in its impressiveness. What can compare to spending hours and hours over the course of many years, immersed in intense concentration, mastering concept after concept until at last the entirety of the work is his?

The giants of *mussar* (ethical teachings) tell us, however, that none of the above is the correct answer. The truly most difficult task in the world is to conquer and change a *middah ra'ah* (negative character trait). The most grueling physical labor, the most intense intellectual toil cannot compare to the endeavor of subduing our natural drives with the aim of changing our very self.

So can it be done? And is it really worth the time and effort? With so much Torah to learn, so many mitzvos to perform, perhaps it would be wiser to simply concentrate on what the Torah discusses explicitly, rather than undertake the herculean task of perfecting our *middos*. Indeed, given the magnitude of the challenge, what is to stop us from throwing in the towel before we even get started?

The Charted Course

The answer to these questions, says the Nesivos Sholom, emerges from a careful reading of a well-known teaching of *Chazal*. This is the mishnah (Sanhedrin 10:1) that is traditionally read as an introduction to the study of *Pirkei Avos*. The mishnah states, כָּל יִשְׂרָאֵל יֵשׁ לָהֶם חֵלֶק לָעוֹלָם הַבָּא — *All Yisroel has a portion in the World to Come.*

It is noteworthy that the mishnah employs the term *yeish* — "**has** [a portion]," as opposed to *yiheyeh* — "**will have** [a portion]"; after all, isn't *Olam Haba* a future destination? While this issue was addressed in the previous *ma'amar* (discourse), we advance here yet another understanding, one that will also serve to clarify another apparent difficulty with the mishnah's wording.

Take another look at the mishnah: כָּל יִשְׂרָאֵל יֵשׁ לָהֶם חֵלֶק לְעוֹלָם הַבָּא. Translated literally, it is saying that every Jew has a portion **to** the World to Come. Now, what can that possibly mean? Shouldn't the mishnah have stated, *b'Olam Haba* — "**in** *Olam Haba*" instead? What is a portion **to** *Olam Haba*? *Chazal*, always supremely deliberate in their phrasing, must have had in mind some deeper meaning when choosing such curious language.

The Maggid MiKozhnitz *ztz"l* explains the mishnah as alluding to a tremendously powerful *yesod* (fundamental principle), relevant to the life of every Jew. Each one of us is unique, having individual strengths and talents to apply to *avodas Hashem*. By the same token, we each have areas of weakness and issues with which we struggle. Something that one person may find very easy to deal with may present a terrific challenge to someone of a different temperament. A person with an easygoing nature may have little trouble keeping his *ka'as* (anger) in check, yet struggle mightily with feelings of haughtiness. Another person may be naturally humble, but at the same time be overcome by an overwhelming *ta'avas hamamon* (desire for wealth). The Maggid explains that, while it is true that the Jewish people are destined for *Olam Haba*, the mishnah is saying much more than that; in fact, it is making a vital point about the here and now. *Kol Yisroel* — "**every single** Jew," *yeish lahem cheilek* — "**has** his own personal **portion** (that is, area of *avodah*)," *l'Olam Haba* — that serves as his pathway **to** the World to Come. In other words, each of us — with our specific strengths, and through the unique challenges that Hashem sends our way — is allotted an individualized portion of *avodah* as our life's work. Applying ourselves to this task is what sets us on the way to *Olam Haba*! No two people are alike, and therefore no two paths to *Olam Haba* are alike. Each Jew at birth receives a ticket; the tickets are specific and unique, and also non-transferable.

So how do we know what our particular *avodah* is? Here is where we use the *yetzer hara* (evil inclination) to our advantage. We know what the *yetzer hara's* main goal is: to prevent us from fulfilling ours! The last thing in the world it wants is for us to fulfill our *tachlis* (purpose); it directs all its strength and wiliness in an effort to thwart the completion of our mission. Its attentions thus present us with the greatest clue as to just what our specific jobs are! When we see that we have a particularly difficult time overcoming a certain *middah*, it is a clear indication that we have been charged with precisely this mission: to overcome that very *middah*! That is exactly why the *yetzer hara* is expending all of its energy towards this specific target. And so this shows what it is we have to accomplish in order to advance on our path to *Olam Haba*.

This idea provides much insight into why it is that we read this specific mishnah prior to learning *Pirkei Avos*. *Maseches Avos* is the guide to *middos*, the manual for perfection of character. As stated, such an undertaking is a daunting task; how can a person change even one *middah*? The mishnah of *Kol Yisroel* provides us with a timely reminder as we contemplate embarking on this tremendous endeavor. True, the mishnah tells us it is very difficult to change, but the difficulty itself reassures us that we are on the right track. The very fact that the going is not easy is what reveals to us that we are doing what is necessary to accomplish the ultimate and unique *tachlis* Hashem designed for each of us.

Is it really worth the time and effort to concern ourselves with mere *middos*? As we shall see, the mishnah of *Kol Yisroel* answers this question as well.

The Nesivos Sholom offers a novel insight into the function of the inner *mizbei'ach* (altar) in the Mishkan (Tabernacle). We know that the outer *mizbei'ach*, on which the *korbanos* (sacrifices) were brought, served as a tool for *kapparah* — eliciting atonement for the sins of Bnei Yisroel. The inner *mizbei'ach*, which was used for *ketores* (incense offering), did not deal with the outright sins of Bnei Yisroel. Rather, its function was to cleanse them from those indiscretions that cause a *rei'ach ra* — a bad (spiritual) odor, so to speak, one that renders a person unfit to stand in the presence of Hashem. From the burning of the *ketores*, then, would arise a *rei'ach nicho'ach laHashem* — an aroma that is "pleasant" to Hashem as He beholds His children, who are now clean and ready to draw close to Him.

And what is it that causes a person to emit this spiritually foul odor? Bad *middos* are chiefly responsible. As we've seen in the previous *ma'amar*, Hashem does not wish to be in close proximity to someone who exhibits negative character traits. Only through pristine *middos* can we actually come close to Him.

Olam Haba is a place where tzaddikim sit and enjoy the presence of Hashem. Such proximity is only possible for an individual who possesses good *middos*. So, is it truly worth the trouble to work on *middos*? You had better believe it! To drive the point home, we recite the mishnah of *Kol Yisroel* before learning *Pirkei Avos*, thereby reminding ourselves exactly how high the stakes are in refining our character.

Identity Check

Take a moment to try the following thought exercise. Ask yourself the simple question, "Who am I?" Of course, you know your name, occupation, and address. But ask yourself, "At the deepest level, who am I really? What defines me, my essence, my place in the infinite cosmos?" When we really dig deep, fundamental self-definition can be a surprisingly daunting task.

The truth is that every member of Klal Yisroel has a singular identity, and it is incumbent upon us to familiarize ourselves with it. In a later mishnah in *Avos* (3:1), Akavya ben Mahalalel presents a series of questions in which he exhorts us to practice self-awareness in three principal areas in order to ensure a lifetime of purity. He states: הִסְתַּכֵּל בִּשְׁלשָׁה דְבָרִים וְאֵין אַתָּה בָא לִידֵי עֲבֵרָה. דַּע, מֵאַיִן בָּאתָ, וּלְאָן אַתָּה הוֹלֵךְ, וְלִפְנֵי מִי אַתָּה עָתִיד לִתֵּן דִּין וְחֶשְׁבּוֹן. מֵאַיִן בָּאתָ, מִטִּפָּה סְרוּחָה, וּלְאָן אַתָּה הוֹלֵךְ, לִמְקוֹם עָפָר רִמָּה וְתוֹלֵעָה. וְלִפְנֵי מִי אַתָּה עָתִיד לִתֵּן דִּין וְחֶשְׁבּוֹן, לִפְנֵי מֶלֶךְ מַלְכֵי הַמְּלָכִים הַקָּדוֹשׁ בָּרוּךְ הוּא — *Focus on three things, and this will prevent you from coming to the hands of sin. Know from where you came, to where you are going, and before Whom you are destined to give an account and reckoning.*

GEMS FROM THE *SEFER NESIVOS SHOLOM*

From where did you come? From a putrid drop. To where are you going? To a place of dust, worms, and maggots. And before Whom are you destined to give an account and reckoning? Before the Highest King of kings, the Holy One Blessed is He. The message of this mishnah seems clear enough. The answers it supplies to the three questions stress a person's lowly physical origins and temporary nature. Heightened awareness of this reality should inculcate enough humility and sobriety within a person to enable him to abstain from sin in the face of temptation.

Yet, the structure of this mishnah appears puzzling. Notice that it lists the set of three questions twice. Akavya ben Mahalalel lists them together at the outset of the mishnah; then, as he proceeds to answer them, he reiterates each question. Why the repetition?

The commentators elucidate Akavya ben Mahalalel's intent. They explain that, in reality, the first half of the mishnah stands alone in its own right. In other words, there are actually two distinct ways in which these questions may be addressed. One way is spelled out by the second half of the mishnah, in which the responses to the questions reveal man's lowly, ephemeral nature. But by treating the questions in the beginning as a stand-alone entity, the mishnah is alluding to the fact that there is another approach. The very questions themselves are a reminder of an even higher ideal, speaking to the sublime identity of every individual as a member of *Hakadosh Baruch Hu's* holy nation. In this sense, the questions lend themselves to a different set of answers. From where do I come? I am a holy *neshamah* taken from Hashem's special storehouse, a member of Klal Yisroel, intrinsically connected to Hashem Himself! There can be nothing more special and pure than that; it is an identity of spiritual beauty that behooves its bearer to always live up to its stature. To where am I going? I am engaged in a lifelong struggle to return myself to those highest spheres in a state that befits my origins. I must actively seek holiness and purify myself to be worthy of standing with the One before Whom I will ultimately give a final reckoning.

This mishnah thus reveals the crucial role a healthy knowledge of self-worth plays in a Jew's *avodah*. Every Jew is, at the core, defined by his status as a member of the royal family, a precious child of the King of kings. This alone should fill us with a sense of purpose and confidence, as well as an awesome feeling of responsibility. We must live up to this identity and behave only in ways befitting our status as Hashem's children.

This responsibility goes further than avoiding sins and performing mitzvos. There is a subtle difference between even the mundane acts of a prince and those of a commoner. A Jew's attitude toward every aspect of life, the way he approaches any action or challenge, should reflect his regal lineage. This idea is reflected in the following commandment (*Vayikra* 18:3): כְּמַעֲשֵׂה אֶרֶץ־מִצְרַיִם אֲשֶׁר יְשַׁבְתֶּם־בָּהּ לֹא תַעֲשׂוּ וּכְמַעֲשֵׂה אֶרֶץ־כְּנַעַן אֲשֶׁר אֲנִי מֵבִיא אֶתְכֶם שָׁמָּה לֹא תַעֲשׂוּ וּבְחֻקֹּתֵיהֶם לֹא תֵלֵכוּ — *Do not perform the practice of the land of Egypt in which you dwelled, and do not perform the practice of the land of Canaan to which I will bring you, and do not walk in their statutes.* The *sefarim* understand this *passuk* not as referring to the outright sins that the Egyptians and Canaanites committed; for the Torah warns elsewhere about all of these practices. Rather, they perceive herein an exhortation to something more subtle. The *passuk* is conveying a message concerning one's everyday activities, stating that even these should bear a marked distinction from that of a non-Jew. A Jew is different, special, and sacred. It does not behoove him to act — in any situation — in the same manner as one who lacks this heritage and essence.

The *yetzer hara* works very hard to prevent us from recognizing our intrinsic holiness. Reb Baruch of Mezibuz would quote his grandfather, the holy Ba'al Shem Tov, as saying that it is impossible to explain to a gentile what a Jew really is; he is simply incapable of grasping the concept of a human being built entirely from holiness. Reb Baruch would add that, in his experience, it is even more difficult to explain to a Jew what a Jew is. Since this inner recognition is so crucial to proper *avodah*, the *yetzer hara* concentrates intense efforts on suppressing it.

This inner battle was played out in the conversation between Yosef Hatzaddik and his master's wife. In her attempt to coerce Yosef into sin, the Torah tells us about Potiphar's wife: *Vatispeseihu b'vigdo* —

"and she grabbed him by his garment" (*Bereishis* 39:12). The word *bigdo*, "his garment," can also be read *begido*, "his treachery." This alludes to yet another mode of attack, a further attempt to cause Yosef to stumble. Potiphar's wife seized upon whatever faults in his *avodah* she could find; she "grabbed him by (these) 'treacheries.'" In essence, she was telling him, "Look, your personal *avodah* is flawed as it is. You already are impure. So what is stopping you from sinning just one more time?" But Yosef had cultivated an attitude which anticipated this approach; he had a stark and ready response: אֵינֶנּוּ גָדוֹל בַּבַּיִת הַזֶּה מִמֶּנִּי — *There is no one in this house greater than I* (*ibid.* v. 9). This was not merely arrogance or a display of bravado; rather, it was an important mindset, one in which he recognized his true identity. He was proclaiming: "I am a Jew. I am holy. This act is antithetical to my innermost nature." In the end, it was this realization that helped him to avoid dying a spiritual death.

As we embark on the journey of character refinement that is *Pirkei Avos*, our first step is to remind ourselves of the definition of the character on which we are working. And so we begin, כָּל יִשְׂרָאֵל יֵשׁ לָהֶם חֵלֶק לָעוֹלָם הַבָּא. The Toldos Yaakov Yosef explains that there are three levels to a person's spiritual makeup: *nefesh*, *ruach*, and *neshamah* (various dimensions of the soul). Each of these aspects has a corresponding portion in *Olam Haba* that it attempts to attain. The "lower Gan Eden" is the *Olam Haba* of the *nefesh*; the "upper Gan Eden" is the domain of the *ruach*; and the *Olam Haba* corresponding to the *neshamah* is beyond any possible description.

Obviously, it is really beyond our capacity to understand any of these arenas in any type of depth. What can be said on a superficial level, at least, is the following: The higher levels of the World to Come can only be attained through intense efforts of self-rectification. However, the "lower Gan Eden," the *Olam Haba* of the *nefesh*, is guaranteed to every Jew. We need not even "earn" it through specific actions; each Yid has a portion there simply by being a member of Klal Yisroel. But this concept itself can prove to be quite powerful. Simply knowing of our uniqueness — the fact that we are the holy people, who have a portion in *Olam Haba* just by virtue of who we are — should galvanize us to put in the necessary exertions to accomplish our true purpose, thereby advancing to those higher levels. Know from where you come — and use that knowledge to understand where you are going and before Whom you will give the final accounting. And then you will be prepared to live your life accordingly.

Doing the Right Thing — for the Right Reasons

Having discussed the introductory mishnah of *Kol Yisroel*, the Nesivos Sholom now turns his attention to the mishnah (*Makkos* 3:16) we recite upon the conclusion of each *perek* (chapter) of *Pirkei Avos*: רַבִּי חֲנַנְיָא בֶּן עֲקַשְׁיָא אוֹמֵר, רָצָה הַקָּדוֹשׁ בָּרוּךְ הוּא לְזַכּוֹת אֶת יִשְׂרָאֵל, לְפִיכָךְ הִרְבָּה לָהֶם תּוֹרָה וּמִצְוֹת — *Rabbi Chananya ben Akashya says: Hashem wished to bestow merit upon Yisroel; He therefore gave them Torah and mitzvos in abundance.* At first glance the idea seems basic enough; Hashem loves the Jewish people, desires their ultimate welfare, and so bestowed upon them the greatest of all gifts — Torah and mitzvos. An analysis of the mishnah in context, however, can reveal even deeper meaning. It will also help us understand how this statement relates to *Pirkei Avos*.

The mishnah originally appears at the very end of *Maseches Makkos*. In the mishnah that immediately precedes it, Rabbi Shimon bar Rebbi discusses the prohibition against consuming blood. Who would even want to do such a thing? It is an act almost anyone would find revolting. Nevertheless, it is one of the commandments; one who refrains from this "dish" thus merits reward. How much more so, Rabbi Shimon derives, is a person deserving of reward for refraining from such things as theft and immorality — prohibitions for which people do have a natural inclination!

It is on the heels of this teaching that Rabbi Chananya delivers his statement. Why, in fact, is there an explicit directive against consuming blood? If no one would do it anyway — why bother issuing an apparently superfluous prohibition? Rabbi Chananya supplies the answer: *L'zakos es Yisroel* — "to grant even more benefit to Klal Yisroel"! The abundance of Torah and mitzvos, which includes the "superfluous" ones, is a remarkable display of Hashem's great kindness to His people. Now reframed in the form of a command, a person gets rewarded for refraining from something he would have abstained from in any event.

The Nesivos Sholom broadens this concept through a discussion of the mitzvah of honoring parents. Everyone intuitively understands that parents deserve our respect by virtue of the fact that they brought us into the world and sacrificed so much to raise us. Even gentiles, who don't have a mitzvah in this regard, generally realize that they should honor their parents. Thus, even without a specific commandment, honoring parents is a logical imperative. But once enshrouded in an explicit mitzvah, the act takes on a new dimension entirely. The Kabbalah masters teach that when a Jew respects his parents in light of Hashem's instruction to do so, his deed sets in motion a spiritually potent chain of events of epic proportions. He draws down from on High the Heavenly emanations associated with the mystical concepts known as *Abba* and *Ima* that are built into the mitzvah of *kibbud av v'eim*.

(A full treatment of these elevated concepts — cited by the Nesivos Sholom in the name of the *sefer Divrei Moshe* by Rav Moshe MiDulina — is obviously well beyond the scope of this particular essay. Readers inclined to follow up on this thread are referred to the *Divrei Moshe, Parshas Kedoshim*, pages 45b-50a.)

What Rabbi Chananya ben Akashya is revealing to us, then, is that the mitzvos Hashem gave us are much more than mere rules and regulations. Rather, they are powerful tools, the ramifications of which reverberate throughout the universe. The very fact that Hashem commanded them serves to transform mundane deeds — even those which we would have done on our own — into meaningful acts of *avodah* and *tikkun olam* (rectification of the world).

Pirkei Avos begins with a history of the *mesoras haTorah* (transmission of the Torah) from Moshe Rabbeinu down to the *Anshei Knesses Hagedolah* (Men of the Great Assembly). The *mefarshim* (commentators) explain why this particular overview was included here: to preempt a potential misimpression. The study and cultivation of proper character traits is such a worthwhile endeavor, yet there is also a certain danger associated with it. That is, one may develop a fallacious and shallow view of the whole idea. He may make the mistake that proper *middos* are imperative from a purely logical standpoint — and that is all. After all, there are many people from the length and breadth of society who are "nice guys" and naturally affable and easygoing; they also practice good *middos*.

And so, right at the start, *Pirkei Avos* introduces the notion of *mesoras haTorah*. It does this to stress the real impetus behind the cultivation of good *middos*. It is not just because it gives us a warm feeling inside, but because it is a mitzvah handed down from Hashem to Moshe, and so on through the generations. It is important to have smooth-functioning and peaceful societies, but the Torah view of *middos* goes well beyond that. As these, too, are derived from Sinai, the practice of proper *middos* carries with it the same cosmic ramifications as do other areas of *avodas Hashem*.

This is also the reason for appending the mishnah of Rabbi Chananya ben Akashya to each *perek*. It reminds us of this crucial point — emphasizing the fundamental difference between doing something because it seems like a nice idea and doing it because it is the will of the Master of the Universe.

In Summary

One of the characteristics of the study of *Pirkei Avos* is the inclusion of "extras." That is, when learning a chapter of this *masechta*, there is a mishnah appended to the beginning, preceding the body of the chapter itself, as well as an additional mishnah after the conclusion of the *perek*. The Nesivos Sholom elucidates the meaning of these "additional" mishnayos, and their relevance to the subject matter of *Pirkei Avos* itself.

The mishnah that precedes the study of *Avos*, which is a selection from *Maseches Sanhedrin*, lays down a fundamental *yesod*. It states: כָּל יִשְׂרָאֵל יֵשׁ לָהֶם חֵלֶק לָעוֹלָם הַבָּא — *All Yisroel has a portion in the World*

to Come, apparently conveying the basic principle that *Yidden* are destined for the bliss of the Afterlife. But certain textual anomalies point to the fact that this mishnah contains a more subtle message. When speaking of Yisroel's portion in the World to Come, why does the mishnah speak in the present tense, *yeish lahem*, and not the future, *yiheyeh lahem*? And why does it speak of a *cheilek la'Olam Haba*, which literally denotes "a portion **to** the World to Come"? Wouldn't it have been appropriate to speak in terms of a *cheilek ba'Olam Haba* — "a portion **in** the World to Come"?

Citing the Maggid of Kozhnitz, the Nesivos Sholom explains that the mishnah is, in fact, speaking of the here and now. It is referring to the individual mission of each and every Jew; the specific area unique to every person, who has some defect of character or other that requires correction. Each of us, as a member of Klal Yisroel, right now, has a *cheilek* — our own "portion," which comprises our particular area of *avodah*. It is our purpose in life to rectify and perfect this area; and this is our ticket, which will lead us *to* our ultimate destination — *Olam Haba*.

Thus, at the outset of the study of *Avos*, this selection from *Sanhedrin* delivers a timely and powerful message. *Pirkei Avos* is the study of character refinement — an endeavor so inherently difficult, the *ba'alei mussar* (masters of ethics) consider it the hardest task in the world. As such, we may almost get discouraged from the get-go; how are we to tackle this herculean project? The mishnah of *Kol Yisroel* offers succor and direction. True, the task is daunting and difficult — but this is no reason for despair. On the contrary, the difficulty itself is the clearest indication that you are on the right track. Every Jew has a "portion" with which he must deal, one which will enable him to enter *Olam Haba*. But how are we to know what our particular mission is? The answer is that the *yetzer hara* is inordinately interested in ensuring that we fail specifically in the area that is our purpose in life. That is, it puts up the biggest fight exactly in the area that is the Yid's "portion" of *avodah*. And so, by identifying the aspect of our character that presents the greatest challenge, we find therein our individualized "portion" and our ticket to the World to Come.

הקדמת כל ישראל יש להם חלק לעולם הבא

There is an additional message contained in this mishnah, which bears particular relevance to the study of *Avos*. The mishnah reminds us of our intrinsically elevated identity, emphasizing that we are Hashem's beloved children. The fact that we belong to the nation that is guaranteed a portion in (at least the initial levels of) *Olam Haba* indicates that we are members of the royal family. This realization can be quite beneficial in our spiritual pursuits, as we must match our character to this lofty status. Such knowledge is quite apropos as we embark on the journey of character refinement, for which *Pirkei Avos* is our guide. Aware of the nobility of our souls, we may be spurred on to attain even greater heights.

The mishnah appended to the end of the chapter — a selection from *Maseches Makkos* — places the whole notion of refining our character in the proper perspective. The mishnah speaks of Hashem's great kindness in granting Yisroel a preponderance of mitzvos with which to earn merit. From the context, it is clear that the mishnah is referring to the fact that we have many mitzvos in which we are commanded to refrain from something we would have naturally done on our own; thus, with a formal command, we receive reward for what we would have observed in any event.

But an even broader concept is being described here, and that is the overall role that a mitzvah plays. Had the action been left at the "natural" level, it would have been adhered to — but would have remained just that. But because of being commanded by Hashem, the action takes on a whole new light; it is now infused with sanctity, and its reverberations are felt, in some spiritual sense, throughout the Heavens and the earth.

Thus, this mishnah provides a timely message as well, one quite relevant to the study of *Pirkei Avos*. As we embark on this study, and the concomitant exercise in character refinement, there does exist a potential pitfall. The practice of good *middos* is a very logical endeavor, one recognized even by proper and decent gentiles. Let us make no mistake — in the Torah's perspective, it goes well beyond just the art of good neighborliness and being nice. The imperative to perfect one's character is also a product of Sinai. As such, the notion of engendering good *middos* is imbued with a special sanctity, a manifestation of the will of Hashem.

כל ישראל יש להם חלק לעולם הבא
All Yisroel Has a Portion in the World to Come

כָּל יִשְׂרָאֵל יֵשׁ לָהֶם חֵלֶק לָעוֹלָם הַבָּא, שֶׁנֶּאֱמַר וְעַמֵּךְ כֻּלָּם צַדִּיקִים לְעוֹלָם יִירְשׁוּ אָרֶץ נֵצֶר מַטָּעַי מַעֲשֵׂה יָדַי לְהִתְפָּאֵר: (סנהדרין פרק י' משנה א')

All Yisroel has a portion in the World to Come, as it states (*Yeshayah* 60:21): "And your nation are all righteous, they shall inherit the land forever; they are a branch of My planting, the work of My hands in which to be glorified" (*Sanhedrin* 10:1).

הקדמה

SOURCES:

אַל תִּהְיוּ כַּעֲבָדִים הַמְשַׁמְּשִׁין אֶת הָרַב עַל מְנָת לְקַבֵּל פְּרָס. (אבות א׳)

Do not be as servants who serve their master for the sake of reward. (*Avos* 1)

צַדִּיקִים יוֹשְׁבִין וְעַטְרוֹתֵיהֶם בְּרָאשֵׁיהֶם וְנֶהֱנִים מִזִּיו הַשְּׁכִינָה. (ברכות י״ז.)

The righteous sit, with their crowns (of glory) upon their heads, basking in the splendor of the *Shechinah* (Divine Presence). (*Berachos* 17a)

דְעָלָךְ סְנֵי לְחַבְרָךְ לֹא תַעֲבֵיד. (שבת ל״א.)

What is hateful to you, do not do to your friend. (*Shabbos* 31a)

כל ישראל יש להם חלק לעולם הבא

Wouldn't it be wonderful if everywhere we went, we encountered only righteous people? If the average fellow in the street would exude piety and sterling character? This utopian ideal may actually be a reality! At least, so it seems from an initial reading of the mishnah that serves as the introduction to *Maseches Avos*. The mishnah (from *Sanhedrin* 10:1) states: כָּל יִשְׂרָאֵל יֵשׁ לָהֶם חֵלֶק לָעוֹלָם הַבָּא שֶׁנֶּאֱמַר וְעַמֵּךְ כֻּלָּם צַדִּיקִים לְעוֹלָם יִירְשׁוּ אָרֶץ — *All Yisroel has a share in the World to Come, as it states* (*Yeshayah* 60:21), *"And all your people are righteous, they shall forever inherit the land."*

To uncover the true meaning and deeper message of this mishnah, some puzzling points must first be clarified:

- There seems to be an issue with verb tense in the mishnah's wording of כָּל יִשְׂרָאֵל יֵשׁ לָהֶם חֵלֶק לָעוֹלָם הַבָּא — *All Yisroel* **has** *a portion in the World to Come*. Why does the mishnah speak in the present tense? *Olam Haba*, it would seem, pertains to the future, the reward a Yid accesses at the appointed time. Why does the mishnah talk as if our relation to *Olam Haba* is in the here and now?

- To be realistic, the mishnah's prognosis does seem a bit overly optimistic. *All* Yisroel are such tzaddikim? True, the mishnah brings a source to back up its claim; but the *passuk* itself appears mystifying. *V'ameich **kulam** tzaddikim*; **kulam** — "**all** of them"? Is this actually the case — the entire nation is comprised solely of righteous people? Have we not encountered, unfortunately, at least some individuals of unsavory character? What, in fact, does the *passuk* mean with this categorical assertion?

- To be sure, there are exceptions; as the mishnah itself proceeds to relate (in its continuation, following the selection that we read). The contrast between those who retain their portion in *Olam Haba* and those who forfeit it is worthy of note. Regarding the above selection, which discusses those who do have a share in the World to Come, the commentators explain that this includes even those individuals who have transgressed heinous crimes and incurred the death penalty — murderers and the like. After receiving their punishment, they remain eligible to enter *Olam Haba*.

Who loses their portion? This list includes people who, at first glance, seem to be guilty of relatively minor offenses. For example, the mishnah places into this category someone who denies the Biblical source for the concept of *techiyas hameisim*. That means that this individual acknowledges the notion that *techiyas hameisim* will take place; it is only in the matter of the Biblical source for this idea that his faith is lacking. Also listed is one who reads *sefarim chitzonim* — an "outer" book. The commentators explain this to mean a book that was authored by a heretic. This, too, appears somewhat inconsequential, as the implication is that the book itself may not contain any heresy. The simple fact that he reads a book penned by a questionable author is the main offense.

So, how exactly are we to understand this phenomenon? Murderers or adulterers may still be candidates for *Olam Haba*, but one who reads a benign book that happened to be written by a non-believer is denied a portion? What could possibly account for this arrangement?

The Nesivos Sholom discusses these points one by one. In so doing, he sheds much light both on the mishnah's lessons and on the reason for its selection as an introduction to *Pirkei Avos*.

Individual or Communal?

We live in a culture that is fiercely individualistic, where each person clings tenaciously to his "rights." Woe to the authority figure who dares to suggest that one make sacrifices on behalf of the greater good! The much-touted value of personal independence seems to trump one's responsibilities as a member of society.

What does *Yiddishkeit* say about this attitude? Is individual opportunity indeed more important than communal responsibilities? The Nesivos Sholom asserts that not only does this approach constitute a dereliction of duty, it in fact runs counter to the best interests of the individual! So much more can be gained as contributing members of the *tzibbur* (community) than as individuals striking out on our own. This concept, so critical for spiritual growth, is an underlying message of the mishnah of *Kol Yisroel*.

When the mishnah says that **Kol Yisroel**, **all** of Yisroel, will have a portion in the World to Come, it is not necessarily referring to each individual in Klal Yisroel. Rather, the mishnah's intent is for the unit known as *Kol Yisroel*. When it functions as a group, the nation Yisroel certainly has a portion in *Olam Haba*. This reflects the tremendous *ko'ach hatzibbur* (communal strength). Individuals may be flawed; when judged on their own merits, these flaws are quite apparent and relevant. However, when appearing before the Almighty as a cohesive nation, each person's qualities fill in for the others' faults. In this complementary relationship no sinners are perceived; it is a unification that exudes unadulterated perfection and holiness. It is to this phenomenon the *passuk* is referring when it states, *V'ameich* **kulam** *tzaddikim*; the compound entity known as *ameich kulam* — "your nation in its entirety" — is purely righteous.

How foolish is one who trades in the incredible power and protection of the *tzibbur* for the dubious ideal of individualism! It is for this reason that *chassidus* (chassidism) places such emphasis on healthy communal relationships. It is imperative to view ourselves as part of a larger group bound together by the common goal of *avodas Hashem*. By submitting our "self" to the communal ideal, we can thereby shed our own personal faults and failings. By thus appearing before Hashem as a component of *Kol Yisroel*, we may likewise be included in the communal promise of כָּל יִשְׂרָאֵל יֵשׁ לָהֶם חֵלֶק לָעוֹלָם הַבָּא.

Seizing the Future

It is a well-known fact of human nature that people tend to exchange future happiness for immediate (and comparatively insignificant) pleasure. We live in the here and now, and the allure of instant gratification can often outshine what we know to be in our long-term interests.

As a result, sometimes even the promise of eternal reward in *Olam*

Haba may prove insufficient as a motivational tool to successfully navigate our present struggles. On an intellectual level, we may very well understand that today's temporal pleasures, when compared to the prospect of eternal bliss, are nothing more than childish pettiness. Nevertheless, it is still hard to translate this knowledge into practice and to trade away the present for the sake of the future. However, a careful reading of our mishnah may reveal that no such trade-off is actually necessary. Let us take a closer look.

Elsewhere in *Avos* (1:3), Antignos Ish Socho states, אַל תִּהְיוּ כַּעֲבָדִים הַמְשַׁמְּשִׁין אֶת הָרַב עַל מְנָת לְקַבֵּל פְּרָס — *Do not be as servants who serve their master for the sake of reward*. The Noam Elimelech explains that the intent of this mishnah is to apprise us of the true worth of a mitzvah. When involved in a mitzvah, it is important that we fully appreciate the magnitude of what we are doing. In essence, the performance of a mitzvah is a unique opportunity to come close to the King of all kings. We thereby elevate our mundane, earthly existence to levels that are the envy of even the Heavenly angels. No act is so pure, no endeavor so sublime, as the act of involving ourselves in the mitzvos of Hashem.

Of course, there is reward beyond our wildest dreams in the World to Come for every mitzvah we perform. What Antignos is telling us, though, is that by focusing only on the reward at the time of a mitzvah, we miss the forest for the trees. The true benefit of performing the mitzvah is both immediate and enduring: it is *d'veikus baHashem*, attaining closeness with our Heavenly Father.

Although we may not be able to comprehend it fully, this is the true meaning of *Olam Haba*. *Chazal* describe *Olam Haba* in these terms: צַדִּיקִים יוֹשְׁבִין וְעַטְרוֹתֵיהֶם בְּרָאשֵׁיהֶם וְנֶהֱנִים מִזִּיו הַשְּׁכִינָה — *Tzaddikim sit, with their crowns (of glory) upon their heads, basking in the splendor of the* Shechinah (*Berachos* 17a). The bliss of *Olam Haba* is the attainment of the ultimate closeness with the *Shechinah* (Divine Presence).

This is why the mishnah, in speaking of Yisroel's portion in *Olam Haba*, speaks specifically in the present tense: **Yeish** lahem cheilek — "They **have** a portion." Every mitzvah that we perform, in the here and now, affords us the opportunity to experience *Olam Haba* right here in This World. It is up to us to recognize this, appreciate it, and seize the future in the moment.

Don't Lose the Connection

The primary role of *d'veikus* (attachment to Hashem) in *avodas Hashem* is an underlying theme of this entire mishnah. It is manifest in the second half of the mishnah, as well, where the discussion focuses on those sins that remove a person from *Olam Haba*, R"l.

As mentioned, the contrast between the two sections of the mishnah is quite noteworthy. Among the sinners who forfeit their share we find one who denies the Biblical source for *techiyas hameisim*, although he acknowledges the actual concept. One who reads a book written by a heretic is also a part of this group; this is apparently so even if the actual contents contain no heresy. Yet the first half of the mishnah, in discussing those who do receive a share in the World to Come, includes some perpetrators of the most heinous crimes. As the Bartenura points out, even those who incurred the death penalty may still be eligible for *Olam Haba*.

What accounts for these apparently surprising outcomes? The Nesivos Sholom explains that, indeed, it is not necessarily sinful acts that cause a person to lose his share in *Olam Haba*, no matter how dire they are. What does cause someone to be rendered ineligible for *Olam Haba*? The severing of his connection with Hashem on a fundamental level. *Emunah* is the fabric underlying the essence of the Klal Yisroel entity. Anything affecting one's core *emunah* — be it as subtle as reading a book of dubious authorship — redefines a person. He is no longer fully a member of the Klal Yisroel that is assured a place in the World to Come. Since his ability to attain *d'veikus* is stunted, he can no longer access the promise of כָּל יִשְׂרָאֵל יֵשׁ לָהֶם חֵלֶק לָעוֹלָם הַבָּא.

The Gemara (*Shabbos* 31a) records the well-known episode of the potential convert who attempted to antagonize Hillel. In response to his demand to be taught the whole Torah while standing on one leg, Hillel famously declared, דְּעֲלָךְ סַנִי לְחַבְרָךְ לֹא תַעֲבֵיד — *What is hateful to*

you, do not do to your friend. This, Hillel explained, is the essence of the entire Torah; the rest can be viewed as offshoots of this rule.

The Maggid of Mezeritch *ztz"l* offers a homiletic interpretation of Hillel's words, reflecting the underlying theme of *avodas Hashem*. The term *chaver* is from the same root as *chibbur* — "connection" (as one has a connection with his friend). Thus, Hillel's statement can be understood as referring to a connection with Hashem. "What is hateful to your *attachment* — i.e., to your closeness with Hashem — do not do." This is the guiding principle in life. The only real goal is *d'veikus*; anything that potentially interferes with its attainment conflicts with our entire *raison d'être*. The entire Torah is merely application of and commentary to this concept, as the mitzvos are the means through which we attain *d'veikus* with Hashem.

And so, by maintaining our relationship with Hashem, we are guaranteed a share in *Olam Haba*, regardless of the specific sins we may have perpetrated. For as long as the foundations for a relationship with the Almighty are present, there exists the realistic opportunity for us to rectify our poor choice of actions. Ultimately, the message of our mishnah is לְבִלְתִּי יִדַּח מִמֶּנּוּ נִדָּח — *no Jew can stray so far as to be entirely lost* (*Shmuel II* 14:14). The direst of sins do not necessarily cause a Jew to lose his innermost identity — that of a member of Hashem's holy nation.

There is another prime area crucial to the endeavor of attaining *d'veikus*: that of *middos* (character) improvement. When we sit down to study *Pirkei Avos*, we are embarking on a battle to refine our *middos*. This involves a fundamental change to our innermost character — something the *ba'alei mussar* tell us is the most difficult task in the world. How can we even approach this monumental undertaking? And so, as an introduction, we recite: כָּל יִשְׂרָאֵל יֵשׁ לָהֶם חֵלֶק לָעוֹלָם הַבָּא. Essentially, we are declaring, "Don't think that my character flaws define who I really am. At the core, I am a Jew. I have an intimate relationship with Hashem and a guarantee of eternal existence. I am not, in reality, changing my character, rather I am uncovering, polishing, and living up to my true essence." With this thought, success in this endeavor becomes a possibility. Let us begin this exhilarating process.

כל ישראל יש להם חלק לעולם הבא

In Summary

In serving as the introduction to *Avos*, the mishnah of *Kol Yisroel* must contain a message most fundamental to the study of this *masechta*. We may discover this message by closely examining key aspects of this mishnah.

The mishnah begins with quite an optimistic pronouncement: "All Yisroel have a share in the World to Come...(for) they are all tzaddikim." Indeed! That would be truly wonderful; but does it concur with the reality? Aren't there at least some people who don't seem to fit the bill?

The Nesivos Sholom perceives here an emphasis on the *ko'ach hatzibbur*. Of course, there are flawed individuals who don't measure up to the standard of a tzaddik. It is by negating our "self" in favor of the overall *tzibbur*, to the communal entity known as "*Kol Yisroel*," that we are guaranteed a portion in *Olam Haba*. When standing apart, our faults and misdeeds are scrutinized and judged. When we become part of the *tzibbur*, the qualities of others can fill in for our shortcomings as individuals.

Another noteworthy feature of the mishnah is the fact that it speaks in the present tense: **Yeish** lahem cheilek — "They **have** a portion." When discussing *Olam Haba* — "the World **to Come**," one may have assumed that the future tense is more appropriate, as it is then that one will enter *Olam Haba*.

However, explains the Nesivos Sholom, the mishnah means to accentuate a fundamental principle by employing such phrasing. The mishnah's message is that, yes, there is a concept of *Olam Haba* right now, in the present, a fact that can be appreciated the more one is aware of the ultimate purpose of life and mitzvah performance. For the thrust of all aspects of *avodas Hashem* is to attain *d'veikus*, that ultimate state of attachment to Hashem. And this, in essence, is what *Olam Haba* is all about: where the tzaddikim sit, so close to Hashem, delighting as they gaze at His radiant Presence. As such, one whose *avodah* is properly focused, as he aims for achieving *d'veikus* through

הקדמה

67

mitzvah observance, can experience a semblance of *Olam Haba* in the present tense, right here, in This World.

This notion informs another phenomenon of our mishnah. The first half of the mishnah revolves around those who do receive a portion in *Olam Haba*, including even perpetrators of transgressions so severe they were liable for the death penalty. By contrast, the second half of the mishnah lists those people who forfeit their share in *Olam Haba*, and the list contains some surprising entries. For example, one who believes in *techiyas hameisim*, but merely denies its Biblical source, loses his share in *Olam Haba*. How could this be? Once again, explains the Nesivos Sholom, we see the centrality of *d'veikus* in *avodas Hashem*. Of course, deeds are important, but so long as a Yid maintains the foundations of a connection with Hashem, he is always able to rectify his actions. But faltering in the area of *emunah* is a different story altogether. By tampering even slightly with those basic fundamentals that serve as the backbone of the entity of Klal Yisroel, a person has redefined his very essence. The foundations of *d'veikus* have been severed, and this individual loses his connection to the *Kol Yisroel* unit. Thus severed, he no longer has the guarantee that Klal Yisroel possesses — a claim to *Olam Haba*.

And this accounts, as well, for the connection between this mishnah and the overall study of *Avos*. As we approach this area of study, we are confronted with a monumental task. *Avos* focuses on the topic of *middos* refinement, which the *ba'alei mussar* deem to be the most challenging endeavor in the world. Yet it is a crucial endeavor, essential to the attainment of *d'veikus*.

Thus, the mishnah of *Kol Yisroel* reminds us that, after all, the task is vastly achievable. It strengthens our recognition of who we are — a part of the Klal Yisroel entity, one that is inherently perfect and pristine. Our faults as individuals need not blind us to the fact that we can belong to this entity after all. What is key is maintaining the inherent connection with Hashem. We need only polish our character; for underneath lurks a pristine essence, destined for eternal life.

Gems from the ספר נתיבות שלום
NESIVOS SHOLOM

פרק א'

פרק א' משנה א'
משה קבל תורה מסיני
Moshe Received the Torah from Sinai

מֹשֶׁה קִבֵּל תּוֹרָה מִסִּינַי, וּמְסָרָהּ לִיהוֹשֻׁעַ, וִיהוֹשֻׁעַ לִזְקֵנִים, וּזְקֵנִים לִנְבִיאִים, וּנְבִיאִים מְסָרוּהָ לְאַנְשֵׁי כְנֶסֶת הַגְּדוֹלָה. הֵם אָמְרוּ שְׁלֹשָׁה דְבָרִים, הֱווּ מְתוּנִים בַּדִּין, וְהַעֲמִידוּ תַלְמִידִים הַרְבֵּה, וַעֲשׂוּ סְיָג לַתּוֹרָה:

Moshe received the Torah from Sinai, and transmitted it to Yehoshua, and Yehoshua to the Elders, and the Elders to the Prophets, and the Prophets transmitted it to the Men of the Great Assembly. They said three things: Be deliberate in judgment, develop many students, and make a fence for the Torah.

GEMS FROM THE *SEFER NESIVOS SHOLOM*

SOURCES:

לָמָּה תְּרַצְּדוּן הָרִים גַּבְנֻנִּים הָהָר חָמַד אֱלֹקִים לְשִׁבְתּוֹ אַף־ה' יִשְׁכֹּן לָנֶצַח. (תהלים ס"ח י"ז)

Why do you dance, high mountains? The mountain that G-d desires for His dwelling – even there Hashem will reside eternally. (*Tehillim* 68:17)

וְהַחָכְמָה מֵאַיִן תָּבוֹא. (איוב כ"ח כ')

And wisdom – from where does it come? (*Iyov* 28:20)

וְאֵלֶּה הַמְּלָכִים אֲשֶׁר מָלְכוּ בְּאֶרֶץ אֱדוֹם... וַיִּמְלֹךְ בֶּאֱדוֹם בֶּלַע בֶּן־בְּעוֹר וְשֵׁם עִירוֹ דִּנְהָבָה. וַיָּמָת בָּלַע וַיִּמְלֹךְ תַּחְתָּיו יוֹבָב בֶּן־זֶרַח מִבָּצְרָה. וַיָּמָת יוֹבָב וַיִּמְלֹךְ תַּחְתָּיו חֻשָׁם מֵאֶרֶץ הַתֵּימָנִי וַיָּמָת חֻשָׁם... וַיִּמְלֹךְ תַּחְתָּיו הֲדַר וְשֵׁם עִירוֹ פָּעוּ וְשֵׁם אִשְׁתּוֹ מְהֵיטַבְאֵל בַּת־מַטְרֵד בַּת מֵי זָהָב. (בראשית ל"ו ל"א-ל"ט)

And these are the kings who reigned in the land of Edom... And there reigned in Edom Bela ben Be'or, and the name of his city was Dinhavah. And Bala died, and there reigned in his place Yovav ben Zerach from Batzrah. And Yovav died, and there reigned in his place Chusham from the land of the Teimani. And Chusham died... And there reigned in his place Hadar, and the name of his city was Pa'u, and the name of his wife was Meheitavel bas Matreid bas Mei Zahav. (*Bereishis* 36:31-39)

וְהָאִישׁ מֹשֶׁה עָנָו מְאֹד מִכֹּל הָאָדָם אֲשֶׁר עַל־פְּנֵי הָאֲדָמָה. (במדבר י"ב ג')

And the man, Moshe, was exceedingly humble, more than any man on the face of the earth. (*Bamidbar* 12:3)

פֶּה אֶל־פֶּה אֲדַבֶּר־בּוֹ...וּתְמֻנַת ה' יַבִּיט. (שם פסוק ח')

Speaker to speaker I converse with him...and he gazes upon the image of Hashem. (*ibid.* v. 8)

משה קבל תורה מסיני

Am I Humble?

Anivus — humility. The term generally brings to mind someone with his head hanging low, unaware of his own strengths. But is this really an ideal — to cultivate low self-esteem?

Aside from being just plain depressing, this definition of humility is also a bit perplexing. Is it even possible for a truly great person to be humble? Take someone who has spent a lifetime working on himself and as a result has accomplished much, attaining great heights. How does he convince himself that he is no better than any guy off the street? And if he can, is that really what he should do?

Actually, the Torah's concept of *anivus* has nothing to do with ignoring one's achievements. In fact, it is even possible for someone to simultaneously be aware that he is one of the greatest men ever to live and to serve as the epitome of *anivus*.

So, what exactly does it mean to be an *anav* (humble person)? *Chazal* provide the answer in the very first words of the very first mishnah of *Pirkei Avos*. Let us discover what they had to say about Moshe Rabbeinu, the humblest of all men and the model for the Torah's ideal of *anivus*.

מֹשֶׁה קִבֵּל תּוֹרָה מִסִּינַי — *Moshe Rabbeinu received the Torah **from** Har Sinai*. At the outset, the wording appears somewhat peculiar. Did Har Sinai give Moshe the Torah? It was where he received the Torah. Seemingly, the mishnah should have stated, *Moshe kibeil Torah b'Sinai* — "Moshe received the Torah **at** Har Sinai." Or, if the mishnah intended to discuss from Whom Moshe received the Torah, it should have said, *Moshe kibeil Torah mei'Hashem* — "Moshe received the Torah **from Hashem**"!

The Nesivos Sholom explains that, in fact, neither of these possibilities represents the mishnah's intent; presumably, we are all well aware that Hashem gave Moshe the Torah on Har Sinai. Quoting the Toldos Yaakov Yosef, he offers a most illuminating interpretation of the opening words of this mishnah.

The mishnah is informing us of Moshe Rabbeinu's *inspiration* in accepting the mission of receiving the Torah on behalf of Klal Yisroel.

פרק א'

In truth, the fact that he so readily acquiesced should give us pause. When Hashem sent Moshe to lead the Jews out of Mitzrayim, Moshe was adamantly opposed to the idea, insisting for days on end that he wasn't worthy of the task. But when chosen to bring down the Torah from on High for the Jewish people — not one word of protest! Why the amazing turnabout?

According to the Toldos Yaakov Yosef, the answer lies in *Chazal's* well-known characterization of Har Sinai. They inform us that when selecting the site for giving the Torah, Hashem passed over the tall and mighty mountains and chose instead the smallest — Har Sinai. Moshe Rabbeinu saw this and learned from it. He understood that the giving of the Torah was inextricably linked not to the high and mighty, but specifically to the unobtrusive. Since he viewed himself in the smallest possible light, he realized, by extension, that he was perfectly suited for this particular role.

The Zenith: Nothing

The Be'er Avraham of Slonim expands on this idea, seeing it expressed in *Tehillim* (68:17): לָמָּה תְּרַצְּדוּן הָרִים גַּבְנֻנִּים הָהָר חָמַד אֱלֹקִים לְשִׁבְתּוֹ אַף־ה׳ יִשְׁכֹּן לָנֶצַח — *Why do you dance, high mountains? The mountain that G-d desires for His dwelling, even there Hashem will reside eternally.* He understands the *passuk* as referring to that element of the story of *Mattan Torah*, with which even schoolchildren are familiar. The *harim gavnunim* are the majestic mountain peaks, which vied to be selected as the favored location. But their boastfulness was to no avail, as Hashem instead settled on **hahar** — **the** mountain, tiny Har Sinai. Or so the song goes.

In actuality, explains the Be'er Avraham, this was not a case of simple braggadocio, but a contest of a much more sublime and noble sort. These *harim gavnunim*, towering peaks, are none other than the *Avos* (Patriarchs), and the *middos* (attributes) that they perfected over their lifetime. Avraham excelled in the *middah* of *chessed*, Yitzchak personified *gevurah* (strength and might in Divine service), and Yaakov embodied *tiferes* (splendor). Each of these *middos* can be utilized to foster sanctity and closeness with the Almighty. The high mountains "jostling for position" can thus be understood as a reference to these *middos*, the pristine qualities of which, one may think, could serve as the foundation for the giving of the Torah.

And yet, great and mighty as these other peaks may be, Hashem chose another as the base for His eternal abode. *The* mountain, the one granted pre-eminence, was the small one, for it is specifically this quality that renders it as the prime receptacle for Torah. As the *passuk* says in *Iyov* (28:20): *Hachachmah* **mei'ayin** *tavo*. While usually translated as, "**From where** does wisdom come?", the verse can be read homiletically as providing an answer to that very question. *Chachmah*, Divine wisdom, comes from *ayin*, nothing! This is the *middah* that Hashem deems the best vehicle for giving over His wisdom: *ayin*, self-negation.

Why is this *middah*, above all others, the prime candidate for the giving of the Torah? What is it about this trait that makes it supreme? And — what, exactly, is it?

The Be'er Avraham provides a profound explanation. All other traits, as noble and worthy as they may be, don't have the same potential as *ayin*. That is, as positive entities, they are susceptible to *shevirah*, breakage, and can eventually be so affected. But as a non-entity — *ayin*, after all, is nothing — nothing can affect it. Paradoxically, then, this *middah* has to it an element of sustainability the other *middos* simply don't have. In a sense, it is eternal — which accounts for its selection by *Hakadosh Baruch Hu*. He sought to deliver His Torah through an attribute that will live on forever.

The Be'er Avraham's explanation of the *passuk* in *Tehillim* can now be appreciated on a much deeper level. The "high mountains" — the other traits — may have been worthy candidates for the giving of the Torah. But in the end, the "mountain that G-d desired for His dwelling" was the *middah* of *ayin*, for that is everlasting — "Hashem will reside eternally."

Yet another allusion to the supremacy of this *middah* appears elsewhere in the Torah. Ironically, the teaching is revealed through some unlikely sources — the kings of the nation of Edom.

GEMS FROM THE *SEFER NESIVOS SHOLOM*

The end of *Parshas Vayishlach* contains a somewhat mysterious section, consisting mainly of names. The Torah devotes much space to listing the genealogy and chieftains of the nation of Edom, the descendants of Eisav. Towards its conclusion (*Bereishis* 36:31-39), eight generations of Edom's kings are delineated.

An interesting detail is contained therein. The listing of the monarchs follows a basic pattern: וַיִּמְלֹךְ...בֶּלַע בֶּן־בְּעוֹר...וַיָּמָת...וַיִּמְלֹךְ תַּחְתָּיו יוֹבָב בֶּן־זֶרַח — *And Bela ben Be'or reigned...and he died...and Yovav ben Zerach reigned in his place.* The ruler is identified, it states that he reigned, that he died, and then his successor is named. And so on for all successive kings — except the final one, whose wife is also identified: וַיִּמְלֹךְ תַּחְתָּיו הֲדַר...וְשֵׁם אִשְׁתּוֹ מְהֵיטַבְאֵל — *And Hadar reigned in his place...and the name of his wife was Meheitavel.* And there the narrative ends — this time, curiously omitting mention of this king's death.

Why does the phrase "and he died" appear in reference to all the other kings, while it is omitted from the last? The Be'er Avraham explains the significance based on a mechanism of interpretation known as *notreikun* (acronym), which uncovers hidden meaning through breaking up a term. The first seven kings represent the seven principal attributes. As such, they each include a mention of "death," reflecting their "mortality" and susceptibility to *shevirah*, as mentioned above. The eighth and final listing, however, represents the supreme *middah*, the only one immune to *shevirah*. This is the *middah* of *ayin*, which endures forever; hence, no mention of "and he died." It is embodied in the name **Meh**eitavel, as isolating its beginning yields the term **mah**, "what." This is the ultimate declaration of *anivus*, implying that there is "nothing" there.

Meheitavel, the term from which the *middah* is derived, sheds much light on the nature of this ultimate embodiment of humility. At the outset, we contemplated the definition and source of humility, wondering if it entailed obliviousness to one's true worth and accomplishments. This *passuk* demonstrates otherwise, as an examination of this name reveals. Broken still further, it yields the following: **Mah-tav-Keil**; **tav** (derived from *tov*, good) implying that there is a "good" *mah* and a "bad" *mah*. Denial of self-worth, a general discouragement that breeds low self-esteem, is by no means the *mah* that the Torah promotes. The self-negation Hashem desires — the "*mah*" which is "*tav-Keil*" (good in Hashem's eyes) — is of a much different sort (as will be further elaborated upon below).

The absolute master of the trait of *ayin* — the "preferred" *mah* — was Moshe Rabbeinu. It was he who declared, *V'nachnu* **mah** — "**What** (after all) are we?" (*Shemos* 16:8). And so it was only through him — the quintessential embodiment of this everlasting force — that the Torah could be given.

Definition of Humility

What, then, is this signature *middah* of Moshe Rabbeinu? What is the definition of the *middah* of *ayin*? And what about it makes it so uniquely suited for the giving of the Torah? Let us more closely examine his employment of this trait to gain a clearer picture of its true essence.

וְהָאִישׁ מֹשֶׁה עָנָו מְאֹד מִכֹּל הָאָדָם אֲשֶׁר עַל־פְּנֵי הָאֲדָמָה — *And the man, Moshe, was the most humble of all men on the face of the earth* (*Bamidbar* 12:3). The truth is that this statement should raise some eyebrows. No man before or since has reached the level of prophecy attained by Moshe Rabbeinu. He was the only person to actually talk to Hashem *peh el peh*, speaker to speaker (*ibid.* v. 8). And of him it states further (*ibid.*), *U'semunas Hashem yabit* — "He gazed upon Hashem's image." While the exact meaning of these phrases lies beyond our ability to fully grasp it, one thing is clear: Moshe enjoyed an intimate relationship with Hashem entirely unparalleled in the annals of human history.

How, then, could Moshe be humble? Was he not aware that he had reached heights beyond the comprehension of most human beings? Does humility entail self-delusion?

The answer is that Moshe was fully cognizant of his unprecedented achievements. He knew that he saw the "image of Hashem," spoke to Him *peh el peh*, and operated on a different plane from most any other person. But such awareness did not detract from his *middah*

of *ayin*. On the contrary — *it contributed to it*. The very fact that Moshe enjoyed such closeness with Hashem is what helped him to be the *anav* that he was. True *anivus* does not require us to ignore our accomplishments. What it means is to recognize them, and then to surrender our entire Self — talents and all — to Hashem's unmitigated greatness.

The point is subtle, and the Nesivos Sholom provides an analogy to help us better understand. Imagine standing by the vast ocean holding a cup. You bend over, fill it with seawater, and hold it up for a closer look. Now, the cup contains something, which has individuality. But what happens when the contents are poured back into the ocean; are we still struck by those particular few ounces of seawater at which we had been gazing just a moment before? Of course not! They haven't changed their individual characteristics, but have been subsumed within the parent body of water. The sea level hasn't risen as a result — nor would it, even if tankers full of water were to be emptied into the sea. This does not at all take away from the intrinsic value of the original ounces in the cup. But by surrendering their own individuality to the greater whole, they have become one with the vastness of the ocean.

So, too, Moshe Rabbeinu. The fact that he had such intimate knowledge of Hashem did not result in pride. The connection actually worked the other way; his crystal-clear awareness of Hashem *enabled* him to attain *ayin*. For the more one recognizes the awesomeness and Infinite greatness of Hashem, the more he will be able to submit to His will, dedicating his Self and abilities to Him alone. *V'ha'ish Moshe* — specifically the one who beheld the *temunas Hashem*, and knew it — *he* was the *anav me'od mi'kol ha'adam*.

The Yom Kippur Connection

Thus, this *middah* of *ayin* has enhanced our understanding of *Mattan Torah* — where it was given, through whom it was given — all underscoring how the enduring trait of proper self-negation is fundamental to Torah observance.

It also informs the notion of *when* the Torah was given. After the unfortunate episode of the *Eigel Hazahav* (Golden Calf), Moshe's intercession on behalf of the people and his return to receive the *Luchos* (tablets) a second time — the completion of the giving of the Torah took place on Yom Kippur. And this is no coincidence. On this day, Klal Yisroel — then and now — experience a level of humility greater than almost any other time, as they stand in Hashem's Presence in sublime contrition. What more appropriate venue for giving the Torah than a day noted for such communal and individual submission to the Almighty?

Actually, the relationship between Yom Kippur and the *middah* of *ayin* runs quite deep. This is reflected in the well-known statement of Reb Levi Yitzchak of Berditchev in *Kedushas Levi*, concerning the ability to tap into the atonement power of the day. "Yom Kippur does not effect atonement for a person," he asserted, "unless and until one places himself within the *geder* (rubric) of *ayin*. That is, he must feel and declare, 'I, all I possess, and all my abilities — all are the Creator's.'"

This declaration cuts to the heart of this notion of *ayin* and the closely related *middah* of *hisbatlus* (utter self-negation), so necessary and foundational to achieving closeness with Hashem. In fact, the *Kedushas Levi's* formulation reflects the vast difference that exists between the different ways in which people tend to approach Yom Kippur, and Hashem in general. This is the distinction between *yeish* (something) and *ayin* (nothing). Those who perceive themselves as possessing *yeish* — that is, their own entity, attributing their abilities and accomplishments to themselves — will have a different Yom Kippur experience indeed. They perceive of themselves as able to manage their own affairs. Thus, the focus of their prayers basically amounts to a request of Heaven not to interfere. "Please don't let anything spoil our plans," they pray. "We'll handle the rest." Such an attitude, obviously, is an outright impediment to achieving *hisbatlus* to Hashem, relegating them to remain distant from Him.

But for those who aspire to *ayin*, it is a different story entirely. So much more attuned to the overarching presence and greatness of Hashem, they recognize the extent to which they are utterly dependent on Him. "Please don't conceal Your guidance from us," they beseech. "Without it — even for a moment — we are completely lost." These *Yidden* realize that, without Hashem, they are truly nothing. And this "nothingness" is their ultimate salvation. Through such *hisbatlus*, they are able to be subsumed within the sanctity of Hashem's Presence. Regarding the laws of ritual purity, the Mishnah tells us (*Keilim* 12:2): כָּל הַמְחֻבָּר...לַטָּהוֹר, טָהוֹר — *Whatever is attached...to a source of purity, obtains that purity.* For those who have cultivated the *middah* of *ayin*, there is nothing to stand between them and attachment to the Creator. They can cleave to Him, in effect become one with Him. Attached to His pristine essence, the ultimate source of purity, they achieve complete purity and atonement, entirely cleansed of sin.

It should be noted that the words of the *Kedushas Levi* were very deliberate. Moshe Rabbeinu attained the "height" of *ayin*, completely and utterly subsuming himself to *Hakadosh Baruch Hu*, obtaining unprecedented closeness. In stating that *hisbatlus* is a prerequisite to Yom Kippur, however, the *Kedushas Levi* was not referring to such an extreme; such a level is not necessarily expected, or even feasible, for us to reach. All that is necessary to merit atonement is to enter within the *geder*, the category, of *hisbatlus*. Whatever strides, however minimal, we make in the direction of *ayin* are an immeasurable achievement and a step that much closer towards Hashem.

This, then, is the profundity of the opening words of *Avos*. It was **mi**Sinai — **from** the lessons in *ayin* that Moshe learned and epitomized, based on this quality of Har Sinai — that he served as the perfect conduit for the giving of the Torah.

And with this foundation, we may be ready for the rest of *Avos* and the journey of character refinement that leads ultimately to *hisbatlus* and *d'veikus* to Hashem.

In Summary

The very first words of *Avos* convey a vital lesson, laying the very foundation of Torah itself. מֹשֶׁה קִבֵּל תּוֹרָה מִסִּינַי, the mishnah states; not *at* Sinai or *from Hashem*, but ***from*** *Sinai*. What could this mean?

The Nesivos Sholom clarifies the mishnah's intention. It was "from Sinai" — that is, viewing and learning from Sinai — that Moshe drew inspiration to become the most suitable vessel to receive the Torah. He noticed that the majestic peaks were passed over, and the smaller Har Sinai was selected by Hashem. Moshe thereby discerned that "smallness" — humility — was the paramount quality for the giving of the Torah. Cultivating this trait, Moshe became the most humble man on the planet, the perfect candidate to accept the Torah.

Chachmah mei'ayin tavo, the *passuk* states in *Iyov*; Divine wisdom is achieved through *ayin*. Why is this trait so crucial, more so than any other? The *passuk* in *Tehillim* elucidates:

הָהָר חָמַד אֱלֹקִים לְשִׁבְתּוֹ...יִשְׁכֹּן לָנֶצַח. Har Sinai, reflecting the quality of *ayin*, serves as the "eternal base" of the Torah. This is what separates it from all other noble qualities. *Middos*, in general, important as they are, are subject to *shevirah*, as any entity possessing substance is susceptible to deterioration of some sort. *Ayin*, however, is immune in this regard; as inherently "nothing," it cannot be adversely affected by anything. Thus, this *middah* has a quality of eternity, which made Hashem desirous of utilizing it as a base for the giving of the Torah.

In discussing the essentiality of the *middah* of *ayin*, nothingness, it is important to draw distinctions. "Humility" borne from blatant lack of self-esteem is not the Torah's view of what *anivus* is all about. Even Moshe Rabbeinu, the quintessential *anav*, was certainly aware of his remarkable and unprecedented spiritual accomplishments; his *ayin* was not a product of self-delusion or denying his attainments. True humility entails a clear recognition of the greatness of Hashem; the clearer and more developed our awareness of His awesome Presence, the more we will be able to negate our Self to Him. Thus we may recognize our own achievements and talents while realizing at the same time that they all ultimately belong to and originate from the Creator. As such, we may surrender our Self, talents and all, to Hashem, subsuming our Self within Hashem's Presence, and attaining, in the process, the ultimate closeness to Him.

This idea also helps to explain why the Torah was given specifically on Yom Kippur. This day is the quintessential day of *ayin*, as we stand humbled before Hashem in genuine contrition. Thus, the *Kedushas Levi* remarks that one may only obtain atonement on this day through achieving at least a measure of *hisbatlus*. Such a state is impossible for someone who considers himself a *yeish*, that is, who has a mistaken impression that the individual himself is his own entity, able to wield his own power and abilities. But one who recognizes that he is totally beholden to Hashem, and that without His constant beneficence and supervision he is essentially nothing — such a person personifies the *middah* of *ayin*. As opposed to the *yeish* individual, the true *anav* has no barriers impeding his connection to Hashem. He can therefore exercise *hisbatlus*, becoming subsumed within His sacred Presence. Attached to the ultimate source of purity, his sins and imperfections disappear, and he obtains atonement and *d'veikus* with Hashem.

פרק א' משנה ב'
על שלשה דברים העולם עומד
The World Stands on Three Things

שִׁמְעוֹן הַצַּדִּיק הָיָה מִשְּׁיָרֵי כְנֶסֶת הַגְּדוֹלָה. הוּא הָיָה אוֹמֵר, עַל שְׁלשָׁה דְבָרִים הָעוֹלָם עוֹמֵד, עַל הַתּוֹרָה וְעַל הָעֲבוֹדָה וְעַל גְּמִילוּת חֲסָדִים:

Shimon the Righteous was from the remaining members of the Great Assembly. He would say: The world stands on three things: on Torah, Divine service, and acts of kindness.

GEMS FROM THE *SEFER NESIVOS SHOLOM*

SOURCES:

עַל שְׁלֹשָׁה דְבָרִים הָעוֹלָם קַיָּים, עַל הַדִּין וְעַל הָאֱמֶת וְעַל הַשָּׁלוֹם. (אבות א׳)

On three things the world endures – on justice, truth, and peace. (*Avos* 1)

וַיַּרְא אֱלֹקִים אֶת־הָאוֹר כִּי־טוֹב. (בראשית א׳ ד׳)

And G-d saw the light that it was good. (*Bereishis* 1:4)

וַיַּרְא אֱלֹקִים כִּי־טוֹב. (שם פסוקים י׳, י״ב, י״ח, כ״א, כ״ה)

And G-d saw that it was good. (*ibid.* v. 10, 12, 18, 21, 25)

וַיַּרְא אֱלֹקִים אֶת־כָּל־אֲשֶׁר עָשָׂה וְהִנֵּה־טוֹב מְאֹד וַיְהִי־עֶרֶב וַיְהִי־בֹקֶר יוֹם הַשִּׁשִּׁי. (שם פסוק ל״א)

And G-d saw all that He had made, and behold, it was very good. And it was evening and it was morning – the sixth day. (*ibid.* v. 31)

על שלשה דברים העולם עומד

The Three Pillars

Have you ever had a bad day? Most everyone has. What's the ideal method for dealing with one? Sometimes, when nothing is going right, the best idea seems to be to just crawl back into bed and try again tomorrow. This is human nature. If not literally going back to sleep, a person at times may feel like giving up, or at least — on an emotional level — not trying. Why fight your way through a day that you can feel will simply not be one marked by success and accomplishment?

In fact, this may very well be true. Some days we are going to accomplish less than others; ups and downs are an inevitable part of life. Nevertheless, from a Torah perspective, no concept could be considered more foreign than that of a simply useless, "throw-away" day. No matter how frustrating, it is imperative to try to achieve some goal, regardless how small, each and every day.

Moreover, *Chazal* have provided us with an actual guidepost of what is to be accomplished on a daily basis. The Nesivos Sholom reveals this "checklist" through a novel reading of the famous axiom of Shimon Hatzaddik in our mishnah: עַל שְׁלשָׁה דְבָרִים הָעוֹלָם עוֹמֵד, עַל הַתּוֹרָה וְעַל הָעֲבוֹדָה וְעַל גְּמִילוּת חֲסָדִים — *On three things the world stands: on Torah, Divine service, and acts of kindness.*

A major issue with which the *mefarshim* grapple is how this mishnah relates to a similar one that appears later. In the final mishnah of this *perek*, Rabban Shimon ben Gamliel also provides a list of three items essential to the world: עַל שְׁלשָׁה דְבָרִים הָעוֹלָם עוֹמֵד, עַל הַדִּין וְעַל הָאֱמֶת וְעַל הַשָּׁלוֹם — *On three things the world endures: on justice, truth, and peace.* In addition to listing different items, Rabban Shimon ben Gamliel's choice of wording also deviates from that of our mishnah. Shimon Hatzaddik speaks of those things upon which the world *omeid*, stands, while Rabban Shimon ben Gamliel discusses the things upon which the world *kayam*, endures. What is the difference, and to what exactly does each mishnah refer? The Nesivos Sholom clarifies the issue by offering an entirely new understanding of the word *olam* in our mishnah.

Mission Statement

The Arizal, quoted in the *sefer Yesod Ha'avodah* (section 4, chapter 1), relates a truism that is both sobering and empowering. Each and every person placed on this earth, from Adam Harishon until today, has been charged with a certain *tafkid*, a specific mission in *avodas Hashem* that can be carried out by him alone. This notion is not limited just to our overall lifetime; in addition to a Yid's general task, there is a new mission to accomplish for *each new day that dawns*. In this sense, each day, for every Jew, can be looked at as a *world* in and of itself, with its own duties, objectives, and accompanying challenges.

The concept is breathtaking to behold. Every day, another world to build! Miss one day, miss out on an entire world! An overwhelming thought indeed!

But on the other hand, consider the implications. Once a person realizes that each day has its own specific mission, there's no longer any reason to give up when encountering a day that seems not to be going as well as others. It can still be salvaged and transformed into a day of accomplishment. All that is expected of us is to achieve what we can in fulfillment of today's special *tafkid*.

What is the plan of action to ensure that no day is entirely wasted, and that the particular goals of each day are reached to whatever extent possible? The Nesivos Sholom explains that our mishnah is presenting us with a checklist, the three absolute musts, to which we may refer every single day. With these three tools, we can ensure that the *olam* — the miniature world we must daily construct within ourselves — will *stand* in the face of the attempted sabotage of the *yetzer hara*.

The mishnah's listing of *three* essentials is no arbitrary matter. They correspond to the three major elements which make up the human being, through which we function and serve our Creator. The brain controls our intellectual activities, processing and analyzing information, as we try to understand the world around us. The heart controls our emotions, directing how we feel about ourselves, others, and every scenario we encounter in our lives. And the limbs serve to translate our thoughts and feelings into concrete action.

These three personal elements can be molded and directed toward the service of Hashem by following the three dictates of our mishnah. In-depth Torah study is, of course, the highest possible use of the mind. The emotions can be directed toward Hashem by crying out and clinging to Him through sincere prayer. And the limbs can be perfected in His service by using them for acts of loving-kindness.

And while the three items of our mishnah each principally relate to and elevate one aspect of a person, their effect is not limited to that aspect alone. Torah study is primarily a function of the mind and thus infuses it with especial sanctity, but it sheds its light on a person's remaining components, as well. As the Maharal writes (*Derech Chaim*, ch. 2), true devotion to Torah transforms one's entire essence, down to one's very flesh. So, too, *tefillah* (prayer) affects the entire body, not limiting its reach to a person's heart. As the *passuk* states in *Tehillim* (63:2), צָמְאָה לְךָ נַפְשִׁי כָּמַהּ לְךָ בְשָׂרִי — *My soul thirsts for You (Hashem), my **flesh** yearns for You*. When the heart and soul are fully dedicated to connecting with Hashem, even the flesh joins in the yearning. And the use of the limbs for *gemilus chassadim* likewise has an effect on the intellect and emotions.

It must be noted, however, that the three items do not operate independently of each other. To attain true *shleimus* (completeness), all three must be present and working in tandem. Without the intellectual aspect of Torah, for example, even the heart and limbs cannot function at their full spiritual capacity. And the aspects of *tefillah* and *gemilus chassadim* are likewise necessary to form the complete unit of an *oveid Hashem* (servant of Hashem). This idea is similar to the *Chovos Halevavos's* characterization (*Sha'ar Haprishus*, chapter 5), in which the various *middos* are likened to a string of pearls. If just one of them becomes detached, the others will fall off along with it. For the structure to be sound, all interdependent parts must be firmly in place. This is true of the makeup of a person's character and of the implementation of the three elements, as well.

This unity of the three elements is essential not just in the long-term, but must be manifest each and every day. The Shl'ah remarks that if a Jew goes one day without performing an act of *chessed* on behalf of his fellow, he has skipped a day in his life. This is derived from the *passuk* that states (*Tehillim* 52:3), חֶסֶד קֵל כָּל־הַיּוֹם — *Hashem's kindness is every day.* Our lives depend on Hashem's everlasting kindnesses, which He bestows upon us every day. The conduit through which Hashem's kindness is channeled to us is the emulation of this trait — that is, engaging in kindness ourselves. Thus, to be worthy of "Hashem's kindness every day," we must likewise perform kindness every day.

The Nesivos Sholom explains that this is true of all the elements sustaining the personal world that is each day of a Jew's life. It is imperative for us to find, on a daily basis, at least one small issue about which to *daven* with all our heart, thereby drawing closer to Hashem. And of course, we must find time every day for learning Torah. We can thus enlist the intellect, emotions, and actions in Hashem's service, and through them work to complete our individual, daily *tafkid*.

This, then, is the full import of Shimon Hatzaddik's teaching. At the end of the *perek*, Rabban Shimon ben Gamliel lists the items that enable the world to *kayam*, endure. That is, for the world's inhabitants to function as a harmonious society, it is essential that they adhere to the dictates of justice, truth, and peace. Shimon Hatzaddik, on the other hand, is discussing the personal world of every Jew, the formula that guides each of us on our day's mission, setting the stage for its fulfillment. He relates those elements upon which the world "stands"; that is, our personal world will be established on a firm and complete foundation, ready for us to build upon, strengthen, and accomplish. Through following Shimon Hatzaddik's formula for success, we can literally create worlds!

The World Is Good

An even deeper layer of meaning can be perceived in Shimon Hatzaddik's teaching.

The story is told of Aristotle, the famous Greek philosopher: His disciple once chanced upon him as he was engaged in some unseemly behavior. Disturbed by the unpleasant discovery, the disciple questioned the master about it. How can the great ethicist, who spent a lifetime contemplating and lecturing on the proper modes of conduct, stoop to such levels in his personal life? Aristotle did not deny the hypocrisy inherent in his actions, but excused himself with the following pronouncement, "If you can show me a mathematician who is a parallelogram, then I, too, will practice what I preach!"

In truth, Aristotle's rationalization is not entirely off the mark. Why must there be a connection between pondering and teaching ethics as a science, and applying the results of one's study to one's private behavior? Regarding any secular science, the conceptual need not have any relevance for the actual. One can spend a lifetime on any particular subject without it affecting one's inner essence or behavior — no more than a mathematician will ever become one with his work.

When it comes to Torah, however, the opposite is true. Whereas secular disciplines are entirely abstract, Torah is inner-directed. *Chazal* teach us (*Avos D'Rebbi Nosson* 24:4) that when we learn Torah in our youth, it actually becomes absorbed into our bloodstream, sanctifying our very essence. This is because learning Torah is not merely an intellectual pursuit, but an exercise in connecting with the Divine. When we dedicate ourselves to Torah, we are exposed to the ultimate *Tov*, Good. Thus, by absorbing its teachings, we can bring out our best, actually transforming ourselves into the essence of Good.

In truth, the transformation of a human being into *Tov* goes against the laws of nature. The *passuk* tells us that man is born with a natural predisposition toward evil: כִּי יֵצֶר לֵב הָאָדָם רַע מִנְּעֻרָיו — *For the inclination of a man's heart is for evil, from his youth* (*Bereishis* 8:21). Yet this is itself our obligation and life's work: to change our core tendency from bad to good. In so doing, we not only uplift our individual souls, but we bring the entire purpose of the creation of the world to fruition.

The Nesivos Sholom expounds on this idea, demonstrating how our personal struggles and efforts of transformation fulfill the purpose of Creation. It was for the good that exists within it that the world was created in the first place. Thus we see at the completion of each step of *ma'aseh bereishis*, the Torah records, *Vayar Elokim ki tov* — "Hashem saw that it was good." Every single aspect of the created world — every hill, stream, penguin, and tree — was put here for one purpose only: to contribute in some way to the realization of good in This World.

Let us take this notion one step further. At the completion of the entirety of *ma'aseh bereishis*, the Torah proclaims (*Bereishis* 1:31), *V'hinei tov me'od* — "and behold, it was very good." The Midrash (*Bereishis Rabbah* 9:12) points out that the Hebrew letters that make up the word **me'od** — *mem, aleph, daled* — when rearranged, can also form the word **Adam** (Man). The ultimate, end result of creation is Man; as the goal of creation is to bring out the *Tov* in the world, perforce the primary objective is to bring out the spark of good within Man.

This is no simple feat, however. Man is not born with his good nature inherently predominant, as we've discussed. What, indeed, is the method for changing the natural order, and transforming a person into an intrinsically good entity? The answer is provided through Shmuel Hakatan's teaching.

The process may be long and arduous, and it must be thorough. But it is a crucial undertaking, and it can be done. Through the three dictates of the mishnah, a person can effect this monumental transformation in every aspect of his being. The Maharal explains that for *avodah* to be complete, it must relate to three areas: our self, our fellow, and our Creator. We have already noted above the transformative power on our self that is effected through Torah. Through sincere *tefillah*, we attain *d'veikus* to the Creator before Whom we pour out our heart. By thus clinging to Hashem, the ultimate entity of Good, we likewise become an essence of good. As such, we have perfected and brought out the good in the aspect of our relationship with the Creator. And through the performance of acts of kindness, we likewise achieve inherent goodness in this aspect of relating to our fellow Jews.

על שלשה דברים העולם עומד

Furthermore, as mentioned previously, the three items of our mishnah correspond to and elevate the three components of human functionality. The Torah sanctifies our intellect, *tefillah* affects our heartfelt emotions, and the acts of kindness elevate our limbs, which performed those acts.

Thus, Shimon Hatzaddik provides the formula through which we can so thoroughly and completely transform our self into an essence of good, in all of our various aspects. Thereby, we perfect and solidify our self, our personal *olam*. And in bringing out our inherent goodness, we thereby validate the existence of the entire world! The purpose of the world's creation is the good within it, and humanity is the end result of creation. Therefore, when Man is Good — the goal has been reached!

In Summary

It is interesting how nearly identical is the format at the beginning and the end of the first *perek* of *Pirkei Avos*. Mishnayos towards the beginning and end of the *perek* both deal with a list of three items that are essential to the *olam*. In truth, however, they focus on different messages. At the end of the *perek*, Rabban Shimon ben Gamliel discusses the three things upon which the world *kayam*, endures, relating the items necessary for a stable, functioning society: justice, truth, and peace. Shimon Hatzaddik, in our mishnah, speaks of the elements upon which the world *omeid*, stands, and, as the Nesivos Sholom explains, he refers to a different "world" entirely.

The focus of our mishnah is the task of the individual, himself a "miniature world" of sorts. We each are sent to This World with a mission to fulfill. Each and every day, we are charged with a new, unique mission. Thus, every new day is transformed into a new "world" for the *oveid Hashem* to construct and perfect. And the guidelines for the fulfillment of this mission — the elements upon which each new "world" stands — is the formula Shimon Hatzaddik provides in our mishnah.

How can we complete our day's mission? Even if things seem to have started off on the "wrong foot," is there something that can be done to salvage that day and ensure that it will be productive and full of accomplishments? If we are careful to apply the dictates of our mishnah — to engage in Torah, *avodah*, and *gemilus chassadim* each and every day — we will be assured of a mission accomplished.

It is important to keep in mind, however, that for the mission to be successfully completed in all of its fullness, all three elements must be manifest. For the items of the mishnah correspond to the three aspects of a person, and sanctify and elevate these components. Torah is primarily associated with the mind, infusing the intellect with a Divine light. The same is accomplished for the emotions through heartfelt *tefillah*, and for the limbs through the acts of kindness they perform.

And through the fulfillment of these three elements, a Yid — and all aspects of his person — can undergo a complete transformation, emerging as the essence of good. For such is the nature of the elements of Hashem's service. As opposed to the secular disciplines, the aspects of Torah have an effect on the inner essence of a person. This is true, as well, of the elements of *tefillah* and *chessed*. These three entities can help transform the mind, heart, and physicality of a Yid into inherent goodness.

This, in fact, is the very purpose of creation — to bring out the good within it. Man is the pinnacle and ultimate purpose of creation. Thus, by perfecting and transforming the "personal world" of a Yid into the essence of goodness, the entire purpose and goal of creation is fulfilled.

פרק א׳ משנה ג׳
הוו כעבדים המשמשין שלא על מנת לקבל פרס
Be Like Servants Who Serve Not for the Sake of Receiving a Reward

אַנְטִיגְנוֹס אִישׁ סוֹכוֹ קִבֵּל מִשִּׁמְעוֹן הַצַּדִּיק. הוּא הָיָה אוֹמֵר, אַל תִּהְיוּ כַעֲבָדִים הַמְשַׁמְּשִׁין אֶת הָרַב עַל מְנָת לְקַבֵּל פְּרָס, אֶלָּא הֱווּ כַעֲבָדִים הַמְשַׁמְּשִׁין אֶת הָרַב שֶׁלֹּא עַל מְנָת לְקַבֵּל פְּרָס, וִיהִי מוֹרָא שָׁמַיִם עֲלֵיכֶם:

Antignos of Socho received from Shimon the Righteous. He would say: Do not be like servants who serve the master in order to receive a reward, rather be like servants who serve the master not in order to receive a reward. And the fear of Heaven should be upon you.

GEMS FROM THE *SEFER NESIVOS SHOLOM*

SOURCES:

הָעוֹלָם הַבָּא אֵין בּוֹ לֹא אֲכִילָה וְלֹא שְׁתִיָּה וְלֹא פְּרִיָּה וּרְבִיָּה וְלֹא מַשָּׂא וּמַתָּן וְלֹא קִנְאָה וְלֹא שִׂנְאָה וְלֹא תַחֲרוּת, אֶלָּא צַדִּיקִים יוֹשְׁבִין וְעַטְרוֹתֵיהֶם בְּרָאשֵׁיהֶם וְנֶהֱנִים מִזִּיו הַשְּׁכִינָה. (ברכות י״ז.)

In the future world there is neither eating, drinking, propagation, business activity, jealousy, hatred, nor competition. Rather, the righteous sit with their crowns upon their heads, and delight in the radiance of the *Shechinah* (Divine Presence). (*Berachos* 17a)

עוֹלָמְךָ תִּרְאֶה בְּחַיֶּיךָ. (שם)

You shall witness your world in your lifetime. (*ibid.*)

אָנֹכִי ה׳ אֱלֹקֶיךָ אֲשֶׁר הוֹצֵאתִיךָ מֵאֶרֶץ מִצְרַיִם מִבֵּית עֲבָדִים. לֹא־יִהְיֶה לְךָ אֱלֹהִים אֲחֵרִים עַל־פָּנָי. (שמות כ׳ ב׳, ג׳)

I am Hashem your G-d Who took you out from the land of Egypt, from the house of bondage. You shall have no other gods before Me. (*Shemos* 20:2, 3)

הוו כעבדים המשמשין שלא על מנת לקבל פרס

What's the Prize?

One of the starkest distinctions manifest between Yisroel and the nations is the perspective on life. By and large — and especially in current times — the world around us is steeped in materialism, with pleasure and "getting ahead" as the foremost of goals. In contrast, the *ma'aminim bnei ma'amanim* (believers, children of believers) have quite a different set of priorities. The immortal words of the *Mesillas Yesharim* ingrained on their consciousness, they are well aware that This World is not "it." It is eternal life in the World to Come that is paramount, while this life is regarded chiefly as an arena for preparation through mitzvah observance.

These two worlds, of course, are separated by a wide gulf. This World, the domain of the living, is the world we know and experience, of course. The nature of the Next World is largely a concealed matter, which no mortal eye has beheld. While firm in our faith of the infinite delight awaiting the righteous in the Next World, our knowledge of this entity perforce remains limited.

But the blissful existence of the Next World need not remain a thing entirely beyond our current reach. The mishnah discloses how these two worlds can actually intersect, to be experienced and enjoyed by the true servant of Hashem.

The mishnah in *Pirkei Avos* (1:3) sets forth a most compelling goal in our service of Hashem. Antignos of Socho states, אַל תִּהְיוּ כַּעֲבָדִים הַמְשַׁמְּשִׁין אֶת הָרַב עַל מְנָת לְקַבֵּל פְּרָס, אֶלָּא הֱווּ כַּעֲבָדִים הַמְשַׁמְּשִׁין אֶת הָרַב שֶׁלֹּא עַל מְנָת לְקַבֵּל פְּרָס, וִיהִי מוֹרָא שָׁמַיִם עֲלֵיכֶם — *Do not be as servants who serve their master for the sake of reward; rather be like servants who serve their master not for the sake of reward. And the fear of Heaven should be upon you.*

The Nesivos Sholom *ztz"l* raises several questions on these sage words.

The mishnah's message seems fairly self-evident. What, after all, is it advocating? That one's *avodah* should be pristine. Is that something we didn't already know? Anyone with even minimal sense could tell you that the prime reason a Jew must serve Hashem is because Hashem told him to, not because there is a reward in store for him. Why is it necessary to stress this point?

Antignos's final statement, וִיהִי מוֹרָא שָׁמַיִם עֲלֵיכֶם — *And the fear of Heaven should be upon you*, appears similarly superfluous. The Oral Torah, as embodied in the Mishnah, serves to interpret the laws and meaning of the Written Torah; it does not merely repeat what is already stated explicitly. The commandment to fear Hashem is stated numerous times throughout Tanach, such as, אֶת־ה' אֱלֹקֶיךָ תִּירָא — *Hashem, your G-d, you should fear* (Devarim 10:20), and, יִשְׂרָאֵל מָה ה' אֱלֹקֶיךָ שֹׁאֵל מֵעִמָּךְ כִּי אִם־לְיִרְאָה אֶת־ה' אֱלֹקֶיךָ — *What does Hashem your G-d ask of you; only to fear Hashem...* (ibid. v. 12). What new understanding is provided by these words of Antignos?

In order for our *avodas Hashem* to be complete, it must be comprised of both fear *and* love of Hashem. Why does Antignos instruct us only to fear Hashem, omitting the other essential component?

Through some illustrative examples, the Noam Elimelech (*Parshas Terumah*) sheds much light on the mishnah. He portrays two different *Yidden*, each one meticulous in his observance. The *avodas Hashem* of the first one is marked by a quality of dryness. He fulfills all the mitzvos with great care, leaving no room for error. But he fails to achieve the ultimate goal of connecting to Hashem, for which strict observance alone is insufficient. Of course, he will merit abundant reward in the World to Come for his loyal service. Lacking a true love for and enjoyment of the mitzvos, however, he derives no inherent pleasure from his observance in This World. It was such an individual the mishnah was referring to when it spoke of *avodah* "for the sake of a reward." For this was the prime impetus — and indeed, sole benefit — this *oveid* received from his *avodah*.

There is another path in *avodas Hashem* described by the Noam Elimelech; that is, serving Hashem with a focus on cultivating a relationship with Him, to cleave to Him through the fulfillment of His will. Every mitzvah presents a remarkable opportunity to become that much closer to his Creator. For an individual with this type of outlook, serving Hashem will be an enthralling and fulfilling experience even in the here and now. It will serve as a reward in and of itself, a pleasure of the greatest magnitude.

Seeing "the World"

In effect, then, this latter type of servant will experience *Olam Haba* already in *Olam Hazeh* (This World). For what, ultimately, is the reward in the World to Come?

הָעוֹלָם הַבָּא אֵין בּוֹ לֹא אֲכִילָה וְלֹא שְׁתִיָּה וְלֹא פְּרִיָּה וּרְבִיָּה וְלֹא מַשָּׂא וּמַתָּן וְלֹא קִנְאָה וְלֹא שִׂנְאָה וְלֹא תַחֲרוּת, אֶלָּא צַדִּיקִים יוֹשְׁבִין וְעַטְרוֹתֵיהֶם בְּרָאשֵׁיהֶם וְנֶהֱנִים מִזִּיו הַשְּׁכִינָה.

In the future world there is neither eating, drinking, propagation, business activity, jealousy, hatred, nor competition. Rather, the righteous sit with their crowns upon their heads, **and delight in the radiance of the Shechinah** (*Berachos* 17a).

While only a *neshamah* can completely bask in the *Shechinah* with no other thoughts or needs, it is possible for a living human to achieve a real semblance of this very phenomenon. Our ultimate purpose and mission in This World is to cleave to Hashem, a state of being attained through the particular form of *avodah* championed by the mishnah. When a person does mitzvos with the singular aim of forging a lasting connection with Hashem, he creates a lifetime of reward for himself; one that precedes the final reward waiting for him in *Olam Haba*, as even now he is attached to the Divine Presence. *Olamcha sir'eh b'chayecha* — "You will see your world in your lifetime," *Chazal* say further (*ibid.*), referring to this remarkable opportunity to experience the ultimate bliss of *Olam Haba* right here in *Olam Hazeh*.

With this insight, we find that the teaching of Antignos is astounding indeed. Consider the incredible irony manifest in the contrast between these varying paths in *avodas Hashem*. In using the term *pras*, Antignos refers only to the reward attained in *Olam Haba*. If we serve עַל מְנָת לְקַבֵּל פְּרָס we will receive that — and only that. We will live a life of scrupulous observance, replete with *chumros* (stringencies), but ultimately without much meaning or vitality. But if we serve שֶׁלֹּא עַל מְנָת לְקַבֵּל פְּרָס, to cleave to Hashem in the present, we will experience a Gan Eden-like existence while our body yet lives — in addition to the ultimate *pras* that awaits us in the Afterlife.

In fact, in this latter circumstance, the whole notion of "reward" is hardly applicable. What is there even to discuss? No reward could possibly surpass our achievement and current bliss! Through our *d'veikus*, we bask in the *Shechinah*, the ultimate imaginable pleasure; any other "reward" pales in comparison. Such *avodah* can truly be characterized as "not for the sake of reward," for there is no greater delight than this form of *avodah*. We serve Hashem with every fiber of our being, deriving in turn immeasurable benefit from our relationship with Him every moment of our life.

Contradiction or Complement?

This remarkable insight carries through to the end of the mishnah. Antignos's final statement, וִיהִי מוֹרָא שָׁמַיִם עֲלֵיכֶם — *May the fear of Heaven be upon you*, appeared puzzling. Why simply repeat a familiar and explicit Biblical exhortation? And what happened to *ahavah* (love)? In light of the above, we see that, in fact, the entire first half of the mishnah was advocating the most exalted level of *ahavas Hashem* (love of Hashem), reflecting a form of service so infused with love of Hashem as to intimate a blissful-like existence. And it is for this very reason Antignos *had* to bring *yirah* (fear) into the picture. With the focus on the intense love we must cultivate in order to feel pleasure in serving Hashem, we could mistakenly conclude that this exalted quality is paramount — to the exclusion of all else. Granted, the mitzvah of fearing Hashem is written in the Torah; but perhaps *yirah* is not necessary for one who has climbed to the much higher rung of supreme *ahavah* highlighted in the mishnah so far. Thus, Antignos had to remind us that love is still only half the equation. In order to serve Hashem perfectly, we must feel awe and fear, as well as love, in following His Torah.

These two emotions — *ahavah* and *yirah* — may seem to contradict each other. Yet they are paired together numerous times throughout Tanach. *Akeidas Yitzchak* (binding of Yitzchak) serves as a prime example. Through Avraham's successful completion of the previous trials, Hashem was satisfied with Avraham's joy in serving Him through love. Hashem then felt the time had come for Avraham to demonstrate the completeness of his *avodas Hashem* through the added element of fear. Thus, Hashem issued him the almost inconceivable command to sacrifice his son. And so when Avraham showed his willingness to do even this, Hashem declared: עַתָּה יָדַעְתִּי כִּי־יְרֵא אֱלֹקִים אַתָּה — *Now I know that you are G-d-fearing* (*Bereishis* 22:12).

The truth is that neither element is more important or more necessary for *avodas Hashem* than the other. Their equality is emphasized in the first two of the *Aseres Hadibros* (Ten Commandments). The positive commandment of אָנֹכִי ה׳ — *I am Hashem* (*Shemos* 20:2), refers to serving Hashem through *ahavah*, while the prohibition of לֹא־יִהְיֶה לְךָ אֱלֹהִים אֲחֵרִים — *You shall not have other gods* (*ibid.* v. 3), represents service through fear. These directives were uttered simultaneously, illustrating that they are equally essential aspects in serving the Creator.

Thus far, the Nesivos Sholom has interpreted the mishnah's final statement as a reaction to the theme espoused in the first part. He concludes his discourse on this mishnah with an alternate explanation, in which the end of the mishnah delivers its own message, not connected with the beginning.

There are two aspects of fear that can be used to adhere to Hashem's commandments. A person could be afraid of the consequences he will have to face for committing an *aveirah*, or he could fear the *aveirah* itself. Either form of fear could be utilized to overcome his *yetzer hara* and refrain from sin.

It would seem to follow that, in this respect, *yirah* differs from *ahavah*. *Yirah*, it appears, is only necessary as a tool with which to fight the *yetzer hara*. It need not be ever-present, but merely called upon periodically whenever temptation presents itself. This is contrary to the emotion of love, which we know must be constantly sensed, present in our minds and hearts at all times. While both love and fear are equally necessary, there is an inherent difference — one may assume — in the manner in which they are employed: love must be a permanent part of a Jew's conscience, while fear is a tool to be wielded as necessary.

This is far from the truth.

It is true that the ultimate level of *ahavas Hashem* is an intense, constant love that does not diminish with time. In *Hilchos Teshuvah*, the Rambam describes true love of Hashem as an unending yearning for a relationship with Him, to the point where one pines for Hashem's love as a sick person does for a cure. Serving Hashem with love means to do so — בְּשִׁבְתְּךָ בְּבֵיתֶךָ וּבְלֶכְתְּךָ בַדֶּרֶךְ וּבְשָׁכְבְּךָ וּבְקוּמֶךָ — *When you sit in your house, when you go on your way, when you lie down and when you rise* (*Devarim* 6:7), as we recite in the *Shema* twice daily.

The mishnah comes to teach us that contrary to what we may have thought, *yirah* also shares this aspect of constancy. Therefore, Antignos specifically spoke of *mora Shamayim*, the fear of Heaven. In so doing, he was introducing another facet of *yirah*, the fear of Heaven. Previously we discussed *yiras cheit* (fear of sin) and *yiras onesh* (fear of punishment), worthy and necessary elements whose utility is basically limited to the periodic bouts with the *yetzer hara*. *Mora Shamayim*, on the other hand, is not time- or circumstance-dependent. It is the fear of Hashem Himself, of Whose Presence one must always be aware and in awe. This is what Antignos aimed to remind us: as with *ahavas Hashem*, this type of *yirah* must constantly be upon us, not allowing it to leave our consciousness.

Through this unique combination of love and fear of Hashem — a constant awe of His Presence and an unending yearning — we may be able to forge a strong connection with Him. And this lifetime relationship can be maintained and strengthened through the same fear and love that created it in the first place.

In Summary

In exhorting us to serve Hashem altruistically, Antignos Ish Socho also reveals a tremendous secret. He demonstrates how we may acquire and experience *Olam Haba* while still living in This World.

הוו כעבדים המשמשין שלא על מנת לקבל פרס

The Nesivos Sholom cites the Noam Elimelech, who understands the mishnah in this light.

The decisive factor is the aim and focus of our service of Hashem. We can observe all the mitzvos meticulously, even adhering to numerous stringencies. But if our *avodah* lacks the proper purpose and heart, it will remain a dry exercise. If our prime impetus is to obtain reward — to the exclusion of focusing on our relationship with the Creator — we will merit *Olam Haba*, but our life of service in This World will lack real meaning. However, if we serve Hashem in order to cleave to Him, setting our connection with Hashem as our primary objective, we will find that our very life in This World will be transformed. The delight of the World to Come takes the form of basking in the radiance of the *Shechinah*; through *d'veikus* to Hashem in This World, we experience a real foretaste of what awaits us in the World of *neshamos*. And this is true fortune indeed, as we merit *Olam Haba* in the World to Come and in this life as well!

Following such a compelling description of pure delight — a life of reveling in the service to Hashem, fulfilling His will with joy and intense love — we may have concluded that our *avodah* is complete. Antignos reminds us that all the same, the true *oveid* must not neglect the other essential component of *avodas Hashem*. Thus he concludes his teaching with an exhortation that וִיהִי מוֹרָא שָׁמַיִם עֲלֵיכֶם — *and the fear of Heaven should be upon you.*

פרק א' משנה י"ב, י"ג, י"ד
ג' המימרות דהלל
Hillel's Three Statements

הִלֵּל וְשַׁמַּאי קִבְּלוּ מֵהֶם. הִלֵּל אוֹמֵר, הֱוֵי מִתַּלְמִידָיו שֶׁל אַהֲרֹן, אוֹהֵב שָׁלוֹם וְרוֹדֵף שָׁלוֹם, אוֹהֵב אֶת הַבְּרִיּוֹת וּמְקָרְבָן לַתּוֹרָה:

הוּא הָיָה אוֹמֵר, נְגַד שְׁמָא, אֲבַד שְׁמֵהּ. וּדְלָא מוֹסִיף, יָסִיף. וּדְלָא יָלֵיף, קְטָלָא חַיָּב. וּדְאִשְׁתַּמֵּשׁ בְּתַגָּא, חָלָף:

הוּא הָיָה אוֹמֵר, אִם אֵין אֲנִי לִי, מִי לִי. וּכְשֶׁאֲנִי לְעַצְמִי, מָה אֲנִי. וְאִם לֹא עַכְשָׁיו, אֵימָתַי:

Hillel and Shamai received from them. Hillel says: Be from the disciples of Aharon: Loving peace, pursuing peace, loving people, and drawing them close to Torah.

He would say: One whose name becomes great, his name will be lost; one who does not increase (his learning), it will decrease; one who does not learn incurs the death penalty; and one who makes use of the crown, will pass on.

He would say: If I am not for me – who is for me? And if I am for myself – what am I? And if not now – when?

GEMS FROM THE *SEFER NESIVOS SHOLOM*

SOURCES:

סוּר מֵרָע וַעֲשֵׂה־טוֹב. (תהלים ל״ד ט״ו)

Turn from evil, and do good. *(Tehillim 34:15)*

עֲשֵׂה לְךָ רַב, וּקְנֵה לְךָ חָבֵר. (אבות א׳)

Make for yourself a *rav*, and acquire for yourself a friend. *(Avos 1)*

אַל תֹּאמַר לִכְשֶׁאֶפָּנֶה אֶשְׁנֶה, שֶׁמָּא לֹא תִפָּנֶה. (שם ב׳)

Do not say, "I will learn when I am not preoccupied," for you may always be preoccupied. *(ibid. 2)*

הֵיכִי דָמֵי בַּעַל תְּשׁוּבָה? ... בְּאוֹתָהּ אִשָּׁה, בְּאוֹתוֹ פֶּרֶק, בְּאוֹתוֹ מָקוֹם. (יומא פ״ו:)

What is a proper *ba'al teshuvah*? ... (One who, after stumbling the first time, is confronted with) the same woman, the same circumstance, and the same location. *(Yuma 86b)*

ג' המימרות דהלל

This famous adage of Hillel Hazakein certainly appears quite cryptic. What is meant by being "to oneself"? And is Hillel advising us to embrace this attitude or distance ourselves from it? An initial reading seems to give us contradictory messages. "If I am not for myself, who am I?" This implies that a failure to be "for oneself" is problematic. But the next statement seems to indicate the opposite: "If I am to myself, what am I?"

The Nesivos Sholom sheds light on the matter. He explains that the two opposite viewpoints each have their place, depending on which area of *avodas Hashem* is our focus. When correctly applied, the attitude of *ani li* is crucial to success; when misapplied, it brings failure in its wake. But we are getting ahead of ourselves. Let us work through his thought process one enlightening step at a time.

Together and Alone

Certain underlying principles regarding Hashem's guidance of the world serve as the backdrop for Hillel's teaching. The *Ribono Shel Olam* set up This World to function through a system of *mashpia* and *mekabel*, bestowing and receiving. That is to say, two interrelated processes must be working together for any productive growth to take place. There must be an entity that gives forth and another that receives the bounty and utilizes it constructively. We can behold a prime example of this phenomenon by simply observing the plant world. A tree doesn't spontaneously appear and grow by itself, but follows a specific pattern. The heavens (as the *mashpia*) send forth rain, the soil (the *mekabel*) accepts it, and together they create a living, majestic being. It is easy to see how each on their own would be useless. To merely give, with no receiver on the other end, is futile; to accomplish, without an outside source providing raw material and nutrients, is impossible.

This complementary relationship, the *mashpia* and the *mekabel*, is a necessary element in all fields of accomplishment. No growth can take place in a vacuum; multiple factors are required for the construction of anything useful. The reason this is so is that there is only one Being in the world who is truly One and so entirely self-sufficient — the *Ribono Shel Olam* Himself. All of His creations, on the other hand, are compound entities, needing the assistance of others in order to thrive.

This same unavoidable fact of life holds true, as well, in the area that is our primary mission in life — growth in *avodas Hashem*. On our own, it is not possible to climb the spiritual ladder, to amass any notable achievements in the lifelong endeavor of coming nearer to the Creator. For this, it is necessary to seek guidance and encouragement from other qualified trailblazers. In other words, exactly what Hillel was conveying in the second part of his statement: *U'ch'she'ani l'atzmi, mah ani.* When I am "to myself," going it totally alone and relying solely on my personal input — "what am I," really?

To properly appreciate the full statement of Hillel, we introduce another elementary notion. In *Tehillim* (34:15), Dovid Hamelech sets forth two major components — category headings, if you will — that define the lifelong mission of an *oveid Hashem*. He states succinctly: סוּר מֵרָע וַעֲשֵׂה־טוֹב — *Turn from evil, and do good.* The former is an exhortation to avoid all actions prohibited by the Torah; the latter urges us to continuously reach higher, striving to increase the scope and intensity of our proactive *avodah*.

Now we can understand the dichotomy of our mishnah. When it comes to *sur meira*, a person actually *is* entirely on his own. He is the target the *yetzer hara* seeks to vanquish, and so only he himself can successfully fend it off. Of course, he can gain inspiration by observing other great *yirei Shamayim* (G-d-fearing individuals), or be motivated by a forceful *mussar shmuess*. But ultimately, when temptation seeks to ensnare an individual, no one else can defeat his *yetzer hara* for him. *Sur meira* is an intensely personal affair; the battle is for each of us to win or lose on our own. Hillel declares as much when he states, *Im ein ani li, mi li?* If I don't fight the good fight for myself, no one else can do it for me.

The next part of Hillel's teaching concerns the other aspect of *avodah* — *aseih tov*. Here, the opposite approach holds true, and the input and assistance of others is paramount. While self-reliance has its place, here is where the *mashpia/mekabel* nexus really comes into play. A person cannot build himself up, reaching higher levels of *kedushah* (sanctity), without tapping into the recourse that a *mashpia* has to offer — any more than the earth can produce a tree without rain supplied by the heavens. *U'ch'she'ani l'atzmi, mah ani?* If I remain on my own, what, indeed, may I become?

And so, *Chazal* instruct anyone with an aspiration for growth: עֲשֵׂה לְךָ רַב, וּקְנֵה לְךָ חָבֵר — *Make for yourself a rav, and acquire for yourself a friend*. When we set out to improve ourselves, our first step must be to look towards our network of family, *rabbeim*, and friends for guidance and encouragement. When we see a *ma'alah* (virtue) in someone else — a friend who excels in *chessed*, a family member whose *tefillah* is exemplary, a *chavrusa* (study partner) who learns with *hasmodah* (diligence), or a *rebbi* who teaches with passion — we can acquire new goals and aspirations. Then we can turn to this same network for advice and strategies for developing into what we now know we want to become.

By seeking outside inspiration, our aims can be crystallized. Without it, it becomes very difficult to visualize what it is we are striving for, let alone actually fulfill our lofty ambitions entirely by ourselves. What will be the result of "going it alone"? What will the final product end up looking like? Hillel sums it up: *U'ch'she'ani l'atzmi, mah ani?* Without the input of others, what am I, indeed?

"Kosher" Procrastination

V'im lo achshav, eimasai — "If not now, when?"

This pithy statement sums up what may very well be one of the most essential — yet most easily overlooked — principles of *avodah*. An appreciation of the depth of its message can literally inspire an entirely new approach to life.

Does that sound hyperbolic? You be the judge. Let us take a closer look at the mishnah through the Nesivos Sholom's point of view.

The tendency to put things off is part of the natural human condition. Some fortunate individuals may be somewhat less afflicted than others, but, by and large, it's a fairly universal phenomenon.

Obviously, Hillel's exhortation warns against this behavior, as he implores a person to seize the initiative for positive action.

Truth be told, however, there are different forms of procrastinating. It is common to push things off simply out of a lack of motivation — we're "not in the mood." If not now, when? Well, maybe later. Tomorrow. Or next week.

But sometimes the temptation to delay is of a much "loftier" variety. Rather than the product of simple laziness, a person at times — or often — has a legitimate complication, one that frames the delay as a somewhat reasonable prospect. If not now, when? When my headache goes away. When the deal goes through. When the kids get older. When it is not so very difficult!

This attitude is quite natural and can even sometimes seem justifiable. We all go through stages that make it very difficult to concentrate on our true goals. It doesn't even necessarily have to be for a bad reason. Perhaps someone is busy preparing for a child's wedding. A day marked by the stress of planning, making phone calls, and addressing invitations; under these circumstances, it is very easy to rationalize collapsing into bed at night without having fulfilled one's daily learning protocol. He may even make up his mind to learn extra later on — to catch up on what he missed when he doesn't have so much on his mind. Sounds reasonable, and if he indeed follows through, what harm has been done?

Or imagine someone on his way home, exhausted from a particularly difficult day. Suddenly, an opportunity to perform a *chessed* for another Yid presents itself. This commuter truly wants to help others and, in fact, does so all the time. Right now, however, he is just too tired. What's wrong with passing up on the *chessed* just this once and leaving it for someone else to do? After all, it's just too difficult right now.

These are not examples of garden-variety dallying, but the result of seemingly legitimate issues! However, explains the Nesivos Sholom, there is an inherent problem with this mindset. The challenges depicted above are certainly understandable, but what these individuals don't realize is that they are entirely missing out on a major aspect of their particular *avodah*! True, this one might be able to accomplish the same learning later, when the *chasunah* (wedding) is safely in the rear-view mirror; the other can do other *chassadim* a different time. But they never will have fulfilled the *avodah* of learning under stress! We don't look to make it more difficult — but when the occasion arises of its own, it is actually a remarkable opportunity. *Im lo achshav — eimasai?* Perhaps Hashem desired for these individuals to perform *chessed* specifically while exhausted! Pushing off the mitzvah until later — even if, theoretically, they were to fulfill it then — misses the point completely. For then they missed out on the opportunity of performing *avodah* even under difficult conditions.

This idea may be reflected in another statement of Hillel's elsewhere in *Avos* (2:5): אַל תֹּאמַר לִכְשֶׁאֶפָּנֶה אֶשְׁנֶה, שֶׁמָּא לֹא תִפָּנֶה — *Do not say, "I will learn when I am not preoccupied," for you may always be preoccupied.* This adage is usually understood to be a simple reproach against procrastination; if one waits until he's "freed-up," it may well never happen. But the Slonimer Rebbe *ztz"l* had another take on it, in line with the sentiment expressed above. He understood Hillel here to be encouraging a person to serve Hashem and accept the yoke of Torah even in the midst of his many pressures. But not necessarily because of the danger of losing the mitzvah; rather, even if, theoretically, he will end up having free time later on, it still won't be the same *avodah*. *Shema lo sipaneh* — maybe this is exactly what Hashem is mandating of this particular individual. He desires a *lo sipaneh* type of *avodah*, one wherein the individual exerts himself to learn and serve Hashem in the face of his constraining circumstances.

A certain young man once consulted with the Beis Avraham *ztz"l* concerning his progress in *avodah*. The Beis Avraham explained to the young man, "When you were a *bachur*, you felt it was premature to work on improving your *avodah*. You preferred to wait until you became a little more mature, getting married and 'settling down'; that would be the optimum time to work on yourself. Well, here you are, in the role of a *yungerman*, married and more seasoned, and yet you still desire to put off improving your *avodah* until you become even older!" The Beis Avraham, with an overwhelming sense of humility, then added the following, "Take it from me — in the senior years, it's the *zelber ma'aseh* (same business)." His point was to emphasize the aforementioned sentiment. We have to realize that Hashem desires our service in whatever circumstance or time period we currently find ourselves. Pushing it off to a different time should not be part of our menu of options.

In this respect, the message of *Im lo achshav, eimasai* is not limited to *aseih tov*; it could be equally applicable to *sur meira*. A person may be confronted with a surge of temptation; he may feel that, this time, the *yetzer hara* has him cornered. It appears that he has no choice but to succumb. In response, the mishnah delivers a resounding, "No! If not *now*, when?" Perhaps it is specifically *now*, specifically through this "impossible" circumstance that Hashem is testing the individual, hoping and expecting him to emerge victorious. In fact, this is the principal form of serving Hashem, the mark of a true *oveid* — to fulfill His will precisely when we think we "can't."

In fact, it is to just such a situation that *Chazal* were referring when they issued their well-known definition of a *ba'al teshuvah* (penitent). "What is a proper *ba'al teshuvah*? ... (One who, after stumbling the first time, is confronted with) the same woman, the same circumstance, and the same location" (*Yuma* 86b). Why is it necessary for the potential *ba'al teshuvah* to have to face all of these conditions? For that is precisely the point. He may feel that under these circumstances, it is not possible for him to do *teshuvah*. *Chazal* thus encourage him to re-orient his thinking. It is *specifically* these conditions that Hashem desires of you — same place, same time, etc. He desires that you demonstrate your innate ability to overcome the *yetzer hara* and fulfill Hashem's will even when — or specifically when — you may have deemed it impossible. If not now, when?

In Summary

In a few succinct sentences, Hillel provides a wealth of crucial counsel, touching on vital areas in *avodas Hashem*. The challenge is

to unlock the meaning of these somewhat cryptic, pithy statements, which the Nesivos Sholom proceeds to do.

The two statements at the beginning of Hillel's teaching almost seem to contradict each other. Referring to the notion of being/acting on one's own, we appear to be receiving mixed messages about the desirability of doing so. "If I am not to myself, who is for me?" seems to imply that one should be "to one's self." But the next phrase — "If I am for myself, what am I?" — indicates disapproval of a "go-it-alone" attitude.

The truth is that Hillel is addressing two different aspects of *avodas Hashem*. These are comprised, as Dovid Hamelech informs us, of the elements of *aseih tov* and *sur meira*. Thus, in the beginning, Hillel speaks of the *sur meira* aspect. When it comes to overcoming one's *yetzer hara* and refraining from its invitation to sin, a person really does need to be *l'atzmo*. At the end of the day, it is he alone who can defeat his *yetzer hara* — no one else can do so for him.

But regarding the aspect of *aseih tov*, it is a different matter entirely. There is a principle informing the workings of the universe, which states that Hashem set up a system whereby everything in the world works through a *mashpia/mekabel* relationship; this is how productive growth and accomplishment comes about. The sky gives rain, and the earth receives it: thus, a tree develops. With one but without the other, nothing would even start. This is the operating principle when it comes to *avodas Hashem*, as well, specifically in the area of *aseih tov*. For a Yid to grow spiritually and attain new heights, he must garner assistance and encouragement from the models of greatness around him. *Aseih lecha rav, u'keneih lecha chaver* reflects the notion that a person needs a qualified *rebbi* to offer teaching and guidance, and appropriate, virtuous *chaveirim* whose behavior he may emulate.

Hillel concludes his teaching with a familiar exhortation: *Im lo achshav, eimasai*. To appreciate the true depth of this comment, we must realize that Hillel was saying a lot more than simply, "Don't procrastinate." This is true, of course; but Hillel was conveying that we should not procrastinate even in the face of what seems to be a legitimate, justifiable reason. A person may find himself in a difficult situation — perhaps even a series of ongoing challenges. He should nevertheless set out on a path of *avodah* right away — not only *despite* the circumstances, but *because of them*. There is a danger that the situation may not improve so fast, and he may never have the opportunity to learn or fulfill a certain mitzvah if he waits for things to "calm down." But even aside from this concern — even if, theoretically, he were to be assured that he will "get the chance" later on — he still should seize the mitzvah moment. This is because it is often the case that Hashem specifically orchestrated the situation as that is precisely what He desired: that is, that the individual should serve Him *while* there is pressure and *while* it is difficult. Should he wait until later, even if things do clear up for him to fulfill the mitzvah from leisure — he has missed the golden opportunity of serving Hashem from a situation of *lo sipaneh*, where there is no leisure.

פרק א' משנה י"ב
הוי מתלמידיו של אהרן
Be of the Disciples of Aharon

הִלֵּל וְשַׁמַּאי קִבְּלוּ מֵהֶם. הִלֵּל אוֹמֵר, הֱוֵי מִתַּלְמִידָיו שֶׁל אַהֲרֹן, אוֹהֵב שָׁלוֹם וְרוֹדֵף שָׁלוֹם, אוֹהֵב אֶת הַבְּרִיּוֹת וּמְקָרְבָן לַתּוֹרָה:

Hillel and Shamai received from them. Hillel says: Be from the disciples of Aharon: Loving peace, pursuing peace, loving people, and drawing them close to Torah.

GEMS FROM THE *SEFER NESIVOS SHOLOM*

SOURCES:

מִקְדָּשׁ רִאשׁוֹן מִפְּנֵי מָה חָרַב? מִפְּנֵי שְׁלֹשָׁה דְבָרִים שֶׁהָיוּ בּוֹ: עֲבוֹדָה זָרָה, וְגִלּוּי עֲרָיוֹת, וּשְׁפִיכוּת דָּמִים... אֲבָל מִקְדָּשׁ שֵׁנִי, שֶׁהָיוּ עוֹסְקִין בַּתּוֹרָה וּבַמִּצְוֹת וּגְמִילוּת חֲסָדִים מִפְּנֵי מָה חָרַב? מִפְּנֵי שֶׁהָיְתָה בּוֹ שִׂנְאַת חִנָּם. לְלַמֶּדְךָ שֶׁשְּׁקוּלָה שִׂנְאַת חִנָּם כְּנֶגֶד שָׁלֹשׁ עֲבֵירוֹת: עֲבוֹדָה זָרָה, וְגִלּוּי עֲרָיוֹת, וּשְׁפִיכוּת דָּמִים. (יומא ט:)

Why was the first Temple destroyed? Because of three practices of that era: idolatry, immorality, and murder... But the second Temple, wherein they were involved in Torah study, mitzvos, and acts of kindness – why was it destroyed? Because there was baseless hatred during that era. This teaches you that baseless hatred is equal to three (cardinal) sins: idolatry, immorality, and murder. (*Yuma* 9b)

עֹשֶׂה שָׁלוֹם בִּמְרוֹמָיו. (איוב כ"ה ב')

He makes peace in His heights. (*Iyov* 25:2)

אַתָּה אֶחָד וְשִׁמְךָ אֶחָד, וּמִי כְּעַמְּךָ יִשְׂרָאֵל גּוֹי אֶחָד בָּאָרֶץ. (מנחה לשבת)

You are One, and Your Name is One, and who is like Your people, Yisroel – one nation in the land! (Minchah for Shabbos)

פרקי אבות

Let's Be Friends

Shalom — peace. This is probably one of the most universally familiar terms in the Hebrew language.

Truly a beautiful sentiment. But what does it really mean? When we see the volume of Torah teachings surrounding this concept, its frequent recurrence as a theme in the daily prayers, and, indeed, the central role it seems to play in our lives and in the world — we come to the realization that it contains much more depth than we may have initially realized.

Hillel's call for peace is perhaps one of the more famous samplings of the sage teachings of *Pirkei Avos*. It is interesting how Hillel chose to introduce his idea: הֱוֵי מִתַּלְמִידָיו שֶׁל אַהֲרֹן, אוֹהֵב שָׁלוֹם וכו׳ — ***Be** like the disciples of Aharon: loving peace...* The Nesivos Sholom finds the imperative phraseology — "**Be** a student of Aharon" — somewhat surprising. Inherently, there is nothing problematic with it; Hillel could very well make an unequivocal statement, highlighting the importance of the matter by stressing that it's not simply "optional." The issue is that it deviates from the usual pattern the mishnah follows in such instances.

Elsewhere in *Pirkei Avos* (5:22), the mishnah encourages the emulation of Avraham Avinu, who possessed עַיִן טוֹבָה, וְרוּחַ נְמוּכָה, וְנֶפֶשׁ שְׁפָלָה — *a good eye, a meek spirit, and a humble soul*. Yet instead of a directive — "**Be** like Avraham" — the mishnah adopts a more passive stance. It merely states: כָּל מִי שֶׁיֵּשׁ בְּיָדוֹ שְׁלֹשָׁה דְבָרִים הַלָּלוּ, מִתַּלְמִידָיו שֶׁל אַבְרָהָם אָבִינוּ — *Whoever cultivates these three traits is a disciple of Avraham Avinu*. Why, then, when it comes to following the lead of Aharon, did the mishnah issue its teaching in the form of a command: הֱוֵי מִתַּלְמִידָיו שֶׁל אַהֲרֹן — ***Be** a disciple of Aharon*? What is it about the pursuit of peace that calls for such a powerful tone?

"Great Is *Shalom*"

The primacy of the *middah* of *shalom* is glaringly evident from numerous places — not the least of which is our mishnah. This mishnah begins a series of three mishnayos featuring Hillel's teachings, each conveying profound and lofty concepts. If he chose in his opening statement to discuss *shalom*, it is obvious that he accorded this *middah* the utmost urgency and importance.

Let us also recall with whom we are dealing. In his *sefer Yesod Ha'avodah*, the first Slonimer Rebbe reminds us not only of Hillel's towering spiritual stature, but that of his *talmidim*, as well. They lived in the post-prophetic era during the time of the second Beis Hamikdash; inherently, however, many of them were worthy of receiving *nevuah* (prophecy) on a level reminiscent of Moshe Rabbeinu. If Hillel so strongly advocates peace to us, his *talmidim* surely practiced this *middah*. And they achieved the highest possible levels of *kedushah*! It is no wonder, then, why the *middah* of peace is written as a directive, for it can be the vehicle of such intense greatness.

There is a *masechta* — one of the *Masechtos Ketanos* (Minor Tractates) — known as *Derech Eretz Zuta*. The final chapter of this *masechta*, referred to as *Perek Hashalom* (Chapter of Peace), is devoted entirely to this subject. *Chazal* were so emphatic about reinforcing the message of peace that they began every mishnah in the *perek* with the words, *Gadol hu hashalom* — "Great is peace."

In one of the mishnayos there, Rabbi Yehoshua points out that Hashem's Name is *Shalom*. Could there be a greater demonstration of how this *middah* is so closely linked with ultimate perfection? Many descriptive titles are employed to refer to Hashem — *Rachum* (Merciful One), *Chanun* (Compassionate One), etc. But of all of His attributes, it is *Shalom* that is chosen to represent His essence and serve as His very Name.

In the daily *tefillos* (prayers), we make frequent reference to the numerous *brachos* (blessings) that Hashem will shower upon those who keep His Torah. It is noteworthy — as mentioned by the Midrash (*Bamidbar Rabbah* 21) — that in so many sections of the *davening*, the final and ultimate *brachah* is that of *shalom*. The *brachos* surrounding *Krias Shema* (recital of *Shema*) conclude with a reference to *shalom*: וּפְרוֹשׂ עָלֵינוּ סֻכַּת שְׁלוֹמֶךָ — *Spread over us Your canopy of **peace***. The words of *Birkas Kohanim* (Priestly Blessing) we intone every day likewise end with this reference: יְבָרֶכְךָ ה'...וְיָשֵׂם לְךָ שָׁלוֹם — *May Hashem bless you...and grant you **peace***. Similarly, the last of the nineteen *brachos* of *Shemoneh Esrei* is the *Sim **Shalom*** (Grant Peace) blessing, which concludes with the phrase, הַמְבָרֵךְ אֶת עַמּוֹ יִשְׂרָאֵל בַּשָּׁלוֹם — *Who blesses His people, Yisroel, with **peace***. Rashi explains the intent in ending *brachos* with "*shalom*"; in so doing, Hashem is telling us that peace is the "mega-*brachah*," equal to all other *brachos* combined. *Shalom* outweighs all other good in the world; without it, there is no good.

Peace is so essential to life that, to protect it, Hashem will even allow His Name to be obliterated. This is evidenced by the procedure involving the *sotah*, the wife suspected of unfaithfulness. This ritual entails writing a special scroll containing the Name of Hashem, which is then dissolved in water. The *sotah* drinks the water to prove her innocence, thereby restoring domestic harmony.

Antithesis of Peace

The opposite of peace is *machlokes*, strife. It is an ugly *middah* and a destructive force, capable of ruining people and their relationships. To truly understand the beauty and necessity of peace, one must contrast it with the unpleasantness of strife and the damage it causes.

One particularly severe instance of *machlokes* involved Korach, whose campaign — terminating with his spectacular death — disrupted and damaged Klal Yisroel to an unprecedented extent. Throughout Bnei Yisroel's travels, the *mann* (manna) fell consistently, regardless of circumstances. Even on the day on which the *Eigel Hazahav* was fashioned, the *mann* still made its daily appearance. But on the climactic day of the Korach affair, Hashem withheld the *mann* — a demonstration of the intensity of His grief.

The destruction of the second Beis Hamikdash serves as another clear illustration of the gravity of *machlokes* between Jews. Compare the causes of the destruction of both the first and second Beis Hamikdash. The Gemara (*Yuma* 9b) states that the first was destroyed on account of the rampant violation of the three cardinal sins (idolatry, immorality, and murder), while the second was lost due to the single *aveirah* of baseless hatred.

Read that sentence again. The *three* most terrible *aveiros* — for each of which a person should die rather than transgress (*yeihareig v'al ya'avor*) — are equal to hatred-based *machlokes*? Apparently, hatred and strife are such potent entities that they have the same effect as the most egregious of sins.

By now, it should be abundantly clear that peace and strife are far more powerful than we may have initially realized. Which begs the next question: why? What exactly is it about *shalom* and its counterpart, *machlokes*, that makes them so significant and formidable?

Peace, Strife, and I

On this point, the Nesivos Sholom elucidates the true meaning and nature of *shalom*. People often think that peace is a more or less passive entity — when there is no strife, there is peace. Actually, there is a lot more to *shalom* than the mere absence of *machlokes*. This we see from the *passuk* (which has been incorporated at numerous places in our daily prayers), *Oseh shalom bimromav* — "He makes peace in His heights" (*Iyov* 25:2). What need is there for peace-making in the Celestial Abode? *Malachim* (angels) don't squabble! It must be, then, that the concept of *shalom* contains a real, positive element, of a most pristine and elevated nature.

Peace goes well beyond simply enhancing *bein adam lachaveiro* (interpersonal) relationships. Real *shalom* enables a person to strengthen his relationship with Hashem, as well, and become closer to Him. Likewise, *machlokes* distances one from Hashem and damages that relationship.

An analysis of the *middah* of *machlokes* helps simplify this connection. A person gets into a fight with someone else based on an offense (real or perceived). The insulted party feels that his honor has been slighted, and a verbal (or physical) *machlokes* ensues. Thus we discover what is ultimately at the root of *machlokes*: an inflated sense of self. Had this element been lacking, he would not be so focused on the (perceived) degradation to his honor.

This self-image is mistaken, since a person is truly nothing in comparison to Hashem, the One and Only perfect entity. The stronger a person's relationship with Hashem, the more aware he will be of his own inherent lack of importance and the less he will be affected by someone else's insulting behavior. Thus a person who has truly internalized the reality of Hashem's perfection and greatness will feel much less negativity toward his fellow humans.

This happy phenomenon can work the other way, as well. The Nesivos Sholom goes on to explain that one can achieve this recognition of Hashem, and cultivate an *ahavah* for Him, through genuine *ahavas Yisroel* (love of fellow Jews). This correlation is not like a *segulah* (spiritual charm), which pulls on sources of *kedushah* and *hashgachas Hashem* (Divine Providence) that are unknown to us. Rather, it is a direct cause and effect. The more one asserts his own wishes and demands, the more he will conflict with those around him. To get on well with others, one must, to a large extent, relinquish his own sense of self. *Ahavas Yisroel* entails a degree of discounting our personal stakes, nullifying our self before the greater needs of the *klal* (collective body). When someone realizes that he himself is not as remarkable as he first thought, his love and respect for others will automatically increase.

The more we cultivate *ahavas Yisroel*, the more habituated we will become to the exercise of *bitul atzmo*, self-nullification. This tremendous accomplishment can thus translate into the next step — negating our self before Hashem, the ultimate, perfect and powerful Being.

This notion is reflected in the words recited in the Minchah *Shemoneh Esrei* of Shabbos: אַתָּה אֶחָד וְשִׁמְךָ אֶחָד, וּמִי כְּעַמְּךָ יִשְׂרָאֵל גּוֹי אֶחָד בָּאָרֶץ — *You are One, and Your Name is One, and who is like Your people, Yisroel — one nation in the land!* We become unified as "one nation" when we prevail over selfishness and relinquish our individual sense of self-importance. Then we can come to a crystallized realization of Hashem's true greatness. Recognizing our own deficiencies and powerlessness, we see Hashem for what He is — the sole force and entity in the universe; אַתָּה אֶחָד וְשִׁמְךָ אֶחָד — *You are One, and Your Name is One.*

And this, in reality, is the very foundation of creation. The existence of the world is predicated on the notion that *Ein od milvado* — "There is no other beside Him" (*Devarim* 4:35). From the smallest pebble to the biggest elephant to the most accomplished of men, everything is entirely dependent on *Hakadosh Baruch Hu's* life-giving force: וְאַתָּה מְחַיֶּה אֶת־כֻּלָּם — *And You maintain the lives of them all* (*Nechemiah* 9:6). The principal function of creation is to recognize Hashem as its sole Creator. When the world's creatures acknowledge that Hashem is the sole Power and subjugate themselves to His allegiance, then Creation has fulfilled its true purpose. At that point, it has achieved its most harmonious state — and this is the ultimate *shalom*.

This understanding sheds new light on the issue of the *churban* (destruction) of the second Beis Hamikdash. How could one seemingly "standard" *aveirah* be the source of such colossal and far-reaching devastation? The truth is that, in and of itself, *sin'as chinam* (baseless hatred) was not the actual cause. Rather, its presence indicated a total lack of recognition of Hashem's greatness. This is what occasioned such grave consequences. As we have seen, the acknowledgment of and subservience to Hashem's Oneness and power is the ultimate manifestation of *shalom*, indicating a world functioning to perfection. If such a realization is the foundation of the world, the converse is also true — a lack thereof will wreak destruction.

Hillel's teaching — and the way he conveyed it — can be appreciated more fully in light of the above. The delivery of the message of peace is certainly deserving of such a direct and forceful tone. For we are not simply discussing an admirable trait; rather, it is the very purpose of creation that is at stake. Peace is not just essential for perfecting one's *middos* but is a critical step in coming close to Hashem and ensuring that the world fulfills its prime function.

The Peace-Maker

Hillel directs us to learn from Aharon, the quintessential lover and pursuer of peace. Bnei Yisroel were aware of and appreciated this fact, as is so apparent from their response to his passing. The entire nation, including women and children, mourned for this beloved figure, as the Torah tells us, "The entire Bnei Yisroel wept for Aharon for thirty days" (*Bamidbar* 20:29). Eighty thousand young children, all named Aharon, attended his funeral. What caused this naming phenomenon? Whenever a man contemplated divorce, Aharon would come to the rescue. Through his wise and caring intervention, husband and wife would be reconciled and would carry on in their marriage with peace and respect. When the woman would subsequently give birth to a son, the grateful couple would name him Aharon, for, essentially, Aharon had brought about his birth.

Following this model will benefit not only the harmony of Klal Yisroel, but also their very essence. Only peace can bring us closer to Hashem and give our *neshamos* (souls) the G-dly relationship they crave.

May we be *zocheh* to the *brachah* of עֹשֶׂה שָׁלוֹם בִּמְרוֹמָיו, הוּא יַעֲשֶׂה שָׁלוֹם עָלֵינוּ וְעַל כָּל יִשְׂרָאֵל, וְאִמְרוּ אָמֵן — *He Who brings peace among His high places, may He make peace among us and all of Yisroel; and answer: amen!*

In Summary

Peace, as should be well known, is a wonderful and important attribute. In *Perek Hashalom*, a chapter of *Maseches Derech Eretz*, every mishnah begins with the words: *Gadol hashalom* — Great is peace. This sentiment is universally acknowledged. But — what is it? Do we really have a firm grip on the definition of *shalom*?

One might think that this question elicits a simple answer. *Shalom* — that's easy; when things are quiet, and there's no *machlokes*, well, that's "peace." In actuality, however, there is much more profundity to the concept than that. The *passuk* speaks of *shalom* in Heaven — even though there is no room to contemplate a concept of strife among the angels. Apparently, more than just an absence of discord, *shalom* is an actual, positive entity.

Insight as to what truly lies behind *shalom* can be gained by examining the nature of its counterpart, *machlokes*. What is the root cause of this pernicious trait? The Nesivos Sholom attributes its existence to a fundamental flaw: a person's sense of self. That is, it usually begins through injured pride, whereby someone feels (justified or not) that another has slighted his honor. But this slight only registers on a person who gives significant credence to his own standing; one who negates himself, recognizing that, in essence, he is nothing before *Hakadosh Baruch Hu*, will not be so bothered by insults, real or perceived.

Thus, this truly remarkable concept reveals just what *shalom* is and to where it can lead. *Shalom* is the manifestation of this clear recognition, whereby the created beings recognize that they themselves are ultimately nothing and that their existence is entirely dependent on the one true Power, the Creator of the Universe. A world that recognizes this is a world at harmony. In any event, in order to avoid *machlokes* and get along with others, a person must exercise this trait of self-negation. As this mindset is so clearly linked with recognition of Hashem's greatness, one who cultivates it will not only be at peace with his fellow man but will be able to draw close to Hashem, before Whom he subjugates himself.

Thus we discover that, in effect, *shalom* is the fulfillment of the purpose of creation. At the root of *shalom* is our nullification before and recognition of Hashem as the sole and ultimate Power in the world He created. A world that accedes to this realization is a world that has fulfilled the purpose for which it was brought into existence.

All of the above informs our understanding of the mishnah in *Avos* which discusses "*shalom*." In uncharacteristically emphatic language, the mishnah instructs us — in the imperative — to be like Aharon: הֱוֵי מִתַּלְמִידָיו שֶׁל אַהֲרֹן, אוֹהֵב שָׁלוֹם וְרוֹדֵף שָׁלוֹם. Based on the above, it should be clear why the mishnah puts such a stress on the cultivation of this trait, to the point of issuing a command. For *shalom* is not merely a nice quality, a helpful state that facilitates good relations. These are important, but *shalom* goes well beyond that. It is the entity by which a person can draw close to his Creator, and it serves as the fulfillment of the purpose of creation.

פרק א׳ משנה י״ד
אם אין אני לי מי לי
If I Am Not for Me – Who Is for Me?

הוּא הָיָה אוֹמֵר, אִם אֵין אֲנִי לִי, מִי לִי. וּכְשֶׁאֲנִי לְעַצְמִי, מָה אֲנִי. וְאִם לֹא עַכְשָׁו, אֵימָתַי:

(Hillel) would say: If I am not for me – who is for me? And if I am for myself – what am I? And if not now – when?

GEMS FROM THE *SEFER NESIVOS SHOLOM*

SOURCES:

וְהַצְנֵעַ לֶכֶת עִם־אֱלֹקֶיךָ. (מיכה ו' ח')

And to walk discreetly with your G-d. (*Michah* 6:8)

כְּשֶׁחָלָה רַבִּי אֱלִיעֶזֶר, נִכְנְסוּ תַּלְמִידָיו לְבַקְּרוֹ. אָמְרוּ לוֹ: רַבֵּינוּ, לַמְּדֵנוּ אוֹרְחוֹת חַיִּים וְנִזְכֶּה בָּהֶן לְחַיֵּי הָעוֹלָם הַבָּא. אָמַר לָהֶם: הִזָּהֲרוּ בִּכְבוֹד חַבְרֵיכֶם... (ברכות כ"ח:)

When Rabbi Eliezer became ill, his disciples came to visit him. They said to him: "Our Master! Teach us the ways of life, that we may merit through them the life of the World to Come." He said to them: "Be careful with the honor of your fellows..." (*Berachos* 28b)

הָעוֹלָם הַבָּא אֵין בּוֹ לֹא אֲכִילָה וְלֹא שְׁתִיָּה וְלֹא פְּרִיָּה וּרְבִיָּה וְלֹא מַשָּׂא וּמַתָּן וְלֹא קִנְאָה וְלֹא שִׂנְאָה וְלֹא תַחֲרוּת, אֶלָּא צַדִּיקִים יוֹשְׁבִין וְעַטְרוֹתֵיהֶם בְּרָאשֵׁיהֶם וְנֶהֱנִים מִזִּיו הַשְּׁכִינָה. (ברכות י"ז.)

In the future world there is neither eating, drinking, propagation, business activity, jealousy, hatred, nor competition. Rather, the righteous sit with their crowns upon their heads, and delight in the radiance of the *Shechinah* (Divine Presence). (*Berachos* 17a)

עוֹלָמְךָ תִּרְאֶה בְּחַיֶּיךָ. (שם)

You shall witness your world in your lifetime. (*ibid.*)

שְׂכַר מִצְוָה, מִצְוָה. וּשְׂכַר עֲבֵרָה, עֲבֵרָה. (אבות ד')

The reward of a mitzvah is a mitzvah, and the result of a sin is a sin. (*Avos* 4)

דַּעֲלָךְ סְנֵי לְחַבְרָךְ לֹא תַעֲבֵיד. (שבת ל"א.)

What is hateful to you, do not do to your friend. (*Shabbos* 31a)

פרקי אבות

124

אם אין אני לי מי לי

Me, Who and When

Few maxims from *Pirkei Avos* are as familiar to us as this teaching of Hillel — and not just because of the popular song. To young and old, these classic words and their timely message have been repeated and cherished throughout the generations.

What may not be so familiar to us, however, is the eye-opening approach of the Nesivos Sholom to this mishnah. Basing his rendering on the *Yesod Ha'avodah* (vol. IV, ch. 1), he opens up an entirely new vista within the mishnah's words.

To be sure, the words of this mishnah are few, short, and succinct. Unquestionably, though, they are laden with meaning. First, consider the stature of the author of this teaching, the great *Tanna*, Hillel. Not only did he live in an elevated era when the Beis Hamikdash yet stood, but he occupied the position of *nasi*, leader of the entire generation. An office of such magnitude, of course, could not be occupied by just anyone; a prerequisite was the acquisition of the loftiest levels of Torah scholarship and piety. Hillel, steadfastly, had reached them all.

Furthermore, the opening words of the mishnah are very informative. *Hu hayah omer* — "He would say…" Hillel had a lot of worthwhile things to say; the knowledge he possessed and transmitted was awesome in its volume. This particular message was not merely one of the many teachings he conveyed; the phrase *Hu hayah omer* indicates that he conferred especial emphasis on this teaching, stressing and repeating it frequently. Obviously, he felt it contained a critical lesson for those of his generation and the generations to follow.

For Me or Not for Me?

On its most basic level, the mishnah's statement exhorts us to do our part. אִם אֵין אֲנִי לִי, מִי לִי — *If I am not for myself, who is for me?*; the implication is that, to some extent, one should be "for himself." Failure to do so will leave one at a disadvantage — "who will be for me?" While this is the conventional understanding, the *Yesod Ha'avodah* takes an opposite tack. It sees the mishnah as actually

פרק א'

125

dissuading a person from acting "for himself," as this shall give rise to the optimal results.

People study Torah, observe mitzvos, and serve Hashem for any one of a number of reasons. For some, the primary motivator is the promise of the immeasurable reward awaiting them upon their arrival in the Next World; others seek thereby public approval and glory, focusing on their advancement in the here and now; someone else may simply be inclined towards spirituality, deriving enjoyment from elevated living. There is, of course, the option of genuine altruism, serving Hashem with no motive other than that it gives Him *nachas ruach* (pleasure). The latter, of course, constitutes the highest level in *avodas Hashem*. Now, there may also be other benefits the *oveid* obtains in following the Torah; but to one who serves *lishmah* (for its own sake), the other considerations are purely peripheral. His prime (and actually only) focus is to serve the Creator. It is not for me; it is for Him!

According to the *Yesod Ha'avodah*, it is this highest level of serving Hashem that Hillel is describing. Thus Hillel's words are interpreted with fresh insight. "If I am not for myself" is actually the preferred course of action, referring to the altruistic *oveid*. That is, he serves not "for myself," with my own personal interests in mind, but solely for *Hakadosh Baruch Hu*. To underscore the stature of this form of *avodah*, Hillel concludes, *mi li*. While usually understood to mean "who is for me?", the *Yesod Ha'avodah* renders the *passuk* differently. If I perform mitzvos without selfish interest — "If I am not for myself" — then *mi li*, "who is *like* me?" Who can compare to this type of *oveid*, who discounts personal benefit, being invested solely in pleasing his Creator? Hillel thereby wants us to realize that this is the ultimate level of serving Hashem.

At the other end of the spectrum, of course, is one whose primary focus is "myself." He may do everything he is told; possibly even studying Torah every free minute, fulfilling mitzvos meticulously, and serving Hashem with fervor. All the same, he completely misses the boat. All that he does is for his own personal benefit and gain. He may enjoy the honor and prestige that his code of conduct affords him; he may enjoy leading such a pure life; he may earn his livelihood from his study of Torah. He may be driven by any of these or any other reason; the issue is that he neglects the real reason. For such an individual, giving Hashem pleasure may not register on his radar. Thus, his actual performance may be of the highest level, but the purpose of his performance is of the lowest.

Hillel was addressing his next words to such an individual. *U'ch'she'ani l'atzmi* — "If I am only for myself," meaning, if I am acting on behalf of "myself," to my own benefit, then *mah ani* — "what am I?" The implication, of course, is that I am really nothing. It is not an actual question; it is what one should see is the result of his underlying motivation. Missing, as it is, what should be the primary focus, what I do can almost be considered a waste.

In an insightful interpretation to a well-known *passuk*, the Divrei Shmuel delivers a similar message. The *navi* in *Sefer Michah* (6:8) says, וְהַצְנֵעַ לֶכֶת עִם־אֱלֹקֶיךָ — *and to walk discreetly with your G-d.* The Divrei Shmuel breaks up the *passuk* differently, reflecting Hillel's same sentiment. He renders: *V'hatznei'a* — "That which is done discreetly, hidden from public view," *leches im Elokecha* — "goes and ascends before Hashem." Thus the *navi* informs us that it is those deeds performed without fanfare that are readily accepted by Hashem. But when one serves Hashem principally so that others will see and know — that is an entirely different matter.

The Nesivos Sholom shares another interpretation of the first parts of the mishnah from the *sefer Ahavas Dodim*. While echoing a message similar to that of the *Yesod Ha'avodah*, it presents a nuanced reading of Hillel's words. The *Ahavas Dodim* explains that the word *ani* — normally translated as "I" — can also serve as a general term referring to materialistic and earthly matters. Thus, Hillel is discussing the way in which we employ the earthly bounty at our disposal. Once again, the most praiseworthy path is when that bounty is used altruistically. *Im ein ani li* encourages us not to use the *ani*, material goods, solely for our personal benefit. If we discount our own interests and view earthly items merely as vehicles with which to serve Hashem, the result will be most optimal. For we will then achieve *Mi li* — "'Who' is to me," with *Mi* in this context serving as a title for the Almighty. The *navi* tells us (*Yeshayah* 40:26), שְׂאוּ־מָרוֹם עֵינֵיכֶם וּרְאוּ מִי־בָרָא אֵלֶּה — *Lift up your eyes on High and see,* **Who** *created these.*

What Hillel is informing us is profound indeed. By utilizing the conventions of This World with the sole focus of fulfilling Hashem's will, we may attain the ultimate spiritual level in This World. **Mi li**, **Hashem** will be to me, and I will be attached to Him in utmost *d'veikus*. But, *U'ch'she'ani l'atzmi*: if I use *ani*, materialism, *l'atzmi* — "for myself," with my own benefit in mind, then, *mah ani* — "what am I?" I live, but a life devoid of anything meaningful.

The Final Lesson — Preserve the "Friendship"

This is further understood based on the explanation of the Noda B'Yehudah in his *Tzlach*.

The Gemara in *Maseches Berachos* (28b) relates an important dialogue that took place between a *rebbi* and his *talmidim*. When Rabbi Eliezer fell ill, his students came to visit him. They used the opportunity to extract some crucial knowledge from the bedridden scholar. "Master!" they said. "Teach us the paths of life, so we can thereby merit life in the World to Come!" Rabbi Eliezer responded by imparting the following maxim: *Hizaharu b'chavod chavreichem* — "Be mindful of the respect due your fellows."

The narrative, as depicted above, represents the simple, superficial understanding of the Gemara's text. In *Tzlach*, his commentary to the Gemara, the Noda B'Yehudah reveals how this teaching, as well, actually says a lot more than appears on the surface. His innovative explanation dovetails with the message expounded above concerning our mishnah.

Dealing first with the *talmidim's* question, the Noda B'Yehudah explains that they were not simply asking how one merits *Olam Haba*. The formula for this is simple and well known: do mitzvos and you will have a beautiful portion in *Olam Haba*. What the students really wanted to know was something completely different: Is there a way, they asked, to merit and experience the bliss of the World to Come *even while still alive in This World*?

Such a notion, as unlikely as it may seem, is not an entirely foreign concept. Elsewhere, *Chazal* allude to the concept of enjoying the reward prescribed for the World to Come while still residing in the domain of the living. The Gemara speaks of a wonderful blessing: *Olamcha sir'eh b'chayecha* — "May you behold your world in your lifetime" (*Berachos* 17a). While normally taken to mean that your needs should be provided in your lifetime, it could alternatively be understood along the lines of our discussion. "May you behold your world" — that is, the existence of the World to Come — "yet in your lifetime."

This idea can best be understood in light of how *Chazal* describe the eternal bliss of the World to Come: "Tzaddikim sit and delight in the radiance of the *Shechinah*" (*ibid.*). This is the immense pleasure of attachment to *Hakadosh Baruch Hu*, basking in the Light of His Essence. In truth, we may experience a sense of this paradisiacal encounter each time we perform a mitzvah. As it states elsewhere in *Avos* (4:2): *S'char mitzvah mitzvah* — "The reward of a mitzvah is (the fulfillment of) a mitzvah." When we fulfill a mitzvah in the proper manner and with the appropriate intention, attaining a level of *d'veikus* through our service, we may derive such Heavenly pleasure that we taste a semblance of the World to Come. Thus, the sweetness of this close association with Hashem through mitzvah performance is itself one of the chief benefits and rewards of mitzvos — right here on this earth.

The *talmidim* of Rabbi Eliezer understood this great truth; and it is this that they sought. They knew it was possible to obtain a measure of the *Olam Haba* experience already here in *Olam Hazeh*. And so, explains the Noda B'Yehudah, they asked of their master to provide them with guidance in obtaining this ultimate connection with the *Shechinah* right away. "Teach us, our master, what are the paths of life through which to merit — right here and now — a semblance, at least, of the ultimate reward reserved for the World to Come?"

In light of this question, however, Rabbi Eliezer's reply may appear unusual. "Be mindful of the respect due your friends." An important concept, no doubt; but how is it that this is the key to an "immediate" *Olam Haba* experience?

The Noda B'Yehudah continues by explaining that in this instance, the word *chavreichem* is to be translated differently. Yes, it usually denotes friends. Rabbi Eliezer's intent here, however, was somewhat different. He was utilizing the same root, but wasn't referring to interpersonal friendships. *Chaver* intimates closeness; *chibbur* is an attachment of two entities. Rabbi Eliezer was speaking of the cultivation of a relationship with *Hakadosh Baruch Hu*. The secret is single-minded purpose: as Hillel imparted, we must ensure that the sole impetus of our *avodah* is simply that — *d'veikus* with Hashem, and not self-interest. He related to his *talmidim* that this type of service will preserve and enhance their connection with Him, enabling them to experience here on earth a measure of the joy of the *d'veikus* of *Olam Haba*.

Thus, Rabbi Eliezer's lesson mirrors the sentiment of our mishnah. The Noda B'Yehudah demonstrates the extent to which Rabbi Eliezer sought to emphasize this point. In his carefully worded statement, Rabbi Eliezer chose the term *hizaharu* — "be careful (with your *chibbur*)." This signifies an added dimension to the mishnah's message. Until this point, we have discussed mainly the importance of performing *deeds* with the proper intention: not for receiving personal reward in This or the Next World, but for cleaving to Hashem. But *hizaharu* implies a warning, and a warning is usually a statement for what one should *not* do.

Here, Rabbi Eliezer is taking the idea a step further. It may not be so difficult to do the positive mitzvos of the Torah with the goal of developing a relationship with Hashem. The real challenge is to adhere to the warnings of Hashem, when He bids us to refrain from transgression. One may follow those rules, and avoid violating these negative commandments. But even here, the question of motive comes in to play. Why am I refraining from *aveiros* — is fear of punishment my prime motivation? Rabbi Eliezer stresses that all facets of *avodas Hashem* — both what to do and what *not* to do — should be done for *kavod chavreichem* — the sake of your attaining closeness with Hashem. As such, it is crucial to avoid whatever attitudes or actions may jeopardize this sacred relationship.

Another teaching from *Avos* was cited previously: *S'char mitzvah mitzvah* — "The reward for a mitzvah is (itself the performance of) a mitzvah." The end of that teaching states, *s'char aveirah aveirah*; and the meaning is the same. The reward of a mitzvah is its performance, for when undertaken properly, the ensuing *d'veikus* from fulfilling Hashem's will is a taste of Heavenly delight. A transgression works similarly — but, obviously, in the opposite direction. The commission of an *aveirah* weakens our connection with Hashem, distancing ourselves from Him. It may even be a minor failing, moving us back just a small distance. But any further lessening of our attachment to Hashem, any slight increase in the distance, is itself the harshest of punishments.

The Nesivos Sholom presents yet another teaching of *Chazal* in this light, this time in the name of the Maggid of Mezeritch. The Gemara in *Shabbos* (31a) relates the familiar exchange between Hillel and the prospective convert. The latter issued his ridiculous request that Hillel teach him the entire Torah as he stood on one foot. But the wise Hillel was up to the challenge and delivered his famous answer. He asserted that the essence of the entire Torah can be encapsulated in the following idea: דְּעָלָךְ סַנִי לְחַבְרָךְ לֹא תַעֲבֵיד — commonly rendered as: "That which is hateful to you, don't do to your friend."

This answer seems perplexing. Granted, *ahavas Yisroel* is a crucial aspect of observance. But how are we to understand that this comprises the essence of the whole Torah?

The Maggid of Mezeritch solves this dilemma with simplicity and brilliance, interpreting these words of Hillel in a manner reminiscent of the Noda B'Yehudah's teaching. The Maggid also explains *chavrech* not as a "friend" but in reference to one's *chibbur*, relationship. He thus renders these words of Hillel as follows: דְּעָלָךְ סַנִי לְחַבְרָךְ לֹא תַעֲבֵיד — *Those actions of yours which threaten your relationship, do not do.*

In other words, Hillel was not talking of human relationships here, but rather a relationship with Hashem. What is the crux of the entire Torah? *That which is hateful to Hashem and jeopardizes your relationship with Him — do not do!* In the same vein as above, Hillel was instructing the would-be convert that the ultimate goal is obtaining closeness with Hashem. As such, every action must be evaluated in this light, to determine how it will affect his relationship with *Hakadosh Baruch Hu*. This credo will thus encompass everything: mitzvos, *aveiros*, and even mundane activities. If it furthers his attachment to Hashem, the path should be embraced; but if it places further distance between him and his Creator — if it is *sani* to his *chibbur* — then, *lo sa'avid*.

This is our overarching mission in life: to get as close as we possibly can to the glory and absolute truth that is Hashem. And the path to this nearness is illuminated for us in 613 steps. The mitzvos, every word and nuance of the Torah, is our traveler's guide, with which to navigate This World. Some of the instructions are things we should do, some point to things we must avoid at all costs. We may have some understanding of the reasons behind a portion of these instructions, while others remain beyond our limited grasp. But we do know without a shadow of a doubt that they constitute the only path that can lead us to *d'veikus* with Hashem, which is the ultimate goal and the ultimate pleasure.

The Maggid of Mezeritch's understanding of *D'alach sani*, and the *Tzlach's* interpretation of Rabbi Eliezer's lesson, both echo the sentiment expressed by Hillel: *Im ein ani li* — If I am not doing anything (positive, negative, or even neutral) for my own personal benefit, but to get closer to Hashem, then *mi li*, who can compare to me.

Now Is the Time

Hillel concludes this mishnah with a final note of encouragement.

Encouragement, that is, in the face of what may appear as insurmountable challenges. *Chazal* tell us that a person's *yetzer hara* is *misgaber* (exerts power) over him every day, and is *mischadeish* (renewed) upon him every day. What this means, explains the Nesivos Sholom, is that today's *yetzer hara* is never the same as yesterday's;

whatever it was one day, it becomes even stronger and more wily the next.

In the face of these odds, we may begin to feel discouraged (another of the *yetzer hara's* strategies). Oftentimes, we may be inclined to say that it's just too hard. Maybe somewhere or sometime down the line, we'll muster the fortitude to do real battle against our nature and really rectify our shortcomings. But in our current situation, being pressed for time, under financial duress, and whatever other contributing factors, we may feel that the time is not right to turn things around.

Addressing just this type of attitude, Hillel comes to say: "On the contrary. Now is the perfect time to do *teshuvah*, to increase your Torah study, to work on your *davening*, to improve that certain *middah*.

"You may feel too constricted or overburdened by your circumstances. But it is precisely within such an environment that Hashem desires your *avodah*; that is why He presented it to you in the first place!" Hillel urges us. We know that our forefather Avraham had to undergo ten trials. The *Me'or Einayim* points out that in doing so, Avraham was performing his role as progenitor of the entire Jewish nation; that is, all of his offspring — every single Yid — also must undergo their personal series of "ten trials." And it is the particular set of life circumstances, and the challenges and struggles we each face, that comprise the setting of our trials.

As such, whatever situation we may find ourselves in — even the most daunting — has been tailor-made to advance our *avodah*, presenting the opportunity to endure and ultimately emerge victorious from the struggle. The challenges are in reality the vehicle through which to become closer to Hashem.

And so, instead of waiting for a more "favorable" time, Hillel exhorts us to seize the opportunity. As he puts it: וְאִם לֹא עַכְשָׁיו, אֵימָתָי — *If not now, when?*

In Summary

The great *Tanna* Hillel provided the Jewish people with some of the most memorable Torah maxims by which to live. Many of us may be most familiar with the words and basic idea of the classic teaching of this particular mishnah, but the Nesivos Sholom uncovers new layers of meaning to these well-worn words.

אִם אֵין אֲנִי לִי, מִי לִי. This is usually understood to be a call for a certain amount of self-reliance, translated as, "If I am not for myself, who will be for me?" But the Nesivos Sholom renders it in an entirely different light; he perceives this statement as an exhortation to purify our intentions in serving Hashem. People fulfill mitzvos for many reasons; often, the cause is self-serving, be it thoughts of reward in the World to Come, or for prestige and glory in This World. Hillel calls this *li*, and encourages us to serve Hashem without these calculations, and, instead, with a single focus on fulfilling His will for His sake. "If I eschew my own personal interests, and serve Hashem just to give Him pleasure — who can compare to me?" For this form of service is the most lofty and pleasing to the Creator. Conversely, however, if I do become self-invested — "If I am for myself" — then what, really, is the value of my service? *Mah ani?*

Hillel further reminds us that it is best not to be embittered or discouraged by our circumstances. We may feel that we struggle with our *yetzer hara* and that we are losing the battle against this powerful adversary. The temptation may be great to postpone efforts of improvement, to wait until the challenges abate and circumstances appear more favorable for a strengthened *avodah*.

And so Hillel sets out to correct this mistake. "If not now, when?" Whatever struggles we may face, it is not coincidence, nor need they be viewed as insurmountable impediments to growth. On the contrary, Hashem's desire is that specifically now — in the midst of our circumstances — we rise to the occasion and succeed in our trials to come closer to Him.

פרק א' משנה י"ח
על שלשה דברים העולם קיים
The World Endures on Three Things

רַבָּן שִׁמְעוֹן בֶּן גַּמְלִיאֵל אוֹמֵר, עַל שְׁלשָׁה דְבָרִים הָעוֹלָם קַיָּם, עַל הַדִּין וְעַל הָאֱמֶת וְעַל הַשָּׁלוֹם, שֶׁנֶּאֱמַר אֱמֶת וּמִשְׁפַּט שָׁלוֹם שִׁפְטוּ בְּשַׁעֲרֵיכֶם:

Rabban Shimon ben Gamliel says: The world endures on three things: on justice, truth, and peace; as it states (*Zechariah* 8:16): "Truth and peaceful justice shall you judge in your gates."

GEMS FROM THE *SEFER NESIVOS SHOLOM*

SOURCES:

עַל שְׁלֹשָׁה דְבָרִים הָעוֹלָם עוֹמֵד, עַל הַתּוֹרָה וְעַל הָעֲבוֹדָה וְעַל גְּמִילוּת חֲסָדִים. (אבות א')

On three things the world stands: Torah, Divine service, and acts of kindness. (*Avos* 1)

מוֹדָה אֲנִי לְפָנֶיךָ, מֶלֶךְ חַי וְקַיָּם, שֶׁהֶחֱזַרְתָּ בִּי נִשְׁמָתִי בְּחֶמְלָה, רַבָּה אֱמוּנָתֶךָ. (תפלת השכמת הבקר)

I give thanks before You, O Living and Enduring King, for You have returned my soul within me with compassion; great is Your faithfulness. (Prayer upon arising in the morning)

אַתָּה נְפַחְתָּהּ בִּי, וְאַתָּה מְשַׁמְּרָהּ בְּקִרְבִּי. (ברכות השחר)

You have breathed (my soul) inside of me, and You preserve it within me. (Morning benedictions)

שִׁיקְרָא לֹא קָאִי. (שבת ק"ד.)

Falsehood cannot be sustained. (*Shabbos* 104a)

לְעוֹלָם יַעֲסוֹק אָדָם בַּתּוֹרָה וּבַמִּצְוֹת אַף עַל פִּי שֶׁלֹּא לִשְׁמָהּ, שֶׁמִּתּוֹךְ שֶׁלֹּא לִשְׁמָהּ – בָּא לִשְׁמָהּ. (פסחים נ:)

A person should, in any event, occupy himself with Torah and mitzvos even if not for its own sake; for from doing so not for its own sake, he will (eventually) come to do so for its own sake. (*Pesachim* 50b)

על שלשה דברים העולם קיים

Universal Life Support

Each human being constitutes an entire world.

While this may initially sound hyperbolic, it is a statement of our Sages, that, like all their words, is grounded in the Torah's infinite wisdom. The truth is that Torah literature is replete with such references, characterizing man as an *olam katan* (microcosm of the world), an idea with immense philosophical and mystical ramifications.

This concept, as we shall see, can help inform our understanding of the intriguing mishnah that closes the first *perek*.

Rabban Shimon ben Gamliel informs us of the world's foundational principles: justice, truth, and peace. This is somewhat mystifying, as Shimon Hatzaddik, in the mishnah at the beginning of the *perek* (1:2), already identified the pillars of the world: עַל שְׁלֹשָׁה דְבָרִים הָעוֹלָם עוֹמֵד, עַל הַתּוֹרָה וְעַל הָעֲבוֹדָה וְעַל גְּמִילוּת חֲסָדִים — *On three things the world stands: Torah, Divine service, and acts of kindness*. What, indeed, *does* the world stand on?

Our mishnah actually comprises the very first words with which the *Tur* begins the *Choshen Mishpat* volume of his *halachic* code, addressing this very issue right from the start. He cites the explanation of Rabbeinu Yonah, who notes a distinction in the wording of the two mishnayos. In the beginning of the *perek*, Shimon Hatzaddik uses the word **omeid** — "The world **stands** on three things..." Here, Rabban Shimon ben Gamliel discusses on what the world **kayam** — the three things through which the world **exists**.

In other words, Shimon Hatzaddik was speaking of the world's purpose — the three reasons for which it was created in the first place: Torah, *avodah*, and *gemilus chassadim*. Rabban Shimon ben Gamliel was not dealing with the question of why the world was created; rather, he listed those elements responsible for *maintaining its existence*.

Having resolved the apparent contradiction, there remain certain points in this mishnah in need of further clarification, as the Nesivos Sholom delineates:

פרק א'

GEMS FROM THE SEFER NESIVOS SHOLOM

What exactly is it about these three items — *din*, *emes*, and *shalom* — that makes them uniquely qualified for "holding up" the world, more so than any other admirable quality?

We find other "trios" listed elsewhere in *Avos* as having significant impact on our existence in the world. עַיִן הָרָע, וְיֵצֶר הָרָע, וְשִׂנְאַת הַבְּרִיּוֹת, מוֹצִיאִין אֶת הָאָדָם מִן הָעוֹלָם — *An evil eye, the evil inclination, and hatred of people remove a person from the world* (2:11); הַקִּנְאָה, וְהַתַּאֲוָה, וְהַכָּבוֹד, מוֹצִיאִין אֶת הָאָדָם מִן הָעוֹלָם — *Envy, desire, and (lusting for) glory remove a person from the world* (4:21). These mishnayos are cast in the negative, displaying what traits can terminate existence. By contrast, Rabban Shimon ben Gamliel utilized a "positive" approach, speaking of the traits or principles that "hold up" the world. While optimism is always admirable, Rabban Shimon ben Gamliel presumably was guided by more concrete considerations. Why, then, did he express himself in this way? In line with the other mishnayos, why not teach us about the three pernicious qualities that would "destroy" the world: a corrupt justice system, falsehood, and strife?

Lifeblood of the Universe

An allusion was made at the outset to the effect that man is a microcosm of the world. This foundational idea can work both ways. That is, we can learn much about the inner workings of man by observing the world. We can also learn a lot about the world by examining man's essence.

The life of a person, as we know, is inextricably linked with his *neshamah*, his soul. A Yid's very first act upon awakening in the morning and discovering that he is alive, is to proclaim his thanks to Hashem for returning his soul: מוֹדֶה אֲנִי לְפָנֶיךָ...שֶׁהֶחֱזַרְתָּ בִּי נִשְׁמָתִי — *I give thanks before You...for having returned my soul within me*. And this theme appears repeatedly in our blessings and prayers. We express our heartfelt gratitude that אַתָּה נְפַחְתָּהּ בִּי, וְאַתָּה מְשַׁמְּרָהּ בְּקִרְבִּי — *You have breathed (my soul) inside of me, and You preserve it within me*, for we are aware of the consequences were the *neshamah* to depart, G-d forbid.

The retention of this spiritual entity within the confines of the opposing force of the physical body is nothing short of remarkable. It is miraculous, but at the same time, essential. Man, with his material tendencies fueled by his innate evil inclination, would be wholly given over to the fulfillment of his base passions. Hashem therefore imbued him with a sacred and pristine *neshamah*, a spark of the Divine. Only through this power does he have the capability to withstand and overcome his sinful nature and chart a course to righteousness.

The Nesivos Sholom explains that the world operates in the same fashion as the *olam hakatan*. There are forces with the capacity to tear the world apart; left to their own devices, this is exactly what would happen. These are the qualities mentioned above: falsehood, corruption, and strife. But Hashem desires not only that the world be maintained; His purpose in creating it was to establish for Himself a dwelling place in the lower spheres. Thus, to counteract the pull exerted by these evil forces upon the very foundations of the world, He imbued it with a special sanctity. This infusion of holiness was comprised of none other than *din*, *emes*, and *shalom*.

These qualities actually serve as the "*neshamah*" of the world, enabling it to survive and to thrive. Indeed, in their absence, the world — no longer able to contain the *Shechinah* — would cease to exist. A world rampant with lawlessness and corruption cannot function; strife tears at the very fabric of society. And, as *Chazal* tell us (*Shabbos* 140a), *Shikra lo ka'i* — "Falsehood cannot be sustained."

The Nesivos Sholom explains further that these three qualities are uniquely suited to serve as the *neshamah*, the life-force of creation, for they reflect the essence of the Creator Himself, as evidenced by the fact that they comprise the Names of Hashem. "The seal of *Hakadosh Baruch Hu* is *Emes*," the Gemara in *Shabbos* (51a) informs us; in our prayers, we refer to Hashem as the פּוֹעֵל אֱמֶת שֶׁפְּעֻלָּתוֹ אֱמֶת — *Performer of Truth, Whose acts are truth* (Kiddush Levanah). Hashem refers to Himself in this way: אֲנִי ה' אֹהֵב מִשְׁפָּט — *I am Hashem, Lover of Justice* (Yeshayah 61:8). We likewise refer to Him this way in the conclusion of the blessing in *Shemoneh Esrei*: מֶלֶךְ אוֹהֵב צְדָקָה וּמִשְׁפָּט — *The King Who loves righteousness and justice*, sharpening the focus even more during the crucial judgment period between Rosh Hashanah and

Yom Kippur: *Hamelech Hamishpat* — "The King of Justice." And of course, the Gemara states explicitly that Hashem's Name is *Shalom* (*Shabbos* 10b).

We have thus seen what it is about these specific items that make them responsible for the upkeep of the world. Through them, Hashem imbued the universe with the prestige and life-giving force of His very own Name. Likewise, we now understand why Rabban Shimon ben Gamliel adopted the "positive" approach, instead of delineating the vices that destroy the world. In so doing, he was stressing this crucial aspect that the world also needs a *neshamah* to survive, and it has one — in the form of *din*, *emes*, and *shalom*. Inherently the antithesis of truth — dubbed by *Chazal* as the *alma d'shikra* (world of falsehood) — the world simply cannot endure without its counterbalancing *neshamah* of *emes*, as *sheker*, by itself, will not stand.

Din likewise functions as a creative force, as evidenced by the remarkable statement of *Chazal* (*Shabbos* 10a): "Any judge who rules truthfully becomes a partner with *Hakadosh Baruch Hu* in fashioning creation." (It is noteworthy to compare this with *Chazal's* characterization of the role of parents in the creation of a child: "Three partners collaborate in man's creation: *Hakadosh Baruch Hu*, a father, and a mother" [*Kiddushin* 30b]. In fulfilling the procreation directive, one participates in fashioning a single, living being, whereas the magnitude of *din* is such that it serves to maintain the entire creation.)

And of course, *shalom* rounds out this universal *neshamah*. It is a quintessential life-giving force, comprising, as it does, the essence of the entire Torah: דְּרָכֶיהָ דַרְכֵי־נֹעַם וְכָל־נְתִיבוֹתֶיהָ שָׁלוֹם — *Its ways are ways of pleasantness, and all of its paths are peace* (*Mishlei* 3:17). The priestly blessing concludes with *shalom*, the principal prayers (*Shemoneh Esrei*) conclude with a blessing for (and the actual word) *shalom* — all reflecting how *shalom* is the cornerstone on which all existence is based. As the Midrash sums up (*Bamidbar Rabbah* 21:1): "Great is *shalom*, for the world operates only through the medium of *shalom*."

It's a Small World…

It is not just the overall universe in which *din*, *emes*, and *shalom* play such a vital role in maintaining existence. The private "world" of each and every Yid must also be predicated upon these principles to foster a healthy and harmonious coexistence with his fellows.

Din: We must serve as a constant judge over our own interactions with others. Are we profiting unfairly, capitalizing on the naiveté of our fellow Jew? Will the action we are about to take, or the comment we are about to dispense, be the cause of pain or distress?

Emes: Truth must permeate all aspects of our lives as Jews, including the "pillars" of our personal world: our Torah learning, our Divine service, and our acts of kindness. Care must be taken that our motives remain pure and our focus genuine. Otherwise, even a small measure of *sheker* that creeps into our observance can undermine and topple the stoutest foundations.

This notion is illustrated quite starkly by the Divrei Shmuel, who described the following scenario at one of his *tischen*: A Yid who observed Torah and mitzvos throughout his life passed away, entering into the Next World. Having expected to be showered with the reward for his years of service, he was dismayed to find that no reward was forthcoming. Upon inquiring on the matter from the Heavenly tribunal, he was told the following: "Whom were you really serving? It sure wasn't *Hakadosh Baruch Hu*. Go to whoever were your real targets in your observance, and let *them* provide you with your reward!"

Here an important distinction must be drawn. The ideal, of course, is to serve Hashem at all times exclusively for altruistic reasons; for many people, however, this is no simple task. The real question is: do we even yearn to get there? Someone for whom the notion of selfless *avodas Hashem* doesn't even register on his radar screen may be the subject of the Admor Bada"sh's admonition. But someone who is desirous of and strives to attain the preferred level may fall into an entirely different category.

The Nesivos Sholom quotes an interpretation of the well-known statement of *Chazal*, which sheds much light on the issue. The Gemara states, "A person should engage in Torah study and mitzvah observance even if not for its own sake (i.e., he has ulterior motives); for from non-altruistic observance, he will (eventually) come to altruistic observance" (*Pesachim* 50b). *Chazal* are not speaking of someone who is truly and wholly self-absorbed; one whose thoughts are so distant from *Hakadosh Baruch Hu* may in fact remain in such a state forever. What the Gemara refers to is someone who learns Torah for many hours — albeit with ulterior motives — but with the hope and intent that at least some small fraction of his study session will be undertaken purely for its own sake. While recognizing that he's not there yet, the stated and sincere goal of this *oveid* is for pristine observance. Thus, this underlying sliver of *emes* can support and sustain his *avodah*.

Shalom: The truth is that this point needs little elaboration, as most people recognize how foundational peace is in their personal lives: at home, with others, or internally.

Thus, Rabban Shimon ben Gamliel has imparted a fundamental lesson. In all matters — general and specific, spiritual and physical, in the "big" world or the "small" one — *din*, *emes*, and *shalom* comprise the soul that sustains all.

In Summary

The first *perek* of *Pirkei Avos* seems to begin and end on a very similar note. At almost the very beginning, Shimon Hatzaddik declares that the world stands on three things: Torah, *avodah*, and *gemilus chassadim*. The issue is that at the end of the *perek*, Rabban Shimon ben Gamliel provides what appears to be an alternate list, stating that the world stands on *din*, *emes*, and *shalom*.

However, as the *Tur* points out, there really is no contradiction. Shimon Hatzaddik's list dealt with the three pillars on which the world *omeid* (stands) — Torah, *avodah*, and *gemilus chassadim*.

על שלשה דברים העולם קיים

Rabban Shimon ben Gamliel was dealing with the *kiyum* (upkeep) of the world, achieved through the entities of *din*, *emes*, and *shalom*.

In explaining the mechanics of how exactly these items fulfill their mission, the Nesivos Sholom provides much insight. Just as the human body is dependent for its existence on the soul imbued in it by its Creator, so, too, the world has its *neshamah*. And just as a person's *neshamah*, of pristine and sacred quality, serves to counteract the natural tendencies of the physical body, the *neshamah* of the universe is likewise a counterbalance to the forces of evil that seek to tear the world asunder. Rabban Shimon ben Gamliel informs us that it is *din*, *emes*, and *shalom* that make up this universal *neshamah*, so crucial in maintaining the world's existence in the face of strife, corruption, and falsehood.

Of course, Rabban Shimon ben Gamliel did not select random qualities, laudable as they are. It is specifically these entities that sustain the world, as they share a common denominator of immeasurable magnitude and potency: each one comprises a Name by which Hashem is known, and reflects His pristine attributes. It is no wonder, then, that *Chazal* convey through various teachings that the world is upheld through *din*, *emes*, and *shalom*. And this holds true not only of the world at large; but also of the *olam hakatan*, the private world of each and every individual Yid, which likewise is so dependent on these integral qualities.

פרק א'

Gems from the
ספר
נתיבות שלום
NESIVOS
SHOLOM

פרק
ב'

פרק ב' משנה א'
איזוהי דרך ישרה שיבור לו האדם
What Is the Upright Path That a Man Should Choose for Himself

רַבִּי אוֹמֵר, אֵיזוֹהִי דֶרֶךְ יְשָׁרָה שֶׁיָּבוֹר לוֹ הָאָדָם, כֹּל שֶׁהִיא תִפְאֶרֶת לְעוֹשֶׂיהָ וְתִפְאֶרֶת לוֹ מִן הָאָדָם. וֶהֱוֵי זָהִיר בְּמִצְוָה קַלָּה כְּבַחֲמוּרָה, שֶׁאֵין אַתָּה יוֹדֵעַ מַתַּן שְׂכָרָן שֶׁל מִצְוֹת. וֶהֱוֵי מְחַשֵּׁב הֶפְסֵד מִצְוָה כְּנֶגֶד שְׂכָרָהּ, וּשְׂכַר עֲבֵרָה כְּנֶגֶד הֶפְסֵדָהּ. וְהִסְתַּכֵּל בִּשְׁלֹשָׁה דְבָרִים וְאֵין אַתָּה בָא לִידֵי עֲבֵרָה, דַּע מַה לְּמַעְלָה מִמְּךָ, עַיִן רוֹאָה וְאֹזֶן שׁוֹמַעַת, וְכָל מַעֲשֶׂיךָ בַּסֵּפֶר נִכְתָּבִים:

Rebbi says: What is the upright path a man should choose for himself? Whatever is honorable for the one who does it, and that accords him honor from man. Be as careful regarding a simple mitzvah as with a severe one, for you do not know the reward given for mitzvos. Calculate the loss of a mitzvah against its reward, and the reward of a sin against its loss. Look at three things and you will not come to the hands of sin: Know what is above you – an eye that sees, an ear that hears, and that all of your deeds are being inscribed in a book.

פרק ב'

GEMS FROM THE *SEFER NESIVOS SHOLOM*

SOURCES:

חֲמִשָּׁה תַלְמִידִים הָיוּ לוֹ לְרַבָּן יוֹחָנָן בֶּן זַכַּאי... אָמַר לָהֶם, צְאוּ וּרְאוּ אֵיזוֹהִי דֶרֶךְ טוֹבָה שֶׁיִדְבַּק בָּהּ הָאָדָם. רַבִּי אֱלִיעֶזֶר אוֹמֵר, עַיִן טוֹבָה. רַבִּי יְהוֹשֻׁעַ אוֹמֵר, חָבֵר טוֹב. רַבִּי יוֹסֵי אוֹמֵר, שָׁכֵן טוֹב. רַבִּי שִׁמְעוֹן אוֹמֵר, הָרוֹאֶה אֶת הַנּוֹלָד. רַבִּי אֶלְעָזָר אוֹמֵר, לֵב טוֹב. (אבות ב׳)

Rabban Yochanan ben Zakkai had five (primary) disciples... He said to them: "Go out and see which is the good path to which a person should adhere." Rabbi Eliezer says: A good eye. Rabbi Yehoshua says: A good friend. Rabbi Yose says: A good neighbor. Rabbi Shimon says: Foreseeing the outcome. Rabbi Elazar says: A good heart. (*Avos 2*)

מִקְדָּשׁ רִאשׁוֹן מִפְּנֵי מָה חָרַב? מִפְּנֵי שְׁלֹשָׁה דְבָרִים שֶׁהָיוּ בוֹ: עֲבוֹדָה זָרָה, וְגִלּוּי עֲרָיוֹת, וּשְׁפִיכוּת דָּמִים... אֲבָל מִקְדָּשׁ שֵׁנִי, שֶׁהָיוּ עוֹסְקִין בַּתּוֹרָה וּבְמִצְוֹת וּגְמִילוּת חֲסָדִים מִפְּנֵי מָה חָרַב? מִפְּנֵי שֶׁהָיְתָה בּוֹ שִׂנְאַת חִנָּם. לְלַמֶּדְךָ שֶׁשְּׁקוּלָה שִׂנְאַת חִנָּם כְּנֶגֶד שָׁלֹשׁ עֲבֵירוֹת: עֲבוֹדָה זָרָה, וְגִלּוּי עֲרָיוֹת, וּשְׁפִיכוּת דָּמִים. (יומא ט:)

Why was the first Temple destroyed? Because of three practices of that era: idolatry, immorality, and murder... But the second Temple, wherein they were involved in Torah study, mitzvos, and acts of kindness – why was it destroyed? Because there was baseless hatred during that era. This teaches you that baseless hatred is equal to three (cardinal) sins: idolatry, immorality, and murder. (*Yuma* 9b)

אוֹהֵב לִפְרוֹק וְשׂוֹנֵא לִטְעוֹן – מִצְוָה בְּשׂוֹנֵא...לָכוֹף אֶת יִצְרוֹ עָדִיף. (בבא מציעא ל״ב:)

(One is simultaneously presented with two opportunities to offer assistance, providing a choice to either) help his friend unload, or help his enemy to load; (helping) the enemy takes precedence... for it is better to (engage in an act which entails) coercing one's (evil) inclination. (*Bava Metzia* 32b)

פרקי אבות

148

איזוהי דרך ישרה שיבור לו האדם

רַבִּי חֲנַנְיָא בֶּן עֲקַשְׁיָא אוֹמֵר, רָצָה הַקָּדוֹשׁ בָּרוּךְ הוּא לְזַכּוֹת אֶת יִשְׂרָאֵל, לְפִיכָךְ הִרְבָּה לָהֶם תּוֹרָה וּמִצְוֹת. (מכות ג' ט"ז)

Rabbi Chananya ben Akashya says: Hashem wished to bestow merit upon Yisroel; He therefore gave them Torah and mitzvos in abundance. (*Makkos* 3:16)

הֲלֹא הִיא כְתוּבָה עַל סֵפֶר הַיָּשָׁר. מַאי סֵפֶר הַיָּשָׁר? א"ר חִיָּיא בַּר אַבָּא א"ר יוֹחָנָן: זֶה סֵפֶר אַבְרָהָם יִצְחָק וְיַעֲקֹב שֶׁנִּקְרְאוּ יְשָׁרִים. (ע"ז כ"ה.)

"Is it not written in the Book of the Just?" (*Yehoshua* 10:13). What is the "Book of the Just"? Rabbi Chiya bar Aba said in the name of Rabbi Yochanan: This (refers to) the book of Avraham, Yitzchak, and Yaakov (i.e., *Sefer Bereishis*), for they were referred to as "Just." (*Avodah Zarah* 25a)

וְעָשִׂיתָ הַיָּשָׁר וְהַטּוֹב בְּעֵינֵי ה'. (דברים ו' י"ח)

And you shall do what is upright and good in the eyes of Hashem. (*Devarim* 6:18)

כִּי תַעֲשֶׂה הַטּוֹב וְהַיָּשָׁר בְּעֵינֵי ה'. (שם י"ב כ"ח)

When you shall do that which is good and upright in the eyes of Hashem. (*ibid.* 12:28)

הַטּוֹב - בְּעֵינֵי הַשָּׁמַיִם. וְהַיָּשָׁר - בְּעֵינֵי אָדָם. (רש"י שם)

"That which is good" – in the eyes of Heaven. "And upright" – in the eyes of man. (*Rashi, ibid.*)

סוֹף דָּבָר הַכֹּל נִשְׁמָע אֶת־הָאֱלֹקִים יְרָא וְאֶת־מִצְוֹתָיו שְׁמוֹר כִּי־זֶה כָּל־הָאָדָם. (קהלת י"ב י"ג)

In the final analysis, all is heard: Fear G-d and keep His commandments; for this comprises the complete man. (*Koheles* 12:13)

פרק ב'

149

GEMS FROM THE *SEFER NESIVOS SHOLOM*

כִּי־תִרְאֶה חֲמוֹר שׂנַאֲךָ רֹבֵץ תַּחַת מַשָּׂאוֹ...עָזֹב תַּעֲזֹב עִמּוֹ. (שמות כ״ג ה׳)

When you see the donkey of your enemy crouching under its load...assist in the unloading with him. (*Shemos* 23:5)

לֹא־תִרְאֶה אֶת־חֲמוֹר אָחִיךָ אוֹ שׁוֹרוֹ נֹפְלִים בַּדֶּרֶךְ וְהִתְעַלַּמְתָּ מֵהֶם הָקֵם תָּקִים עִמּוֹ. (דברים כ״ב ד׳)

You may not simply watch passively as the donkey of your brother, or his ox (or their burden) have fallen in the way; (rather) you shall assist with him in picking them up. (*Devarim* 22:4)

איזוהי דרך ישרה שיבור לו האדם

Straight or Good

How should a Jew live his life?

That may seem like an odd question. The answer is easy: just learn Torah and do mitzvos. Right?

While definitely true, the question still needs further probing. In fact, *Pirkei Avos* raises this very issue and addresses it extensively — in a number of ways.

One example is found right here, at the beginning of the second *perek*, as Rebbi (Rabbi Yehudah Hanasi) tackles the question: What is the proper path?

The issue is brought up yet again later on (2:10), when Rabban Yochanan ben Zakkai presents almost the identical question to his five prime *talmidim*: — אָמַר לָהֶם, צְאוּ וּרְאוּ אֵיזוֹהִי דֶרֶךְ טוֹבָה שֶׁיִּדְבַּק בָּהּ הָאָדָם He said to them: Go and search out: what is the good path to which a person should adhere?

There are, however, some subtle differences in the way in which Rebbi and Rabban Yochanan ben Zakkai pose their questions. The holy *Tanna'im* were supremely deliberate and sparing in their choice of wording. As such, accounting for these variations should prove to be quite edifying.

First, it should be noted that there exists a variant textual version of Rabban Yochanan's question. Rebbi asked what the *derech* **yesharah** (**proper/upright** path) is. According to the version of the *Machzor Vitry*, Rabban Yochanan asked: What is the *derech* **tovah** (**good** path)?

Another difference in the language occurs with the term for choosing. Rebbi asked: "What is the path...*sheyavor lo ha'adam* (that a person should **select**)?" Rabban Yochanan stated: "What is the path...*sheyidbak bah ha'adam* (to which a person should **adhere/ attach himself**)?"

Perhaps even more significant is the difference in the substance of the direction the *Tanna'im* provide. In his answer, Rebbi seems to emphasize a path of action: *Kol she'hi tiferes l'oseha* — "That

פרק ב'

151

which is harmonious for the one who **does** it." In their replies, Rabban Yochanan ben Zakkai's *talmidim* spoke more of matters that constitute the inner makeup of a person — his intellect and emotions (a good heart, a good eye, etc.).

Thus we find that Rebbi and Rabban Yochanan were actually each addressing different fundamental aspects of *avodas Hashem*. Rebbi was dealing more with the practical facets of fulfilling the commandments in the most complete and pre-eminent manner. The Bartenura elaborates on Rebbi's action-based approach, explaining it as promoting a middle-of-the-way path, in which extremes at either end should be avoided. Take the issue of how one allocates his resources, for example. A spendthrift, in showering his bounty indiscriminately on others, most certainly will acquire many friends. In the area of *tiferes lo min ha'adam*, agreeable to people, he has done quite well. But in the area of *tiferes l'oseha*, agreeable to the one who does it, he comes up quite short, as he will soon find himself penniless. On the other hand, a miser who hoards his fortune, spending precious little — and that on himself only — may be benefitting his own person in the long run. Obviously, however, his actions don't earn him many admirers. And so, Rebbi instructs us that the best course of action is to choose a path that is honorable for oneself and one's peers at the same time. Be neither stingy nor extravagant, but take care to do right by yourself and by others.

Spreading Goodness

Rabban Yochanan's focus, explains the Nesivos Sholom, was on a person's *essence*; he aimed to ensure that one's makeup will be entirely infused with *tov*, goodness. This may sound like a tall order, as a person is actually born with an inherent predilection towards evil. As the *passuk* tells us (*Bereishis* 8:21): כִּי יֵצֶר לֵב הָאָדָם רַע מִנְּעֻרָיו — *For from his youth, the inclination of man's heart is towards wickedness.* But Rabban Yochanan understood that we were brought down upon this earth for this very purpose: we are charged with the mission of addressing and working on our inherent evil, converting our essence into one of goodness. And the mission is not the same for each person;

on the contrary, we each have our own unique set of character flaws and negative tendencies that need be corrected.

Rabban Yochanan, however, realized that there is a key to accomplishing what appears to be a monumental feat. As Rabbeinu Yonah explains, it is possible to attain mastery of all pristine traits by *initially* focusing on a single, overarching *middah*. That is, through dedicating oneself to the perfection of one *middah*, that goodness will infuse his entire being. This was the essence of Rabban Yochanan's question: What is that singular *middah* **sheyidbak** *bah ha'adam*, to which a person should **cling** (that is, perfect)? For this will enable his entire essence to be permeated with *tov*.

The first response to their *rebbi's* question came from Rabbi Eliezer, who selected *ayin tovah*, a good eye. Rabbi Eliezer felt that cultivating a favorable outlook towards others would be the source of developing all other positive traits.

It could be that Rabbi Eliezer's source for centering on this particular *middah* was the tragic history of the destruction of the Beis Hamikdash; he perceived from this the consequences engendered by the opposing force.

The Nesivos Sholom explains: There appears to be a remarkable aspect in *Chazal's* identification of the causes of the Temples' destruction. The Gemara tells us (*Yuma* 9b) that the first and second Beis Hamikdash were each destroyed for a different reason. The first was lost due to the weakness of the Jewish people in the areas of idol worship, immorality, and murder. The destruction of the second came about as a result of *sin'as chinam*, baseless hatred.

It is the equivalency factor that appears most perplexing. It is understandable that rampant perpetration of the sins of idolatry, immorality, and murder would bring about the destruction of the Beis Hamikdash. After all, these are extremely heinous transgressions, widely and accurately referred to as the three cardinal sins of all Torah prohibitions. But *sin'as chinam*? While certainly a deplorable trait, it still seems to pale in comparison to the violations that characterized the First Temple era. Technically speaking, *sin'as chinam* entails nothing more than the violation of a single prohibition, and while transgressing any one of the "big three" incurs the death penalty, for *sin'as chinam* the perpetrator does not even receive lashes (as it is an action-less prohibition)! How can it be that one Beis Hamikdash is destroyed as the result of the three most serious violations, which carry such grave consequences, while the other is destroyed as a result of a single prohibition for which the *Beis Din* (Rabbinical Court) does not even administer any punishment!

The Nesivos Sholom clarifies the issue by examining both extremes — *sin'as chinam* and *ahavas chinam* (unconditional love). While they are opposites, they are both the result of the principal makeup and guiding force emanating from within the individual. Loving your neighbor, as Rabbi Akiva taught us, is a great and overriding principle of Torah. This statement reflects the fact that not only do we fulfill a mitzvah thereby; but such love reveals a heart that is refined and good, as love emanates from internal goodness. That is, when we view our fellows with favor and bear unmitigated love for them all, it is a clear indication that the force of good is asserting primary control in us.

On the other end of the spectrum, the same holds true for hatred. Hateful behavior results when it is the bad that controls an individual's essence. The destruction of the second Beis Hamikdash was not so much the result of the technical violation of a prohibition. Rather, it was brought on by a more severe and sinister entity that lay beneath this violation: an evil and corroded essence, by which the power of hate and evil controls the individual.

Rabbi Eliezer learned this lesson, and this understanding informed his response. From the devastation wrought by its absence, he discerned the power of an *ayin tovah*. Thus he submitted that it is an *ayin tovah* that is the primary *middah*, as it indicates the presence of an internal essence of good. When the power of good is in control, all other positive traits can emerge.

While providing alternate answers, the other *talmidim* were guided by essentially the same principle of cultivating a source of good from which goodness will pervade all areas. Rabbi Yehoshua's answer was a *chaver tov*, a good friend; as a person is generally drawn to imitate his peers, a good friend will serve as the prime motivator and influence for one to develop positive traits. Rabbi Elazar explicitly promotes the development of a *lev tov*, a good heart; and so forth.

Taken together — Rabban Yochanan ben Zakkai's emphasis on the essence of goodness asserting control, and Rebbi's approach to practical and complete fulfillment of mitzvos — these teachings provide a potent and important guide in perfecting *avodas Hashem*. It could very well be, in fact, that the Torah promotes both approaches, alluding to them in *Parshas Va'eschanan*: וְעָשִׂיתָ הַיָּשָׁר וְהַטּוֹב בְּעֵינֵי ד׳ — *And you shall do what is upright and good in the eyes of Hashem* (*Devarim* 6:18). *Hayashar*, the upright, refers to Rebbi's set of directives; that is, the straight, middle path one should adopt in refining and performing all actions perfectly and completely. *V'hatov*, and the good, reflects Rabban Yochanan's teaching, as he encouraged the cultivation of an essence of good to overpower and assert control over one's inherent inclination towards evil.

Acting *L'sheim Shamayim*, Sanctifying *Sheim Shamayim*

Returning to Rebbi's exposition on mitzvah performance, we find that the Maharal adds another dimension to his teaching. Rebbi was instructing us on the path of action — the optimal way to fulfill Hashem's precepts. He stresses two conditions: that the actions be considered *tiferes* both from the standpoint of the doer himself and from the standpoint of others. In his commentary to this mishnah, the Maharal clarifies Rebbi's intent. *Tiferes l'oseha* entails that the mitzvah be performed entirely *l'sheim Shamayim* (for the sake of Heaven), without any element of personal interest. If one's primary aim is to impress his onlookers, he obviously has missed the boat regarding this aspect. Rather, the deed should be inherently *tiferes* — praiseworthy and pristine — even though the intent is revealed only *l'oseha*, to the one who performs it, for only he is privy to his innermost thoughts.

While the first *tiferes* relates to the person performing the act, the focus of the second *tiferes* reference in Rebbi's instruction is on the splendor accorded to Hashem through man's actions. This is attained through actions that create a *kiddush Hashem* (sanctification of Hashem's Name). When a Yid's behavior is proper and refined, he thereby brings glory to G-d Whom he serves. In effect, a faithful Jew functions as an ambassador in the Name of Hashem, Who commanded him to act in the way he does. And so his behavior must reflect positively on his Master. That is, his deeds must have the effect of eliciting *tiferes Lo min ha'adam* — "splendor to Him in the eyes of others."

This explanation sheds further light on the particular wording chosen by Rebbi. He did not state *tiferes lo min **haberiyos*** (literally: creatures), employing the term commonly used to refer to the general populace. Rather, the mishnah utilizes the word ***ha'adam***. The Maharal explains the significance, asserting that the mishnah is conveying the extent to which one's actions must be refined and admirable. *Beriyos* refers to people of little depth, who are basically unqualified and incapable of discerning true value. They may easily conclude that someone is considered praiseworthy when, in fact, the individual is really fooling society. As such, winning the admiration of the *beriyos* is no impressive feat. The character of these people themselves is none too exemplary; as such, they are easily taken in, and their standards in the first place are not too substantial. A person of true character, however, is one who earns the approval of people of true quality and discernment. This group represents people of real substance, the quintessential *adam*. They themselves possess and appreciate real character, and so are able to identify what is truly refined behavior. Thus, one who is able to garner *tiferes* from *adam* has truly made a *kiddush Hashem* by displaying genuinely admirable behavior.

We mentioned previously that the Torah makes reference to the qualities of *tov* and *yashar*. These terms appear together yet again, in *Parshas Re'eh*: כִּי תַעֲשֶׂה הַטּוֹב וְהַיָּשָׁר בְּעֵינֵי ד' — *When you shall do that which is* tov *and* yashar *in the eyes of Hashem* (Devarim 12:28). The Maharal perceives this couplet as reflecting the two qualities expounded by Rebbi — *tiferes l'oseha* and *tiferes Lo min ha'adam*.

איזוהי דרך ישרה שיבור לו האדם

The Maharal (in his commentary to our mishnah, as well as in *Gur Aryeh*, *Devarim ibid.*) bases his comments on Rashi's interpretation of the *passuk*. Rashi (*Devarim ibid.*) identifies exactly to what these two terms refer. He explains *tov* as being good in the eyes of Hashem, and *yashar* as straight and upright in the eyes of man.

There appears to be an issue with Rashi's rendering; seemingly, he should have interpreted the verse in the opposite order. In the *passuk*, the word *yashar* is adjacent to the phrase *b'einei Hashem* — "in the eyes of Hashem." Seeing that the *passuk* connects them, wouldn't it have made more sense to interpret *yashar* as "straight *in the eyes of Hashem*" and render *tov* as "good *in the eyes of man*"? Why does Rashi deviate from the interpretation apparently suggested by the order of the *passuk* itself (and instead explain *yashar* as "straight in the eyes of *man*," and *tov* as "good in the eyes of *Hashem*")?

The Maharal explains that, in truth, Rashi's interpretation squares quite well with the ideas mentioned above. Note that *yashar*, straightness, is a quality perceivable by the human eye. That is, through his own vision, a person can discern if a line is straight or crooked. This is why Rashi felt that *yashar* was better matched with "in the eyes of man." In other words, the Torah is referring to behavior that people can discern as proper and upright; those actions which will cause a *kiddush Hashem*, as men behold and identify the *oveid Hashem* as an upright and pleasant individual. This is the *tiferes Lo min ha'adam* of which Rebbi spoke. *Tov*, on the other hand, is something which is inherently good, albeit this fact may be concealed from onlookers who cannot discern one's innermost thoughts. Only Hashem knows if one's action was performed completely for His sake, with no trace of ulterior motive — *tiferes l'oseha*. For this reason, Rashi attributed *tov* in the *passuk* to that which is "good in the eyes of Hashem." Thus, *tov v'yashar* mirror the two attributes emphasized by Rebbi.

Easy Mitzvos and Hard Mitzvos

The Nesivos Sholom relates an alternate explanation to Rebbi's statement, quoting the Saba Kadisha of Slonim *ztz"l* (*Toras Avos*).

Most people find that the various mitzvos relate to their inherent natures in differing ways. That is, there are certain mitzvos which seem to come somewhat easily to the individual. No harm in that, of course; in fact, it is a great kindness Hashem grants to us. There is a mitzvah, for example, to delight in good foods on Shabbos. Many people may find they don't need too much coaxing to partake of this mitzvah.

But then there are many mitzvos that not only don't automatically comply with one's inherent nature, but are actually at odds with it. These mitzvos entail real toil, in that a Jew must expend much effort to fight against and conquer his *yetzer hara* in order to fulfill them properly.

In his teaching, Rebbi was addressing both types of precepts, stressing that *shleimus* in *avodas Hashem* requires complete dedication to the fulfillment of both types. This is the way to pursue the *derech hayashar*, so that one's mitzvah observance will be optimal. It involves the proper fulfillment of those acts which are *tiferes l'oseha*, agreeable to the doer, in that they are in keeping with his nature and hence easy to comply with. But it also demands complete adherence to the other class of mitzvos, those which he must go against his grain to fulfill. In fact, this type of *avodah* is paramount, and may actually take precedence.

It is to this latter form of *avodah* that Rebbi refers when speaking of actions which are *tiferes lo min ha'adam*. As mentioned previously, the term *"adam"* is perhaps the most complimentary manner of referring to a person. It connotes a sense of *shleimus*, as manifest in the conclusion of *Koheles*. Having examined all facets of existence, and discovering that the world's pleasures essentially amount to *hevel havalim* (vanity of vanities), Shlomo Hamelech closes his work with the following exhortation: סוֹף דָּבָר הַכֹּל נִשְׁמָע אֶת־הָאֱלֹקִים יְרָא וְאֶת־מִצְוֹתָיו שְׁמוֹר כִּי־זֶה כָּל־הָאָדָם — *In the final analysis, all is heard: Fear G-d and keep His commandments; for this comprises the complete* **adam** (*Koheles* 12:13). The method by which an individual attains that status of *shleimus* implied by the title *adam* is through the subjugation of his natural tendencies. And the principal way this is achieved is through

איזוהי דרך ישרה שיבור לו האדם

the performance of those mitzvos for which he must exert himself and work against his nature. In this way, he will attain *tiferes*, the glorified status of *adam*.

We find this idea manifest in the precepts of **perikah u'te'inah** (helping one's fellow to **unload** or **load** his animal). When confronted with both prospects — that is, two individuals requiring assistance: one to load his donkey, the other to unload — it is usually unloading which takes precedence (to relieve the animal's discomfort). Although *perikah* is normally accorded more urgency, there is an exception. If one's friend needs help unloading, while his enemy needs help loading, one should give precedence to helping his enemy. Why the shift in priority? Why abandon the standard protocol of attending first to *perikah* and only then to *te'inah* when suddenly one's enemy is involved? *Chazal* explain: לָכוֹף אֶת יִצְרוֹ עָדִיף — *Subjugation of one's inclination takes precedence* (*Bava Metzia* 32b). To grant assistance to one's enemy requires one to summon real willpower and act against one's inherent tendencies. So much did the Torah value this exercise, that when the opportunity arises, the regular priority order for assistance is suspended.

The Saba Kadisha explains the next part of Rebbi's teaching as a continuation of this theme, as the aforementioned notion is expressed in its words. הֱוֵי זָהִיר בְּמִצְוָה קַלָּה כְּבַחֲמוּרָה, שֶׁאֵין אַתָּה יוֹדֵעַ מַתַּן שְׂכָרָן שֶׁל מִצְוֹת — *Be as careful to fulfill a less severe mitzvah as a severe one, for ultimately you do not know the magnitude of reward given for particular mitzvos*. One would assume that, by and large, a mitzvah of especial severity would take precedence over a much "lighter" one. However, the reward given for mitzvos is deeply affected by the level of difficulty entailed in its performance. Thus, as in the case of *te'inah* — which under normal circumstances is not viewed in the category of a "severe" mitzvah — if it involves subduing one's *yetzer hara* (such as when one's enemy needs help), it gets first priority.

With this understanding, we can perceive another well-known statement of *Chazal* in a new light. The mishnah in *Makkos* states: רַבִּי חֲנַנְיָא בֶּן עֲקַשְׁיָא אוֹמֵר, רָצָה הַקָּדוֹשׁ בָּרוּךְ הוּא לְזַכּוֹת אֶת יִשְׂרָאֵל, לְפִיכָךְ הִרְבָּה לָהֶם תּוֹרָה וּמִצְוֹת — *Rabbi Chananya ben Akashya says:* Hakadosh Baruch

Hu *desired to grant Yisroel merit; therefore, He increased for them Torah and mitzvos.* This is the standard rendering of this teaching. However, *l'zakos* can also be understood in light of the root word *zakeich*, meaning "to purify." For this is the principal task for which a Yid was brought to This World: to refine his soul, a feat achieved specifically through the fight against and subjugation of his evil inclination. Each mitzvah corresponds to another aspect or limb of a person; by toiling to fulfill these many mitzvos, one purges his materialistic tendencies and refines his inherent nature. "Hashem desired to *purify* Yisroel; therefore, He granted them much Torah and mitzvos."

The *Derech* to *D'veikus*

Earlier, the Nesivos Sholom had clarified the different areas of focus between the teachings of Rebbi and Rabban Yochanan ben Zakkai. Rebbi was seeking the *derech yesharah*, addressing the practical approach of performing a mitzvah in the optimal manner, such that all his actions are upright and proper. Rabban Yochanan dealt with the *derech tovah*, the way by which one can transform his inner nature so that the good gains mastery, and his essence becomes one of goodness.

There is another approach to account for the differences between the two *Tanna'im*. The Nesivos Sholom presents this alternate explanation, predicated on a nuanced view of the concepts of *tov* and *yashar*.

These terms — as they appear in the *passuk* — were respectively explained by Rashi (quoting the teaching of the Sifri) as "good in the eyes of Hashem" and "upright in the eyes of man." This had been previously understood as reflecting the difference between actions and intent. *Yashar* was referring to actions, as these are perceivable "in the eyes of man." *Tov* referred to pure intent, an entity which can only be detected by "the eyes of Hashem."

Here, the Nesivos Sholom takes a slightly different tack in understanding this teaching of the Sifri. He perceives these two entities as actually reflective of the two well-known categories

איזוהי דרך ישרה שיבור לו האדם

into which all mitzvos are divided: *bein adam laMakom* (between man and Hashem, such as Shabbos and kashrus), and *bein adam lachaveiro* (interpersonal mitzvos, such as loving one's fellow man).

When the *passuk* instructs us to do *tov* and *yashar*, it is emphasizing these two aspects. "Good in the eyes of Hashem" can refer to *mitzvos bein adam laMakom*, as Hashem Himself is the Source of all good. "Upright in the eyes of man" is a reference to *mitzvos bein adam lachaveiro*. The *navi* makes mention of the *Sefer* **Hayashar**, Book of **the Just** (*Shmuel II* 1:18). The Gemara (*Avodah Zarah* 25b) identifies this as *Sefer Bereishis*, titled *Sefer Hayashar* after the *Avos* who are featured in this *sefer*. The *Avos* are referred to as *Yesharim* (Upright Ones), for their excellence in the area of *bein adam lachaveiro* was legendary. *Sefer Bereishis*, which recounts their deeds, is, in effect, a *sefer* of *middos* (proper conduct).

The Nesivos Sholom explains the difference between the teachings of Rebbi and Rabban Yochanan based on this division. Rebbi focused on the *derech* **yesharah** — that is, actions and behaviors in the area of *bein adam lachaveiro*. He emphasized that to attain perfection, a Jew must strive to deal uprightly both with himself, *tiferes l'oseha*, and with his fellow man, *min ha'adam*.

Rabban Yochanan, on the other hand, addressed the area of *bein adam laMakom*. He sought out the *derech* **tovah** to which a person should be **misdabeik** (attached). He solicited ideas from his prime disciples as to the path by which one can achieve that ultimate state of perfection — *d'veikus* to Hashem, the supreme Source of goodness.

The responses of his *talmidim* all revolved around this crucial point — what is the optimal way whereby a Yid can attain *d'veikus*. Rabbi Eliezer advocated an *ayin tovah*, a good eye. By viewing everything through a lens of goodness — perceiving the good qualities of others, rejoicing in their success, being satisfied with our own lot, discerning Hashem's benevolent hand in everything that occurs — we each become an entity of good will. As individuals whose essence is one of pure goodness, we will thus be able to cleave to *Hakadosh Baruch Hu*, the Source of goodness.

Rabbi Yehoshua submitted that priority should be granted

towards obtaining a *chaver tov*, a good friend. He sought to achieve the same aim as above, but through different means. By *chaver tov*, Rabbi Yehoshua meant an individual who has attained the level of *d'veikus* to Hashem. By forming a bond with such a person, one will be influenced in a positive way and led to a state of *d'veikus* as well.

And so forth with the remaining responses. It was the suggestion of Rabbi Elazar that Rabban Yochanan favored, as he explained to his disciples, "For your ideas are subsumed within his." Rabbi Elazar had put forth that one cultivate the attribute of *lev tov*, a good heart. In truth, Rabbi Elazar's response is quite similar to that of Rabbi Eliezer who promoted an *ayin tovah*, as they both seek to internalize goodness within the individual. The difference lies in the fact that — in the final analysis — a positive outlook, while admirable and important, is primarily a function of the intellect. What Rabbi Elazar perceived (and Rabban Yochanan ultimately concurred) was that one must go even deeper to root out the evil within. One's inherent evil tendencies are not confined to the mind alone, but form one's very makeup; in a sense, it resides within his very blood. Therefore, to truly eradicate the evil from within and transform oneself into an entity of good, the goodness must permeate the very marrow of one's bones. All one's innermost drives and feelings must radiate *tov*. This is the essence of a *lev tov*, and through it a Yid becomes an inherent entity of *tov*. Only when the roots of one's soul are the essence of goodness, will one be able to achieve *d'veikus* with the One Who is the Ultimate Source of goodness.

In Summary

In a series of teachings literally packed with a wealth of crucial lessons, the *Tanna'im* outline the path through which a Jew can attain *shleimus* in *avodas Hashem*.

Our mishnah at the beginning of the second *perek*, as well as one later in this same chapter, both ask similar questions, with slight but notable linguistic differences. These deviations reflect different (but not opposing) approaches, with each *Tanna* addressing an alternate path of reaching perfection. Rebbi speaks of the *derech* **yesharah** a person should select, while Rabban Yochanan ben Zakkai seeks the *derech* **tovah** to which one should attach himself (*sheyidbak bah ha'adam*).

These differences can be accounted for by examining the answers the *Tanna'im* supply to the overarching question of choosing a path. In the continuation of the mishnah, Rebbi is clearly addressing the area of actions; he speaks of a path that is *tiferes l'oseha*, to the one who **does**. The other qualification Rebbi mentions is that it be *tiferes lo min ha'adam* — one garnering favor from others. The Bartenura understands Rebbi as promoting a middle path, whereby his actions are calibrated to avoid extremes. Thus, for example, he should adopt such a path when it comes to spending money. Were he to be free-spending with his friends, he would win their praise but do himself harm. If he were overly stingy, though protecting his own assets, he would not be much loved by those around him who could otherwise have benefitted from his generosity. Instead, he should aim for the middle, whereby he would please his peers while avoiding self-destruction.

Alternatively, Rebbi's action-centered approach could be understood as differentiating between intent and purposeful exposure. The Maharal interprets the mishnah in this way: *Tiferes l'oseha* refers to the performance of a mitzvah with pristine intentions, done solely for the sake of Hashem without any trace of ulterior motive. The act is inherently pure, but relates solely to the doer and remains unknown to his peers. *Tiferes Lo min ha'adam* refers to Hashem. That is, Rebbi exhorts one to create a *kiddush Hashem* through his actions, behaving in a way that is befitting of an *oveid Hashem*, and that will bring honor to Him in the eyes of man. *Tiferes* **Lo** *min ha'adam*.

Rebbi's words can also be taken as referring to the varying levels of difficulty associated with mitzvos. There are those that are *tiferes l'oseha*; that is, inherently agreeable to the doer, as they fit with his personal nature. He need not fight to fulfill this type of mitzvah, and may actually derive some natural enjoyment from it. One's primary task, however, is to perform those mitzvos that require exertion, for which one must subdue his inclination in order to fulfill them. Rebbi refers to this type of mitzvah when speaking of *tiferes lo min ha'adam*. For it is specifically by engaging in this type of *avodah* — subjugating his passions — that a person purifies his nature and emerges thereby as an *adam hashaleim*. It is for this purpose that he was placed on this earth.

While Rebbi had focused primarily on actions, Rabban Yochanan ben Zakkai addressed the inherent makeup of a person. Thus he presented to his disciples the question of how to attach oneself to goodness to the point that it will affect his entire essence. He understood that through selecting the proper good attribute and cleaving to it, the goodness would permeate and grow within the person, leading him to excel in all other positive traits. His *talmidim* submitted what they felt was the *middah* most capable of having this effect: an *ayin tovah*, a *lev tov*, etc.

There is yet another approach to understanding the different areas of focus expounded by Rebbi and Rabban Yochanan. The Nesivos Sholom explains further that they were addressing, respectively, the two common categories of mitzvos: *bein adam lachaveiro* and *bein adam laMakom*. In expounding on the *derech yesharah*, Rebbi was dealing with interpersonal mitzvos, those actions which govern one's relationship with his fellows. The *Avos*, who attained perfection in the arena of *bein adam lachaveiro*, were referred to as **Yesharim** for their achievement. It is for this reason that the *sefer* that features their accomplishments — *Sefer Bereishis* — is also known as *Sefer* **Hayashar**.

Rabban Yochanan's focus was on *bein adam laMakom*, as he sought the way in which one can achieve *d'veikus* with *Hakadosh Baruch Hu*, the Source of all **Tov**. His *talmidim* offered responses demonstrating what they felt was the optimal way whereby a person could transform his essence into one of goodness, thereby becoming a prime candidate for cleaving to the Ultimate Source of goodness. The response most favored by Rabban Yochanan was the promotion of a *lev **tov***. This represents a real sea change within the individual, the only bona fide method for expunging one's evil tendencies from the very fibers of his being. A *lev tov* implies that our goodness is not confined to the intellect, but permeates to the very essence of our being. Having transformed into an entity of inherent goodness, we will thus be able to attain *d'veikus* with Hashem, the true Source of good.

פרק ב' משנה א'
שהיא תפארת לעושיה ותפארת לו מן האדם
(One) That Is Honorable to the One Who Does It, and Accords Him Honor from Man

רַבִּי אוֹמֵר, אֵיזוֹהִי דֶרֶךְ יְשָׁרָה שֶׁיָּבוֹר לוֹ הָאָדָם, כֹּל שֶׁהִיא תִפְאֶרֶת לְעוֹשֶׂיהָ וְתִפְאֶרֶת לוֹ מִן הָאָדָם. וֶהֱוֵי זָהִיר בְּמִצְוָה קַלָּה כְּבַחֲמוּרָה, שֶׁאֵין אַתָּה יוֹדֵעַ מַתַּן שְׂכָרָן שֶׁל מִצְווֹת. וֶהֱוֵי מְחַשֵּׁב הֶפְסֵד מִצְוָה כְּנֶגֶד שְׂכָרָהּ, וּשְׂכַר עֲבֵרָה כְּנֶגֶד הֶפְסֵדָהּ. וְהִסְתַּכֵּל בִּשְׁלֹשָׁה דְבָרִים וְאֵין אַתָּה בָא לִידֵי עֲבֵרָה, דַּע מַה לְּמַעְלָה מִמְּךָ, עַיִן רוֹאָה וְאֹזֶן שׁוֹמַעַת, וְכָל מַעֲשֶׂיךָ בַּסֵּפֶר נִכְתָּבִים:

Rebbi says: What is the upright path a man should choose for himself? Whatever is honorable for the one who does it, and that accords him honor from man. Be as careful regarding a simple mitzvah as with a severe one, for you do not know the reward given for mitzvos. Calculate the loss of a mitzvah against its reward, and the reward of a sin against its loss. Look at three things and you will not come to the hands of sin: Know what is above you – an eye that sees, an ear that hears, and that all of your deeds are being inscribed in a book.

GEMS FROM THE *SEFER NESIVOS SHOLOM*

SOURCES:

סוֹף דָּבָר הַכֹּל נִשְׁמָע אֶת־הָאֱלֹקִים יְרָא וְאֶת־מִצְוֹתָיו שְׁמוֹר כִּי־זֶה כָּל־הָאָדָם. (קהלת י״ב י״ג)

In the final analysis, all is heard: Fear G-d and keep His commandments; for this comprises the complete man. (*Koheles* 12:13)

אוֹהֵב לִפְרוֹק וְשׂוֹנֵא לִטְעוֹן – מִצְוָה בְּשׂוֹנֵא...לָכוֹף אֶת יִצְרוֹ עָדִיף. (בבא מציעא ל״ב)

(One is simultaneously presented with two opportunities to offer assistance, providing a choice to either) help his friend unload, or help his enemy to load; (helping) the enemy takes precedence... for it is better to (engage in an act which entails) coercing one's (evil) inclination. (*Bava Metzia* 32b)

כְּמַעֲשֵׂה אֶרֶץ־מִצְרַיִם אֲשֶׁר יְשַׁבְתֶּם־בָּהּ לֹא תַעֲשׂוּ... אִישׁ אִישׁ אֶל־כָּל־שְׁאֵר בְּשָׂרוֹ לֹא תִקְרְבוּ לְגַלּוֹת עֶרְוָה... אַל־תִּטַּמְּאוּ בְּכָל־אֵלֶּה... לְבִלְתִּי עֲשׂוֹת מֵחֻקּוֹת הַתּוֹעֵבֹת אֲשֶׁר נַעֲשׂוּ לִפְנֵיכֶם וְלֹא תִטַּמְּאוּ בָּהֶם אֲנִי ה' אֱלֹקֵיכֶם. (ויקרא פרק י״ח)

Do not do like the practice of the land of Egypt in which you have dwelled... No man shall approach the relations of his flesh to uncover nakedness... Do not become defiled through any of these... Refrain from doing the abominable practices which had been done prior to (your arrival), and do not become defiled through them – I am Hashem your G-d. (*Vayikra* ch. 18)

קְדֹשִׁים תִּהְיוּ כִּי קָדוֹשׁ אֲנִי ה' אֱלֹקֵיכֶם. (שם י״ט ב׳)

You shall be holy, for I, Hashem your G-d, am holy. (*ibid.* 19:2)

אַךְ אֶת־זֶה לֹא תֹאכְלוּ...אֶת־הַגָּמָל...וְאֶת־הַחֲזִיר... וְכֹל אֲשֶׁר אֵין־לוֹ סְנַפִּיר וְקַשְׂקֶשֶׂת בַּמָּיִם... וְאֶת־אֵלֶּה תְּשַׁקְּצוּ מִן־הָעוֹף לֹא יֵאָכְלוּ... אַל־תְּשַׁקְּצוּ אֶת־נַפְשֹׁתֵיכֶם בְּכָל־הַשֶּׁרֶץ הַשֹּׁרֵץ וְלֹא תִטַּמְּאוּ בָּהֶם. (שם פרק י״א)

שהיא תפארת לעושיה ותפארת לו מן האדם

But this you shall not eat...the camel...and the swine... And all that do not have fins or scales in the seas... And of the following fowl, you shall consider an abomination, they shall not be eaten... Do not cause your souls to become abominable through any swarming thing that swarms, and do not defile yourselves through them. (*ibid.* ch. 11)

וְהִתְקַדִּשְׁתֶּם וִהְיִיתֶם קְדֹשִׁים כִּי קָדוֹשׁ אָנִי וְלֹא תְטַמְּאוּ אֶת־נַפְשֹׁתֵיכֶם בְּכָל־הַשֶּׁרֶץ הָרֹמֵשׂ עַל־הָאָרֶץ. (שם פסוק מ״ד)

And you shall become holy, and be holy, for I am holy; and do not defile your souls through any swarming thing that crawls on the earth. (*ibid.* v. 44)

פרק ב׳

169

Path of Ease, a Path of Struggle

There are days we would chalk up as "good days" — from a *ruchniyus* point of view. Perhaps we attended a particularly inspiring *shiur* (Torah lecture); maybe we were involved in some ambitious project of communal *chessed*, where we were buoyed with the warm feeling of our significant contribution to the public good; perhaps it was even a day where we had experienced significant success in the realm of *davening*, or an intriguing, exhilarating Torah study session.

But then there are other days and periods we may characterize as simply "blah." Nothing particularly special occurred, nor were any noteworthy accomplishments added to our record. The *davening* was "average" (at best), as was the learning; no extraordinary inspiration here. We may even consider these times as a waste, periods through which we must merely "get by" and slog along.

Towards the end of his life, the Rebbe of Kobrin *ztz"l* reflected on his many days of *avodas Hashem*. He made a surprising remark that seems to conflict with the sentiment stated above. He placed particular value on those "uninspiring" days of drudgery. Those times in which he experienced feelings of powerful inspiration, he now felt, were of a comparatively lower quality. But the days that had seemed plain at the time, he now realized, were actually of much more potent spiritual value.

This assessment actually holds a crucial and powerful message for each and every one of us. Its full depth is brought out through the Nesivos Sholom's treatment of this mishnah in *Avos*. In the previous *ma'amar*, the same mishnah was dealt with at a number of levels. One of the aspects mentioned there now receives further elaboration, providing further insight into the powerful lessons contained therein.

Of Greater Value

In outlining the path a Yid should take in *avodas Hashem*, Rebbi here discusses two different kinds of mitzvos.

The Saba Kadisha *ztz"l*, in *Toras Avos*, explains: There are certain

שהיא תפארת לעושיה ותפארת לו מן האדם

mitzvos a person simply finds easier to do. These may differ from person to person, depending on one's particular makeup and natural tendencies. The common denominator is that an individual tends to gravitate towards those mitzvah acts that conform to his specific nature and personality. This is quite understandable, as he finds them much easier to perform. And so he generally will invest more time and effort in these types of mitzvos, practicing them with all their intricacies and *hiddurim* (added stringencies).

These mitzvos, of course, should not be eschewed. It is to this category that Rebbi refers when he speaks of performing deeds that are *tiferes l'oseha*, glorious and cherished by the one who does them. This is a fitting description, as he has a natural inclination to this type of *avodah* and so takes pride in and derives pleasure from their fulfillment.

The truth is, however, that it is not from this kind of activity that a person will develop his true *shleimus* (completeness in *avodas Hashem*). Rebbi refers to the *avodah* that engenders such *shleimus* in the next phrase, when he encourages the performance of deeds which are *tiferes lo min ha'adam* (translated literally: "from which he derives honor from people"). In elucidating what this means, the Saba Kadisha points to the well-known statement of Shlomo Hamelech: סוֹף דָּבָר הַכֹּל נִשְׁמָע אֶת־הָאֱלֹקִים יְרָא וְאֶת־מִצְוֹתָיו שְׁמוֹר כִּי־זֶה כָּל־הָאָדָם — *In the final analysis, all is heard: Fear G-d and keep His commandments; for this comprises the complete* **adam** (*Koheles* 12:13). When our mishnah mentions **ha'adam**, it likewise refers to "the complete man" mentioned in *Koheles*. Rebbi is instructing us to put a premium on those deeds which are *tiferes lo min ha'adam*; that is, they relate to his acquisition of *shleimus*.

So, what are these deeds that contribute to our *shleimus*, shaping us into a complete person? The mitzvos that come naturally to us may be more enjoyable, and are also praiseworthy. But to attain true completeness, and to refine our essence, it is necessary to work *against* our inherent nature, which has its roots in materialistic tendencies. That is, it is those mitzvos that we find more difficult to

פרק ב'

perform, for which we must toil in their fulfillment, which ultimately rectify our character and facilitate our rise to *shleimus*.

This notion is manifest in the *parshah* (section of the Torah) that deals with the related mitzvos of *perikah u'te'inah*. A fellow is dealing with his donkey's load. The assistance he requires may be in the form of *te'inah* (loading the donkey) or *perikah* (unloading). In either instance, the Torah mandates that one not merely stand by but lend a hand to the owner.

The issue becomes somewhat more involved when one is confronted with *two* separate donkey owners, each one in need of assistance. One needs help loading his donkey, the other has to unload. To whom should one turn his attention first? *Perikah* takes precedence over *te'inah*, as by lightening its load, one thereby alleviates the suffering of the struggling animal.

But there is one notable exception, where one is bidden to help out the one involved in *te'inah* over the one involved in *perikah*, the suffering of the animal notwithstanding. What is so important that it trumps the regular concerns of *tza'ar ba'alei chaim* (animal suffering)? The Gemara establishes the case, accounting as well for the overriding factor: If the one involved in *perikah* is his friend, while the individual involved in *te'inah* is his *enemy* — he must grant priority to *te'inah*. Why? לָכוּף אֶת יִצְרוֹ עָדִיף — *Subjugation of one's inclination takes precedence* (*Bava Metzia* 32b).

Here's an instance where one's natural inclinations and *the normal procedure of prioritization* intersect. His friend needs help, so does his enemy. His friend is involved in *perikah* (characterized by the additional factor of *tza'ar ba'alei chaim*), his enemy needs assistance with *te'inah*. The standard priority rules state that one should first deal with *perikah* to lighten the animal's burden, which is what the prospective helper would like to do in any event, as it is his friend who is involved with *perikah*. This would seem to be a "no-brainer," as all signs point here towards helping with unloading first. But the Torah says, "No. Not so fast." Because here a different opportunity presents itself, as well: that of *lachuf es yitzro*, working against one's natural inclination. A person wants to help his friend and has an aversion to

שהיא תפארת לעושיה ותפארת לו מן האדם

the prospect of helping his enemy. And so the Torah directs him to do just that. You have a chance to actually work on yourself — grab it. The opportunity is so golden, it overrides the otherwise pressing concern of *tza'ar ba'alei chaim*.

Thus we see the premium the Torah places on deeds where we must push against our *teva* (nature), as opposed to those deeds to which we are naturally inclined. This idea is reflected, as well, in the continuation of the mishnah. הֱוֵי זָהִיר בְּמִצְוָה קַלָּה כְּבַחֲמוּרָה, שֶׁאֵין אַתָּה יוֹדֵעַ מַתַּן שְׂכָרָן שֶׁל מִצְוֹת — *Be as careful to fulfill a less severe mitzvah as a severe one, for ultimately you do not know the magnitude of reward given for particular mitzvos.* An example of a *mitzvah kalah* would be *te'inah*; as we have seen, under usual circumstances, this mitzvah must yield to *perikah*, its more pressing counterpart. But that is only insofar as it remains an "easy" mitzvah. Once the element of "difficulty" is introduced (such as when one's enemy is involved in *te'inah*), then this "less severe" mitzvah takes on sudden urgency. And its *mattan s'char*, its given reward, increases in turn. As *Chazal* tell us (*Avos* 5:23): *L'fum tza'ara agra* — "The reward is in proportion to the effort involved." Since one has to subjugate his *yetzer hara* in order to fulfill this particular mitzvah, it becomes that much more valuable in Hashem's eyes and contributes that much more in transforming one into an *adam hashaleim* (complete person).

Fulfilling the *Tachlis*

There is yet another component to choosing the "more difficult" path, in which emphasis is placed on working *against* our *teva*, as opposed to conforming to it. As mentioned above, the very act of opposing and vanquishing our innate tendencies serves to purge our materialistic nature and attain *shleimus*. This venture also enables us to fulfill the very purpose of our overall *avodas Hashem*. And this purpose is *d'veikus baHashem*.

The *sefarim hakedoshim* (sacred volumes), in explaining the notion of *d'veikus*, assert that it is in fact the goal and result of mitzvah fulfillment. How, indeed, does a mortal man, a physical being, attach himself to *Hakadosh Baruch Hu*, the Source of all sanctity and purity?

פרק ב'

For this reason, man was granted the 613 mitzvos, the fulfillment of which serves to purify his essence. In other words, they are essentially 613 ways and opportunities to facilitate *d'veikus baHashem*.

This is yet another dimension to Rebbi's teaching. הֱוֵי זָהִיר בְּמִצְוָה קַלָּה כְּבַחֲמוּרָה — *Be as careful to fulfill a less severe mitzvah as a severe one*, especially if that "lesser" mitzvah contains the element of opposing one's *yetzer*. A dedication to this type of *avodah* will enable the *oveid* to reach the level of *d'veikus*. And what greater reward could a human attain than to be able to cleave to Hashem? It is to such a phenomenal opportunity that Rebbi refers when he cautions against underestimating the potential for outstanding reward: שֶׁאֵין אַתָּה יוֹדֵעַ מַתַּן שְׂכָרָן שֶׁל מִצְוֹת — *You may not be aware of the magnitude of the reward given for particular mitzvos*.

This, as well, is the profundity of the Rebbe of Kobrin's statement, which was mentioned at the outset. There may have been days when he experienced a strong sense of inspiration, which propelled him to great deeds. But in these instances, it was not particularly difficult to perform *avodas Hashem*, assisted, as he was, by the presence of special spiritual yearnings. What he truly valued were those times when the inspiration seemed lacking, when he had to "force himself" to do what was right. He recognized that these were opportunities to serve Hashem from the standpoint of *lachuf es yitzro* — the more desirable option. In the end, it was instances such as these that brought true illumination to his life, as he was thereby enabled to achieve the ultimate purpose of the entirety of his *avodah* — *d'veikus baHashem*.

The Saba Kadisha *ztz"l* expressed a similar sentiment. He urged that, every day, a Jew should engage in at least one spiritual activity for which he has no real passion — just to act contrary to his inherent nature. A day that goes by with no act of *lachuf es yitzro*, he asserted, is considered one day of life that was completely wasted. While the statement may almost sound harsh, it is perfectly understandable in light of the above. The very purpose of our *avodah*, the purpose of life, is to come closer to Hashem. As explained, it is the act of opposing one's *yetzer* that enables a Yid to achieve this *d'veikus*. A day without

שהיא תפארת לעושיה ותפארת לו מן האדם

any *lachuf es yitzro* is a day in which we did not make any headway in achieving the goal of our existence. A day not utilized for the purpose for which it was granted is thus essentially a waste of a day.

A Preponderance of *Kedushah*

The Nesivos Sholom uncovers yet another layer of understanding to the statement of our mishnah.

A number of times in *Sefer Vayikra*, the Torah exhorts us to exhibit *kedushah*. This is obviously a sublime and lofty ideal, but what does it mean? The mitzvah of *Kedoshim tiheyu* — "You shall be holy" — appears at the beginning of *Parshas Kedoshim* (*Vayikra* 19:2). The Ramban explains that this entails acting with restraint even in permissible areas: קַדֵּשׁ עַצְמְךָ בְּמוּתָּר לָךְ — *Sanctify yourself by (refraining even from things) which are permissible to you*.

This is a recurring phenomenon in *Sefer Vayikra*. *Parshas Kedoshim* follows on the heels of *Parshas Acharei Mos*, which ends with a section containing an extensive list of forbidden unions. Thus, following these prohibitions against immorality, the Torah (at the beginning of *Parshas Kedoshim*) instructs us to be holy — *Kedoshim tiheyu*. As the Ramban explained, the implication is that not only must one refrain from the various forbidden forms of immorality, but even after all that — *Kedoshim tiheyu*, show restraint even in permissible areas. Just because something is allowed, it doesn't mean that one should overindulge. No explicit prohibition may be operative here, but a Yid still should not enslave himself to wanton passion. We find a similar instance in *Parshas Shemini*. The Torah records, in great detail, the various aspects of forbidden foods — the animals, fish, birds, etc. — whose consumption is proscribed. How does the section end? Again, with an exhortation to *kedushah*: *V'hiskadishtem v'heyisem kedoshim* — "And you shall sanctify yourselves, and you shall be holy" (*Vayikra* 11:44). Once again, the Torah is urging us not to be satisfied with merely observing the actual prohibitions against *treif* (non-kosher) food. Even when it comes to permissible food, a Yid must still exhibit self-control. Kosher certification is not a license to gorge oneself.

Which of these two entities — actual prohibitions vs. moderation in permissible areas — is more difficult to observe? It would appear that the latter presents more of a challenge. When it comes to explicit prohibitions, it is quite clear that we are dealing with a forbidden entity; as such, there is present an element of *yiras ha'onesh* (fear of Divine punishment), which could serve as an effective deterrent. But exercising restraint from permissible pleasures — that's not a simple matter at all! Here is something we might desire, with no clear-cut prohibition involved, and hence no real "fear factor"; and we are still expected to refrain?! Yet, this is precisely the category of observance that is the favored course of *avodah*. That is, we are serving Hashem with the element of *lachuf es yitzro*, fighting against our inherent nature. This is the path whereby we acquire *kedushah*, and it is the way that brings a Yid to *d'veikus*.

And so we discover even more depth to Rebbi's profound words. הֱוֵי זָהִיר בְּמִצְוָה קַלָּה — What is the *mitzvah kalah* of which Rebbi speaks? It is this very element of our discussion — the permissible items — which, in a sense, are not really mitzvos at all. Yet it is precisely our conduct regarding these areas that takes on such monumental importance. By refraining from permitted excesses, we demonstrate that we are *kadosh* (holy), attaining closeness to Hashem by subjugating our *yetzer*.

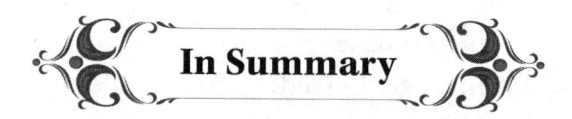

In Summary

The Torah places a great premium on subduing our natural inclinations — *lachuf es yitzro*. The Nesivos Sholom perceives this teaching of Rebbi as reflective of this all-important principle.

A key area where this notion appears is the section of the Torah dealing with the mitzvos of *perikah u'te'inah* — unloading and loading. Inherently, *perikah* takes precedence over *te'inah*, as the former involves the added element of *tza'ar ba'alei chaim*. In this respect, then, *perikah* could be considered, of the two, the mitzvah that is more *chamurah* (severe), while *te'inah* is the *mitzvah kalah*. But when an enemy is involved, the order can be reversed: if one's friend needs help with the *chamurah* (*perikah*), but his enemy needs

שהיא תפארת לעושיה ותפארת לו מן האדם

someone to help him with the *kalah* (*te'inah*), *Chazal* instruct that we should help the enemy. The reason is that we now have the opportunity to perform an act which goes against our nature, an opportunity the Torah does not want us to pass over. And so Rebbi exhorts us to give our attention, in such an instance, to the *mitzvah kalah*; when it entails coercion of our *yetzer*, the *mattan s'char* increases exponentially.

Another important aspect of the practice of subduing our *yetzer* relates to the very purpose of the 613 mitzvos — *d'veikus baHashem*. If a person does not toil, but remains satisfied with those mitzvos which "agree" with his natural tendencies, he will remain in a state of spiritual stagnation. It is specifically those acts where he must coerce his *yetzer* and fight against his nature that enable him to come closer to Hashem. The effort involved purges his materialistic nature, facilitating his attainment of *d'veikus* — and this is the greatest form of *mattan s'char*.

Mitzvah kalah can likewise refer to the endeavor of self-sanctification; that is, showing restraint even in permissible matters. In a few sections of the Torah — in *Sefer Vayikra*, specifically — we find an interesting juxtaposition. The Torah lists numerous prohibitions — in the area of immoral behavior, or the dietary laws — and then follows these with an exhortation to *kedushah*. In fact, adherence to the latter directive presents much more of a challenge to a person. When confronted with explicit prohibitions, one has the element of *yiras onesh* to keep him in check. But this factor is largely absent when it comes to refraining from the permissible; as such, observing such restraint goes against one's inherent nature. That is exactly what makes this form of *avodah* so precious and powerful.

פרק ב׳

פרק ב' משנה א'
הסתכל בג' דברים ואין אתה בא לידי עבירה
Look at Three Things and You Will Not Come to the Hands of Sin

רַבִּי אוֹמֵר, אֵיזוֹהִי דֶרֶךְ יְשָׁרָה שֶׁיָּבוֹר לוֹ הָאָדָם, כֹּל שֶׁהִיא תִפְאֶרֶת לְעוֹשֶׂיהָ וְתִפְאֶרֶת לוֹ מִן הָאָדָם. וֶהֱוֵי זָהִיר בְּמִצְוָה קַלָּה כְּבַחֲמוּרָה, שֶׁאֵין אַתָּה יוֹדֵעַ מַתַּן שְׂכָרָן שֶׁל מִצְוֹת. וֶהֱוֵי מְחַשֵּׁב הֶפְסֵד מִצְוָה כְּנֶגֶד שְׂכָרָהּ, וּשְׂכַר עֲבֵרָה כְּנֶגֶד הֶפְסֵדָהּ. וְהִסְתַּכֵּל בִּשְׁלֹשָׁה דְבָרִים וְאֵין אַתָּה בָא לִידֵי עֲבֵרָה, דַּע מַה לְּמַעְלָה מִמָּךְ, עַיִן רוֹאָה וְאֹזֶן שׁוֹמַעַת, וְכָל מַעֲשֶׂיךָ בַּסֵּפֶר נִכְתָּבִים:

Rebbi says: What is the upright path a man should choose for himself? Whatever is honorable for the one who does it, and that accords him honor from man. Be as careful regarding a simple mitzvah as with a severe one, for you do not know the reward given for mitzvos. Calculate the loss of a mitzvah against its reward, and the reward of a sin against its loss. Look at three things and you will not come to the hands of sin: Know what is above you – an eye that sees, an ear that hears, and that all of your deeds are being inscribed in a book.

פרק ב'

GEMS FROM THE SEFER NESIVOS SHOLOM

SOURCES:

אַתָּה הָרְאֵתָ לָדַעַת כִּי ה' הוּא הָאֱלֹקִים אֵין עוֹד מִלְבַדּוֹ. (דברים ד' ל"ה)

You have been shown in order to know that Hashem is G-d; there is no other aside from Him. (*Devarim* 4:35)

הָרְאֵתָ – כְּתַרְגּוּמוֹ: אִתְחֲזֵיתָא. (רש"י שם)

"You have been shown" – as the Targum renders: "You have been made to see." (*Rashi, ibid.*)

אַתֶּם רְאִיתֶם כִּי מִן־הַשָּׁמַיִם דִּבַּרְתִּי עִמָּכֶם. (שמות כ' י"ט)

You have seen that I spoke to you from the Heavens. (*Shemos* 20:19)

הסתכל בג' דברים ואין אתה בא לידי עבירה

Danger: Be Aware

Emunah — faith. Most of us are aware of the central role it plays in our lives, serving as the cornerstone of our *avodas Hashem*.

Yet, are we truly cognizant of what *emunah* entails? Of course, we must believe in Hashem, and believe strongly. But how solid, in reality, is our faith? If a person, G-d forbid, were confronted with some challenge or danger — would he not experience an element of fear? Then again, one who literally feels the Divine Presence watching him at all times and directing his affairs would feel security in the face of peril. What degree of belief is expected of us, and what level could we possibly attain? The surprising answers to these questions emerge from the teaching of Rabbi Yehudah Hanasi.

The second *perek* of *Maseches Avos* begins with a seemingly simple strategy for avoiding *aveiros*. As Rabbi Yehudah Hanasi teaches, one need merely: הִסְתַּכֵּל בִּשְׁלשָׁה דְבָרִים וְאֵין אַתָּה בָא לִידֵי עֲבֵרָה: דַּע מַה לְמַעְלָה מִמְּךָ, עַיִן רוֹאָה וְאֹזֶן שׁוֹמַעַת, וְכָל מַעֲשֶׂיךָ בַּסֵּפֶר נִכְתָּבִים — *Look at three things, and you will not come to the hands of transgression: Know what is above you — a seeing eye, a listening ear, and the inscribing of all your deeds in a book.*

Rebbi's advice appears straightforward enough. A person who is aware that Hashem is always watching, listening, and recording his deeds will be naturally less inclined to violate His will.

However, on closer examination, his teaching contains numerous perplexities. In conveying his message, Rebbi's choice of wording raises several questions, as the Nesivos Sholom delineates:

- The mishnah encourages us to *look* at "an eye that sees, an ear that hears, and all your deeds being inscribed in a book." Now, these items are imperceptible to the human eye; while we could reflect on these abstract concepts, we certainly can't *see* them. Wouldn't it have been more appropriate for Rebbi to have instructed us to *contemplate* these intangibles instead of *looking* at them?

- The mishnah asserts that one who follows its advice will not come *lidei aveirah* — literally, to the *hands* of an *aveirah*. This

פרק ב'

GEMS FROM THE *SEFER NESIVOS SHOLOM*

is the mishnah, not poetry; why the embellishment? Let the mishnah simply state, "You will not come to sin."

- In its introductory statement, the mishnah mentions that there are three items that demand our attention: "Look at *three* things..." But it then proceeds to list four! 1) Know what is above you, 2) a seeing eye, 3) a listening ear, and 4) the inscribing of all your deeds in a book. How many areas of focus are there — three or four?

- It is noteworthy that the mishnah zeroes in on the individual: "Know what is above *you*." But the celestial items of which the mishnah speaks are not merely above this or that person; they are above the entire world. Why doesn't the mishnah simply state, "Know what is above?"

- By using the word *da*, know, the mishnah implies that a person can overcome his *yetzer hara* through intellect alone. How can this be? The *yetzer hara* is not merely an intellectual foe, but manifests its power through passion and emotions. Simply knowing the consequences of one's action does not seem to be enough to stop a person from committing an *aveirah*.

Rebbi's choice of phraseology, of course, was quite deliberate, and in fact reflects great profundity. Before clarifying his intent, however, the Nesivos Sholom provides some critical background by discussing the concept of *emunah*.

Believing Is Seeing

The Nesivos Sholom explains that, in fact, there are four basic levels through which people perceive Hashem's existence and involvement in the world. The most basic level of *emunah* is achieved through intellect, whereby a person comes to understand that there is a G-d. He may reach this conclusion after a personal life experience in which Divine involvement was plainly evident, through contemplation of the world's creation and continuing existence, or perhaps by pondering the general purpose and function of life.

This level is the most common. While an excellent vehicle for

הסתכל בג' דברים ואין אתה בא לידי עבירה

emunah, it still leaves room for much development. It is hard to say of those whose belief is solely intellectual in nature that their faith is complete. Do they know with a thousand percent certainty that Hashem exists? Not really, since no one actually sees Hashem. It's just the logical, sensible conclusion that Hashem must exist. But such individuals don't necessarily sense His Presence.

The second level of *emunah* is a belief in Hashem that a person actually *feels in his heart*. Yet even here the climb is not over. This level can describe those who express their *Yiddishkeit* as "I feel G-d in my heart, and I am Jewish at heart, but not always in practice." Such individuals may believe in Hashem's creating and running of the world, and may even hold a deep belief. But their faith does not always translate into action.

The third level entails a belief in Hashem that begins in our heart and *radiates out to our limbs*. While this may appear somewhat oxymoronic — how could a physical body *feel* the existence of an abstract entity — it is nevertheless achievable. We say weekly in the *Nishmas* prayer (quoting Dovid Hamelech): כָּל עַצְמֹתַי תֹּאמַרְנָה ה' מִי כָמוֹךָ — *All my limbs declare, "Hashem, who is like You?"* (*Tehillim* 35:10). While not easily attained, it is possible for us to reach such a level, whereby our *emunah* is so internalized that our very limbs can feel and attest to the existence of Hashem.

The fourth and highest level of *emunah* is predictably the most difficult to achieve. At this level, a person's sense of *emunah* is so developed that he perceives Hashem with utmost clarity — as clearly as if he beholds Him with his own eyes. This does not mean that one sees His actual Presence; Moshe Rabbeinu was the only human to have merited a vision approaching such a degree of revelation. The form of seeing referred to here is not a physical perception obtained through the faculties of vision; rather, it is an absolute understanding of something, one normally attainable through sight alone.

This level of *emunah* may appear, at first glance, completely beyond our realm. The truth is, however, that it is entirely within the reach of each and every Jew to obtain such clarity of vision. The Nesivos Sholom explains that it is actually an inherent part of our essence, infused within us from the collective, national experience of the revelation at Har Sinai.

In *Sefer Devarim* (4:35), Moshe tells Bnei Yisroel, אַתָּה הָרְאֵתָ לָדַעַת כִּי ה׳ הוּא הָאֱלֹקִים אֵין עוֹד מִלְבַדּוֹ — *You have been* **shown** *in order to know that Hashem is G-d; there is no other aside from Him.* Rashi, quoting the *Targum*, explains the word *hareisa* to mean "you were made to see," teaching us that Bnei Yisroel were granted the unequivocal ability to perceive Hashem's existence. At the time of the giving of the Torah, Hashem opened up the seven heavens and showed them that He was the only One. This was previously described in *Shemos* (20:19), when Moshe Rabbeinu was instructed to tell Bnei Yisroel, אַתֶּם רְאִיתֶם כִּי מִן הַשָּׁמַיִם דִּבַּרְתִּי עִמָּכֶם — *You have* **seen** *that I spoke to you from the Heavens.*

To develop such an acute sense of *emunah* — as strong as if he had beheld with his eyes — may very well be a near-impossible task, but only for someone who was not privy to the revelations of *Mattan Torah*. However, there is no Jew who ever lived, now lives, or will live, who was not present at Har Sinai and who did not experience that which gave Bnei Yisroel the rock-solid knowledge of and *emunah* in Hashem's existence and power. And the impact of this event was imprinted into our very makeup. Thus, every Yid, deep within, possesses an internal reservoir of unshakeable faith. Through perseverance, we can tap in to this latent treasure and develop our *emunah* to the extent described above — where, literally, it is as if our eyes have beheld the Divine.

Against this backdrop, we can appreciate the mishnah's teaching and its particular choice of wording. *Histakel b'shloshah devarim...* Rabbi Yehudah Hanasi did not discuss a need to "think about," "contemplate," or "understand," but quite specifically instructed us to *look* at the three essential elements. In so doing, he was referring to this level of *emunah*, imploring us to develop a belief in Hashem that is as powerful as sight. Only then is a person guaranteed to be able to stay away from *aveiros* entirely.

With the lesser levels of *emunah*, a person fulfills his obligation to believe in Hashem's existence and will likely control his impulse in the case of most *aveiros*. But there are permissible actions as well that pose a danger. While appearing innocuous on the surface, they can easily lead up to an *aveirah*. These actions, often difficult to avoid, can be considered *yedei aveirah*, the "hands" of an *aveirah*, as they serve as the *yetzer hara's* vehicle for drawing a person closer to sin.

One's *emunah* must be solid indeed to avoid even these pitfalls. Thus the mishnah tells us, הִסְתַּכֵּל...וְאֵין אַתָּה בָא לִידֵי עֲבֵרָה. If a person has the **seeing** level of *emunah*, he will have the fortitude to refrain from even those actions which are *lidei aveirah*.

Behind the Scenes

In teaching us how to avoid *aveiros*, the mishnah advises: "Know what is above *you*." The phraseology appears puzzling, as the items mentioned are not merely above one individual, but stand in the loftiest spiritual realms, high above the entire world. To account for this curious term, the Nesivos Sholom shares a story involving the Rebbe, Reb Elimelech of Lizhensk.

A certain individual who had been steeped in sin came to realize the weight of his actions. To atone for his numerous transgressions, he had undertaken a course of frequent fasts and self-afflictions. This man approached Reb Elimelech, begging for guidance on the path of *teshuvah*.

Surprisingly, Reb Elimelech told the *ba'al teshuvah* to halt his afflictions and to return after partaking of sufficient food and drink. When the man came back at the appointed time, Reb Elimelech began expounding on the secrets and order of the universe. In precise detail, he described the far-reaching effects of a person's every deed: how both positive and negative actions reverberate throughout the lower and upper spheres, spreading either light or destruction.

After this profound lesson, Reb Elimelech began saying *vidui* (confession) with the *ba'al teshuvah*. But he soon discovered that it was slow-going. Together they recited, "*Ashamnu* — we have been guilty." Immediately, the *ba'al teshuvah* fainted. When he came to, they proceeded to the second word: "*Bagadnu* — we have been disloyal." Again, he collapsed. And so it proceeded throughout the recitation, due to his newfound appreciation for the enormity of his deeds.

The mishnah's exhortation is directed to this phenomenon as well. By imploring each person to "know what is above *you*," the mishnah is not referring to a physical presence in the sky but to the power of every single action. The message is not to "know what is above you" as much as it is to "know what is *caused* by you and your actions." Only when you have the knowledge to recognize what emanates from you — the sheer magnitude of your deeds, both positive and negative — can you begin to truly fulfill the directive of *histakel b'shloshah devarim...*

This also explains why the mishnah announces three *devarim* and then states four. "Knowing what is above you (i.e., what your actions cause)" is not one of the *devarim*, but rather a *prerequisite* and introduction for the trio. Only once a person fully understands the consequences of his actions can he properly contemplate the *ayin ro'ah...*

Regarding the *shloshah devarim*, the Nesivos Sholom demonstrates that they share a common thread. He explains that each signifies an aspect of human life that may initially seem innocuous to us, but in reality is far from harmless.

- The eye that sees: We are instructed not to follow our eyes and view inappropriate sights. Nevertheless, we often falter, justifying our looking with one of many excuses.

- The ear that hears: We know that our ears are not allowed to hear words of *lashon hara* (evil gossip) and other forbidden forms of speech. Nevertheless, we find excuses why we can't restrict our ears from hearing, claiming that we can't just clog up our ears with plugs.

- *All* your deeds (even permitted ones) are inscribed in a book: We are bidden to temper our pursuit of earthly desires, not merely giving in to every permissible temptation. Nevertheless, we rarely curb our indulgences, justifying our conduct by stating that eating that extra dish, drinking that desirable drink, driving a fancier car, etc., is not an *aveirah* in itself.

In warning us of these behaviors, Rabbi Yehudah Hanasi counters our erroneous notions. "You may have thought that these are not such weighty matters," he tells us. As such, you must "know what is above you." As mentioned previously, the consequences of your actions throughout all the worlds — "what is caused by *you*" — is monumental. Only once you truly understand the colossal import of your deeds, both positive and negative, will you be able to avoid falling into the lure and trap of the "hands of sin."

In Summary

Rabbi Yehudah Hanasi supplies a formula to avoid the pitfalls of sin. The basic strategy is to be aware of Divine surveillance. All that one does is seen, heard, and recorded.

But Rebbi phrases his message in a most interesting way. Instead of instructing us to "contemplate" or "reflect" on the eye that sees, the ear that hears, and the inscribing of our deeds in a book, he actually tells us to "look" at these three things; a feat which, at first glance, seems impossible. How does one "see" these invisible entities?

The mishnah is actually reflecting a certain degree of *emunah*, exhorting us to attain the highest of its four levels. There are those whose faith begins and ends with their intellect; others "feel it in their hearts" but don't necessarily match their actions with their sentiments. A yet higher level of internalized belief is where a person's belief actually penetrates his very limbs. But the ultimate accomplishment is a clarity of vision, whereby one's belief in Hashem is so strong, it is as if he has beheld the Divine with his own eyes. And it was to such a level that Rebbi was referring. One's belief in Hashem's scrutiny of our deeds should not be marked with any degree of superficiality; rather, it should be as strong as if we had beheld with our eyes. *Look* at these three things; then you will not come to sin.

Rebbi further stated that you will not even come to "the hands" of sin. This intimates refraining from even permissible actions, the indulgence in which may lead to sin.

A prime aspect of this effort entails a focus on "what is above *you*." In this statement, the mishnah points to the hidden reality, the astronomical impact our deeds have in the upper and lower realms of the universe. In order to truly steer clear of the "hands of sin," we must be aware of the import and power of our actions.

פרק ב' משנה ד'
עשה רצונו כרצונך
Make His Will as Your Will

הוּא הָיָה אוֹמֵר, עֲשֵׂה רְצוֹנוֹ כִּרְצוֹנְךָ, כְּדֵי שֶׁיַּעֲשֶׂה רְצוֹנְךָ כִּרְצוֹנוֹ. בַּטֵּל רְצוֹנְךָ מִפְּנֵי רְצוֹנוֹ, כְּדֵי שֶׁיְּבַטֵּל רְצוֹן אֲחֵרִים מִפְּנֵי רְצוֹנֶךָ:

(Rabban Gamliel) would say: Make His will as your will, so that He will make your will as His will. Nullify your will before His will, so that He will nullify the will of others before your will.

GEMS FROM THE *SEFER NESIVOS SHOLOM*

SOURCES:

רִבּוֹנוֹ שֶׁל עוֹלָם, כְּמוֹ שֶׁכָּבַשׁ אַבְרָהָם אָבִינוּ אֶת רַחֲמָיו מֵעַל בֶּן יְחִידוֹ לַעֲשׂוֹת רְצוֹנְךָ בְּלֵבָב שָׁלֵם, כֵּן יִכְבְּשׁוּ רַחֲמֶיךָ אֶת כַּעַסְךָ מֵעָלֵינוּ. (תפלת שחרית)

Master of the Universe: Just as Avraham Avinu conquered his mercy, withholding it from his only son in order to perform Your will with a full heart, so may Your mercy conquer and withhold Your anger from us. (Morning prayers)

רַחֲמָנָא לִבָּא בָּעֵי. (זהר, רעיא מהימנא, כי תצא)

Hashem desires the heart. (*Zohar, Raya Mehemna, Parshas Ki Seitzei*)

וַיְהִי אַחַר הַדְּבָרִים הָאֵלֶּה וְהָאֱלֹקִים נִסָּה אֶת־אַבְרָהָם וַיֹּאמֶר אֵלָיו אַבְרָהָם וַיֹּאמֶר הִנֵּנִי. וַיֹּאמֶר קַח־נָא אֶת־בִּנְךָ אֶת־יְחִידְךָ אֲשֶׁר־אָהַבְתָּ אֶת־יִצְחָק וְלֶךְ־לְךָ אֶל־אֶרֶץ הַמֹּרִיָּה וְהַעֲלֵהוּ שָׁם לְעֹלָה. (בראשית כ"ב א', ב')

And it was after these things, and G-d tested Avraham, and He said to him: "Avraham," and he answered: "Here I am." And He said: "Take, please, your only son, that you have loved – Yitzchak, and go for you to the Land of Moriah, and offer him up there as a sacrifice." (*Bereishis* 22:1, 2)

אָנֹכִי עֹמֵד בֵּין־ה' וּבֵינֵיכֶם. (דברים ה' ה')

I was standing between Hashem and you. (*Devarim* 5:5)

שְׁמַע יִשְׂרָאֵל ה' אֱלֹקֵינוּ ה' אֶחָד. וְאָהַבְתָּ אֵת ה' אֱלֹקֶיךָ, בְּכָל לְבָבְךָ, וּבְכָל נַפְשְׁךָ, וּבְכָל מְאֹדֶךָ. (שם ו' ד', ה')

Hear, Yisroel, Hashem is our G-d, Hashem is One. And you shall love Hashem your G-d, with all of your heart, all of your soul and all of your might. (*ibid.* 6:4, 5)

עשה רצונו כרצונך

בְּשָׁעָה שֶׁהוֹצִיאוּ אֶת רַבִּי עֲקִיבָא לַהֲרִיגָה זְמַן קְרִיאַת שְׁמַע הָיָה, וְהָיוּ סוֹרְקִים אֶת בְּשָׂרוֹ בְּמַסְרֵקוֹת שֶׁל בַּרְזֶל, וְהָיָה מְקַבֵּל עָלָיו עוֹל מַלְכוּת שָׁמַיִם. אָמְרוּ לוֹ תַּלְמִידָיו: רַבֵּינוּ, עַד כָּאן? אָמַר לָהֶם: כָּל יָמַי הָיִיתִי מִצְטַעֵר עַל פָּסוּק זֶה בְּכָל נַפְשְׁךָ - אֲפִילוּ נוֹטֵל אֶת נִשְׁמָתְךָ, אָמַרְתִּי: מָתַי יָבֹא לְיָדִי וַאֲקַיְּמֶנּוּ, וְעַכְשָׁיו שֶׁבָּא לְיָדִי לֹא אֲקַיְּמֶנּוּ? הָיָה מַאֲרִיךְ בְּאֶחָד עַד שֶׁיָּצְתָה נִשְׁמָתוֹ בְּאֶחָד. יָצְתָה בַּת קוֹל וְאָמְרָה: אַשְׁרֶיךָ רַבִּי עֲקִיבָא שֶׁיָּצְאָה נִשְׁמָתְךָ בְּאֶחָד.
(ברכות ס"א)

When Rabbi Akiva was being taken out to be executed (by the Romans), it was the time to recite *Shema*. As (the tormentors) raked his flesh with iron combs, he was accepting the yoke of Heaven upon himself (in reciting the *Shema*). His disciples said to him: "Our Master – even to this extent?" He said to them: "All of my life, I was troubled regarding the verse which states, '(And you shall love Hashem) with all of your soul,' (which is expounded to mean:) 'Even as He removes your soul.' I had said (to myself): 'When will (the opportunity) come to my hand, that I may fulfill (this dictum)?' And now, that it has (finally) come to my hand – will I not fulfill it?" (Rabbi Akiva) elongated the recital of the word '*Echad* – One,' until his soul expired (during the recital of this word). A Heavenly voice resounded and proclaimed: "Fortunate are you, Rabbi Akiva! For your soul expired (while reciting the word) '*Echad*'!" (*Berachos* 61b)

וְהָאִישׁ מֹשֶׁה עָנָו מְאֹד מִכֹּל הָאָדָם אֲשֶׁר עַל-פְּנֵי הָאֲדָמָה. (במדבר י"ב ג')

And the man, Moshe, was exceedingly humble, more than any person on the face of the earth. (*Bamidbar* 12:3)

מָתַי יַגִּיעוּ מַעֲשַׂי לְמַעֲשֵׂי אַבְרָהָם יִצְחָק וְיַעֲקֹב. (תנא דבי אליהו רבה כ"ג א')

When will my deeds reach those of Avraham, Yitzchak, and Yaakov? (*Tanna D'vei Eliyahu Rabbah* 23:1)

פרק ב'

Where There's a Will

The well-worn adage "Where there's a will, there's a way" was actually pre-empted by thousands of years. Rabban Gamliel had already discussed the importance of will and want in the mishnah in *Avos*. Not only was he way ahead in addressing this theme, but his message is infinitely more profound than the pithy statement above, as we shall soon discover.

The Nesivos Sholom begins with a foundational understanding of this idea. The *wants* of a person are at the root of every thought we have, of every word we speak, and of every action we take. Throughout our life, all decisions — good or bad, meritorious or evil — begin with the central question: What do we want? What is our will?

This translates into *avodas Hashem* in a most sobering way; it emerges that our service to Him is intrinsically bound up with and dependent on this single factor: *ratzon* (will). This underscores the importance, regarding one's *ratzon*, of "getting it right." Whether one is observing the mitzvos out of fear of punishment or out of rote, if he is missing that main ingredient of *an inherent will to fulfill Hashem's dictates*, his entire *avodah* is wanting.

This principle is manifest in an oft-quoted *halachah*. While a transgressor is held accountable for his misdeed, there is a key exception: if the act was done *b'oneis* (under unavoidable coercion). Perhaps, for example, a person was forced to commit a particular sin (of the overwhelming majority of prohibitions for which he is not required to sacrifice his life) in order to avoid death. In this case, he is rendered blameless and completely exonerated, as *Chazal* state: *Oneis Rachmana patrei* — "In an instance of *oneis*, the Torah exempts" (*Avodah Zarah* 54a). Thus we see just how crucial the concept of *ratzon* is to a given act. When the deed is devoid of actual *ratzon* — such as in the case of *oneis* — it is as if it was never performed in the first place.

This is the precious message of Rabban Gamliel in this mishnah. *Aseih retzono k'retzoncha* — "Make His will your will." Hashem desires from a Yid that he perform His mitzvos not for other considerations, but chiefly because this is what one really wants to do. A Yid's true and earnest *ratzon* should be to do the *ratzon* of Hashem.

Rabban Gamliel then takes the matter to the next level. He states: *Batel retzoncha mip'nei retzono* — "Nullify your will from before His will." A person may be faced with temptation; he may even have a burning desire to commit a particular sin, but his *seichel* (intellect) prevails; he resists the enticement and refrains from sin. This is a tremendous show of spiritual fortitude, an act for which this Yid will surely be credited and rewarded. But there is a higher *madreigah* (level) — and it is to this that Rabban Gamliel refers. It is far more preferable if we were to *completely nullify our independent desire*. That is, instead of merely overpowering an innate urge, a Yid is exhorted to negate it completely, rendering it as if it doesn't exist. Our will and desire should be solely for one thing: what Hashem wants. Anything else pales into insignificance, and virtually disappears.

The *Akeidah* — a Sacrifice?

One of the most powerful and dramatic examples of devotion to and self-sacrifice for Hashem is undoubtedly the episode of *Akeidas Yitzchak*. Avraham had waited so long for a child to continue his legacy of *avodas Hashem* and was finally granted this enduring wish with the miraculous birth of Yitzchak to two very elderly parents. And then one day Avraham was told to offer him as a sacrifice to Hashem. Avraham endured the ordeal and proved his readiness to fulfill Hashem's will even to the extent of slaughtering his beloved son. At the critical moment, he was prevented from doing so by the *malach* (angel), who informed him that he had sufficiently demonstrated his loyal devotion.

A truly emotional scene, yet it raises the question: How, indeed, was this really a "test"? Let us recall that this was not Avraham's own idea; rather, *Hashem appeared to him and instructed him to do so*. Under these circumstances, wouldn't anybody have acted accordingly? If even an average Yid received a personal appeal from Hashem to sacrifice his son, would he hesitate to respond? After all, look at Jewish history and see how many people gave away their lives and the lives of their children even without the benefit of receiving a communication from Hashem Himself; they nevertheless proved themselves ready to die *al kiddush Hashem* (for the sanctification of His Name). What, then, is so unique to Avraham's behavior during the episode of the *Akeidah* that he is credited to such an extent throughout the generations?

Insight to this issue can be gleaned from one of the *tefillos* we recite in connection to the *Akeidah*. (The *parshah* of the *Akeidah* in the Torah is incorporated into the morning prayers. The following text is taken from the prayer recited immediately following the reading of the *Akeidah*.) רִבּוֹנוֹ שֶׁל עוֹלָם, כְּמוֹ שֶׁכָּבַשׁ אַבְרָהָם אָבִינוּ אֶת רַחֲמָיו מֵעַל בֶּן יְחִידוֹ לַעֲשׂוֹת רְצוֹנְךָ בְּלֵבָב שָׁלֵם, כֵּן יִכְבְּשׁוּ רַחֲמֶיךָ אֶת כַּעַסְךָ מֵעָלֵינוּ — *Master of the Universe:* **Just as Avraham Avinu conquered his mercy, withholding it from his only son in order to perform Your will with a full heart**, so may Your mercy conquer and withhold Your anger from us.

This factor, explains the Nesivos Sholom, is what set Avraham apart through his deed. The Midrash relates (*Bereishis Rabbah* 56) that the event of the *Akeidah* was indeed fraught with deep emotion. The angels wept, and trembling seized the beings of both the upper and lower worlds. There was only one individual who — in the midst of this great outpouring of awe and desperation — retained his composure and was actually in high spirits. This individual was Avraham. He was on his way to fulfill Hashem's will; nothing could give him greater satisfaction. And so he approached the *Akeidah* with a spring in his step and joy in his heart.

This is the significance of the words of the *tefillah*. Avraham was known for his kind and gentle nature; *rachamim* (mercy) was a hallmark of his. And yet, when it came to fulfilling Hashem's will through the *Akeidah*, what was his response? כָּבַשׁ...אֶת רַחֲמָיו...לַעֲשׂוֹת רְצוֹנְךָ בְּלֵבָב שָׁלֵם — *He conquered his mercy...in order to perform Your will with a full heart*. In other words, he fulfilled the dictum of the mishnah!

This was the true greatness Avraham displayed in the trial of the *Akeidah*. True, almost any Jew would be willing to duplicate Avraham's act of self-sacrifice (and in fact many have). But the main "credit" due Avraham is not so much for the deed of sacrificing his son; rather, it is for the fact that he did so with a full *ratzon*. He literally nullified his personal feelings on the matter, and his sole impetus was a burning desire to do what Hashem wanted. The notion is reminiscent of the well-known statement of the Rebbe of Kobrin, who characterized Avraham's innate sense of devotion to Hashem: "It is not such a *chiddush* (new idea) that Avraham Avinu was unscathed by the fiery furnace into which he was cast (for refusing to relinquish his belief in the One True Hashem); the real *chiddush* was the fact that the surroundings were not burned up by the great fire of Avraham's love for *Hakadosh Baruch Hu*!"

The Ba'al Shem Tov understands the mishnah in the manner expounded above and would often stress its message. Meticulousness and stringencies in fulfillment of the mitzvos are important and have their place, but they are not the principal factor of mitzvah observance. That characteristic goes to the notion that *Rachmana liba ba'i* — "Hashem desires the heart" (*Zohar, Raya Mehemna, Parshas Ki Seitzei*). What Hashem desires most from a Yid is the *neshamah* that he invests in a mitzvah, serving Hashem with a full heart, and making His will into his own. And so, we should negate our own will before that of Hashem. That is, when refraining from sin, it should not be an exercise in wishing to succumb to the urge, but resisting the urge. It is preferable that we totally nullify that urge, making our only desire that of fulfilling Hashem's will.

Above and Beyond

Continuing with his exposition of the mishnah, the Nesivos Sholom introduces another dimension to the statement of *Aseih retzono k'retzoncha*. The idea is illustrated in the following story about the Rebbe of Lublin *ztz"l*.

The Rebbe of Lublin once had to undergo a somewhat unique *nisayon* (test of faith). While the exact details of the situation may not be known, what has come down to us is that he was tested with a form of confusion. That is, he was confronted with a situation in which he had to decide if something was permissible or forbidden. It was later confirmed that the matter did, indeed, involve a prohibition. At the time, however, the whole issue was somehow unclear in his mind. This was the *nisayon* — for one reason or another, his usually clear assessment abilities were just not getting into gear, and he could see no reason that anything forbidden was involved.

And so he was faced with a quandary of sorts: What to do? He could detect no reason to be stringent in the matter. And yet…he just was hesitant to go ahead and permit it. And so he relied upon a rule that governed his every move. The Rebbe of Lublin would only participate in a given activity if it clearly provided some *nachas ruach* to *Hakadosh Baruch Hu*. Otherwise, he would abstain, even though there was no clear prohibition involved. He allowed himself to be guided by this principle once again. In the matter at hand, while he could discover no prohibition, he also could not see how any *nachas ruach* to Hashem would emerge from it, and so he abstained. Which turned out to be a good thing. Later, when his memory returned to full capacity, he recognized that there was a clear prohibition involved after all. Had he not had a standing rule to refrain from whatever did not definitively constitute an act that would please Hashem, he would have transgressed, albeit unintentionally, an explicit prohibition.

This attitude that governed the Rebbe of Lublin's life is another facet of the mishnah's teaching. There are some people who are very meticulous to observe all of the mitzvos, but their *avodah* ends there. Whatever is mandatory or forbidden, they keep to the letter. Beyond that, however, is completely out of their purview. But the truth is that there are things that — while not covered by an explicit prohibition — still fall within the category of Hashem's will. A person may be exempt from taking a certain action, but it would still please his Creator if he would undertake it. And so the mishnah puts an emphasis on fulfilling Hashem's *ratzon*. That is, sometimes going beyond the letter of the law, simply because that is what Hashem would prefer.

The singularity of Avraham's successful effort in the ordeal of the *Akeidah* could also be understood in light of this idea. We had wondered what, indeed, was so extraordinary about Avraham's feat;

wouldn't anyone who was visited and instructed by Hashem have acted likewise? While this issue was addressed earlier with one approach, there is another explanation that emerges from a most remarkable revelation of the *Derashos Haran* (*D'rush* 6). The Ran contends that, in fact, *Avraham was never commanded to sacrifice his son*. That is, he was never obligated to do so. When Hashem first communicated the idea to Avraham, He said: קַח נָא אֶת־בִּנְךָ...וְהַעֲלֵהוּ שָׁם לְעֹלָה — **Please** *take your son...and offer him as a sacrifice* (*Bereishis* 22:2). The Ran understands from here that Hashem was really only stating His preference: "It would grant Me *nachas ruach* if you would do this act." But Avraham had the option of declining and would have done nothing wrong had he done so.

Yet Avraham offered up his son anyway, and it was in this way that his act was indeed unique. It is true that Jews throughout the ages heroically forfeited their lives and those of their children to sanctify Hashem's Name. But these were principally instances that involved an actual prohibition, such as being forced to convert to a foreign faith. What was singular about Avraham's self-sacrifice was that it involved an act for which he was under no obligation but did so solely because it would please Hashem. The words of the aforementioned *tefillah* are quite exact in this regard. It does not state, כְּמוֹ שֶׁכָּבַשׁ אַבְרָהָם אָבִינוּ אֶת רַחֲמָיו...לַעֲשׂוֹת מִצְוָתְךָ בְּלֵבָב שָׁלֵם — *As Avraham Avinu conquered his mercy...to perform* **Your commandment** *with a full heart*; but rather, לַעֲשׂוֹת רְצוֹנְךָ בְּלֵבָב שָׁלֵם — *to perform* **Your will** *with a full heart*. Although it was only Hashem's wish, and not a full-fledged command, Avraham did not hesitate. He was lovingly ready to sacrifice all for Hashem's desire.

The second half of the mishnah's teaching, בַּטֵּל רְצוֹנְךָ מִפְּנֵי רְצוֹנוֹ — *Nullify your will from before His will*, can be understood along similar lines. The intent here is not just regarding explicit prohibitions, stating that if one desires to sin, he should negate this urge in order to comply with Hashem's command. Rather, the emphasis, once again, is on Hashem's *ratzon* — i.e., things that may fall outside the boundaries of an explicit prohibition but would nonetheless please Hashem if one were to refrain from them. This reflects the notion of being *Mekadesh atzmo b'mutar* — "Sanctifying oneself in even permissible areas" (cf. Ramban, Vayikra 19:2). There is no explicit prohibition, for example, against excessive eating, but such behavior runs counter to Hashem's *ratzon*.

The mishnah then lays out the outcome of nullifying one's will for that of *Hakadosh Baruch Hu*: כְּדֵי שֶׁיְּבַטֵּל רְצוֹן אֲחֵרִים מִפְּנֵי רְצוֹנֶךָ — *So that He will nullify the will of* **others** *from before your will*. Who are these "others" of whom the mishnah speaks? The Nesivos Sholom understands this as a reference to that ultimate "other" — the *Sitra* **Achra**, the evil force of the "**Other** Side." For the *yetzer hara* is delighted when a person overindulges in even permissible pleasures. As Reb Menachem Mendel of Vitebsk explains, the main purpose of a Yid's *avodah* is to become closer and attached to Hashem. But indulging in pleasure for its own sake has the opposite effect, separating a person from Hashem. The *yetzer hara* is well aware of this, which is why it encourages and entices a Yid to seek and partake of worldly pleasures. In this way, it can prevent a Yid from attaining his purpose in life, which is *d'veikus baHashem*. And so, by refraining from even these permissible pleasures — by being *mevatel* (negating) one's desires, simply for the sake of Hashem's *ratzon* (even where no actual prohibition is involved) — the end result will be the thwarting of the *yetzer hara's* design: כְּדֵי שֶׁיְּבַטֵּל רְצוֹן אֲחֵרִים מִפְּנֵי רְצוֹנֶךָ — *So that He will nullify the will of* **the "other one"** *from before your will*. His desire to keep a Yid far from his Creator will be frustrated, as instead the earnest *oveid Hashem* who abstained from these pleasures will be able to achieve *d'veikus*.

Disappearing Act

The Nesivos Sholom uncovers yet another layer of meaning to the second half of the mishnah. He understands that the emphasis on nullification reflects a central aspect of *avodas Hashem*: the concept of *bitul hayeishus* (nullification of "entities"). That is, the mishnah is stating that to attain the higher levels in serving Hashem and fulfilling His will, a Yid must be willing to engage in earnest self-nullification. The assertion of "self" leads a person to be constantly absorbed with his own self-interest; as such, the notion of *yeishus* is the root of chasing one's desires and other negative tendencies. For a Yid to become truly close to Hashem, he must first cleanse himself of the influence of his ego and adopt the course of *bitul hayeishus*.

The Ba'al Shem Tov makes a similar exhortation through one of his well-known teachings. When Moshe Rabbeinu recounted the events at Har Sinai, he described his role in the following manner: אָנֹכִי עֹמֵד בֵּין־ה׳ וּבֵינֵיכֶם — *I was standing between Hashem and you* (*Devarim* 5:5). According to the simple understanding of this *passuk*, Moshe was referring to his serving as the intermediary between Hashem and the nation, relating His words to the people. The Ba'al Shem Tov supplies a homiletic rendering of this *passuk*, reflecting the notion discussed above. He interprets: "'*Anochi*' — that is, the *middah* of '*anochi'us*' (assertion of one's sense of 'I') — is what stands between a Yid and Hashem," keeping him far from attaining *d'veikus*. This is the depth of the exhortation of בַּטֵּל רְצוֹנְךָ מִפְּנֵי רְצוֹנוֹ — to completely nullify one's self and one's innate *ratzon* before Hashem, to the extent that, in effect, these entities no longer exist.

Reb Menachem Mendel of Vitebsk *ztz"l* expounded on the notion of *bitul hayeishus*, elaborating at some length on just what this endeavor entails. He describes how the individual views himself as a virtual non-entity, as if his personal concerns simply have no bearing. Thus, he completely relinquishes any claim to self-interest. Not to act recklessly, of course, but utter negation and subservience to Hashem's majesty. One who has perfected this trait has so completely submitted his essence to Hashem that he feels ready to allow his own self, body and soul, to be completely eradicated from both This World and the Next if (theoretically) that would please Hashem. Such is the mindset of the truly devoted; he has completely abandoned any thoughts of self, instead focused completely and solely on sanctifying Hashem's Name and bringing Him satisfaction. In this almost unimaginably elevated plane, the *oveid* truly feels that there is nothing aside from Hashem — not even his very own self.

There is a beautiful and well-known narrative recorded in the Gemara recounting the final moments of Rabbi Akiva's life (*Berachos* 61b). The last thing he related to his disciples, as he was being led to die a martyr's death, concerned the *passuk* from *Krias Shema* that states: וְאָהַבְתָּ אֵת ה׳ אֱלֹקֶיךָ...בְּכָל־נַפְשְׁךָ — *And you shall love Hashem your G-d...**with all of your soul*** (*Devarim* 6:5). The phrase "with all of your soul" is interpreted to mean, "Even as He is taking your soul away." Rabbi Akiva explained that he spent his whole life worrying if he would ever have the opportunity to fulfill this dictum — and now it finally came. And so, as the enemy commenced their murderous torture of the sage, he recited the *Shema*: שְׁמַע יִשְׂרָאֵל ה׳ אֱלֹקֵינוּ ה׳ אֶחָד — *Hear, Yisroel, Hashem is our G-d, Hashem is One* (ibid. v. 4). His soul departed as he intoned the word *echad* (one). The Gemara then relates: יָצְתָה בַּת קוֹל וְאָמְרָה: אַשְׁרֶיךָ רַבִּי עֲקִיבָא שֶׁיָּצְאָה נִשְׁמָתְךָ בְּאֶחָד — *A Heavenly voice came forth and proclaimed: "How fortunate are you, Rabbi Akiva, for your soul exited during (the recital of the word)* echad*!"*

Truly a moving account — but mysterious, as well. For the climax of the narrative almost appears incongruous. Rabbi Akiva had so yearned to fulfill the directive of loving Hashem *b'chol nafshecha*, and he finally was able to do so. Wouldn't it have been most appropriate, then, for his soul to have departed while reciting these words? Why all the focus on his soul leaving while declaring *echad*?

Based on the Maharal (*Nesivos Olam, Nesiv Ahavas Hashem*, ch. 1), the Nesivos Sholom demonstrates that this teaching of *Chazal* is echoing the sentiment described above. Rabbi Akiva had attained — throughout his life, and climaxing at that moment — a supreme level of *d'veikus baHashem*. *D'veikus* with Hashem is a completely different notion than the *d'veikus* experienced between two dear friends, for example. In this latter instance, there are two separate entities attaching themselves to each other. They may become exceedingly close, but they still remain two different units. True *d'veikus baHashem*, however, means that there are no two entities here, but only one. That is, the person completely negates himself before Hashem, becoming completely subsumed by His Presence.

Thus, it emerges that *b'chol nafshecha* and *echad* are really one and the same. Once again, we could ask what makes Rabbi Akiva so unique; while his deed was truly heroic, was he not only one of many martyrs throughout the annals of Jewish history? Why does he deserve such particular focus, to the extent that from the Heavens was declared, "How fortunate are you, Rabbi Akiva!" The answer is that the singling out of Rabbi Akiva was not so much for the act of dying *al kiddush Hashem*, but for what he achieved at that moment. As his soul departed, Rabbi Akiva had attained the most supreme levels of *d'veikus baHashem*. He was not his own entity, graciously and heroically allowing that entity to be killed for Hashem's sake. Instead, he had made himself into a *non-entity*, thereby able to cleave to Hashem in the most elevated fashion. His *neshamah* truly did depart in a state of *echad*; having completely nullified his *yeishus*, there remained only One entity.

In a similar vein, this notion was also demonstrated by Moshe Rabbeinu. The *passuk* refers to him in the following way: וְהָאִישׁ מֹשֶׁה עָנָו מְאֹד מִכֹּל הָאָדָם אֲשֶׁר עַל־פְּנֵי הָאֲדָמָה — *And the man, Moshe, was exceedingly humble, more than any person on the face of the earth* (Bamidbar 12:3). The Nesivos Sholom explains that the level of *anivus* referred to here is not simply an absence of *ga'avah* (arrogance). Rather, it reflects the very trait of our discussion — an actual sense of humility comprised of active self-nullification. Having actually been able to gaze upon the Divine Presence in a way that no other human has, Moshe was awed by what he beheld to such a remarkable extent that he became solely focused on Hashem's greatness, achieving thereby both total self-negation and supreme submission to Hashem.

The mishnah concludes: כְּדֵי שֶׁיְּבַטֵּל רְצוֹן אֲחֵרִים מִפְּנֵי רְצוֹנֶךָ — *So that He will nullify the will of others from before your will*. The term "others" was previously interpreted as a reference to the *yetzer hara*. The Nesivos Sholom continues with that idea here, but with a slight nuance. He explains the mishnah as referring to the reciprocal benefit that accrues to someone who attains the state of *bitul hayeishus*. Having nullified his sense of self, Hashem will aid his further elevation by nullifying from his essence any residual tendencies towards evil. These are the wishes and desires that are the products of the *yetzer hara*.

The above certainly represents some very lofty ideals. Nevertheless, a Yid should not feel discouragement but must realize that — to some extent, at least — these ideals are definitely attainable. *Chazal* instruct us that every Yid must declare of himself: מָתַי יַגִּיעוּ מַעֲשַׂי לְמַעֲשֵׂה אַבְרָהָם יִצְחָק וְיַעֲקֹב — *When will my deeds reach those of Avraham, Yitzchak, and Yaakov?* (*Tanna D'vei Eliyahu Rabbah* 23:1). The tzaddikim interpret the term *yagi'u* of this teaching according to its literal meaning of "touching." That is, even if we cannot literally duplicate the levels attained by our saintly forefathers, we should be able to attain levels that at least make some peripheral contact with those of the Patriarchs.

In Summary

The Nesivos Sholom uncovers the profundity contained within this relatively short mishnah. He does so by interpreting Rabban Gamliel's teaching in a number of ways.

The first approach centers around the well-known principle that *Rachmana liba ba'i* — Hashem's primary interest is our heart, the *neshamah* that we invest in our deeds. As such, our service of Hashem should not be done for other considerations, such as fear of retribution, or by rote. Rather, the most important factor is that we should do it *because we want to do it*. *Aseih retzono k'retzoncha* — "Your will should be to do His will." Furthermore, *Batel retzoncha mip'nei retzono* — "Nullify your will before His will." The implication here is that it is not necessarily enough, when confronted with temptation, to simply overpower that temptation and refrain from sin. Ideally, we should completely *nullify our will before Hashem's will*; that is, we should banish it completely, leaving no *ratzon* of our own other than to fulfill Hashem's will.

Another dimension to this teaching relates to a focus on the term *ratzon* — that is, Hashem's "will" as opposed to "command." According to this approach, the mishnah is exhorting a Yid not to be satisfied with simply adhering to those practices that are obligatory. Rather, his aim should be to fulfill Hashem's will, performing those deeds that will bring Him satisfaction even where there may not be an explicit directive. Similarly, the second half of the mishnah conveys a like sentiment: *Batel retzoncha mip'nei* **retzono**. Once again, the stress is on the *ratzon*, referring to a need to refrain even from permissible indulgence. Although there is no explicit prohibition involved, it is Hashem's will that we practice a measure of restraint even in permissible areas. The result of adopting this path is most significant: כְּדֵי שֶׁיְּבַטֵּל רְצוֹן אֲחֵרִים מִפְּנֵי רְצוֹנֶךָ — *so that He will nullify the will of others before your will.* The *acheirim* referred to here is the *Sitra Achra*, who seeks to entice a person to indulge in pleasures; for such conduct will keep a Yid far away from Hashem. As such, by refraining from such pleasures, the designs of the *yetzer hara* are rendered null and void, and the Yid can attain *d'veikus baHashem*.

The notion of *Batel retzoncha mip'nei retzono* can also be understood as referring to the all-important endeavor of *bitul hayeishus*. For it is the ego and self-absorption that serves as a barrier between a Yid and his Creator; by nullifying our self and our personal desires, the barrier is removed and we can attain *d'veikus* with Hashem. And Hashem will reciprocate and aid our ascension, rendering our negative tendencies and urges — the desires that are products of the *yetzer hara* (*ratzon acheirim*) — null and void. This is the full depth of the teaching כְּדֵי שֶׁיְּבַטֵּל רְצוֹן אֲחֵרִים מִפְּנֵי רְצוֹנֶךָ.

פרק ב' משנה ו'

אין בור ירא חטא ולא עם הארץ חסיד
A Boor Cannot Be Sin-Fearing, an Ignoramus Cannot Be Pious

הוּא הָיָה אוֹמֵר, אֵין בּוּר יְרֵא חֵטְא, וְלֹא עַם הָאָרֶץ חָסִיד, וְלֹא הַבַּיְשָׁן לָמֵד, וְלֹא הַקַּפְּדָן מְלַמֵּד, וְלֹא כָל הַמַּרְבֶּה בִסְחוֹרָה מַחְכִּים. וּבִמְקוֹם שֶׁאֵין אֲנָשִׁים, הִשְׁתַּדֵּל לִהְיוֹת אִישׁ:

(Hillel) would say: A boor cannot be sin-fearing, an ignoramus cannot be pious, a bashful person cannot be well-learned, an impatient person cannot be a teacher, nor can anyone who deals excessively in business become wise. And in a place where there are no men, strive to be a man.

GEMS FROM THE *SEFER NESIVOS SHOLOM*

SOURCES:

אָ"ר פִּנְחָס בֶּן יָאִיר: תּוֹרָה מְבִיאָה לִידֵי זְהִירוּת, זְהִירוּת מְבִיאָה לִידֵי זְרִיזוּת, זְרִיזוּת מְבִיאָה לִידֵי נְקִיּוּת, נְקִיּוּת מְבִיאָה לִידֵי פְּרִישׁוּת, פְּרִישׁוּת מְבִיאָה לִידֵי טָהֳרָה, טָהֳרָה מְבִיאָה לִידֵי קְדוּשָׁה, קְדוּשָׁה מְבִיאָה לִידֵי עֲנָוָה, עֲנָוָה מְבִיאָה לִידֵי יִרְאַת חֵטְא, יִרְאַת חֵטְא מְבִיאָה לִידֵי חֲסִידוּת. (עבודה זרה כ:)

Rabbi Pinchas ben Yair says: Torah leads to scrupulousness, scrupulousness leads to alacrity, alacrity leads to cleanliness, cleanliness leads to abstinence, abstinence leads to purity, purity leads to sanctity, sanctity leads to humility, humility leads to fear of sin, fear of sin leads to piety... (*Avodah Zarah* 20b)

כְּשֶׁיָּשִׂים הָאָדָם אֶל לִבּוֹ שֶׁהַמֶּלֶךְ הַגָּדוֹל הַקָּבָּ"ה אֲשֶׁר מָלֵא כָל הָאָרֶץ כְּבוֹדוֹ עוֹמֵד עָלָיו וְרוֹאֶה בְּמַעֲשָׂיו...מִיַּד יַגִּיעַ אֵלָיו הַיִּרְאָה. (רמ"א, אורח חיים א' א')

When a person takes to heart that the great King – *Hakadosh Baruch Hu*, Whose glory fills the entire world – stands over him and peers at his deeds...immediately, he achieves awe. (*Rama, Orach Chaim* 1:1)

יֶאֱהַב אֶת ה' אַהֲבָה גְדוֹלָה יְתֵרָה עַזָּה מְאֹד עַד שֶׁתְּהֵא נַפְשׁוֹ קְשׁוּרָה בְּאַהֲבַת ה' וְנִמְצָא שׁוֹגֶה בָּהּ תָּמִיד כְּאִלּוּ חוֹלֶה חוֹלִי הָאַהֲבָה שֶׁאֵין דַּעְתּוֹ פְּנוּיָה...וְהוּא שׁוֹגֶה בָּהּ תָּמִיד בֵּין בְּשִׁבְתּוֹ בֵּין בְּקוּמוֹ בֵּין בְּשָׁעָה שֶׁהוּא אוֹכֵל וְשׁוֹתֶה. (רמב"ם פרק י' מהלכות תשובה הל' ג')

He should love Hashem with a love which is great, immense, and extremely strong, to the point where his soul is bound up in love with Hashem. It shall thus emerge that he will be constantly preoccupied with (the object of his love), as one who is lovesick, whose mind is never free... He is constantly preoccupied with (the object of his love): when he sits, stands, eats and drinks. (*Rambam, Hilchos Teshuvah* 10:3)

וְנִרְגָּן מַפְרִיד אַלּוּף. (משלי ט"ז כ"ח)

A complainer causes a friend to keep his distance. (*Mishlei* 16:28)

פרקי אבות

206

אין בור ירא חטא ולא עם הארץ חסיד

דְּעָלָךְ סַנֵי לְחַבְרָךְ לֹא תַעֲבֵיד. (שבת ל״א)

What is hateful to you, do not do to your friend. (*Shabbos* 31a)

קְדֹשִׁים תִּהְיוּ כִּי קָדוֹשׁ אֲנִי ה' אֱלֹקֵיכֶם. (ויקרא י״ט ב')

You shall be holy, for I, Hashem your G-d, am holy. (*Vayikra* 19:2)

...הִנֵּה יִהְיֶה נָבָל בִּרְשׁוּת הַתּוֹרָה, לְפִיכָךְ בָּא הַכָּתוּב, אַחֲרֵי שֶׁפֵּרַט הָאִסוּרִים שֶׁאָסַר אוֹתָם לְגַמְרֵי, וְצִוָּה בְּדָבָר כְּלָלִי שֶׁנִּהְיֶה פְּרוּשִׁים מִן הַמּוּתָרוֹת. (רמב״ן שם)

...(Through overindulgence in [even] permissible pleasures,) a person could conduct himself as a "scoundrel with the (supposed) authorization of the Torah"; therefore, the verse – after having delineated those prohibitions involving a completely forbidden matter – now comes with a general commandment that we should practice abstinence in even permissible areas (*Ramban ibid.*)

אַךְ אֶת־שַׁבְּתֹתַי תִּשְׁמֹרוּ כִּי אוֹת הִוא בֵּינִי וּבֵינֵיכֶם לְדֹרֹתֵיכֶם לָדַעַת כִּי אֲנִי ה' מְקַדִּשְׁכֶם. וּשְׁמַרְתֶּם אֶת־הַשַּׁבָּת כִּי קֹדֶשׁ הִוא לָכֶם מְחַלְלֶיהָ מוֹת יוּמָת כִּי כָּל־הָעֹשֶׂה בָהּ מְלָאכָה וְנִכְרְתָה הַנֶּפֶשׁ הַהִוא מִקֶּרֶב עַמֶּיהָ... וְשָׁמְרוּ בְנֵי־יִשְׂרָאֵל אֶת־הַשַּׁבָּת לַעֲשׂוֹת אֶת־הַשַּׁבָּת לְדֹרֹתָם בְּרִית עוֹלָם. בֵּינִי וּבֵין בְּנֵי יִשְׂרָאֵל אוֹת הִוא לְעֹלָם כִּי־שֵׁשֶׁת יָמִים עָשָׂה ה' אֶת־הַשָּׁמַיִם וְאֶת־הָאָרֶץ וּבַיּוֹם הַשְּׁבִיעִי שָׁבַת וַיִּנָּפַשׁ. (שמות ל״א י״ג, י״ד, ט״ז, י״ז)

But My *Shabbosos*, you shall observe; for it is a sign between Me and you for your generations, for you to know that I am Hashem Who sanctifies you. And you shall observe the Shabbos, for it is holy to you; those who desecrate it shall surely die, for anyone who performs labor in it – that soul shall be cut off from the midst of its nation... And Bnei Yisroel shall observe the Shabbos, to make the Shabbos an eternal covenant, for their generations. Between Me and between Bnei Yisroel, it is an eternal sign that in six days Hashem made the heavens and the earth, and on the seventh day, He stopped and rested. (*Shemos* 31:13, 14, 16, 17)

פרק ב'

GEMS FROM THE *SEFER NESIVOS SHOLOM*

רָזָא דְשַׁבָּת, אִיהִי שַׁבָּת. (ערבית לליל שבת)

The secret of Shabbos – is Shabbos itself. (Evening service for Shabbos night)

אין בור ירא חטא ולא עם הארץ חסיד

What Is a Chassid?

People like to think they know what they're talking about. And often, this is indeed the case. We express our feelings, make certain assertions, and try to back up our claims with facts. And of course, at the very least, we know the meanings of the words we utilize in our speech.

But every so often, we get stumped. A particular assumption we had taken as a given becomes suddenly less clear when we are pressed to confront it. Or even, on occasion, we may realize that there is a certain term we are wont to use — but we don't have a clear picture of what it *really* means.

"Chassid" is one of these terms. One may respond that it's not so difficult to define. After all, a chassid is… Well, what is a chassid, exactly? Of course, in conventional thought, it refers to a member of the chassidic community. But that is not its original meaning, as the term existed well before the spread of this form of *avodas Hashem*; the disseminators of this approach adopted the term to reflect their philosophy. But the word was already in use in the Mishnah — in *Pirkei Avos*, in fact. So…what is a "chassid," in the original sense of the word? Someone who is pious? Nice? Something else?

The answer should become clearer as we delve into the mishnah in which it appears. Other commonly used terms, as well, will have to be defined. But the exercise is well worth the effort, as we glean from the mishnah the timeless message it seeks to impart.

One or Two?

In his analysis of the mishnah, the Maharal zeroes in on a few key points. This section of the mishnah is composed of two brief statements: אֵין בּוּר יְרֵא חֵטְא, וְלֹא עַם הָאָרֶץ חָסִיד — *A* bur *(boor) cannot fear sin, an* am ha'aretz *(ignoramus) cannot be a chassid (rendered, at least for the time being, as "pious")*. While broken up into two parts, the mishnah does appear to be conveying essentially the same point: a lack of Torah knowledge will impede one's spiritual development. Why, then, was the mishnah divided into two apparently synonymous phrases? We may conclude, therefore, that there must be some difference between them. The obvious issue needing to be addressed is, well, what *is* the difference between a boor and an ignoramus?

Even with the distinction between them uncovered, the matter would require further clarification. Why is a deficiency in *yiras cheit* (fear of sin) associated specifically with a *bur*, and an inability to be a chassid a property of an *am ha'aretz*? The implication seems to be that an *am ha'aretz*, while unable to become a chassid, can nevertheless attain the fear of sin which eludes the *bur*. How are we to understand this phenomenon?

The Maharal explains the mishnah's intent. Indeed, the mishnah is discussing a single individual, whose primary fault is his lack of Torah learning. However, two different consequences ensue for the individual due to this state of affairs. One primarily affects his mind, while the other affects his body. These are the two factors that the mishnah is addressing.

Torah study facilitates the forging of a powerful connection to Hashem. Of course, this is only possible for one who immerses himself in its study. Since a boor does not study Torah, he remains distant from Hashem. And that is why he does not have *yirah*.

This notion can be understood by considering the relationship of subjects to their king. Who truly fears the king? Those ministers and attendants who are in the king's immediate proximity. Standing close to their king, they have ample occasion to be in awe of him. But one who is distant from the king, hardly ever encountering him, has much less reason to be afraid. Likewise, fear of Hashem is the consequence of being close to Him. When one studies Torah, Hashem is nearby; in such close quarters, one automatically will fear Hashem. The boor doesn't have this privilege. He doesn't have Torah, and therefore it's as though the King is distant from him. "A boor," therefore, "doesn't fear sin."

But not only does a dearth of Torah knowledge affect one's mindset; one's body is also affected. The Maharal explains that just as a person's body is more dignified than that of an animal, so, too, the physical essence of a Torah scholar is more refined and elevated than that of the average human. Torah is a purifying power. As such, it can purge the *guf* (body) of the latent impurities that are part of its inherent nature. It can transform a natural tendency towards callousness to one of compassion, a cruel nature to one of kindness. Devoid of Torah, the *am ha'aretz* doesn't have this benefit. The mishnah reflects this aspect by stating that the ignoramus will not develop into a chassid.

How, exactly, does Torah study cause the physical body to become uplifted? The Maharal elaborates: Inherently, the entire *beri'ah* (creation) is infused with natural goodness. Thus we find a common refrain throughout the Creation narrative in the first *perek* of *Parshas Bereishis*: וַיַּרְא אֱלֹקִים כִּי־טוֹב — *And G-d saw that it was good*.

But all of this changed through the first sin of Adam Harishon, who ate from the forbidden fruit. The effects of this deed were devastating. Now, the force of evil was inculcated into the *beri'ah*, obscuring the inherent good. From now on, the materialism of creation was a source for *ra* (evil), and the good would somehow need to be extracted from deep within. How was this to be accomplished? This is where the *ko'ach haTorah* (power of Torah) comes in; for it is through the medium of Torah that one would draw out the latent *tov*. Thus, when a person dedicates himself to Torah study, he reawakens the good within, and transforms his essence from one that craves evil to one that gravitates towards and desires to perform good.

And this, according to the Maharal, is the definition of a chassid — one whose natural tendencies have been refined and transformed; a person who is now naturally drawn towards opportunities to perform *chessed* for others. But, as mentioned, this is only possible through the *ko'ach haTorah*. For one who is devoid of Torah, who never underwent this "cleansing" process, the forces of evil will remain dominant. He cannot develop this pristine goodness, an inclination towards *chessed*. As the mishnah declares: לֹא עַם הָאָרֶץ חָסִיד.

This, asserts the Maharal, is the essence of the mishnah's message. It speaks of one person — one ignorant in Torah. And the mishnah outlines the two main areas whereby the individual is affected by this ignorance. One consequence relates to the mind (he does not acquire *yirah*), and the other to the body (he is not a chassid). In any event, this approach to the mishnah avoids a major issue that was mentioned before. We need not examine how or why it is that an *am ha'aretz* can achieve the *yirah* that a boor cannot, yet is still excluded from the category of chassid. According to the Maharal, there are not two different people under discussion here, but a single person — one who neither has *yirah* nor is a chassid.

However, Rashi and the other commentaries differ with this understanding. They take the more conventional approach, interpreting the mishnah as referring to two different individuals of progressive levels: The first, a *bur*, is devoid of *yirah*. The second, an *am ha'aretz* — while capable of attaining *yirah* — still falls short in the area of being a chassid. This understanding is further borne out by the well-known teaching of Rabbi Pinchas ben Yair, who outlines the progressive levels the earnest *oveid Hashem* attains in his quest for spiritual elevation. He states (*Avodah Zarah* 20b), תּוֹרָה מְבִיאָה לִידֵי זְהִירוּת, זְהִירוּת מְבִיאָה לִידֵי זְרִיזוּת...עֲנָוָה מְבִיאָה לִידֵי יִרְאַת חֵטְא, יִרְאַת חֵטְא מְבִיאָה לִידֵי חֲסִידוּת — *Torah leads to scrupulousness, scrupulousness leads to alacrity...humility leads to fear of sin, fear of sin leads to* chassidus. Even barring any definitive definition of this latter term, one thing seems clear from this statement: among the varying gradations of *avodas Hashem*, *chassidus* ranks higher than *yiras cheit*.

As such, the original perplexities remain in place: what is the fundamental difference between a *bur* and an *am ha'aretz*, and what accounts for the varying levels and outcomes of their divergent paths?

The Learned *Am Ha'aretz*

A novel approach to the mishnah is offered by the Kedushas Levi. It appears that he understood the first part of the mishnah's teaching in a straightforward manner, along the lines of what was mentioned before. A *bur* did not learn and does not know Torah; as such, he does not fear sin. *Yiras cheit* is also a *madreigah*; but without a connection to Torah, one does not attain it. By contrast, the *am ha'aretz* does attain this *madreigah*; it is only the higher level of *chassidus* from which he is blocked. While an *am ha'aretz* usually connotes a person who has not learned, here, that cannot possibly be the case; otherwise, how would he have achieved the level of *yiras cheit*? It must be, then, that in its second half, our mishnah speaks of someone who *has* learned Torah. So, what makes him an *am ha'aretz*?

The *am ha'aretz* of our mishnah, the Kedushas Levi explains, must mean something other than the conventional understanding. The literal translation of *am ha'aretz* is "people of the land." That is, they are land-oriented people. Not necessarily in the agrarian sense, but rather in terms of their nature. These are materialistic people, immersed in the "earthly" aspect of their makeup. Thus, the mishnah speaks of someone who readily indulges in the pleasures of This World. He may even know a lot of Torah, and might therefore have a fine sense of *yirah*. It is in the area of indulgence where he does not have control, and this is what impedes him from attaining *chassidus*.

In other words, the Kedushas Levi explains, this section of the mishnah may even be speaking of someone who is a *ba'al madreigah* (elevated person) of sorts. The Rama, in the very beginning of *Shulchan Aruch*, outlines how a person acquires *yirah*: כְּשֶׁיָּשִׂים הָאָדָם אֶל לִבּוֹ שֶׁהַמֶּלֶךְ הַגָּדוֹל הקב״ה אֲשֶׁר מְלֹא כָל הָאָרֶץ כְּבוֹדוֹ עוֹמֵד עָלָיו וְרוֹאֶה בְּמַעֲשָׂיו...מִיַּד יַגִּיעַ אֵלָיו הַיִּרְאָה — *When a person takes to heart that the great King* — Hakadosh Baruch Hu, *Whose glory fills the entire world* — *is standing over him and peering at his deeds...immediately, he will achieve fear*. One who learns Torah is certainly capable of coming to this realization. And this fear will induce him to meticulously observe Hashem's commandments, always keeping an eye out to see if this or that matter conforms to the laws of the Torah or is something that must be avoided. Due to the care and precision with which he approaches his service of Hashem, he can even be considered a tzaddik, who walks in righteous ways. He is a faithful servant of Hashem. But due to his indulgent nature, a chassid he is not.

What emerges is that the *am ha'aretz* of our mishnah is a tzaddik who keeps all the mitzvos, yet isn't a chassid. Let us define these terms: who is a tzaddik and who is a chassid, and in what way does a chassid "outrank" the tzaddik?

A chassid is someone who does *chessed* for his Maker. That is, he constantly yearns to do good for Hashem in fulfillment of His will. In fact, this is his sole preoccupation; to the point that it constitutes a (healthy) obsession. The Rambam (*Hilchos Teshuvah* 10:3) paints a similar picture when describing what true love for Hashem should look like: יֶאֱהַב אֶת ה׳ אַהֲבָה גְדוֹלָה יְתֵירָה עַזָּה מְאֹד עַד שֶׁתְּהֵא נַפְשׁוֹ קְשׁוּרָה בְּאַהֲבַת ה׳ וְנִמְצָא שׁוֹגֶה בָּהּ תָּמִיד כְּאִלּוּ חוֹלֵה חוֹלִי הָאַהֲבָה שֶׁאֵין דַּעְתּוֹ פְּנוּיָה... וְהוּא שׁוֹגֶה בָּהּ תָּמִיד בֵּין בְּשִׁבְתּוֹ בֵּין בְּקוּמוֹ בֵּין בְּשָׁעָה שֶׁהוּא אוֹכֵל וְשׁוֹתֶה — *He should love Hashem with a love which is great, immense, and extremely strong, to the point where his soul is bound up in love with Hashem. It shall thus emerge that he will be constantly preoccupied with (the object of his love), as one who is lovesick, whose mind is never free... He is constantly preoccupied with (the object of his love): when he sits, when he stands, when he eats and drinks...*

These fiery words aptly depict a chassid, who serves Hashem from love. He stands in contrast to a tzaddik, as described above. For, while the tzaddik is meticulous in following the commandments, he does so primarily out of fear. Stated another way, the chassid is in love with Hashem. The *am ha'aretz* — who, as we said, may be a tzaddik, but has tendencies towards *artzi'us* (materialism) — is in love with himself.

And while the tzaddik serves Hashem in the capacity of a faithful *eved* (servant), a chassid takes on the persona of a *ben* (son), a prince who serves his father, the king. Whereas the former aims to abide by all the royal decrees and fulfill the king's demands, he does not necessarily do so out of any sense of strong connection with the monarch. But the prince is motivated by his undying love for his father; his goal and aspiration is simply to give him pleasure.

The difference between them is truly manifest when the opportunity arises to do something that would please the king, though no formal request had been made. The prince, whose main objective is to make his father happy, will eagerly do the deed. But the servant may very well hold back. He does whatever the king asks for, but does not go beyond his official duties.

אין בור ירא חטא ולא עם הארץ חסיד

A Little Self-Control Goes a Long Way

This idea rounds out the definition of a chassid: one who goes "above and beyond" for Hashem. The *am ha'aretz* declares, "If it's permitted, that's good enough for me." But the chassid realizes that indulgence — even in areas of permissibility — is not what Hashem desires from us. The chassid's guiding philosophy is: "I seek to make Hashem happy, and I am not interested in enjoyments that do not in any way promote this objective."

This notion, however, deserves some examination. What is wrong with physical pleasures? If it is permitted, why should we refrain?

At the heart of the matter is an issue of priority. That is, a human being is limited and can only have a single priority. By adopting a primary objective, he automatically consigns all other concerns to secondary importance. And so, a person must decide the primary object of his concern: is it Hashem, or himself? It can't be both.

A chassid's main desire is to bring pleasure to Hashem. This is his primary ambition in life, and all of his activities are ultimately directed towards the fulfillment of this ideal. Before he eats, for example, he asks himself: "What will Hashem derive from this activity? Does it further His honor in some way, or not?" He may decide that Hashem indeed desires that he partake of this particular dish; perhaps it is necessary for his health, it will grant him strength to serve Hashem, it promotes his emotional well-being, etc. The chassid may also enjoy the physical pleasures of life; it is only that he does so through the lens of fulfilling Hashem's will. And so, he first decides that this is indeed what Hashem wants. His goal is to please Hashem, not himself.

The *am ha'aretz*, with his bent towards materialism, is primarily interested in personal pleasure. He may also serve Hashem because he knows that he must. It is not, however, his principal aspiration. That is reserved for pleasure-seeking. When the opportunity arises to enjoy himself, he grabs it immediately, and then goes searching for more.

In this regard, the Rambam writes (*Peirush Hamishnayos*,

פרק ב'

עִנְיָן הָאָסוּר וְהַמּוּתָּר אֵינָן בְּעִנְיָן הַמְרוּחָק וְהַשָּׂנוּא וְהַמְרוּצָה וְהָאָהוּב :(Sanhedrin, ch. 7) וּמָה שֶׁרָאוּי לַעֲשׂוֹת וכו׳ — *The matter of (what is explicitly) prohibited and permitted is not necessarily the identical issue as what constitutes what is repulsive and despised or preferred, loved, and appropriate to do...* In other words, there are deeds which are permissible according to the strict letter of the law; but they still may be abominable in the eyes of Hashem.

In his commentary to the Torah (*Vayikra* 19:2), the Ramban accentuates this point. He speaks of an individual who is a *naval b'reshus haTorah*, a person who conducts himself in a debased manner, all within the boundaries of the Torah. He thinks that he is not doing anything wrong, since he has indulged only in permitted matters. But it is not the "permitted or forbidden" that is the issue here, but the indulgence itself. Acting in a permissible but hedonistic manner, he separates himself from Hashem.

This same idea is expressed in a teaching of the *Pri Ha'aretz*. He cites a phrase appearing in *Mishlei* (16:28): *Nirgan mafrid Aluf.* In the context of the *passuk*, this refers to the fact that a complainer causes Hashem to separate from him (*cf. Rashi, ibid.*). The *Pri Ha'aretz* applies the phrase to enjoyment-seekers as well, contending that "any pleasure in life is *mafrid Aluf* (forges a division between a Yid and Hashem)." This refers to someone who enjoys pleasures for himself, unrelated to Hashem's service. By doing so, he separates himself from Hashem.

It is noteworthy that the *Tanna* of our mishnah, which warns against *artzi'us*, is Hillel (the mishnah begins, *Hu hayah omeir* — "He used to say," referring to Hillel, whose name appears in preceding mishnayos). This is the same Hillel featured in the well-known episode recorded in the Gemara (*Shabbos* 31a), in which a prospective convert approached him with an odd request. He asked Hillel to teach him the entire Torah while standing on one foot. Hillel famously replied, דַּעֲלָךְ סַנֵי לְחַבְרָךְ לֹא תַעֲבֵיד — *What is hateful to you, do not do to your friend.* That, he asserted, is the essence of the entire Torah. The rest is explanation.

The truth is that Hillel's answer seems puzzling; how did he

אין בור ירא חטא ולא עם הארץ חסיד

address the question, exactly? What Hillel said is the basic idea of a single mitzvah — that of *ahavas Yisroel*. But the man had requested to be taught the entire Torah! How, indeed, does Hillel's teaching encompass the entirety of Torah?

The Maggid of Mezeritch renders Hillel's answer somewhat different than is usually understood. *L'chavrach*, to your friend, can also be understood as *l'chavrusach*, your connection "to the connection." In other words, Hillel was not just talking about the single mitzvah of loving one's fellow but was in fact laying down an overarching principle. He was telling the potential convert to avoid any action that may weaken his connection with Hashem. This short lesson is essentially the entire Torah, for it highlights the purpose of the entire Torah: creating a bond between a Yid and Hashem. Hillel told the convert, "Never sever this connection." Included in this lesson is, "don't even enjoy pleasures solely for yourself, without Hashem's service in mind," because all of these separate the Yid from Hashem.

Thus it emerges that Hillel's instruction to his visitor is essentially the same lesson he is imparting in our mishnah. In discouraging *am ha'aratzus*, Hillel was warning against over-indulgence in even the permissible aspects of materialism. Doing so is a contradiction to being a chassid and — as the *Pri Ha'aretz* teaches — it *mafrid Aluf*, separates a Yid from Hashem. Exactly what Hillel told the potential convert: "Do not do any action that is detrimental to your connection with Hashem."

The path of *chassidus* is not simply a "bonus"; in a sense, it constitutes the highest level of *avodas Hashem*. The Torah enjoins a Yid to cultivate holiness: *Kedoshim tiheyu* — "Be holy" (*Vayikra* 19:1). How, indeed, is this possible? The answer emerges from the continuation of Rabbi Pinchas ben Yair's teaching (mentioned previously). In outlining the ascending levels of *avodas Hashem*, he concludes the list: יִרְאַת חֵטְא מְבִיאָה לִידֵי חֲסִידוּת, חֲסִידוּת מְבִיאָה לִידֵי רוּחַ הַקּוֹדֶשׁ — *Fear of sin leads to* chassidus. Chassidus *leads to* ruach hakodesh *(a spirit of holiness). Chassidus* leads a Yid to the highest attainments. It enables him to become *kadosh*.

פרק ב׳

217

The Shabbos-Chassid Connection

There is another area wherein the difference between these two entities — the tzaddik/*am ha'aretz* and the chassid — is readily apparent. It is manifest in their relationship to the Shabbos Kodesh.

The Kedushas Levi continues his dissertation by expounding upon the section in *Parshas Ki Sisa* dealing with Shabbos. Adopting his approach to these *pesukim* with some minor variations, we can arrive at some very profound ideas.

There appears to be some redundancy in these *pesukim*. In the beginning of this section, the *passuk* states (*Shemos* 31:13): אֶת־שַׁבְּתֹתַי תִּשְׁמֹרוּ כִּי אוֹת הִוא בֵּינִי וּבֵינֵיכֶם לְדֹרֹתֵיכֶם לָדַעַת כִּי אֲנִי ה' מְקַדִּשְׁכֶם — *Keep my Shabbosos, for it is a sign between Me and between you, for all your generations, to know that I am Hashem Who sanctifies you.* The very next verse seems to repeat much of the material just stated: וּשְׁמַרְתֶּם אֶת־הַשַּׁבָּת כִּי קֹדֶשׁ הִוא לָכֶם מְחַלְלֶיהָ מוֹת יוּמָת וכו' — *Keep the Shabbos, because it is holy to you. Those who profane it will be put to death...* Why does the Torah require two *pesukim* in a row, each exhorting us to "keep the Shabbos"?

We may gain some insight into the issue by examining the general nature of all mitzvos. In fact, there are essentially two different components of a mitzvah. Every mitzvah is comprised of the "technical" aspect, the portion of the mitzvah relating to the practical mechanics of its performance. Additionally, the mitzvah has a "soul," if you will, the deeper, underlying "spirit" of the mitzvah, the sublime power residing within the overall effort to please *Hakadosh Baruch Hu*, which serves to connect the *oveid* to Him. Each of these components are essential to the mitzvah as a whole; every mitzvah must be performed to the utmost, and the importance of forging a connection thereby cannot be overstated. The only question is: which aspect is paramount, serving as the primary force of the mitzvah? In this respect, the mitzvos differ. There are mitzvos whose primary aspect is the actual performance of the mitzvah, with all of its attendant details. However, other mitzvos — while all of the technical details need be scrupulously adhered to — are characterized by a prime focus on *d'veikus*.

אין בור ירא חטא ולא עם הארץ חסיד

Shabbos is an example of this latter type of mitzvah, whereby the inner profundity of the mitzvah is paramount. Those who follow the liturgical tradition known as *Nusach Sefard* recite every Friday night a passage from the Zohar, known for its opening word: *Kegavna*. This passage contains the phrase: רָזָא דְשַׁבָּת, אִיהִי שַׁבָּת — *The secret of Shabbos, is Shabbos itself*. The Rebbe of Lechovitz points out that the numerical value of the word רָז (secret) is 207 — the same as אוֹר (light). Thus, the Zohar is telling us, "The 'light' of Shabbos is the Shabbos." That is to say, the primary aspect of Shabbos is the holiness, the spiritual light, the connection we develop with Hashem on this day.

This idea is also reflected in a remarkable statement of Reb Shlomo Karliner. He reported of hearing a Heavenly announcement, which highlighted the importance of relating to the inner, spiritual bliss of Shabbos. The Heavenly voice said something to the following effect: "Whoever is careful to keep all the details of the Shabbos laws, but does not strive to experience the light and spiritual joy of Shabbos, will be forever affected. He will surely merit to enter Gan Eden, but his delight there will be somewhat mitigated. He will experience the same pleasure as if he were merely a bench placed in the Garden." On Shabbos, it is essential that we strive to experience its great light and joy.

It is to this crucial aspect of Shabbos that the first of the two *pesukim* alludes. אֶת־שַׁבְּתֹתַי תִּשְׁמֹרוּ כִּי אוֹת הוּא בֵּינִי וּבֵינֵיכֶם — *Keep my* Shabbosos **for it is a sign between Me and you**. Here the *passuk* refers to the spiritual connection with Hashem that is developed on Shabbos. The observance of Shabbos serves as a proclamation of the covenant and the bond that exists between Hashem and the Jewish nation.

The *passuk* therefore concludes: לָדַעַת כִּי אֲנִי ה' מְקַדִּשְׁכֶם — *So that you* **know** *that I am Hashem Who sanctifies you*. Actually, the word *da'as* carries another, deeper connotation than merely "knowing." As evidenced by its usage in *Parshas Bereishis* (4:1) — וְהָאָדָם יָדַע אֶת־חַוָּה אִשְׁתּוֹ — *And Adam "knew" Chavah, his wife* — it refers to a much more special, intimate connection. Thus, we see this first *passuk*

פרק ב'

219

highlighting the spirit of Shabbos — it is a day of *d'veikus* with Hashem.

The following *passuk* discusses the practical aspect of adhering to the Shabbos laws. One manifestation of the practicality aspect is the punishment meted out to those who violate the Shabbos: *Mechalelehah mos yumas*. The actual "doing" component of Shabbos warrants its own exhortation to "keep Shabbos," and so the *shemirah* (observance) directive is repeated here.

One *passuk* discusses the *d'veikus* of Shabbos; the other, its actual performance. Both are essential, neither can be ignored. But which is considered the focal point of Shabbos? The answer is alluded to a few *pesukim* later, in the familiar passage recited by all congregations in the Shabbos *davening*. It begins (v. 16): וְשָׁמְרוּ בְנֵי־יִשְׂרָאֵל אֶת־הַשַּׁבָּת — *And Bnei Yisroel shall keep the Shabbos*. Yet another mention of the *shemirah* of Shabbos! The Rebbe of Kobrin thus interpreted this reference as alluding to the *shemirah* of Shabbos for the Jewish people; that is, when Yidden keep Shabbos, Shabbos "reciprocates" and protects them.

But which aspect of the Shabbos is responsible for providing this measure of protection? The *pesukim* continue (v. 17): בֵּינִי וּבֵין בְּנֵי יִשְׂרָאֵל אוֹת הוּא — *Between Me and between Bnei Yisroel, it is a sign*. Here, the *passuk* speaks of the connection with Hashem that is strengthened through Shabbos. Apparently, it is this element of Shabbos observance — the *d'veikus*, the "light" of Shabbos — that is paramount to the day, and chiefly responsible for the reciprocal protection it affords.

And it is here we see the difference between a chassid and an *am ha'aretz* reflected in the Shabbos. After all, isn't this the essence of a chassid, as we explained earlier? A chassid is one who goes above and beyond, because he loves Hashem and yearns for a connection with Him. And so a chassid can relate well to the "light" of Shabbos, the primary focus of the day. This stands in contrast to the *am ha'aretz/tzaddik*. The main thrust of his *avodah* is limited to what the laws demand; he adheres loyally to them, but does not delve deeper or beyond. As such, he relates more to that aspect of Shabbos, which, in relative terms, is of secondary standing.

אין בור ירא חטא ולא עם הארץ חסיד

The Nesivos Sholom takes this idea one step further, based on the teachings of *Chazal*. The Zohar (vol. 3, page 29) contrasts a *talmid chacham* with an *am ha'aretz*, actually according a *talmid chacham* with a *bechinah* (component) of Shabbos. That is to say, a *talmid chacham* (even throughout the week) exists in a state of spiritual elevation, in the manner that Shabbos towers above the other days of the week. This notion is particularly apropos in light of all that has been elaborated on above. The *talmid chacham*/chassid stands in contrast to an *am ha'aretz*/tzaddik. As stated, the chassid is given over to *d'veikus* — the main essence of Shabbos. And so, for the *talmid chacham*/chassid, who exists in a permanent state of *d'veikus*, every day is like a Shabbos.

It was mentioned further that the *am ha'aretz*/tzaddik serves Hashem primarily from a sense of *yirah*. It is noteworthy how the *Yerushalmi* (*Demai* 4:1) characterizes the state of an *am ha'aretz* on Shabbos. It speaks of the fact that **eimas Shabbos alav** — **"the fear** of Shabbos is upon him," preventing him from sinning on Shabbos. This reflects the fact that the "earthly" *am ha'aretz* serves Hashem not from love, like his counterpart the chassid, but out of fear. As such, even on Shabbos he attains at most the level of *yiras cheit*, keeping the Shabbos laws from a sense of duty. But that is as far as it goes; enjoying the spiritual light of Shabbos is beyond their capacity, as long as they retain their predilection for materialism.

It should be noted that, whereas they are distant from the true spirit of Shabbos and the preferred *avodah* of the chassid, all is certainly not lost for the *am ha'aretz* of our mishnah. *Yiras cheit* is still a *madreigah* in its own right and can ultimately lead to love of Hashem. As Rabbi Pinchas ben Yair taught, יִרְאַת חֵטְא מְבִיאָה לִידֵי חֲסִידוּת — *Fear of sin leads to* chassidus; the latter being characterized by a burning love for Hashem. The Zohar (in its introduction) emphasizes the fact that *yirah* is essentially a prerequisite to the attainment of *ahavah*. The *am ha'aretz* is not yet a chassid. But if he so desires, he can grow from level to level: from an *am ha'aretz* to a chassid; from *yirah* to *ahavah*; from *yiras cheit* to *chassidus*. He can go from being a servant who fulfills his duty, to the King's caring and loving son, whose primary desire is to bring pleasure to his Father in Heaven.

In Summary

In the course of elucidating this mishnah, the Nesivos Sholom not only defines some common, key terms in a most innovative way, but reveals great profundity in the mishnah's teaching.

One primary issue that requires attention is clarifying the difference between a *bur* and an *am ha'aretz*; at first glance, these seem to be the same thing. The first cited approach is that of the Maharal. He explains that the mishnah is actually speaking of a single individual and that these two entities are essentially the same: they both refer to someone who has not learned Torah. The mishnah is comprised of two separate teachings because there are in fact two harmful consequences to one's lack of learning: both the mind and the body are affected. A person with no connection to Torah cannot cultivate a sense of *yirah*, just as one who is distant from a king will not be afraid of him. This is the thrust of the mishnah's first statement: אֵין בּוּר יְרֵא חֵטְא. The mishnah continues: לֹא עַם הָאָרֶץ חָסִיד. Here, the mishnah speaks of the effects on the *guf*, whose inherent goodness can only be brought out through the power of Torah. As such, the *guf* of an *am ha'aretz* will by habit remain mired in its tendency towards *ra*. This is in contrast to the chassid, whose natural tendencies have been purged through the *ko'ach haTorah*. Such a refined individual will now seek to perform *chessed* towards others.

The other commentators, however, understand the mishnah as referring to two different people. Accordingly, the difference between a *bur* and an *am ha'aretz* can be accounted for through the novel explanation of the Kedushas Levi. The definition of a *bur* is straightforward: he is a boor, unlearned and devoid of Torah. As such, he cannot even attain the comparatively lower *madreigah* of *yiras cheit*. But the *am ha'aretz* can attain *yirah*. For the Kedushas Levi understands that the *am ha'aretz* of our mishnah is not necessarily ignorant. In fact, he is learned, and can even be a tzaddik; that is, one who faithfully carries out the Torah's laws, as a loyal servant performs his duty to the king. But he is not a chassid, an individual who, by dint of his overwhelming love for Hashem, seeks to go beyond the letter of the law, just like the king's son who, out of love for his father, seeks only to give his father pleasure.

A key area where the difference between a tzaddik and a chassid is displayed is the notion of refraining from permissible activities. The tzaddik/*am ha'aretz* is characterized by *artzi'us*, a gravitational pull towards materialism. While fear propels him to adhere to the commandments, he does not go beyond; rather, he feels free to indulge in permissible items. Why not? he contends. Thus, he may readily slip into the category referred to by the Ramban as a *naval b'reshus haTorah*. A chassid, on the other hand, is careful even with the prospect of the permissible. His primary focus in life is not his own pleasure, but granting Hashem pleasure. As a result, every action is weighed with consideration of how it looks in the eyes of Hashem: does this serve His purposes, or does it not? And he is likewise aware of the characterization of the *Pri Ha'aretz*, that every indulgence in pleasure places a wedge between a Yid and his Creator. The chassid's main concern is maintaining his *d'veikus* with Hashem and eschewing that which may interfere with this all-important goal.

Shabbos is another area where the distinction is manifest. As with all mitzvos, Shabbos has two components. There is the practical aspect of adhering to its laws, and there is the inner essence of the mitzvah, the joy and light of Shabbos through which a Yid develops an attachment to Hashem. In the case of Shabbos, it is this latter component that is paramount. The chassid, whose overall service of Hashem is characterized by love for Him and *d'veikus* to Him, obviously relates to the light of Shabbos, which signifies *d'veikus*. In fact, *Chazal* state that a *talmid chacham*/chassid enjoys a semblance of Shabbos throughout the week, a notion that is most understandable in light of the fact that a chassid's whole essence is one of *d'veikus*. An *am ha'aretz*, on the other hand, does not attain the light of Shabbos. His *avodah* is characterized by mere adherence to the bounds of the law, with little focus on forming a connection with Hashem. Driven primarily by fear, his Shabbos experience is likewise characterized by sufficing with the basic letter of the law. *Chazal* thus describe the relation of the *am ha'aretz* to Shabbos as *eimas Shabbos alav* — the fear of Shabbos is upon him.

But there is hope even for the *am ha'aretz*. Having attained *yirah*, he is at least on the road towards climbing higher. In fact, in Rabbi Pinchas ben Yair's delineation of the levels of *avodas Hashem*, *chassidus* is next on the list: *Yirah* leads to *chassidus* and love of Hashem.

פרק ב' משנה י"ג
איזוהי דרך טובה שידבק בה האדם
What Is the Good Path to Which a Person Should Attach Himself

אָמַר לָהֶם, צְאוּ וּרְאוּ אֵיזוֹהִי דֶרֶךְ טוֹבָה שֶׁיִּדְבַּק בָּהּ הָאָדָם. רַבִּי אֱלִיעֶזֶר אוֹמֵר, עַיִן טוֹבָה. רַבִּי יְהוֹשֻׁעַ אוֹמֵר, חָבֵר טוֹב. רַבִּי יוֹסֵי אוֹמֵר, שָׁכֵן טוֹב. רַבִּי שִׁמְעוֹן אוֹמֵר, הָרוֹאֶה אֶת הַנּוֹלָד. רַבִּי אֶלְעָזָר אוֹמֵר, לֵב טוֹב. אָמַר לָהֶם, רוֹאֶה אֲנִי אֶת דִּבְרֵי אֶלְעָזָר בֶּן עֲרָךְ מִדִּבְרֵיכֶם, שֶׁבִּכְלָל דְּבָרָיו דִּבְרֵיכֶם.

(Rabban Yochanan ben Zakkai) said to (his five disciples): Go out and see what is a good path to which a person should attach himself. Rabbi Eliezer said: A good eye. Rabbi Yehoshua said: A good friend. Rabbi Yose said: A good neighbor. Rabbi Shimon said: Projecting the outcome. Rabbi Elazar said: A good heart. (Rabban Yochanan) said to them: I prefer the words of Elazar ben Arach to your words, for his words include all of yours.

GEMS FROM THE *SEFER NESIVOS SHOLOM*

SOURCES:

אֵיזֶהוּ עָשִׁיר הַשָּׂמֵחַ בְּחֶלְקוֹ. (אבות ד')

Who is wealthy? One who is happy with his portion. (*Avos* 4)

דַּעֲלָךְ סַנֵי לְחַבְרָךְ לֹא תַעֲבֵיד. (שבת ל"א)

What is hateful to you, do not do to your friend. (*Shabbos* 31a)

מַה הַמָּקוֹם...רַחוּם וְחַנּוּן אַף אַתָּה הֱוֵי רַחוּם וְחַנּוּן... מָה הקב"ה...נִקְרָא חָסִיד...אַף אַתָּה הֱוֵי חָסִיד. (ספרי עקב י"ג)

Just as Hashem...is merciful and compassionate, so should you be merciful and compassionate... Just as Hashem...is called, "The Pious One"...so should you be pious. (*Sifri, Eikev* §13)

לְאַהֲבָה אֶת ה' אֱלֹקֵיכֶם לָלֶכֶת בְּכָל דְּרָכָיו וּלְדָבְקָה בוֹ. (דברים י"א כ"ב)

To love Hashem your G-d, to walk in all His ways, and to cleave to Him. (*Devarim* 11:22)

רַבִּי אוֹמֵר, אֵיזוֹהִי דֶרֶךְ יְשָׁרָה שֶׁיָּבוֹר לוֹ הָאָדָם. (אבות ב')

Rebbi said: Which is the straight path that a person should choose? (*Avos* 2)

איזוהי דרך טובה שידבק בה האדם

The GPS of Old

Directions! It used to be that traveling from Bnei Brak to Yerushalayim, from New Jersey to New York, or all points in between, could be something of a mild nightmare. How do you go? What are the directions? Oftentimes, whatever planning went into the trip didn't exactly pan out as intended. The journey could end up including numerous stops at gas stations, phone calls, asking passersby, and so on, all in the hopes of finding one's very lost way.

Modern technology has presented us with advanced GPS systems, devices that obviate the need for directions and traffic reports. Not only does a GPS provide accurate, step-by-step detailed directions, but it even informs of traffic delays, construction, and everything that one needs to know to reach his destination.

Life is also a journey, one of obviously much greater significance. But the road is not necessarily smooth, and we don't always know where we're supposed to be going. Even if we have some idea, it's not altogether clear at times how to get there. How to get from point A to point B is one of the greatest — if not the greatest — of challenges. Rabban Yochanan ben Zakkai, with the help of his students, provides us with a GPS for the journey of our life.

Before hearing what Rabban Yochanan ben Zakkai had to say, it is worthwhile to reflect for a moment on his stature. One of the leading scholars of his generation, he was a primary link in the chain of Sages who transmitted the Torah from Har Sinai until the present day. Therefore, if Rabban Yochanan ben Zakkai posed this query to his august *talmidim*, we can be sure that it is one of profound meaning and importance, affecting the *avodah* of every Jew. It is also quite certain that, in asking his question, Rabban Yochanan was quite deliberate in his choice of words.

And so, when asking אֵיזוֹהִי דֶּרֶךְ טוֹבָה שֶׁיִּדְבַּק בָּהּ הָאָדָם — *What is a good path to which a person should* **attach** *himself*, he was referring to the notion of *d'veikus baHashem*, cleaving to Hashem. This is the purpose for which a person was created, and it is the thrust of the mitzvos, as

פרק ב׳

well. The Zohar refers to the 613 mitzvos as the "613 *ittin*" (strategies). That is, they are the means through which we can attain our *tachlis*; they comprise 613 different ways to achieve *d'veikus*.

This is the heart of the matter that Rabban Yochanan ben Zakkai presented to his *talmidim*. Together with these 613 specific strategies, there must be a basic, overall approach to life that will direct a person to *d'veikus*. Rabban Yochanan ben Zakkai was asking his students to discover this road. In some detail, the Nesivos Sholom elucidates the entirety of Rabban Yochanan's question along the following lines.

Rabban Yochanan told them, ***Tze'u u're'u*** — "**Go out** and discern." The commentaries explain that the master was apprising his students that, in order to contemplate how to help others, they may need to "go out" temporarily from their exalted levels. These five *talmidei chachamim* (Torah scholars) had certainly by now found their path to union with Hashem, but the routes they took could prove too strenuous for the average person to follow. Therefore, Rabban Yochanan ben Zakkai bade them to consider a method whereby even someone of lesser stature could attain the lofty level of *d'veikus*.

אֵיזוֹהִי דֶרֶךְ טוֹבָה שֶׁיִּדְבַּק בָּהּ הָאָדָם — *What is a **good** path to which a person should attach himself.* This is a further indication that *d'veikus* was the subject of Rabban Yochanan's discussion. For that is essentially what *d'veikus baHashem* is — the pinnacle of goodness in the world. Thus we repeatedly find this term *tovah* used in connection with *d'veikus*. For example, in reference to Eretz Yisroel, the *passuk* states (*Bamidbar* 14:7), טוֹבָה הָאָרֶץ מְאֹד מְאֹד — *The land is very, very good.* Eretz Yisroel is called a very good land because its atmosphere of holiness is most conducive to forming a connection with Hashem. And that is the utmost good.

The Responses

Rabban Yochanan presented his students with a monumental challenge, for their discoveries would serve as the approach to life for all future generations. Each student replied according to his own individual essence and understanding, providing five different approaches in all.

Rabbi Eliezer said: "A good eye."

What exactly is an *ayin tovah* (good eye)? The Nesivos Sholom understands it as referring to one who is *samei'ach b'chelko*, happy with his lot. He accepts whatever Hashem sends his way with a happy heart. Because of his firm faith that Hashem has supplied him with all that he needs, he suffers no disappointment over what he lacks. Likewise, he does not begrudge others their own wealth and success. He is supremely confident that Hashem always has his best interests in mind. Thus, if he lacks something, that is the surest sign that he's better off without it.

The *Toras Avos* describes the added benefit of this approach: it engenders favor in the eyes of Hashem. When a Yid is satisfied with his life, content with whatever Hashem bestows upon him, Hashem will reciprocate in kind. This follows the overriding principle of *middah k'negged middah* (measure for measure), in which Hashem's conduct towards a person mirrors that person's conduct to Him. This individual was happy with Hashem; Hashem will be satisfied with him, as well. What mortal can withstand a heightened scrutiny of his deeds? And so, by displaying satisfaction with what Hashem has apportioned to him, this Yid will merit that Hashem will likewise be pleased with his service towards Him.

This is the crux of Rabbi Eliezer's response. It is the *middah* of being *samei'ach b'chelko* that brings a Yid to *d'veikus baHashem*. This can be understood in light of the teaching of the Saba Kadisha of Slonim, who said that all good *middos* are derivatives of being *samei'ach b'chelko*. This ideal attitude grants a person both *Olam Hazeh* (This World — which he enjoys because he is happy with his lot) and *Olam Haba* (the World to Come — because he is always united with Hashem through love).

Rabbi Yehoshua said: "A good friend."

Rabbi Yehoshua doesn't disagree with Rabbi Eliezer; he accepts the view that a good eye is essential for coming close to Hashem. He feels, however, that it isn't sufficient. One also needs a good friend because a good friend can support him when he falls.

This is especially so in light of what was taught in the *Me'or Einayim* regarding the *nisyonos* of Avraham Avinu. It asserts that just as Avraham Avinu had to undergo ten trials, so, too, do all of his descendants. Every single Yid has his personal set of ten *nisyonos*, life-challenges to be successfully overcome. As the tests are demanding and difficult, the risk of failure is real. To endure these challenges and shore up his ability to successfully withstand them, a person needs a "good friend" for support. It is much easier for the *yetzer hara* to overpower someone who is completely on his own. A close friend can help sustain a person, even during the darkest moments of life.

A "good friend" is not necessarily so easy to find, but Rabbi Yehoshua urges us that acquiring one should be a priority. What constitutes a "good friend"? Someone from whom one can learn, a positive influence on his endeavor to serve Hashem. A person should befriend good *Yidden* who fear Hashem, and should likewise become close to tzaddikim. These relationships will supply him with spiritual support and guidance at a time when he needs them most. His friends will encourage him and prevent him from slacking off in his obligations. With their help, he will remain *dovuk* (attached) to Hashem, throughout all the trials and tribulations of life.

Rabbi Yose said: "A good neighbor."

As expressed by the commentators, Rabbi Yose's counsel is very similar to that of Rabbi Yehoshua; he just goes a step further. A good friend, Rabbi Yose claims, isn't enough, because friends aren't always available. What should a person do if he's going through a crisis when his best friend is overseas? Therefore, Rabbi Yose advocates for the continuous presence of good neighbors. It is advantageous to live in a neighborhood where there are G-d-fearing people, and where there is a communal atmosphere of people helping each other. This environment will supply the support a person needs when challenges arise, and help him maintain his *d'veikus* to Hashem at all times.

Rabbi Shimon said: "One who foresees the outcome."

Rabbi Shimon's teaching also focuses on maintaining a state of *d'veikus baHashem*. And so he instructs that, before taking any action, one must first think about the outcome. He should ask himself: "Will this deed help bring me closer to Hashem — or set me further back?" If it will result in a closer connection, by all means, he should grasp it. But if he foresees that it will have the opposite effect, he should keep away. This is the assessment Rabbi Shimon encourages us to constantly replay in our minds. Clearly, by following this counsel, a Yid will always remain close to Hashem.

This same sentiment was echoed by Hillel in the familiar episode involving the would-be convert (*Shabbos* 31a). In an attempt to antagonize the sage, the gentile asked Hillel to teach him the entire Torah on one foot. But Hillel proceeded to do just that, "summing up" the Torah in one pithy statement. This idea, Hillel said, is the core of the Torah; the rest is an offshoot of this key principle. The statement Hillel offered was דְּעֲלָךְ סַנִי לְחַבְרָךְ לֹא תַעֲבֵיד, which is ordinarily translated as, "What is hateful to you, do not do to your friend." The Maggid of Mezeritch, however, renders it homiletically; he understands Hillel's teaching as a reference to *d'veikus*. "That which is *sani l'chavrach* — detrimental to your **chibbur**, your *attachment* to Hashem — do not do." In other words, Hillel is counseling that one must scrupulously avoid any act or behavior that could interfere with one's *d'veikus baHashem*.

This short counsel encapsulates the entire Torah, and all other aspects of the Torah are offshoots of it — for the ultimate purpose of all mitzvos is to create a connection with Hashem. And so, in order to always remain attached to Hashem, one must constantly be looking ahead, assessing the potential outcome of whatever opportunities present themselves. The bottom line is to consistently determine: "Will this bring me closer to, or lead me further from, Hashem?"

Rabbi Elazar ben Arach said: "A good heart."

A "good heart" includes many things. It means to be kind, compassionate, helpful, and caring. In short, it entails cultivating good *middos*.

A person who develops pristine *middos* attains closeness with

Hashem. *Chazal* instruct us to be *doveik* (attach ourselves) to His ways: מָה הַמָּקוֹם...רַחוּם וְחַנּוּן אַף אַתָּה הֱוֵי רַחוּם וְחַנּוּן... מָה הַקָּבָ"ה...נִקְרָא חָסִיד...אַף אַתָּה הֱוֵי חָסִיד — *Just as Hashem...is merciful and compassionate, so should you be merciful and compassionate... Just as Hashem...is called, "The Pious One"...so should you be pious* (*Sifri, Eikev* §13; cf. *Rashi, Devarim* 13:5). A similar notion appears in the *passuk* (*Devarim* 11:22): לְאַהֲבָה אֶת ה' אֱלֹקֶיךָ לָלֶכֶת בְּכָל־דְּרָכָיו וּלְדָבְקָה־בּוֹ — *To love Hashem your G-d, to walk in all His ways, and* **to cleave to Him**. The *passuk* is outlining two approaches through which to attain closeness to Hashem. One method is to love Hashem; by loving Hashem, one certainly feels a special closeness to Him. The other approach is "to walk in all His ways." As we have seen, this entails emulating His pristine attributes and acquiring good *middos*. A person should train himself to be good, compassionate, and kind. When there is someone in need, be ready to help. When someone has a sorrow, feel their pain. Developing the ideal character traits, the *passuk* informs us, is also a way to achieve לְדָבְקָה־בּוֹ.

Rabban Yochanan ben Zakkai declared his preference for the approach of Rabbi Elazar ben Arach. For he understood that, whatever else he may do, if one retains poor *middos* then *d'veikus* will be impossible to attain. The more one asserts his sense of "self," granting priority to his base and selfish needs, the greater will be the wedge he drives between him and his Creator. Selfishness and haughtiness are the polar opposites of Hashem's attributes of compassion and caring. Conversely, however, the more one purges his inner essence and refines his character, the closer to Hashem he will become.

It should be noted that Rabban Yochanan ben Zakkai's quest seems very similar to the question posed earlier by Rebbi. This appears at the beginning of our chapter (2:1): רַבִּי אוֹמֵר, אֵיזוֹהִי דֶרֶךְ יְשָׁרָה שֶׁיָּבוֹר לוֹ הָאָדָם — *Rebbi said: "Which is the straight path that a person should choose?"* Close attention to the words, however, reveals that they were discussing two different issues: Rebbi sought the "straight path," while Rabban Yochanan ben Zakkai sought the "good path" which involves *d'veikus* (שֶׁיִּדְבַּק בָּהּ הָאָדָם). The "straight path" searched out by Rebbi is the "golden mean," the delicate balance of living moderately in This World. Rabban Yochanan ben Zakkai sought the road that leads to the ultimate goodness — a connection to Hashem. His five holy students offered us five different approaches to follow to achieve this goal.

It is true that all of these ways may be "easier said than done." Each path requires immense toil before reaching the goal. Nevertheless, it is so crucial that we do what we can. When that is the case, Hashem will help. And then we may discover that ultimate goodness of being close to Hashem.

In Summary

While Rebbi at the beginning of the chapter spoke of the straight, middle road of moderation, Rabban Yochanan ben Zakkai addresses here a different issue. He sought the way to acquire *d'veikus baHashem*, the ultimate goodness in the world, and consulted with his five disciples on the matter. They each presented what they felt was a prime method for achieving *d'veikus*.

Rabbi Eliezer favored the cultivation of a "good eye." This refers to mastery of the trait of being *samei'ach b'chelko*, satisfied with one's lot. If we are content with whatever Hashem bestows upon us, we will be spared both disappointment over lack of wealth and the envy of others. Happy with our share, we will not begrudge others what they have, as we are confident in our faith that we, ourselves, were given everything that we need. As the *Toras Avos* explains, the *middah* of *samei'ach b'chelko* effectively leads to all good things; it enables the individual both to enjoy This World, and inherit the Next. Likewise, it leads him close to Hashem; as such, it is Rabbi Eliezer's selection for the path to *d'veikus*.

Rabbi Yehoshua was concerned about the various trials we must face throughout life. There exists the risk that these tribulations will serve as a distraction, causing us to deviate from the path of *d'veikus*. As such, Rabbi Yehoshua encouraged the acquisition of a "good friend," a G-d-fearing companion to serve as a positive and buttressing influence. With a good friend, a Yid will gain the necessary support to withstand his *nisyonos*; his encouragement will help maintain *d'veikus baHashem*.

Rabbi Yose goes one step further. A good friend is surely a tremendous asset; the only drawback is that he's not always around. Therefore, Rabbi Yose advocates settling among "good neighbors." Their constant presence will serve as a steady bulwark, fostering an environment that facilitates consistent *d'veikus*.

Rabbi Shimon was forward-looking. He encourages a person to be constantly on the lookout, "seeing the outcome" of every potential action. The question we must always ask is: "Will this deed bring me closer to Hashem, or lead me further away?" This cautious approach will enable us to make *d'veikus* our priority.

The approach ultimately championed by Rabban Yochanan ben Zakkai was that offered by Rabbi Elazar ben Arach — a "good heart." This refers to the cultivation of pristine *middos*, a crucial prerequisite to obtaining *d'veikus*. To a large extent, *d'veikus* itself entails the emulation of Hashem's perfect attributes of mercy, kindliness, etc. A person who retains negative *middos* will never be able to attain *d'veikus*, as his emphasis on self erects an impenetrable wall between himself and Hashem. Thus, in order to achieve *d'veikus*, a Yid must purify himself and his character. Through the cultivation of a "good heart," he will be able to attain the ultimate ends of *d'veikus baHashem*.

פרקי אבות

פרק ב' משנה ט״ז, י״ז
יהי כבוד חברך חביב עליך כשלך
The Honor of Your Fellow Should Be as Precious to You as Your Own

הֵם אָמְרוּ שְׁלֹשָׁה דְבָרִים. רַבִּי אֱלִיעֶזֶר אוֹמֵר, יְהִי כְבוֹד חֲבֵרְךָ חָבִיב עָלֶיךָ כְּשֶׁלָּךְ, וְאַל תְּהִי נוֹחַ לִכְעוֹס. וְשׁוּב יוֹם אֶחָד לִפְנֵי מִיתָתְךָ. וֶהֱוֵי מִתְחַמֵּם כְּנֶגֶד אוּרָן שֶׁל חֲכָמִים, וֶהֱוֵי זָהִיר בְּגַחַלְתָּן שֶׁלֹּא תִכָּוֶה, שֶׁנְּשִׁיכָתָן נְשִׁיכַת שׁוּעָל, וַעֲקִיצָתָן עֲקִיצַת עַקְרָב, וּלְחִישָׁתָן לְחִישַׁת שָׂרָף, וְכָל דִּבְרֵיהֶם כְּגַחֲלֵי אֵשׁ:

רַבִּי יוֹסֵי אוֹמֵר, יְהִי מָמוֹן חֲבֵרְךָ חָבִיב עָלֶיךָ כְּשֶׁלָּךְ. וְהַתְקֵן עַצְמְךָ לִלְמוֹד תּוֹרָה, שֶׁאֵינָהּ יְרֻשָּׁה לָךְ. וְכָל מַעֲשֶׂיךָ יִהְיוּ לְשֵׁם שָׁמָיִם:

(Rabban Yochanan ben Zakkai's five disciples) each said three things. Rabbi Eliezer said: The honor of your fellow should be as precious to you as your own, and do not anger easily; repent one day before your death; warm up before the flames of the Sages, and be cautious with their coals that you not get singed – for their bite is the bite of a fox, their sting is the sting of a scorpion, their hiss is the hiss of a fiery serpent, and all of their words are coals of fire.

Rabbi Yose said: The property of your fellow should be as precious to you as your own; prepare yourself to learn Torah, for it is not bequeathed to you as an inheritance; and all of your deeds should be for the sake of Heaven.

יהי כבוד חברך חביב עליך כשלך

SOURCES:

וְאָהַבְתָּ לְרֵעֲךָ כָּמוֹךָ. (ויקרא י״ט י״ח)

Love your neighbor as yourself. (*Vayikra* 19:18)

וְאָהַבְתָּ לְרֵעֲךָ כָּמוֹךָ – רֶבִּי עֲקִיבָא אוֹמֵר זֶהוּ כְּלָל גָּדוֹל בַּתּוֹרָה. (ירושלמי נדרים ט׳ ד׳)

"Love your neighbor as yourself" – Rabbi Akiva says: This is a great, essential principle of the Torah. (*Talmud Yerushalmi, Nedarim* 9:4)

אָנֹכִי עֹמֵד בֵּין־ה׳ וּבֵינֵיכֶם. (דברים ה׳ ה׳)

I was standing between Hashem and you. (*Devarim* 5:5)

וְאָהַבְתָּ אֵת ה׳ אֱלֹקֶיךָ בְּכָל־לְבָבְךָ וּבְכָל־נַפְשְׁךָ וּבְכָל־מְאֹדֶךָ. (שם ו׳ ה׳)

You shall love Hashem your G-d, with all of your heart, with all of your soul, and with all of your wealth. (*ibid.* 6:5)

תָּנָא דְּבֵי רֶבִּי יִשְׁמָעֵאל: אִם רָאִיתָ תַּלְמִיד חָכָם שֶׁעָבַר עֲבֵירָה בַּלַּיְלָה, אַל תְּהַרְהֵר אַחֲרָיו בַּיּוֹם, שֶׁמָּא עָשָׂה תְּשׁוּבָה. (ברכות י״ט.)

D'vei Rabbi Yishmael taught: If you witness a Torah scholar commit a sin in the nighttime, do not even cast aspersions on him by day, for it is quite possible that he has repented. (*Berachos* 19a)

תַּלְמִידֵי חֲכָמִים מַרְבִּים שָׁלוֹם בָּעוֹלָם. (שם ס״ד.)

Torah scholars increase peace in the world. (*ibid.* 64a)

אֵין דִּבְרֵי תּוֹרָה מִתְקַיְּמִין אֶלָּא בְּמִי שֶׁמֵּמִית עַצְמוֹ עָלֶיהָ. (שם ס״ג.)

Torah is firmly established only through one who "kills himself" over it. (*ibid.* 63b)

GEMS FROM THE *SEFER NESIVOS SHOLOM*

Precious

To put it simply, the Jewish people have it great.

Consider the state of mankind today as compared to past eras. Scientific knowledge is astounding. Technological advances take place at an astonishing rate. The average person has resources and abilities at his fingertips that not too long ago were the stuff of science fiction. Access to information, global communication and connectivity — the whole scenario could boggle the mind.

And yet, let us pose one simple question. Are people happier today than they were in those "primitive" times? In an advanced and privileged society on such an unprecedented scale, replete with conveniences and sophistication, one would think that the answer would be undoubtedly "yes." As extreme as it may sound to say it, though, the truth is that — unfortunately — the answer is undoubtedly "no." If anything, the opposite seems to be the case. The world has become a much more confusing and challenging place — both for individuals and for continents. Where there are no mass upheavals and strife, there are individuals who feel lost and directionless. The breakdown of both families and morals has no doubt contributed to this pervasive feeling of instability and uncertainty.

And so, *baruch Hashem*, the Jewish people are blessed. In the midst of this confusing and often contradictory world, we possess the one constant and great truth — the Torah. It is the guidepost that dispels all uncertainty, showing the way and clarifying our life goals. Thus we each can know with confidence exactly where our focus should be, to attain the greatest success in This World and the Next. And the Torah informs us what the ultimate aim is, to which we should direct our efforts: cultivating a strong relationship with *Hakadosh Baruch Hu*. For this is the ultimate goal of all life: to forge a connection with Hashem that can withstand the intensity of the physical world. The pinnacle of this relationship is the state known as *d'veikus*, attachment to Hashem. While a constant and daunting challenge, the results of its attainment are immeasurably rewarding. And it can only be attained through the commandments in the

יהי כבוד חברך חביב עליך כשלך

Torah, which have the ability to unlock the barriers that separate man from his Creator.

The only remaining question is — how exactly to get there. What are the first steps, the key to begin the journey towards successfully completing this ultimate goal in life? The answer may come as somewhat of a surprise. There is an idea that, at first glance, seems to have little to do with the relationship between man and Hashem but can nevertheless have a tremendous impact in this area. The mitzvah of וְאָהַבְתָּ לְרֵעֲךָ כָּמוֹךָ — *Love your neighbor as yourself* (*Vayikra* 19:18), appears to serve as the epitome of mitzvos that solely concern human-to-human relationships. But, as we shall see, it has the power not only to create a connection with Hashem, but to strengthen this relationship to the highest extent possible. Thus, a careful scrutiny of the mitzvah and its particulars can shed much light on the enormity of its effect on *d'veikus*.

Getting Out of Your Own Way

A clear manifestation of the mitzvah of loving and caring for others occurs in the mishnah in *Avos* (2:10, 12): רַבִּי אֱלִיעֶזֶר אוֹמֵר: יְהִי כְבוֹד חֲבֵרְךָ חָבִיב עָלֶיךָ כְּשֶׁלָּךְ... רַבִּי יוֹסֵי אוֹמֵר: יְהִי מָמוֹן חֲבֵרְךָ חָבִיב עָלֶיךָ כְּשֶׁלָּךְ — *Rabbi Eliezer says: The honor of your friend should be as precious to you as your own... Rabbi Yose says: The property of your friend should be as precious to you as your own.*

So reminiscent is this statement of the mitzvah that it almost appears redundant. We know that the Torah, both Written and Oral, does not engage in senseless repetition; every statement is precise and calculated, intended for some new teaching. Why, then, did Rabbi Eliezer feel the need to mention this particular piece of advice? The directive to love others as oneself naturally includes regarding the honor of another as equal to one's own. What, then, is Rabbi Eliezer adding?

The Rambam provides a key in clarifying this issue. In *Hilchos Dei'os* (6:3), the Rambam comments on this mitzvah, even including a few examples. He points out that the mitzvah of *v'ahavta l'rei'acha kamocha* is not merely an internal mitzvah of loving others and perhaps acting kindly towards them, but includes certain actions not immediately apparent from an initial reading of the *passuk*. To fulfill the mitzvah of *v'ahavta l'rei'acha kamocha* in its fullest sense, writes the Rambam, we must relate the praise of others and display the same care for the property and honor of our fellow as we would for our own.

From where did the Rambam learn to include these elements in his explanation of the mitzvah? It seems obvious that he derived this from our mishnah. That is, he understood that this is what Rabbi Eliezer and Rabbi Yose were coming to "add"; they were not merely restating the mitzvah but elucidating what it entails. And they inform us that proper fulfillment of the mitzvah includes these "extra" elements of displaying honor through praise and caring for others' possessions.

But this itself requires further clarification. Why, indeed, did the *Tanna'im* single out these particular aspects? *V'ahavta l'rei'acha kamocha* entails any number of things. Is there something specific to the examples of praising others and safeguarding their money that is particularly illuminating regarding the mitzvah as a whole? Why did they warrant special attention? Clearly, to gain a complete understanding of the mishnah and the Rambam, we must delve into the essence of the mitzvah of loving others.

Perhaps one of the best known statements about this mitzvah, conveying its centrality to observance, is the teaching of Rabbi Akiva (*Talmud Yerushalmi, Nedarim* 9:4): וְאָהַבְתָּ לְרֵעֲךָ כָּמוֹךָ – רַבִּי עֲקִיבָא אוֹמֵר: זֶהוּ כְּלָל גָּדוֹל בַּתּוֹרָה. Rabbi Akiva characterizes this mitzvah as "a great, essential principle of the Torah." The implication is that not only is it a mitzvah of its own, but *v'ahavta l'rei'acha kamocha* is a stepping-stone to achievement in all areas. It is the means through which we can come to a fulfillment of the entire Torah and attain the all-important goal of forging a sincere relationship with Hashem.

How can such a seemingly simple and straightforward mitzvah carry such tremendous repercussions? The matter can be understood through a fundamental teaching of the Besh"t (Ba'al Shem Tov). The critical factor is mentioned in the *passuk* where Moshe Rabbeinu

יהי כבוד חברך חביב עליך כשלך

recounts the events at Sinai: אָנֹכִי עֹמֵד בֵּין ה' וּבֵינֵיכֶם — *I was standing between Hashem and you* (*Devarim* 5:5). While the narrative refers literally to Moshe's serving as the intermediary between Hashem and Yisroel, the Besh"t supplies a homiletic interpretation. He renders: "It is *anochi* — 'I' — that stands between you and Hashem." Human nature is that, above all else, a person's interests are focused mostly (or solely) on himself. Yet, the message of the *passuk* is that this ego stands as an impenetrable barrier between us and Hashem. With the ego in place, we have no chance of attaining real *d'veikus* with Hashem. The only way to break down the barrier created by our sense of self-importance is to completely re-orient our thinking. That is, we must *negate* our self and our ego, rendering our self completely subservient to Hashem.

Obviously, this is easier said than done. Counteracting and negating our ego is far from a simple task, requiring strenuous and sustained efforts. Many levels must be traversed before it is possible to attain complete *d'veikus*. But *v'ahavta l'rei'acha kamocha* is step one, and it has the power to propel us along the path of our ascent.

How does loving our fellow accomplish this? The more importance we grant to other people, and the more our thoughts and actions become centered on others — the less, by default, we will be focused on ourselves and our own egotistical needs. By increasing our *ahavas Yisroel*, the more will our *anochi* be reduced. As this barrier is mitigated, the path opens wider to foster a relationship with Hashem. Our *ahavas Yisroel* will end up translating into *ahavas Hashem* and eventually complete *d'veikus* to Him.

This, in fact, is the purpose of all the mitzvos of the Torah: to lead ultimately to *d'veikus baHashem*. But this is impossible so long as the ego-barrier is in place. The process of negating our ego begins by loving and raising our esteem of others. Indeed, *V'ahavta l'rei'acha kamocha — zeh klal gadol baTorah!* This endeavor is the key to the rest of Torah, as it provides us with the means through which to achieve *Yiddishkeit's* ultimate goal.

The *Pri Ha'aretz* demonstrates the profundity of this notion of self-negation. He asserts that it is not enough to serve Hashem only

פרק ב'

through fear and love. These qualities are admirable and essential, and will of course provide some level of connection with Hashem. But it is still not enough for creating true *d'veikus*. Attaining the ultimate closeness to Hashem entails a level of subjugation to Him which is thoroughly and utterly complete; that is, one must achieve one-hundred-percent clarity that — on his own — he is ultimately nothing and no one.

In what way, in fact, does a person possess true value? Strip him of his accomplishments, his thoughts, needs, and desires, his possessions and human relationships, and what is he left with? He is only something worthy by virtue of the fact that he is an extension of *Hakadosh Baruch Hu*, a *tzelem Elokim* (a being fashioned in Hashem's image). Through this realization, a person sheds the human qualities and barriers from his soul and is left with nothing save a connection to Hashem. And in reality, this is the greatest form of emancipation possible. All of a sudden, he has a real and unfettered relationship with Hashem; irrevocably attached to Him, he achieves true *d'veikus*.

The Nesivos Sholom compares this relationship between man and Hashem to a branch on a tree. The branch may bear leaves, flowers, and fruits. It may be proud of its foliage, believing it to be the product of its own efforts, a testament to its abilities. But is the branch really its own entity? Ultimately, it derives its life and nutrition from the tree. Were it to become detached from the tree, it would shrivel up and die. Stripped of the fruits of its labor and left with no leaves, flowers, or fruits, the branch is nothing, its existence entirely dependent on its connection to the main trunk.

This is the level of negation necessary to achieve the highest level of true *d'veikus*. Fearing and loving Hashem are certainly prerequisites in this climb. Yet, it is only through nullification of one's self and total subjugation to Hashem that a true bond between a human and his Creator can be solidified.

The *Ahavas Yisroel-Ahavas Hashem* Continuum

While we are speaking of the loftiest of levels, attained through intensive efforts and contemplation, it is important to bear in mind that the beginning entails a *comparatively* smaller and quite attainable step. *V'ahavta l'rei'acha kamocha* is not a formula for *d'veikus* that speaks only to those who have already achieved the higher levels of connection to Hashem, ready to intensify their relationship to the utmost.

In fact, from the very word *kamocha*, as yourself, we gain an indication of just who it is that the Torah is addressing. In order for a person to fulfill the directive of loving another "as he loves himself," he must first have a sense of self. Otherwise, how could he actually love another as himself? If the individual has already nullified himself, having completely subjugated his ego to Hashem, then loving another as himself doesn't mean very much. After all, he thinks nothing of himself. Evidently, the Torah's message is intended for those who have not yet climbed the ladder of *d'veikus*, those who still retain a sense of love and ego for themselves. Thus, the Torah instructs to love another Jew *kamocha*, as yourself, attaching to others the same amount of natural concern and devotion that we feel toward ourselves.

This being the case, the assertion made previously bears revisiting. *V'ahavta l'rei'acha kamocha* breeds self-negation; how so, exactly? We are dealing with people who still possess a real sense of self. Does caring for another Jew automatically mean that I care less about myself? Isn't there enough love to "go around"? A parent does not love each of his children less and less as more are born! How does loving others *kamocha* result in self-nullification?

The illuminating words of the Rambam, gleaned from our mishnah, are instrumental in clarifying this issue. In elucidating this mitzvah, the Rambam demonstrated just what *kamocha* entails, stating that it includes the acts of praising others and treating their monetary possessions with great care. These aspects are key to self-negation, as they generally go directly against the grain of a person.

The reality is that it is human nature to derive satisfaction from the belittling of others. The multi-billion-dollar industry known as "the media" is predicated largely on unearthing and magnifying the foibles and failures of other people. By undertaking an endeavor of raising others up instead of tearing them down, we take aim right at the core of our nature and fight against it. Normally, we would be disinclined to insult our ego by praising someone else; by elevating another person — the ego says — you essentially are lowering yourself. When others suffer degradation, it makes you look all the better. As such, actively praising others is an exercise in reversing our innate inclinations and base, selfish nature.

The approach to other people's money follows along similar lines. It is far more common to care first and foremost about our own material standing, securing for ourselves the better end of the deal. We tend to care less about the possessions of others, even when entrusted to our care. Therefore, merely treating others as *kamocha* — raising them up, being concerned for their money — entails a re-orientation of sorts, a push against our inherent nature. When we are able to surpass our natural ego in these ways, we have fulfilled the mitzvah of *v'ahavta l'rei'acha kamocha* in optimal fashion. Compared to the ultimate goal, it may appear as a relatively small achievement; but it is a significant step. We have begun to diminish our *anochi*, thereby climbing the first rung on the ladder of *d'veikus*.

Once we have begun to quash our ego sufficiently to view others as *kamocha*, giving away a little bit of our "self" in order to raise others, we gain a greater capacity to love Hashem. The less room our ego occupies, the more room there is for *ahavas Hashem*. Once the *mitzvah* of *v'ahavta l'rei'acha kamocha*, representing *ahavas Yisroel*, has been fulfilled, the mitzvah of *ahavas Hashem* can begin to develop.

It is edifying to examine the Torah's requirements regarding *ahavas chaveirim* (loving our fellows) in comparison to *ahavas Hashem*. The demands with regards to the latter are significant indeed. We recite in *Krias Shema*, וְאָהַבְתָּ אֵת ה' אֱלֹקֶיךָ בְּכָל־לְבָבְךָ וּבְכָל־נַפְשְׁךָ וּבְכָל־מְאֹדֶךָ — *You shall love Hashem your G-d, with all of your heart, with all of your soul, and with all of your wealth* (Devarim 6:5). This entails a level of absolute love for and dedication to Hashem, whereby we divest ourselves of everything that makes us human, devoting ourselves entirely to Hashem. We do not find the same all-encompassing love demanded of us regarding our fellow men; the requisite level is merely that we love him *kamocha*. This highlights the nature of the path to the ultimate goal. We begin with the initial step of lessening our ego. This makes room for love of Hashem, putting us on the path of complete and utter love and subservience to Him, the qualifications for achieving true *d'veikus*.

On the Path to *Kabbalas HaTorah*

The above ideas set the stage for understanding what may be one of the most mystifying aspects of the time period of *sefiras ha'omer*. During this time we mark and recall that incomparable tragedy wherein the twenty-four thousand *talmidim* of Rabbi Akiva lost their lives. This calamity resulted, *Chazal* tell us, from the lack of *kavod* (respect) they displayed for one another. It is noteworthy that it is not stated that they belittled each other; rather, they simply did not accord each other sufficient respect. It seems difficult to understand how the punishment fit the crime. Why did they deserve such severe consequences for what doesn't appear, at first glance, to have been the most egregious of transgressions?

On the other hand, the very fact that the failure of this particular band of men took place in this specific area seems somewhat ironic. These were individuals of great stature; did they not know or care to cultivate proper respect for each other? For that matter, they were the *talmidim* of Rabbi Akiva, the very sage noted for promoting mutual respect! וְאָהַבְתָּ לְרֵעֲךָ כָּמוֹךָ – רַבִּי עֲקִיבָא אוֹמֵר: זֶהוּ כְּלָל גָּדוֹל בַּתּוֹרָה.

A teaching of Reb Mendel of Premyshlan, a prime disciple of the Besh"t, sheds much light on the issue. He provides a novel interpretation of the following statement of *Chazal* (*Berachos* 19a): תָּנָא דְּבֵי רַבִּי יִשְׁמָעֵאל: אִם רָאִיתָ תַּלְמִיד חָכָם שֶׁעָבַר עֲבֵירָה בַּלַּיְלָה, אַל תְּהַרְהֵר אַחֲרָיו בַּיּוֹם, שֶׁמָּא עָשָׂה תְּשׁוּבָה — *D'vei Rabbi Yishmael taught: If you witness a Torah scholar commit a sin in the nighttime, do not even cast aspersions on him by day, for it is quite possible that he has repented.* This seems somewhat strange; are we supposed to delude ourselves? Why can't we consider him as having done an *aveirah*, even if he later repented; after all, didn't we behold his very act?

Reb Mendel explains the Gemara in a most eye-opening way: "For he may have repented." The Gemara is not speaking of *teshuvah* he performed after the fact; rather, it refers to *teshuvah* he had undertaken even *before* he succumbed to sin. Not that this Torah scholar adopted the sinister approach of declaring, "I will sin and then do *teshuvah* for it," which *Chazal* deplore (stating that such an approach will not succeed anyway). Rather, the Gemara speaks of an individual whose efforts in improving his *avodas Hashem* were completely sincere.

What happened was this: This earnest *oveid* perceived an area in need of strengthening. He resolved to invest his efforts in this endeavor; that is, in this aspect of service, he undertook to do *teshuvah* and improve. In response, the *yetzer hara* geared up for battle in precisely this area. For it is exactly where a Yid seeks to elevate himself that the *yetzer hara* redoubles its efforts, placing stumbling block after stumbling block to ensure that the *oveid* will fail.

This is the Gemara's intent: If you see a tzaddik fail, do not cast aspersions upon him. What happened does not necessarily reflect inherent failings within him; on the contrary, it is quite feasible that his succumbing to sin reveals the sincere intentions and earnest efforts to improve. Terrified at the prospect of his imminent, spiritual elevation, the *yetzer hara* did everything in its power to thwart him, possibly even presenting him with a trial that was indeed quite hard to overcome. But the message for all concerned — the onlookers, as well as the *talmid chacham* himself — is not to assume that all is lost. Actually, what occurred could very well be a sign of the *yetzer's* desperation, as it realizes that with a little more time and effort, it is soon to be vanquished.

In any event, this provides much insight in the matter of Rabbi Akiva's *talmidim*. It was specifically because of who they were and from whom they received instruction and inspiration that they were faced with such a challenge. They absorbed their master's teaching about the vital role played by *v'ahavta l'rei'acha kamocha*; how, through the medium of negating the aspect of *anochi*, it serves as

יהי כבוד חברך חביב עליך כשלך

a conduit to *d'veikus*, the goal of the entire Torah. The *yetzer hara* thus geared up to prevent the realization of this goal at all costs. It tripped them up specifically in this area, dissuading them from raising the prestige of their colleagues. That is, it ensured that their egos retained a measure of robustness, instead of becoming lessened by according honor to their fellows.

Coming as it did during this time period, the overall failure was accorded especial gravity. This pre-Shavuos period is a time of preparation for *Kabbalas HaTorah*. As such, it is a particularly auspicious time to cultivate the trait of *ahavas Yisroel*. After all, this is the very door which leads to the most important and loftiest levels, the very goal of all the mitzvos — *zeh klal gadol baTorah*! As such, a breach at this time in this area is perforce a matter of utmost severity.

In this vein, *Chazal* present a picture of what a *talmid chacham* should look like. This is conveyed specifically through two central teachings. The Gemara at the end of *Berachos* (64a) states: תַּלְמִידֵי חֲכָמִים מַרְבִּים שָׁלוֹם בָּעוֹלָם — Talmidei chachamim *increase peace in the world*. How do they achieve this? The Gemara says earlier in *Berachos* (63b): אֵין דִּבְרֵי תוֹרָה מִתְקַיְּימִין אֶלָּא בְּמִי שֶׁמֵּמִית עַצְמוֹ עָלֶיהָ — *Torah is firmly established only through one who "kills himself" over it*. The meaning of this enigmatic statement is in keeping with the above ideas. It is by diminishing one's sense of self — his aspect of *anochi* — that one can achieve the ultimate goal of the mitzvos of the Torah. Those who do so are men of true stature. The source of all strife and confrontation in the world can ultimately be traced to one source: ego. Those who have succeeded in uprooting it from within themselves are true purveyors of peace in the world.

In this time between Pesach and Shavuos, we focus on the teachings of *Pirkei Avos* as we prepare to receive the Torah anew. As such, this particular mishnah exhorting us to accord our fellows proper respect is especially relevant. For, as we have seen, this is the gateway to the entirety of Torah.

In Summary

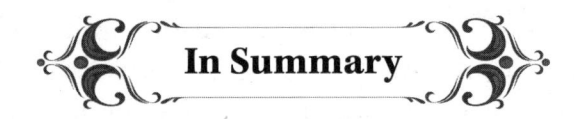

This mishnah conveys the importance of valuing our fellow's honor and his possessions as we would our own. As such, the mishnah encapsulates the mitzvah of *v'ahavta l'rei'acha kamocha*. This is apparent from the words of the Rambam, who, in elucidating this mitzvah, reflects the teachings of our mishnah. He states that loving one's fellow as himself entails the acts of relating the praise of others and treating their property with care.

These elements and their relation to *v'ahavta l'rei'acha kamocha* can best be understood by examining this mitzvah. The well-known teaching of Rabbi Akiva is most illuminating in this regard. Rabbi Akiva declared that the mitzvah of *v'ahavta l'rei'acha kamocha* plays a most central role in *Yiddishkeit* — it is a *klal gadol baTorah*. Obviously, all mitzvos of the Torah are of paramount importance. What Rabbi Akiva seeks to convey is that the proper fulfillment of *v'ahavta l'rei'acha kamocha* can be a stepping-stone to the entirety of Torah, as it is the door that leads eventually to the attainment of the ultimate goal of all the mitzvos. The most coveted and lofty level we can reach is complete *d'veikus* with Hashem, and the mitzvos of the Torah are intended to facilitate the realization of this central goal. *V'ahavta l'rei'acha kamocha* is that important first step, the mitzvah that points us in the direction of achieving *d'veikus*.

How does one lead to the other? The Besh"t reveals that the primary barrier standing between us and our Creator is none other than us — that is, our sense of *anochi*. Diminishing our ego is imperative to attaining *d'veikus*. And so the mitzvah of loving others takes on such urgency, as by focusing more on others, we focus less on ourselves. By fostering a love for our fellow, we will be able to pass on to greater levels, developing a greater capacity for loving Hashem. Eventually, we may climb to august heights, loving Hashem with literally our entire self, our entire heart. Having negated our sense of self, we may come to realize how we are inherently nothing without our Creator. Through complete subjugation before Him, we may thus attain *d'veikus baHashem*.

יהי כבוד חברך חביב עליך כשלך

This is why the qualities mentioned in our mishnah are so crucial. In practicing them, we must work directly against our inherent nature, our inner *anochi*, which revels in the denigration of our fellow — not in raising him up. By treating our friend with honor, we cut to the core of our egotistical nature and fight against it. Thus, it is an important aspect of nullifying our *anochi* and clearing the way for ascending to greater heights — and eventually to achieving real *d'veikus*.

This is a particularly pertinent lesson for the *sefirah* period, as we gear up for *Kabbalas HaTorah*. In fact, this is a prime reason why the *talmidim* of Rabbi Akiva suffered such severe consequences for failing to accord their colleagues the proper respect. It is specifically at this time that we must prepare for accepting the Torah, and — as their *rebbi* taught — the key to the entirety of Torah is through *v'ahavta l'rei'acha kamocha*. The mitigation of the ego achieved through the act of praising and regarding our fellow is what sets us on the path of attaining *d'veikus*, the Torah's goal. Neglecting to engage at this time in this exercise of weakening the ego — and instead, granting it new life by not honoring other people — was regarded with the utmost gravity. It is a time of *hachanah* (preparation) to receive the Torah; as such, the *chovas hasha'ah* (obligation of the hour) is to open the door that leads us on the path of *d'veikus*, the ultimate goal of the entirety of Torah. *Zeh klal gadol baTorah*.

פרק ב' משנה ט"ז
עין הרע ויצר הרע ושנאת הבריות
The Evil Eye, Evil Inclination, and Hatred of People

רַבִּי יְהוֹשֻׁעַ אוֹמֵר, עַיִן הָרָע, וְיֵצֶר הָרָע, וְשִׂנְאַת הַבְּרִיּוֹת, מוֹצִיאִין אֶת הָאָדָם מִן הָעוֹלָם:

Rabbi Yehoshua says: The evil eye, evil inclination, and hatred of people remove a person from the world.

GEMS FROM THE *SEFER NESIVOS SHOLOM*

SOURCES:

וַיַּרְא אֱלֹקִים כִּי־טוֹב. (בראשית פרק א' פסוקים י', י"ב, י"ח, כ"א, כ"ה)

And G-d saw that it was good. (*Bereishis* 1:10, 12, 18, 21, 25)

כַּבֵּד אֶת־אָבִיךָ וְאֶת־אִמֶּךָ לְמַעַן יַאֲרִכוּן יָמֶיךָ עַל הָאֲדָמָה אֲשֶׁר ה' אֱלֹקֶיךָ נֹתֵן לָךְ. (שמות כ' י"ב)

Honor your father and mother in order that your days be lengthened on the land that Hashem your G-d is giving to you. (*Shemos* 20:12)

כַּבֵּד אֶת־אָבִיךָ וְאֶת־אִמֶּךָ כַּאֲשֶׁר צִוְּךָ ה' אֱלֹקֶיךָ לְמַעַן יַאֲרִיכֻן יָמֶיךָ וּלְמַעַן יִיטַב לָךְ עַל הָאֲדָמָה אֲשֶׁר ה' אֱלֹקֶיךָ נֹתֵן לָךְ. (דברים ה' ט"ז)

Honor your father and mother as Hashem your G-d commanded you, in order that your days be lengthened and in order that it be good for you on the land that Hashem your G-d is giving to you. (*Devarim* 5:16)

מִפְּנֵי מָה בְּדִבְּרוֹת הָרִאשׁוֹנוֹת לֹא נֶאֱמַר בָּהֶם טוֹב, וּבְדִבְּרוֹת הָאַחֲרוֹנוֹת נֶאֱמַר בָּהֶם טוֹב? ... הוֹאִיל וְסוֹפָן לְהִשְׁתַּבֵּר. (בבא קמא נ"ד.)

Why is it that in the original (text of the) commandments it does not make mention of "tov," but in the latter commandments it does state "tov"? ... (The answer is:) Since the (original tablets) were destined to be shattered. (*Bava Kamma* 54b)

אֵיזֶהוּ עָשִׁיר הַשָּׂמֵחַ בְּחֶלְקוֹ. (אבות ד')

Who is wealthy? One who is happy with his portion. (*Avos* 4)

וְכָל־יֵצֶר מַחְשְׁבֹת לִבּוֹ רַק רַע כָּל־הַיּוֹם. (בראשית ו' ה')

And all the inclination of his heart is only for evil, the entire day. (*Bereishis* 6:5)

עין הרע ויצר הרע ושנאת הבריות

אָנֹכִי עֹמֵד בֵּין־ה' וּבֵינֵיכֶם. (דברים ה' ה')

I was standing between Hashem and you. (*Devarim* 5:5)

וְהָאִישׁ מֹשֶׁה עָנָו מְאֹד מִכֹּל הָאָדָם אֲשֶׁר עַל־פְּנֵי הָאֲדָמָה. (במדבר י"ב ג')

And the man, Moshe, was exceedingly humble, more than any man on the face of the earth. (*Bamidbar* 12:3)

פֶּה אֶל־פֶּה אֲדַבֶּר־בּוֹ...וּתְמֻנַת ה' יַבִּיט. (שם פסוק ח')

Speaker to speaker I converse with him...and he gazes upon the image of Hashem. (*ibid.* v. 8)

גָּדוֹל שֶׁנֶּאֱמַר בְּמֹשֶׁה וְאַהֲרֹן יוֹתֵר מִמַּה שֶּׁנֶּאֱמַר בְּאַבְרָהָם. דְּאִילוּ בְּאַבְרָהָם כְּתִיב וְאָנֹכִי עָפָר וָאֵפֶר, וְאִילוּ בְּמֹשֶׁה וְאַהֲרֹן כְּתִיב וְנַחְנוּ מָה. (חולין פ"ט.)

What is said about Moshe and Aharon is even greater than that which is said about Avraham. By Avraham, it is written (the following declaration which reveals his inherent modesty): "And I am but dust and ashes" (*Bereishis* 18:27). However, by Moshe and Aharon, it is written (that they proclaimed) (*Shemos* 16:8): "And what, after all, are we?" (*Chullin* 89a)

פרק ב'

253

GEMS FROM THE *SEFER NESIVOS SHOLOM*

A World of Good

From an initial glance at this mishnah, it almost appears not to be telling us much. What, actually, is it that Rabbi Yehoshua seeks to convey — that bad is bad? That doesn't seem to be something of which we needed to be informed.

The Maharal uncovers the depth behind this mishnah, which is actually imparting a profound concept: It's not just that bad is "bad" and good is "good." Rather, the *state of existence is intertwined with these forces*. Any entity is sustained to the extent that it is associated with the *ko'ach hatov* (force of good), whereas an involvement with *ra* leads inevitably to *heder* (mitigation and removal). In a sense, the *ko'ach hatov* is to the *beri'ah* what the *neshamah* is to the *guf*; the body can only survive as long as the *neshamah*, its life-giving force, remains within it. Once the *neshamah* exits, the body will perish. It is for this reason we find this refrain throughout the Creation narrative (*Bereishis*, ch. 1): וַיַּרְא אֱלֹקִים כִּי־טוֹב — *And G-d saw that it was good*. When *Hakadosh Baruch Hu* saw that the *beri'ah* was infused with goodness, He knew that it would endure.

This notion also emerges from the arrangement regarding the *Luchos*. As we know, there were two sets: The first was destroyed by Moshe on account of the sin of the Golden Calf. Klal Yisroel was later presented with a second set of *Luchos*. And while each contained the *Aseres Hadibros*, there were some textual differences between them. One of these concerns the term *tov*. When contrasting the formulation of the commandment to honor our parents in both sets of *Luchos*, we discover that this term appears only in the second set. Compare the mention of the reward for fulfilling this mitzvah. In the first *Luchos*, the *passuk* states (*Shemos* 20:12): כַּבֵּד אֶת־אָבִיךָ וְאֶת־אִמֶּךָ לְמַעַן יַאֲרִכוּן יָמֶיךָ — *Honor your father and mother, so that your days will be lengthened*. In the second rendition, however, the following phrase is appended (*Devarim* 5:16): לְמַעַן יַאֲרִיכֻן יָמֶיךָ וּלְמַעַן יִיטַב לָךְ — *In order that your days be lengthened, and in order that it be* **good** *for you*. This difference prompts the following reaction from *Chazal* (*Bava Kamma* 54b): מִפְּנֵי מָה בַּדִּבְּרוֹת הָרִאשׁוֹנוֹת לֹא נֶאֱמַר בָּהֶם טוֹב, וּבַדִּבְּרוֹת הָאַחֲרוֹנוֹת נֶאֱמַר בָּהֶם טוֹב? ... הוֹאִיל וְסוֹפָן לְהִשְׁתַּבֵּר — *Why is it that in the original (text*

of the) commandments it does not make mention of "tov," but in the latter commandments it does state "tov"? ... (The answer is) since the (original tablets) were destined to be shattered. It seems that, knowing their fate, Hashem withheld the mention of the word *tov* in the first *Luchos*, for only without this element was it possible that they would not last.

This, then, is the message of our mishnah: Good perseveres. Good is the root of all existence. Therefore, those who are connected to goodness endure and exist in This World. But those who are connected to *ra* — such as through an *ayin hara*, the *yetzer hara*, and *sin'as haberi'os* — are subject to *heder* and are taken out of the world.

The Evil Eye and the Satisfied Soul

What, exactly, is this "evil eye" of which the mishnah speaks? The Bartenura explains that the reference is to someone who is deficient in his *middos*, specifically in the area of being satisfied with his lot. This characterization may seem somewhat puzzling. Being *samei'ach b'chelko*, no doubt, is an admirable quality. But if one is wanting in this area, is it really so tragic that he becomes removed from the world as a result? How are we to understand what accounts for such drastic consequences?

A fuller appreciation of this trait can shed much light on the issue. The Saba Kadisha of Slonim *ztz"l* expounded on this particular attribute, stating quite emphatically that it is much more than just a nice *middah*. In fact, it is an all-encompassing and overwhelmingly valuable trait. It envelops all pristine qualities, elevates a person tremendously, and enables him to attain great benefit in both This World and the Next.

The Nesivos Sholom provides insight as to how this comes about. This World is inherently a world of pure goodness. *Hakadosh Baruch Hu*, Who is completely good, created the world for the sole purpose of bestowing goodness upon His creatures.

The only issue is that the reality may not seem to square with this characterization. Looking around, we seem to behold a world filled with sorrow and strife. How is this a manifestation of goodness? And how, then, is the purpose of creation being fulfilled?

This is where the urgency of the *middah* of *samei'ach b'chelko* is most apparent. For the world is unquestionably a place of inherent goodness, but we must take the first step to recognize this and search out the goodness in all situations. When we aim to be happy with our lot, life will become truly good for us.

In effect, this is a two-step process. A positive attitude helps us to overcome hardships. We focus on all that is good in life; despite the troubles and challenges, we feel satisfied. But more than that, when we are happy with the way Hashem leads us, our actual situation will undergo real changes for the better. This is a phenomenon known as *hamtakas hadinim* (sweetening of the judgments), whereby Heaven responds to our attitude with an increase in blessing and beneficence. A positive view on life makes the hardships more bearable and effects their ultimate annulment.

This is the full import of the words of the Saba Kadisha. He asserted that the *middah* of being *samei'ach b'chelko* leads to all good things in *Olam Hazeh* and *Olam Haba*. We have the ability to affect our surroundings for the better by adopting a mentality of being satisfied with our lot. Thus we see that this *middah* can ensure that our reality will in fact be in tune with the characterization of the world as a place filled with goodness for its inhabitants.

This is precisely why the concept of *ayin hara* can be so wholly detrimental. Since satisfaction with one's lot makes This World a better, happier place — bringing a person to achieve bliss in This World and the Next, as the Saba Kadisha proclaimed — a lack thereof, as manifested in the *middah* of *ayin hara*, will consequently lead to the exact opposite. Instead of leading a person to the blessings of This World and the Next, it will remove him from the world.

The other two concepts listed in our mishnah round out the picture. The Nesivos Sholom explains that while the *yetzer hara* leads a person to sin, it is not necessarily synonymous with sin. That is, when Rabbi Yehoshua attributes to the *yetzer hara* the ability to remove a person from the world, it is not necessarily because of the sins that a person perpetrates at the *yetzer's* behest. Rather, Rabbi Yehoshua is referring to a general indulgence of one's desires, a constant quest for more and more pleasure. As the *passuk* states regarding the generation of the Flood (*Bereishis* 6:5): וְכָל־יֵצֶר מַחְשְׁבֹת לִבּוֹ רַק רַע כָּל־הַיּוֹם — *And all the **inclination** of his heart is only for evil, the entire day*. Such a total preoccupation with and subservience to the desires of his *yetzer* indicates that one is wholly given over to the power of *ra*. The results at the time of the Flood were devastating, as is well known, constituting the ultimate "removal from the world." But so it is with anyone over whom *ra* is dominant; lacking the *ko'ach hatov*, he loses his right and ability to endure. And so it is with the entity of *sin'as haberi'os*, referring to one who is literally in arrears with the entire world. This situation is likewise rooted in the *ko'ach hara*, thus leading to *heder*. And so, one who is stricken with these maladies is consigned to a fate of removal from the world.

The gravity of these three traits can be appreciated on yet another level, in light of another principle expounded by the Maharal. Discussing the essential endeavor of achieving *shleimus* in *avodas Hashem*, the Maharal defines just what it entails. He speaks of attaining *shleimus* in three key areas: with Hashem, with his fellow man, and with himself. One who cultivates *shleimus* in these three dimensions has truly acquired perfection.

The three qualities listed in our mishnah stand in direct contradiction to the *shleimus* of these three areas. A person afflicted with an *ayin hara* — a lack of satisfaction with his lot — is not *shaleim* (complete and at peace) with himself, as he is constantly feeling that he doesn't have enough and doesn't measure up to his neighbors. Someone governed by his *yetzer hara* is quite obviously far from Hashem, and nowhere near the ideal of being *shaleim* with Him. And it is quite apparent how *sin'as haberi'os* stands in contradiction to the notion of being *shaleim* with one's fellow men. Instead of obtaining the heights of perfection, such an individual is not even worthy to remain in the world.

GEMS FROM THE *SEFER NESIVOS SHOLOM*

It All Comes Down to "Me"

The commonality among these three traits can be understood on another level. They can be described as all emanating from the same root: the *middah* of *anochi'us*, characterized by an emphasis on *anochi* ("I"). Since a self-absorbed person views himself as a *yeish* — a "something," meaning an entity in and of itself — he asserts his self-perceived superiority, feeling that he is deserving of all manner of privileges and honor. Thus, he ends up adopting the three qualities listed in the mishnah. Such a person will certainly not be satisfied with what he has and can't accept the fact that someone else may possess more wealth or talent than he. His *yetzer hara* will likewise shift into high gear; since his needs and wants are front and center in his universe, why shouldn't he seek to fulfill every whim and desire? And of course, an inflated sense of self is a prescription for discord with those around him. In his haughtiness, he has little or no respect for other people, seeing them as mere obstacles to the attainment of his own success and happiness.

The role of the ego as a prime factor in one's spiritual deterioration is highlighted by an exposition of the Ba'al Shem Tov. He references the *passuk* in which Moshe Rabbeinu was recounting the events at Har Sinai (*Devarim* 5:5): אָנֹכִי עֹמֵד בֵּין־ה׳ וּבֵינֵיכֶם — *I was standing between Hashem and you*. In its literal sense, the *passuk* is speaking of Moshe Rabbeinu's acting as intermediary at Har Sinai, relating Hashem's words to the people. The Ba'al Shem Tov renders a homiletic interpretation of the verse: "'*Anochi*' — that is, the *middah* of *anochi'us* — is what stands between a Yid and Hashem." In other words, it is the assertion of one's own supremacy that drives a wedge between a person and his Creator, causing one to be distant from Him. Conversely, however, this idea also contains the counterpart: By engaging in *bitul hayeishus* — negating one's ego and sense of self-importance — the barriers are removed, and a Yid can come close to Hashem, attaining elevated levels of spirituality.

An examination of the seminal figure of Moshe Rabbeinu encapsulates this crucial point; he serves as the quintessential model of what *bitul hayeishus* can effect. In relatively close proximity to each other, the Torah lists two primary qualities of Moshe Rabbeinu — qualities which, at first glance, may seem to be contradictory in nature. One relates to his unprecedented (and never to be matched) level of prophecy, attaining levels of closeness with the Divine, more so than any other mortal. Hashem describes His interactions with Moshe in the following way: פֶּה אֶל־פֶּה אֲדַבֶּר־בּוֹ...וּתְמֻנַת ה' יַבִּיט — *Speaker to speaker I converse with him...and he gazes upon the image of Hashem* (*Bamidbar* 12:12). Just a few *pesukim* earlier (v. 3), the Torah says about Moshe: וְהָאִישׁ מֹשֶׁה עָנָו מְאֹד מִכֹּל הָאָדָם אֲשֶׁר עַל־פְּנֵי הָאֲדָמָה — *And the man, Moshe, was exceedingly humble, more than any person on the face of the earth.* How is this even possible? As modest as he was, surely Moshe was not oblivious to the fact that he had also attained the most august spiritual heights! How could one remain so exceedingly humble while simultaneously being — in a spiritual sense — on top of the world?

The truth is, however, that these attributes are not contradictory, but complementary. Attaining an unprecedented level of modesty contributed to Moshe's attainment of the heights of sanctity and spiritual grandeur. The Saba Kadisha had stated that the *middah* of *samei'ach b'chelko* is the vehicle that brings a person to ever-greater heights in *avodas Hashem*. We have seen, moreover, that *anochi'us* and *yeishus* prevent a person from being satisfied with his lot, intensifying, instead, the *middah* of *ayin hara*. Conversely, *bitul hayeishus* enables one to be satisfied with his portion, a crucial attribute leading to the greatest spiritual attainments. Since Moshe Rabbeinu developed his sense of *bitul hayeishus* to an unprecedented extent, he was thus able to climb the spiritual heights to a place no man has ever been — before or since.

A Drop in the Ocean

Highlighting the extent of Moshe Rabbeinu's self-negation, *Chazal* (*Chullin* 89a) compare his achievement in this matter to that of another figure renowned for his humility — Avraham Avinu: גָּדוֹל שֶׁנֶּאֱמַר בְּמֹשֶׁה וְאַהֲרֹן יוֹתֵר מִמַּה שֶּׁנֶּאֱמַר בְּאַבְרָהָם. דְּאִילּוּ בְּאַבְרָהָם כְּתִיב וְאָנֹכִי עָפָר וָאֵפֶר, וְאִילּוּ בְּמֹשֶׁה וְאַהֲרֹן כְּתִיב וְנַחְנוּ מָה — *What is said about Moshe and Aharon is*

even greater than that which is said about Avraham. By Avraham, it is written (the following declaration which reveals his inherent modesty): "And I am but dust and ashes" (Bereishis *18:27). However, by Moshe and Aharon, it is written (that they proclaimed): "And what, after all, are we?"* (Shemos *16:8).*

In the final analysis, the difference between the two may seem insignificant. Avraham compared himself to dust; Moshe Rabbeinu went a step further, indicating that he was simply a non-entity: "What are we?" The Nesivos Sholom explains that the distinction is indeed significant. While Avraham's humility was indeed legendary, that of Moshe Rabbeinu represented a whole different level.

The Nesivos Sholom elucidates this point by portraying a scenario by the ocean. Imagine that someone were to dip a cup into the ocean, filling it with water. Compared to the vast ocean, what appears in this cup is truly minuscule. But, having been separated from this body of water, it does represent an entity in and of itself; it has its own identity, no matter how insignificant. When the water is subsequently poured back into the ocean, then its identity effectively disappears. The water is now simply subsumed within the greater body that is the sea.

This picture represents the different levels of how one may view himself. Given this particular allegory, most people may consider themselves the ocean. Compared to this, Avraham's attitude was that he was but a cup filled with water beside this vast body. This is truly a monumental step forward in terms of achieving modesty, diminishing his own stature in his eyes in a manner so vastly more profound than the rest of the population. But there is yet another level, the one attained by Moshe Rabbeinu: He rendered himself literally a non-entity, as the water poured back into the ocean. He was simply nullified in the greater body of water.

Yet, this very notion can help us to understand even better how it is that the listed characteristics of Moshe Rabbeinu — unprecedented prophetic levels and supreme humility — are complementary qualities. It was *because* Moshe had reached such astounding levels of spiritual grandeur *that he was able to be so humble.* That is, he had attained such closeness to Hashem, becoming *dovuk* to Him, that complete self-negation and subjugation to Him followed. Moshe was as the cup of water spilled back into the ocean. In this way, through his unprecedented closeness to Hashem, Moshe became "nullified" before the boundless greatness of Hashem.

The Nesivos Sholom employs another allegory to illustrate this concept. In a given kingdom, there are many subjects who fear and respect their monarch. But who really trembles in awe before the king? It is specifically those who are closest to him. They see royalty up close; how everyone in his presence is filled with trepidation and reverence. They behold the glory and grandeur that surrounds the king, how his attendants stand before him in respectful silence and admiration. Witnessing such august subservience and nullification before him — how everything and everyone in his proximity pales in significance before his majesty — those who surround the king are most likely to negate themselves to him. By contrast, the far-away subjects, the common folk who hardly ever see the king, view him as some abstract entity. So far removed, they are much less likely to be awed and nullified by his greatness.

And so it was with Moshe Rabbeinu. It was *because* he experienced פֶּה אֶל־פֶּה אֲדַבֶּר־בּוֹ, *because* he gazed upon Hashem's Presence, that he excelled in humility. Of course Moshe knew that he had attained unprecedented closeness with Hashem; this is what intensified his feelings of self-negation. So close was he to the King, cleaving to Him with such passionate *d'veikus*, that he was able to nullify himself to Him more so than any other person. And so he became the quintessential practitioner of *bitul hayeishus*, making himself — before Hashem's Presence — into literally nothingness. And this was the apex of greatness.

In Summary

The Maharal explains that good is a sustaining force; for this reason, the Torah repeatedly emphasizes in the Creation narrative that Hashem saw that "it was good." In order for the *beri'ah* to endure, it must be infused with goodness. Whatever is associated with the *ko'ach hara*, by contrast, is subject to *heder* and loss. This is the backdrop to Rabbi Yehoshua's teaching. A person who possesses the negative traits of *ayin hara*, *yetzer hara*, and *sin'as haberi'os* — all predicated on *ra* — will be removed from the world.

Ayin hara, as explained by the Bartenura, is a lack of satisfaction with one's lot. One who does possess the attribute of *samei'ach b'chelko* is in a very advantageous position in life. The Saba Kadisha of Slonim explained that this particular trait is an all-encompassing *middah* that includes all positive qualities, and it brings blessing to a person in This World and the Next. By contrast, one who is never content with his portion will be removed from the world. The same holds true for someone enslaved to his passions or at odds with his fellow men. The involvement with *ra* as manifested in these traits will, unfortunately, be his undoing and remove him from the world.

The gravity of these traits can also be understood in light of the Maharal's explanation of *shleimus*. He speaks of *shleimus* in three main areas, advocating that a person be *shaleim* with himself, with his fellow man, and with Hashem. The three elements of the mishnah stand in direct contrast to these qualities. Someone with an *ayin hara*, constantly unhappy with what he has, is not *shaleim* with himself; one who chases his passions in contradiction to Hashem's will is obviously not *shaleim* with Him; and, of course, a person immersed in *sin'as chinam* is not *shaleim* with his fellow man.

At another level, these three elements revolve around a single issue: that of *anochi'us* and *yeishus*; one who asserts his self-importance sees himself as a separate entity, "deserving" of having his wishes fulfilled. Of course, such a person will not be satisfied with what he has but will pine for more. And he'll have a very hard time deferring to and getting along with others.

As a general rule, the sense of ego is a most serious impediment to serving Hashem and becoming close to Him. By contrast, one who develops a sense of *bitul hayeishus*, self-negation, removes such barriers. As such, he will become close to Hashem, and, of course, excel in the area of *samei'ach b'chelko*. In this way, as the Saba Kadisha explained, he will have access to the blessings of goodness in This World and the Next.

פרק ב' משנה י"ח
הוי זהיר בקריאת שמע ובתפלה
Be Meticulous with the Reading of Shema and Prayer

רַבִּי שִׁמְעוֹן אוֹמֵר, הֱוֵי זָהִיר בִּקְרִיאַת שְׁמַע וּבִתְפִלָּה. וּכְשֶׁאַתָּה מִתְפַּלֵּל, אַל תַּעַשׂ תְּפִלָּתְךָ קֶבַע, אֶלָּא רַחֲמִים וְתַחֲנוּנִים לִפְנֵי הַמָּקוֹם בָּרוּךְ הוּא, שֶׁנֶּאֱמַר כִּי חַנּוּן וְרַחוּם הוּא אֶרֶךְ אַפַּיִם וְרַב חֶסֶד וְנִחָם עַל הָרָעָה. וְאַל תְּהִי רָשָׁע בִּפְנֵי עַצְמְךָ:

Rabbi Shimon says: Be meticulous with the reading of *Shema* and prayer; and when you pray, do not make your prayer burdensome, but rather a plea for mercy and compassion before Hashem, as it states (*Yoel* 2:13): "For He is compassionate and merciful, long-suffering and abundant in kindness, and will retract from retribution"; and do not consider yourself as wicked.

GEMS FROM THE *SEFER NESIVOS SHOLOM*

SOURCES:

וָאֶתְחַנַּן אֶל ה' בָּעֵת הַהִוא. (דברים ג' כ"ג)

And I beseeched Hashem at that time. (*Devarim* 3:23)

בָּנִים אַתֶּם לַה' אֱלֹקֵיכֶם. (שם י"ד א')

You are children of Hashem your G-d. (*ibid.* 14:1)

בָּנִים אַתֶּם לַה' אֱלֹקֵיכֶם - בִּזְמַן שֶׁאַתֶּם נוֹהֲגִים מִנְהַג בָּנִים אַתֶּם קְרוּיִם בָּנִים, אֵין אַתֶּם נוֹהֲגִים מִנְהַג בָּנִים אֵין אַתֶּם קְרוּיִם בָּנִים; דִּבְרֵי ר' יְהוּדָה. רַבִּי מֵאִיר אוֹמֵר בֵּין כָּךְ וּבֵין כָּךְ אַתֶּם קְרוּיִם בָּנִים. (קידושין ל"ו.)

"You are children of Hashem your G-d" – When you conduct yourselves in a manner befitting (Hashem's) children, you are called "(His) children"; if you do not conduct yourselves in a manner befitting children, you are not called "children"; these are the words of Rabbi Yehudah. Rabbi Meir says: In all events, you are still called "(My) children." (*Kiddushin* 36a)

אֱלֹקַי בְּךָ בָטַחְתִּי אַל־אֵבוֹשָׁה. (תהלים כ"ה ב')

My G-d, I have trusted in You; let me not be ashamed. (*Tehillim* 25:2)

אֱלֹקַי אֶקְרָא יוֹמָם וְלֹא תַעֲנֶה וְלַיְלָה וְלֹא־דוּמִיָּה לִי... בְּךָ בָּטְחוּ אֲבֹתֵינוּ בָּטְחוּ וַתְּפַלְּטֵמוֹ. אֵלֶיךָ זָעֲקוּ וְנִמְלָטוּ בְּךָ בָטְחוּ וְלֹא־בוֹשׁוּ. (שם כ"ב ג',ה',ו')

My G-d, I call out by day and You do not reply; and at night I do not keep silent. Our fathers trusted in You; they trusted, and You saved them. They cried out to You, and were rescued; they trusted in You, and were not ashamed (*ibid.* 22:3, 5, 6)

פרקי אבות

Before Whom You Stand

To choose the path of least resistance — that is part of human nature. In approaching a given task, people tend to fulfill it in a manner that requires the least possible expenditure of time and effort.

This phenomenon helps explain why it is that virtually everyone struggles with *tefillah*, an activity we attend to at least three times a day, every day of the year. The basest part of the human mind tries to block out the gravity of this endeavor, and human nature kicks in. This leads to a situation whereby *davening* becomes an exercise of chanting by rote words that really have the potential to change lives and move mountains.

Rabbi Shimon echoes this concept in *Pirkei Avos* (2:13): רַבִּי שִׁמְעוֹן אוֹמֵר, הֱוֵי זָהִיר בִּקְרִיאַת שְׁמַע וּבִתְפִלָּה, וּכְשֶׁאַתָּה מִתְפַּלֵּל אַל תַּעַשׂ תְּפִלָּתְךָ קֶבַע, אֶלָּא רַחֲמִים וְתַחֲנוּנִים לִפְנֵי הַמָּקוֹם... וְאַל תְּהִי רָשָׁע בִּפְנֵי עַצְמָךְ — *Be meticulous with the reading of the* Shema *and with prayer. When you pray, do not make your prayers routine, but (an entreaty of) mercy and a supplication before Hashem... And do not be wicked in your own eyes.*

It is interesting that of all the 613 mitzvos of the Torah, Rabbi Shimon chose to issue his warning *hevei zahir*, be careful, concerning these two specific mitzvos of *Krias Shema* and *tefillah*. What tremendous power lies inside these two that he granted them priority in this respect over others?

A further point to ponder about this mishnah is that, at first glance, it seems a bit disjointed. Rabbi Shimon first discusses the appropriate way to *daven*; i.e., as a plea for mercy, and not simply by rote. He then adds that one should not view himself as a *rasha*. What could possibly be the connection between these seemingly unrelated ideas?

Even putting aside the issue of its relevance to the beginning, this final statement of the mishnah, on its own, is somewhat perplexing. Why shouldn't a person view himself as wicked? Isn't humility a concept greatly stressed in *Yiddishkeit*? Ostensibly, seeing oneself as a *rasha* could spur a person to reverse his negative trends and improve his attitude and behaviors. Why does Rabbi Shimon discourage this approach?

Who — and What — Is a Jew?

The Nesivos Sholom begins his elucidation of these issues by relating an essential element of *Yiddishkeit*. Humans have laws by which they must abide — namely, the *sheva mitzvos bnei Noach*, the seven commandments applicable to Noach's progeny (which is the whole world). The mitzvos of the Torah, however, were issued with only the Jewish people in mind. They are designed to take a Jew from the level of ordinary human to become a true vehicle for *ratzon Hashem* (Hashem's will).

And while the Torah's mitzvos apply only to Jews, the real question is — who, indeed, is a Jew? Jewish blood itself does not qualify one as a Jew in the full sense of the word. A real Yid is someone whose *very essence* is Jewish, whose being is dedicated to Hashem's service and forming a real connection with Him.

This is the crucial role fulfilled by *Krias Shema* and *tefillah*. Other mitzvos like Shabbos, kashrus, or *taharas hamishpachah* (family purity), of course have their place and are fundamental to *Yiddishkeit* in their own right. But in the aspect of infusing our inner self with *Yiddishkeit*, to the extent that our very essence becomes a "Jewish essence" — *Krias Shema* and *tefillah* are key. They bear a particular impact on the development of a special relationship with Hashem. When a Yid recites שְׁמַע יִשְׂרָאֵל ה׳ אֱלֹקֵינוּ ה׳ אֶחָד, he lovingly accepts upon himself the *ol Malchus Shamayim* (yoke of Heaven's Kingdom). In so doing, he subjugates himself completely to his Master, committing one hundred percent of his abilities to fulfilling His will. And through *tefillah* (referring primarily to the *Shemoneh Esrei* prayer), he achieves that ultimate state of *d'veikus baHashem*.

This is why Rabbi Shimon emphasizes *Krias Shema* and *tefillah* over all other mitzvos. Not that they are more important, per se, but they reflect the *essence* of a Jew. Their proper fulfillment can make the difference in determining one's status as a genuine Jew as opposed to a person who is simply a member of the Jewish people through blood.

(It is noteworthy that in the mishnah, Rabbi Shimon includes a much more elaborate warning regarding *tefillah* than *Krias Shema*. His opening statement refers equally to both: הֱוֵי זָהִיר בִּקְרִיאַת שְׁמַע וּבִתְפִלָּה — *Be careful regarding* Krias Shema *and* tefillah. But he then continues to address *tefillah* alone: וּכְשֶׁאַתָּה מִתְפַּלֵּל אַל תַּעַשׂ תְּפִלָּתְךָ קֶבַע, אֶלָּא רַחֲמִים וְתַחֲנוּנִים לִפְנֵי הַמָּקוֹם — *And when you pray, do not make your prayer one of rote, but, rather, a plea for mercy and compassion before Hashem*. The reason for this disparity is that, by definition, an authentic recitation of *Krias Shema* requires an intense amount of focus. As such, it can't possibly be by rote. And so Rabbi Shimon directed his main warning against rote recital to *tefillah* alone.)

Tefillah: An Exercise in Connectivity

The goal of *tefillah* is for Bnei Yisroel to be able to connect to Hashem and create the basis of a sincere relationship with Him. Even if a person does not actually feel as if he needs something from Hashem, he must act as if he does by begging for mercy from Hashem to grant his requests. For through such entreaties, he creates the beginnings of a potentially life-changing relationship.

The true nature of what *tefillah* should be is depicted in the *Chovos Halevavos*, which explains (*Sha'ar Cheshbon Hanefesh*, ch. 3) that the quintessential *tefillah* is one that comes from the pristine essence of a Yid. At its root, this essence is pure spirituality, untouched by human interference in the form of emotions, materialism, and external motivations. All that remains is the *neshamah*, aching to connect to its Maker. When *tefillah* comes from a place as pure and deep as the *neshamah*, it can enable a Yid to achieve true *d'veikus*.

Echoing this thought, the Maharal further demonstrates how *tefillah* breeds *d'veikus*. He states (*Nesivos Olam, Nesiv Ha'avodah*, ch. 3) that a prime element of *tefillah* is the utter dependency on Hashem the supplicant reveals through his pleading. He realizes that there is nothing within his own power to do, and it is only through Hashem's benevolent salvation that he can carry on. Thus, one who *davens* properly actually gains a clearer awareness of his own lack of capability. This acknowledgment that he is like nothing before Hashem is a crucial step to achieving the ultimate level of *d'veikus* to Him; having nullified himself, he is ripe to attach himself to the Creator. *Tefillah*, we discover, is the tool through which we can harness the power of connection; it combines the negation of our "human" qualities with the ability to bond, creating thereby an unstoppable force of *d'veikus* with Hashem.

Once we appreciate this concept, we come to understand the critical role *tefillah* plays in our life. When *davening*, we realize that if not for the specific words we are uttering at that very moment, we would not be able to exist. The appropriate mindset in this regard is to think: "I have life because I am connected to Hashem, and *tefillah* is the way in which I become connected to Him. If I don't *daven* properly, I can't be connected to my Source. I must take my *davening* quite seriously; my very right and ability to exist depend on it."

We can thus see what happens when our *tefillos* become automatic, recited merely by rote. We lose the ability to reaffirm our connection to Hashem, and any measure of connection that we had previously achieved diminishes as a consequence.

The matter is comparable to a cell-phone battery. As the phone is used throughout the day, the battery's energy is depleted. Most people realize that it must be recharged often, to full capacity, in order to continue using it. Imagine someone who connects the charger to the phone but neglects to plug the other end into the wall socket. Obviously, if he's expecting it to work the next day, he's in for a disappointment. Nor can one assume that if he charged the phone last week, it will have enough "juice" to last for another week. There simply is no substitute for a regular actual connection to a source of electricity. Otherwise, the phone will not charge and its current energy will continue to dwindle.

Most of us realize — on an intellectual level, at least — that *tefillah* is a very necessary component in obtaining and maintaining life and its blessings. That is, we recognize the need for "recharging." However, by treating *tefillah* as mere lip service, a task to be completed three times daily without active *kavanah* (focus), we thereby deny ourselves the genuine connection to the vital Source. Our charger may be connected to the phone — but it's not plugged in to the wall. As such, the spiritual energy slowly dwindles from our lives.

This notion helps to account, as well, for the imperative of recognizing our "nothingness." When we adopt a tone of true desperation, we demonstrate that we indeed think of ourselves as nothing. We are not merely asking Hashem to connect, but begging for our life. Such a mindset paves the way for the attainment of the highest levels of *d'veikus*; by realizing our own nothingness, we can easily attach to Hashem as our power source. However, if we view our human qualities and abilities as a source of life and power, how can we truly connect to Hashem? Only when we reach the "rock bottom" of our humanity can we recognize that all that is left is our spiritual essence. As this essence is itself an aspect of Hashem, we can now reattach our self to our Maker.

Many *sefarim* explain that the mitzvos of the Torah share a common purpose: they comprise 613 ways of developing *d'veikus* to Hashem. And so, in our mishnah, Rabbi Shimon singles out the two areas that serve as the strongest and most effective method of achieving this purpose: *Krias Shema* and *tefillah*. Through these elements, a Yid accepts the sovereignty and omnipotence of Hashem and connects to Him as an eternal source of life and strength. If done by rote, however, both of these aspects remain essentially unfulfilled, leaving a person empty of true *Yiddishkeit*.

Deserving or Not

Elaborating on the *avodah* of *tefillah*, the Rashba identifies three mindsets that are essential for this *avodah* to be successfully performed.

At the root of any *tefillah* must be the absolute knowledge that whatever Hashem gives us is pure *chessed* on His part — we do not deserve anything of our own accord. Moshe Rabbeinu provides one of the most powerful examples of *tefillah* in Tanach. He offered a series of constant and heartfelt pleas in which he begged Hashem to allow him to lead his flock into Eretz Yisroel. The Torah describes these prayers with a somewhat unusual term: **Va'eschanan el Hashem** — "and I beseeched Hashem" (*Devarim* 3:23). *Chazal* explain that the root of this word is *chinam*, free. This was the essence of Moshe's prayer: he was not asking for something he felt he had earned or deserved, but rather for a free gift, as it were, that would come solely from the goodness of Hashem.

The *Avodas Yisroel* sees this notion manifest in the first *brachah* (blessing) of *Shemoneh Esrei*. This *brachah* describes *Hakadosh Baruch Hu* as the *Gomeil chassadim tovim* — "One Who bestows benevolent kindnesses," reflecting the fact that whatever we have in life, even life itself, is not what we deserved but a result of the Creator's largesse. As such, we must beg Hashem for every breath of air and every penny of income, with the complete understanding that receiving these gifts is an outpouring of Hashem's *chessed*. We must appeal to Hashem's boundless mercy and literally beg for every second of life and morsel of sustenance.

Begging Hashem for each aspect of life is meaningless without a firm belief that Hashem is the Creator of all and is capable of providing everything for anyone in the entire universe. This, explains the Rashba, is the second aspect of *tefillah*: it must be accompanied by an unwavering *emunah* in the power of Hashem. The *Avodas Yisroel* demonstrates how this concept is reflected in the words of the second *brachah*: מְחַיֶּה מֵתִים...סוֹמֵךְ נוֹפְלִים, וְרוֹפֵא חוֹלִים, וּמַתִּיר אֲסוּרִים — *He revives the dead...supports those who fall, heals the sick, frees the imprisoned, etc.* This is the supplicant's affirmation of the omnipotence of *Hakadosh Baruch Hu*, a very necessary prerequisite to asking Hashem to bestow kindness upon him.

Finally, proper *tefillah* requires a clear recognition that it is Hashem, and only Hashem, that can deliver. This, explains the *Avodas Yisroel*, is the essence of the third *brachah* of *Shemoneh Esrei*: אַתָּה קָדוֹשׁ וְשִׁמְךָ קָדוֹשׁ, וּקְדוֹשִׁים בְּכָל יוֹם יְהַלְלוּךָ סֶּלָה — *You are holy, Your Name is holy, and the holy ones praise You every day, Selah*. Throughout the universe and its various spheres, all praise is directed only towards You, Hashem. Ultimately, it is not the doctor who finds a cure, or a business partner who comes through with a large transaction. Hashem is the Source of all goodness and bounty; only He can help, not the professional or the person signing the check. Every *tefillah* must emanate from the recognition that Hashem is the only provider.

This insight into the makeup of *tefillah* may present a particular problem for a certain person — namely, one who views himself as unworthy due to his own wickedness. In light of the understanding that every moment of life is a *chessed* from Hashem, one who views himself in this way feels no hope. How could he — a *rasha* in his own eyes — possibly merit the unlimited *chassadim* of Hashem if he has flouted Hashem's will?

It was such an individual that Rabbi Shimon was addressing in his final words in the mishnah. וְאַל תְּהִי רָשָׁע בִּפְנֵי עַצְמְךָ — *Do not see yourself as a* rasha. How could one possibly ask for the millions of gifts that make up human existence if he sees himself in such a light? He will logically conclude that he should abandon *tefillah* completely, as he has no right to ask for sustenance from the One he has forsaken. As one may have drawn this (erroneous) conclusion after having contemplated the essence of *tefillah*, Rabbi Shimon seeks to prevent such a mistake. "Don't view yourself this way," he urges.

Why not take this view? The Torah tells us, בָּנִים אַתֶּם לַה' אֱלֹקֵיכֶם — *You are children of Hashem your G-d* (Devarim 14:1). All Jews must see themselves as sons and daughters of Hashem, as children who deserve infinite kindness and gifts; not because of their own deeds, but simply as a result of their beloved status in the eyes of their Father. As such, every Jew should be able to approach Hashem as the Creator and Beneficiary of the universe, and beg for His mercy and kindness.

The Rebbe of Kobrin takes this idea a step further. He asserts that if someone feels like he cannot approach Hashem due to the numerous sins he has transgressed, that person obviously does not understand what *Yiddishkeit* is about. Being a Jew by definition means that we can always approach Hashem, no matter what actions have been done. *Chazal* tell us that this appellation of *banim* applies at all times, regardless of the Jews' actions. בֵּין כָּךְ וּבֵין כָּךְ אַתֶּם קְרוּיִים בָּנִים — *In*

all events, you are still called "(My) children" (*Kiddushin* 36a). A child is beloved, no matter what he has done. He can always approach his father.

The truth of the matter is, though, that the assumption itself is flawed. Rabbi Shimon tells us not to view ourselves as wicked because a Jew is intrinsically good. On the surface, his misdeeds may be apparent; but deep down, a Yid, by nature, is programmed to follow the Torah and desires to do so. It is just that, for the time being, his *yetzer hara* has overpowered his inherent *yetzer hatov* (good inclination). Therefore, a Jew is never wicked; sometimes he just does wicked things. He may have made a terrible mistake but is never a terrible person.

Echoing this concept, the *pesukim* in *Sefer Tehillim* introduce another element. אֱלֹקַי בְּךָ בָטַחְתִּי אַל־אֵבוֹשָׁה — *My G-d, I have trusted in You; let me not be ashamed* (25:2). בְּךָ בָטְחוּ אֲבֹתֵינוּ...בָּטְחוּ וְלֹא־בוֹשׁוּ — *Our fathers trusted in You...they had trust, and were not ashamed* (22:5, 6). A Yid need not be embarrassed to approach Hashem because he has *bitachon* that Hashem knows his true essence; despite his actions, inherently, he is not wicked.

This element of *bitachon* can prove quite beneficial in this regard. It provides a Yid with the knowledge that Hashem does not regard him as a *rasha*. But even more than that — the very fact that he has *bitachon* arms him with the power of *tefillah*. He may have faltered and committed *aveiros*, producing prosecuting angels in the process. However, the *bitachon* he cultivates is very potent and causes the accusers to be silenced. And so he may continue to stand with confidence before Hashem. The *bitachon* itself brought the salvation, granting him the *zechus* (merit) to stand before Hashem without shame.

The *passuk* preceding the verse quoted above states the following: אֱלֹקַי אֶקְרָא יוֹמָם וְלֹא תַעֲנֶה וְלַיְלָה וְלֹא־דוּמִיָּה לִי — *My G-d, I call out by day and You do not reply; and at night I do not keep silent* (*Tehillim* 22:3). Here, Dovid Hamelech speaks of a person who cries out to Hashem — but it seems like He is not listening! That is, he feels that he cannot possibly stand before Hashem in *tefillah* due to his numerous sins. How dare he ask Hashem for his needs? This is the backdrop to the solution provided by the continuation of the *mizmor* (chapter): בְּךָ בָטְחוּ...וְלֹא־בוֹשׁוּ. He must put his trust in Hashem; through that absolute trust, he may earn the prize of being able to *daven* to Hashem. This is the only way to break through the cloud of desperation in the darkest of times: to achieve the level of *bitachon* that silences the prosecutors and allows for *tefillah*.

Thus we see that both sections of Rabbi Shimon's teaching are inextricably linked. Be careful with *Shema* and with *tefillah* — but don't get caught in the trap of thinking that you are worthless and have no right to stand before Hashem. One must know that he is not a *rasha*. If one could only place his trust in Hashem, he would gain the ability to *daven*. Through the intimate connection which *tefillah* fosters, he will achieve his needs and desires.

In Summary

Rabbi Shimon singles out — from all other mitzvos — two elements that he deems to need special attention: *Krias Shema* and *tefillah*. While this may seem extraordinary, Rabbi Shimon is imparting an important lesson about the nature of these entities.

Obviously, Rabbi Shimon does not mean that these are the most "important" mitzvos, as all 613 are equally as binding. The reason Rabbi Shimon focuses specifically on these is that they are particularly suited to achieve a certain desired result. These two mitzvos accomplish the refinement of a person's essence into one that is an inherently "Jewish" essence. That is, rather than remaining merely a "Jew by birth," he transforms his whole being into a Jewish being, with Jewish flesh, Jewish insides, etc.

What is it about these two activities that account for this ability? Through the recital of *Shema*, a Yid thereby accepts upon himself the *ol Malchus Shamayim* with love. In so doing, he succeeds in negating himself before Hashem, subjugating himself completely to the Sovereign Creator of the Universe. And through *tefillah*, he completes the process of achieving *d'veikus* with Him. After all, the 613 mitzvos are in effect vehicles by which to attain *d'veikus*; *tefillah* is particularly powerful for achieving this end.

It is chiefly on account of the connection with Hashem engendered by sincere *tefillah* that Rabbi Shimon felt the need to warn against *davening* by rote. It is through this connection with the Source of all life that a person gains life. But forging such a connection requires focus and purposeful attention. By merely reciting familiar words as a habit, the connection becomes much more tenuous, thus depleting a Yid's spiritual energy.

Rabbi Shimon further stressed the need for one's *tefillah* to be a supplication for mercy. This reflects the fact that every *tefillah*, in essence, is an acknowledgment that we do not deserve anything but must entreat Hashem to perform undeserved kindness for us and maintain our existence.

This message, however, may have produced unintended consequences. A person who views himself as a *rasha* — upon learning that all of what he has are really "gifts" from Hashem — may become discouraged. "What good is it for me to *daven*," he may think, "if everything in life is a gift from Hashem — what right do I have to even approach Him and ask for anything?" To forestall this attitude, Rabbi Shimon is quick to add, "Do not be a *rasha* in your eyes." In all events, you are a child of Hashem, who may always approach his loving Father. A Jew's wickedness is essentially only skin deep; it is crucial to develop *bitachon* that Hashem knows that his essence is essentially good. And this *bitachon* itself has the power to silence the accusers, enabling the Yid to approach his Father in prayer.

פרקי אבות

GEMS FROM THE
ספר נתיבות שלום
NESIVOS SHOLOM

פרק ג'

פרק ג׳ משנה א׳
דע מאין באת וכו׳
Know from Where You Came, etc.

עֲקַבְיָא בֶּן מַהֲלַלְאֵל אוֹמֵר, הִסְתַּכֵּל בִּשְׁלֹשָׁה דְבָרִים וְאֵין אַתָּה בָא לִידֵי עֲבֵרָה. דַּע, מֵאַיִן בָּאתָ, וּלְאָן אַתָּה הוֹלֵךְ, וְלִפְנֵי מִי אַתָּה עָתִיד לִתֵּן דִּין וְחֶשְׁבּוֹן. מֵאַיִן בָּאתָ, מִטִּפָּה סְרוּחָה, וּלְאָן אַתָּה הוֹלֵךְ, לִמְקוֹם עָפָר רִמָּה וְתוֹלֵעָה. וְלִפְנֵי מִי אַתָּה עָתִיד לִתֵּן דִּין וְחֶשְׁבּוֹן, לִפְנֵי מֶלֶךְ מַלְכֵי הַמְּלָכִים הַקָּדוֹשׁ בָּרוּךְ הוּא:

Akavya ben Mahalalel says: Reflect upon three things and you will not come to the hands of transgression. Know from where you came, to where you are going, and before Whom you are destined to give a judgment and accounting. From where you came – from a putrid drop; to where you are going – to a place of dust, maggots and worms; and before Whom you are destined to give a judgment and accounting – before the Supreme King of kings, the Holy One, Blessed is He.

GEMS FROM THE *SEFER NESIVOS SHOLOM*

SOURCES:

בָּרָאתִי יֵצֶר הָרָע וּבָרָאתִי לוֹ תּוֹרָה תַּבְלִין. (קידושין ל:)

I have created the evil inclination; and I have also created Torah as its remedy. (*Kiddushin* 30b)

רַבִּי אוֹמֵר... הִסְתַּכֵּל בִּשְׁלֹשָׁה דְבָרִים וְאֵין אַתָּה בָא לִידֵי עֲבֵרָה, דַּע מַה לְמַעְלָה מִמָּךְ, עַיִן רוֹאָה וְאֹזֶן שׁוֹמַעַת, וְכָל מַעֲשֶׂיךָ בַּסֵּפֶר נִכְתָּבִים. (אבות ב')

Rebbi states... Focus on three things, and you will not come to the hands of sin: Know what is above you – an eye that sees, an ear that hears, and a book in which all your deeds are recorded. (*Avos* 2)

אֵין צַדִּיק בָּאָרֶץ אֲשֶׁר יַעֲשֶׂה־טּוֹב וְלֹא יֶחֱטָא. (קהלת ז' כ')

There is no righteous man on earth who does only good, and does not sin. (*Koheles* 7:20)

Caution — Avoid the Sins

Journeying down any road comes with an inherent risk — a person may trip and fall.

And so it is with our journey through life. The *yetzer hara* is constantly on the lookout to ensnare us. It places innumerable stumbling blocks and lures in the way in a never-ending attempt to make us stumble and stray from the path of Torah and mitzvos.

How, indeed, do we deal with such a cunning and persistent enemy? How do we avoid falling into the many traps it sets for us? A crucial factor, of course, is to utilize the power of Torah study. *Chazal* tell us (*Kiddushin* 30b) that Hashem declares: בְּרָאתִי יֵצֶר הָרָע וּבְרָאתִי לוֹ תּוֹרָה תַּבְלִין — *I have created the* yetzer hara; *and I have also created Torah as its remedy.*

Pirkei Avos supplies additional and specific strategies for combating the *yetzer hara* and avoiding its pitfalls in the form of a list of areas of focus to aid in this endeavor. In fact, there is more than one teaching in *Avos* featuring the same introduction: הִסְתַּכֵּל בִּשְׁלֹשָׁה דְבָרִים וְאֵין אַתָּה בָא לִידֵי עֲבֵרָה — *Focus on (the following) three things, and you will not come to the hands of sin*. This occurs at the beginning of the second *perek*, where Rebbi provides such a list, as well as here at the beginning of the third *perek* in the name of Akavya ben Mahalalel.

The two lists are not identical. In the second *perek* (2:1), Rebbi states: הִסְתַּכֵּל בִּשְׁלֹשָׁה דְבָרִים וְאֵין אַתָּה בָא לִידֵי עֲבֵרָה, דַּע מַה לְמַעְלָה מִמְּךָ, עַיִן רוֹאָה וְאֹזֶן שׁוֹמַעַת, וְכָל מַעֲשֶׂיךָ בַּסֵּפֶר נִכְתָּבִים — *Focus on three things, and you will not come to the hands of sin: Know what is above you — an eye that sees, an ear that hears, and a book in which all your deeds are recorded.* Akavya ben Mahalalel's teaching here is somewhat lengthier and includes a series of questions to contemplate — such as one's origin, his destination, etc.

Obviously, these strategies will be best employed the better we understand them. To gain clarity in these teachings, there are a number of points that warrant scrutiny:

- The most apparent factor, of course, is the difference: Rebbi and Akavya ben Mahalalel don't include the same items on their lists. What accounts for these variations, and what are the distinct messages they seek to convey?

- Another point of interest is the sequence of these mishnayos; for some reason, they don't follow chronological order. Akavya ben Mahalalel, who appears in the third *perek*, was a much earlier scholar than Rebbi, who appears in the second *perek*. Why, indeed, were the mishnayos arranged in such a way that Rebbi, who came much later, is the first to offer his advice?

- Focusing on the teaching of Akavya ben Mahalalel, the Noam Elimelech points out a most perplexing facet of this mishnah's presentation. The mishnah appears to contain much unwarranted repetition. Consider: הִסְתַּכֵּל בִּשְׁלֹשָׁה דְבָרִים וְאֵין אַתָּה בָא לִידֵי עֲבֵרָה. דַּע מֵאַיִן בָּאתָ, וּלְאָן אַתָּה הוֹלֵךְ, וְלִפְנֵי מִי אַתָּה עָתִיד לִתֵּן דִּין וְחֶשְׁבּוֹן. מֵאַיִן בָּאתָ, מִטִּפָּה סְרוּחָה, וּלְאָן אַתָּה הוֹלֵךְ, לִמְקוֹם עָפָר רִמָּה וְתוֹלֵעָה. וְלִפְנֵי מִי אַתָּה עָתִיד לִתֵּן דִּין וְחֶשְׁבּוֹן, לִפְנֵי מֶלֶךְ מַלְכֵי הַמְּלָכִים הַקָּדוֹשׁ בָּרוּךְ הוּא — *Focus on three things, and you will not come to the hands of sin. Know from where you came, to where you are going, and before Whom you are destined to give a judgment and accounting. From where you came — from a putrid drop; to where you are going — to a place of dust, worms, and maggots; and before Whom are you destined to give a judgment and accounting — before the Supreme King of kings, the Holy One, Blessed is He.*

Notice that the mishnah begins by listing three questions without, initially, supplying the answers. These are provided in the next half of the mishnah, which also reiterates each of the three questions (simultaneously answering each one: "From where you came — from a putrid drop," etc.)! Wouldn't it have been more sensible to simply delete that initial listing of the three questions? The mishnah could simply tell us to look at three things, and then list, in turn, each question with its attendant answer. As things stand, the first half of the mishnah is almost completely superfluous. What is the meaning of this arrangement?

The High Way and the Low Way

Addressing this latter issue, the Noam Elimelech explains that the mishnah is reflecting two different paths utilized by the tzaddikim in their approach to *avodas Hashem*. One way employs a contemplation of Hashem's greatness and the loftiness associated with serving Him. The other path entails a more somber outlook, in which a person reflects on his own lowly state.

Which is the proper path? The answer is that both are necessary, and this is the mishnah's intent. The reiteration of the set of questions is actually no redundancy at all but was done quite deliberately. Akavya ben Mahalalel is conveying, thereby, that there are two different ways to address these crucial questions. That is, through a focus on Hashem's exalted glory and, alternatively, through a recognition of man's inherent insignificance.

The first half of the mishnah — which presents the initial listing of the three questions — is addressing the "elevated" path. While not explicitly stating the answers, the mishnah's seemingly redundant inclusion of the questions at this point indicates that there are implied answers, different in tone from those mentioned expressly in the second half of the mishnah.

"From where do you come?" The mishnah presses a Yid to recognize his exalted origins. Do you realize from where you hail? Your pristine and elevated *neshamah* was hewn from under Hashem's very Throne of Glory! As such, it is critical to realize the inestimable value inherent within you, and how incumbent on you it is to serve Hashem in a manner that befits one of such exalted roots. "To where are you going?" Eventually, your *neshamah* will return to its high station in *Shamayim* (Heaven), back to its abode among the grandeur and holiness of the court of Hashem. As such, it behooves you to protect your soul in this lifetime from accruing even the slightest blemish, such that it may be returned, in the proper time, in its pristine state of perfection.

This is one method of setting the tenor of one's *avodas Hashem*. The other method — quite different, but also essential — is dealt with in the second half of the mishnah. Here the emphasis is on the lowly origins and makeup of man. The realization that, after all, one stems from a foul seed and is destined for an ignominious end in the grave should have the effect of striking haughtiness from one's heart. Instead, a person will feel humility and submissiveness, as he stands — a lowly being — before the Creator of the entire universe. As such, he will conclude: How could a mere mortal dare to oppose the word of the mighty and awesome Hashem?

The *Avodas Yisroel* explains the mishnah along similar lines, describing the first half of the mishnah as addressing a Yid's *neshamah*, his spiritual side, while the second half is directed towards his *guf*. The primary point of both the Noam Elimelech and the *Avodas Yisroel* is that both of these approaches — contemplation of the exalted, as well as the lowly — form a potent and essential combination that prevents a Yid from succumbing to sin.

While these are poignant interpretations of the mishnah, a central element is still left unaccounted for. The explanations above primarily addressed the first two questions concerning one's origin and destination. But what about the final question regarding the future reckoning one must provide before Hashem? Why was this repeated?

Two Paths, Two Stories

The Nesivos Sholom demonstrates that this query, as well, can be understood on the two levels: one contemplating Hashem's greatness, the other dwelling on the lowliness of man.

The first level is illustrated by the following story related by the Beis Avraham:

When Reb Pinchas of Koritz was *niftar* (passed away), his son, Reb Yaakov Shimshon, was worried and depressed. A tzaddik asked him, "Why are you so distraught? You know that your father was a great tzaddik who reached very lofty levels. Surely you needn't worry about his judgment."

The son replied, "What you say is true. But in front of Whom will he stand in judgment!"

Reb Yaakov Shimshon wasn't worried about the outcome of his father's court case. He was certain that his father would emerge with a favorable judgment and receive endless reward for his good deeds. Still in all, he was aware that the Heavenly judgment is awesome. This was the essence of his answer: "Can you imagine what it means to stand before Hashem in judgment?!" Even the greatest tzaddikim tremble at the very thought. This is the reason Reb Yaakov Shimshon was anxious. He knew that his father must be frightened at this moment; empathically, he joined him in experiencing this fear.

This is the import of the mishnah's statement: וְלִפְנֵי מִי אַתָּה עָתִיד לִתֵּן דִּין וְחֶשְׁבּוֹן — *Before Whom you are destined to give a judgment and accounting*. In this first rendition, the mishnah is delivering the following message: Don't forget that one day you will be standing before Hashem in judgment. Even if you ultimately receive a favorable judgment, the experience itself is awesome beyond words. Contemplate this moment, and you will be dissuaded from sinning.

Thus, this statement reflects the notion of contemplating the awesome greatness of Hashem, using this as a motivator to remain steadfast in righteousness. The second half of the mishnah repeats the contemplation: "Before Whom you will stand in judgment." This time, however, it is in reference to the lowliness of man, a notion which is illustrated by another story, also related by the Beis Avraham.

A certain chassid of Reb Shlomo Karliner was, unfortunately, a man of low character. Upon his *petirah*, he was brought before the Heavenly tribunal with little prospect for a favorable outcome. But the man had one request: "In my lifetime, I traveled to be in the company of my saintly Rebbe, Reb Shlomo Karliner. As such, I would like to ask that he judge my case." The unusual request was granted.

The saintly Rebbe later reported on the proceedings. "I pronounced on this Yid the following sentence: When the tzaddikim shall gather together in the Upper World, this man should be summoned before them. Before this august group, he must list all of the *aveiros* he committed in his lifetime.

"When the chassid heard this," Reb Shlomo Karliner continued, "he was resistant. He preferred any number of extremely harsh punishments, anything but this. He simply could not bear the immense shame of having to disclose all of his misdeeds in front of such elevated people. But I was adamant. I realized that this would be the most excruciating experience imaginable. Nevertheless, I understood that this was the preferable path. In this way, he would receive all of his retribution at once and be immediately cleansed of all of his sins. He would then be able to proceed to the bliss of eternal life."

This account highlights the other method of contemplation: considering man's lowly state and the great shame experienced when his unworthiness is exposed before the Heavenly Court. It is with this in mind that the mishnah reiterates a second time: וְלִפְנֵי מִי אַתָּה עָתִיד לִתֵּן דִּין וְחֶשְׁבּוֹן — *Before Whom you are destined to give a judgment and accounting*. If people are embarrassed to tell their sins in front of tzaddikim, how much greater will the shame be when doing so before the Supreme King of kings.

Everything in Order

The overall arrangement of the mishnayos, as well as the differences between them, should be apparent in light of the above. While Rebbi and Akavya ben Mahalalel were both supplying points of contemplation to deter sin, they were, in a sense, addressing different audiences in different ways.

In the second *perek*, Rebbi was fulfilling a crucial task: providing instruction to the average Yid to enable him to simply avoid transgressions. The *yetzer hara* is constantly at work in its attempts to entice us to sin. And so Rebbi supplied the bare-bones basics, the formula for all to employ in resisting the *yetzer's* temptations. The solution is clear and straightforward *emunah*. Every Yid must be cognizant that there is a judgment, and that all deeds are seen, heard, and recorded. Would that we only remember! For if we did, we would not sin.

It is for this reason as well that Rebbi's teaching was presented before that of Akavya ben Mahalalel — despite the fact that this does not accord with the chronology. Rather, the teachings were delivered in the sensible order of sophistication level. That is, Rebbi was delivering a vital and straightforward message for the average

Yid, supplying the basics to combat simple sins. Akavya's teaching is of a more subtle form, addressing even the greatest tzaddikim. Even they need encouragement and strategic thinking, as Shlomo Hamelech states (*Koheles* 7:20): אֵין צַדִּיק בָּאָרֶץ אֲשֶׁר יַעֲשֶׂה־טּוֹב וְלֹא יֶחֱטָא — *There is no tzaddik on earth who does only good, and does not sin.* Thus, Akavya implores the tzaddikim to engage in deep and meaningful contemplation — on a range of levels — to shore up their resistance to the wiles of the *yetzer*. These include a focus on both the greatness of the Creator and the pristine nature of the soul, as well as the inherent lowliness and weakness of man.

Together, these two mishnayos form a unit which speaks to every Yid — from the greatest tzaddikim to the regular person — teaching them how to remain free from sin.

In Summary

Pirkei Avos features not one, but two separate listings of points on which to focus to avoid sin. Rebbi provides a list in the second *perek*, exhorting us to recall the eye that sees, the ear that hears, and that all of our deeds are recorded. In the third *perek*, Akavya ben Mahalalel offers a list of questions for us to contemplate. Interestingly, after listing the questions, he repeats each one before supplying the answers. These are: From where do you come — a putrid drop; to where are you going — to the grave; and before Whom will you stand in judgment — before *Hakadosh Baruch Hu*.

The Noam Elimelech and the *Avodas Yisroel* provide similar explanations to account for the apparent redundancy in Akavya's teaching. In truth, there are really two sets of answers — that is, an extra set aside from the answers that are stated explicitly in the mishnah. For Akavya is really presenting two areas of focus — one is spelled out, the other is implied. The first area of focus is the "high road," so to speak. That is, a Yid derives inspiration by contemplating the greatness of Hashem and the pristine nature of his soul. Given his elevated stature and eventual return before the glory of Hashem — how could he sully himself with sin? The other method takes the opposite tack, focusing on the *guf* and man's lowliness. Both methods are necessary to shore up one's defenses against the *yetzer hara*.

The third item of contemplation — the eventual judgment before the Heavenly tribunal — can likewise be understood on these two levels. We can focus on the august greatness of the Supreme King of kings before Whom we will have to stand in judgment; even the greatest tzaddik would tremble at such a prospect. Likewise, we can contemplate the utter shame and disgrace of having sins and flaws revealed in this revered forum.

In essence, Rebbi was addressing even the simple Yid, providing the basic formula to avoid sin; that is, to gain clear awareness and strengthen our faith that all of our deeds are observed and recorded. Akavya supplied encouragement to even the greatest tzaddikim, who also need to be constantly vigilant. Together, their teachings address the breadth of Klal Yisroel — from the lowliest member to the greatest tzaddik — instructing and encouraging all of us in this most crucial endeavor: the avoidance of transgressing the will of Hashem.

פרק ג' משנה ג', ד', ה'
שנים שיושבין ויש ביניהם דברי תורה
Two Who Sit Together and There Are Words of Torah Between Them

רַבִּי חֲנִינָא בֶּן תְּרַדְיוֹן אוֹמֵר, שְׁנַיִם שֶׁיּוֹשְׁבִין וְאֵין בֵּינֵיהֶן דִּבְרֵי תוֹרָה, הֲרֵי זֶה מוֹשַׁב לֵצִים, שֶׁנֶּאֱמַר וּבְמוֹשַׁב לֵצִים לֹא יָשָׁב. אֲבָל שְׁנַיִם שֶׁיּוֹשְׁבִין וְיֵשׁ בֵּינֵיהֶם דִּבְרֵי תוֹרָה, שְׁכִינָה שְׁרוּיָה בֵינֵיהֶם, שֶׁנֶּאֱמַר אָז נִדְבְּרוּ יִרְאֵי ה' אִישׁ אֶל רֵעֵהוּ וַיַּקְשֵׁב ה' וַיִּשְׁמָע וַיִּכָּתֵב סֵפֶר זִכָּרוֹן לְפָנָיו לְיִרְאֵי ה' וּלְחֹשְׁבֵי שְׁמוֹ. אֵין לִי אֶלָּא שְׁנַיִם. מִנַּיִן שֶׁאֲפִלּוּ אֶחָד שֶׁיּוֹשֵׁב וְעוֹסֵק בַּתּוֹרָה, שֶׁהַקָּדוֹשׁ בָּרוּךְ הוּא קוֹבֵעַ לוֹ שָׂכָר, שֶׁנֶּאֱמַר יֵשֵׁב בָּדָד וְיִדֹּם כִּי נָטַל עָלָיו:

רַבִּי שִׁמְעוֹן אוֹמֵר, שְׁלֹשָׁה שֶׁאָכְלוּ עַל שֻׁלְחָן אֶחָד וְלֹא אָמְרוּ עָלָיו דִּבְרֵי תוֹרָה, כְּאִלּוּ אָכְלוּ מִזִּבְחֵי מֵתִים, שֶׁנֶּאֱמַר כִּי כָּל שֻׁלְחָנוֹת מָלְאוּ קִיא צֹאָה בְּלִי מָקוֹם. אֲבָל שְׁלֹשָׁה שֶׁאָכְלוּ עַל שֻׁלְחָן אֶחָד וְאָמְרוּ עָלָיו דִּבְרֵי תוֹרָה, כְּאִלּוּ אָכְלוּ מִשֻּׁלְחָנוֹ שֶׁל מָקוֹם בָּרוּךְ הוּא, שֶׁנֶּאֱמַר וַיְדַבֵּר אֵלַי זֶה הַשֻּׁלְחָן אֲשֶׁר לִפְנֵי ה':

רַבִּי חֲנִינָא בֶּן חֲכִינַאי אוֹמֵר, הַנֵּעוֹר בַּלַּיְלָה וְהַמְהַלֵּךְ בַּדֶּרֶךְ יְחִידִי וְהַמְפַנֶּה לִבּוֹ לְבַטָּלָה, הֲרֵי זֶה מִתְחַיֵּב בְּנַפְשׁוֹ:

Rabbi Chanina ben Teradyon says: Two people who sit together and there are no words of Torah between them, it is a sitting of scoffers; as it says (*Tehillim* 1:1): "In a sitting of scoffers he did not sit." But two people who sit together and there are words of Torah between them, the Divine Presence rests among them; as it says (*Malachi* 3:16): "Then those who fear Hashem spoke one to another, and Hashem listened and heard, and a book of remembrance was written before Him, for those who fear Hashem and consider His Name. (So far,) I only know this as applying to two (who sit together); from where (do we learn) that if even a single individual sits (alone) to engage in Torah study, Hashem sets aside reward for him? For it states (*Eichah* 3:28): "Let him sit alone, and be silent; for he has taken for it."

Rabbi Shimon says: Three people who ate at one table and didn't speak over it words of Torah, it is as if they ate of sacrifices to the dead; as it states (*Yeshayah* 28:8): "For all tables are filled with vomitus filth, lacking the Omnipresent One." But three people who ate at one table and spoke over it words of Torah, it is as if they ate from Hashem's table; as it states (*Yechezkel* 41:22): "And he spoke to me, 'This is the table that is before Hashem.'"

Rabbi Chanina ben Chachinai says: One who is awake at night – or walks alone on the road – and thinks empty thoughts, is liable for his life.

שנים שיושבין ויש ביניהם דברי תורה

SOURCES:

שֶׁהַכֹּל בָּרָא לִכְבוֹדוֹ. (שבע ברכות)

All He created for His glory. (*Sheva Brachos*)

קְדֹשִׁים תִּהְיוּ כִּי קָדוֹשׁ אֲנִי ה' אֱלֹקֵיכֶם. (ויקרא י״ט ב׳)

You shall be holy, for I, Hashem your G-d, am holy. (*Vayikra* 19:2)

וְאַתֶּם תִּהְיוּ־לִי מַמְלֶכֶת כֹּהֲנִים וְגוֹי קָדוֹשׁ. (שמות י״ט ו׳)

And you shall be for Me a kingdom of priests and a holy nation. (*Shemos* 19:6)

מִנְחָה הִוא שְׁלוּחָה לַאדֹנִי לְעֵשָׂו. (בראשית ל״ב י״ט)

It is an offering sent to my master, Eisav. (*Bereishis* 32:19)

אִישׁ וְאִשָּׁה, זָכוּ – שְׁכִינָה בֵּינֵיהֶן, לֹא זָכוּ – אֵשׁ אוֹכַלְתָּן. (סוטה י״ז.)

A husband and wife: If they are meritorious – the Divine Presence rests among them; if they are not meritorious – they are consumed by fire. (*Sotah* 17a)

Turn on the Lights

Life entails a series of choices; a set of options presents itself before an individual, and he must select one of the offerings. It could be as inconsequential a matter as deciding what to order in a restaurant or as weighty as choosing a spouse.

More often than not, the options are measured. For example, if one is outside and it starts to rain, the options are to remain outside and get wet or come inside and avoid getting wet. The second option may not be earth-shattering but seems pretty logical. Perhaps a certain business venture presents itself. If he invests, he stands to earn substantial profits; if he doesn't, he won't. Much less common is a scenario where the two options are in stark opposition, where if option "A" is chosen, the consequences will be magnificent, while option "B" will result in horrific circumstances.

Yet that is exactly what this series of mishnayos seems to offer. A glorious picture is painted of those who come together and speak words of Torah. Neglecting to do so, however, turns their gathering into a most deplorable event.

This concept is difficult to understand. What did these people do? Notice that the mishnah did not state that they came together to discuss anything so terrible; it doesn't mention that they spoke evil gossip or other forbidden topics. Perhaps it was even a quiet affair, where no one said a word! Nevertheless, the very fact that they didn't share Torah thoughts transforms the get-together into a "sitting of scoffers" or a feasting on idolatrous sacrifices to the dead! On the other hand, if they did exchange words of Torah, their meeting resembles the *avodah* in the Beis Hamikdash! Such seemingly extreme differences for what appears to be so relatively benign. What could it all mean?

Perhaps the underlying issue is the *aveirah* of *bitul Torah* (neglect of Torah study). To be sure, *Chazal* do refer to this as an extraordinarily severe transgression, warning strongly against even a moment of *bitul Torah*. But, as grievous as it is, this does not seem to be the focus of these mishnayos. If it were, the mishnah would have been structured quite differently, dealing with the issue head-on. It would have opened by explicitly mentioning the weighty obligation to study Torah at every moment, as well as the grave sin of remaining idle from this great endeavor. Only then would it have proceeded to elaborate on the merits and demerits of the various types of gatherings.

And so, it does not appear that the main thrust of the mishnah is to address the specific prohibition of *bitul Torah*. The basic question remains, then: What *is* the underlying message of these mishnayos? What accounts for these drastic extremes, and why are seemingly innocuous events being referred to in the harshest of terms?

The answer to the above, the Nesivos Sholom explains, touches on the very fabric of the purpose of the universe and what our role is within it.

To Make It Holy

In fact, the purpose and function of the *beri'ah* is summed up succinctly in one of the blessings we recite in celebration of a marriage. The first blessing of *sheva brachos* concludes: *Shehakol bara lichvodo* — "All He created for His glory." For this is the aim of the *beri'ah*: to bring glory to *Hakadosh Baruch Hu*. And it is primarily the responsibility of the Jewish people to ensure that this goal is achieved. As such, the prime task of every Yid is to elevate the elements of creation by dedicating their usage towards fulfillment of His will.

This idea is inherent in the oft-repeated exhortation, *Kedoshim tiheyu* — "You shall be holy" (*Vayikra* 19:2). In order to glorify the Name of Hashem, a Jew's mission is to sanctify his deeds and subjugate his utilization of the world's pleasures to His will.

This notion brings us a step closer to gaining clarity in the mishnayos above. As stated, it does not seem that the particular focus of these mishnayos is the specific transgression of *bitul Torah*. However, aside from the all-important aspect of the particular obligation of Torah study, there is an additional component. In the lead-up to Hashem's presentation of the Torah to Bnei Yisroel on

GEMS FROM THE *SEFER NESIVOS SHOLOM*

Har Sinai, He delivered a statement by way of introduction. Hashem instructed: וְאַתֶּם תִּהְיוּ־לִי מַמְלֶכֶת כֹּהֲנִים וְגוֹי קָדוֹשׁ — *And you shall be for Me a kingdom of priests and a holy nation* (*Shemos* 19:6). Thus, aside from the actual study of Torah, there is the element of the aim and end-purpose of Torah: to elevate a Jew to an entity of sanctity, worthy for the *Shechinah* to rest upon.

This, then, is the focus of the mishnayos. *Bitul Torah* is a severe transgression indeed, but this is not the subject of this particular discussion. Rather, these teachings revolve around the concept of the power of Torah's holiness, the *kedushas haTorah*. For this is the life-mission of a Yid and the purpose of creation: to provide for Hashem's glory through sanctifying ourselves and our usage of Hashem's world, and to thereby make ourselves into vessels capable of containing the *Shechinah*. As the mishnah states: שְׁנַיִם שֶׁיּוֹשְׁבִין וְיֵשׁ בֵּינֵיהֶם דִּבְרֵי תוֹרָה, שְׁכִינָה שְׁרוּיָה בֵּינֵיהֶם — *Two who sit and words of Torah are exchanged between them, the Shechinah rests among them.*

We can also begin to appreciate the heightened severity with which *Chazal* view someone who neglects to fulfill the mishnah's dictum. What were they doing? we wonder. The individuals featured in the mishnah did not necessarily engage in forbidden speech; they just didn't speak words of Torah. But now we see that they weren't merely refraining from doing a "nice thing." The very purpose of creation, the goal of *Yiddishkeit*, is at stake here. Two people sat together to enjoy each other's company — a natural, normal thing in the course of everyday life. But it is also an opportunity to consign this simple worldly pleasure towards the effort of glorifying His Name; the event can be elevated and sanctified by introducing words of Torah. By neglecting to do so, they essentially spurned the importance of this endeavor, constituting an affront to the *kedushas haTorah*.

It is for this reason, as well, that this get-together is considered a *moshav leitzim*, a gathering of scoffers. What is scorn, after all, if not the denial and degradation of some inherent value? The *Chassid Ya'avetz* provides an illustrative example: An extremely wealthy and generous person decided to bestow a remarkable gift upon someone. He leads this individual into the treasure house, which is overflowing with gold pieces. "Start counting gold pieces," the rich man instructs. "Whatever you are able to count within the span of one hour is yours to keep." Then imagine that the recipient of this largesse turns around and, for the duration of this hour, sits idle, twiddling his thumbs! This is not just a squandering of a "golden" opportunity; it is a stark statement of ingratitude and scorn. The intended recipient has basically communicated to the generous giver that his gift holds no value in his eyes; he has taken something inherently wonderful and demonstrated that, to him, it is meaningless. And so, if someone is aware of the astronomical reward granted for Torah study and of the great import of sanctifying his everyday affairs and nevertheless rejects the opportunity — this is nothing less than an act of disgracing the *kedushas haTorah*; the greatest form of scorn imaginable.

Thus it is that the missed opportunities represented in these mishnayos are in fact indicative of one's contempt for sanctity. Three people come together to partake of a meal. Once again, an instance of enjoying the pleasures of This World, and once again, an opportunity to dedicate these worldly pleasures to the honor of His Name, to elevate the event by infusing the occasion with Torah thoughts. Once again, a failure to do so can be attributed to little else than an attitude that the endeavor, in their eyes, is simply not worthwhile. And this is a grave affront to that which is inherently priceless and critically important in the eyes of Hashem. These individuals took an act that could have been as holy as partaking of sacrificial meat and turned it, instead, into a debased encounter, tantamount to some sordid ceremony of idolatrous content.

The final mishnah can likewise be viewed in this light. הַנֵּעוֹר בַּלַּיְלָה וְהַמְהַלֵּךְ בַּדֶּרֶךְ יְחִידִי וְהַמְפַנֶּה לִבּוֹ לְבַטָּלָה, הֲרֵי זֶה מִתְחַיֵּב בְּנַפְשׁוֹ — *One who stays awake at night or traverses the roads alone, and turns his heart to idle thoughts, he thereby is liable for his life.* Why does the mishnah speak specifically of someone dwelling on idle thoughts during the nighttime? Is that any more egregious than doing so during daylight hours? Actually, to a certain extent, the offense is indeed compounded at that time. Night is a time more prone to danger; certain evil spiritual forces have dominion then. Therefore, a person is in need of added protection, which would be provided to him through accessing the power of *kedushas haTorah*. Thus, if he would sanctify his thoughts at this time of peril by contemplating Torah topics, he would be elevated, as well as protected. Once again, his resistance to do so is indicative of a scornful attitude, one in which he does not perceive the holiness and value of the Torah. Traveling alone is likewise fraught with danger. His neglecting to avail himself of the power of *kedushas haTorah* at this time is an affront of the highest order, as he spurns an opportunity of inestimable value, denying thereby the august status and potency of Torah's sanctity.

We have discovered, then, that these essentially are the only two options, and the distance between them is extreme, indeed. We have the opportunity to fulfill the purpose of creation and our primary mission as Jews, to sanctify and elevate our everyday occurrences and dedicate them to the Almighty, by introducing *kedushas haTorah* into our life. If we recognize the value of this endeavor, we will certainly attach ourselves to Torah at every available opportunity. But a person who withholds from this endeavor demonstrates that it holds no importance in his eyes. And this is nothing less than an utter disgrace to the Torah and to Hashem. Instead of glorifying His Name in the world, this individual grants Him nothing but scorn.

Default and Transformation

There is another dimension to the "extreme positions" delineated in these mishnayos. Indeed, it is noteworthy how their message is conveyed. One may have assumed that by exchanging words of Torah in a gathering, for example, one elevates the occasion thereby, but if one neglects to do so, the event simply remains plain and mundane. But the mishnayos state emphatically that this is not the case; if not elevated through *divrei Torah* (words of Torah), the event is nothing less than scornful or idolatrous.

To help clarify the issue, the Nesivos Sholom provides some insight concerning the workings of the universe. *Hakadosh Baruch Hu*, in His infinite wisdom and with great purpose, set up the *beri'ah* to function in a specific way. That is, He fashioned This World as a realm for materialism, of dark forces and latent urges and desires. In this way He challenges us and tasks us, for our benefit, with bettering ourselves and bettering the world. And, of course, He provides us with all of the necessary tools to fulfill this crucial mission.

Thus it is that the "default" of This World is a status quo of inherent impurity. That doesn't mean that it is a thoroughly evil place. On the contrary, Hashem likewise infused within the *beri'ah* components of inherent goodness, and it is the mission of a Yid to access the goodness and transform the world into a place of goodness.

This eye-opening notion informs many of the practices listed in the Torah. We find numerous mitzvos that seem to share a common thread; many of these have to do with "firsts." That is, a Yid is enjoined to designate the initial offerings of a given endeavor to the service of Hashem. When his crops grow, he brings the first fruits, in the form of *bikkurim*, to the Beis Hamikdash; one's *bechor*, first-born son, is sanctified, and needs be redeemed; *reishis hagez* comprises the first portion of the wool from his shearing that is granted to the *kohen* (priest); and so on. All of these practices demonstrate the way in which a Yid confronts the features and pleasures of This World. Within each aspect — food, sustenance, children, resources, etc. — he hones in on the inherent goodness and presents an offering to Hashem, thereby elevating these very elements, and transforming the material and the mundane into a manifestation of holiness.

But, of course, this transformation only takes place through the active initiative of a Yid. Were he to neglect to take such actions, all of the elements of This World would remain within their former status, one of materialistic impurity. A dark, windowless room is just that — dark. One can turn on a lamp or light a candle, bathing the room in a luminous glow. In the absence of any such initiative, however, the room remains as is — dark and gloomy. This is not a punishment; it's just simple and stark reality. If one wishes to dispel the darkness and impurity, it is necessary to employ the light of mitzvos and the torch of Torah.

This is the message of these mishnayos. Of course, these teachings are not employing some random and extreme imagery, speaking of harsh punishments for seemingly innocuous events. It is simply reflecting the reality and the status quo. The aspects of This World are of an inherently low nature, suffused with impurity. But the opportunity is there, through the power of sanctity of Torah, to elevate and transform it, spreading much light. By infusing our lives and encounters with Torah, we introduce the *Shechinah* to our environs and transform our meals into Temple service. But if we leave the "lights" off, the world remains in the dark. It reverts to its default status of inherent impurity.

The options presented by the mishnayos may seem to lie between two extremes, but that is because, in truth, those are the only options. When Yaakov Avinu was preparing to meet his arch-rival, his brother Eisav, he sent forth gifts in an attempt to appease him. His agents were instructed to deliver this message to his brother when presenting the gifts: מִנְחָה הִוא שְׁלוּחָה לַאדֹנִי לְעֵשָׂו — *It is an offering sent to my master, Eisav* (*Bereishis* 32:19). The Beis Avraham *ztz"l* renders these last two words homiletically, reflecting the idea at the crux of our discussion: "To my L-rd" — referring to Hashem; "to Eisav" — representing the forces of evil. All of our deeds and actions fall into one of these categories. A particular act or mode of conduct will present a "gift" either to Hashem or to the *Sitra Achra*. There are no neutral options, and it behooves us, of course, to make the right choice.

This is why we find, for example, a similar range expressed in relation to the dealings between husband and wife. *Chazal* point out an interesting linguistic anomaly that has far-reaching ramifications. The words for man and woman — אִישׁ and אִשָּׁה — are linguistically alike, both containing the letters *aleph* and *shin*; the only difference is that "man" also has a *yud* and "woman" has a *heh*. Together, these two letters comprise one of the Names of Hashem (*yud-heh*). If these letters were to be deleted, what remains is merely the *aleph* and *shin* — *eish*. Commenting on this phenomenon, the Gemara states (*Sotah* 17a), אִישׁ וְאִשָּׁה, זָכוּ – שְׁכִינָה בֵּינֵיהֶן, לֹא זָכוּ – אֵשׁ אוֹכַלְתָּן — *A husband and wife: If they are meritorious, the* Shechinah *rests between them* (as evidenced by the appearance of Hashem's Name among their "letters"); *if they are not meritorious, they are consumed by fire* (*eish*, as only the *aleph* and *shin* remain when the *yud-heh* of the *Shechinah* departs).

Once again, we seem to be faced with this dichotomy. There is no outright mention here of the perpetration of any egregious deeds; *Chazal* speak generally only of a difference between having "merit" or not. The Nesivos Sholom explains, however, in light of the above. Through his conduct, a Yid supplies "gifts" either to Hashem, or, Heaven forbid, to "Eisav," the *Sitra Achra*. To whom these gifts are sent depends on the individual's approach to his mission in life and his utilization of Hashem's world. Is he trying to sanctify it and bring glory to His Name? Is he designating and dedicating his enjoyment of worldly matters to His service? If so, he is "meritorious"; the "gift" goes to Hashem, the Yid and his world are elevated, and the *Shechinah* can dwell among them. If his actions are directed primarily at satisfying his own selfish desires, his "gift" has nowhere else to go; there is no neutrality — it is presented to Eisav. When there is no *Shechinah*, the default is *eish ochalason* (consumption by fire).

In Summary

In this series of three mishnayos, we have what appears to be a dramatic swing between two extreme outcomes. If two sit together and exchange words of Torah, their meeting serves as a resting place for the *Shechinah*. If they omit *divrei Torah*, they are considered as a sitting of scoffers. Jews eat together; if they include Torah, they are eating sacrificial offerings. If not, they are partaking in some morbid and idolatrous ceremony. And someone awake at night or walking on the way who engages in idle musings incurs the death penalty. How can we account for such dramatic shifts and seemingly harsh characterizations for what doesn't appear, on the surface at least, to constitute any egregious activity?

According to the Nesivos Sholom, the matter can be understood in two slightly different ways. While it is true that the companions mentioned above may actually be silent and not engaging in forbidden speech, their conduct nevertheless has severe consequences. This becomes evident the more clarity one has about the purpose of creation and the role of a Yid in This World. The purpose is to glorify the Name of Hashem by sanctifying all aspects of This World. This entails dedicating our enjoyments of This World in fulfillment of His will.

This is what these mishnayos represent — opportunities to utilize these worldly pleasures in a sanctified manner. People enjoy camaraderie, partaking of food, etc. By introducing words of Torah to these occasions, we demonstrate our acknowledgment of the power of *kedushas haTorah* to elevate our world and bring honor to His Name. As a result, the simple acts of enjoying company or having a meal become lofty experiences in *avodas Hashem*, enabling the *Shechinah* to dwell with us. But one who neglects to adopt this approach is not simply refraining from a laudable action; he is spurning this wondrous and transformative opportunity, thereby revealing his disdain for *kedushas haTorah*. As such, his conduct is egregious indeed, filled with scorn for inherent sanctity. This constitutes a despicable act, an affront and scoffing of the highest order.

These teachings can also be understood as reflecting reality. The harsh descriptions mentioned are not necessarily punitive in nature, but an accurate description of the status quo. This World was fashioned purposefully to serve as the realm of lowliness and desires; as such, it is inherently an impure environment. But Hashem gave *Yidden* the ability and the mission to transform this situation, to focus on the positive and pristine aspects of creation and thereby elevate the world. Mitzvos such as *bikkurim* and *bechoros* reflect this idea, as a Yid approaches his material bounty by first dedicating a portion of these worldly enjoyments to Hashem. Just as we can light up a dark room with a candle or a lamp, so, too, the darkness of This World can be dispelled by employing the power of Torah and mitzvos. But this only holds true, of course, insofar as we actually utilize this power. If we do not "turn on the lights," the world will remain a place of darkness and impurity, a *moshav leitzim*.

Especially as we approach the festival of Shavuos and prepare ourselves for *Kabbalas HaTorah*, the message of these mishnayos takes on added urgency. Now is a most appropriate time to internalize the sentiments expressed above, to ensure that we properly value the *kedushas haTorah* and utilize it to illuminate and elevate ourselves and the world around us.

פרק ג' משנה ו'
כל המקבל עליו עול תורה
Whoever Accepts the Yoke of Torah upon Himself

רַבִּי נְחוּנְיָא בֶּן הַקָּנָה אוֹמֵר, כָּל הַמְקַבֵּל עָלָיו עוֹל תּוֹרָה, מַעֲבִירִין מִמֶּנּוּ עוֹל מַלְכוּת וְעוֹל דֶּרֶךְ אֶרֶץ. וְכָל הַפּוֹרֵק מִמֶּנּוּ עוֹל תּוֹרָה, נוֹתְנִין עָלָיו עוֹל מַלְכוּת וְעוֹל דֶּרֶךְ אֶרֶץ:

Rabbi Nechunia ben Hakanah says: Whoever accepts the yoke of Torah upon himself is relieved of the yoke of government and worldly matters. Whoever throws off the yoke of Torah from himself, is burdened with the yoke of government and worldly matters.

SOURCES:

אֵין לְךָ בֶּן חוֹרִין אֶלָּא מִי שֶׁעוֹסֵק בַּתּוֹרָה. (אבות ו׳)

The only one considered truly free is someone who involves himself with Torah. (*Avos* 6)

כָּל בְּנֵי אָדָם עַבְדֵי תַּאֲוֹת הָעוֹלָם. (אבן עזרא, במדבר ו׳ ז׳)

The entirety of humankind are slaves to worldly desires. (*Ibn Ezra, Bamidbar* 6:7)

דּוֹרוֹת הָרִאשׁוֹנִים עָשׂוּ תּוֹרָתָן קֶבַע וּמְלַאכְתָּן עֲרַאי... דּוֹרוֹת הָאַחֲרוֹנִים עָשׂוּ מְלַאכְתָּן קֶבַע וְתוֹרָתָן עֲרַאי. (ברכות ל״ה:)

The earlier generations established Torah as the primary factor (in their lives), relegating their occupation as secondary... The latter generations established their occupations as primary, while their (dedication to) Torah was secondary. (*Berachos* 35b)

בָּא לִטַּמֵּא - פּוֹתְחִין לוֹ, בָּא לִטַּהֵר - מְסַיְּעִים אוֹתוֹ. (שבת ק״ד.)

One who comes to defile himself – (the way) will be opened for him (to do so). One who comes to purify himself – will receive (Divine) assistance. (*Shabbos* 104a)

אוֹ־הוֹדַע אֵלָיו חַטָּאתוֹ. (ויקרא ד׳ כ״ג)

Or his sin be made known to him. (*Vayikra* 4:23)

אוֹרַיְיתָא קָא מוֹדְעָא לֵיהּ חוֹבֵיהּ. (זוהר)

It is the Torah that makes known to him his sin. (*Zohar*)

אֵיזֶהוּ עָשִׁיר הַשָּׂמֵחַ בְּחֶלְקוֹ. (אבות ד׳)

Who is wealthy? One who is happy with his portion. (*Avos* 4)

Escape from Slavery

Freedom. A beautiful word, a lofty concept, the dream of humanity. The stark reality, however, is that hardly anyone attains it.

What is freedom? A common mistake is to equate the notion of freedom with a loosening and abandonment of any and all restrictions. A person may be at liberty to partake of a certain harmful and addictive substance. Is that freedom? Now he is imprisoned within his own deleterious urges. In a sense, one may argue, he is free to destroy his life. But is this the freedom to which mankind aspires?

Chazal enlighten us on the subject, teaching us a truth that may initially seem somewhat difficult to assimilate. אֵין לְךָ בֶּן חוֹרִין אֶלָּא מִי שֶׁעוֹסֵק בַּתּוֹרָה — *The only one considered truly free is someone who involves himself with Torah* (*Avos* 6:2). Conventional wisdom would balk at this idea: A restrictive lifestyle of scholarly pursuits is *freedom*? Yet, as we shall see, those who scoff at the notion are themselves enslaved, in more ways than one. The teaching of Rabbi Nechunia ben Hakanah demonstrates the inherent falsity of the "conventional wisdom." Yes, in truth, what may appear to many as freedom and indulgence in pleasure is in effect a form of slavery and drudgery, while subjugation to Torah is what provides one with true freedom and happiness.

A Matter of Substitution

The universe is an orderly affair, conducted on the basis of a number of systems. The Maharal delineates three ways in which Hashem has arranged the operation of the world. These three ways actually fall into one of two categories.

Hanhagas derech eretz, the "worldly matters system," is the first of these entities. It covers those efforts in which man must engage to obtain his sustenance, and usually entails strain and toil. Thus, he must work the land by the sweat of his brow or otherwise make strenuous attempts to earn his bread. *Hanhagas ol malchus*, the next system, refers to the implementation of governmental systems. These are necessary to ensure a safe and functioning society, but its maintenance likewise entails a significant toll on the individual in the form of taxes and other obligations. As is well known, these two forms of *hanhagos* encompass basically every living person. They are, in many respects, "necessary evils," and there is little one can do to avoid them.

But there is a third measure established by Hashem through which the world may be governed, and this system falls into a category all of its own. As opposed to the first two forms of *hanhagah*, this one is not necessarily bound by natural dictates. This is the *hanhagah* of Torah, an operation that takes place on another plane entirely.

As the Maharal explains, these "systems" are all reflected in the teaching of Rabbi Nechunia ben Hakanah, where he reveals that they function in a mutually exclusive fashion. As part of the natural world, a person will be subsumed under the "yoke" of *derech eretz* and *malchus*, but there actually is a path to freedom. כָּל הַמְקַבֵּל עָלָיו עֹל תּוֹרָה, מַעֲבִירִין מִמֶּנּוּ עֹל מַלְכוּת וְעֹל דֶּרֶךְ אֶרֶץ — *Whoever accepts the yoke of Torah upon himself is relieved of the yoke of government and worldly matters.* What exactly "accepting the yoke of Torah" entails is a subject we will return to later, G-d willing. But one prudent enough to do so will have his affairs taken care of through a system that works beyond the natural scheme of things. One who neglects to do so will remain subservient to the other, rigorous systems: וְכָל הַפּוֹרֵק מִמֶּנּוּ עֹל תּוֹרָה, נוֹתְנִין עָלָיו עֹל מַלְכוּת וְעֹל דֶּרֶךְ אֶרֶץ — *Whoever casts off the yoke of Torah from himself, will be burdened with the yoke of government and worldly matters.*

The Maharal explains further that the *ol Torah* (yoke of Torah) method does not necessarily involve miraculous means; it is merely that one who adopts this path will have a much simpler time fulfilling his needs. This sentiment is expressed by Rabbi Shimon ben Elazar at the end of *Kiddushin* (82a). He makes the observation that the birds and animals of the field are not trained professionals. They possess no especially complex, lucrative skills, but are nevertheless able to obtain their sustenance with relative ease. Now, their function in This World is to serve man, and man's function is to serve the Creator. If creatures of inferior status are able to "make a living" without undue toil, certainly their human superiors should be able to do the same. Why, then, does the bulk of humankind have to endure so much and still barely "get by"? This is simply a result of their having committed misdeeds.

Apparently, notes the Maharal, it is inherent in the *beri'ah* that man, like the animals, should be able to subsist without much effort — had he not gone astray. And so, in a sense, the *ol Torah* system is actually the pristine and natural system, reflecting the way things really ought to be. One who properly adheres to this path, while still having to make some efforts to acquire sustenance, will find that the results will come with relative ease. Subjugating himself to the Heavenly yoke, the worldly one will all but disappear.

The above represents the "simple" understanding of the concepts dealt with by the mishnah. The ideas are relatively straightforward, and at the same time quite powerful. Yet, Rabbi Nechunia's teaching can be understood on a number of different levels. In fact, as the Nesivos Sholom proceeds to demonstrate, the "worldly matters" under discussion are not necessarily limited to the material realm.

The Yoke of the *Yetzer Hara*

Not only does a firm acceptance of the *ol Torah* free us from struggles regarding our physical needs, but it can even liberate us from the attempts of the *yetzer hara* to impede our spiritual growth.

The *Toras Avos* interprets the mishnah in this light. There are any number of ways and areas in which the *yetzer hara* seeks to distract and dissuade us from the right path. One key aspect is in that of *emunah*. While we should have clear and firm belief in Hashem's dominion, the *Malchus Shamayim* (Heavenly Kingdom), the *yetzer hara* seeks to muddle our mind and cloud our vision. It tries to sow doubts and thus weaken our *emunah*. But by accepting upon ourselves the yoke of Torah, aiming to attach ourselves to Hashem through His Torah, we attain clarity in this arena. Our thoughts are purified and our belief strengthened. We are relieved of the *ol malchus*, that is, the burden of doubts in matters of belief in the *Malchus Shamayim* that the *yetzer hara* seeks to impose.

Likewise, we may be relieved of the yoke of *derech eretz*, a phrase *Chazal* often employ as a benign way of referring to matters of *ta'avah* (desire). The Ibn Ezra (*Bamidbar* 6:7) declares somewhat starkly: כֹּל בְּנֵי אָדָם עַבְדֵי תַּאֲוֹת הָעוֹלָם — *The entirety of humankind are slaves to worldly desires*. Yet by accepting the *ol Torah*, we become spiritually fortified, able to overcome the passions fueled by the *yetzer hara*.

The key in this endeavor is that the *kabbalah* (acceptance) be comprehensive and all-pervading. We must accept the yoke of Torah on all aspects of ourselves, subjugating every facet of our being to the Torah. We must make our mind subservient to Torah: in the areas of *hashkafos* (outlook) and *emunah*, and decisions of conduct — all must be aligned to comply with the will of Hashem as expressed in the Torah. We must accept the Torah upon our heart; that is, our emotions and passions must likewise be subsumed under the dominion of Torah. And we must accept the yoke of Torah upon our limbs — our eyes, hands, all parts of us — that they should all act in accordance with the Torah. And in so doing, Hashem will reciprocate in kind. The Torah is an entity that exists above and beyond the plane of the natural world. By striving to conform to this great ideal, Hashem will remove from us the pressures and facets of the natural world that prevent our upward climb.

Simple Mathematics

The Beis Avraham *ztz"l* provides further insight into the mechanics of this phenomenon, explaining how it is that accepting the *ol Torah* will result in relief from the *ol malchus* and the *ol derech eretz*. Based on his explanation, in fact, it appears to be quite a logical affair.

The notion is based on the fact that included in Hashem's decree governing human affairs is an apportionment of pleasant and difficult experiences. In other words, for every person, Hashem sets the amount of both suffering and enjoyment that individual will undergo. By and large, however, He leaves it up to each individual to decide how to "spend" one's pleasure and pain dividends.

As such, a person really has a choice to set himself up in a very comfortable and happy situation — if he chooses wisely. No one said

כל המקבל עליו עול תורה

that *avodas Hashem* is supposed to come easily. Battling and resisting the *yetzer hara*, rectifying one's character, toiling in Torah — these can be quite strenuous endeavors! But if one dedicates his efforts to these lofty causes, having to undergo struggles of a pristine nature, he has made a tremendous investment. For in so doing, a person can virtually use up his "share" of suffering on these worthwhile pursuits. He thereby serves Hashem, fulfills His will, and, at the same time, empties his account of pain and difficulty. Thus he will be left with nothing but pleasantness and ease, to further bulwark his service of Hashem.

The converse, of course, is true as well. Consider a person who dedicates himself to pursuing pleasure; as the Ibn Ezra put it, being a slave to his passions. He thereby empties out his "enjoyment account" on frivolity and is left, in the end, with nothing but a huge store of suffering yet to come.

This is the equation that our mishnah delineates. Dedicating oneself to Torah is not necessarily a simple matter; as stated, it transcends the bounds of nature, and one must likewise lift himself above his nature to properly accept the *ol Torah*. But the difficult struggle is ultimately so beneficial. By expending one's "difficulty account" on this endeavor, he will thus be spared from other forms of suffering. מַעֲבִירִין מִמֶּנּוּ עֹל מַלְכוּת וְעֹל דֶּרֶךְ אֶרֶץ. Relieved from these pressures, he will be left to serve Hashem from a position of ease and grandeur. But one who rejects this path, choosing instead to expend his entire measure of enjoyment on worldly pleasures, will have a large tab to settle to account for the suffering. As such, he will be burdened with the *ol malchus* and the *ol derech eretz*.

In an ironic twist, what emerges is exactly the opposite of the common perception. Those who dedicate themselves to Torah do not have to suffer through life, eyeing the rest of the population who are "living it up." On the contrary, even in This World, those who accept the *ol Torah* are afforded the ability to enjoy life, while their counterparts are left to face difficulty and struggle. The Rebbe of Kobrin *ztz"l* summed up this state of affairs: "It is such a bright and sweet world — for those who do not involve themselves in it. For those who do, it is a dark and bitter place."

The Letter and the Spirit

The Nesivos Sholom uncovers yet a whole other dimension to this mishnah. Careful examination reveals, he notes, that Rabbi Nechunia does not necessarily speak here of someone who violates the Torah. Rather than portraying the difference between one who "observes" the Torah and one who does not, the mishnah mentions only that one "accepts the *ol Torah*" while the other neglects to do so. This intimates more of a distinction between levels of dedication; but both individuals featured in our mishnah do, in fact, observe the commandments of the Torah.

So what, exactly, is the difference between them? What does the *madreigah* of accepting the *ol Torah* entail? The notion can be illustrated on the basis of an idea that appears in the *sefarim hakedoshim*. They portray a scenario in which a certain Yid is careful to keep all of the commandments throughout his life. Upon his passing, he ascends before the Heavenly tribunal, who comment to him, "We see that you have observed all of the commandments of the Torah; well and good. But why have you not conducted yourself in accordance with the *ruach* of the Torah?"

This, explains the Nesivos Sholom, is the difference between simply adhering to the Torah and subjugating oneself to the *ol Torah*. That is, in addition to the basic *madreigah* of keeping the laws of the Torah themselves, there is also the matter of the higher purpose of the Torah. Where this added dimension manifests itself is in those areas for which there may not be a specific, explicit commandment, matters where, according to the letter of the law, one may have discharged his duty. But the *ruach haTorah* demands additional effort. A complete acceptance of the *ol Torah* entails a firm commitment to ensure that all of one's deeds, conduct, and qualities will conform even to the spirit of the Torah, as befitting a member of the מַמְלֶכֶת כֹּהֲנִים וְגוֹי קָדוֹשׁ — *kingdom of priests and holy nation* (*Shemos* 19:6).

Another stark manifestation of this difference occurs in the area of priority. *Chazal* compared the loftier status of the earlier generations to the lower status of the later ones in these terms: דורות הָרִאשׁוֹנִים עָשׂוּ — תּוֹרָתָן קֶבַע וּמְלַאכְתָּן עֲרָאִי... דּוֹרוֹת הָאַחֲרוֹנִים עָשׂוּ מְלַאכְתָּן קֶבַע וְתוֹרָתָן עֲרָאִי *The earlier generations established Torah as the primary factor (in their lives), relegating their occupation as secondary... The latter generations established their occupations as primary, while their (dedication to) Torah was secondary* (*Berachos* 35b). This difference is a function of an adherence to the *ruach haTorah*. Those who are concerned that all aspects of their conduct and character conform even to the spirit of the Torah, make Torah the centerpiece of their lives. But those who just get by with the barest minimum, concerned chiefly with only the letter of the Law, and nothing more — such people will inevitably grant highest priority to their worldly affairs. For them, Torah will have to yield center stage to their material pursuits.

And so our mishnah informs us that both groups will end up having their wishes fulfilled (though not everybody will merit that this happen in the manner they envisioned). *Chazal* tell us: בָּא לִיטַמֵּא – פּוֹתְחִין לוֹ, בָּא לִיטַהֵר – מְסַיְּעִים אוֹתוֹ — *One who comes to defile himself, (the way) will be opened for him (to do so). One who comes to purify himself will receive (Divine) assistance* (*Shabbos* 104a). This is an eye-opening concept, revealing that Heaven will enable the individual to succeed on the path he has chosen — for good, or otherwise. And we see this outlined in our mishnah. A person who accepts upon himself the *ol Torah*, seeking to adhere to the *ruach haTorah* and making the Torah his top priority — the Torah will in fact become the mainstay of his life. All other worldly distractions will fade into the distance; as the mishnah states: כָּל הַמְקַבֵּל עָלָיו עֹל תּוֹרָה, מַעֲבִירִין מִמֶּנּוּ עֹל מַלְכוּת וְעֹל דֶּרֶךְ אֶרֶץ. Likewise, one who relegates Torah to second place, elevating worldly matters to front and center, will get his wish. Such a person will in fact become preoccupied and bogged down with the yoke of worldly matters, as the mishnah concludes: וְכָל הַפּוֹרֵק מִמֶּנּוּ עֹל תּוֹרָה, נוֹתְנִין עָלָיו עֹל מַלְכוּת וְעֹל דֶּרֶךְ אֶרֶץ.

The Gift of Pain

As harsh as it may seem, the consequence awaiting the individual who fails to make Torah his priority — becoming burdened by the *ol*

malchus and *ol derech eretz* — need not necessarily be viewed solely as punitive. In a sense, it is a remarkable gift. The Rebbe of Kobrin infers as much from the precise wording employed by the mishnah: נוֹתְנִין עָלָיו עַל מַלְכוּת וְעַל דֶּרֶךְ אֶרֶץ. The term for "gift" (מתנה) derives from the root word נתן (place, give).

How, exactly, can taxes and hard labor be a "gift"? Once again, the "equation factor" of the mishnah proves enlightening on this matter. Subjugating oneself to the *ol Torah* has a most important effect: a person's character is refined thereby. The Torah has the power to enable a person to become self-aware, directing him to those areas of his character that need rectification. Commenting on the words of the *passuk* (*Vayikra* 4:23), אוֹ־הוֹדַע אֵלָיו חַטָּאתוֹ — *Or his sin be made known to him*, the Zohar clarifies who it is that enables him to realize his misdeed: אוֹרַיְיתָא קָא מוֹדְעָא לֵיהּ חוֹבֵיהּ — *It is the Torah that makes known to him his sin*. Thus we see that the Torah helps one to identify blemishes of the soul and spur him on to correct them.

The rigors of *malchus* and *derech eretz* can likewise have such a purging effect on a person. But one who already has accepted the yoke of Torah upon himself — utilizing this method to perfect his character — does not have to deal with the *ol malchus* and *ol derech eretz*, being thus relieved of these travails. But someone who did not accept the *ol Torah* — and, as such, still lacks character refinement — will then require the "offices" of the *ol malchus* and *ol derech eretz*. So we see that this is not just a punishment, but an actual necessity, and a gift of sorts. It would have been preferable, for all concerned, had this individual accepted the *ol Torah*; he would have spared himself much heartache. But he still needs to perfect his character, and this opportunity is provided him — in the form of *ol malchus* and *ol derech eretz*. It is a gift because it still affords him a most beneficial effect: the purging of his character from negative traits and tendencies.

This aspect is likewise a function of accepting to abide by the *ruach haTorah*. A person who seeks to conform to the *ruach haTorah*, ensuring that his conduct and character will be aligned with the spirit of the Torah, will attain just that. His *kabbalah* of the *ol Torah*

serves to purge his character, so that he need not avail himself of the other "yokes." But someone who casts off the *ol Torah* — who may keep the commandments but does not concern himself with *middos* and other aspects of the *ruach haTorah* — will become burdened by the *ol malchus* and *ol derech eretz*. That is a shame, but it is also a gift. Through these yokes, at least, he may also gain character perfection.

Now, of course, a person considering such a gift may be tempted to decline the offer. He may not be so partial to gifts of this sort.

But this is a grave mistake. The *sefarim hakedoshim* tell us that the main purpose for which Hashem created the world is *l'heitiv l'beru'av*, to bestow goodness upon His creations. One may be puzzled, then, about the seeming preponderance of misery and suffering that occur in This World, to the extent that the *ba'alei mussar* refer to the world as the *Neveh Hatela'os* (Vale of Travails). However, the *Mesillas Yesharim* clarifies the error. Of course Hashem's greatest desire is to bestow goodness upon His creatures, and this is exactly what He does. But He wants to supply them with real goodness, not something fake and ephemeral. The true goodness is that which is experienced by connecting to Hashem and basking in His Presence in the World of Truth. The travails of This World are the means through which a person undergoes certain trials and purifications that enable him to attain the ultimate goal of the goodness of the World to Come. It is well worthwhile to endure a lifetime of travail in order to attain this ultimate goodness.

This issue can be clarified in light of the very remarkable phenomenon that we witness on a daily basis, the interaction with the medical world. Consider a person suffering, *R"l*, from a debilitating and life-threatening disease. Such a person will seek out the best medical treatment. And so he engages a doctor who proceeds to take a knife and rip open his body to purge it of the toxic substances. The patient awakes to intense pain, weakness, and a prolonged and difficult recovery process. And for all of this, he feels intense gratitude to the doctor and hands him a large sum of money for the whole ordeal! On the one hand, the whole notion may almost seem ridiculous; here he was put through abject physical torture, and he goes ahead and pays his tormentor! But this scenario plays itself out numerous times every day around the country and around the world!

Of course, we know why. People are mature enough to realize that everything that was done in this instance was intended for the patient's benefit. All of the pain, the discomfort, the expense — it was all worth it for the sake of the cure. And so it may be said of the *ol malchus* and *ol derech eretz*. While far from pleasant, they are indeed "gifts," as they enable a person to refine his character and be worthy of entering the eternal bliss of the life of the World to Come.

The recognition that everything that Hashem does is calculated to benefit His creations is an essential component of *avodas Hashem*. It characterizes the all-important *middah* of *hasamei'ach b'chelko*, one who is happy with whatever circumstances and encounters he is presented with, for he has strong faith and trust in Hashem that it is all done with his welfare in mind. In fact, the tzaddikim inform us that developing such an attitude can go a long way towards relieving a difficult situation. This is a concept known as *hamtakas hadinim* (literally, "sweetening of the judgments"); when Hashem sees that despite the suffering, this Yid is firm in his belief and trusting that everything ultimately provides benefit, He responds in kind and lessens the travails.

This idea leads us to yet another layer of understanding to our mishnah. As stated, accepting the *ol Torah* entails a commitment to abide by the *ruach haTorah*. Undoubtedly, this endeavor requires a Yid to cultivate this essential attribute of *hasamei'ach b'chelko*, viewing even harsh circumstances as necessary and beneficial; and hence, rejoicing in them. In turn, this will effect a *hamtakas hadinim*, which will alleviate his suffering. In other words, the acceptance of the *ol Torah* will result in relief from the *ol malchus* and *ol derech eretz*.

In Summary

Rabbi Nechunia ben Hakanah establishes an interrelationship between different factors — different "yokes," to be exact. They operate in a mutually exclusive fashion. When a person accepts upon himself the *ol Torah*, he is relieved of the *ol malchus* and the *ol derech eretz*. And when casting off the *ol Torah*, it is replaced with the *ol malchus* and the *ol derech eretz*.

This calculus can be understood on a number of levels. The most basic understanding seems to be to recognize the mishnah as referring to material matters. That is, one who accepts the *ol Torah*, a "supernatural" entity, will be spared the struggles of the natural order of This World, as represented by the yoke of pursuing a livelihood and the yoke of government. One who does not seek the *ol Torah* but instead gravitates towards material pursuits will receive just that — a significant dosage of struggling to obtain his material needs.

The mishnah can also be understood as referring to spiritual endeavors. One who accepts the *ol Torah* will be aided in overcoming and avoiding the *yetzer hara*, which seeks to bring him down. He will be relieved of the *ol malchus*, referring to matters of belief in the *Malchus Shamayim*. This is an area the *yetzer hara* normally seeks to involve itself with, by trying to cloud one's *emunah*. One who seeks to attach himself to Hashem through His Torah will be freed from the *yetzer hara's* attempts at distraction in this regard, and his *emunah* will be firm. He will also be relieved of the *ol derech eretz*, referring to base desires and passions fueled by the *yetzer hara*.

The aspect of mutual exclusivity of the mishnah can also be viewed in a number of ways. On a basic level, we see here a manifestation of the *middah k'negged middah* concept. By acceding to the *ol Torah*, one is essentially undertaking to conform to an entity that exists beyond the normal bounds of the rules of nature. As such, Hashem reciprocates, relieving him of those aspects of the natural world that prevent his spiritual growth and keep him lowly.

On yet another level, the mishnah can be understood as the logical outcome of a person's choices. That is, the Heavenly decree regarding the affairs of each individual also relate to his pleasant and difficult experiences; that is, it is pre-ordained how much enjoyment one will receive, as well as how much suffering. If one expends his allotted difficulty by struggling to accept and conform to the *ol Torah*, he does himself a tremendous service, for he depletes his store of suffering and is left with a substantial measure of enjoyment to utilize in *avodas Hashem*. Conversely, if a person dedicates himself to the pursuit of worldly pleasures, he will use up his allotted enjoyment in this way. Then he will be left with an account of suffering, which will be meted out to him in the form of *ol malchus* and *ol derech eretz*.

The equation could be viewed through yet another dimension. Difficulties and travails do carry with them a certain benefit, in that they help to purge and refine one's character. Thus, if a person accepts the *ol Torah* and accesses the Torah's power to perfect his character, he will have no need of the *ol malchus* and *ol derech eretz*. However, if one does not utilize the *ol Torah*, he will be burdened from Heaven by the *ol malchus* and *ol derech eretz*. This is actually for a person's benefit, for while it would have been preferable to refine his character through the *ol Torah*, at the very least he is receiving this service through the *ol malchus* and *ol derech eretz*.

It should be noted that the mishnah does not speak of a difference between one who *observes* the Torah and one who does not. It appears that both parties discussed in the mishnah do, in fact, observe the Torah. The main difference is that one accepts the *ol Torah*, referring to a desire to fulfill even the *ruach haTorah*, while the other suffices with the bare letter of the Law. A Yid who is concerned with having all aspects of his life conform to the *ruach haTorah* will make the Torah his primary occupation in life. Consequently, he will be freed from the other yokes. But one who seeks to restrict his Torah commitment to the bare minimum will obviously not make it the centerpiece of his existence. Since he places worldly matters front and center, these indeed will become his primary occupation, as he will be burdened by the *ol malchus* and *ol derech eretz*.

The Nesivos Sholom concludes with one other approach to the mitzvah, focusing on the primary attribute of *hasamei'ach b'chelko*. One who is concerned with conforming his *middos* to the *ruach haTorah* will certainly concentrate on this trait, which carries the added benefit of effecting a *hamtakas hadinim*. Thus, by accepting the *ol Torah* and cultivating this *middah*, we can be confident in our

כל המקבל עליו עול תורה

belief that everything Hashem does is ultimately for our supreme benefit. This satisfaction with our situation will ultimately yield a relieving of our difficulties. In this way, as well, our acceptance of the *ol Torah* will relieve us of the *ol malchus* and *ol derech eretz*.

פרק ג'

פרק ג' משנה ח'
תן לו משלו שאתה ושלך שלו
Give Him What Is His, for You, and What Is Yours, Are His

רַבִּי אֶלְעָזָר אִישׁ בַּרְתּוֹתָא אוֹמֵר, תֶּן לוֹ מִשֶּׁלּוֹ, שֶׁאַתָּה וְשֶׁלְּךָ שֶׁלּוֹ. וְכֵן בְּדָוִד הוּא אוֹמֵר כִּי מִמְּךָ הַכֹּל וּמִיָּדְךָ נָתַנּוּ לָךְ:

Rabbi Elazar of Bartosa says: Give Him what is His, for you, and what is yours, are His. And so it states by Dovid (*Divrei Hayamim I* 29:14): "For everything is from You; and we have given You from Your hand."

GEMS FROM THE *SEFER NESIVOS SHOLOM*

SOURCES:

שֶׁהַכֹּל בָּרָא לִכְבוֹדוֹ. (שבע ברכות)

All He created for His glory. (*Sheva Brachos*)

קָדוֹשׁ, קָדוֹשׁ, קָדוֹשׁ, ה' צְבָקוֹת, מְלֹא כָל הָאָרֶץ כְּבוֹדוֹ. (ישעיה ו' ג')

Holy, holy, holy is Hashem of Hosts; His glory fills the whole world. (*Yeshayah* 6:3)

אִם־יִתֵּן אִישׁ אֶת־כָּל־הוֹן בֵּיתוֹ בָּאַהֲבָה בּוֹז יָבוּזוּ לוֹ. (שיר השירים ח' ז')

Should a person give all the wealth of his house for love, they would denigrate him. (*Shir Hashirim* 8:7)

ה' נָתַן וַה' לָקָח יְהִי שֵׁם ה' מְבֹרָךְ. (איוב א' כ"א)

Hashem has given, and Hashem has taken; may the Name of Hashem be blessed. (*Iyov* 1:21)

יִצְרוֹ שֶׁל אָדָם מִתְגַּבֵּר עָלָיו בְּכָל יוֹם וּמְבַקֵּשׁ הֲמִיתוֹ...וְאִלְמָלֵא הַקָּבָּ"ה עוֹזְרוֹ, אֵין יָכוֹל לוֹ. (קדושין ל:)

A person's inclination surges against him every day, seeking his demise...and if not for Hashem's help, that person would be unable to prevail. (*Kiddushin* 30b)

פרקי אבות

תֵּן לוֹ מִשֶּׁלוֹ שֶׁאַתָּה וְשֶׁלְּךָ שֶׁלּוֹ

Mission Accomplished!

A common theme runs through Tanach and the works of *Chazal*: All of our abilities and assets are a gift from Hashem, to be utilized for His purposes. Ideally, all schoolchildren, ardent seminary girls, young *kollel avreichim* (members of a *kollel*), mothers, wealthy businessmen, and so on, are to lead their lives and direct their activities with this aim in mind: doing their utmost to serve Hashem with their given talents and gifts.

This idea of utilizing one's strengths for *avodas Hashem* is a well-known principle. Nevertheless, few people realize the true magnitude of their G-d-given capabilities or use them to their full extent. The Nesivos Sholom explores the depths of Hashem's expectations from us in this regard, highlighting the necessity of dedicating every aspect of our lives to His service.

Pass It Along

It is this very concept Rabbi Elazar imparts to us when he states, תֵּן לוֹ מִשֶּׁלוֹ, שֶׁאַתָּה וְשֶׁלְּךָ שֶׁלּוֹ — *Give Him from what is His, because you and yours are His*. On the most basic level, the mishnah is delivering a succinct message: Everything that you have really belongs to Hashem — since it is He Who gave it to you in the first place. As such, it is only fitting to employ these gifts to serve Him.

Rabbeinu Yonah explains that this directive extends to our body, possessions, and all capabilities. *Everything* that we have is to be enlisted in fulfilling Hashem's will. Thus, when using our gifts for Hashem's purposes, we are not actually giving of *ourselves*. Hashem is the true Producer, Giver, and Owner of all of these gifts. As the *passuk* (cited by the mishnah) states, *Ki mimcha hakol* — "It all comes from You, Hashem." As such, *u'miyadcha nasanu Lach* — "we are obligated to give it back to You." How is this accomplished? By using it all — to its full extent — in the service of the One Who gave it.

To really drive the message home, the Nesivos Sholom employs the following *mashal* (parable). A king removes one thousand coins from his treasury, handing them to a trusted servant. He informs the servant that he can keep one hundred coins but must deliver the remaining nine hundred to nine specific people, giving them one hundred coins each.

Let's do some simple math. How many coins does this messenger actually have? During his journey, there are one thousand coins in his possession; but most of them are not his! Nine hundred are to be conveyed to other people. Until the time of delivery, these nine hundred coins remain the absolute property of the king. When the servant reaches his destination, the coins are transferred into the possession of the recipients. The messenger, in effect, is nothing but an extension of the king's will. One hundred coins remain with him to sustain him on his journey and otherwise enable him to continue to perform royal errands. Similarly, our strengths, capabilities, and possessions do not truly belong to us. We have been given "nine hundred coins," and are charged with their conveyance and transfer, to be converted into the fulfillment of Hashem's will. A certain measure of these gifts, by necessity, must be used for "maintenance" purposes — itself a manifestation of serving Hashem. We, as messengers, must be kept healthy and able to continue with the all-important task of dedicating all resources to His service.

This is how the Torah views "success." A wealthy person is Hashem's banker; he holds on to the money Hashem gave him until he ascertains how to best make use of it — to which pressing *tzedakah* (charity) cause it should go. Doctors, teachers, *rabbanim*, accountants, makeup artists, lawyers, mothers, businessmen — in fact anyone who utilizes his or her talents to benefit others — are not giving away from their personal assets. They are simply using the gifts for the express purpose for which they were given — that is, to pass along to others!

Anyone who has talent, money, or ability is in reality a mere vehicle through which Hashem can pour His *chessed* upon others. Thus, we discover a crucial aspect of *avodas Hashem* beyond a meticulous adherence to mitzvos. To serve Hashem in the most complete manner, a person must *identify* the gifts that Hashem has granted him and "distribute" these gifts to others.

תן לו משלו שאתה ושלך שלו

There Is Nothing but His Glory

The Maharal adds another dimension to this idea. In one of the blessings that comprise *sheva brachos* (the special blessings recited in celebration of a marriage), we say, *Shehakol bara lichvodo* — "He created everything for His glory." In fashioning the entire world in His honor, He bequeathed of His glory to the earth's inhabitants. This comes in the form of individual talents and capabilities, to be used to distribute to others. Yeshayah Hanavi alludes to this concept when he states: מְלֹא כָל־הָאָרֶץ כְּבוֹדוֹ. This is usually translated as, "His glory fills the entire world." However, the Maharal renders, "What fills the entire world (i.e., everything that exists) is for His glory." Not only is the entire world filled *with* Hashem's glory, but the world *is* Hashem's glory! As such, whatever Hashem gave us of Himself is not intended to be used simply as we see fit; rather, all G-d-given talents and possessions must be utilized *to reflect the glory of Hashem in the world*. By putting these gifts to their intended, proper usage, the glory of Hashem's Presence becomes revealed in the world — which is the purpose of creation in the first place.

The Maharal then focuses on the *passuk* quoted by the mishnah: כִּי מִמְּךָ הַכֹּל וּמִיָּדְךָ נָתַנּוּ לָךְ — *For everything comes from You,* **and from Your hand** *we give to You.* The implication of this verse is startling. At the end of the day, wasn't it our hands that "released" these gifts back to *Hakadosh Baruch Hu*? Shouldn't the *passuk* have stated that we gave back to Him "from **our** hand"? But this is precisely the point, asserts the Maharal. The *passuk* studiously avoided the impression that these items were in our possession even for a second! They never belonged to us — not even *while they were in "our" hands*. Since our hands, in essence, are mere conveyor belts through which these gifts are to be channeled towards their proper destination, it would be inaccurate to state that we had given "from our hands." They were always Hashem's possessions; we are but the stewards.

It is interesting to note how this *passuk* describes an act such as giving *tzedakah*. Not only do we give "from Your hand," but even what we give, we give "to You." This highlights the fact that even the *recipient* does not possess what is given to him as that, too, ultimately

פרק ג'

belongs to Hashem. This idea is so profound that we can spend a lifetime contemplating it, yet only gain the slightest glimpse into its depth. What *Chazal* are saying is, in effect, that any act of giving is nothing less than Hashem giving to Himself, for *Ein od milvado* — "There is nothing other (than Hashem)" (*Devarim* 4:35). It is actually a display of Hashem's intense loving-kindness that He has allowed us to take part in this act of Divine benevolence.

The extent to which this principle holds true is remarkable — as evidenced by the words of Shlomo Hamelech. In *Shir Hashirim* (8:7), he states, אִם־יִתֵּן אִישׁ אֶת־כָּל־הוֹן בֵּיתוֹ בָּאַהֲבָה בּוֹז יָבוּזוּ לוֹ — *Should a person give all the wealth of his house for love, they would denigrate him.* At first glance, the *passuk* seems perplexing. If someone demonstrates such love for Hashem that he gives away all of his possessions on His behalf — for this, he deserves to be ridiculed? Shouldn't he be lavished with praise for his dedication? The Saba Kadisha of Slonim *ztz"l* explained the *passuk* along the above lines. Shlomo Hamelech, quite deliberately, was speaking of someone who gave away the wealth of *beiso*, **his** house. That is, while performing a great charitable act, the giver viewed himself as giving away from his own possessions; he perceived that he, himself, was the ultimate giver. But as stated above, the reality is not that way. Even when temporarily residing near us, the wealth is merely in our safekeeping. But it never actually belongs to us — not even for a second. This individual is worthy of scorn for adopting the mistaken attitude that he was giving away something that was *his*.

The medieval classic, *Mivchar Peninim*, tells of a wise man who apparently never suffered disappointment. Whatever happened, he seemed not to be bothered or upset. "How are you able to remain unflustered, no matter the situation?" he was asked. To which the wise man replied, "Why should I be bothered? It's not like anything happened to me or anything of mine. If something truly belonged to me, I would be upset were it to be taken away. But in any event, whatever I deal with — my health, family, pride, possessions — is not mine anyway; it all belongs to Hashem. And so, regarding all of these things, I know to apply the *passuk* (*Iyov* 1:21), ה' נָתַן וַה' לָקָח יְהִי שֵׁם

תן לו משלו שאתה ושלך שלו

ה׳ מְבֹרָךְ — Hashem has given, and Hashem has taken; may the Name of Hashem be blessed."

This concept — ה׳ נָתַן וַה׳ לָקָח — while fairly well known, is nevertheless a *madreigah* that we must exert significant effort to reach. This is true not only regarding major life events but even when confronting mundane challenges; many of us have yet to develop this attitude. Who can claim to be unaffected upon receipt of an unexpected, expensive repair bill, or when they're skipped over for an honor they feel they deserved? Nevertheless, it does behoove us to try to cultivate the realization that whatever we "have" — money, pride, and the like — is not truly ours. As such, the suspension of all or part of these resources need not necessarily be viewed with the gravity we sometimes accord them.

In the same vein, since our abilities are not truly "ours," we must avoid feeling undue pride in these attributes. This is true in both the physical and spiritual realms. Were you given a beautiful voice, great wealth, or a special talent in business, science or the arts? Perhaps you have the ability to sit and learn and understand Torah? If this is the case, it is still important not to draw the wrong conclusions. Do you feel pleased with yourself because of your special skills? Do you feel that they somehow make you better than other people, or that they came into existence due to certain efforts on your part? A person with such an attitude is gravely mistaken.

As mentioned, even our spiritual accomplishments cannot be attributed entirely to our own efforts. One of the previous Slonimer Rebbes had an interesting, motivational routine he would follow each morning. Upon awakening, he would shout, "It is difficult to be a Jew!" The difficulty to which he referred was not a result of the physical requirements of the mitzvos; rather, it was due to the interference of the *yetzer hara*. The *yetzer hara* is, after all, a *malach* of Hashem, and we are mere mortals. This, obviously, puts us at a tremendous disadvantage in fighting its myriad wiles.

What can be done? After this pronouncement, the Rebbe would continue, "Nevertheless, Hashem grants us the power to overcome our *yetzer hara*." The Rebbe's statement mirrors what *Chazal* relate in

Kiddushin (30b): יִצְרוֹ שֶׁל אָדָם מִתְגַּבֵּר עָלָיו בְּכָל יוֹם וּמְבַקֵּשׁ הַמִיתוֹ...וְאִלְמָלֵא הַקָּבָּ"ה עוֹזְרוֹ, אֵין יָכוֹל לוֹ — *A person's inclination surges against him every day, seeking his demise...and if not for Hashem's help, that person would be unable to prevail.* This is a crucial point for even a very committed individual to keep in mind to prevent undue haughtiness. Even our spiritual accomplishments are not entirely attributable to us. Just as Hashem is the source of every single aspect of our lives, He also gives us the power, the means, and the opportunities to overcome the *yetzer hara* as well.

Deserving of Praise?

Now, a certain degree of pride in one's achievements is understandable. But there is a world of difference between the following two scenarios. One talented individual thinks to himself, "Look at me! I am so special and gifted! See how they applaud me and my life's work!" Compare this with the attitude of a more thinking person, who says, "I feel so grateful that I am able to heal/entertain/teach others through the gift with which Hashem has blessed me. *Baruch Hashem* (Thank G-d)!" In truth, it is nothing short of absurd to be filled with pride and brag about abilities that are not truly yours. From a Torah perspective, there really is only one thing for which a talented person deserves accolades: for seeing through the veils of illusion promoted by the *yetzer hara* and recognizing his gifts for what they are — wonderful gifts that Hashem, in His wisdom, has bestowed on that individual to be used to serve Hashem and help others. And, of course, he is praiseworthy for doing just that: applying these talents in the manner in which Hashem intended.

Imagine that you are traveling from one city to another. A friend asks you to deliver an envelope full of cash to a colleague at your destination city; you faithfully carry out the request. Though you may very well be thanked for your efforts, should you expect to be praised for not keeping the money? Such a thought probably would not even cross your mind. Ideally, we should view our talents and abilities in the same light as a package that we have been asked to deliver.

Unfortunately, the *yetzer hara* gets in the way and convinces us that everything we have — our possessions, our talents, our personality traits — are ours to do with as we see fit.

This mishnah, when fully understood and applied to our thoughts and actions, can have a tremendous impact on the life of every Yid. Look at yourself, your belongings, your family, your talents and abilities. The crucial question we must ask is: Am I using them for Hashem's glory and honor, or "stealing" borrowed goods for my personal use and gratification? Are you creative or charismatic? Or do you have a gift for interpersonal relationships? Don't squander your talents on personal pursuits; rather make sure that you are distributing Hashem's gifts to those who need them.

If you can look at your gifts and know that you are utilizing them properly and acting as Hashem's messenger to give of His glory to others, you can rest assured that your mission in life is being accomplished.

In Summary

People may generally be aware of the importance of using their abilities to serve Hashem. However, the Nesivos Sholom asserts, most people are unaware of how great those abilities actually are. Still fewer utilize them fully in their *avodas Hashem*. The Nesivos Sholom understands the underlying message of our mishnah as an exhortation to concentrate all of our resources to Divine service.

To explain the essence of our mishnah, the Nesivos Sholom employs a parable. A king gives his servant a large volume of coins, instructing him to deliver them to various people. Would anyone consider that these coins belong to the messenger? The same is true regarding our possessions and abilities. Things that we think we possess, in actual fact, belong solely to *Hakadosh Baruch Hu*. We are simply the messengers, agents of His will charged with imparting to others those gifts with which He entrusts us.

The Maharal explains the mishnah based on the words of Yeshayah Hanavi: מְלֹא כָל־הָאָרֶץ כְּבוֹדוֹ. He understands this *passuk* to mean not merely that "the whole world is filled *with* Hashem's glory," but that "the whole world *is* Hashem's glory." As such, whatever Hashem bequeaths to a person must be utilized for the purpose of increasing His glory in the world. The Maharal further explains the *passuk* quoted by our mishnah: *U'miyadcha nasanu Lach* — "from Your hand we give to You," as highlighting the notion mentioned above. The *passuk* is stressing our role as "intermediaries" in conveying Hashem's gifts to the proper destination. In this sense, we are not giving anything from "our hands"; although they were temporarily placed in our safekeeping, not even for a moment were these possessions considered anyone's but Hashem's. Thus, when we "return" them, we are giving to Hashem what has always been His.

With all this in mind, we should better be able to understand and apply the principle that, *Hashem nassan, Hashem lakach* — "Hashem gives and Hashem takes away." There is essentially no need to be overly concerned when things don't go as planned. After all, these items don't belong to us; why should we experience consternation at their absence?

Furthermore, as everything anyway belongs to Hashem, it is simply absurd for us to be filled with pride at our G-d-given abilities. True honor is due only when we see through the many veils of the *yetzer hara* and understand that we are merely a medium through which Hashem's gifts are transmitted to others.

Even our spiritual accomplishments are facets not entirely attributable to our own efforts. As a *malach* of Hashem, the *yetzer hara* is truly a formidable adversary. Without Hashem's help, it would be absolutely impossible to defeat him.

The Nesivos Sholom concludes by encouraging us to constantly assess the way we use our attributes and abilities: Are we using them to glorify Hashem? If we succeed in doing this, we will fulfill thereby the very purpose for which we have come to This World.

פרק ג' משנה י'
הַשּׁוֹכֵחַ דָּבָר אֶחָד מִמִּשְׁנָתוֹ
One Who Forgets a Single Item from His Studies

רַבִּי דוֹסְתַּאי בְּרַבִּי יַנַּאי מִשּׁוּם רַבִּי מֵאִיר אוֹמֵר, כָּל הַשּׁוֹכֵחַ דָּבָר אֶחָד מִמִּשְׁנָתוֹ, מַעֲלֶה עָלָיו הַכָּתוּב כְּאִלּוּ מִתְחַיֵּב בְּנַפְשׁוֹ, שֶׁנֶּאֱמַר רַק הִשָּׁמֶר לְךָ וּשְׁמֹר נַפְשְׁךָ מְאֹד פֶּן תִּשְׁכַּח אֶת הַדְּבָרִים אֲשֶׁר רָאוּ עֵינֶיךָ. יָכוֹל אֲפִלּוּ תָקְפָה עָלָיו מִשְׁנָתוֹ, תַּלְמוּד לוֹמַר וּפֶן יָסוּרוּ מִלְּבָבְךָ כֹּל יְמֵי חַיֶּיךָ, הָא אֵינוֹ מִתְחַיֵּב בְּנַפְשׁוֹ עַד שֶׁיֵּשֵׁב וִיסִירֵם מִלִּבּוֹ:

Rabbi Dostai ben Rabbi Yannai says in the name of Rabbi Meir: Anyone who forgets (even) a single item from his studies, the Torah considers it as if he is liable for his life; as it is stated (*Devarim* 4:9): "Just be careful, and guard your soul very much, lest you forget the things that your eyes have seen." It could be (that this applies) even if (the cause of his forgetfulness was that) his studies proved too difficult for him; (to negate this possibility,) the verse tells us (*ibid.*): "And lest they be removed from your heart throughout all the days of your life." Hence, one does not become liable for his life until he deliberately sets himself to remove them from his heart.

GEMS FROM THE *SEFER NESIVOS SHOLOM*

SOURCES:

וְשַׁבְתֶּם וּרְאִיתֶם בֵּין צַדִּיק לְרָשָׁע בֵּין עֹבֵד אֱלֹקִים לַאֲשֶׁר לֹא עֲבָדוֹ. (מלאכי ג׳ י״ח)

And you will go back and discern between a righteous man and a wicked one, between one who serves G-d, and one who does not serve Him. (*Malachi* 3:18)

אֵינוֹ דוֹמֶה שׁוֹנֶה פִּרְקוֹ מֵאָה פְּעָמִים לְשׁוֹנֶה פִּרְקוֹ מֵאָה וְאֶחָד. (חגיגה ט:)

The one who reviews his learning one hundred times is incomparable to one who reviews his learning one hundred and one (times). (*Chagigah* 9b)

הַמְהַלֵּךְ בַּדֶּרֶךְ וְשׁוֹנֶה וּמַפְסִיק מִמִּשְׁנָתוֹ וְאוֹמֵר, מַה נָּאֶה אִילָן זֶה וּמַה נָּאֶה נִיר זֶה, מַעֲלֶה עָלָיו הַכָּתוּב כְּאִלּוּ מִתְחַיֵּב בְּנַפְשׁוֹ. (אבות ג׳)

One who reviews his learning as he walks along the way, and interrupts his studying to say: "How nice is this tree! How nice is this plowed field!" – Scripture accounts it to him as if he is liable with his life. (*Avos* 3)

פרקי אבות

השוכח דבר אחד ממשנתו

Memory

A *yeshivah bachur* once approached his Rosh Yeshivah, looking dejected. "Rebbi," he said, "I'm just not getting into my learning. I'm not feeling it. What should I do?" The Rosh Yeshivah looked at the *bachur* with concern. He asked him pointedly, "Did you think about *Hakadosh Baruch Hu* at all today?" The *bachur* was momentarily nonplussed. "Well," he began, "it's been a bit hectic so far. I had to get up early for Shacharis. There was a longer *davening* due to *krias haTorah*. I then rushed through breakfast to make it to morning *seder*; I learned, after which I had to wash for lunch, *bentch*, go to Minchah, and then afternoon *seder*. And now, here I am. So I didn't really have a chance to think about Hashem yet today."

Obviously, this is a perfect example of someone who has completely missed the boat. It is clear that the *bachur* featured in this account is going through the day's activities totally oblivious to the true meaning of his actions. If only he would just give the matter a little thought! It is ironic how he is so *shtark* (strongly religious) on the outside, while his inside is so empty.

But at the very least he goes through the motions; his admirable actions are at least his saving grace. Contrast this with a different *bachur*, who spends his day in yeshivah muddling around, schmoozing, talking on the phone, hanging out, napping; basically killing time. Who is more flawed? It would seem simple to point to the second *bachur*, who completely neglected to engage in productive activity. While the learning of the first *bachur* may have lacked real substance, at least he was *learning*.

But as is apparent from the mishnah in *Pirkei Avos*, the matter may not be so simple. While neither *bachur's* performance is stellar, it is the first one — as we shall see — whose offense is particularly egregious.

Fitting the Punishment to the Crime

In the mishnah, Rabbi Dostai bar Yannai addresses the "sin" of forgetting one's learning, according it unusual severity. It is not merely one who forgets *all* that he has learned who is subject to censure; but, הַשּׁוֹכֵחַ דָּבָר אֶחָד מִמִּשְׁנָתוֹ מַעֲלֶה עָלָיו הַכָּתוּב כְּאִלּוּ מִתְחַיֵּב בְּנַפְשׁוֹ — *He who forgets* **one** *item of his study, the Torah regards him as though he was liable for his life*. A person forgets one thing that he learned, and his life is forfeit?!

Now, the mishnah does make clear that one is not held responsible for things he was simply unable to retain; that one word must be forgotten *deliberately* in order to qualify for the grave consequences. To fortify this point, the mishnah cites a supporting *passuk* (*Devarim* 4:9): וּפֶן־יָסוּרוּ מִלְּבָבְךָ כֹּל יְמֵי חַיֶּיךָ — *Lest they be removed from your heart all the days of your life*. The mishnah concludes: הָא אֵינוֹ מִתְחַיֵּב בְּנַפְשׁוֹ עַד שֶׁיֵּשֵׁב וִיסִירֵם מִלִּבּוֹ — *Thus we see, he is not liable unless he sets himself to remove them from his heart*.

But even with this qualification, the demands are still substantial. How does one define "deliberate forgetfulness" and go about "removing the words from his heart"? In his explanation, the Maharal makes a poignant observation. The *passuk* quoted by the mishnah does not use the term, *U'fen* **tesireim** — "Lest **you** remove them," implying a forceful, active endeavor. Rather, it merely states, *U'fen* **yasuru** — "Lest they **be removed**," intimating a more passive, automatic process. In other words, the mishnah speaks of one who forgets due to neglect. Not bothering with *chazarah* (review), his learning was lost.

Yet it still seems that the punishment far exceeds the crime. The importance of *chazarah* is no secret; real retention and understanding are only achieved thereby. But it is difficult to see how even the deliberate neglect of review, while harmful to the learning process, should make one liable to such severe consequences as listed in the mishnah.

Given the Torah's inherent and absolute justness, there must be a deeper meaning to the mishnah's words. What was the hidden message that Rabbi Dostai wished to convey?

Who Knows "One"?

In addressing this issue, the Nesivos Sholom highlights another aspect. Curiously, the mishnah here does not discuss the broader offense of *bitul Torah*, neglecting Torah. One would imagine that abject time-wasting, whereby one does not even engage in Torah study, would be a cause for harsh recrimination. But the mishnah instead chose to critique the individual who learned without sufficient review! How could it be that one who took the trouble to learn, but merely forgot "one item" is worse off than the loafer who did not even crack open a *sefer*?!

Based on the words of the Maggid (quoted in *Sefer Pri Hachaim*), the Nesivos Sholom interprets the mishnah in an entirely new light. The mishnah states that a person incurs guilt for forgetting *davar echad* (one matter) from his learning. The simple understanding is that this refers to forgetting a single item that one has learned. But the Nesivos Sholom learns otherwise. He translates *davar echad* as meaning "the matter of One" — that is, the ONE AND ONLY. Therefore, it is not a person who forgets one *word* that is the subject of Rabbi Dostai's teaching; rather, it is someone who deletes Hashem from his learning that is liable for such harsh punishment.

A person may be learning day and night; truly an outstanding endeavor. At the same time, however, he must ensure that he remains loyal to the ideal of *talmud Torah* (Torah study). There are some who learn Torah because the material is intellectually stimulating, not because it is Hashem's Torah and they wish to draw closer to Him and His commandments. A person such as this will close his Gemara at night and leave the *limud* (learning) right where it is — between the pages of the *sefer*.

In the ideal situation, a person would close his Gemara at night after his learning session and, in effect, bring the Torah home with him. Such an individual acts upon the lessons he learns and carries the *limud* with him throughout the day. Fully cognizant that the Torah comprises Hashem's teachings, he allows it to become part and parcel of his existence. This is the ideal the mishnah advocates.

The *bachur* described at the outset seems to fit the profile outlined by the mishnah of one who has deleted Hashem from his learning and thus is liable for his life. In his particular circumstance, however, there may be room for some leeway. As much as that hapless *bachur* is essentially wrong in not applying his *talmud Torah* to his life, he does not seem to be learning solely as an intellectual exercise. As such, he does not deserve *misah* (death) as much as a guiding hand. The mishnah is not targeted to individuals like him, who at the core are searching for Hashem. Rather, it addresses those who mimic his actions without any interest in refining their ways. Such individuals have truly banished Hashem from their learning.

The Nesivos Sholom perceives a similar message in the oft-quoted teaching in *Maseches Chagigah* (9b). The Gemara focuses on the statement of the *navi*: וּרְאִיתֶם...בֵּין עֹבֵד אֱלֹקִים לַאֲשֶׁר לֹא עֲבָדוֹ — *And you shall discern between one who serves G-d, and one who does not serve Him* (*Malachi* 3:18). Hillel explains the *passuk* as referring to *chazarah*: The "one who serves G-d" has reviewed his learning 101 times; the "one who has not" has done so only 100 times.

Again, the cause and effect seem out of proportion. Someone reviewed his learning 100 times; because it was one less time than his colleague, he is not considered a servant of Hashem? How could what appears to be such a minimal difference in actuality be considered so vast?

The Nesivos Sholom thus applies his understanding of "one" to this instance as well. The Gemara's precise wording is: אֵינוֹ דוֹמֶה שׁוֹנֶה פִּרְקוֹ מֵאָה פְּעָמִים לְשׁוֹנֶה פִּרְקוֹ מֵאָה וְאֶחָד — *The one who reviews his learning 100 times is incomparable to one who reviews his learning 101 (times).* Accordingly, it may very well be that both studied their lessons the same *number* of times — an even one hundred. When Hillel praised the student who reviewed "one hundred *and one*," he meant someone who learned his 100 times "with the ONE" — *Hakadosh Baruch Hu.*

A person can review his learning numerous times; but his level of *avodah* is not complete if he leaves Hashem out of the equation. Only through a conscious awareness that one's learning is being done for a specific purpose — to draw closer to Hashem — can he be considered a true *oveid Hashem*. These two scholars both reviewed 100 times, but only one of them learned his 100 with "the ONE." The gulf between them is wide indeed.

When one brings Hashem along with his studies, the learning experience is completely transformed. He studies with the awareness that this is not just another subject; rather, he is delving into Hashem's Torah. He therefore understands that his learning should have a powerful impact on every aspect of his being — from his deepest thoughts to his most public actions. The Torah he imbibes will affect and guide every step of his journey through life.

Forgetting vs. Neglecting

We can now understand Rabbi Dostai's intent more clearly; he specifically directed his comments towards one who forgets "the One" from his learning, as opposed to the standard *batlan* (one who neglects Torah study). Someone who neglects to learn in the first place is certainly not in the right, but his main offense can be characterized as a plain dereliction of duty. But one who is involved in learning yet deletes Hashem from the exercise — this is an egregious affront. Failure to acknowledge that the purpose of one's Torah study is to affect one's thoughts and actions is essentially a denial of Torah's *kedushah* and an unforgivable disregard of Hashem Himself. Such an offense is severe indeed.

This understanding can also shed light on a related teaching. The previous mishnah discusses a scenario whereby a man reviews his studies as he walks along the road. He suddenly interrupts his learning to comment on the scenery: מַה נָּאֶה אִילָן זֶה וּמַה נָּאֶה נִיר זֶה — *How pleasant is this tree; how pleasant is this field*. Rabbi Yaakov pronounces on this individual the identical verdict of our mishnah: he has virtually become liable for death.

Again, we are faced with the same perplexity. Why is one who learns but interrupts treated much more severely than one who doesn't learn in the first place?! The matter is even more mystifying in light of the nature of his interruption; after all, his comments about the tree and the field are also a positive reflection of the works of Hashem.

The Nesivos Sholom clarifies the issue with a brief allegory, comparing the situation to one conversing with a king. Would a subject suddenly terminate the conversation with his monarch, turning to share a word or two with a passerby? Doing so would constitute the ultimate display of disrespect to his illustrious company. He would well deserve the death penalty.

One who interrupts his learning acts in similar fashion. When learning "with Hashem," one dare not terminate the conversation! Our *chachamim* (wise men) delineate the difference between *davening* and learning. When you *daven*, you are talking to Hashem; when you learn, Hashem is talking to you. A person who recognizes that when he learns, he is studying Hashem's Torah, and understands that Hashem is with him at that moment, will not interrupt his learning for anything — even to comment on His masterful creations.

There are many sources in *Chazal* that stress the true purpose of Torah study. It is supposed to change a person, raise a person, and make him a true *oveid Hashem* in every sense of the word. If you want your study of Torah to meet its purpose, you must bring Hashem into your learning and not view it as a mere body of study. One who focuses on the true purpose and elevated nature of Torah study will never forget that his learning is an encounter with the Divine.

In Summary

At first glance, the mishnah's admonishment may almost appear overly harsh. It attributes the greatest severity to one whose Torah study was lacking in a certain area, considering him liable for his life. And what was his offense? He forgot his learning. And we are not even speaking of one who lost all of his learning, but one who forgot merely *davar echad*.

The mishnah's intent becomes much clearer through the Nesivos Sholom's innovative interpretation. He understands the mishnah not as referring to someone who forgot "one item" from his studies. Rather, the "*echad*" refers to the loftiest entity — "the ONE AND ONLY." That is, the mishnah was speaking of one who — although engaged in learning — forgets about *Hakadosh Baruch Hu* Himself.

And this indeed is a grievous affront to Hashem and His Torah. One who learns for mere intellectual stimulation, viewing the material not as sacred but as just another subject, denies thereby the true nature and purpose of the Torah. Torah, the Word of Hashem, is capable of transforming and elevating the individual who delves into it. Thus, the awareness that Torah is designed to bring one closer to Hashem is a prerequisite to its proper study. When one brings Hashem into his learning, his learning experience is dramatically transformed. One who leaves Hashem out is deserving of the mishnah's grave pronunciation of his guilt.

פרק ג' משנה י"א

כל שיראת חטאו קודמת לחכמתו
Anyone Whose Fear of Sin Precedes His Wisdom

רַבִּי חֲנִינָא בֶּן דּוֹסָא אוֹמֵר, כֹּל שֶׁיִּרְאַת חֶטְאוֹ קוֹדֶמֶת לְחָכְמָתוֹ, חָכְמָתוֹ מִתְקַיֶּמֶת. וְכֹל שֶׁחָכְמָתוֹ קוֹדֶמֶת לְיִרְאַת חֶטְאוֹ, אֵין חָכְמָתוֹ מִתְקַיֶּמֶת:

Rabbi Chanina ben Dosa says: Anyone whose fear of sin precedes his wisdom, his wisdom endures. But anyone whose wisdom precedes his fear of sin, his wisdom does not endure.

GEMS FROM THE *SEFER NESIVOS SHOLOM*

SOURCES:

רֵאשִׁית חָכְמָה יִרְאַת ה׳. (תהלים קי״א י׳)

The beginning of wisdom is fear of Hashem. (*Tehillim* 111:10)

אֵין בּוּר יְרֵא חֵטְא. (אבות ב׳)

An ignoramus cannot fear sin. (*Avos* 2)

רַבִּי אֶלְעָזָר בֶּן עֲזַרְיָה אוֹמֵר...אִם אֵין חָכְמָה, אֵין יִרְאָה, אִם אֵין יִרְאָה, אֵין חָכְמָה. (שם ג׳)

Rabbi Elazar ben Azaryah said...if there is no wisdom, there is no fear; if there is no fear, there is no wisdom. (*ibid.* 3)

אָמַר לוֹ הַקָּדוֹשׁ בָּרוּךְ הוּא לְמֹשֶׁה: מַתָּנָה טוֹבָה יֵשׁ לִי בְּבֵית גְּנָזַי, וְשַׁבָּת שְׁמָהּ. (שבת י.)

Hashem said to Moshe: "I have ready, stored in My treasure house, a great gift – Shabbos is its name." (*Shabbos* 10a)

לְיִרְאָה אֶת־הַשֵּׁם הַנִּכְבָּד וְהַנּוֹרָא הַזֶּה אֵת ה׳ אֱלֹקֶיךָ. (דברים כ״ח נ״ח)

To fear this honored and awesome Name – Hashem your G-d. (*Devarim* 28:58)

כל שיראת חטאו קודמת לחכמתו

What Comes First

In life, the specific order of things may not always be paramount. The legendary puzzle of "which came first, the chicken or the egg?" may be interesting to contemplate, but bears no real application in the practical world.

There are other situations, however, where sequence and order are essential. The *Tanna* of this mishnah seems to be identifying just such an area; when it comes to wisdom and fear of sin, the order can make all the difference. "Rabbi Chanina ben Dosa says: He whose fear of sin precedes his wisdom, his wisdom will last, and he whose wisdom precedes his fear of sin, his wisdom will not last." It appears to be a clear message that regarding these two qualities, fear must come first, and the rewards of following this order are substantial indeed.

There is a well-known *passuk*, incorporated into the morning *davening*, which at first glance seems to be expressing the identical sentiment. Each morning, we recite the verse, רֵאשִׁית חָכְמָה יִרְאַת ה׳ — *The beginning of wisdom is fear of Hashem* (*Tehillim* 111:10). Seemingly, this *passuk* could have served as an excellent Scriptural reference for Rabbi Chanina's statement. However, he did not cite this as proof. We must conclude, therefore, that Rabbi Chanina must have perceived that this statement of Dovid Hamelech must be addressing something else, instead. What, exactly, is the difference between these two nearly identical statements?

The truth is that there are different types, and different levels, of *yirah*. Notice that the *passuk* refers to **yiras Hashem** (fear of Hashem), while Rabbi Chanina discusses **yiras cheit** (fear of sin). The distinction between these two entities is outlined in the Zohar (introduction, p. 11), which explains that fear of sin and punishment is not the primary form of *yirah*. The principal type of *yirah* is *yiras Hashem*, wherein a person is simply awed by Hashem's dominion and mastery over the universe.

Having identified the subject of Rabbi Chanina's teaching — fear of sin — we may now turn towards understanding the depth of his

פרק ג׳

message. Rabbi Chanina conveys that fear of sin must precede the accumulation of wisdom. The commentaries question how such a feat is even possible. Hillel had stated in an earlier mishnah (2:5): אֵין בּוּר יְרֵא חֵטְא — *An ignoramus cannot fear sin.* This is quite an understandable concept; if a person doesn't have background in the laws, knowing what is permitted and what is forbidden, how could he possibly fear sin? He doesn't even know what sin is that he should fear transgressing it! How, then, could Rabbi Chanina require that one *first* cultivate fear of sin and only then proceed to increase his wisdom?

Rabbeinu Yonah clarifies the mishnah's intent. In fact, it was not speaking of precedence in terms of time and order but rather in thought. A person is readying to undertake a major and vital endeavor — the acquisition of wisdom. What is his overarching purpose in this pursuit? Rather than a mere intellectual exercise, Rabbi Chanina teaches that the primary goal must be fear of sin. Regarding the sequence, one may begin with Torah study; but his purpose in this study should be that the Torah will protect him from sin. But were his wisdom to "precede" his fear — that is, his aim was confined to intellectual challenge, pursuit of livelihood, or the like — his goal may never be reached. His wisdom will not endure, for the Torah will not help him in this type of endeavor.

This same idea is demonstrated in the aforementioned *passuk*, which speaks of *yirah* and *chachmah*. The *Avodas Yisroel* notes that it does not state, **Techilas** *chachmah yirah*, which would intimate a sequence, with fear coming **before** wisdom. Rather, the *passuk* used an alternate term, **Reishis** *chachmah yirah* — "fear is the **beginning** of wisdom." This intimates a matter of priority and purpose — that fear is what must drive our pursuit of wisdom.

Later on in this chapter (3:17), we encounter another teaching discussing the qualities of Torah and *yirah*: ...רַבִּי אֶלְעָזָר בֶּן עֲזַרְיָה אוֹמֵר אִם אֵין חָכְמָה, אֵין יִרְאָה. אִם אֵין יִרְאָה, אֵין חָכְמָה — *Rabbi Elazar ben Azaryah said...if there is no wisdom, there is no fear; if there is no fear, there is no wisdom.* Rabbi Elazar is speaking here of the higher level of fear of Hashem. Here, there is no issue of precedence; Rabbi Elazar simply lists the ingredients that are essential to the attainment of *shleimus* (perfection). Perfection in Torah cannot be achieved without fear, and this highest level of fear of Hashem is not possible without Torah.

Shabbos and Torah, Love and Fear

How does one attain this highest level of fear — the fear of Hashem? The *Me'or Einayim* (*Likutim, Beha'aloscha*) states that Shabbos is the conduit to achieving perfection in this area. The *Tikkunei Zohar* points out that the letters of the first word in the Torah, בראשית, when rearranged, form the acrostic ירא שבת. This implies a connection between this sacred day and the attainment of *yirah*. Indeed, the *Yerushalmi* tells us that an *am ha'aretz*, whose word is usually suspect, gains more trust on Shabbos. Why? Because "the awe of Shabbos is upon him" (*Demai* 4:1). Thus we see that the power of Shabbos is such that it can infuse even someone of a low stature with a measure of *yirah*.

This idea is further demonstrated by *Chazal's* description of Hashem presenting the Jewish people with the gift of Shabbos: אָמַר לוֹ הַקָּדוֹשׁ בָּרוּךְ הוּא לְמֹשֶׁה: מַתָּנָה טוֹבָה יֵשׁ לִי בְּבֵית גְּנָזַי, וְשַׁבָּת שְׁמָהּ — *Hashem said to Moshe: "I have ready, stored in My treasure house, a great gift; Shabbos is its name"* (*Shabbos* 10a). What is Hashem's "treasure house"? Another statement of *Chazal* sheds light on this concept. The Gemara in *Berachos* mentions Hashem's special treasure, stating that nothing in Hashem's world is valued more than the *otzar* (store) of fear of Heaven. This, then, was the "storeroom" from which Hashem extracted the gift of Shabbos: it came right from the treasure house of *yiras Hashem*, further emphasizing the deep connection between Shabbos and fear of Hashem.

The compelling proofs notwithstanding, the notion of associating Shabbos with fear appears mystifying. Shabbos is known primarily as a day of love for and *d'veikus* to Hashem; how, then, can it be such a primary instrument in instilling *yiras Hashem*? The comments of the *Pri Ha'aretz* (*Parshas Eikev*) may prove quite edifying in this regard; based on its words, we discover that *yirah*, in fact, can be a conduit to *d'veikus*.

At first glance, the very notion seems counterintuitive. How can fear be a catalyst for drawing close? The normal reaction of a person, when experiencing fear, is to back away from the source of his fear! The *Pri Ha'aretz* explains, however, that there is a degree of *yiras Hashem* that has the opposite effect. This is the level the Zohar refers to as *Yiras Hashem L'chaim*, "Fear of Hashem for Life," and it is the supreme level of *yiras Hashem*. This form of *yirah* is uniquely potent; it has the power to propel us *towards* Hashem — to the point that we achieve *d'veikus* to an even greater degree than could be attained through *ahavah*. Through Shabbos — the day of *d'veikus*, which draws from the power of Hashem's treasured *yirah* — a Yid can attain the complete form of *d'veikus*, borne out of the highest level of *yiras Hashem*.

While *yirah* is generally understood as occupying a level below that of *ahavah*, we see here that there is a form of *yirah* that surpasses it. In a similar vein, the *Yesod Ha'avodah* speaks of a degree of *yirah* considered to be of a higher level than *ahavah*, for it derives from the love itself. This is the hallmark of an *oveid Hashem* whose degree of *ahavah* is supreme. So much does he cherish his loving bond with Hashem that he fears and is on guard lest anything, G-d forbid, interfere with his relationship in even the slightest way. This brand of love-based fear is referred to by the *passuk* (*Devarim* 28:58) that states: לְיִרְאָה אֶת־הַשֵּׁם הַנִּכְבָּד וְהַנּוֹרָא הַזֶּה אֶת ה' אֱלֹקֶיךָ — *To fear this honored and awesome Name, Hashem your G-d*. The concluding phrase — Hashem your G-d — implies a closeness; He is *your* G-d, with Whom you have a close and special relationship. And this is the basis of "fearing His Name" — that is, that the loving relationship you enjoy with Him should always be maintained, never to be diminished in the slightest.

Thus we have discovered a great secret by which we can obtain the highest levels, as an outgrowth of just how intertwined these crucial elements are. The Zohar revealed the close association of Shabbos and *yirah*, as contained together in the word בראשית — ירא שבת. Rabbi Elazar ben Azaryah taught that Torah and *yiras Hashem* are both indispensable entities, as one cannot be attained without the other.

כל שיראת חטאו קודמת לחכמתו

And so, through the power of Shabbos and the power of Torah, we can reach the highest levels of *yiras Hashem* and *d'veikus* with Him.

In Summary

Through various teachings, especially as appearing in the mishnayos of this *perek*, *Chazal* reveal the multi-faceted nature of the attribute of *yirah*, as they elucidate its many levels.

In our mishnah, Rabbi Chanina ben Dosa addresses the comparatively lesser — but crucial — level of *yiras cheit*. This form of *yirah* is essential not only for avoiding sin, but for Torah learning to be meaningful and enduring. When stating that *yiras cheit* must precede our learning, Rabbi Chanina is not speaking so much in terms of the order of the process; technically speaking, we may learn "first." Rather, his intent is on priority and purpose: what is the goal of our learning? If it is merely as an intellectual pursuit — with no thought towards spiritual advancement — our wisdom will not endure. Rabbi Chanina teaches that learning must include an element of *yiras cheit*, whereby we study with the intent that the Torah should affect us and protect us from sin.

Later on in this *perek*, Rabbi Elazar ben Azaryah addresses the more lofty form of *yirah*: *yiras Hashem*. He supplies a basic prescription, identifying the interrelated elements that are essential for acquiring *shleimus*. To acquire *shleimus* in Torah, we need *yiras Hashem*, as well. Conversely, without Torah, it is impossible to acquire *shleimus* in *yiras Hashem*.

There are levels of *yiras Hashem* that are considered to be of the highest order. The supreme level is that form of *yirah* known in the Zohar as *Yiras Hashem L'chaim*; it represents a level so elevated that it surpasses the level of *ahavah*. In a similar vein, there is a *yiras Hashem* that *results* from *ahavas Hashem*. This *oheiv Hashem* has such love for his Creator that he actually fears lest this love be diminished in any way. Deriving from *ahavah*, this type of *yirah* is likewise considered to be on a higher level than love.

GEMS FROM THE *SEFER NESIVOS SHOLOM*

As we have seen from the teaching of Rabbi Elazar ben Azaryah, Torah has the power to facilitate the attainment of *yiras Hashem* at the greatest levels. Another element that leads to such achievement is the gift of Shabbos. Although known primarily as a day of *ahavah* and *d'veikus*, Shabbos is closely associated with the highest levels of *yirah*. The word בראשית actually contains this hidden truth; its letters can be rearranged to read ירא שבת. Through the power of Torah and Shabbos, we can ascend the heights of *yiras Hashem*, through which we can attain the greatest degree of *d'veikus* with Hashem.

פרק ג' משנה י"ב
כל שמעשיו מרובין מחכמתו
Anyone Whose Deeds Exceed His Wisdom

הוּא הָיָה אוֹמֵר, כֹּל שֶׁמַּעֲשָׂיו מְרֻבִּין מֵחָכְמָתוֹ, חָכְמָתוֹ מִתְקַיֶּמֶת. וְכֹל שֶׁחָכְמָתוֹ מְרֻבָּה מִמַּעֲשָׂיו, אֵין חָכְמָתוֹ מִתְקַיֶּמֶת:

(Rabbi Chanina ben Dosa) would say: Anyone whose deeds exceed his wisdom, his wisdom endures. But anyone whose wisdom exceeds his deeds, his wisdom does not endure.

GEMS FROM THE *SEFER NESIVOS SHOLOM*

SOURCES:

כֹּל שֶׁחָכְמָתוֹ מְרֻבָּה מִמַּעֲשָׂיו, לְמָה הוּא דוֹמֶה, לְאִילָן שֶׁעֲנָפָיו מְרֻבִּין וְשָׁרָשָׁיו מֻעָטִין, וְהָרוּחַ בָּאָה וְעוֹקַרְתּוֹ וְהוֹפַכְתּוֹ עַל פָּנָיו... אֲבָל כֹּל שֶׁמַּעֲשָׂיו מְרֻבִּין מֵחָכְמָתוֹ, לְמָה הוּא דוֹמֶה, לְאִילָן שֶׁעֲנָפָיו מֻעָטִין וְשָׁרָשָׁיו מְרֻבִּין, שֶׁאֲפִלּוּ כָּל הָרוּחוֹת שֶׁבָּעוֹלָם בָּאוֹת וְנוֹשְׁבוֹת בּוֹ אֵין מְזִיזִין אוֹתוֹ מִמְּקוֹמוֹ. (אבות ג׳)

Anyone whose wisdom exceeds his deeds – to what is he compared? To a tree whose branches are many, but whose roots are few. The wind will come, uproot (the tree), and turn it on its face... But anyone whose deeds exceed their wisdom – to what is he compared? To a tree whose branches are few, but whose roots are many. Even if all the winds in the world would come and blow at (this tree), they would be unable to budge it from its place. (*Avos* 3)

וַיֹּאמְרוּ כֹּל אֲשֶׁר־דִּבֶּר ה׳ נַעֲשֶׂה וְנִשְׁמָע. (שמות כ״ד ז׳)

And they said: "All that Hashem has spoken – we will do and we will hear." (*Shemos* 24:7)

בְּשָׁעָה שֶׁהִקְדִּימוּ יִשְׂרָאֵל נַעֲשֶׂה לְנִשְׁמַע יָצְתָה בַּת קוֹל וְאָמְרָה לָהֶן מִי גִילָה לְבָנַי רָז זֶה שֶׁמַּלְאֲכֵי הַשָּׁרֵת מִשְׁתַּמְּשִׁין בּוֹ. (שבת פ״ח.)

When Yisroel preceded the word "*nishma*" (we will hear) with that of "*na'aseh*" (we will do), a Heavenly voice emanated and proclaimed: "Who revealed to My children this secret that is employed by the ministering angels?" (*Shabbos* 88a)

אָז תִּתְעַנַּג עַל ה׳. (ישעיה נ״ח י״ד)

Then you shall take pleasure in Hashem. (*Yeshayah* 58:14)

לְאוּקְמֵי גִירְסָא סַיַּעְתָּא מִן שְׁמַיָּא הִיא. (מגילה ו:)

Retention of one's learning is dependent on special Divine assistance. (*Megillah* 6b)

The Power of Acceptance

We tend to admire and respect brilliance. Often, if someone is a "whiz," we may overlook deficiencies in character or deeds.

Pirkei Avos presents a different perspective. While *Chazal* place a premium on Torah learning, they understand that such wisdom must be reflected in one's actions. In this mishnah, Rabbi Chanina ben Dosa appears to undertake a comparative analysis of wisdom and deeds: כֹּל שֶׁמַּעֲשָׂיו מְרֻבִּין מֵחָכְמָתוֹ, חָכְמָתוֹ מִתְקַיֶּמֶת. וְכֹל שֶׁחָכְמָתוֹ מְרֻבָּה מִמַּעֲשָׂיו, אֵין חָכְמָתוֹ מִתְקַיֶּמֶת — Anyone whose deeds exceed (literally, are more numerous than) his wisdom, his wisdom will endure. But anyone whose wisdom exceeds his deeds, his wisdom will not endure.

On the surface, Rabbi Chanina's message seems clear enough. He warns against neglecting one's deeds while focusing solely on academic achievement; if one does so, his learning itself is worth little.

But a closer examination reveals some very significant perplexities surrounding this mishnah. As the Nesivos Sholom notes:

- Towards the end of this *perek*, Rabbi Elazar ben Azaryah expresses a most similar sentiment. He states (3:17): כֹּל שֶׁחָכְמָתוֹ מְרֻבָּה מִמַּעֲשָׂיו, לְמָה הוּא דוֹמֶה, לְאִילָן שֶׁעֲנָפָיו מְרֻבִּין וְשָׁרָשָׁיו מֻעָטִין, וְהָרוּחַ בָּאָה וְעוֹקַרְתּוֹ וְהוֹפַכְתּוֹ עַל פָּנָיו... אֲבָל כֹּל שֶׁמַּעֲשָׂיו מְרֻבִּין מֵחָכְמָתוֹ, לְמָה הוּא דוֹמֶה, לְאִילָן שֶׁעֲנָפָיו מֻעָטִין וְשָׁרָשָׁיו מְרֻבִּין, שֶׁאֲפִלּוּ כָּל הָרוּחוֹת שֶׁבָּעוֹלָם בָּאוֹת וְנוֹשְׁבוֹת בּוֹ אֵין מְזִיזִין אוֹתוֹ מִמְּקוֹמוֹ... — *Anyone whose wisdom exceeds his deeds, to what is he compared? To a tree whose branches are many, but whose roots are few. The wind will come, uproot (the tree), and turn it on its face... But anyone whose deeds exceed his wisdom, to what is he compared? To a tree whose branches are few, but whose roots are many. Even if all the winds in the world would come and blow at (this tree), they would be unable to budge it from its place.*

So reminiscent is Rabbi Elazar ben Azaryah's teaching of that of Rabbi Chanina, that one wonders what new facet he introduced. In fact, it is basically identical, as both extol the virtue of one whose deeds exceed his wisdom, and deplore the opposite. Aside from providing an illustrative allegory, what, indeed, did Rabbi Elazar add to the discussion?

- This whole notion of "wisdom exceeding one's deeds" or vice-versa is likewise quite puzzling. These two elements don't seem to be comparable, or measured on the same "scale." Let us consider, for example, the two elements of *yiras Shamayim* and *tzedakah*. Could you say of someone that "he gives more *tzedakah* than he has *yiras Shamayim*" (or vice-versa)? *Tzedakah* is a matter of quantity, literally measurable in dollars and cents. *Yiras Shamayim*, on the other hand, is an issue of quality; it is not something that can be counted. Thus, it doesn't make much sense to state that someone has more of one over the other. It's a much worse comparison than the proverbial apples and oranges, in this respect.

   The same is true of the subject of our mishnah. "Deeds" are a measurable quantity; "wisdom" is a matter of quality. As such, describing a person as having more wisdom than deeds doesn't seem to have much meaning.

- From the wording of the mishnah, one can almost get the sense that, not only should one's deeds exceed one's wisdom, but there is something inherently wrong with an abundance of wisdom! Notice that the mishnah does *not* say, "Anyone whose deeds are less than his wisdom, his wisdom will not endure"; rather, the stress is on an over-abundance of wisdom: "Anyone whose wisdom exceeds his deeds, his wisdom will not endure." How could it be said that an increase in Torah wisdom is *not* a good thing?!

- The Maharal makes a similar point regarding the later mishnah. It is problematic when one's wisdom exceeds his deeds. Logic would dictate, seemingly, that the ideal situation would be a person whose deeds are numerous, and his wisdom substantial (just not exceeding his deeds). But the implication of the mishnah, with its example of wind-battered trees, suggests otherwise. Given two trees, each with many roots (that exceed its branches), which would be better able to cope with the gale winds: one with few branches or many? Of course, the fewer the branches, the better. The more one has, the more likely it is to be blown over. What emerges, then, is that even if one's deeds/roots are in the majority, the one who has less branches/wisdom is better off! Is the mishnah trying to convey that it pays to be an ignoramus?

- How, in fact, is it even possible for one's deeds to exceed his Torah wisdom? After all, a person can't perform mitzvos he's never heard of. Amassing Torah knowledge is a prerequisite to proper performance. So, how could one's deeds be greater than the extent of one's knowledge?

This last point is raised by Rabbeinu Yonah. He answers it by introducing another well-known element and by advancing a most interesting phenomenon. And, as we shall see, many of the other questions are resolved by his comments.

Secret of the Angels

To shed light on our mishnah, Rabbeinu Yonah cites a passage from *Avos D'Rebbi Nosson* (ch. 22). It basically reiterates our mishnah, but with one key addition: הוּא הָיָה אוֹמֵר: כֹּל שֶׁמַּעֲשָׂיו מְרֻבִּין וְכוּ' שֶׁנֶּאֱמַר נַעֲשֶׂה וְנִשְׁמָע — He would say: Anyone whose deeds exceed...**as it states** (**Shemos** 24:7), "**We will do and we will hear.**"

This pronouncement — *Na'aseh v'nishma* — is the very one uttered by Bnei Yisroel when Hashem offered them the Torah. Declaring their readiness in this fashion was a monumental achievement, as *Chazal* relate (*Shabbos* 88a): בְּשָׁעָה שֶׁהִקְדִּימוּ יִשְׂרָאֵל נַעֲשֶׂה לְנִשְׁמַע יָצְתָה בַּת קוֹל וְאָמְרָה לָהֶן מִי גִּילָה לְבָנַי רָז זֶה שֶׁמַּלְאֲכֵי הַשָּׁרֵת מִשְׁתַּמְּשִׁין בּוֹ — When Yisroel **preceded the word** *nishma* **(we will hear) with that of** *na'aseh* **(we will do)**, a Heavenly voice emanated and proclaimed: "Who revealed to My children this secret that is employed by the ministering angels?"

From this teaching of *Chazal*, it is clear that the greatness inherent in the Jews' reply was the order in which they arranged their response, placing *na'aseh* before *nishma*. What was so remarkable about this was that they were in essence proclaiming their readiness to fulfill

Hashem's command even before hearing about it or knowing what it was.

So how, indeed, is such a thing possible? As admirable a display of willingness as it was, it doesn't appear to make much sense. "We will do even before we hear what to do." How does one do that?

Rabbeinu Yonah clarifies the intent of this teaching of *Chazal*: they are demonstrating the power of *kabbalah*, acceptance and commitment. True, they did not know yet *what* to do; but they were accepting upon themselves to do whatever they would be told, including Hashem's commandments and the instructions of the *chachamim*. And the effects of such a *kabbalah* are astounding. Rabbeinu Yonah asserts that by merely accepting right now, in an earnest way, to do all that will be forthcoming, it is accounted to the individual as *if he already fulfilled everything*.

This, explains Rabbeinu Yonah, is the meaning of our mishnah, as well. How does one achieve a state of *ma'asav merubin meichachmaso* — having his deeds exceed his wisdom — if he doesn't know what to do? The secret is: through a heartfelt *kabbalah*. As of this moment, he may not know all of the mitzvos and all of their attendant details and *halachos* (laws). But by accepting to fulfill in the future whatever it is that he will discover, he is considered as of this moment to have fulfilled *everything*; even though he knows far less than everything. *Ma'asav merubin meichachmaso.*

In this light, explains the Nesivos Sholom, the aforementioned questions regarding our mishnah are resolved. Based on the comments of Rabbeinu Yonah, the mishnah can be interpreted as referring to *precedence* as opposed to volume. How can wisdom and deeds be measured on the same scale? Why is there an implication that a lot of wisdom is problematic? The answer is that we are not discussing "amount." *Ma'asav merubin meichachmaso* means that he places his deeds *before* the acquisition of wisdom, in the manner of Bnei Yisroel at Har Sinai. Recall that the *Avos D'Rebbi Nosson* applied the *na'aseh v'nishma* proclamation to our very mishnah. When Rabbi Chanina ben Dosa speaks of one who achieves a state of *ma'asav*

merubin meichachmaso, he refers to a Yid who follows in the footsteps of his forefathers, fulfilling the *na'aseh v'nishma* dictum.

What remains to be clarified is the meaning of the "similar" mishnah concerning the wind-battered trees. The Nesivos Sholom proceeds to do just that — in the process shedding further light on our mishnah, as well.

The Dual Nature of *Na'aseh V'nishma*

There is more than one aspect to the monumental proclamation of *na'aseh v'nishma*. On one level, it represents a supreme display of loyalty and resignation. A Yid declares before Hashem, "Although I don't know what lies ahead, I am 100 percent ready to do it all; be it hard or easy, something I understand or something I don't understand — all that has no bearing on the question of whether or not I shall fulfill it. And regarding that issue, there is no doubt, for I am resolute to perform Your service to the utmost, come what may."

Such a resolution is a manifestation of one of the key foundations in *avodas Hashem*: the notion of *hisbatlus*, self-negation before Hashem. Here is a Yid who is relinquishing himself in complete dedication to Hashem's will, ready to go through thick and thin just to serve Him. And it is on account of this quality that Bnei Yisroel were compared to *malachim*. For this is the nature of these celestial servants; they have no selfish interest or ego and don't deliberate whether the various commandments square with their own view of "morality." Rather, they are beings completely subservient to *Hakadosh Baruch Hu*; if it is His will, it is right and just and something to be immediately fulfilled.

There is another aspect to the *na'aseh v'nishma* mindset, one that relates to the element of pleasure. Not material pleasure, but a more sublime sort. This is the delight experienced by those *Yidden* of an elevated stature — the pleasure derived from mitzvah performance, as encapsulated in the *passuk* (Yeshayah 58:14): אָז תִּתְעַנַּג עַל ה' — *Then you shall take pleasure in Hashem*. This, as well, comes in two varieties.

One form of deriving pleasure from mitzvos relates to *hasagos*

(attainments). The study and contemplations of a thinking, earnest *oveid* may have borne fruit. As a result, this individual has attained a singular understanding or appreciation for a particular area of *avodas Hashem*; he may relate in a unique way to certain aspects of a mitzvah. Thus, when performing these deeds, he takes especial pleasure in this service, reflecting his deep connection to it, the unique feeling that he has towards this facet of serving Hashem. And while the *Mesillas Yesharim* states that there is no greater pleasure in the world than what was just described, it does not necessarily reflect the highest levels of serving Hashem. For there is still an element here of focusing on one's self; this individual has not mastered the art of *hisbatlus*, as his main concern is still his own pleasure based on his personal understanding.

But then there is a form of *tisaneig al Hashem* (pleasure in Hashem) that is even more lofty and pristine. One who reaches this level indeed demonstrates *hisbatlus*. The essence of this type of delight is that the *oveid* takes singular pleasure simply and purely from *the fact that he is fulfilling Hashem's will*. That is, whether he has a special "feeling" for this or that aspect of service, whether he understands or does not understand, all of these considerations fade into the background. He is serving Hashem, doing what He wants. And that is his greatest pleasure.

A special *piyut* (hymn) is included in the *birchos Krias Shema* (blessings before reciting the *Shema*) on Shabbos morning, known as *Keil Adon*. This *piyut* contains the verse, צָהֳלָה וְרִנָּה לְזֵכֶר מַלְכוּתוֹ — *(There is) joy and exultation at the mention of His Kingship*. The Divrei Shmuel *ztz"l* explains this as a reference to the boundless exhilaration a Yid should feel simply for being granted the privilege to make mention of the *Malchus* of Hashem. That a mere mortal is able to refer with his own lips to the greatness of His Dominion is awesome in its own right and should fill him with indescribable joy.

And this is simply for just mentioning that Hashem is the King. Imagine the tremendous fortune at being able to actually serve the King of the Universe! What an unprecedented and unparalleled

כל שמעשיו מרובין מחכמתו

privilege this must be! The ability to serve Hashem and fulfill His mitzvos — truly a supreme delight!

When we consider these two forms of spiritual delight — the pleasure associated with understanding of and feeling for the mitzvos versus the pleasure of simply fulfilling Hashem's will — it becomes apparent that only this second form is applicable to *malachim*. Emotional considerations, intellectual pursuits — these items are not the domain of the angelic beings. Their fiery pleasure derives solely from this aspect of fulfilling Hashem's word in complete *hisbatlus* to His will.

It was in this way that Klal Yisroel resembled the *malachim* when they declared *na'aseh v'nishma*. For this august proclamation can be understood as reflecting this very aspect of *tisaneig al Hashem*. From where do you derive your principal delight? From your understanding and feeling for the mitzvah — the *nishma*; or from the actual doing, the mere fact that you are performing Hashem's will — the *na'aseh*? Klal Yisroel responded by placing the *na'aseh* before the *nishma*; that is, their principal pleasure and focus was simply on performing the will of Hashem. Through this response, they demonstrated that they had discovered the secret of the angels, prompting the Heavenly Voice to resound in proud wonderment, "Who revealed to My children the secret employed by the ministering angels?"

Thus we discover that *na'aseh v'nishma* can be understood on two different levels. One aspect of this mindset of servitude reflects a firm resolve, a commitment to subservience before Hashem. Through this declaration, a Yid proclaims his readiness to serve Hashem in any and all circumstances, no matter what lies ahead. The *na'aseh v'nishma* declaration also serves as a statement and display of priorities. A Yid reveals thereby where his main desire lies and from where he derives spiritual pleasure. He places the *na'aseh*, the pleasure associated with simply fulfilling His will, before the *nishma*, the hearing, understanding, and relating to the mitzvah. Both aspects of *na'aseh v'nishma* reveal a sense of *hisbatlus* before Hashem, and both are principal characteristics of the *malachim* themselves.

פרק ג'

The Nesivos Sholom proceeds to outline the differences between the teachings of Rabbi Chanina in our mishnah and Rabbi Elazar ben Azaryah in the later mishnah. He understands that these two mishnayos, which initially appear to be so similar, are actually reflecting the two different aspects of *na'aseh v'nishma*.

No Matter What

Rabbi Chanina ben Dosa considers the notion of deeds in connection with study. In so doing, he is actually drawing upon the first aspect of *na'aseh v'nishma* as outlined above. As the *Yidden* stood at Har Sinai contemplating the prospect of *Kabbalas HaTorah*, they stated emphatically — even before hearing and knowing what the mitzvos were — that they were ready to do it all. In fact, the subject of our mishnah does the same exact thing. Before sitting down to learn and involve himself in the wisdom of the Torah, he places the element of deeds first. That is, as stated previously, *ma'asav merubin meichachmaso* means that the doing comes *before* the engagement in wisdom. Before he even knows what to do, he already accepts upon himself that whatever he will discover in his quest for Torah wisdom, he is ready and prepared to put it into practice. As such, he achieves a state of *ma'asav merubin meichachmaso* in the literal sense; that is, his accredited deeds outnumber the deeds he knows about! For such is the power of this form of *kabbalah*; when accepting upon oneself to fulfill Hashem's will in its entirety, one is immediately granted the reward for having fulfilled all the mitzvos — even those he still has to discover!

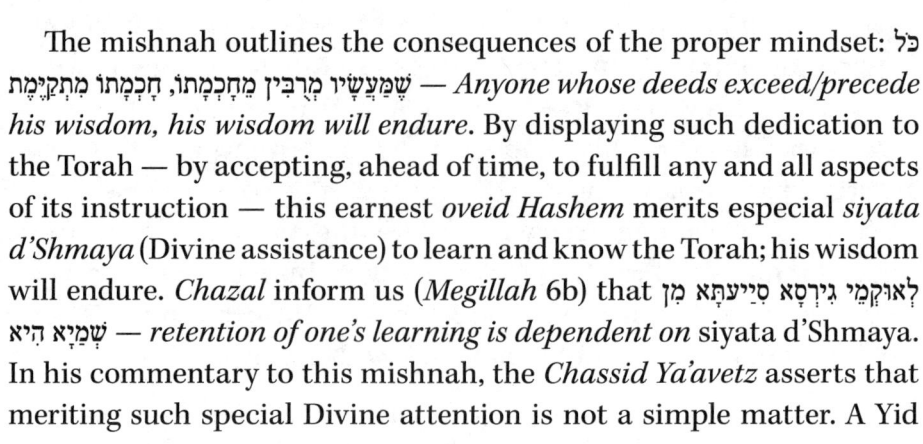

The mishnah outlines the consequences of the proper mindset: כל שֶׁמַּעֲשָׂיו מְרֻבִּין מֵחָכְמָתוֹ, חָכְמָתוֹ מִתְקַיֶּמֶת — *Anyone whose deeds exceed/precede his wisdom, his wisdom will endure.* By displaying such dedication to the Torah — by accepting, ahead of time, to fulfill any and all aspects of its instruction — this earnest *oveid Hashem* merits especial *siyata d'Shmaya* (Divine assistance) to learn and know the Torah; his wisdom will endure. *Chazal* inform us (*Megillah* 6b) that לְאוּקְמֵי גִּירְסָא סִיַּעְתָּא מִן שְׁמַיָּא הִיא — *retention of one's learning is dependent on* siyata d'Shmaya. In his commentary to this mishnah, the *Chassid Ya'avetz* asserts that meriting such special Divine attention is not a simple matter. A Yid must be found worthy, for Hashem only reveals His wisdom to those who find favor in His eyes. This is achieved, however, by one who declares *na'aseh v'nishma*; that is, his *kabbalah* precedes his pursuit of wisdom. Such an attitude will earn him the favor of Hashem, Who will then grant him the *siyata d'Shmaya* necessary for his wisdom to endure. One who is more wary, neglecting to make such a blanket acceptance prior to his discovery of the commandments, will not be privy to Hashem's special favor and guidance. His wisdom will not endure.

Thus, this mishnah dealt with this first facet of *na'aseh v'nishma*, the *kabbalah* aspect. Previously, we had wondered about the mishnah featuring Rabbi Elazar ben Azaryah's teaching: was he adding anything to what Rabbi Chanina had already said? It did not appear as such, save for providing a poignant allegory of wind-battered trees to illustrate Rabbi Chanina's point. The truth is, however, that Rabbi Elazar ben Azaryah is adding quite a bit to our previous knowledge. In fact, he is introducing to us an entire other aspect of the *na'aseh v'nishma* principle.

The second aspect of *na'aseh v'nishma* centered on the notion of deriving spiritual pleasure from serving Hashem and performing His mitzvos. It pitted two different forms of this pleasure against each other: the pleasure associated with understanding and relating to a certain mitzvah for which he has a particular feel versus the pleasure of simply being able to fulfill Hashem's will. We had demonstrated that this second form of pleasure is a much loftier form and is manifest in the *na'aseh v'nishma* declaration. That is, one places his premium on the delight of *na'aseh*, the simple "doing," over that of the *nishma*, the understanding and appreciating on an emotional level.

A significant ramification emerges between these two forms of *tisaneig al Hashem*. Most every Yid undergoes different and varying periods in his experience of performing mitzvos. There may be times of illumination and inspiration, where one feels moved to reach ever higher. But there are also periods where such inner inspiration seems to vanish. In a spiritual sense, these are periods of "blandness," where the illumination has worn off and the drive to excel has been muted. Obviously, these times provide a much stiffer challenge in one's *avodas Hashem* than when moved by some inner excitement for spirituality.

It is during these "bland" and dreary periods that the difference between the two forms of *tisaneig al Hashem* will be especially accentuated. If one's *avodah* is based, in large part, on an emotional component, a feeling of connection to an aspect to which one particularly relates — then one exposes himself to a type of spiritual danger. That is, his *avodah* will be strong and full of light and meaning — as long as the emotions hold up. But when those dark days hit, that is where the challenge becomes especially pronounced. The "spiritual high" that had so defined his *avodah* in the past has suddenly gone missing. Fulfilling the mitzvos under these conditions will really require some "heavy lifting."

The situation is entirely different, however, for one whose primary pleasure is derived from the simple fact that he is serving Hashem. This mindset is not dependent on such outside factors as mood and ambience. Even when the "dark days" hit, the reality has not changed. He is a Yid who is still privileged to be able to serve Hashem in all circumstances, under all conditions.

Rabbi Elazar ben Azaryah compared the different approaches in serving Hashem to trees battered by the wind. To what exactly does this "storm wind" refer? The Nesivos Sholom attributes it to this very phenomenon: those periods of darkness, when innate inspiration is scarce. That is, he interprets Rabbi Elazar ben Azaryah's teaching in light of this second aspect of *na'aseh v'nishma* — prioritizing and deriving pleasure in *avodas Hashem*.

One who favors the *chachmah* approach over that of *ma'asim* (deeds) — that is, he places *nishma* before *na'aseh* — is opening himself up to a difficult time. This refers to the individual whose principal pleasure is the understanding and meaning he discovers in various aspects of the mitzvos. This is well and good — until the "wind" comes along. In Rabbi Elazar ben Azaryah's parable, his "tree" has substantial foliage — plenty of meaning and inspiration — but is short on roots. When the winds of difficult and dark times blow, he will be shaken to the core. Deprived of his usual "feelings" for the mitzvos, he will be devastated and his *avodah* will suffer. He will be uprooted by the "wind."

It will be quite a different story for one whose *ma'asim* precede his *chachmah*, who places *na'aseh* before *nishma*. Deriving pleasure solely from fulfilling the will of Hashem, he is strongly rooted to the ground. In all situations of all levels of difficulty, he remains the loyal servant so grateful to serve his Master. Even when the storm winds blow, he will not be budged; his mission and purpose remain steadfast.

Is Rabbi Elazar ben Azaryah adding anything significant? The truth is that he is providing us with a lesson whose significance cannot be overstated. It is a lesson we can take with us throughout our life, to enhance our life. For he is revealing to us the secret of the prime method of serving *Hakadosh Baruch Hu* — reflective of the very secret employed by the *malachim*!

The reality is that these dark, bland days comprise most of a person's life! One whose mitzvah fulfillment is based primarily on finding meaning and constant inspiration may be in for a rough time of things. The nature of the *yetzer hara* is such that periodically — often, in fact — the emotions and feeling may just not be there. How much better would it be for a person and his *avodah* if he adopts the *na'aseh v'nishma* approach. By cultivating an appreciation of the tremendous privilege of serving Hashem, and deriving pleasure from the simple fact that you can fulfill Hashem's will, the experience of *avodas Hashem* will be elevated and transformed. And it won't be dependent on the weather, either. Rather, in all circumstances and all conditions, the joy of simply doing the will of Hashem will always be there.

In Summary

In the third *perek* of *Pirkei Avos*, Rabbi Chanina ben Dosa (mishnah 9) and Rabbi Elazar ben Azaryah (mishnah 17) both appear to deliver nearly identical teachings. Both are centered on the calculus of deeds in relation to wisdom, and both favor the individual whose "deeds exceed his wisdom." Rabbi Chanina says about such a person that his wisdom will endure; the opposite is true of one whose wisdom exceeds his deeds. The only discernible addition Rabbi Elazar ben Azaryah brings to the discussion is an illustrative allegory. He portrays the individual whose wisdom exceeds his deeds as a tree with many branches but few roots; when a strong gust blows, the tree will be uprooted and fall over. In contrast, the one whose deeds exceed his wisdom has few branches but many roots; all the winds in the world will not make the tree budge.

The Nesivos Sholom, however, demonstrates that the two teachings do, in fact, convey different ideas. He explains that the two are reflective of different aspects of the *na'aseh v'nishma* declaration.

The *Avos D'Rebbi Nosson* indicates that *na'aseh v'nishma* is the source of Rabbi Chanina's teaching. Rabbeinu Yonah explains the mishnah in light of this proclamation. The singularity of Klal Yisroel's legendary response is that they preceded the "hearing" with the "doing." That is, they agreed to fulfill all of the mitzvos before they knew what the mitzvos were. What emerges from this is a wonderful principle, pointing to the power of *kabbalah*. How does a person "do" something he wasn't yet told about? Apparently, by merely committing to fulfill all mitzvos of Hashem and instructions of the Sages, it was immediately accredited to Bnei Yisroel as if they had already done everything. In our mishnah, as well, when we place deeds before wisdom — agreeing to fulfill everything even though we do not yet know everything — it is accorded to us as if we had already fulfilled it all. In this way, our deeds "outnumber" the extent of our wisdom. And since we displayed such loyalty, Hashem will grant us special *siyata d'Shmaya* that our learning and wisdom will endure.

Delving somewhat deeper into the issue of *na'aseh v'nishma*, the Nesivos Sholom explains that the phrase can be understood on two different levels. The first aspect relates to this notion of *kabbalah*; that is, a Yid declares his readiness to fulfill all that Hashem commands, no matter how difficult and no matter if he understands it or not. This notion is reflected in Rabbi Chanina's teaching, as was explained above.

The other aspect of *na'aseh v'nishma* deals with spiritual delight, the way in which one derives pleasure from *avodas Hashem* — אָז תִּתְעַנַּג עַל ה׳. This can come about in one of two ways. There are those who put the emphasis on *chachmah*; that is, they revel in the meaning and understanding they find in regard to a particular mitzvah or aspect of *avodas Hashem*. The other method is not dependent on any specific emotional attachment to a specific component of the mitzvah. Rather, the emphasis is on the *ma'asim*, the simple act of serving Hashem. That is, the individual derives tremendous pleasure from the fact that he is privileged to be able to fulfill Hashem's will. This is another level of understanding to the notion of *na'aseh v'nishma*: where does one place his emphasis, and what is the source of his spiritual pleasure? By placing *na'aseh*, the "doing," before the *nishma*, the understanding, a Yid demonstrates thereby that his ultimate pleasure is simply doing Hashem's bidding, regardless of whatever feelings or understanding he may have in relation to particular mitzvos.

This latter aspect is reflected in the teaching of Rabbi Elazar ben Azaryah. One who places the emphasis on *chachmah* — the emotional attachment and intellectual appreciation of aspects of the mitzvos — over *ma'asim*, may be setting himself up for failure. As long as the inspiration endures, all may be well and good; but when the "wind" blows and darkness descends — that is, the fleeting inspirational feelings wear off — then mitzvah fulfillment will become a great challenge. But one who places *ma'asim* — the pleasure of simply doing the will of Hashem — before the facet of *chachmah*, will be in a much sturdier position. His *avodah* is not dependent on any specific feelings or intellectual understanding; as such, when the "wind" of dreariness begins to blow, he is not in danger of becoming uprooted and broken. No matter what the circumstance, whether he is undergoing a period of spiritual inspiration or lack thereof — a common occurrence throughout one's lifetime — his primary purpose in serving Hashem remains constant. He still is a most privileged soul, able and ready to fulfill Hashem's will. As such, this joy may remain with him throughout his life, and can likewise remain a constant — just as his *avodah* will be consistently strong and filled with delight in Hashem.

פרק ג׳ משנה י״ג
כל שרוח הבריות נוחה הימנו
Anyone with Whom People Are Pleased

הוּא הָיָה אוֹמֵר, כֹּל שֶׁרוּחַ הַבְּרִיּוֹת נוֹחָה הֵימֶנּוּ, רוּחַ הַמָּקוֹם נוֹחָה הֵימֶנּוּ. וְכֹל שֶׁאֵין רוּחַ הַבְּרִיּוֹת נוֹחָה הֵימֶנּוּ, אֵין רוּחַ הַמָּקוֹם נוֹחָה הֵימֶנּוּ:

(Rabbi Chanina ben Dosa) would say: Anyone with whom people are pleased, Hashem is also pleased with him. Anyone with whom people are not pleased, Hashem is also not pleased with him.

GEMS FROM THE *SEFER NESIVOS SHOLOM*

SOURCES:

כָּל מִי שֶׁיֵּשׁ בְּיָדוֹ שְׁלֹשָׁה דְבָרִים הַלָּלוּ, מִתַּלְמִידָיו שֶׁל אַבְרָהָם אָבִינוּ...עַיִן טוֹבָה, וְרוּחַ נְמוּכָה, וְנֶפֶשׁ שְׁפָלָה. (אבות ה׳)

Whoever possesses these three items is considered to be a disciple of Avraham Avinu...a good eye, a humble spirit, and a tempered soul. (*Avos* 5)

לֹא־יִהְיֶה בְךָ אֵל זָר. (תהלים פ״א י׳)

There shall be no foreign god among (literally: within) you. (*Tehillim* 81:10)

לֹא־יִהְיֶה בְךָ אֵל זָר... אֵיזֶהוּ אֵל זָר שֶׁיֵּשׁ בְּגוּפוֹ שֶׁל אָדָם, הֱוֵי אוֹמֵר זֶה יֵצֶר הָרָע. (שבת ק״ה:)

"There shall be no foreign god among (literally: within) you" – Which "foreign god" is found within a person's body? Conclude that this must be a reference to the evil inclination. (*Shabbos* 105b)

וַיַּעַן אַבְרָהָם וַיֹּאמַר... וְאָנֹכִי עָפָר וָאֵפֶר. (בראשית י״ח כ״ז)

And Avraham answered, and he said... "I am but dust and ashes." (*Bereishis* 18:27)

וְהָאִישׁ מֹשֶׁה עָנָו מְאֹד מִכֹּל הָאָדָם אֲשֶׁר עַל־פְּנֵי הָאֲדָמָה. (במדבר י״ב ג׳)

And the man, Moshe, was exceedingly humble, more than any man on the face of the earth. (*Bamidbar* 12:3)

וְנַחְנוּ מָה כִּי תַלִּינוּ עָלֵינוּ. (שמות ט״ז ז׳)

And what are we, that you should complain against us? (*Shemos* 16:7)

כל שרוח הבריות נוחה הימנו

אָנֹכִי עֹמֵד בֵּין ה׳ וּבֵינֵיכֶם. (דברים ה׳ ה׳)

I was standing between Hashem and you. (*Devarim* 5:5)

וְאָהַבְתָּ לְרֵעֲךָ כָּמוֹךָ – **רַבִּי עֲקִיבָא אוֹמֵר** זֶהוּ כְּלָל גָּדוֹל בַּתּוֹרָה. (ירושלמי נדרים ט׳ ד׳)

"Love your neighbor as yourself" (*Vayikra* 19:18) – Rabbi Akiva says: This is a great, essential principle of the Torah. (*Talmud Yerushalmi, Nedarim* 9:4)

הַקִּנְאָה וְהַתַּאֲוָה וְהַכָּבוֹד מוֹצִיאִין אֶת הָאָדָם מִן הָעוֹלָם. (אבות ד׳)

Envy, desire, and pursuing honor remove a person from the world. (*Avos* 4)

פרק ג׳

Beyond a Popularity Contest

One of the beautiful aspects of a Torah life is that it affords the opportunity to separate truth from falsehood. Whereas most of the world lusts after money and material success, we are able to look to the Torah for guidance as to what is truly important and what is not, what constitutes an enriched life and what is just a mirage.

But then we come to this teaching and, at first glance, everything seems to be turned on its head. A cursory reading of this mishnah seems to suggest that popularity is everything, something we would not have expected from a Torah-true perspective. The message of the mishnah appears to be that if you want to be liked by Hashem, become an all-around popular guy.

Could this really be so? Is that what's important? What happened to *middos*, to earnestness in *avodas Hashem*? Does the Torah really promote that the main thing is merely to be "popular"?

The Nesivos Sholom uncovers the true meaning of the mishnah, demonstrating that its message is infinitely more profound than a superficial reading would have suggested.

The Root of *Middos*

We find a curious statement in a later mishnah regarding our forefather, Avraham Avinu. We would expect that any basic treatment of Avraham would mention that particular trait in which he excelled: the *middah* of *chessed*. The Torah itself devotes much space to delineating Avraham's acts of kindness; the opening section of *Parshas Vayeira*, depicting the extent to which he would go in offering hospitality to wayfarers, is one case in point. Interestingly enough, however, when the mishnah (5:19) discusses the characteristics of Avraham Avinu, it completely omits any reference to Avraham's *chessed*, concentrating instead on some (seemingly) unrelated traits: כָּל מִי שֶׁיֵּשׁ בְּיָדוֹ שְׁלֹשָׁה דְבָרִים הַלָּלוּ, מִתַּלְמִידָיו שֶׁל אַבְרָהָם אָבִינוּ...עַיִן טוֹבָה, וְרוּחַ נְמוּכָה, וְנֶפֶשׁ שְׁפָלָה — *Whoever possesses these three items is considered to be a disciple of Avraham Avinu...a good eye, a humble spirit, and a tempered*

soul. Why does the mishnah seem to avoid mentioning the things for which Avraham was most known, selecting other traits instead?

The Nesivos Sholom explains that underlying this teaching is the fact that, in essence, there are two aspects to *middos*, both good and bad. Many of the traits we encounter and discuss are actually an outgrowth of something much deeper. That is, all *middos* stem from a particular root, something that lies at the core of a person. When the leaves on a tree, for example, begin to wilt or experience some abnormality in their growth and appearance, the issue may not actually rest with the leaves themselves. Often, what we perceive as unhealthy leaves is just a symptom pointing to the fact that some rot or disease may have settled into the trunk or roots of the tree.

So it is with a person's *middos*. When we see, for example, a person who displays envy or anger, these traits by themselves do not constitute the core problem. These are merely outer manifestations of a *shoresh*, a root, which at its core is *ra*.

What is that foundational attribute, the *shoresh hara*, from which spring all *middos ra'os* (poor character traits)? The Nesivos Sholom identifies it as the quality of *yeishus*, from the word *yeish* (literally, "there is"). In our parlance, this refers to the notion of ego, whereby a person asserts his sense of self, viewing himself as deserving of special care and attention. Someone with an overdeveloped sense of self has a sense of entitlement, as if everything is coming to him and everyone around him should cater to his whims and desires. Thus, a person with *yeishus* at his core will be a *ba'al ta'avah*, one who chases after desires, constantly seeking to satiate his urges. The negative traits of *kinah* (envy), *redifas hakavod* (pursuit of honor), and the like are all outward manifestations of his sense of *yeishus*. This is what is really at the root of his character.

Chazal discuss this aspect of *yeishus* in very stark terms. Commenting on the *passuk* in *Tehillim* (81:10) that states, לֹא־יִהְיֶה בְךָ אֵל זָר — *There shall be no foreign god among (literally, within) you*, the Gemara identifies this as referring to the evil root within, the אֵל זָר שֶׁיֵּשׁ בְּגוּפוֹ שֶׁל אָדָם — *foreign entity within a person's body* (*Shabbos* 105b). In some respects, viewing oneself as one's own, separate entity is a form of idolatry. The only real power is Hashem; who are you to assert yourself, as if you are entitled to honor and to have your whims fulfilled? Thus we find that *Chazal* equate one who exhibits arrogance or anger with an idol-worshipper. For these *middos* are outward manifestations of a *shoresh* of *yeishus* deep within a person. Asserting one's self as a separate and deserving entity is a form of "competing" with the One True Entity.

But the converse is also true. While the quality of *yeishus* is the foundation for all negative traits, *bitul hayeishus* is the root for all *middos tovos*. This is not to be confused with the unhealthy trait of low self-esteem, which can serve as a key impediment to a successful and productive life. Those who suffer from low self-esteem often view themselves as "bad," unlovable anomalies. They tend to feel inferior to those around them and hence take insults very to heart, and crave approval and validation from others. True *bitul hayeishus* stems from a clear recognition of the *gadlus haBorei*, the greatness of the Creator, and how everyone and everything else is *k'ayin v'efes*, like nothing, in comparison to His absolute Majesty. One who truly inculcates this idea will, for example, be impervious to insults; what does he care what some person says, if anyway both he and the other person are nonentities in the first place. What matters is only what the *Ribono Shel Olam* thinks.

And so, honing one's sense of *bitul hayeishus* can actually lead a person to tremendous accomplishments. A perfect example is none other than Avraham Avinu, who excelled in this *middah*. As he stated, *Va'anochi afar v'eifer* — "And I am but dust and ashes" (*Bereishis* 18:27). And look what he became! But the truth is that it should come as little surprise. Since *bitul hayeishus* is the root of all good *middos*, one who excels in this area will become truly great.

This is why the mishnah, when speaking of the traits of Avraham Avinu, did not mention the characteristic of *chessed*. All of Avraham's positive qualities stemmed from the all-important root of *bitul hayeishus*; to accentuate this point, the mishnah lists those *middos* where this connection is most apparent. One who engages in self-negation has essentially cured himself of airs and arrogance, and hence views everyone and everything with an *ayin tovah*. He doesn't feel that every whim or fancy he has deserves to be catered to, and hence he develops a *nefesh shefalah*. And, of course, he is the embodiment of a *ruach nemuchah*.

The Torah testifies that there was one individual who personified this attribute of Avraham Avinu to an even greater degree. וְהָאִישׁ מֹשֶׁה עָנָו מְאֹד מִכֹּל הָאָדָם אֲשֶׁר עַל־פְּנֵי הָאֲדָמָה — *The man, Moshe, was exceedingly humble, more than any person on the face of the earth* (*Bamidbar* 12:3). Moshe Rabbeinu's complete self-negation is demonstrated by the response to his and his brother's detractors, when he stated (*Shemos* 16:7), *V'nachnu mah* — "What are we?" This expression — "what are we" — represents a greater degree of humility than Avraham's declaration of "I am but earth and ashes," since earth and ashes have some substance, while "what" is the equivalent of nothing.

Foundation of the Torah

In a fairly well-known dissertation, Rav Chaim Vital (*Shaarei Kedushah* 1:2) makes the following observation. The importance of *middos* is known to all; yet, we do not find a specific commandment in the Torah regarding the cultivation of proper character traits! Why is that? Rav Chaim explains that this itself underscores the importance of *middos*, revealing just what a vital role they play in *avodas Hashem*. *Middos* cannot be listed in the form of an individual mitzvah in the Torah because they serve as the *foundation* and *basis* for the Torah. That is, for the Torah to rest within an individual, that individual must first fashion himself into a worthy receptacle by purifying his character.

We have already seen that *bitul hayeishus* — otherwise known as the *middah* of *ayin* (opposite of *yeish*) — is the source of all *middos tovos*. Based on the formulation of Rav Chaim Vital — that *middos* are the basis of the entire Torah — it thus emerges that the *middah* of *ayin* is essentially the foundation of the entire Torah.

For all intents and purposes, this sentiment is expressed by Rabbi Akiva when he declares, וְאָהַבְתָּ לְרֵעֲךָ כָּמוֹךָ זֶה כְּלָל גָּדוֹל בַּתּוֹרָה — "*You shall love your neighbor as yourself*" (*Vayikra* 19:18): *This is a great,*

overarching rule of the Torah (*Bereishis Rabbah* 24:7). The reason why Rabbi Akiva singled out the specific mitzvah of *v'ahavta l'rei'acha kamocha* as the encapsulation of the whole Torah is that it is the embodiment of the *middah* of *ayin*. In order to fulfill this mitzvah properly, a person must free himself from the influences of the quality of *yeishus*. Loving one's neighbor as oneself entails being happy in his success; the Rambam writes that the mitzvah includes an obligation to speak the praises of one's fellow (*Hilchos Dei'os* 6:3). This is very hard to do if someone has an inflated sense of self!

A person inflicted with *yeishus* can hardly tolerate when other people are in the limelight; if success is to be had, he feels, it should come to him! This very sentiment drives the pernicious practice of speaking *lashon hara* against one's fellow, itself a grievous sin. As he cannot bear that someone else be considered "greater" than he, he derives great satisfaction in tearing down his perceived rivals. To be truly interested in the welfare and success of one's fellow man, a Yid must acquire the *middah* of *ayin*; for only by negating the sense of *yeishus* can he truly fulfill the requirements mandated by the mitzvah of *v'ahavta l'rei'acha kamocha*. Since it is predicated on the quality that is the basis for all good *middos* — and hence, the entire Torah — Rabbi Akiva refers to this mitzvah as the *klal gadol baTorah*.

In summation, it can be said about this quality of *ayin* that it serves as one of the most essential factors in *avodas Hashem*, as one's very relationship with *Hakadosh Baruch Hu* is dependent on it. This notion is brought out through the oft-repeated exposition of the Ba'al Shem Tov on the *passuk* (*Devarim* 5:5): אָנֹכִי עֹמֵד בֵּין ה' וּבֵינֵיכֶם — *I (Anochi) am standing between Hashem and you*. In its literal sense, this statement was made by Moshe Rabbeinu when recounting the events of Har Sinai. He was stating how he acted as the intermediary between Hashem and the Jewish people. Homiletically, however, it contains a message of another sort, relating to the nefarious quality of the *middah* of *yeishus*. A person's ego can serve to distance him from his Creator: *Anochi* is what stands between Hashem and a Yid, erecting an iron wall that blocks one's ability to become close to Hashem. It is only to the degree that an individual diminishes his *Anochi* that he can be connected with Hashem.

Fringe Benefits

We can return to the elucidation of our mishnah based on the above. Did the mishnah really mean that so long as a person is popular, then Hashem will be pleased with him? Is this all that really matters?

The answer is that the notion expressed by the mishnah resembles the great truth we have discovered regarding *middos*. As stated, most *middos* are in reality just a symptom, an outer manifestation of a foundational core. If that core is *ra*, infested with *yeishus*, that individual will display a whole range of *middos ra'os*. But if at the root, a Yid is essentially *ayin*, then his *middos* will likewise be pristine and good.

This, explains the Nesivos Sholom, is the true intent of our mishnah. It is not that popularity is inherently important; rather, it is a symptom and signal of one's inner essence. Jews have sensitive antennae for spirituality and holiness; they can detect when they are in the presence of someone whose essence is genuinely pristine. They naturally enjoy the company of unpretentious folk; at the same time, they find themselves feeling uncomfortable around an inherently self-centered individual. As *Chazal* relate (*Bava Basra* 98a): הַאי מַאן דְיָהִיר אֲפִילוּ אֲאִינְשֵׁי בֵּיתֵיהּ לֹא מִקַּבַּל — *One who is haughty is rejected even by members of his own family.*

Thus it emerges that רוּחַ הַבְּרִיוֹת נוֹחָה הֵימֶנּוּ is a good yardstick of a person's core essence. Someone who is self-effacing is looked upon favorably by his fellow man. It is for this reason that Hashem is pleased with him. Not inherently because of his popularity, but because of the true source of that popularity: his mastery of self-negation, the highest of all core character traits. By and large, a person earns the displeasure of his fellow man because they detect that his core is comprised of a sense of *yeishus*, resulting in an outward display of poor *middos*. And it is because of this rotten core that he has also earned the displeasure of Hashem. As the mishnah states (*Avos* 4:21): הַקִּנְאָה וְהַתַּאֲוָה וְהַכָּבוֹד מוֹצִיאִין אֶת הָאָדָם מִן הָעוֹלָם — *Envy, desire, and pursuing honor remove a person from the world.* "Removal from the world" entails a removal from both worlds: from This World, as people will not tolerate him, and the World to Come, for he has earned Hashem's displeasure.

It should be pointed out that popularity is not necessarily a blanket barometer of finding favor in Hashem's eyes. The Gemara in *Kesubos* (105b) makes a very telling remark. It states that when a Torah scholar is particularly well-liked by the people of his locale, it is not necessarily a testament to his pristine character. Rather, it is because he neglects to offer them rebuke. Had he fulfilled this responsibility, his constituents may not have been as enthused.

How do we reconcile this idea with the message of our mishnah? Haven't we learned that popularity is a sign that one's core is solid and pure? The truth is that the mishnah, with its precise language, actually anticipated this issue. Notice, it does not state, כָּל שֶׁהַבְּרִיּוֹת נוֹחָה הֵימֶנּוּ — *Anyone with whom **people** are pleased*, but rather כָּל שֶׁרוּחַ הַבְּרִיּוֹת נוֹחָה הֵימֶנּוּ — *Anyone with whom **the spirit of people** are pleased*. The implication is that the mishnah is speaking of people who possess true "spirit." This is a reference to individuals of a more elevated stature, as the *passuk* states of Yehoshua bin Nun: אִישׁ אֲשֶׁר רוּחַ בּוֹ — *A man within whom the spirit rests* (*Bamidbar* 27:18). If one is well-liked among people who are not growth-oriented, it is not necessarily a good sign; on the contrary, it may point to the fact that one is shirking his duties to foster growth among the people. It is when one is well-liked among the "men of spirit" that we may conclude that he has likewise found favor in the eyes of Hashem.

In Summary

Good *middos* are manifestations of a pristine and worthy root. The core *middah* from which the others are derived is the quality of *bitul hayeishus*. As *middos* are the prerequisites to Torah and mitzvos, and they stem from this notion of *ayin*, it thus emerges that *bitul hayeishus* is, in fact, foundational for the entirety of Torah. This is the reason that *v'ahavta l'rei'acha kamocha* is considered the *klal gadol baTorah*, for its fulfillment hinges on a developed sense of *ayin*.

This is also the reason why Moshe Rabbeinu, the most humble of men, was able to achieve such greatness in his lifetime.

Yeishus is the antithesis of the *middah* of *ayin*, and hence it is literally the root of all evil. The Ba'al Shem Tov explains that the concept of *Anochi* serves as an iron wall between a Jew and Hashem. When a Yid asserts his sense of self, viewing himself as a deserving entity, he is in effect granting credence and value to an entity other than Hashem. In a sense, this is a form of idol worship, a violation of the *passuk* לֹא־יִהְיֶה בְךָ אֵל זָר — *There shall be no strange god within you.*

People can readily discern whether a person is self-effacing or self-aggrandizing. The yardstick of "if the spirit of one's fellows is pleased with him" correctly gauges self-negation, the highest of all core character traits. This, of course, assumes that we are dealing with "men of spirit." If one finds favor in their eyes, Hashem, as well, is certainly pleased with this individual. Not necessarily because of his popularity, but because of the root of self-negation that caused it. On the other hand, one who does not negate his *yeishus* is an undesirable neighbor. He will thus become disconnected from people in This World — and from Hashem in the World to Come.

פרק ג' משנה ט"ז
הוי קל לראש ונוח לתשחורת
Be Light in the Beginning and Easy in Old Age

רַבִּי יִשְׁמָעֵאל אוֹמֵר, הֱוֵי קַל לְרֹאשׁ וְנוֹחַ לְתִשְׁחֹרֶת, וֶהֱוֵי מְקַבֵּל אֶת כָּל הָאָדָם בְּשִׂמְחָה:

Rabbi Yishmael says: Be light in the beginning and easy in old age; and greet every man with joy.

GEMS FROM THE *SEFER NESIVOS SHOLOM*

SOURCES:

שַׁמַּאי אוֹמֵר... הֱוֵי מְקַבֵּל אֶת כָּל הָאָדָם בְּסֵבֶר פָּנִים יָפוֹת. (אבות א׳)

Shamai says... Greet each person with a radiant, pleasant countenance. (*Avos* 1)

מִי־יַעֲלֶה בְהַר ה׳ וּמִי־יָקוּם בִּמְקוֹם קָדְשׁוֹ, נְקִי כַפַּיִם וּבַר לֵבָב. (תהלים כ״ד ג׳, ד׳)

Who shall ascend the mountain of Hashem, and who shall stand in the place of His holiness? The one who has clean hands, and purity of heart. (*Tehillim* 24:3, 4)

יְהוּדָה בֶן תֵּימָא אוֹמֵר, הֱוֵי עַז כַּנָּמֵר, וְקַל כַּנֶּשֶׁר, וְרָץ כַּצְּבִי, וְגִבּוֹר כָּאֲרִי לַעֲשׂוֹת רְצוֹן אָבִיךָ שֶׁבַּשָּׁמָיִם. (אבות ה׳)

Yehudah ben Teima says: Be as fierce as a leopard and swift as an eagle, quick as a deer and mighty as a lion, to do the will of your Father in Heaven. (*Avos* 5)

הוי קל לראש ונוח לתשחורת

Oh, those youthful years! How much fun and freedom; how much free-spirited adventure with little pressure. "Take it easy" is the mantra of youth. There will be plenty of time to get serious when I "grow up." When I have achieved maturity of years, I will be much better positioned to vanquish my *yetzer hara* and improve and perfect my *avodas Hashem*. In the meantime, I might as well take advantage and enjoy life.

Surprisingly, at first glance it almost appears that Rabbi Yishmael in the mishnah agrees with this sentiment, at least as interpreted by Rashi. He explains the opening message of the mishnah as referring to the time of youth: the *rosh* or beginning (of one's life-path). At this point in life, he should be *kal*, light; that is, he should perform his Creator's will with ease. This will result in *no'ach l'sishchores* — it will be easy for him in old age.

If this is the mishnah's intent, however, it seems almost counterintuitive. The reality is that a person's *yetzer hara* is at peak strength in his youth. How could the *Tanna* recommend a path of "taking it easy," being "light" in one's *avodas Hashem* at that point? Reason would seem to dictate that the very opposite approach is preferable. If one works hard earlier in life, that should set him up for smooth riding later on down the road. What, then, is the mishnah really telling us?

The wording at the end of the mishnah likewise needs some clarification. This is not the first time the mishnah comments on extending a proper greeting to people, as the same idea was mentioned earlier in *Avos* (1:15). But there is a difference. Previously, in describing the need to present a joyous greeting, the mishnah used the expression *b'seiver panim yafos* — "with a radiant, pleasant countenance." Here, however, the mishnah deviates from this language, stating merely, "Greet each person *b'simchah* — with gladness," seemingly the less expressive of the two options. Why the change?

The interpretation of the Toldos Yaakov Yosef (*Parshas Vayigash*) sheds much light on the issue. Following Rashi's lead, it understands the mishnah's beginning as referring to a person's youth. Its insightful

פרק ג'

377

explanation is based on some key *pesukim* in *Tehillim* (24:3, 4): מִי־יַעֲלֶה בְהַר ה' וּמִי־יָקוּם בִּמְקוֹם קָדְשׁוֹ, נְקִי כַפַּיִם וּבַר לֵבָב — *Who shall ascend the mountain of Hashem, and who shall stand in the place of His holiness? The one who has clean hands and purity of heart.*

Mountain Climbing

These verses compare a person's principal mission in his younger years to the act of scaling a mountain. A basic rule of mountain climbing (which can be logically deduced even by those who lack expertise in this area) is to limit one's baggage. It is obviously detrimental to lug heavy packages along on one's climb; the extra weight will weigh the climber down, making his endeavor much more difficult, if not outright perilous. To ease the way up, the best advice is to travel light.

The same holds true of our effort to grow and "ascend the mountain of Hashem" in a spiritual sense. There are factors that could weigh us down, holding us back from attaining *kedushah*. What is the way forward — "Who will ascend the mountain of Hashem?" The answer is to cast off all impediments to further spiritual advancement. We must cultivate "clean hands and purity of heart," for a lack of these attributes will heavily weigh us down, thwarting our climb to higher levels in *avodas Hashem*.

This is the message the mishnah seeks to convey. It is not stating that in our youth, we should "take it easy" and coast through life. When the *Tanna* speaks of being "light," he is referring to the notion mentioned in *Tehillim*. That is, the mishnah's focus is on the spiritual climb that one must undertake while yet young. It advises the youth to "lighten his load"; that is, to cast off those factors that impede his spiritual growth. In order to ascend the mountain, he must rid himself at this time of the material influences that add to his weight and withhold him from ascending higher.

Thus we see that the matter is not as "simple" as we may have thought at first. The youthful years, in a spiritual sense, are perhaps the most difficult. It is then that one's *yetzer hara* is in its prime, exerting its strongest influence. Yet, the mishnah tells us that it is precisely at this time that one must gear up to climb the mountain and shake off the shackles and influence of This World. At first glance, this may seem like a tall order. How is this mission to be approached?

The human body actually has much to teach us about *avodas Hashem*; as it states (*Iyov* 19:26): מִבְּשָׂרִי אֶחֱזֶה אֱלוֹק — *From my flesh, I am able to perceive Hashem*. The Nesivos Sholom sheds light on our subject through an observation about the human condition. He notes two major differences concerning the incidence of sickness among the youth and later adulthood. First, it appears that children are more susceptible to contracting illness than their more seasoned counterparts; some kids seem to be in an almost perpetual state of coming down with some ailment or another. Another key distinction is resilience; while youth may be more subject to sickness, they seem, by and large, to recover somewhat quickly. An older individual, on the other hand, can find even a minor illness to be long-lasting and debilitating.

This arrangement is not coincidental, as the first aspect is directly responsible for the second. Young people are more prone to contract an illness; as such, Hashem imbued them with heightened resistance, enabling them to better withstand the onslaught of various ailments. This "extra-strength" fighting power was not granted to the older population, who are faced less frequently with such illnesses.

The Nesivos Sholom perceives in this phenomenon a great lesson, which carries over to the spiritual realm, as well. The identical situation is in effect for man's life-long spiritual climb. True, the youthful years can be the most challenging, as it is then that the *yetzer hara* wields such extraordinary power. As such, it is specifically during this period that Hashem grants us an extra measure of *siyata d'Shmaya*, supplying us with added strength to resist the *yetzer's* temptations and to rise above whatever elements seek to drag us down. Later on in life, the *yetzer* may have cooled somewhat. On the other hand, it is likewise much more difficult to undertake a spiritual climb at that late date.

The Nesivos Sholom elaborates further with an illustrative example:

Imagine if someone were thrust into an untenable and dangerous situation. He finds himself in perilous terrain, replete with abundant snakes and scorpions, and a tangle of piercing thorns wherever he treads. It is virtually impossible for him to emerge unscathed; at best, he can hope to simply remain alive while keeping his wounds and injuries to a minimum. His only real salvation would be to somehow lift himself out of this pit, rising above the reach of these harmful elements.

This is the actual situation in which we *Yidden* find ourselves. Our pristine and sacred *neshamah*, having originated from on High, has been sent down to This World to reside within a physical body. We are surrounded by potential dangers, elements that seek to sully our soul and prevent any elevation towards greater sanctity. Our sole recourse is to lift ourselves up: *Mi ya'aleh b'har Hashem*. Elsewhere in *Avos* (5:20), *Chazal* advise that to be successful in *avodas Hashem*, a Jew must conduct himself "as light as an eagle." An eagle's light composition enables it to overcome the gravitational pull of the earth and attain buoyancy to soar through the air. So, too, we must strive to "ascend the mountain of Hashem," to withstand the strong pull of the forces of materialism of This World and rise above the various pitfalls set for us by our *yetzer hara*.

This is the notion Rabbi Yishmael emphasizes in our mishnah. One may have thought that the optimal time for great spiritual advancement is in the older years, when the influence of the *yetzer* has waned (to an extent). Rabbi Yishmael sets out to correct this misimpression. On the contrary, he declares; it is specifically in our youth that we should scale Hashem's mountain, for it is then when we are fortified with the strength and vigor to reach the heights. It is true that, as long as we have a breath of life, we can always do *teshuvah*; *Ad yom moso techakeh lo* — "You wait for him (to repent) until the day of his death" (*Mussaf* for Yamim Nora'im). But the reality is that trying to forge an entirely new path in our later years is a difficult prospect indeed. Thus, it is incumbent that during the *rosh*, the younger years, with their freshness and strength, we should shake off the shackles of the material world and rise above it.

הוי קל לראש ונוח לתשחורת

One who follows this prescription — of climbing up the mountain of Hashem while yet young — will find that his path will be all the more stable and easy to adhere to as he matures. This idea is reflected both in the *passuk* as well as the mishnah. "Who will ascend the mountain of Hashem," the *passuk* states, exhorting the youth to make the climb. It continues, "And who will stand in the place of His holiness?" For one who ascends in the beginning will continue to stand firmly in Hashem's holy place throughout his life. As Rabbi Yishmael expresses, *Hevei kal l'rosh* — "Be 'buoyant' in youth" for this will facilitate *v'no'ach l'sishchores*; in the later years, it will be possible and comparatively easy to remain on this path.

The Greatest Burden

When speaking of the need to cast off the heavy packages to enable our ascent, there is, perhaps, one aspect that is more significant than the rest. For the burden that seems to act as the greatest impediment to spiritual elevation can be summed up in two letters: יש (literally, "there is"). This refers to a person's ego, the force that asserts itself within a person and serves as the basis for a host of spiritual maladies. The "*yeish*" within a person is the source of jealousy, desire, and lusting for honor, the traits that "remove a person from This World" (*Avos* 4:21). And one of the greatest of dangers of this quality is that one's "*yeish*" tends to accompany him throughout his life, constantly rearing its head and wreaking spiritual havoc.

That is, of course, unless one can purge himself of this entity right from the start. *Yeish* is *mamashus*, substantial in its influence, and it thus weighs heavily on one who would attempt to climb. But if one can minimize and cast away his ego — developing instead the quality of *ayin* (nothingness) — he will thus be rid of any extra baggage. Now, unencumbered by dead weight, the *oveid* will be able to reach the heights. One who fulfills *hevei kal l'rosh* to the maximum extent, relieving himself of his ego from the beginning of his path, will be able to enjoy the fruits of this all-important endeavor. Having successfully ascended the mountain of Hashem, he will realize the *no'ach l'sishchores*, retaining his elevated status in his older years as well.

Conversely, however, the longer one waits to address this trait, the more difficult and entrenched it will become. Ego tends to strengthen and grow as the years go on. One who does not uproot it in his younger years will have a very tough time trying to deal with it when he's older.

Thus we come full circle; the meaning of the mishnah's concluding message becomes apparent in light of the above. A person afflicted by his ego will find that it hampers his relations with other people. As he is primarily focused on his own benefit and advancement, he tends to view others as potential rivals. To his egotistical mindset, other people pose a threat: the spotlight may shift from focusing on him to shine on them instead. Such a person will find it very difficult to fulfill that crucial directive to "love your neighbor." Instead of feeling joy upon seeing others, he may experience consternation.

And so, the mishnah instructs us on greeting others. This should be done not only *b'seiver panim yafos*, with an outward, pleasant countenance, but *b'simchah*, feeling true, inner joy. This lesson follows naturally from the mishnah's preceding teaching. After casting off the burden of ego while yet in one's youth, it is now possible — with this impediment removed — to proceed to greet others with genuine *simchah*.

In Summary

Rabbi Yishmael's teaching that one should be "light" in youth, and the older years will be pleasant, reflects the *pesukim* in *Tehillim* (chapter 24). These verses state, "Who will ascend the mountain of Hashem, and who will stand in the place of His holiness? One who has clean hands and purity of heart." The mishnah and the *pesukim* share a common theme. And they both aim to clarify a misconception.

One may have assumed that the endeavor to attain spiritual elevation is best left for the time when one is more mature in years.

הוי קל לראש ונוח לתשחורת

At such a period, one's *yetzer hara* is significantly weakened — much more so than in one's youth, when the *yetzer hara* is in its prime. But the truth is just the opposite. Young people get sicker much more often; as a result, Hashem has imbued them with greater strength and resiliency to withstand the frequent occurrence of illness. This holds true in the spiritual arena, as well. While the force of the *yetzer hara* is greatest in one's youth, it is specifically then that Hashem grants a Yid special Divine assistance to resist his temptations.

"Who shall ascend the mountain of Hashem?" The time to do so is precisely while one is young, as he then has added strength. It is therefore the optimal time to cast off the drag of the material pull and rise above the temptations of This World to reach the heights of sanctity. He must develop clean hands and purity of heart, unloading the heavy burdens and impediments to his elevation. Having thus attained a spot in the place of His holiness, there he will stand and remain, even during his older years.

Rabbi Yishmael expresses this idea. When encouraging a Jew to be "light" in his youth, he doesn't mean, *chas v'shalom*, that youth is the time to "take it easy." Rather, Rabbi Yishmael is reflecting the same sentiment as contained in the *pesukim* from *Tehillim*. That is, he should be "light" in his youth, referring to the casting off of the impediments that weigh him down and keep him from climbing higher. If he follows this path and undertakes the ascent from his earliest years, then his spiritual success will continue in his older years with relative ease. He will experience *no'ach l'sishchores*.

Perhaps the most significant burden that the youth must shed is the pervasive quality of *yeish*, the ego. And while its weight is substantial and can hold one back from most any spiritual ascent, its removal is likewise empowering. Without the weight of *yeish*, a Jew can be free to leap up to the spiritual heights.

It is the ego that prevents us from opening our heart to our fellow. We view others as potential rivals, barriers to attaining our own selfish goals. But by ridding ourselves of its pernicious effects, we will be able to truly love our fellow and greet others with genuine *simchah*.

פרק ג' משנה י"ח
חביבין ישראל
Beloved Are Yisroel

הוּא הָיָה אוֹמֵר, חָבִיב אָדָם שֶׁנִּבְרָא בְּצֶלֶם. חִבָּה יְתֵרָה נוֹדַעַת לוֹ שֶׁנִּבְרָא בְצֶלֶם, שֶׁנֶּאֱמַר כִּי בְּצֶלֶם אֱלֹקִים עָשָׂה אֶת הָאָדָם. חֲבִיבִין יִשְׂרָאֵל שֶׁנִּקְרְאוּ בָנִים לַמָּקוֹם. חִבָּה יְתֵרָה נוֹדַעַת לָהֶם שֶׁנִּקְרְאוּ בָנִים לַמָּקוֹם, שֶׁנֶּאֱמַר בָּנִים אַתֶּם לַה' אֱלֹקֵיכֶם. חֲבִיבִין יִשְׂרָאֵל, שֶׁנִּתַּן לָהֶם כְּלִי חֶמְדָּה. חִבָּה יְתֵרָה נוֹדַעַת לָהֶם שֶׁנִּתַּן לָהֶם כְּלִי חֶמְדָּה שֶׁבּוֹ נִבְרָא הָעוֹלָם, שֶׁנֶּאֱמַר כִּי לֶקַח טוֹב נָתַתִּי לָכֶם, תּוֹרָתִי אַל תַּעֲזֹבוּ:

(Rabbi Akiva) would say: Beloved is man, for he was created in the image (of G-d). It is a sign of even greater love that it has been made known to him that he was created in the image (of G-d); as it is stated (*Bereishis* 9:6): "For in the image of G-d, He made man." Beloved are Yisroel, for they are called "children of Hashem." It is a sign of even greater love that it has been made known to them that they are called "children of Hashem"; as it is stated (*Devarim* 14:1): "You are children of Hashem your G-d." Beloved are Yisroel, for they were given a precious article. It is a sign of even greater love that it has been made known to them that they were given a precious article; as it is stated (*Mishlei* 4:2): "For I have given you a good purchase; My Torah, do not forsake."

חביבין ישראל

SOURCES:

וַיֹּאמֶר אֱלֹקִים נַעֲשֶׂה אָדָם בְּצַלְמֵנוּ כִּדְמוּתֵנוּ. (בראשית א׳ כ״ו)

And G-d said, "Let Us make man – in Our image and likeness." (*Bereishis* 1:26)

שֹׁפֵךְ דַּם הָאָדָם בָּאָדָם דָּמוֹ יִשָּׁפֵךְ כִּי בְּצֶלֶם אֱלֹקִים עָשָׂה אֶת־הָאָדָם. (שם ט׳ ו׳)

One who spills the blood of (another) man – (then) through man, his (own) blood shall be spilled; for in the image of G-d, He made man. (*ibid.* 9:6)

כֹּה אָמַר ה׳ בְּנִי בְכֹרִי יִשְׂרָאֵל. (שמות ד׳ כ״ב)

So says Hashem: "Yisroel is My first-born son." (*Shemos* 4:22)

בָּנִים אַתֶּם לַה׳ אֱלֹקֵיכֶם לֹא תִתְגֹּדְדוּ וְלֹא־תָשִׂימוּ קָרְחָה בֵּין עֵינֵיכֶם לָמֵת. (דברים י״ד א׳)

You are children of Hashem your G-d; do not lacerate yourselves, nor render baldness between your eyes in mourning. (*Devarim* 14:1)

וְזֹאת הַתּוֹרָה אֲשֶׁר־שָׂם מֹשֶׁה לִפְנֵי בְּנֵי יִשְׂרָאֵל. (שם ד׳ מ״ד)

And this is the Torah that Moshe placed before Bnei Yisroel. (*ibid.* 4:44)

מוּסַר ה׳ בְּנִי אַל־תִּמְאָס. (משלי ג׳ י״א)

Do not despise, my son, the instruction of Hashem. (*Mishlei* 3:11)

כֵּיצַד הֵן עוֹמְדִין? רַבִּי יוֹחָנָן וְר׳ אֶלְעָזָר, חַד אָמַר: פְּנֵיהֶם אִישׁ אֶל אָחִיו, וְחַד אָמַר: פְּנֵיהֶם לַבַּיִת. וּלְמ״ד פְּנֵיהֶם אִישׁ אֶל אָחִיו, הָא כְּתִיב: וּפְנֵיהֶם

פרק ג׳

387

GEMS FROM THE *SEFER NESIVOS SHOLOM*

לַבַּיִת, לֹא קַשְׁיָא: כָּאן בִּזְמַן שֶׁיִּשְׂרָאֵל עוֹשִׂין רְצוֹנוֹ שֶׁל מָקוֹם, כָּאן בִּזְמַן שֶׁאֵין יִשְׂרָאֵל עוֹשִׂין רְצוֹנוֹ שֶׁל מָקוֹם. (בבא בתרא צ״ט.)

How were (the *Keruvim* [Cherubs] in the Holy Temple) positioned? Rabbi Yochanan and Rabbi Elazar (dispute the matter:) One says: They faced each other; and the other says: They faced the edifice. (But) according to the one who says they faced each other – is it not written: "And their faces (were turned) to the edifice" (*Divrei Hayamim II* 3:13)? There is no contradiction: (The statement that they faced each other) refers to when Yisroel were fulfilling the will of Hashem; (the verse that states they faced the edifice) refers to when Yisroel were not fulfilling the will of Hashem. (*Bava Basra* 99a)

The Real You

Historically speaking, modern society is perhaps one of the wealthiest and most prosperous of all time. Of course, situations differ from person to person, from country to country. Overall, however, it may be said that the standard of living among even average citizens far surpasses that of earlier generations. Not to mention, of course, the virtual explosion of technological advancements that enable us to do things that until recently were the stuff of science fiction. And so, from the standpoint of conveniences, creature comforts, and general wealth, existence for today's society is perhaps the most comfortable it has ever been.

Then why is there such a preponderance of misery in the world? One would have thought that with life so streamlined through technology and replete with the most exotic and varied forms of entertainment — available not just to a privileged class but to any average resident — people should be walking around content and relaxed, with great big smiles on their faces. And yet, it often seems that with all of the advancement and prosperity, there is also widespread depression and emotional suffering.

The issue is even more perplexing given prevailing attitudes among the younger generation. In recent times, the world at large has placed a huge emphasis on self-esteem, fostering a sort of widespread "I'm okay, you're okay" mentality. With so many people being told over and over that they are the most important person in the world, that whatever they do or think or feel is wonderful, why isn't there overwhelming, worldwide confidence and contentment? If anything, lack of self-esteem among today's youth (and beyond) seems rampant.

It could be that the failure is attributable to a simple factor: Empty statements. That is, these grand pronouncements that "You are the greatest" or "You are special" are just that — vapid, unexplained, and unsubstantiated statements. Lacking true substance, the message never really penetrated in the way it was intended.

All of this underscores one truly significant notion: how fortunate is the Torah nation! For we are explicitly told of our inherent greatness and are further informed of exactly what it is that makes us great. Instead of just empty sentiments, these are expressions of powerful truth and substance. Let us examine the teaching of Rabbi Akiva to discover what it is that makes us truly special and great — and how much greater we can become.

The Source of the Matter

In this mishnah, Rabbi Akiva mentions three key areas that demonstrate that we are extraordinary in Hashem's eyes: חָבִיב אָדָם שֶׁנִּבְרָא בְצֶלֶם... חֲבִיבִין יִשְׂרָאֵל שֶׁנִּקְרְאוּ בָנִים לַמָּקוֹם... שֶׁנִּתַּן לָהֶם כְּלִי חֶמְדָּה — *Beloved is man, for he was created in the image of G-d... Beloved are Israel, for they are called "children of Hashem"... Beloved are Israel, for they were given a precious article (the Torah).*

Before elaborating on each of these aspects, the Nesivos Sholom raises some salient points. As admirable as the content of Rabbi Akiva's teaching is, its relevancy and place in this *masechta* is somewhat unclear. *Pirkei Avos* is centered on *mussar* and *middos*, defining hundreds of ways to refine our actions and character. But this mishnah appears to switch tracks; instead of focusing on character improvement, it tells us how special we are! How exactly does this idea conform to the principal message of *Maseches Avos*?

For each of the highlighted aspects, Rabbi Akiva cites a supporting *passuk*. In each instance, however, the particular selection is a cause of some puzzlement.

Take the first one, for instance: חָבִיב אָדָם שֶׁנִּבְרָא בְצֶלֶם. חִבָּה יְתֵרָה נוֹדַעַת לוֹ שֶׁנִּבְרָא בְצֶלֶם, שֶׁנֶּאֱמַר כִּי בְּצֶלֶם אֱלֹקִים עָשָׂה אֶת הָאָדָם — *Beloved is man, for he was created in the image (of G-d). It is a sign of even greater love that it has been made known to him that he was created in the image (of G-d); as it is stated, "For in the image of G-d, He made man"* (Bereishis 9:6). While it may appear straightforward enough, this selection is actually only part of the *passuk*. Viewed in its full context, we see that this is not even the main point of the *passuk*: שֹׁפֵךְ דַּם הָאָדָם בָּאָדָם דָּמוֹ יִשָּׁפֵךְ כִּי בְּצֶלֶם אֱלֹקִים עָשָׂה אֶת־הָאָדָם — *One who spills the blood of (another) man, (then) through man, his (own) blood shall be spilled; for in the image*

of G-d, He made man. The main topic of this verse is the prohibition against murder. It mentions the notion of man in Hashem's image only by way of explaining the severity of the prohibition; "Do not kill a human being, for he reflects the Divine."

This is what seems perplexing: Rabbi Akiva had other, perhaps more appropriate, options in providing a source for his teaching. Why not select a *passuk* where this matter serves as the focal point, rather than merely playing a peripheral role? For example, the following *passuk* from the Creation narrative states: וַיֹּאמֶר אֱלֹקִים נַעֲשֶׂה אָדָם בְּצַלְמֵנוּ כִּדְמוּתֵנוּ — *And G-d said, "Let Us make man in Our image and likeness"* (*ibid.* 1:26). Here, the entire *passuk* is devoted to this theme; it is not simply supplying a reason for something else. Why didn't Rabbi Akiva choose this source instead?

The same issue arises in the next aspect Rabbi Akiva mentions: חֲבִיבִין יִשְׂרָאֵל שֶׁנִּקְרְאוּ בָנִים לַמָּקוֹם. חִבָּה יְתֵרָה נוֹדַעַת לָהֶם שֶׁנִּקְרְאוּ בָנִים לַמָּקוֹם, שֶׁנֶּאֱמַר בָּנִים אַתֶּם לַה' אֱלֹקֵיכֶם — *Beloved are Yisroel, for they are called "children of Hashem." It is a sign of even greater love that it has been made known to them that they are called "children of Hashem"; **as it is stated, "You are children of Hashem your G-d"*** (*Devarim* 14:1). Here, again, a viewing of the greater context reveals a similar situation as before: בָּנִים אַתֶּם לַה' אֱלֹקֵיכֶם לֹא תִתְגֹּדְדוּ וְלֹא־תָשִׂימוּ קָרְחָה בֵּין עֵינֵיכֶם לָמֵת — *You are children of Hashem your G-d; do not lacerate yourselves, nor render baldness between your eyes in mourning.* The main focus in this *passuk* is another prohibition, forbidding the emulation of the gentiles' practice of self-mutilation as a show of mourning. The issue of Klal Yisroel being Hashem's children, in this context, is merely the introduction to this particular law: "You are Hashem's children; as such, you must retain your dignity, and refrain from such practices."

Why, then, does Rabbi Akiva once again cite a verse where the idea he aims to highlight figures only in a secondary, supportive capacity? Why not select a source where this idea plays the dominant role? The *passuk* from the episode of the Jews' ordeal in Egypt serves as a perfect illustration. Hashem instructs Moshe to appear before Pharaoh and relate the following: כֹּה אָמַר ה' בְּנִי בְכֹרִי יִשְׂרָאֵל — *So says Hashem: "Yisroel is My first-born son"* (*Shemos* 4:22). This *passuk*

features nothing else other than Hashem's unequivocal declaration that He considers the Jewish people as His children — first-born, no less. Why did Rabbi Akiva prefer a source where this idea plays a more secondary role, providing a reason for the main object of the *passuk* (the prohibition against making lacerations)?

The final aspect featured by Rabbi Akiva likewise follows this intriguing pattern: חֲבִיבִין יִשְׂרָאֵל, שֶׁנִּתַּן לָהֶם כְּלִי חֶמְדָּה. חִבָּה יְתֵרָה נוֹדַעַת לָהֶם שֶׁנִּתַּן לָהֶם כְּלִי חֶמְדָּה שֶׁבּוֹ נִבְרָא הָעוֹלָם, שֶׁנֶּאֱמַר כִּי לֶקַח טוֹב נָתַתִּי לָכֶם, תּוֹרָתִי אַל תַּעֲזֹבוּ — *Beloved are Yisroel, for they were given a precious article. It is a sign of even greater love that it has been made known to them that they were given a precious article;* **as it is stated, "I have given you a good purchase, My Torah; do not forsake it"** (*Mishlei* 4:2). Once again, the idea is stated here only in the course of providing a rationale for the main point: "Do not forsake My Torah — for I have given you a valuable gift." Why not instead cite a source where the idea is stated explicitly in the Torah as a stand-alone declaration, such as in the following *passuk*: וְזֹאת הַתּוֹרָה אֲשֶׁר־שָׂם מֹשֶׁה לִפְנֵי בְּנֵי יִשְׂרָאֵל — *And this is the Torah that Moshe placed before Bnei Yisroel* (*Devarim* 4:44)?

Obviously, Rabbi Akiva's selections are not haphazard; if we can uncover his intent behind the method described above, we may better appreciate the depth of his message.

The Ultimate *Mussar Shmuess*

Initially, the Nesivos Sholom asked how this mishnah relates to the overall *mussar* theme of *Pirkei Avos*. In addressing this issue, he explains that Rabbi Akiva's words constitute a *mussar* discourse of the most powerful sort.

Shlomo Hamelech states (*Mishlei* 3:11): מוּסַר ה' בְּנִי אַל־תִּמְאָס — *Do not despise, my son, the instruction of Hashem.* On its most basic level — following the aforementioned literal translation — this *passuk* is an exhortation not to disregard Hashem's admonishment and to accept His instruction. The Saba Kadisha of Slonim *ztz"l*, however, renders this verse with a homiletic twist. He perceives in it a poignant call to refine our *middos*; a *mussar shmuess* coming from Hashem Himself. *Mussar Hashem* — what is the admonition that Hashem delivers to each and every Yid? In essence, it consists of a single word: *B'ni!* — "You are My son!" This is the ultimate admonition. To drive home the point, the *passuk* continues: *Al timas!* — "Do not become repulsive!" You are My son, son of the King! Far be it from the royal offspring to betray and degrade their inherently elevated status. By virtue of the fact that Klal Yisroel is *B'ni*, it is essential that they not corrupt their character — "*al timas!*" Without rising to the occasion and refining their *middos*, they will thus render themselves repulsive.

It is this aspect of *middos* that distinguishes a Jew from the rest of the nations. To be sure, it is certainly possible for a gentile to be pleasant and polite; indeed, many are. But their refinement does not stem from the same source as does that of a Yid. The civility of the nations is but a product of social convention; as such, their gentility will never reach the same depth as the *middos tovos* cultivated by a Jew. For a Jew's *middos* result from the exhortation of "*B'ni!*"; they reflect the refinement worthy of a child of Hashem.

This notion forms the basis of Rabbi Akiva's teaching. Hashem informs the *Yidden* that they are indeed special. How? "*B'ni!*" You are My children. Rabbi Akiva demonstrates how this exhortation manifests itself in three key areas in the most powerful and profound ways.

Let us examine the first of these elements a bit more closely: חָבִיב אָדָם שֶׁנִּבְרָא בְצֶלֶם — *Beloved is man, for he was created in the image of G-d*. To appreciate the depth of this statement, it is first necessary to attempt to define this concept. What, indeed, is the meaning of *Tzelem Elokim*, the "image of Hashem"? The issue is all the more thorny in light of the fact that, as we know, *Hashem has no body, shape, or form whatsoever*. This principle is one of the thirteen tenets of our faith. Is there any way, then, to grasp what is meant by "the image of Hashem"?

The short answer to this question is "no." This is a concept so deep and esoteric, it is essentially beyond the comprehension of mortals and is certainly beyond the purview of this work. Nevertheless, a semblance of the underpinnings of this idea has come down to us through the Zohar and the Arizal. We present here a truncated version of their sacred revelations, with the understanding that it can in no way be viewed as a full and complete rendition of their true intent. Although the following presentation reflects but a shell of the complete exposition, falling woefully short of the actual essence of this elevated concept, it is nevertheless hoped that the reader will derive some sense of the sheer magnitude of the ideas involved.

The sacred, mystical sources speak of a *Tzelem* that exists in the uppermost spheres. It has no physical characteristics, it is not a body, it has no form. For our purposes, it can be characterized in terms of *Oros Elyonim*; perhaps the best way to translate this is as "Emanations of Celestial Light." It is to this *Tzelem* that Hashem was referring when He stated at the time of Creation: נַעֲשֶׂה אָדָם בְּצַלְמֵנוּ כִּדְמוּתֵנוּ — *Let Us make man in Our image and likeness*. That is, man was fashioned to correspond to and be connected with this Celestial *Tzelem*. His various limbs and characteristics are aligned, in some fashion, with certain aspects of this Upper *Tzelem*.

In a sense, this arrangement works both ways. That is, to get some sense of the workings of this Celestial *Tzelem*, one need only look at a person. For a human being serves almost as a "map" to the *Oros Elyonim* of the *Tzelem* Above. His eyes reflect the "Eye-*Oros*" of Above; his ears mirror the "Ear-*Oros*"; and so forth. Whatever exists in man below is, in some esoteric sense, a facsimile of the Celestial entity.

It is with this backdrop in mind that we return to Rabbi Akiva's teaching, for he alludes to this concept when highlighting that man is created *b'Tzelem*. Based on the above, the ramifications of this fact are truly awe-inspiring. Rabbi Akiva is couching the "*B'ni*" exhortation in the most awesome of terms. He is reminding us, "Do you know what you are? Not just anyone; not just a 'regular' person; but a creature who reflects the *Tzelem Elokim*! Your makeup, your limbs, everything about you is modeled after the most lofty and august of entities; you are literally connected with the upper spheres!"

The mishnah continually stresses the idea of "realization." *Noda'as lahem* — "It was made known to them." For once a person realizes the magnitude of his stature, how he reflects and is connected with the Upper workings of the Celestial spheres, he can respond in kind.

Thus, this knowledge is a superb tool to refrain from sin and to strive for perfection. *"B'ni, al timas!"* For how can a person — patterned after and connected to the Uppermost Realms, whose limbs serve as vehicles for the *Oros Elyonim* — even consider debasing his sacred essence through sin or poor character? And once one is aware of his actual "pedigree," of his inherently elevated status — then imagine the potential to truly reach the heights!

Thus we see that it is truly a display of love, an especial favor that Hashem shared with us this vital knowledge. One who knows that he was created in Hashem's image has a different impression of himself. He has self-worth. He knows that he is the pinnacle of creation. Therefore, he acts differently. He has tremendous self-respect, as well as respect for others, who were also created in Hashem's image. That is the greatness of man. That is our essence.

This particular aspect relates to all humans, for Adam and all of his descendants share this great privilege of reflecting the Divine image. Unfortunately, precious few members of the human race are aware of this portentous fact. But those who are have a tremendous *zechus*. It behooves them to utilize this great knowledge, remain forever cognizant of their worth and potential, and always strive to meet it.

The following aspects, however, relate solely to the Jewish people. How fortunate they are that they have these great privileges — and that they were made aware of them. *"B'ni! Al timas!"* You are literally Hashem's children — *banim laMakom*. How, then, can you even contemplate betraying this august stature by succumbing to the wiles of the *yetzer hara*. And you were granted the *Kli Chemdah* — the precious article that upholds all of creation! Do you realize how powerful you are, how great you are, how fortunate you are to be part of this chosen nation to whom the Torah was entrusted?!

It is worthwhile to simply contemplate the potency of Rabbi Akiva's *mussar*. Consider an individual who may be feeling somewhat low. He may think to himself, "What good is my *avodah* after all? Do my meager deeds really matter so much? It's not like I'm the *gadol hador* (sage and leader of the generation) or anything. Is what I do really so significant in the long run?" To this Rabbi Akiva responds, "Yes! Yes! A thousand times yes! You are great — greater, in fact, than the angels! You were created in and connected with the Celestial *Tzelem*; you are a noble, royal child of Hashem; you have the responsibility to learn and fulfill the Torah — the key to the universe! You are capable of reaching heights that angelic beings could only dream about!" And of course, one who thinks in this manner will take his *avodah* quite seriously and will recognize and appreciate his own worth and contributions.

A Lasting Impression

In light of the above, we can begin to understand the logic behind Rabbi Akiva's selection of sources. Why did he avoid citing those *pesukim* that seemingly would have served as more appropriate sources? Why didn't he select those *pesukim* in which the idea he sought to highlight was the central focus? When we examine each one, however, we discover that his actual selections are exactly on message. They reflect the point he seeks to make even more than the other options. In fact, had he chosen those other "preferable" *pesukim* as his source, we may have formed the wrong impression, as we shall see.

Rabbi Akiva first discussed man's inestimable value in that he was created *b'Tzelem Elokim*. We wondered why he didn't cite, as support, the *passuk* from the Creation narrative: *Na'aseh adam...* — "Let Us make man (in Our image)." Recall, however, the principal reason Rabbi Akiva is speaking of these matters. He is seeking to instill within us a deep appreciation of our inherent greatness and our remarkable potential, and to spur us on to bring this potential to fruition. It is true that the creation of man in the image of Hashem is the central theme of this particular *passuk*. Had he cited it, however, it may not have conveyed the message he was seeking to impart. For it left room for a person to draw an erroneous conclusion. "That is well and good," someone may have said, "as long as a person remained on a certain level. But nowadays, it's too late; we have already sunken to new lows. We have sinned, and our *Tzelem Elokim* has long since been debased. Who are we to think that after behaviors such as we have exhibited, we can still lay claim to such innate potential? How can we talk of a connection to the most elevated Celestial Realms?"

And so, to correct this mistake, Rabbi Akiva had to resort to an alternate source. He therefore selected the *passuk* that appears in our mishnah. The notion of *Tzelem Elokim* is only mentioned in this verse in a somewhat peripheral manner, as an explanation of the *passuk's* main theme (the prohibition against murder), yet this is precisely the point. The prohibition against murder was not a temporary injunction; rather, it is an eternal law, as relevant today as it was since the start. Rabbi Akiva specifically cited this verse, which juxtaposes the notion of *Tzelem Elokim* with the prohibition against murder. By doing so, he is able to illustrate that the lofty ideal of *Tzelem Elokim* is likewise still very much in effect. In other words, he purposely chose a *passuk* that demonstrates the eternal nature of this concept. In the twenty-first century, it is still forbidden to commit murder; likewise, we still retain the astronomical potential for greatness inherent in beings created in G-d's image.

The same holds true for the other aspects mentioned by Rabbi Akiva. When illustrating that we are Hashem's children, why not cite the verse in which Hashem proclaims, *B'ni bechori Yisroel*? Here, too, there is an opening for one to dismiss the vital message. Yes, this *passuk* demonstrates how special we are in Hashem's eyes. But (one may claim) this *passuk* speaks of a bygone era, before the Jews even left Egypt! At that time Hashem considered them His beloved children. But so much has happened since then, both collectively and individually! After sins like the *Eigel Hazahav*, compounded ever since by our many individual failings, we have surely lost this august title. "Not so," says Rabbi Akiva. And so he once again cites a *passuk* where this idea is tied to a particular law, one which applies throughout the generations. בָּנִים אַתֶּם לַה׳ אֱלֹקֵיכֶם; לֹא תִתְגֹּדְדוּ — *You are children of Hashem your G-d; do not lacerate yourselves. Lo sisgodedu* is an eternal law; so is your status as children of Hashem. No matter what has happened to date, you are still Hashem's precious and royal children. You have the same potential for greatness and the ability to attain it.

When speaking of the *Kli Chemdah* bestowed upon Klal Yisroel, Rabbi Akiva delivers the same message. One may have thought that our tremendous privilege as Hashem's chosen nation has diminished; through our sins, perhaps our connection to Torah has been severed. To banish such thoughts, Rabbi Akiva brings a *passuk* that accentuates our eternal bond with this *Kli Chemdah*. "I have given you a valuable gift," Hashem says. "Don't ever abandon it! It was yours then, it is yours now, and so shall it be, forever." The text of the blessing over the Torah reflects this very notion. In it, we refer to Hashem in the present tense, *Nosein HaTorah* — "the One Who gives us the Torah," as opposed to the past tense, *Nasan HaTorah* — "He gave us the Torah." That is, the giving of the Torah was not a one-time event. Even now, every day, Hashem continually teaches and gives us the Torah. Our ability to connect to it and affect the universe is as relevant today as it ever was.

Elsewhere, *Chazal* make a similar point, bringing it out in a most dramatic way. Many wonders were on display in the time and area of the Beis Hamikdash. One of these phenomena involved the *Keruvim*, the angelic figures perched atop the golden *Aron Kodesh* (Holy Ark). Though fashioned from immobile metal, the *Keruvim* were able to shift their positioning, thereby reflecting the current level of Divine favor Klal Yisroel had earned. The Gemara states (*Bava Basra* 99a) that when Yisroel was worthy, the two *Keruvim* faced each other; but when their observance was wanting, the *Keruvim* turned away from each other.

And yet, an amazing thing occurred at one of the most trying times in our history. The Gemara states elsewhere (*Yuma* 54b) that at the time of the *Churban* (Destruction of the Beis Hamikdash), a surprising discovery was made. When the enemy penetrated the Temple and entered the Sanctuary, the *Keruvim* were locked in embrace.

This seems quite puzzling in light of *Chazal's* other statement (in *Bava Basra*). When Klal Yisroel had fallen to disfavor, the *Keruvim* turned away from each other. But the *Churban* was the nadir of Klal Yisroel's history, from which we still suffer to this day. One would have imagined that if ever there was a "low point" whereby Yisroel had lost Divine favor, it was at the time of the *Churban*. How, then, was it that the *Keruvim* indeed were facing one another and embracing?

The Nesivos Sholom explains that *Hakadosh Baruch Hu* chose this specific occasion to deliver a vital message — one that reverberates throughout the generations. He sought to demonstrate to the entire world just how special Klal Yisroel is to Him; and that this special love continues no matter how low they may have fallen. The surprising discovery of the *Keruvim's* embrace was a stark and public display of Hashem's great love for His children, His Chosen People. They may have sinned, but Hashem wanted them to know that, inherently, their special status in His eyes remains for all time.

The constant refrain throughout Rabbi Akiva's teaching is חִבָּה יְתֵרָה נוֹדַעַת לָהֶם — *It is with abundant love that it was made known to them* (that they are *Tzelem Elokim* and *banim laMakom*, and [they have the] *Kli Chemdah*). Why does Hashem make His great love known to His people? Why does anyone let another know of the great love he feels for that person? The answer, says the Nesivos Sholom, is simple: reciprocation. In revealing His great love for us, Klal Yisroel, by informing us of our elevated stature and inherent greatness, Hashem desires that we reciprocate in kind. Hashem greatly wants that we should likewise love Him with a fiery love and serve Him with completeness and out of love for Him.

In Summary

Even from a cursory glance at Rabbi Akiva's three-tiered teaching we can sense that he is relating something of profound significance. Nonetheless, it appears — initially, at least — to be somewhat out of place. How, exactly, is his statement about how precious and fortunate is Klal Yisroel in keeping with the overall *mussar*-theme of *Pirkei Avos*?

The Nesivos Sholom explains that, indeed, Rabbi Akiva's teaching constitutes a masterful *mussar shmuess*. It reflects that ultimate *mussar* admonishment contained in the words of *Mishlei*, מוּסַר ה' בְּנִי אַל־תִּמְאָס. The *passuk* can be interpreted as relating the "*mussar* of Hashem." To each and every Yid, Hashem says, "*B'ni*, you are My son!" As such, you possess inherent, unimaginable greatness. Your worth and stature is beyond measure. And so, you must take care to conduct yourself with dignity, in keeping with your elevated status. That is the admonishment. "*Al timas!*" Don't betray your responsibility and degrade your essence!

This notion is borne out through the three aspects highlighted by Rabbi Akiva. He speaks first of the concept that man was created in the image of Hashem. The profundity of this idea and its precise meaning are beyond human comprehension. It is clear, however, that it reflects the pristine and elevated nature of human beings and their connection to the highest levels of the upper spheres. Those who recognize that they are patterned after the *Tzelem* of Above will surely aim to be worthy of the sheer loftiness of their stature.

While the above holds true for every human being, the remaining aspects Rabbi Akiva mentions are solely the province of Klal Yisroel. And so he reminds us that we are *banim laMakom*, Hashem's children, members of the most august nobility. And we are members of the Chosen People, those who received the *Kli Chemdah* that is the Torah. The Torah enables its adherents to affect and support the entire universe. Rabbi Akiva thus reminds us of our amazing potential, the knowledge of which could prove instrumental in attaining it.

Rabbi Akiva cited Scriptural proofs for each of the aforementioned items, and his selection of sources is quite noteworthy. While he could have chosen to cite *pesukim* that feature these ideas most prominently, he instead seems to have selected verses where the notion is dealt with only peripherally. For example, instead of citing the *passuk* of *Na'aseh adam* to illustrate the concept of *Tzelem Elokim*, he chose the verse where the idea is mentioned in a different context — namely, as a reason for the prohibition against murder.

The Nesivos Sholom explains that the selection process was indeed quite deliberate. For Rabbi Akiva sought not only to convey to us the idea of our true greatness; he also wanted to ensure that we not conclude (erroneously) that this great potential has been forfeited through our misdeeds. Such a mistake would have been possible had he cited some of the other *pesukim*. But he specifically brought in sources that demonstrate that these ideas are eternal. That is why, for example, he chose the *passuk* mentioning the notion of *Tzelem Elokim* in connection with the prohibition against murder. In so doing, Rabbi Akiva was conveying this important message: just as the prohibition against murder lasts for eternity, so does man's elevated status of reflecting the *Tzelem Elokim*.

This is the thrust of Rabbi Akiva's teaching. He exhorts us to be aware of our inherent greatness, as evidenced by these three wondrous truths. And he seeks to ensure that we not err in thinking that perhaps we have forfeited the opportunity, G-d forbid. Even if a person has stumbled, that inherent greatness remains. Throughout all times and situations, no matter what one has done in the past, Hashem still declares, *"B'ni!"* You are My son; you have outstanding potential. Now — *"Al timas!"* Utilize your august status and reach that great potential that is afforded by the *Tzelem Elokim*, by your status as Hashem's children, and by your connection to the Torah.

פרק ג' משנה י"ט
הכל צפוי והרשות נתונה
All Is Foreseen, yet Freedom of Choice Is Granted

הַכֹּל צָפוּי, וְהָרְשׁוּת נְתוּנָה, וּבְטוֹב הָעוֹלָם נִדּוֹן. וְהַכֹּל לְפִי רֹב הַמַּעֲשֶׂה:

All is foreseen, yet freedom of choice is granted; the world is judged with goodness; and all is in accordance with the majority of deeds.

GEMS FROM THE *SEFER NESIVOS SHOLOM*

SOURCES:

אֲנִי מַאֲמִין בֶּאֱמוּנָה שְׁלֵמָה, שֶׁהַבּוֹרֵא יִתְבָּרַךְ שְׁמוֹ יוֹדֵעַ כָּל מַעֲשֵׂה בְּנֵי אָדָם וְכָל מַחְשְׁבוֹתָם. (עיקר י' מי"ג עקרי אמונה)

I believe with a complete faith that the Creator, Blessed be His Name, knows all the deeds of mankind, as well as all of their thoughts. (From the Thirteen Principles of Faith – Tenth Principle)

צַו אֶת־אַהֲרֹן וְאֶת־בָּנָיו לֵאמֹר זֹאת תּוֹרַת הָעֹלָה. (ויקרא ו' ב')

Command Aharon and his sons, saying: This is the law of the burnt-offering. (*Vayikra* 6:2)

צַו אֶת־אַהֲרֹן - אֵין צַו אֶלָּא לְשׁוֹן זֵרוּז מִיַּד וּלְדוֹרוֹת אָמַר ר' שִׁמְעוֹן בְּיוֹתֵר צָרִיךְ הַכָּתוּב לְזָרֵז בְּמָקוֹם שֶׁיֵּשׁ בּוֹ חִסָּרוֹן כִּיס. (רש"י שם)

"Command (*Tzav es*) Aharon" – "*Tzav*" is none other than a term conveying encouragement, for now and for later generations. Rabbi Shimon said: There is an especial need to provide extra encouragement when issuing a command that entails a financial loss (as the entire animal is consigned to the altar). (*Rashi, ibid.*)

אֵין הַקָּדוֹשׁ בָּרוּךְ הוּא בָּא בִּטְרוּנְיָא עִם בְּרִיּוֹתָיו. (עבודה זרה ג.)

Hashem does not impose tasks upon His creatures that are impossible for them to accomplish. (*Avodah Zarah* 3a)

לֹא בָא עַל הָאָדָם אֶלָּא לְפִי כֹּחוֹ. (שמות רבה ל"ד א')

Hashem only confronts a person (with a trial) in accordance with his abilities. (*Shemos Rabbah* 34:1)

פרקי אבות

404

Telling the Future

The rabbi always felt privileged to have Sam Reshevsky (eight-time winner of the US chess championship) as a participant in his weekly Gemara *shiur*. Sam was a Polish Jew who came to the United States as a child chess prodigy with international celebrity status. The rabbi enjoyed Sam's gifted intellect. The two had a congenial relationship, characterized by mutual respect.

"Sam, if we played chess together, could you predict my next move?" the rabbi asked him one day.

"Yes," Sam replied, "if I watched you play for a few minutes."

"And to what degree of certainty could you predict my move?" coaxed the rabbi.

"I'd say 95 percent," replied Sam.

Armed with this information, the rabbi turned to address his congregation. "Sam has absolutely no control over me or my future moves. Yet, because of his expertise, he can predict my move with a 95-percent degree of certainty. This gives us some insight into understanding Hashem's view of the world. He created us and knows us so well, and can easily foresee our next move with 100 percent certainty. At the same time, however, He opts to allow us complete *bechirah* (free choice) in carrying out that move."

The truth is, however, that Hashem's foreknowledge of our deeds is far more profound than simply being able to render an accurate forecast. That is, it is more than a mere "prediction"; rather, Hashem sees and knows right now what (to us) appears to lie in the future. There is no real way for the human mind to accurately relate to the depths of Hashem's Omniscience, a fact which the Rambam seems to attribute to our mishnah.

Everything Is Foreseen...

The Rambam, in his commentary, makes a singular remark regarding this mishnah: "This teaching encompasses matters of great profundity. It is fitting that it comes from Rabbi Akiva." The

Rambam rarely makes a comment of this nature. What are these weighty matters with which the mishnah is dealing?

The Nesivos Sholom perceives herein an emphasis on clarity in *emunah*. Elsewhere in his mishnah commentary, the Rambam, as is well known, lists thirteen articles of faith incumbent on every Jew to know, acknowledge, and internalize. The tenth principle relates to Hashem's scrutinizing of man's activities. As stated in the summarized version: אֲנִי מַאֲמִין בֶּאֱמוּנָה שְׁלֵמָה, שֶׁהַבּוֹרֵא יִתְבָּרַךְ שְׁמוֹ יוֹדֵעַ כָּל מַעֲשֵׂה בְּנֵי אָדָם וְכָל מַחְשְׁבוֹתָם — *I believe with a complete faith that the Creator, Blessed be His Name, knows all the deeds of mankind, as well as all of their thoughts*. The more firm one's belief that his every move and thought are being observed and recorded by the Creator, the more pristine these moves will be.

In fact, the great tzaddikim explain what it is that distinguishes one pious individual from another. It is not so much that one has more deeds to his credit than his neighbor. Rather, what elevates one person above the rest is his level of clarity in *emunah*. The firmer and clearer his level of belief, the greater he will become. Thus, it is solid faith that serves as the *neshamah* for the "body" of one's observance of the Torah and its 613 commandments.

The Birkas Avraham *ztz"l* advances an interesting interpretation, focusing on the notion of Hashem's surveillance of man's thoughts. The beginning of *Parshas Tzav* deals with the sacrifice known as the *olah*, the burnt-offering, which differs from other sacrifices in that no portion of the animal is apportioned to people; it is entirely consumed on the *mizbei'ach*. The *parshah* begins with a special opening: צַו אֶת־אַהֲרֹן וְאֶת־בָּנָיו לֵאמֹר זֹאת תּוֹרַת הָעֹלָה — **Command** *Aharon and his sons, saying: This is the law of the burnt-offering* (Vayikra 6:2). Commenting on the phraseology, *Chazal* note that the *passuk* here uses the term *tzav* (command), as opposed to the more common *emor* (say) or *dabeir* (speak). Thus, they interpret: אֵין צַו אֶלָּא לְשׁוֹן זֵרוּז — *"Tzav" is none other than a term conveying encouragement*. And why here, of all places, was there a need to provide this extra "boost" when delivering these instructions? בְּיוֹתֵר צָרִיךְ הַכָּתוּב לְזָרֵז בְּמָקוֹם שֶׁיֵּשׁ בּוֹ חֶסְרוֹן כִּיס — *There is an especial need to provide extra encouragement*

when issuing a command that entails a financial loss (as the entire animal is consigned to the mizbei'ach) (Rashi, ibid.).

The term for financial loss, *chisaron kis*, means literally "a loss from the wallet," *kis* referring to a money pouch. But the Birkas Avraham offers a homiletic interpretation. *Kis* can also be related to the word *kisuy*, referring to a "covering." And this meaning is particularly pertinent when discussing the *olah* sacrifice. *Chazal* inform us further that this type of sacrifice is brought to atone for a specific sort of sin: that of *hirhur halev*, impure and evil musings, the very things that are *mechusah* (covered up) from view. That is, there is a significant deterrent to performing outright sins, as one may be embarrassed in front of onlookers. But who knows what is going through a person's mind? One can stand among august company while being occupied with the lowliest of thoughts — and no one is the wiser. Thus, the Birkas Avraham explains that *olah* is brought on account of a *chisaron kis*, that is, a blemish of "concealed matters" (evil thoughts).

Yes, one's thoughts are unknown to everyone — except Hashem. This, then, is included among the "profound matters" of our mishnah. It is only the enlightened awareness of the truth that *hakol tzafui*, all is known by Hashem, that enables pure thinking and behavior.

...Yet Free Choice Is Granted

As brief as the mishnah's overall message is, its profundity is bottomless. In a succinct manner, the mishnah presents a concept that, to the limited capacity of mortal man, seems utterly paradoxical in nature. Hashem knows everything of the past, present, and future about everybody. As such, He knows what man will choose when confronted by temptation. And yet, that individual retains free choice.

To underscore the profundity of this issue, it is worthwhile to cite the words of the Rambam from *Hilchos Teshuvah* (5:5) where he addresses this apparent irony:

דַּע שֶׁתְּשׁוּבַת שְׁאֵלָה זוּ אֲרֻכָּה מֵאֶרֶץ מִדָּה וּרְחָבָה מִנִּי־יָם וְכַמָּה עִיקָרִים גְּדוֹלִים וְהָרְרִים רָמִים תְּלוּיִים בָּהּ... וּכְשֵׁם שֶׁאֵין כֹּחַ בָּאָדָם לְהַשִּׂיג וְלִמְצוֹא אֲמִתַּת הַבּוֹרֵא שֶׁנֶּאֱמַר כִּי לֹא־יִרְאַנִי

הָאָדָם וָחָי אֵין כֹּחַ בָּאָדָם לְהַשִּׂיג וְלִמְצוֹא דַעְתּוֹ שֶׁל בּוֹרֵא, הוּא שֶׁהַנָּבִיא אָמַר כִּי לֹא מַחְשְׁבוֹתַי מַחְשְׁבוֹתֵיכֶם וְלֹא דַרְכֵיכֶם דְּרָכָי — Know, that the answer to this question is "longer than the measure of the earth and broader than the sea" (Iyov 11:9), and many great principles and high mountains are intertwined with it... Just as mortal man lacks the ability to fully comprehend the true essence of the Creator, as it states: "For no man shall see Me and live" (Shemos 33:20), similarly, man lacks the ability to fully comprehend the workings of the Creator's knowledge. To this the prophet refers when saying, "For My thoughts are not as your thoughts, nor are your ways as My ways" (Yeshayah 55:8).

This is part and parcel of the extremely weighty matters of our mishnah mentioned by the Rambam in his commentary. These are things that we cannot understand at all, yet we believe with a complete faith. Hashem sees all, yet grants mankind free reign over his destiny.

Never Too Hard

The Nesivos Sholom perceives an additional message and alternate meaning to these words of the mishnah.

A person may at times feel overpowered by his *yetzer hara*, surmising that he is powerless to overcome it. As logical and as tempting as it may seem to draw such a conclusion, the Nesivos Sholom reminds us that this cannot be the case. *Chazal* tell us (*Avodah Zarah* 3a), אֵין הַקָּדוֹשׁ בָּרוּךְ הוּא בָּא בִּטְרוּנְיָא עִם בְּרִיּוֹתָיו — *Hashem does not impose tasks upon His creatures that are impossible to accomplish.* It is crucial for a Yid to realize that Hashem only presents a test or challenge to an individual that He *knows that individual can pass.* To this end, the Midrash adds (*Shemos Rabbah* 34:1): לֹא בָא עַל הָאָדָם אֶלָּא לְפִי כֹּחוֹ — *Hashem only confronts a person (with a trial) in accordance with his abilities.* Before administering such a test, He first scrutinizes a person's strengths; the test is given only if a determination has already been made that this individual has the capacity to withstand it and emerge successfully. Alternatively, there may be instances where the individual actually lacks the inherent fortitude to pass a given test, but then Hashem will grant him the additional, necessary strength to be able to succeed.

The upshot of this situation is that if a person is confronted by a challenge of sorts, that itself is the greatest proof that he is able to successfully overcome it. Had that not been the case, Hashem would never have given him the test in the first place.

Our mishnah conveys this very notion. *Hakol tzafui*, "everything is seen" by Hashem. He knows our strengths and is fully aware of what we can accomplish and what is beyond our reach. Therefore, if He tests us, this is a sure sign that *hareshus nesunah*, the ability is granted. This particular *yetzer hara* may indeed be vexing, but Hashem knows that the individual is up to the task. Otherwise, the test would never have been allowed to proceed.

In Summary

הַכֹּל צָפוּי וְהָרְשׁוּת נְתוּנָה. Commenting on these four words, the Rambam remarks that they comprise "extremely great matters." That is, they involve concepts that may be beyond our ability to fully comprehend but are nevertheless part of our belief system.

We believe with complete faith that Hashem knows everything, including everything about us, our deeds, and our thoughts. To be a truly great Jew, we must recognize the fact that we are perpetually monitored from above in *all* that we do and think. The degree of clarity we possess regarding this fundamental truth is what distinguishes between the great and the truly great. The more we internalize it, the more this belief will be reflected in our actions.

Furthermore, our *emunah* includes even that which appears to be paradoxical. That is, Hashem knows what we will choose even before we choose it. In some way that defies our limited ability to comprehend, we must know that Hashem's foreknowledge of how we will act does not impede the freedom of choice He has granted us.

Another key element of faith that emerges from the words of this mishnah is regarding the issue of *nisyonos* (challenges). In addition to our deeds and thoughts, Hashem knows, of course, our capabilities. He administers only tests that He knows we can pass. As such, we must be clear that we are equipped to master every challenge that enters our life. Hashem knows our fortitude and has provided us with all necessary tools to successfully endure any trial.

This belief serves as the foundation and soul of our observance of Torah and mitzvos. As such, internalizing this knowledge is part of our preparation leading to *Kabbalas HaTorah* in these weeks before Shavuos, the time of the granting of the Torah. We do not operate in a vacuum. Hashem, our King, stands above us, observing all our deeds and thoughts. He enables us to successfully persevere in the face of even the most trying of circumstances.

Gems from the Nesivos Sholom

ספר נתיבות שלום

פרק ד'

פרק ד' משנה א'
בן זומא אומר איזהו וכו'
Ben Zoma Says: Who Is...

בֶּן זוֹמָא אוֹמֵר, אֵיזֶהוּ חָכָם, הַלּוֹמֵד מִכָּל אָדָם, שֶׁנֶּאֱמַר מִכָּל מְלַמְּדַי הִשְׂכַּלְתִּי כִּי עֵדְוֹתֶיךָ שִׂיחָה לִי. אֵיזֶהוּ גִבּוֹר, הַכּוֹבֵשׁ אֶת יִצְרוֹ, שֶׁנֶּאֱמַר טוֹב אֶרֶךְ אַפַּיִם מִגִּבּוֹר וּמוֹשֵׁל בְּרוּחוֹ מִלֹּכֵד עִיר. אֵיזֶהוּ עָשִׁיר הַשָּׂמֵחַ בְּחֶלְקוֹ, שֶׁנֶּאֱמַר יְגִיעַ כַּפֶּיךָ כִּי תֹאכֵל אַשְׁרֶיךָ וְטוֹב לָךְ. אַשְׁרֶיךָ, בָּעוֹלָם הַזֶּה. וְטוֹב לָךְ, לָעוֹלָם הַבָּא. אֵיזֶהוּ מְכֻבָּד, הַמְכַבֵּד אֶת הַבְּרִיּוֹת, שֶׁנֶּאֱמַר כִּי מְכַבְּדַי אֲכַבֵּד וּבֹזַי יֵקָלּוּ:

Ben Zoma says: Who is wise? One who learns from every man. As is stated (*Tehillim* 119:99): "From all my teachers I have grown wise, for Your testimonies are for me a conversation."

Who is mighty? One who conquers his inclination. As is stated (*Mishlei* 16:32): "One slow to anger is superior to a mighty man, and one who dominates his spirit to one who conquers a city."

Who is rich? One who is happy with his portion. As is stated (*Tehillim* 128:2): "When you eat of toil of your hands, you are fortunate, and it is good for you"; "you are fortunate" in This World, "and it is good for you" in the World to Come.

Who is honorable? One who honors people. As is stated (*Shmuel I* 2:30): "For I shall honor those who honor Me; and those who scorn Me shall be demeaned."

בן זומא אומר איזהו וכו׳

SOURCES:

כֹּה אָמַר ה' אַל־יִתְהַלֵּל חָכָם בְּחָכְמָתוֹ וְאַל־יִתְהַלֵּל הַגִּבּוֹר בִּגְבוּרָתוֹ אַל־יִתְהַלֵּל עָשִׁיר בְּעָשְׁרוֹ, כִּי אִם־בְּזֹאת יִתְהַלֵּל הַמִּתְהַלֵּל הַשְׂכֵּל וְיָדֹעַ אוֹתִי כִּי אֲנִי ה' עֹשֶׂה חֶסֶד מִשְׁפָּט וּצְדָקָה בָּאָרֶץ. (ירמיה ט' כ"ב, כ"ג)

So says Hashem: Let not the wise man glory in his wisdom, neither let the mighty man glory in his might, let not the rich man glory in his riches; let him that glories, glory only in this: to understand and know Me, that I am Hashem Who exercises kindness, justice, and righteousness on the earth. (*Yirmiyahu* 9:22, 23)

וְהָאָדָם יָדַע אֶת־חַוָּה אִשְׁתּוֹ. (בראשית ד' א')

And Adam knew Chavah, his wife. (*Bereishis* 4:1)

אִם דּוֹמֶה הָרַב לְמַלְאַךְ ה'...יְבַקְשׁוּ תּוֹרָה מִפִּיהוּ, וְאִם לָאו, אַל יְבַקְשׁוּ תּוֹרָה מִפִּיהוּ. (חגיגה ט"ו:)

If a *rebbi* resembles an angel of Hashem...then one should seek to learn Torah from his mouth. But if he does not, then one should not learn Torah from his mouth. (*Chagigah* 15b)

סוֹף דָּבָר הַכֹּל נִשְׁמָע אֶת־הָאֱלֹקִים יְרָא וְאֶת־מִצְוֹתָיו שְׁמוֹר כִּי־זֶה כָּל־הָאָדָם. (קהלת י"ב י"ג)

In the final analysis, all is heard: Fear G-d and keep His commandments; for this comprises the complete man. (*Koheles* 12:13)

GEMS FROM THE *SEFER NESIVOS SHOLOM*

The Four Questions

One of the most oft-quoted mishnayos in *Pirkei Avos* is that of Ben Zoma, who teaches about the true manifestation of the treasured qualities of wisdom, strength, wealth, and honor. This mishnah seems to hold the secret to a happy life; after all, who could possibly want more than the qualities mentioned above?

However, this is but a superficial understanding of the mishnah's message; after all, is Ben Zoma's intention to promote wealth and honor as desirable entities? In any event, the Nesivos Sholom is not satisfied with such a reading of this mishnah. And so, he uncovers the incredible depth contained in Ben Zoma's words, demonstrating their direct and profound relation to our *avodas Hashem*.

The Nesivos Sholom begins with a question reminiscent of the very first question posed in Talmud Bavli. The first mishnah of the first *masechta* discusses the time for reciting the evening *Krias Shema*. The opening line of the mishnah is: מֵאֵימָתַי קוֹרִין אֶת שְׁמַע בְּעַרְבִית? — *(Starting) from when do we recite the* Shema *in the evening?* The Gemara (*Berachos* 2a) is perplexed by the mishnah's question; isn't it getting a bit ahead of itself? The Gemara thus asks: תָּנָא הֵיכָא קָאֵי דְּקָתָנֵי מֵאֵימָתַי? — *On what is the* Tanna *basing himself that he asks, "From when (do we recite the evening* Shema*)"?* In other words: Before asking about the minute details of *Krias Shema* (such as what time one may begin to recite it), the first order of business should have been to establish that there is such a thing in the first place! Who said that there even is a mitzvah to recite the *Shema* at night? Obviously, the *Tanna* was assuming that this is the case; but in presenting his teaching, the Gemara asserts, the *Tanna* should have begun with the basics. As such, it demands to know the source.

The same manner of questioning could be applied to Ben Zoma's teaching. He comes to explain who it is that fits into the category of "wise," who fits into the category of "wealthy," etc. But who ever said that one should even strive to be strong or wise in the first place? Before analyzing who fits into these categories, it would seem to be reasonable to first establish that they are, indeed, desirable traits. Now, there seems to be no mention in the Torah about the necessity of cultivating these traits. From what source does Ben Zoma draw these qualities?

To Make a Connection

The Nesivos Sholom proceeds to identify what seems to have been Ben Zoma's starting point. It appears he was basing himself on the words of the *navi* Yirmiyahu (9:22-23): כֹּה אָמַר ה׳ אַל־יִתְהַלֵּל חָכָם בְּחָכְמָתוֹ וְאַל־יִתְהַלֵּל הַגִּבּוֹר בִּגְבוּרָתוֹ אַל־יִתְהַלֵּל עָשִׁיר בְּעָשְׁרוֹ, כִּי אִם־בְּזֹאת יִתְהַלֵּל הַמִּתְהַלֵּל הַשְׂכֵּל וְיָדֹעַ אוֹתִי כִּי אֲנִי ה׳ עֹשֶׂה חֶסֶד מִשְׁפָּט וּצְדָקָה בָּאָרֶץ — *Let not the wise man glory in his wisdom, neither let the mighty man glory in his might, let not the rich man glory in his riches; let him that glories glory in this, that he understands and knows Me, that I am Hashem who exercises kindness, justice, and righteousness on the earth.*

Yirmiyahu seems to conclude that there is only one characteristic in which one can glory: *Haskel v'yado'a Osi* — "understanding and knowing Hashem." This advice in itself seems almost impossible to implement; how could one possibly "understand and know" Hashem, Whose essence is so utterly beyond the grasp of human comprehension?

In truth, Yirmiyahu is not speaking of cerebral, factual knowledge. We find that *de'ah*, the root of the word *yado'a*, has another connotation in Tanach. This term is used in *Parshas Bereishis* (4:1) to describe the relationship between Adam Harishon and his wife, Chavah: וְהָאָדָם יָדַע אֶת־חַוָּה אִשְׁתּוֹ. The intimation here is more than simply "Adam knew his wife, Chavah" with peripheral knowledge; rather, it reflects an intimate connection.

The very purpose of creation is to create a connection with Hashem, to strive to become attached to Him and dwell in His shadow. What Yirmiyahu is telling us is that simple, worldly goals — wisdom, strength, etc. — have no inherent value in and of themselves. They bear significance only insofar as they enable us to establish a connection with Hashem: *Haskel v'yado'a Osi*. When utilized towards this end, they are ultimately beneficial.

This notion forms the basis of Ben Zoma's teaching. He goes

through each of the qualities generally pursued by man and demonstrates how, in fact, they are to be channeled towards their ultimate purpose: forming a connection with Hashem.

Holy Wisdom

אֵיזֶהוּ חָכָם, הַלּוֹמֵד מִכָּל אָדָם — *Who is a wise person? One who learns from every man.* This statement of Ben Zoma seems to require some clarification. How does learning from regular humans foster a close connection with *Hakadosh Baruch Hu*? There is one method whereby the achievement of this goal is readily apparent; that is, by following the advice supplied by *Chazal* in *Chagigah* (15b).

The Gemara there states, אִם דּוֹמֶה הָרַב לְמַלְאָךְ ה'...יְבַקְשׁוּ תּוֹרָה מִפִּיהוּ, וְאִם לָאו, אַל יְבַקְשׁוּ תּוֹרָה מִפִּיהוּ — *If a* rebbi *resembles an angel of Hashem... then one should seek to learn Torah from his mouth. But if he does not (resemble an angel of Hashem), then one should not learn Torah from his mouth.* If one learns from a *rebbi* of angelic spiritual stature, it is understandable how this may elevate the disciple and draw him closer to Hashem. But Ben Zoma almost seems to promote an opposite approach, advocating that one learn *mikol adam*, from *every* man!

The Ba'al Shem Tov resolves the apparent contradiction with a brilliant insight into Ben Zoma's words. He explains that Ben Zoma, in fact, did not necessarily intend that one learn from "just anybody." The words *mikol adam* could actually be understood to be referring to a certain type of individual — one who is a *kol adam*, a whole and complete person. In other words, Ben Zoma is also cautioning the student to approach his studies with the proper regard. When choosing someone from whom to learn the golden words of Torah, one must ascertain that the individual is complete — with proper *yiras Shamayim* (fear of Heaven) and respect for Torah. Only one who is *mikol adam* can truly be considered a tzaddik and is hence worthy of being selected as a *rebbi*.

Thus it appears that the *mikol adam* to which Ben Zoma referred has its roots in the classic utterance of Shlomo Hamelech at the conclusion of *Sefer Koheles* (12:13): סוֹף דָּבָר הַכֹּל נִשְׁמָע אֶת־הָאֱלֹקִים יְרָא וְאֶת־

מִצְוֹתָיו שְׁמוֹר כִּי־זֶה כָּל־הָאָדָם — *The end of the matter (is that) everything having been heard, fear Hashem and keep His commandments, for this is* **the entirety of man**. A *kol adam* is a G-d-fearing person who endeavors to keep Hashem's commandments at all times. When Ben Zoma implores us to learn from *kol adam*, he is referring to just such an individual. A real tzaddik who embodies these qualities can impart true *chachmah* (wisdom) to his disciples, facilitating their spiritual advancement and enhancing their connection with Hashem.

Who is wise? He who chooses to learn from one who is a kol adam.

Brain Power

אֵיזֶהוּ גִבּוֹר, הַכּוֹבֵשׁ אֶת יִצְרוֹ — *Who is a man of strength? One who conquers his inclination.* This teaching certainly appears straightforward enough. One might have thought that strength means physical prowess. Ben Zoma corrects this error, pointing out that true strength lies in one's ability to overcome his baser inclinations and conduct himself in accordance with the Torah. Notice, however, that in imparting this teaching, Ben Zoma does not use the generic term *yetzer hara*. Instead, he speaks of one who is *koveish es* **yitzro**, who conquers **his inclination**. The specificity indicates a deeper meaning.

The Nesivos Sholom elucidates Ben Zoma's intent. There is no universal *yetzer hara* that affects every person. That is, everyone is "bothered" by a *yetzer hara* — but the exact manner in which it presents a challenge differs from individual to individual, depending on one's unique characteristics and capabilities. Every Jew has a distinct mission in life, a task to fulfill that cannot be accomplished by anyone else. This unique mission has never been, nor will ever be, assigned to any other *neshamah*.

The *yetzer hara* molds itself to match each person's individualized mission. It presents the exact challenge we each need to overcome in order to accomplish our mission. Our purpose in life is to struggle with and subdue our personal *yetzer hara*, thereby overcoming the impediments to the fulfillment of our life's *tafkid* (appointed task).

GEMS FROM THE SEFER NESIVOS SHOLOM

How do we each identify what our "personal" *yetzer hara* is, and our individualized life mission? The thought of sifting through the mental labyrinths of our conscious and subconscious minds that drive our actions is a daunting prospect. The truth of the matter is, though, that the search need not necessarily be so difficult, as the *yetzer hara*, in this respect, is actually quite revealing; it tends to focus its energies on the very areas that comprise our mandated purpose. When there is a specific *middah*, a particular *aveirah* with which we find ourselves locked in a regular struggle — this is a pretty clear indication of what our life's mission is. By providing so much "trouble" in this area, the *yetzer hara*, in effect, is casting a clear, bright light on what it is we need to fix.

When a *neshamah* appears before the Heavenly tribunal, it must give an account not only of its fulfillment of the mitzvos, but also of the successful completion of its life mission. To be able to answer that we have indeed accomplished, or even attempted to accomplish, our *tafkid* in life, it is necessary to have identified and battled against the "personal" *yetzer hara*.

Who is strong? He who has isolated and conquered the particular barriers preventing him from carrying out his tafkid.

Possessed by Money?

אֵיזֶהוּ עָשִׁיר הַשָּׂמֵחַ בְּחֶלְקוֹ — *Who is rich? One who is happy with his portion*. Empires have risen and been destroyed, kingdoms have been conquered, individuals brought to madness, and families ripped to shreds — all in the pursuit of wealth. Money, gold, jewels, stocks, bonds — in fact, every type of worldly wealth — is as nothing compared to the unlimited spiritual riches contained in the Torah and a life devoted to its fulfillment.

What defines wealth and contentment? Simply possessing money is clearly not it, for the more a person has, the more he wants. A poor person only desires a small amount of money, enough to cover his expenses and lead a somewhat comfortable life. A rich man aims to amass a tremendous sum of money, either to upgrade even further his already luxurious lifestyle or simply for its own sake, as a symbol of his power and success. Thus it emerges that, in a sense, the rich man is needier than his poorer counterpart — since he desires that much more money. It is only one who does not desire anything who is the richest of all. He is wealthy by virtue of the fact that he is not needy in the slightest.

It is very difficult to definitively identify who is really wealthy and who is indigent. Looks can be deceiving. A person may appear to be rich, but at the same time suffer from personal or medical problems, challenges with his children, or any number of issues that cash cannot magically solve.

Ultimately, what is important for any person, rich or poor, to bear in mind, is that we cannot order our preferred life circumstances. Hashem determines the conditions of our lives, though not, of course, in any haphazard fashion. On the contrary, He presents each of us with the precise set of circumstances we need to fulfill our life's mission to the fullest.

The same concept can be applied to spiritual endeavors. Some have an easier time than others with basic spiritual challenges. They may have no problem getting up early to *daven* or learn, are naturally positive people, and feel no aversion to other people. Others may find that these and other areas are a real struggle. It all depends on what *tafkid* Hashem has mandated for each individual; for a certain person, his mission may be just that — to grapple with a particular *yetzer hara*.

The crucial point that Ben Zoma seeks to convey here is that a person must realize that he has been furnished with exactly the tools he needs to fulfill his life's mission. The possessions and characteristics with which Hashem has provided him are the only means with which to conquer his *yetzer hara*. A poor person may long for the luxuries he lacks. In fact, however, he has what he needs to fulfill the purpose for which he was sent to earth; if he had anything more, it would only be to his detriment, detracting from his ability to complete his task. Another person finds no difficulty in maintaining proper boundaries in the workplace but has an overwhelming desire to sample non-kosher food and beverages. He is no better or worse than someone with the opposite set of tendencies; he just has a different goal to achieve in life.

And so we see that wealth is not the acquisition of goods. It is the ability to look at the spiritual and material "package" we have been given and to know unequivocally that we have every necessary tool to fulfill our *tafkid* in life. A person who truly internalizes this idea does not merely "come to terms" with his lot in life. Rather, he is also *samei'ach b'chelko*, overjoyed with his portion. After all, why shouldn't he be? He knows with a serene surety that he has exactly what he needs to fulfill the most important task of all, the one with which he, alone, has been charged. This is genuine wealth — experiencing the joy of understanding that we possess everything we need to perfect our life in This World.

Who is rich? One who is happy with his complete material and spiritual package, delighting in the knowledge that Hashem has given him everything he needs to fulfill his purpose.

Reflected Honor

אֵיזֶהוּ מְכֻבָּד, הַמְכַבֵּד אֶת הַבְּרִיּוֹת — *Who is honorable? He who honors others.* Honor is another one of those concepts that is difficult to define with precision, especially as it depends on how one is perceived by others. Of what value is that type of *kavod* if one must come on to other people to receive it? Rather than honorable, such a person is needy, as he looks to and requires the input of others to feel honored and valued.

Actually, it is just the opposite. True honor depends on how one views others. A friend or companion can be compared to a mirror, in which a person sees a reflection of himself. In fact, two different people can both look at a third and behold a different "image." One looks at this person and sees an ungainly picture, viewing this person as beset with flaws. The other sees a more positive sight, noticing the good qualities of that individual. What accounts for these varying results? It is because, in essence, they latch on to their own essence. One sees the value in his friend, because he, himself, is filled with virtue. The other has a baser essence, which is reflected in the fact that he immediately identifies the flaws of his companion.

In other words, what we see in others is essentially a reflection of ourselves. If we honor others, recognizing their value and that they possess traits to emulate, it is a sure sign of being inherently honorable.

Who is honorable? One who can look at the positive aspects of others and honor those very qualities, reflecting his own pristine essence.

All of our *middos*, from the apparently simple to the most challenging, rest on the foundation set forth by these four qualities. The guiding principle is to channel these qualities towards forging a connection with *Hakadosh Baruch Hu*. Through this connection, a person can achieve heights of *kedushah* that were previously unimaginable.

In Summary

The Nesivos Sholom begins his exposition of this mishnah by questioning if Ben Zoma could truly mean that there is intrinsic value in acquiring wealth and honor. The source for Ben Zoma's words can be found in Yirmiyahu's admonition, which warns against ascribing importance to the very values that Ben Zoma espouses. The *navi* asserts that the only true value is in "knowing" Hashem. This, explains the Nesivos Sholom, must be Ben Zoma's true intent: the qualities he lists are only valuable if they enable a person to build a connection with Hashem.

The Nesivos Sholom then proceeds to elucidate each of these four qualities. What does it mean that true *chachmah* is acquired by learning from every man? The Ba'al Shem Tov explains that the words "every man" can be understood to mean a "complete man" in the spiritual sense. That is, we should learn from a true tzaddik.

The Nesivos Sholom then examines the concept of *gibbor*, a strong man. This refers to the strength we need to battle the *yetzer hara*. The *yetzer hara* itself may be identified precisely through those attributes that we find most difficult to overcome. We first need strength to identify and confront these faults, admitting them to ourselves. We must then muster further strength to work on eradicating these traits and rectifying ourselves.

Following this, the Nesivos Sholom looks at the idea of wealth. True wealth is not necessarily monetary, but a wealth that derives from satisfaction with what Hashem has bestowed upon us. A person who has vast amounts of money may constantly crave more — essentially, he is a very needy man. In contrast, a poor person who is happy with his lot is truly wealthy. He recognizes that he has exactly what he needs to fulfill his mission in life.

Finally, the Nesivos Sholom looks at the quality of honor — something not as easy to define as the previous qualities. A person who needs to be honored by others is as needy as the rich man who is never satisfied with the wealth he already has. True honor is the honor we have for others, for their good *middos* and spiritual accomplishments. The ultimate display of honor is when we incorporate those very traits within ourselves.

In conclusion, the Nesivos Sholom states that all the qualities, traits, and attributes that we may possess can only be perfected if they are used as intended by the One Who bestowed them: to help our fellow *Yidden* and to forge a connection with Hashem.

פרק ד' משנה א'
איזהו גבור הכובש את יצרו
Who Is Mighty? One Who Conquers His Inclination

בֶּן זוֹמָא אוֹמֵר, אֵיזֶהוּ חָכָם, הַלּוֹמֵד מִכָּל אָדָם, שֶׁנֶּאֱמַר מִכָּל מְלַמְּדַי הִשְׂכַּלְתִּי כִּי עֵדְוֹתֶיךָ שִׂיחָה לִי. אֵיזֶהוּ גִבּוֹר, הַכּוֹבֵשׁ אֶת יִצְרוֹ, שֶׁנֶּאֱמַר טוֹב אֶרֶךְ אַפַּיִם מִגִּבּוֹר וּמוֹשֵׁל בְּרוּחוֹ מִלֹּכֵד עִיר. אֵיזֶהוּ עָשִׁיר הַשָּׂמֵחַ בְּחֶלְקוֹ, שֶׁנֶּאֱמַר יְגִיעַ כַּפֶּיךָ כִּי תֹאכֵל אַשְׁרֶיךָ וְטוֹב לָךְ. אַשְׁרֶיךָ, בָּעוֹלָם הַזֶּה. וְטוֹב לָךְ, לָעוֹלָם הַבָּא. אֵיזֶהוּ מְכֻבָּד, הַמְכַבֵּד אֶת הַבְּרִיּוֹת, שֶׁנֶּאֱמַר כִּי מְכַבְּדַי אֲכַבֵּד וּבֹזַי יֵקָלּוּ:

Ben Zoma says: Who is wise? One who learns from every man. As is stated (*Tehillim* 119:99): "From all my teachers I have grown wise, for Your testimonies are for me a conversation."

Who is mighty? One who conquers his inclination. As is stated (*Mishlei* 16:32): "One slow to anger is superior to a mighty man, and one who dominates his spirit to one who conquers a city."

Who is rich? One who is happy with his portion. As is stated (*Tehillim* 128:2): "When you eat of toil of your hands, you are fortunate, and it is good for you"; "you are fortunate" in This World, "and it is good for you" in the World to Come.

Who is honorable? One who honors people. As is stated (*Shmuel I* 2:30): "For I shall honor those who honor Me; and those who scorn Me shall be demeaned."

איזהו גבור הכובש את יצרו

SOURCES:

וַיַּרְא אֱלֹקִים כִּי־טוֹב. (בראשית פרק א' פסוקים י', י"ב, י"ח, כ"א, כ"ה)

And G-d saw that it was good. (*Bereishis* 1:10, 12, 18, 21, 25).

וַיַּרְא אֱלֹקִים אֶת־כָּל־אֲשֶׁר עָשָׂה וְהִנֵּה־טוֹב מְאֹד וַיְהִי־עֶרֶב וַיְהִי־בֹקֶר יוֹם הַשִּׁשִּׁי. (שם פסוק ל"א)

And G-d saw all that He had made, and behold, it was very good. And it was evening and it was morning – the sixth day. (*ibid.* v. 31)

הִנֵּה טוֹב זֶה יֵצֶר טוֹב, מְאֹד זֶה יֵצֶר הָרָע…שֶׁאִילוּלֵי יֵצֶר הָרָע לֹא בָּנָה אָדָם בַּיִת וְלֹא נָשָׂא אִשָּׁה וְלֹא הוֹלִיד בָּנִים. (קהלת רבה ג' ט"ז)

"Behold, it was good" – this refers to the good inclination; "very (good)" – this refers to the evil inclination…for without the evil inclination, no man would build a house, marry a woman, nor bear children. (*Koheles Rabbah* 3:16)

עִיר קְטַנָּה…וּבָא־אֵלֶיהָ מֶלֶךְ גָּדוֹל וְסָבַב אֹתָהּ…וּמָצָא בָהּ אִישׁ מִסְכֵּן חָכָם וּמִלַּט־הוּא אֶת־הָעִיר בְּחָכְמָתוֹ. (קהלת ט' י"ד, ט"ו)

There was a small city…and a great king came against it and besieged it… Therein was found a poor wise man, who saved the city with his ingenuity. (*Koheles* 9:14, 15)

רֵאשִׁית חָכְמָה יִרְאַת ה'. (תהלים קי"א י')

The beginning of wisdom is fear of Hashem. (*Tehillim* 111:10)

וַיִּקְרָא אֵלָיו מַלְאַךְ ה' מִן־הַשָּׁמַיִם וַיֹּאמֶר אַבְרָהָם אַבְרָהָם… אַל־תִּשְׁלַח יָדְךָ אֶל־הַנַּעַר וְאַל־תַּעַשׂ לוֹ מְאוּמָה כִּי עַתָּה יָדַעְתִּי כִּי־יְרֵא אֱלֹקִים אַתָּה וְלֹא חָשַׂכְתָּ אֶת־בִּנְךָ אֶת־יְחִידְךָ מִמֶּנִּי. (בראשית כ"ב י"ב)

And the angel of Hashem called to him from the Heavens, and said: "Avraham! Avraham!… Do not send your hand against the

פרק ד'

lad, nor do anything to him, for now I know that you fear G-d." (*Bereishis* 22:12)

כְּשֶׁיָּשִׂים הָאָדָם אֶל לִבּוֹ שֶׁהַמֶּלֶךְ הַגָּדוֹל הקב"ה...עוֹמֵד עָלָיו וְרוֹאֶה בְּמַעֲשָׂיו...מִיָּד יַגִּיעַ אֵלָיו הַיִּרְאָה. (רמ"א, אורח חיים א' א')

When a person sets his heart to the fact that the Great King – the Holy One, Blessed is He...is standing over him and observing his deeds...immediately, one will be vested with awe. (*Rama, Orach Chaim* 1:1)

Who Is the "*Yetzer*"?

Most people are aware what life in This World is all about — in vague terms, at least. From a spiritual standpoint, it centers on the epic battle characterized by most of the world as Good versus Evil, or, in our terms, the *yetzer hatov* versus the *yetzer hara*.

Which is what makes this statement of the mishnah so interesting. Initially, it seems pretty straightforward, extolling the individual who overpowers his evil inclination. But notice the terminology: the mishnah does not clearly identify the *yetzer hara*. Rather, it adopts a somewhat ambiguous term, speaking generally about conquering one's *yetzer*. What is that exactly? Why doesn't the mishnah simply state *yetzer hara* explicitly?

An Issue of Necessity

For that matter, there are a few other linguistic anomalies in this mishnah that need clarification. The mishnah states that a *gibbor* is one who is *koveish es yitzro*. The word *koveish* intimates a sense of restraint; that is, the *yetzer* is still there, but is held in abeyance. Why does the mishnah advocate specifically this type of strategy against the *yetzer hara*? Wouldn't it be preferable to nullify and eradicate it altogether, as opposed to just practicing "containment"? Furthermore, the mishnah seems to get "personal." *Koveish es yitzro* — "conquers **his** inclination." Why not simply state that a mighty person is one who conquers **the** *yetzer hara*?

The truth is, however, that the *yetzer hara* — in a sense — may not be entirely "bad." In fact, it has its place — and can even be considered quite "good." This view emerges from the Midrash's comments concerning Creation. Throughout the Creation narrative (*Bereishis*, ch. 1), there is a recurring phrase. Hashem observes His works of that particular day, prompting the *passuk* to state that Hashem saw *ki tov* — "that it was good." At one point, the phraseology is even more emphatic, stating, *v'hinei tov me'od* — "behold, it was *very* good" (ibid. 1:31). What prompted such added enthusiasm? Somewhat surprisingly, *Chazal* identify what it was that Hashem was labeling as *tov me'od*; it was none other than the *yetzer hara*: הִנֵּה טוֹב זֶה יֵצֶר טוֹב, מְאֹד זֶה יֵצֶר הָרָע...שֶׁאִילוּלֵי יֵצֶר הָרָע לֹא בָּנָה בַּיִת אָדָם וְלֹא נָשָׂא אִשָּׁה וְלֹא הוֹלִיד בָּנִים — "Behold, it was good," this refers to the good inclination; "very (good)," this refers to the evil inclination...for without the evil inclination, no man would build a house, marry a woman, or bear children (*Koheles Rabbah* 3:16).

Thus we see that the *yetzer hara* plays a very functional role. Without its influence, the world would remain desolate. And so these drives cannot be entirely banished. They must endure within every Jew, but at the same time we must effectively restrain their force for good. In other words, they must be "conquered" and contained. It is somewhat more difficult to restrain and properly channel these drives than it may be merely to nullify them altogether. This is a prospect that requires real *gevurah*, as our mishnah describes.

And especial *gevurah* is called for, for a Yid doesn't have to deal with just "any" *yetzer hara*, but with his personal *yetzer*: *yitzro*. Every one of us is charged with an individualized mission, for which we were sent to This World in the first place. This mission entails grappling with specific *nisyonos*, a particular *yetzer hara* that we, alone, must deal with and rectify. As this is our primary task in life, the *yetzer hara* concentrates the bulk of its energies in an attempt to thwart it. As such, the temptations and challenges in this area are noticeably stronger than usual, requiring us to marshal our forces and act with *mesirus nefesh* (heightened exertion). It is to this situation the mishnah refers when exhorting one to use *gevurah* in conquering "his" *yetzer*.

The Great King

The matter of the mishnah's general terminology — "*yetzer*" as opposed to "*yetzer hara*" — is somewhat complex. We may gain some clarity in the issue by examining certain imagery employed by Shlomo Hamelech.

In *Koheles* (9:14, 15), Shlomo Hamelech relates the following story: עִיר קְטַנָּה...וּבָא־אֵלֶיהָ מֶלֶךְ גָּדוֹל וְסָבַב אֹתָהּ... וּמָצָא בָהּ אִישׁ מִסְכֵּן חָכָם וּמִלַּט־הוּא אֶת־הָעִיר

איזהו גבור הכובש את יצרו

בְּחָכְמָתוֹ — *There was a small city...and a "great king" came against it and besieged it... Therein was found a "poor wise man," who saved the city with his ingenuity.* In interpreting these *pesukim*, *Chazal* (*Nedarim* 32b) identify who and what Shlomo was discussing. The "small city" is the human being, who falls under the dominion of the "great king" — that is, the *yetzer hara*. Only the "wise man," the *yetzer hatov*, can save him, and only through employing *chachmah*.

That the *yetzer hara* is referred to as a "great king" is a testimony to the expansive extent to which it yields dominion over a person. That is, there is so much to a person's composition that falls under its jurisdiction, even (and perhaps especially) those matters that are necessary for one's survival. Eating, pursuing a livelihood, etc. — all fall under the purview of the *yetzer hara*. As mentioned previously, it requires substantial *gevurah* to properly channel all of these tendencies, and it is relatively easy for the *yetzer hara* to use them to coax an individual to excesses and sin.

This is why the mishnah uses the general term *yetzer*; it underscores this state of affairs, highlighting the great difference that exists between the *yetzer hatov* and the *yetzer hara*. Due to the all-pervasive nature of the *yetzer hara*, it is effectively the "status quo" of a person. In other words, it would be a mistake to assume that there is room for passivity and neutrality. The reality is that unless a person exerts considerable efforts to combat it, he will *automatically* fall under its influence. To convey this notion, the mishnah does not even need to identify it; the "default" *yetzer* is the *yetzer hara*.

So, how does one utilize his *yetzer hatov* to vanquish this great king? As Shlomo Hamelech stated, it is only through *chachmah*. And in this endeavor, the crucial component is *yirah*, as the *passuk* states (*Tehillim* 111:10), רֵאשִׁית חָכְמָה יִרְאַת ה' — *The beginning of wisdom is fear of Hashem.*

This component was manifest right from the "beginning of (the path of) wisdom." As *Chazal* relate, the Torah was given בְּאֵימָה בְּיִרְאָה בְּרֶתֶת וּבְזִיעַ — *(amidst an atmosphere of) awe, fear, trembling, and quaking* (*Berachos* 22a). One may have thought this was not the optimal way for the Torah to be granted at Har Sinai; instead of

פרק ד'

such a severe and fearful environment, perhaps the Torah should have been given from *ahavah*. But Hashem knew that *yirah* was the essential factor; when the *yetzer hara* is involved and needs to be vanquished, the only counsel is pristine fear of Hashem. רֵאשִׁית חָכְמָה יִרְאַת ה׳ — *The beginning of wisdom is fear of Hashem.*

This same notion was on display in the episode of *Akeidas Yitzchak*. Inherently, Avraham embodied the attribute of *ahavas Hashem*, even referred to by the *navi* as *Avraham ohavi* — "Avraham who loves Me" (*Yeshayah* 41:8). One may have surmised that Avraham's willingness to offer his beloved son Yitzchak as a sacrifice to Hashem was a function of his great love, and the ultimate display of it. Thus, it is instructive to note what the *malach* remarks upon Avraham's successful completion of this trial: עַתָּה יָדַעְתִּי כִּי־יְרֵא אֱלֹקִים אַתָּה — *Now I know that you are* **G-d-fearing** (*Bereishis* 22:12). Avraham realized that *ahavah* alone would be insufficient to withstand this great test; instead, he needed to access the power of *yirah*, specifically. As the Arizal explains, *akeidah* connotes "binding," referring not only to Avraham's binding of his son to the *mizbei'ach*, but also of Avraham's binding of *himself* to Yitzchak. While Avraham represents *ahavah*, Yitzchak is noted for his *yirah*. Thus, to successfully endure this test, Avraham tied himself to Yitzchak's attribute of *yirah*.

And so it is that only through *yirah* can a Yid fulfill the task for which he was sent to the world. As previously mentioned, our mishnah alludes to a Yid's personalized mission: to be *koveish es yitzro*, **his** specific *yetzer hara*. The Saba Kadisha of Slonim adds that any day that goes by in which one did not engage in some action that counteracts his personal will, is like a day that he has not lived. As such, to ensure that every day counts, a Yid must be sure to live every day by the all-important tenet of רֵאשִׁית חָכְמָה יִרְאַת ה׳.

Will the Real *Yetzer Hatov* Please Stand Up?

There is yet another reason why the mishnah speaks only of a generic *yetzer*, without identifying it as the *yetzer hara*.

The key, explains the Nesivos Sholom, is in understanding how the *yetzer hara* operates. He quotes the *Arvei Nachal* (*Parshas Vayakhel*), which provides much insight as to the effects of an *aveirah*. When a Yid commits an *aveirah*, he thereby provides a prize to the *yetzer hara* — a crown of sorts, in some spiritual sense. The issue for the *yetzer hara*, however, is that this "crown" — derived from an *aveirah* — is laden with filth and impurity. Rather than an adornment that is inherently repulsive, the *yetzer hara* would much prefer an object of beauty. It yearns, instead, for a crown of pure gold and jewels. And it has a plan by which to attain one.

That is, it seeks to "steal" a mitzvah from a Yid, which will provide it with the crown of grandeur it desires. To achieve this aim, it actually entices a Yid not to sin, but to perform a good deed! However — so that the mitzvah will be channeled for the *yetzer hara's* benefit — it "co-opts" the mitzvah by introducing impure motives into the mind of the doer. Having succeeded in "contaminating" the mitzvah with selfish motives, the *yetzer hara* then gets what it wants. As the mitzvah was not performed for the sake of Heaven, the "crown" goes to it; but since the crown is derived from a mitzvah after all, it is a dazzling adornment and not an object of disgust.

It is to warn a Yid about this type of scheme that the mishnah selected its particular wording. To be a *gibbor*, one must be cognizant, ready to defeat not only an overt *yetzer hara*, but even the *yetzer hara* masquerading as a *yetzer hatov*. This is why the mishnah exhorts us simply to conquer "the *yetzer*"; for we must constantly be on the lookout for any type of *yetzer* — one convincing us to do an *aveirah*, or even one spurring us on to do a mitzvah, but for inappropriate reasons.

Here, too, the only effective antidote is *yiras Hashem*. This is especially so in light of the well-known words of the Rama at the beginning of *Shulchan Aruch* (*Orach Chaim* 1:1): כְּשֶׁיָּשִׂים הָאָדָם אֶל לִבּוֹ שֶׁהַמֶּלֶךְ הַגָּדוֹל הַקּבָּ"ה...עוֹמֵד עָלָיו וְרוֹאֶה בְּמַעֲשָׂיו...מִיָּד יַגִּיעַ אֵלָיו הַיִּרְאָה — *When a person sets his heart to the fact that the Great King, the Holy One, Blessed is He...is standing over him and observing his deeds...immediately, one will be vested with* yirah. Notice the Rama did not state that Hashem observes his *ma'asim hara'im*, his evil deeds, but stated simply "his deeds." This would include even good deeds and refers to the sentiment expressed above. That is, when a person realizes that Hashem is scrutinizing his every action, even his good deeds and the attendant motives, then — מִיָּד יַגִּיעַ אֵלָיו הַיִּרְאָה — the result will be that he will immediately be overtaken by *yirah*. And this *yirah* will ensure that his deeds and motives remain pristine, thus keeping even his good deeds from the clutches of the *yetzer hara*.

In Summary

All of us labor each day to overcome the wiles of the *yetzer hara*. Every person is imbued with drives and motivations, which ultimately are necessary for us to live our lives and preserve the world. But they are still the province of the *yetzer hara*, and through them, it draws a person to sin. Addressing this issue, the mishnah exhorts a person to resist and contain this *yetzer hara*: אֵיזֶהוּ גִבּוֹר, הַכּוֹבֵשׁ אֶת יִצְרוֹ. It may serve a necessary purpose, but must be subjugated and properly managed.

We must also be aware that we have a specific mission, a unique task with which we have been charged, to rectify an aspect of our nature with which we must struggle. The way to vanquish the *yetzer* is through the attribute of *yirah*. Any day we do not battle this *yetzer* is like a day of our life that has not been used for its intended purpose. The mishnah alludes to this type of *yetzer hara* by employing the possessive form: אֵיזֶהוּ גִבּוֹר, הַכּוֹבֵשׁ אֶת יִצְרוֹ.

It is likewise noteworthy that the mishnah does not explicitly identify which type of *yetzer* is under discussion. Rather than specifying the *yetzer hara*, the mishnah merely states, אֵיזֶהוּ גִבּוֹר הַכּוֹבֵשׁ אֶת יִצְרוֹ. The Nesivos Sholom provides two approaches to account for this phenomenon. He explains that it was not necessary for the mishnah to identify that we are discussing the *yetzer hara*, for, as previously noted, it already has an extensive hold on an individual through one's natural drives and tendencies. As such, a person automatically is under the influence of his *yetzer hara* — unless he specifically exerts himself to assert his *yetzer hatov* and vanquish the evil.

Furthermore, the mishnah reveals to us the *yetzer hara's* strategy, that it engages us in a two-pronged attack. Not only does it entice us to sin, but it even seeks to corrupt our mitzvos. Thus, we must constantly be on the lookout for the *yetzer* — of any and all types. Only *yiras Shamayim* will enable us to say no to the bad, embrace the good for the right reasons, and focus on fulfilling our destiny as Jews.

פרק ד' משנה א'
איזהו עשיר השמח בחלקו
Who Is Rich? One Who Is Happy with His Portion

בֶּן זוֹמָא אוֹמֵר, אֵיזֶהוּ חָכָם, הַלּוֹמֵד מִכָּל אָדָם, שֶׁנֶּאֱמַר מִכָּל מְלַמְּדַי הִשְׂכַּלְתִּי כִּי עֵדְוֹתֶיךָ שִׂיחָה לִי. אֵיזֶהוּ גִבּוֹר, הַכּוֹבֵשׁ אֶת יִצְרוֹ, שֶׁנֶּאֱמַר טוֹב אֶרֶךְ אַפַּיִם מִגִּבּוֹר וּמשֵׁל בְּרוּחוֹ מִלֹּכֵד עִיר. אֵיזֶהוּ עָשִׁיר הַשָּׂמֵחַ בְּחֶלְקוֹ, שֶׁנֶּאֱמַר יְגִיעַ כַּפֶּיךָ כִּי תֹאכֵל אַשְׁרֶיךָ וְטוֹב לָךְ. אַשְׁרֶיךָ, בָּעוֹלָם הַזֶּה. וְטוֹב לָךְ, לָעוֹלָם הַבָּא. אֵיזֶהוּ מְכֻבָּד, הַמְכַבֵּד אֶת הַבְּרִיּוֹת, שֶׁנֶּאֱמַר כִּי מְכַבְּדַי אֲכַבֵּד וּבֹזַי יֵקָלּוּ:

Ben Zoma says: Who is wise? One who learns from every man. As is stated (*Tehillim* 119:99): "From all my teachers I have grown wise, for Your testimonies are for me a conversation."

Who is mighty? One who conquers his inclination. As is stated (*Mishlei* 16:32): "One slow to anger is superior to a mighty man, and one who dominates his spirit to one who conquers a city."

Who is rich? One who is happy with his portion. As is stated (*Tehillim* 128:2): "When you eat of toil of your hands, you are fortunate, and it is good for you"; "you are fortunate" in This World, "and it is good for you" in the World to Come.

Who is honorable? One who honors people. As is stated (*Shmuel I* 2:30): "For I shall honor those who honor Me; and those who scorn Me shall be demeaned."

איזהו עשיר השמח בחלקו

SOURCES:

אֹהֵב כֶּסֶף לֹא־יִשְׂבַּע כֶּסֶף. (קהלת ה׳ ט׳)

One who loves money will never be satiated by money. (*Koheles* 5:9)

אֵין אָדָם יוֹצֵא מִן הָעוֹלָם וַחֲצִי תַּאֲוָתוֹ בְּיָדוֹ. אֶלָּא אִי אִית לֵיהּ מְאָה בָּעֵי לְמֶעְבַּד יָתְהוֹן תַּרְתֵּין מְאָוָן. (קהלת רבה א׳ ל״ב)

No person leaves This World having fulfilled even half of his desires. If he has acquired one hundred, he yearns to increase the amount to two hundred. (*Koheles Rabbah* 1:32)

גָּדוֹל הַנֶהֱנֶה מִיְּגִיעוֹ יוֹתֵר מִירֵא שָׁמָיִם. (ברכות ח.)

Greater is the one who derives benefit from his labor than one who fears Heaven. (*Berachos* 8a)

וְאָהַבְתָּ אֵת ה׳ אֱלֹקֶיךָ בְּכָל־לְבָבְךָ וּבְכָל־נַפְשְׁךָ וּבְכָל־מְאֹדֶךָ. (דברים ו׳ ה׳)

And you shall love Hashem your G-d, with all of your heart, all of your soul, and all of your resources (your *me'od*). (*Devarim* 6:5)

בְּכָל מְאֹדֶךָ, בְּכָל מִדָּה וּמִדָּה שֶׁהוּא מוֹדֵד לְךָ הֱוֵי מוֹדֶה לוֹ בִּמְאֹד מְאֹד. (משנה ברכות ט׳ ה׳)

"With all of your *me'od*" – with whatever measure Hashem metes out to you, be excessively grateful to Him. (*Mishnah Berachos* 9:5)

כִּי חֵלֶק ה׳ עַמּוֹ. (דברים ל״ב ט׳)

For the portion of Hashem is His nation. (*Devarim* 32:9)

אַשְׁרֵי הָעָם שֶׁכָּכָה לּוֹ אַשְׁרֵי הָעָם שֶׁה׳ אֱלֹקָיו. (תהלים קמ״ד ט״ו)

Fortunate is the nation for whom it is like this; fortunate is the nation that Hashem is its G-d. (*Tehillim* 144:15)

פרק ד׳

439

GEMS FROM THE *SEFER NESIVOS SHOLOM*

אֶחָד הַמַּרְבֶּה וְאֶחָד הַמַּמְעִיט, וּבִלְבַד שֶׁיְּכַוֵּן אָדָם אֶת לִבּוֹ לַשָּׁמָיִם. (משנה מנחות י״ג י״א)

Whether one does a lot or a little, the essential component is that a person direct his heart towards Heaven. (*Mishnah Menachos* 13:11)

איזהו עשיר השמח בחלקו

True Wealth

If you look up "wealthy" in the dictionary, you will most likely find the word defined as one in possession of substantial wealth. Now, one can contemplate if vast riches are really important or not, but that's a different question. Who is considered wealthy? Wealthy means having wealth and riches. So what, exactly, is the mishnah's question? And why deviate from the simple, straightforward answer?

The Maharal addresses this issue. He explains that the mishnah was seeking more than just the definition of a word. Rather, the question is: who is *inherently* wealthy, to the extent that his wealth is considered as emanating from within him? An individual may possess vast holdings in real estate, precious gems, and investments, but all of these are not really part of his essence. Despite all his riches, he may be intrinsically poor.

A Wealth of Attitude

What emerges, then, is that true wealth is really a state of mind. As *Chazal* relate (*Nedarim* 41a), אֵין עָנִי אֶלָּא בְּדֵעָה — *True indigence is exemplified by lack of sense.* This is what the mishnah seeks to convey: אֵיזֶהוּ עָשִׁיר הַשָּׂמֵחַ בְּחֶלְקוֹ — *Who is wealthy? One who is happy with his portion.* A person who is wealthy "in the mind" is the only one who is truly wealthy.

Indeed, how could it be otherwise? Could riches and possession truly determine wealth? Shlomo Hamelech states (*Koheles* 5:9), אֹהֵב כֶּסֶף לֹא־יִשְׂבַּע כֶּסֶף — *One who loves money will never be satiated by money.* *Chazal* state further (*Koheles Rabbah* 1:32), אֵין אָדָם יוֹצֵא מִן הָעוֹלָם וַחֲצִי תַּאֲוָתוֹ בְּיָדוֹ. אֶלָּא אִי אִית לֵיהּ מֵאָה בָּעֵי לְמֶעְבַּד יָתְהוֹן תַּרְתֵּין מָאוָון — *No person leaves This World having fulfilled even half of his desires. If he has acquired one hundred, he yearns to increase the amount to two hundred.* Thus, one who yearns for money will constantly be pining for more of it, no matter how much he already has. A very needy person indeed! This, then, is the key to wealth and happiness: a sense of satisfaction. אֵיזֶהוּ עָשִׁיר הַשָּׂמֵחַ בְּחֶלְקוֹ.

The Nesivos Sholom raises a number of points surrounding this

GEMS FROM THE SEFER NESIVOS SHOLOM

middah, the consideration of which can lead us to a fundamental understanding of its nature:

- While there exist any number of pristine and worthy traits, the Saba Kadisha of Slonim *ztz"l* seems to place the notion of *hasamei'ach b'chelko* in a league all of its own. He considers it not merely an individual trait, but an all-encompassing one that includes all positive attributes. He describes this *middah* as performing wonders within a man's heart, enabling him to greatly succeed in This World and the Next. And he concludes that this trait will help a person grow to the extent that he reaches the level of *teshuvah mei'ahavah* (repentance from love of Hashem). What is it about this *middah* in particular that accounts for its unique status and potency?

- It would seem that the needs of this trait are somewhat demanding. The mishnah does not speak of someone who merely *mashlim* (makes peace) with his portion. Such language would have intimated a state of coming to terms with whatever circumstance one finds himself in. Rather, the emphasis is on being *samei'ach* with one's portion, which indicates a level of much higher intensity. More than just "accepting," a Yid is bidden to actually revel in his situation — no matter how desperate or difficult it really is. How, indeed, is this possible? Can a person achieve such a level that he feels joy when faced with abject poverty and/or suffering?

- *Chazal* issue an intriguing statement on a related issue. Referring to the importance of being satisfied with one's earnings, the Gemara states (*Berachos* 8a), גָּדוֹל הַנֶּהֱנֶה מִיגִיעוֹ יוֹתֵר מִירֵא שָׁמַיִם — *Greater is the one who derives benefit from his labor than one who fears Heaven.* The Gemara derives this from a comparison of the Scriptural statements concerning these two people. Regarding *yiras Shamayim*, the *passuk* states (*Tehillim* 112:1): אַשְׁרֵי־אִישׁ יָרֵא אֶת ה׳ — **Fortunate** *is the man who fears Hashem*. When it comes to benefitting from one's labor, however, the *passuk* includes even more words of praise: יְגִיעַ כַּפֶּיךָ כִּי תֹאכֵל אַשְׁרֶיךָ וְטוֹב לָךְ — *When*

you eat of the labor of your hands, **you are fortunate, and it shall be well with you** (ibid. 128:2).

- How are we to understand this remarkable statement? As praiseworthy as it may be to subsist through one's hard-earned efforts, how can this be considered greater than *yiras Shamayim*? This latter quality appears to be the primary task of a Yid, as the Torah states (*Devarim* 10:12), וְעַתָּה יִשְׂרָאֵל מָה ה' אֱלֹקֶיךָ שֹׁאֵל מֵעִמָּךְ כִּי אִם־לְיִרְאָה אֶת־ה' — *And now, Yisroel, what does Hashem your G-d ask of you, but that you fear Hashem*. And yet, in some respect, merely enjoying one's earnings is superior?!

- What, indeed, is this quality of "enjoying the fruits of one's labor"? As by the description of *hasamei'ach b'chelko*, we see that here, too, it is not enough that one reconcile himself to the fact that he must labor. Rather, he must derive *hana'ah*, active enjoyment. What exactly does this entail?

In order to clarify these issues, it is necessary to examine the whole notion of *samei'ach b'chelko* more closely. As we shall discover, it can be understood on a number of levels.

The *Olam Hazeh-Olam Haba* Continuum

Some idea of how one can actually rejoice in a difficult situation can be gleaned from the comments of the No'am Elimelech. The mishnah quoted a *passuk* in *Tehillim*, יְגִיעַ כַּפֶּיךָ כִּי תֹאכֵל אַשְׁרֶיךָ וְטוֹב לָךְ — *When you eat of the labor of your hands, you are fortunate, and it shall be well with you*, which it interpreted as referring to goodness in both worlds: אַשְׁרֶיךָ, בָּעוֹלָם הַזֶּה. וְטוֹב לָךְ, לָעוֹלָם הַבָּא — *"You are fortunate"* in This World; *"and it shall be well with you"* in the World to Come. The No'am Elimelech explains that these are not two separate outcomes but are actually interrelated. That is, your fortune in This World is based solely on the fact that it facilitates your entry into *Olam Haba*. For the righteous individual, worldly matters bear no significance save for serving as the means to acquire *Olam Haba*.

Further insight into this idea comes from what *Chazal* reveal to us concerning the factors of our life that are predetermined before birth. The Gemara states (*Niddah* 16b) that prior to the formation of a given fetus, a Heavenly voice announces if this individual will be wise or unintelligent, poor or wealthy, and so on during his sojourn on earth. The Nesivos Sholom explains that, of course, these determinations are not made on a random basis; rather, they are the precise conditions necessary for this individual to fulfill his purpose in life. For each one of us is tasked with a specific mission, uniquely tailored for the ultimate benefit and rectification of our soul. The exact Divine calculations involved in this determination are obviously a concealed matter, which in any event would be far beyond our capacity to fully comprehend. Suffice it to say, however, that the characteristics and conditions that are set for our life are essential for the completion of our life mission.

One person may only be able to perfect his soul from a position of poverty; another requires a background of wealth to achieve his purpose. Whatever the case may be, it is crucial for us to realize that the sole means by which we can properly rectify our soul and fulfill our individualized mission is through *the exact circumstances in which we find ourselves.* Otherwise, we would have been presented with an entirely different set of conditions.

This is how we may actually rejoice in the circumstances of our life, for had they been any different, *we would be rendered incapable of fulfilling the very role for which we were placed on this earth.* The consequences of such a failure are too awful to contemplate, but the converse is a joy to consider! *Ashrecha ba'Olam Hazeh* — for every detail of one's life, no matter how difficult, is part of the precise prescription to effect the *tov lach* of *Olam Haba*.

An Expression of Love

The *Toras Avos* points out another dimension and benefit to the cultivation of this *middah*. A Yid who is *samei'ach b'chelko* accepts whatever comes his way, secure and happy in the belief that everything comes from the benevolent Hashem and is intended for his ultimate benefit. The development of such a mindset, in addition to providing happiness and peace of mind, is likewise of immeasurable spiritual

איזהו עשיר השמח בחלקו

benefit. The loving acceptance towards Hashem's management of his affairs is reciprocated, in accordance with the concept of *middah k'negged middah*. Just as this Yid is satisfied with Hashem's "conduct" — in a manner of speaking — so, too, will Hashem be satisfied with the conduct of this individual. His "offerings" and his deeds will find abundant favor in Hashem's eyes.

The notion introduced here by the *Toras Avos* — the loving acceptance of all aspects of one's life — can go a long way toward resolving the outstanding issues mentioned previously. As such, this idea bears some closer examination.

We remind ourselves of and reaffirm our love for Hashem every day when we recite *Krias Shema*, which contains the all-important directive (*Devarim* 6:5), וְאָהַבְתָּ אֵת ה' אֱלֹקֶיךָ בְּכָל־לְבָבְךָ וּבְכָל־נַפְשְׁךָ וּבְכָל־מְאֹדֶךָ — *And you shall love Hashem your G-d, with all of your heart, all of your soul, and all of your resources (your* **me'od**). Elaborating upon this latter phrase, the mishnah (*Berachos* 9:5) expounds it based on its *shoresh* (root): בְּכָל מְאֹדֶךָ, בְּכָל מִדָּה וּמִדָּה שֶׁהוּא מוֹדֵד לְךָ הֱוֵי מוֹדֶה לוֹ בִּמְאֹד מְאֹד — "*With all of your* **me'od**" — *whatever* **measure** *Hashem* **metes out** *to you, be* **excessively grateful** *to Him*. This idea reflects the fact that whatever a person must undergo — even if seemingly difficult — is ultimately from Hashem, and intended solely for one's ultimate benefit. As the Rambam writes (*Hilchos Berachos* 10:3), וּבִכְלַל אַהֲבָה הַיְתֵירָה שֶׁנִּצְטַוִּינוּ בָּהּ שֶׁאֲפִילוּ בְּעֵת שֶׁיֵּיצַר לוֹ יוֹדֶה וִישַׁבֵּחַ בְּשִׂמְחָה — *Included in this excessive love of which we are commanded is to joyfully offer thanks and praise, even amidst trying circumstances*. Thus we see that this directive is the embodiment of the *middah* of *samei'ach b'chelko*.

This *passuk* mentioned other aspects of *ahavas Hashem*: loving Him with all of one's heart and all of one's soul. The Nesivos Sholom understands that not only are these various aspects of *ahavah* interrelated, but the order in which they are listed is deliberate and telling. The implication is that loving Hashem with all of one's heart and all of one's soul will then lead to the ultimate *madreigah*: loving Hashem with all of one's *me'od*, in the manner spelled out by *Chazal*.

This is the *madreigah* of one who is *samei'ach b'chelko*, who loves Hashem even in the midst of difficulties, actually harboring thanks

פרק ד'

445

and love for whatever comes his way. For he is secure in his faith and trust that ultimately, it is all pure goodness.

In light of the above, we can better understand the Saba Kadisha's characterization of this *middah*, how he singled it out as the supreme, all-encompassing *middah*. For as we have just seen, this aspect occupies the highest rung of *ahavas Hashem*, which itself is the pinnacle of *avodas Hashem*. The Saba Kadisha himself stated that being *samei'ach b'chelko* is a gateway to *teshuvah mei'ahavah*.

Chazal's statement concerning one who *neheneh m'yegi'as kapav* (enjoys the labor of his hands) can likewise be interpreted in this light. The Nesivos Sholom explains that this, too, refers to one's loving acceptance of Hashem's conduct of his affairs. Thus, he is happy and satisfied with whatever his lot is, whether he is wealthy and comfortable, or whether he must subsist by the sweat of his brow and the toil of his hands. Either way, he is *neheneh*, experiences genuine satisfaction. In this way, it mirrors the notion of being *samei'ach b'chelko*, which is why it is superior even to *yiras Shamayim*. As important and laudable as *yiras Shamayim* is, there is only one quality which surpasses it: *ahavas Hashem*. And, as we have seen, the embodiment of *ahavas Hashem* is the *middah* of *samei'ach b'chelko*.

Focus on "*Chelko*"

The Nesivos Sholom offers another approach to the mishnah in a somewhat homiletic fashion. *Hasamei'ach b'chelko* can reflect Hashem's **cheilek** — which is what we are. As the *passuk* states (*Devarim* 32:9), כִּי חֵלֶק ה׳ עַמּוֹ — *For the portion of Hashem is His nation*. In other words, the joy referred to by the mishnah is the feeling of great fortune a Yid experiences when he reflects that he is part of Hashem's people, serving as His special portion. As we recite thrice daily: אַשְׁרֵי הָעָם שֶׁכָּכָה לּוֹ אַשְׁרֵי הָעָם שֶׁה׳ אֱלֹקָיו — *Fortunate is the nation for whom it is like this, fortunate is the nation that Hashem is its G-d* (*Tehillim* 144:15).

Being the *cheilek* of Hashem is a very profound notion, one which a Yid should feel deeply each morning when he recites the blessing *Shelo asani goy* (that He has not made me a gentile). For being a member of Hashem's nation, serving as His portion, also entails that he is literally a *cheilek*, a portion of the Divine. The pristine *neshamah* of a Yid has been hewn from under Hashem's very Throne of Glory. This reality accentuates the incredible good fortune a Yid must feel upon contemplating that his soul is a spark of the Divine, signaling that Hashem is always with him. As stated in the Torah (*Devarim* 2:7), ה׳ אֱלֹקֶיךָ עִמָּךְ לֹא חָסַרְתָּ דָּבָר — *Hashem your G-d is with you; you have not lacked for anything.*

At the Very Least — Begin

The discussion above has certainly given us what to be happy for and what to think about. Nevertheless, the prospect may still seem daunting. We have seen how *hasamei'ach b'chelko* occupies the highest levels of *avodas Hashem*; yet it can still appear as a somewhat tall order. Is it really possible? Can a person feel true *simchah* in even the most trying of circumstances?

The Nesivos Sholom counsels that the most important factor is the effort. Try. Make a start of it. Begin, at the very least, with even simple acceptance, to come to terms with whatever challenges may be your portion in life. The overriding principle in *avodas Hashem*, as characterized by the mishnah (*Menachos* 13:11), is אֶחָד הַמַּרְבֶּה וְאֶחָד הַמַּמְעִיט, וּבִלְבַד שֶׁיְכַוֵּן אָדָם אֶת לִבּוֹ לַשָּׁמַיִם — *Whether one does a lot or a little, the essential component is that a person direct his heart towards Hashem.* The goal, of course, should be to reach the heights of feeling joy in our *cheilek* — in all circumstances, in the fact that we are part of Hashem's portion. The immediate task is to start on the path, to firmly make peace with all aspects of our circumstances. When Hashem perceives the earnestness of our efforts, He will aid us as we strive to be servants of Hashem, ascending the rungs of this supreme *middah*, and He will enable us to have fortune and goodness in This World and the Next.

In Summary

The all-familiar mishnah dealing with the attribute of *hasamei'ach b'chelko* can be understood on a number of different levels.

The No'am Elimelech advances an approach that draws on the mishnah's conclusion: יְגִיעַ כַּפֶּיךָ כִּי תֹאכֵל אַשְׁרֶיךָ וְטוֹב לָךְ. אַשְׁרֶיךָ, בָּעוֹלָם הַזֶּה. וְטוֹב לָךְ, לָעוֹלָם הַבָּא — *When you eat of the labor of your hands, you are fortunate, and it shall be well with you.* "You are fortunate" in This World; "and it shall be well with you" in The World to Come. The true servant of Hashem, he explains, views This World as having importance only insofar as it brings him to *Olam Haba*. With this in mind, a Yid can come to feel true *simchah* in all aspects of his life, even the difficulties and challenges. For he recognizes that all the conditions of his life are those prescribed by Hashem with exactitude, to enable him to fulfill his life's mission and rectify his soul. If he would somehow exchange his life's circumstances, he would be unable to fulfill the purpose for which he came to the world. Therefore, he can rejoice in whatever comes his way, as he knows that it represents his ticket to the *tov lach* of *Olam Haba*.

Another dimension to the concept of *hasamei'ach b'chelko* is that it represents the ultimate embodiment of *ahavas Hashem*. Based on the *passuk* from *Krias Shema*, *Chazal* instruct us to love Hashem in the face of whatever measures are meted out to a person. Not only to accept them with equanimity, but — as the Rambam states — to love and praise Hashem for these very circumstances. One who recognizes to such an extent that all that Hashem does is for the good has attained the highest levels of *ahavas Hashem*. This underscores the fact that, as the Saba Kadisha declared, the *middah* of *samei'ach b'chelko* is the supreme *middah* in *avodas Hashem*.

Another aspect to the notion of being *samei'ach b'chelko* is to revel in the fact that a Yid is part of the *cheilek* of Hashem. Klal Yisroel is the portion of Hashem, and the *neshamah* of every Yid is a *cheilek* of Hashem above, hewn from under His Throne of Glory. As such, Hashem is constantly with a Yid, itself a strong reason for one to be

איזהו עשיר השמח בחלקו

samei'ach b'chelko and to declare with exuberance: אַשְׁרֵי הָעָם שֶׁכָּכָה לּוֹ אַשְׁרֵי הָעָם שֶׁה׳ אֱלֹקָיו!

The Nesivos Sholom concludes with a reminder and exhortation. What was spoken of above truly represents the highest levels of *avodas Hashem* but may appear daunting to those of us of average levels. It is important to remember that the main thing is to at least start, to do what we can, and to make an earnest effort. אֶחָד הַמַּרְבֶּה וְאֶחָד הַמַּמְעִיט, וּבִלְבַד שֶׁיְּכַוֵּן אָדָם אֶת לִבּוֹ לַשָּׁמָיִם. While the ultimate goal is to excel in this *middah*, and eventually reach the levels of experiencing true joy from even the most trying circumstances, there is a beginning step we all can take. At the very least, we can work on accepting and coming to terms with the circumstances and challenges of our life, with the aim of striving to perfect this acceptance and increase our happiness and love of Hashem. When Hashem sees us honestly trying, He will offer His assistance in the endeavor, and enable us to attain fortune in This World and true goodness in the World to Come.

פרק ד'

פרק ד' משנה ב'

ששכר מצוה מצוה
For the Reward of a Mitzvah Is a Mitzvah

בֶּן עַזַּאי אוֹמֵר, הֱוֵי רָץ לְמִצְוָה קַלָּה, וּבוֹרֵחַ מִן הָעֲבֵרָה. שֶׁמִּצְוָה גּוֹרֶרֶת מִצְוָה, וַעֲבֵרָה גּוֹרֶרֶת עֲבֵרָה. שֶׁשְּׂכַר מִצְוָה, מִצְוָה, וּשְׂכַר עֲבֵרָה, עֲבֵרָה:

Ben Azzai says: Run to perform a "simple" mitzvah, and flee from sin; for a mitzvah leads to a mitzvah, and a sin leads to a sin; for the reward of a mitzvah is a mitzvah, and the result of a sin is a sin.

GEMS FROM THE *SEFER NESIVOS SHOLOM*

SOURCES:

רַבִּי אוֹמֵר...הֱוֵי זָהִיר בְּמִצְוָה קַלָּה כְּבַחֲמוּרָה, שֶׁאֵין אַתָּה יוֹדֵעַ מַתַּן שְׂכָרָן שֶׁל מִצְוֹת. (אבות ב׳)

Rebbi says: Be as careful with a "simple" mitzvah as with a severe one, for (ultimately) you do not know with certainty the reward given for particular mitzvos. (*Avos* 2)

הַיּוֹם לַעֲשׂוֹתָם, לְמָחָר לְקַבֵּל שְׂכָרָם. (עירובין כ״ב.)

Today, to do them (the mitzvos); tomorrow (in Gan Eden), to receive their reward. (*Eruvin* 22a)

שְׂכַר מִצְוָה בְּהַאי עָלְמָא לֵיכָּא. (קידושין ל״ט:)

The reward for mitzvos is not given in This World. (*Kiddushin* 39b)

וְהָיָה אִם שָׁמֹעַ תִּשְׁמְעוּ אֶל מִצְוֹתַי, אֲשֶׁר אָנֹכִי מְצַוֶּה אֶתְכֶם הַיּוֹם, לְאַהֲבָה אֶת ה׳ אֱלֹקֵיכֶם וּלְעָבְדוֹ בְּכָל לְבַבְכֶם וּבְכָל נַפְשְׁכֶם. וְנָתַתִּי מְטַר אַרְצְכֶם בְּעִתּוֹ, יוֹרֶה וּמַלְקוֹשׁ, וְאָסַפְתָּ דְגָנֶךָ וְתִירֹשְׁךָ וְיִצְהָרֶךָ. וְנָתַתִּי עֵשֶׂב בְּשָׂדְךָ לִבְהֶמְתֶּךָ, וְאָכַלְתָּ וְשָׂבָעְתָּ. הִשָּׁמְרוּ לָכֶם פֶּן יִפְתֶּה לְבַבְכֶם, וְסַרְתֶּם וַעֲבַדְתֶּם אֱלֹהִים אֲחֵרִים וְהִשְׁתַּחֲוִיתֶם לָהֶם. וְחָרָה אַף ה׳ בָּכֶם, וְעָצַר אֶת הַשָּׁמַיִם וְלֹא יִהְיֶה מָטָר, וְהָאֲדָמָה לֹא תִתֵּן אֶת יְבוּלָהּ, וַאֲבַדְתֶּם מְהֵרָה מֵעַל הָאָרֶץ הַטֹּבָה אֲשֶׁר ה׳ נֹתֵן לָכֶם. (דברים י״א י״ג-י״ז)

And it shall be, if you listen to My commandments that I am commanding you today – to love Hashem your G-d and to serve Him with all of your heart and all of your soul. And I will grant the rain of your land in its time, the early and late rains, and you shall gather your grain, grapes, and olives. And I shall place grass in your fields for your animals, and you will eat and be satiated. Beware, lest your heart be led astray, and you turn away and serve other gods, and bow to them. And the wrath of Hashem will flare against you, and He will close the heavens such that there will be no rain, and the earth will not yield its produce; and you will quickly become lost from the good land that Hashem is giving you. (*Devarim* 11:13-17)

ששכר מצוה מצוה

תַּחַת אֲשֶׁר לֹא־עָבַדְתָּ אֶת־ה' אֱלֹקֶיךָ בְּשִׂמְחָה וּבְטוּב לֵבָב מֵרֹב כֹּל וְעָבַדְתָּ אֶת־אֹיְבֶיךָ...בְּרָעָב וּבְצָמָא וּבְעֵירֹם וּבְחֹסֶר כֹּל. (שם כ"ח מ"ז, מ"ח)

Since you did not serve Hashem your G-d with joy and goodness of heart, from amidst such plenty, you will instead serve your enemies...from amidst hunger, thirst, nakedness, and lacking everything. (*ibid.* 28:47, 48)

תֵּן לוֹ מִשֶּׁלּוֹ, שֶׁאַתָּה וְשֶׁלָּךְ שֶׁלּוֹ. (אבות ג׳)

Give Him what is His – for you, and what is yours, are ultimately His. (*Avos* 3)

פרק ד'

GEMS FROM THE *SEFER NESIVOS SHOLOM*

Running to and Away

Anyone remotely familiar with Talmudic learning is well aware that *machlokes* figures prominently in both Mishnah and Gemara study. Nothing untoward about this, of course. On the contrary, following the scintillating give-and-take, back-and-forth discussion adds tremendously to the invigorating challenge of this course of study. Secure in the knowledge that אֵלוּ וְאֵלוּ דִבְרֵי אֱלֹקִים חַיִּים — *These and those are the words of the living G-d* (*Eruvin* 13b), adherents enthusiastically devote their energies in scrutinizing and comprehending each view voiced by one of the sage participants in the debate. Abaye says this, Rava says that, and each one represents his own world of lucid thought and Torah grandeur.

As is usually the case, these disputes are beyond our limited ability to "settle," as the merits to both sides of the argument become even more apparent through increased scrutiny. For the purpose of practical guidance, we turn to the great deciders from earlier eras, who render the final *halachah* to be followed.

Rarely do we have a situation where one side appears, even to our relatively imperfect perception, to have the "advantage," staking out a position that seems to be clearly more sound than that of his opponent. And yet, this teaching of Ben Azzai seems to provide just such a scenario. Somewhat reminiscent of Rebbi's teaching in an earlier mishnah, Ben Azzai at the same time seems to take issue with it. Rebbi had stated (2:1), הֱוֵי זָהִיר בְּמִצְוָה קַלָּה כְּבַחֲמוּרָה, שֶׁאֵין אַתָּה יוֹדֵעַ מַתַּן שְׂכָרָן שֶׁל מִצְוֹת — *Be as careful with a "simple" mitzvah as with a severe one, for (ultimately) you do not know with certainty the reward given for particular mitzvos.* This certainly appears to be a sensible deduction. What mortal is privy to the exact nature of the future reward granted for mitzvos? As such, it is most prudent to be meticulous in the fulfillment of them all.

However, Ben Azzai here seems to take a different tack. He also advocates care with the observance of even the "simple" commandments but supplies an alternative reason. Ben Azzai states, הֱוֵי רָץ לְמִצְוָה קַלָּה...שֶׁמִּצְוָה גּוֹרֶרֶת מִצְוָה — *Run to perform (even) a simple mitzvah...for one mitzvah leads to another mitzvah.* That is, seize even the smallest mitzvah; the nature of mitzvah observance is such that one leads to another, so by performing a simple mitzvah, one eventually will encounter the more weighty ones as well. Notice that Ben Azzai did not state that the weight of mitzvos is unknown to us, as Rebbi pointed out. Rather, he seems to imply that while we may know which is less significant and which is more significant, it still pays to perform the "lesser" mitzvos as the "greater" ones will arrive in their wake.

At first glance, this appears to be an example of an untenable *machlokes*. Clearly, one would think, Rebbi here is in the right. How could a person possibly know with surety what the destined reward for mitzvos is? Could that be the source of their argument — whether or not a person has such finely-tuned spiritual foresight? It certainly seems unlikely.

A close scrutiny of Ben Azzai's overall teaching reveals other points requiring further clarification, as the Nesivos Sholom delineates:

- Ben Azzai's choice of wording is somewhat curious. As he deals with the proper approach to mitzvos and *aveiros*, he does not use the standard terminology of applying *zehirus* (care) to one's observance of mitzvos and avoidance of *aveiros*. Rather, he employs more "activist" wording, advocating that one "run" to do mitzvos and "flee" from *aveiros*. What exactly does he seek to convey with such language?

- Ben Azzai's exhortation to flee from sin is noteworthy for another reason. Notice the contrast with his encouragement to seize mitzvah opportunities: הֱוֵי רָץ לְמִצְוָה קַלָּה, וּבוֹרֵחַ מִן הָעֲבֵרָה. Precisely translated, he instructs us to "run to a simple mitzvah, and flee from **the** sin." *The* sin? Why is one being singled out? And which one, exactly?

- There appears to be a redundancy in Ben Azzai's teaching. The rationale he provides for running to mitzvos and fleeing from *aveiros* is that in *avodas Hashem*, the concept of "one thing leads to another" seems to play a significant role. If you do one mitzvah, you'll end up doing another. The same holds true for the converse: one *aveirah* leads to the next. Yet, Ben Azzai seems to make this point *twice in a row*. He employs a very slight shift in the wording, but otherwise seems to be reiterating the same idea. What is the difference between the statement of שֶׁמִּצְוָה גּוֹרֶרֶת מִצְוָה, וַעֲבֵרָה גּוֹרֶרֶת עֲבֵרָה — *One mitzvah leads to another, and one sin leads to another*, and the following statement of שְׂכַר מִצְוָה, מִצְוָה, וּשְׂכַר עֲבֵרָה, עֲבֵרָה — *The reward for a mitzvah is a mitzvah, and the result of a sin is a sin*?

Do It with a Smile

On the subject of *s'char mitzvos* (reward for mitzvos), we find what appears to be quite a stark contradiction. On the one hand, we know that the arena for receiving reward takes place in the World to Come, as *Chazal* state (*Eruvin* 22a), הַיּוֹם לַעֲשׂוֹתָם, לְמָחָר לְקַבֵּל שְׂכָרָם — *Today, to do them (the mitzvos); tomorrow (in Gan Eden), to receive their reward.* In contrast to the "instantaneous gratification" mentality of large segments of today's society, a Yid knows that Hashem runs His world in a different fashion. Rather than performing a mitzvah and then immediately being handed a pot of gold, a Torah Jew knows that the ultimate reward is reserved for the future. The works of *Chazal* are replete with references to *Olam Hazeh* as a place of toil and preparation, and *Olam Haba* as the destination of ultimate bliss and grandeur.

But we also find another phenomenon, which seems to be at odds with this idea. Take, for example, the familiar passage from *Krias Shema* (*Devarim* 11:13-15): וְהָיָה אִם־שָׁמֹעַ תִּשְׁמְעוּ אֶל־מִצְוֹתַי...וְנָתַתִּי מְטַר־אַרְצְכֶם בְּעִתּוֹ... וְאָסַפְתָּ דְגָנֶךָ וְתִירֹשְׁךָ וְיִצְהָרֶךָ... וְאָכַלְתָּ וְשָׂבָעְתָּ — *And it shall be, if you listen to My commandments...I will grant the rains of your land in its time... You will be able to gather your grain, wine, and oil... And you shall eat and be satiated.* The *pesukim* continue: הִשָּׁמְרוּ לָכֶם פֶּן־יִפְתֶּה לְבַבְכֶם וְסַרְתֶּם וַעֲבַדְתֶּם אֱלֹהִים אֲחֵרִים... וְחָרָה אַף־ה' בָּכֶם וְעָצַר אֶת־הַשָּׁמַיִם וְלֹא־יִהְיֶה מָטָר וְהָאֲדָמָה לֹא תִתֵּן אֶת־יְבוּלָהּ וַאֲבַדְתֶּם מְהֵרָה מֵעַל הָאָרֶץ הַטֹּבָה — *Be careful, lest your hearts be led astray, and you turn away and worship other gods... And Hashem's wrath will flare against you, and He shall close up the heavens, that there shall be no rain; and the earth will not give forth its produce. And you shall quickly become lost from the good land* (*ibid.* v. 16, 17). That sounds like fairly instantaneous cause and effect, right here, right now, in This World! Do mitzvos, everything will be grand; plenty of blessing, plenty to eat. But if you abandon the Torah, everything is lost in short order. And this is not the only instance where such matters appear. There are numerous other sections in the Torah that outline blessings and curses addressed to the Jewish nation, real-world physical consequences resulting directly from their actions.

So — which is it? Is there *s'char* in This World, or isn't there?

The Rambam (*Hilchos Teshuvah*, ch. 9; *Mishnah Commentary, Sanhedrin*, ch. 10) addresses this issue in a most profound way. Of course, the principal arena for *s'char mitzvos* is in the World to Come, as *Chazal* explicitly state (*Kiddushin* 39b), — שְׂכַר מִצְוָה בְּהַאי עָלְמָא לֵיכָּא — *There is no reward for mitzvos given in This World.* So what do we make of the many promises in the Torah that compliance with Hashem's commandments will result in the most favorable conditions? The answer is that these blessings are not supplied in the form of a reward — that will yet come in the future. Rather, they represent the natural response and outgrowth of eagerness in mitzvah fulfillment. Regarding the converse, the *passuk* (*Devarim* 28:47, 48) states the reason why curses are visited upon Yisroel for forsaking the mitzvos: תַּחַת אֲשֶׁר לֹא־עָבַדְתָּ אֶת־ה' אֱלֹקֶיךָ בְּשִׂמְחָה וּבְטוּב לֵבָב מֵרֹב כֹּל. וְעָבַדְתָּ אֶת־אֹיְבֶיךָ...בְּרָעָב וּבְצָמָא וּבְעֵירֹם וּבְחֹסֶר כֹּל — *Since you did not serve Hashem your G-d with joy and goodness of heart, from amid such plenty, you will instead serve your enemies...from amid hunger, thirst, nakedness, and lacking everything.* While directed at the curses, this *passuk* also gives us insight into the incidence of the blessings. Apparently, they come about when *Yidden* fulfill these mitzvos with joy and eagerness.

The basic idea, the Rambam explains, is that these blessings are not intended as "payment" or reward, but as facilitation for the *Yidden* to continue on the very path they themselves have chosen. They demonstrated not only compliance in fulfilling Hashem's will, but an eagerness to do so. As a result, Hashem responds in kind, almost as if He were saying, "You are happy and eager to perform My commandments? Let Me make it easier for you to fulfill even more of them." And so, He rains blessing down upon them to increase their vigor and ability to perform more and more mitzvos. He frees them from those elements that would hinder their performance of mitzvos, such as disease, wars, and other distractions. What emerges, of course, is a sort of double blessing. That is, the *Yidden* receive bounty and blessing in This World (as a facilitating measure, not technically a reward), *and* they are granted the ultimate pleasure and goodness of the World to Come.

In fact, this is the theme of Ben Azzai's teaching. *S'char mitzvah, mitzvah* — "The reward for performing a mitzvah will be another mitzvah." This highlights the "mitzvah continuum"; when Hashem beholds the proper performance of a mitzvah — done with alacrity and joy — He responds by supplying those conditions that will facilitate future mitzvah performance. He grants great bounty and blessing so that the *Yidden*, full of satiation and gratitude, will be able to continue to perform more mitzvos with joy and gusto.

The Toldos Yaakov Yosef adds that this aspect, in fact, is the chief "contribution," if you will, on the part of a Yid when he performs a mitzvah for Hashem. The mishnah earlier in *Avos* (3:7) states, תֶּן לוֹ מִשֶּׁלּוֹ, שֶׁאַתָּה וְשֶׁלְּךָ שֶׁלּוֹ — *Give Him what is His, for you and what is yours are ultimately His.* This mishnah points to the fact that, when viewed in the proper perspective, it emerges that even one who performs a mitzvah in essence is not really giving anything away. If he donates a sum of money to *tzedakah*, was that really his money? Hashem created everything, Hashem orchestrates everything, and Hashem owns everything. If someone has funds in his position, it is only because Hashem arranged that they should be placed there, as they essentially belong to Him. When a person gives *tzedakah*, then he is effectively giving back to Hashem what is already His.

So why, then, is a person entitled to any reward at all for performing a mitzvah? Isn't he merely utilizing what Hashem has entrusted to his care for the purpose for which they were given to him? If he performs a *bris milah* (circumcision) on his son, for example, it was Hashem Who blessed him with the child, and he is merely doing what is expected of him when entrusted with the King's gift! The Toldos Yaakov Yosef explains that when performing a mitzvah, the "contribution" a Yid makes is not that actual mitzvah; rather, it is the *way* in which he performs it, the attitude he adopts in carrying out Hashem's service. The *s'char* that is due him is not so much for having done a specific mitzvah, but for having done it with alacrity and joy.

This helps to account for Ben Azzai's choice of wording. *Hevei ratz l'mitzvah...* Why all the focus on "running"? As the Toldos Yaakov Yosef explained, this is the principal "contribution" on the part of the Yid performing the mitzvah; to do so with *zerizus* (alacrity). Instead of making it seem like a burden, an obligation to "get out of the way," one should be eager and "run" to perform the mitzvah. The result will be a facilitation of even more mitzvos, for such is the nature of the endeavor: *Mitzvah goreres mitzvah* — "One mitzvah leads to another." Roadblocks will be removed and more blessing will come his way, so that the earnest *oveid* can fulfill more mitzvos with excitement and gratitude.

Its Own Greatest Reward

We still need to reconcile the mishnah with what we seem to see with our own eyes. That is, the mishnah puts forward a lofty concept: doing a mitzvah will lead to another. And yet, it appears this may not always be borne out by the facts. Many times we observe an instance where someone performs a mitzvah — and there it ends. No other mitzvah follows right on its heels.

The truth is that there is a good reason for this. And this is why Ben Azzai "repeated" himself. That is, *mitzvah goreres mitzvah* is an absolute truth; one mitzvah brings another in its wake. But there are certain prerequisites to be fulfilled in order for this to happen. The Rambam had cited a *passuk* on which he based the notion of "mitzvah facilitation." The *passuk* noted where Klal Yisroel had gone wrong: תַּחַת אֲשֶׁר לֹא־עָבַדְתָּ אֶת־ה' אֱלֹקֶיךָ בְּשִׂמְחָה — *Since you did not serve Hashem your G-d with joy*. This, explains the Nesivos Sholom, is a key component in effecting the phenomenon of *mitzvah goreres mitzvah*. Mitzvah opportunities will present themselves, but only to someone who views the ability to perform mitzvos as a treasured privilege, who derives tremendous satisfaction from the mere fact that he is able to fulfill Hashem's will. When Hashem sees that a Yid fulfills His mitzvos with this magnitude of *simchah*, He will facilitate further observance and send more mitzvos his way.

This is the meaning of the mishnah's conclusion. ...מִצְוָה גּוֹרֶרֶת מִצְוָה שֶׁשְּׂכַר מִצְוָה, מִצְוָה. Ben Azzai appends *s'char mitzvah, mitzvah* to the end of this statement because it is the precondition for mitzvah facilitation. *Mitzvah goreres mitzvah* occurs for someone who views the opportunity to perform a mitzvah as his greatest reward; someone for whom the *s'char mitzvah* — the greatest reward he derives from the mitzvah — is the mitzvah itself. One mitzvah leads to another. When? If *s'char mitzvah, mitzvah*.

The same applies to *aveiros*, as well. One who loves and runs after mitzvos will find his path streamlined, but so will someone who commits *aveiros* with wanton abandon and relish: *Aveirah goreres aveirah*. But here, too, there are preconditions. Only someone who commits *aveiros* in this fashion, with gusto and eagerness, will continually encounter fresh opportunities of sin. For such a person derives a certain pleasure from the fact that he is engaged in a transgression — his *s'char aveirah* is the *aveirah*. Sometimes, however, a person stumbles in sin, but it is a one-time failing. Perhaps someone who normally walks an upright path had a moment of weakness. For such an individual, his *aveirah* will not be *goreres* another *aveirah*, because for him, there was also no *s'char aveirah, aveirah*. Rather than relishing the thought that he partook of forbidden fruit, he is devastated and full of regret. And this attitude of contrition forestalls the onset of *aveirah goreres aveirah*.

Capitalize on Your "Specialty"

One of the issues still outstanding is the matter of the *machlokes* between Ben Azzai in this *perek* and Rebbi in the second *perek*. Rebbi advocated approaching all types of mitzvos — "simple" as well as severe — with the same care and seriousness, for, after all, אֵין אַתָּה יוֹדֵעַ מַתַּן שְׂכָרָן שֶׁל מִצְוֹת — *You do not know with certainty the reward given for mitzvos*. Ben Azzai did not seem to be bothered by this particular aspect, encouraging one to give equal credence even to "simple" mitzvos for a different reason: it will lead to more. Why did Ben Azzai shy away from Rebbi's reasoning? Did he disagree and feel that one is able to divine the values of different mitzvos?

The Nesivos Sholom explains that Ben Azzai certainly agrees with Rebbi's assertion that mortal man does not have clarity regarding the reward designated for varying mitzvos. The reason he cited an alternate reason is that, in truth, Ben Azzai was discussing *a different aspect altogether*. In other words, there really is no dispute here; the two *Tanna'im* were simply addressing different issues.

In fact, the somewhat nebulous term *mitzvah kalah* can refer to two different things. In what way is a given mitzvah considered "simple"? Are we referring to the level of severity, as one mitzvah may be considered very weighty, the other somewhat less so? Or is the reference to the level of difficulty in fulfilling a mitzvah? Some are easier to perform than others.

These were the two different topics that the *Tanna'im* were addressing. Rebbi dealt with the "severity" issue. He thus declared that, for all intents and purpose, we must treat all mitzvos with the same amount of meticulousness. How can we possibly determine which is truly severe and which is less so? And so, we accord all of them with equal seriousness.

Ben Azzai could very well be in complete agreement with this sentiment; he was merely talking about something else. He offers an interesting bit of advice. Depending on the person, he will find certain mitzvos easier to perform than others. Perhaps he has a naturally giving heart and feels an inclination to run after opportunities of *chessed*. Ben Azzai encourages this tendency. "Run after 'easy' mitzvos," he declares, referring to those mitzvos one finds particularly easy to perform.

What lies behind this approach? Perhaps one should specifically look to do those mitzvos that are more challenging. The Nesivos Sholom explains that, of course, one must fulfill all obligations, despite the level of difficulty. But when it comes to devoting especial attention to a particular type of mitzvah, then one should look to those that come most naturally and easily. Concentrating on these kinds of mitzvah acts increases the chances that he will not only fulfill them, but will do so with *simchah* and *zerizus*. As such, these "easy" mitzvos provide a remarkable opportunity; they are just the type that can effect the grand phenomenon of *mitzvah goreres mitzvah*. For as explained above, the precondition for meriting such mitzvah facilitation is *s'char mitzvah, mitzvah* — one must derive satisfaction from the mitzvah, to the extent that a person feels that the mitzvah itself is his greatest reward. Ben Azzai thus urges that we capitalize on those mitzvos for which we have a particular affinity, as the easier it is to do them, the more joyous we may feel in their performance. And this will lead to many more mitzvos.

The Sin and the Mission

The other issue in our mishnah remaining to be clarified relates to Ben Azzai's precise wording. In exhorting us to seize mitzvos and abandon *aveiros*, he curiously referred to the latter in a very specific fashion. Precisely, he did not say "flee from sin" in the same general sense he used when instructing us to "run after a (simple) mitzvah." Rather, he seemed to emphasize a particular sin: *borei'ach min **ha**'aveirah* — "flee from **the** sin."

The Nesivos Sholom explains that Ben Azzai is referring here to the singular, unique mission on which each Yid is dispatched when descending to This World. There is a specific aspect of each soul that needs rectification, and it is to perfect this blemish that Hashem brings each of us into the world in the first place. How do we know what our personal mission is, and to where we should direct our principal efforts? On this score, the *yetzer hara* actually helps out — in a sense. It seeks to thwart our ability to fulfill our life-mission, and so it devotes all of its energies towards ensuring that we will remain bogged down with this sin, unable to overcome it. And so, this is itself the greatest indication of where we should be directing our efforts. In other words, the area in which the *yetzer hara* reveals a surge of power, presenting the greatest challenge for us — this itself points to our mission, identifying what it is we need to overcome.

This, then, is "the" *aveirah* to which Ben Azzai was referring. It is the area where we find that our *yetzer hara* is most overpowering. How, then, do we escape from its clutches — precisely because the temptation is so apparently overwhelming? Ben Azzai provides the strategy: *Borei'ach* — "Flee!" We include in our daily morning prayers a request of Hashem: וְאַל תְּבִיאֵנוּ לֹא לִידֵי חֵטְא...וְלֹא לִידֵי נִסָּיוֹן — *Do not lead us to the hands of sin...nor to the hands of challenge*. The idea is not to prolong a *nisayon*, but to avoid it as much and as soon as possible. Run away from the *yetzer hara*! Don't stick around! The quicker we leave temptation behind, the lesser the chance that we will succumb.

In Summary

Ben Azzai's teaching enlightens us in no small measure concerning the nature of *s'char mitzvah* — in This World and the Next. In the process, he provides some essential guidance in mitzvah performance.

The notion of *s'char mitzvah* seems to present some thorny issues. On the one hand, *Chazal* seem fairly unequivocal about the matter. They state that שְׂכַר מִצְוָה בְּהַאי עַלְמָא לֵיכָּא, and that the arena for receiving the reward for mitzvos is in the World to Come. However, it also appears from throughout the Torah that our situation in This World is directly and immediately dependent on adherence to mitzvos: fulfill the mitzvos and there will be bounty, abandon the mitzvos and all will be lost. The Rambam reconciles this apparent dichotomy. He explains that *s'char mitzvah* is in fact reserved for the World to Come. What takes place in This World is a different matter entirely. The blessings showered upon the *Yidden* from Above in response to their observance of mitzvos are technically not a form of reward, but rather assistance and facilitation to perform further mitzvos. Hashem declares that this is the natural result of a nation that is loyal to the Torah; Hashem will remove obstacles to mitzvah performance and streamline the path to fulfill even more.

There is, however, a crucial component in this endeavor. In the section regarding the curses, the Torah states the reason things would go wrong: תַּחַת אֲשֶׁר לֹא־עָבַדְתָּ אֶת־ה' אֱלֹקֶיךָ בְּשִׂמְחָה — *Since you did not serve Hashem your G-d with joy*. That is the key. When Hashem sees the *Yidden* serving Him with eagerness and alacrity, He will respond in kind, removing the obstacles and streamlining their path to more and more mitzvos. However, lacking this essential quality, the opposite may occur.

This is a principal theme of Ben Azzai's teaching. "*Run* to mitzvos," he exhorts. This will result in more mitzvos: *Mitzvah goreres mitzvah*. "Running," however, intimates eagerness; running with excitement and alacrity to perform a mitzvah. This is the necessary component to trigger the effect of *mitzvah goreres mitzvah*; a phenomenon that only occurs for someone of whom it may be said, *S'char mitzvah, mitzvah*. That is, he feels that his greatest reward is the opportunity he has to perform Hashem's mitzvah.

This notion helps to explain Ben Azzai's intent when focusing on a *mitzvah kalah*. There are certain mitzvos we each find easier to perform; it is specifically these mitzvos that we have the greatest chance of performing with the proper amount of *simchah* and eagerness. This is why Ben Azzai encourages us to concentrate specifically on them; since they contain the component of *s'char mitzvah, mitzvah*, they have the greatest chance of bringing *mitzvah goreres mitzvah* to fruition.

When discussing the need to avoid sin, Ben Azzai utilized the curious term **ha'aveirah**, **the** sin. This refers to "the" main challenge of each individual; the *yetzer hara* in a specific area that poses the greatest difficulty to overcome. Yet this, itself, is our life's mission. It is specifically because this is the area we have been charged to rectify that the *yetzer hara* devotes all of its strength and strategy here. The way to avoid ensnarement, as Ben Azzai exhorts, is simply to "run away." If presented with a *nisayon*, we must do everything we can to overcome it; but we certainly should not prolong the *nisayon*! Thus, removing ourselves as quickly and as far as possible from temptation is the most effective way to avoid "the" sin.

פרק ד׳ משנה ד׳
מאד מאד הוי שפל רוח
Be Very, Very Humble of Spirit

רַבִּי לְוִיטָס אִישׁ יַבְנֶה אוֹמֵר, מְאֹד מְאֹד הֱוֵי שְׁפַל רוּחַ, שֶׁתִּקְוַת אֱנוֹשׁ רִמָּה:

Rabbi Levitas of Yavneh says: Be very, very, humble of spirit, for the hope of mortal man is worms.

GEMS FROM THE *SEFER NESIVOS SHOLOM*

SOURCES:

כָּל אָדָם שֶׁיֵּשׁ בּוֹ גַּסּוּת הָרוּחַ כְּאִילּוּ עוֹבֵד עֲבוֹדַת כּוֹכָבִים... כָּל אָדָם שֶׁיֵּשׁ בּוֹ גַּסּוּת הָרוּחַ אָמַר הקב"ה: אֵין אֲנִי וָהוּא יְכוֹלִין לָדוּר בָּעוֹלָם... א"ר חִיָּיא בַּר אָשֵׁי אָמַר רַב: ת"ח צָרִיךְ שֶׁיְּהֵא בּוֹ אֶחָד מִשְּׁמוֹנָה בִּשְּׁמִינִית... א"ר נַחְמָן בַּר יִצְחָק: לֹא מִינָהּ וְלֹא מִקְצָתָהּ, מִי זוּטַר דִּכְתִיב בֵּיהּ תּוֹעֲבַת ה' כָּל־גְּבַהּ־לֵב? (סוטה ד:ה.)

Anyone who has within him a prideful spirit is as if he practices idolatry... (Regarding) anyone who has within him a prideful spirit, Hashem declares: "He and I cannot dwell in the world (together)"... Rabbi Chiya bar Ashi said in the name of Rav: A Torah scholar must have within him one-eighth of one-eighth's worth (of pride)... Rabbi Nachman bar Yitzchak said: Not from it, and not from even a small portion of it! Is it a minor matter concerning something of which it states (*Mishlei* 16:5): "Anyone proud of heart is an abomination to Hashem!" (Sotah 4b-5a)

מִי הוּא זֶה מֶלֶךְ הַכָּבוֹד, ה' צְבָאוֹת, הוּא מֶלֶךְ הַכָּבוֹד סֶלָה. (תהלים כ"ד י)

Who is the King of Glory? Hashem of Hosts, He is the King of Glory – *Selah*! (*Tehillim* 24:10)

ה' הוּא הָאֱלֹקִים אֵין עוֹד מִלְּבַדּוֹ. (דברים ד' ל"ה)

Hashem, He is G-d; there is none aside from Him. (*Devarim* 4:35)

וְהָאִישׁ מֹשֶׁה עָנָו מְאֹד מִכֹּל הָאָדָם אֲשֶׁר עַל־פְּנֵי הָאֲדָמָה. (במדבר י"ב ג)

And the man, Moshe, was exceedingly humble, more than any person on the face of the earth. (*Bamidbar* 12:3)

אַל תִּהְיוּ כַּעֲבָדִים הַמְשַׁמְּשִׁין אֶת הָרַב עַל מְנָת לְקַבֵּל פְּרָס, אֶלָּא הֱווּ כַּעֲבָדִים הַמְשַׁמְּשִׁין אֶת הָרַב שֶׁלֹּא עַל מְנָת לְקַבֵּל פְּרָס. (אבות א')

Do not be as servants who serve their master for the sake of receiving a reward; rather be like servants who serve their master not for the sake of receiving a reward. (*Avos* 1)

מאד מאד הוי שפל רוח

יֵשׁ דֵעוֹת שֶׁאָסוּר לוֹ לְאָדָם לִנְהוֹג בָּהֶן בְּבֵינוֹנִית, אֶלָּא יִתְרַחֵק מִן הַקָּצֶה הָאֶחָד עַד הַקָּצֶה הָאַחֵר, וְהוּא גוֹבַהּ לֵב, שֶׁאֵין דֶּרֶךְ הַטּוֹבָה שֶׁיִּהְיֶה אָדָם עָנָיו בִּלְבַד, אֶלָּא שֶׁיִּהְיֶה שְׁפַל רוּחַ וְתִהְיֶה רוּחוֹ נְמוּכָה לִמְאֹד... וְכֵן הַכַּעַס מִדָּה רָעָה הִיא עַד לִמְאֹד וְרָאוּי לְאָדָם שֶׁיִּתְרַחֵק מִמֶּנָּה עַד הַקָּצֶה הָאַחֵר. (יד החזקה פ"ב מהל' דעות הל"ג)

(However,) there are traits with which it is forbidden for a person to conduct himself with moderation. Rather, he must keep his distance – as if from one extreme to the other. This is (applicable to the trait of) haughtiness of heart. It is not sufficient for a person to be merely "humble"; rather, he must be of lowly spirit, such that his spirit is exceedingly diminished... Anger, as well, is an exceedingly wicked trait. A person should (likewise) keep his distance from it, going to the opposite extreme. (*Yad Hachazakah, Hilchos Dei'os* 2:3)

כָּל הַכּוֹעֵס, כְּאִלּוּ עוֹבֵד ע"ז. (זוהר)

Anyone who exhibits anger is as if he is practicing idolatry. (*Zohar*)

לֹא יִהְיֶה בְךָ אֵל זָר... אֵל זָר שֶׁיֵּשׁ בְּגוּפוֹ שֶׁל אָדָם. (שבת ק"ה:)

"There shall not be among you (literally: within you) a foreign god" (*Tehillim* 81:10)... (This refers to) the "foreign god" that exists within a person's body. (*Shabbos* 105b)

פרק ד'

Extreme *Middos*

"You really should try to improve your behavior. Get yourself together, and do some good!"

"Who are you to say what's good? It's all relative. Just do what *feels* good once in a while!"

We tend to think of ourselves as single, unique, independent beings. Yet our thoughts tell a different story, as indicated by the above exchange. This is not an example of a conversation between two people but of the rich inner dialogue that frequently takes place within the minds of basically every person. It often seems that there are two conflicting voices in a person's mind. The truth is, we experience such an endless stream of ideas and perspectives, that without the guidance of our holy Torah and the *gedolim* (sage leaders) of Klal Yisroel, it would be very difficult to determine what is the right thing to do at any given moment. Recognizing the complexity of the human mind, *Chazal* have enabled us to make some sense of our inner dialogue by defining two distinct personas that vie for our attention: the *yetzer hatov* and the *yetzer hara*.

"I really am the best baker on the block; these cinnamon buns are the best I've ever tasted."

"The *rav* should ask *me* to speak between Minchah and Ma'ariv; this guy doesn't know what he's talking about."

"I should get the lead solo in the production this year; I have the best voice in school."

"No doubt about it, I am a better teacher/*rebbi* than half the ones in this school!"

The *yetzer hara* is quite obviously the voice behind all the above statements, telling a person that he is in some way better than other people, that he could do a better job or handle a situation more effectively. In stark contrast to this voice, there is another voice — often much quieter — that tends to surface from time to time. This is the voice of the *yetzer hatov*, which says, "Don't be so *ga'avadik* (arrogant)! That is a terribly destructive *middah*! Hashem has created everyone with their own talents and their own shortcomings; it is an *aveirah* to think you are better than your fellow!"

So Bad, They Named It Twice

That same voice resonates strongly in the words of *Chazal*, particularly in our mishnah. Rabbi Levitas imparts a lesson of *anivus* in strong and unequivocal terms: מְאֹד מְאֹד הֱוֵי שְׁפַל רוּחַ — *Be very, very humble of spirit*. *Ga'avah* is certainly a negative *middah* that we should endeavor to weed out of our personalities. But the mishnah seems to be quite emphatic about it. It could have stated, *Hevei sh'fal ruach* — "Be humble." For emphasis, it could even have stated, *Hevei sh'fal ruach me'od* — "Be very humble." But the mishnah, normally so conservative in its word usage, really went all out this time: **Me'od me'od** *hevei sh'fal ruach* — "Be **very, very,** humble." Is *ga'avah* really so much worse than any other negative *middah* that it warrants such an extraordinary description? Is it really so "very, very" bad? There are so many other profound ideas — fundamentals of Judaism — that *Pirkei Avos* conveys with precision and conciseness. Therefore, it is most unusual for a word to be repeated in this way, unless there is a special lesson we are meant to learn from it.

Apparently, the mishnah is trying to convey that *ga'avah* is, in fact, to be treated differently from all other negative traits. The Rambam explains that, regarding all other *middos*, the key is moderation. A person must strive for a happy medium, avoiding the extreme of either direction. He should be neither a miser nor a profligate spender; and so on. *Ga'avah* is the exception to the rule; here, there is no such thing as walking a middle path. Therefore *Chazal's* emphatic warning against this evil: when it comes to *ga'avah*, a Yid must keep very, very far away!

Throughout the length and breadth of Tanach and *Chazal's* teachings, there are numerous references to the evils of haughtiness. The Rambam cites the well-known statement of the Gemara (*Sotah* 5a) to this effect. Rabbi Chiya bar Ashi says in the name of Rav that a *talmid chacham* is actually supposed to cultivate a "smidgeon" of pride — specifically, an "eighth of an eighth" of *ga'avah*. But Rabbi

Nachman bar Yitzchak vociferously disagrees, declaring that he should have absolutely no connection to this *middah*: "Not from it, and not even from the smallest part of it. Is it a minor matter," he continues, "concerning something of which it states (*Mishlei* 16:5): תּוֹעֲבַת ה׳ כָּל־גְּבַהּ־לֵב — *Anyone proud of heart is an abomination to Hashem!*"

Chazal really do take aim at this particular trait. The Gemara (*ibid.*) issues numerous further statements denigrating the haughty. For example, Hashem Himself declares about an arrogant person that אֵין אֲנִי וָהוּא יְכוֹלִין לָדוּר בָּעוֹלָם — *He and I cannot dwell in the world (together)*. The Gemara further compares a *ba'al ga'avah* (arrogant person) to a worshipper of *avodah zarah* (idolatry), or even *avodah zarah* itself!

Clearly, then, the answer to our original question is "yes." *Ga'avah* really is that terrible. The extra *me'od* in our mishnah accentuating that point is anything but redundant; the absolute worst of all *middos* certainly merits a double *me'od*.

There's Pride...and Then There's Pride

In defining this entity, the Nesivos Sholom provides further insight into our mishnah. He explains that, in fact, there are two forms of *ga'avah* — and this is what alludes to the double wording. Each *me'od* refers to another aspect, implying that — while the two forms may not be of equal consequence — they are both to be avoided.

In its "purest" form, *ga'avah* entails an *inherent belief* that "I" am better than others. Such a person will *demean and hurt* others precisely because he "knows" that he is better than they are. *Chazal's* grave assessments certainly apply to such an individual. By asserting his own sense of self in such a way, he presents a severe affront to *Hakadosh Baruch Hu*, Who is the only real entity of the world that He created. As such, this person is indeed an abomination to Him, and Hashem feels that he has no place in the world.

Then there is a less serious form of *ga'avah*, highlighted by a desire for *kavod* and attention. This does not necessarily emanate from an inherent belief in his own superiority. On the contrary, it often stems from a lack of self-esteem. Since he doesn't perceive his own value, he needs others to think he is special in order to feel good about himself. And so, he craves accolades and *kavod* from those around him.

While perhaps not as appalling as the first kind, the mishnah enjoins us to keep our distance from this type of *ga'avah* as well. For it, too, demonstrates a lack of true awareness of and appreciation for *Hakadosh Baruch Hu*, and as such comprises an affront to Him. For it is only Hashem Who is truly worthy of honor; He is the *Melech Hakavod* — "King of Glory" (*Tehillim* 24:7-10). The *passuk* tells us that *Ein od milvado* — "There is none aside from Him" (*Devarim* 4:35); no other entity, power, nothing; only Hashem deserves honor. Anyone else who seeks this quality is essentially attempting to encroach on Hashem's "territory," which itself constitutes a serious offense.

We find this idea played out in the case of Moshe Rabbeinu, of whom the Torah states: וְהָאִישׁ מֹשֶׁה עָנָו מְאֹד מִכֹּל הָאָדָם אֲשֶׁר עַל־פְּנֵי הָאֲדָמָה — *And the man, Moshe, was **very** humble, more than any man on the face of the earth* (*Bamidbar* 12:3). Once again, the added emphasis implies that he retreated utterly and completely from any form of *ga'avah*. And so it was that, in the very episode from which this verse is taken, Moshe Rabbeinu displayed that he was purged from even the "less severe" form of *ga'avah*. Although his sibling had just spoken ill of him, Moshe did not flinch. So far removed was he from a desire for *kavod* that the insult simply did not register on his consciousness.

In any event, we begin to discover what lies at the root of *ga'avah* that renders it such an anathema to *Hakadosh Baruch Hu*. In essence, it constitutes a lack of recognition for His Oneness, an idolatry of sorts. One who desires *kavod*, and certainly one who feels that he himself is worthy of glory, obviously lacks a fundamental understanding that Hashem is the single power in the universe, the only One truly deserving of *kavod*.

We can understand another well-known mishnah in *Avos* along similar lines. Antignos Ish Socho states (1:3), אַל תִּהְיוּ כַעֲבָדִים הַמְשַׁמְּשִׁין אֶת הָרַב עַל מְנָת לְקַבֵּל פְּרָס, אֶלָּא הֱווּ כַעֲבָדִים הַמְשַׁמְּשִׁין אֶת הָרַב שֶׁלֹּא עַל מְנָת לְקַבֵּל פְּרָס — *Do not be as servants who serve their master for the sake of reward;*

rather be like servants who serve their master not for the sake of reward. The Nesivos Sholom interprets this mishnah as promoting a proper appreciation of Hashem and the opportunity to serve Him. Of course it is true that one who performs Hashem's mitzvos will be amply rewarded, beyond his wildest dreams. But that this should be one's major impetus for serving Him — or should even cross his mind — may indicate an imperfection in his outlook. That is, if a person truly realized how very privileged he is to be selected to serve Hashem, that itself would serve as his greatest reward. "Do not be as servants who serve the Master" with thoughts of recompense; that you merited to perform Hashem's service should be such an exhilarating, engrossing thought that it leaves no room for others. One who does not feel this sense of appreciation obviously does not comprehend the extent of his privilege, presenting an affront to the One Who granted him this singular opportunity.

Arrogant — or Just Plain Dumb?

A certain follower of the Rebbe of Kobrin felt that he was afflicted with the *middah* of *ga'avah*. Fortunately, he at least had the sense to try to do something about it. So he approached the Rebbe for guidance.

"Tell me," asked the Rebbe. "Are you a great *talmid chacham*, steeped in advanced scholarship?" "Not really," the man had to admit. The Rebbe questioned further. "Do you have substantial wealth?" Again the man answered in the negative.

This line of questioning continued for some time. Sizing up the supplicant and knowing what message would hit home, the Rebbe finally declared, "It seems that it is not arrogance from which you suffer. Rather, it is stupidity. For what could you possibly have to be conceited about?"

The Nesivos Sholom clarifies that it was not simply because this individual happened to lack the qualities of wisdom or wealth that there was no room for conceit. Even someone blessed with one or more of these traits likewise has no logical reason to feel that he is better than his fellow. Would one fly feel superior to another fly, just because he was a tenth of a millimeter bigger?

In fact, the whole premise of the mishnah's message can be called into question in light of the above. Why, indeed, is *ga'avah* so, so bad? It would seem to be more foolishness than evil. Then why did *Chazal* denigrate it to such a dramatic extent?

But that, the Nesivos Sholom explains, is precisely the point. It is indeed ridiculous for a person to assume that this or that asset or talent makes him more "worthy" than anyone else. One who makes such a presumption is not only mistaken but is essentially in denial of certain fundamentals of belief. He thinks that these assets come from himself? Was it through his own power that these blessings came to him? The fact that this *ba'al ga'avah* even thinks this way reveals that he is completely missing the boat in a most grievous way. He is blind to the true reality that he himself is effectively a non-entity, for whatever he has and whatever he has accomplished — in both the material and spiritual arenas — are due to the orchestrations of Hashem alone.

Stated another way, the mentality of a *ba'al ga'avah* completely contradicts the most basic foundations of *avodas Hashem*. For the key to coming close to Hashem and submitting to His will is through *hisbatlus*, self-negation before His greatness. The true ideal is for a Yid to consider himself as essentially *ayin* before the Creator. A person's entire existence and capabilities are dependent solely on the good will of the Master of the Universe, Who maintains his life and provides all of his needs. But the *ba'al ga'avah* certainly doesn't think along these lines. On the contrary, he sees himself as a *yeish*, a real entity, a somebody — as if he himself has inherent abilities, as if his accomplishments are attributable to his own power. By asserting himself in this way, he effectively seeks to compete, as it were, with the Creator (Who, in truth, is the only real entity, the Source, Possessor, and Controller of all force and power). It is due to these factors that *Chazal* equate the *ba'al ga'avah* with *avodah zarah*, describing him as someone of whom Hashem says, "He and I cannot dwell in the world together."

It may seem ironic, but following the mishnah's advice is really the only way to become truly "worthy." The *ba'al ga'avah* thinks of himself as a *yeish*, feeling himself to be superior to his fellows. In reality, he is nothing and has nothing of his own. And more than just a fool, his attitude reeks of denial of Hashem's true power, making him despicable in Hashem's eyes. But notice how the Torah perceives one who has truly negated himself, who sees himself as *ayin*. For no one of lesser stature than Moshe Rabbeinu is praised for this very trait: וְהָאִישׁ מֹשֶׁה עָנָו מְאֹד מִכֹּל הָאָדָם אֲשֶׁר עַל־פְּנֵי הָאֲדָמָה. Thus we see that the closer one comes to achieving *hisbatlus*, the greater and more praiseworthy he is.

Ga'avah's Evil Twin

The words of the Rambam in his treatment of this attribute are particularly instructive, providing fresh insight to the topic. In the *Yad Hachazakah*, the Rambam cites the exhortation of Rabbi Levitas to be very, very humble of spirit. In that context, and after having advocated at length the importance of the "middle path," the Rambam states the following (*Hilchos Dei'os* 2:3): יֵשׁ דֵּעוֹת שֶׁאָסוּר לוֹ לְאָדָם לִנְהֹג בָּהֶן בְּבֵינוֹנִית, אֶלָּא יִתְרַחֵק מִן הַקָּצֶה הָאֶחָד עַד הַקָּצֶה הָאַחֵר, וְהוּא גֹּבַהּ לֵב, שֶׁאֵין דֶּרֶךְ הַטּוֹבָה שֶׁיִּהְיֶה אָדָם עָנָיו בִּלְבַד, אֶלָּא שֶׁיִּהְיֶה שְׁפַל רוּחַ וְתִהְיֶה רוּחוֹ נְמוּכָה לִמְאֹד — *(However,) there are traits with which it is forbidden for a person to conduct himself on the middle path. Rather, he must keep his distance, as if from one extreme to the other. This is (applicable to the trait of) haughtiness of heart.* **It is not sufficient for a person to be merely "humble"; rather, he must be of lowly spirit, such that his spirit is exceedingly diminished.**

The Rambam is making a critical point. Previously, we had discussed the two "forms" of *ga'avah*. The Rambam is informing us that there are two levels to *anivus* as well. A "regular" *anav* does not feel any superiority in relation to other people. Thus spared from *ga'avah*, he is certainly on the right track. However, the Rambam tells us, this is not sufficient. We are dealing with one of those few traits that necessitate going to the "extreme." It is not enough to simply lack *ga'avah*. Instead, a Yid must take it to the next level by cultivating actual, "active" humility of spirit. That is, he must develop a truly "broken" spirit. Not in the sense of depression, of course, but in terms of fully recognizing the innate powerlessness of a human being. He is an *ayin*, dependent on the benevolent goodness of Hashem for survival and achievement.

The Rambam continues: וְכֵן הַכַּעַס מִדָּה רָעָה הִיא עַד לִמְאֹד וְרָאוּי לְאָדָם שֶׁיִּתְרַחֵק מִמֶּנָּה עַד הַקָּצֶה הָאַחֵר — *Anger, as well, is an exceedingly wicked trait. A person should (likewise) keep his distance from it, going to the opposite extreme.*

Here the Rambam introduces the fact that *ga'avah* has a "sister" trait: *ka'as*. These two entities have the distinction of being the absolute worst character traits. They form the only exceptions to the rule of moderation, as they necessitate keeping the widest berth possible from them.

It is noteworthy, as well, that both these traits are likened to idolatry. We have previously cited *Chazal's* teaching about *ga'avah* in this regard. Similarly, the Zohar states, כָּל הַכּוֹעֵס, כְּאִלּוּ עוֹבֵד עֲבוֹדָה זָרָה — *When a person exhibits anger, it is as if he is practicing idolatry.* So, what is it about these two traits that they have been so singled out, from all other negative qualities, as the absolute most nefarious ones? Why do they entail such a radically different approach than that mandated for all other attributes?

The Nesivos Sholom explains that the responsible factor emerges from another teaching of *Chazal* (*Shabbos* 105b). Referring to the phenomenon of these traits being equated with idolatry, the Gemara expounds a *passuk* in this regard: לֹא יִהְיֶה בְךָ אֵל זָר... אֵל זָר שֶׁיֵּשׁ בְּגוּפוֹ שֶׁל אָדָם — *(The passuk states,) "There shall not be among you (literally, within you) a foreign god"* (Tehillim 81:10)... *(This refers to) the "foreign god" that exists within a person's body.*

This appears to be the key to understanding the distinction of these two traits: they are blemishes from *within*. Of course, there are other negative traits to which a person can fall prey. By and large, however, they pose more of an "external" threat. When a person succumbs to temptation, for example, while certainly worthy of condemnation, the failing is not necessarily an indication of an inherently corrupted nature. It could be a temporary lapse, in that the individual became ensnared in a trap laid quite craftily by the *yetzer hara*. But *ga'avah* and *ka'as* present a very different picture, for they constitute the *el zar shebekirbecha*, the false god that is within you. The presence of these traits indicates that the *yetzer hara* has been granted reign over a person's inner essence. They are particularly pernicious for they reveal that one's inner workings are in the grips of "idolatrous" qualities.

This notion brought by the Rambam opens a new dimension to the mishnah's words. Rabbi Levitas advocated the cultivation of humility to the extreme — *me'od me'od*. It could very well be that the double diction refers to *ga'avah* and *ka'as*. For these two traits — both of which, as we have seen, simply must be eradicated — essentially stem from the same root. They are both outgrowths of the quality of *yeishus*, the mistaken perception that the individual is a "someone," worthy of accolades in his own right. This assertion of one's "self" carries an inherently idolatrous component; it constitutes the *el zar shebekirbecha*. Its presence serves as a wall preventing one from drawing close to Hashem; of such a person Hashem declares, "I and he cannot dwell in the same world together." And so the mishnah exhorts us to stay far, far away from their awful influence, and to adopt the exact opposite approach. By cultivating a sense of *hisbatlus*, a Yid will thus be ready and able to attain *d'veikus* with Hashem, which, after all, is the primary goal of *avodas Hashem*.

As the *sefarim hakedoshim* relate, the mitzvos of the Torah are essentially vehicles through which a Yid can attain *d'veikus*. As we approach the Yom Tov of Shavuos and prepare to receive the Torah, the topic we have been discussing serves as a most fitting area of focus. As Rav Chaim Vital has stated, the cultivation of pristine *middos* is essential in that it supplies the foundation for the entirety of Torah. His teaching can be understood in light of the above. The ultimate purpose of Torah and *avodas Hashem* is to attain *d'veikus*. But this is only achievable if we first purge ourselves of negative character traits. This is especially true of the ones that we have been discussing, as they constitute a manifestation of *yeishus* within a person, a sure impediment to *d'veikus*. By eradicating this evil root and cultivating *hisbatlus* in its place, we will then be able to fulfill the purpose of our *avodah* — *d'veikus* with Hashem.

In Summary

The mishnah, so normally sparing with its words, becomes suddenly quite emphatic when discussing the need for humility. Rabbi Levitas doesn't simply instruct us to be *sh'fal ruach*. He isn't satisfied to tell us to be "very humble." Instead, he repeats: מְאֹד מְאֹד הֱוֵי שְׁפַל רוּחַ — *Be very, very lowly of spirit*. The implication seems to be that, more so than with other traits, there is a particular urgency to avoid *ga'avah*; that is why Rabbi Levitas punctuates his exhortation in this manner. Indeed, we see this concept reflected in the Rambam's treatment of this topic. While the Rambam advocates a general "middle-of-the-road" approach to *middos*, he states unequivocally that *ga'avah* is the exception. Here, there is no room for moderation; a Yid must go to the very opposite extreme and cultivate an intense sense of humility.

The Nesivos Sholom explains that there are actually two forms of *ga'avah*, of varying levels of severity. At its worst, the *ba'al ga'avah* really feels that he is superior to his fellows. He views himself as responsible for his talents and achievements — ignoring, in the process, the true Source of his blessings — and thus deems himself worthy of adulation. There is another type of *ga'avah* in which the individual does not harbor such a heightened sense of self; on the contrary, he may even suffer from lack of self-esteem. Since he needs others to make him feel special, he craves *kavod*. While less serious, this kind of *ga'avah* must also be avoided. In both instances, the individual encroaches on what is essentially the realm of *Hakadosh Baruch Hu*; the first one asserts his sense of self, presenting an affront to the Creator Who is the only real entity, the One responsible for the blessings enjoyed by all of His creatures. The other, who seeks *kavod*, is likewise affronting Hashem, as it is only He Who, as the *Melech Hakavod*, is truly worthy of *kavod*. And so, Rabbi Levitas warns against both forms by using double terminology: *me'od me'od*.

The repetitive term may be understood as reflecting another

dimension, as well. In truth, the Rambam lists two traits that are exceptions to the general rule of moderation. Not only must one stay completely away from *ga'avah*, but also from its "sister" trait of *ka'as*. Essentially, these two share a common denominator. This is reflected by the fact that *Chazal*, in different teachings, compare both of them to *avodah zarah*. This is indicative of the fact that they both stem from a similar root: the quality of *yeishus*, where the individual asserts himself, seeing himself as an actual entity with inherent abilities and assets. Such thinking is a form of idolatry, in that this individual seems oblivious to the One true Power in the world — Hashem, from Whom comes all blessing and goodness. Thus, the manifestation of these traits within a person is referred to as the *el zar shebekirbecha*, as they infest and affect his very essence.

The mishnah seeks to convey to a person that he would be much better served by completely eschewing this attitude. Rather than adopting a mindset of *yeishus*, he should be "very, very lowly of spirit." Not only should he avoid *ga'avah*, but he should cultivate actual lowliness of spirit. Through a real sense of *hisbatlus* before Hashem, a Yid can attain the goal of all *avodas Hashem*: *d'veikus* with Him.

פרק ד' משנה ז'
ודאשתמש בתגא חלף
He Who Exploits the Crown Shall Perish

רַבִּי צָדוֹק אוֹמֵר, אַל תִּפְרוֹשׁ מִן הַצִּבּוּר, וְאַל תַּעַשׂ עַצְמְךָ כְּעוֹרְכֵי הַדַּיָּנִין, וְאַל תַּעֲשֶׂהָ עֲטָרָה לְהִתְגַּדֵּל בָּהּ, וְלֹא קַרְדֹּם לַחְפּוֹר בָּהּ. וְכָךְ הָיָה הִלֵּל אוֹמֵר, וּדְאִשְׁתַּמֵּשׁ בְּתָגָא, חֲלָף. הָא לָמַדְתָּ, כָּל הַנֶּהֱנֶה מִדִּבְרֵי תוֹרָה, נוֹטֵל חַיָּיו מִן הָעוֹלָם:

Rabbi Tzadok says: Do not separate yourself from the community; and do not play the role of a lawyer. Do not make (the Torah) a crown for self-glorification, nor a spade with which to dig. And so would Hillel say: He who exploits the crown shall perish. From this one may learn that whoever derives personal pleasure from the words of Torah removes his life from the world.

GEMS FROM THE *SEFER NESIVOS SHOLOM*

SOURCES:

כָּל הַשּׁוֹכֵחַ דָּבָר אֶחָד מִמִּשְׁנָתוֹ, מַעֲלֶה עָלָיו הַכָּתוּב כְּאִלּוּ מִתְחַיֵּב בְּנַפְשׁוֹ. (אבות ג׳)

Regarding whoever forgets a single item of his (Torah) studies – Scripture accounts it to him as if he is liable for his life. (*Avos* 3)

קוּבּ״ה אוֹרַיְיתָא וְיִשְׂרָאֵל כּוּלְהוּ חַד. (זוהר)

Hashem, the Torah, and Yisroel are all one. (*Zohar*)

כָּל הַמְחַלֵּל אֶת הַתּוֹרָה, גּוּפוֹ מְחֻלָּל עַל הַבְּרִיּוֹת. (אבות ד׳)

Whoever profanes the Torah, his body will become profaned amongst people. (*Avos* 4)

וְתַלְמוּד תּוֹרָה כְּנֶגֶד כֻּלָּם. (פאה א׳ א׳)

Torah study is equivalent to them all. (*Pe'ah* 1:1)

וּדְלָא יָלֵיף, קְטָלָא חַיָּב. (אבות א׳)

One who does not learn, incurs death. (*Avos* 1)

אֵין לְךָ אַהֲבָה כְּאַהֲבָה שֶׁל תּוֹרָה. (אבות דר׳ נתן כ״ח א)

There is no love like the love for Torah. (*Avos D'Rebbi Nosson* 28:1)

אָנֹכִי ה׳ אֱלֹקֶיךָ אֲשֶׁר הוֹצֵאתִיךָ מֵאֶרֶץ מִצְרָיִם. (שמות כ׳ ב)

I am Hashem your G-d Who took you out from the land of Egypt. (*Shemos* 20:2)

אָנֹכִי נוֹטְרֵיקוֹן: אֲנָא נַפְשִׁי כְּתִיבַת יְהָבִית. (שבת ק״ה)

(The word) "*Anochi* (I)" – through (the acrostic device known as) *notreikun* (contains the following message uttered by Hashem): I

480

have inscribed "My Soul" (into the Torah), and have given this (to Klal Yisroel). (*Shabbos* 105a)

לְעוֹלָם יַעֲסוֹק אָדָם בַּתּוֹרָה וּבַמִּצְוֹת אַף עַל פִּי שֶׁלֹּא לִשְׁמָהּ, שֶׁמִּתּוֹךְ שֶׁלֹּא לִשְׁמָהּ – בָּא לִשְׁמָהּ. (פסחים נ:)

A person should, in any event, occupy himself with Torah and mitzvos even if not for its own sake; for from doing so not for its own sake, he will (eventually) come to do so for its own sake. (*Pesachim* 50b)

GEMS FROM THE *SEFER NESIVOS SHOLOM*

The Crowning Glory of the World

These days, not too many people wear crowns. Even the few monarchs left in the world seem to prefer either military attire or regular business suits. As a result, few of us are familiar with the look of royalty, and we find it difficult to relate to the notion of a "crown." In fact, most people have never even *seen* a real crown.

Nevertheless, the concept is not completely foreign to us. The terminology is part of our lexicon; someone discussing a high point in his life or career, for example, will refer to his "crowning glory." Thus we know, at the very least, to associate it with something noble and august. Torah Jews especially have some exposure to the idea, as we recite daily in the morning blessings, *Oter Yisroel b'sifarah* — "He crowns Yisroel with glory."

Of course, there is a lot more to it than that. As we approach a mishnah in *Avos* where "crown" — the "crown of Torah" — seems to take center stage, we hope to uncover more about the nature of this institution and specifically how it relates to Torah and the world. A prime objective is discovering what exactly this "crown of Torah" is.

To help us achieve this objective and gain clarity in the mishnah's overall message, the Nesivos Sholom raises a number of points:

- The centerpiece of this mishnah seems to be Hillel's three-word statement: *U'd'ishtameish b'saga chalaf* — "One who exploits the crown (of Torah) passes on." It appears to be the source for Rabbi Tzadok's own teaching, and from it we further derive that "One who reaps pleasure..." Focusing on this statement, then, why did Hillel feel the need to invoke the "crown" imagery? Why not simply say, "One who exploits Torah perishes"?

- The last of these three words is likewise curious: *U'd'ishtameish b'saga **chalaf*** — "One who exploits the crown **passes on**." This is a unique term for describing one's demise, one that generally does not appear elsewhere. Technically speaking, it carries more of a connotation of "switching." Why did Hillel specifically select this word here?

- Rabbi Tzadok quotes this statement of Hillel and then infers his

ודאשתמש בתגא חלף

וְכָךְ הָיָה הִלֵּל אוֹמֵר, וּדְאִשְׁתַּמֵּשׁ בְּתַגָּא חֲלָף. הָא לָמַדְתָּ: own teaching from it: כָּל הַנֶּהֱנֶה מִדִּבְרֵי תוֹרָה נוֹטֵל חַיָּיו מִן הָעוֹלָם — And so said Hillel: "One who exploits the crown, passes on." From this, one may learn: Whoever derives personal pleasure from the words of Torah, removes his life from the world. Yet, an "inference" implies that one derives a new thought based on a previous teaching; i.e., that teaching led him to draw some conclusion about a related issue. But here, it doesn't seem that Rabbi Tzadok imparts anything particularly new in his teaching; rather, it seems to be merely a reiteration of Hillel's exact statement using other words. What new idea did Rabbi Tzadok derive from Hillel's teaching?

- Actually, there is one discernible difference in Rabbi Tzadok's own statement, but rather than serving as the solution, it seems to create more problems. While Hillel spoke of "exploiting" the crown of Torah, commandeering it for one's own usage, Rabbi Tzadok discusses someone who is *neheneh midivrei Torah* — "deriving pleasure from words of Torah." The terminology employed by Hillel intimates one who truly uses Torah for selfish purposes — to enrich himself or for self-aggrandizement. But Rabbi Tzadok's *neheneh midivrei Torah*, at first glance, doesn't sound like such a nefarious thing at all. In fact, it connotes that someone learned Torah and thoroughly enjoyed his learning. That doesn't sound like something to be condemned; on the contrary, it sounds like a praiseworthy endeavor! So, how is it compared to Hillel's admonition that, for enjoying one's learning, one "removes his life from the world"?!

- Once again, when referring to the consequences, the mishnah seems to employ some rather original language. In fact, throughout *Pirkei Avos*, we encounter a recurring phrase: הֲרֵי זֶה מִתְחַיֵּב בְּנַפְשׁוֹ — *Behold, he has rendered himself liable to lose his life* (cf. 3:4, 7, 8). Rabbi Tzadok, however, avoids this usage, employing instead the unfamiliar expression of נוֹטֵל חַיָּיו מִן הָעוֹלָם — *He removes his life from the world*. What accounts for the shift?

פרק ד'

Torah and Selflessness

Prior to a full elucidation, the Nesivos Sholom demonstrates two ways in which the approach to Torah study differs from that of other mitzvos; both of these aspects, however, require further examination.

The *Yesod Ha'avodah* (vol. I, ch. 87) draws the following distinction. All mitzvos, ideally, should be performed for altruistic reasons — simply to fulfill Hashem's will. If one does fulfill mitzvos for ulterior motives — say, to gain honor from others — his act is considered *meguneh* (unsavory), but not forbidden. This is with regard to standard mitzvos. According to the Rambam, however, when it comes to Torah study, learning in order to gain accolades from others is *strictly forbidden*. Why the added severity when it comes to the mitzvah of Torah study? The Bartenura explains that learning for self-glorification is comparable to violating the prohibition of *me'ilah*, profaning sacred items by subjecting them to mundane use. This notion, however, is likewise somewhat difficult to understand. We may perceive, metaphorically, that "using" Torah for one's own benefit is akin to profaning the sacred, but, at the end of the day, no actual *me'ilah* occurred. How, then, do we account for the added severity of learning for selfish reasons?

The *Avodas Yisroel* (*Avos*) advances a novel interpretation of our mishnah, further solidifying the unique status of Torah learning. The statement אַל תַּעֲשֵׂהָ עֲטָרָה לְהִתְגַּדֵּל בָּהּ — *Do not make it a crown to become great thereby* is usually understood as an admonition against learning for self-aggrandizement. But the *Avodas Yisroel* renders it completely differently, presenting the term לְהִתְגַּדֵּל not as relating to *gadol* (great), but as stemming from a word of the same *shoresh*: *gedil*, meaning "knots" or "fringe." That is, through the Torah, a Yid is able to become "tied" and connected to *Hakadosh Baruch Hu*, attaining *d'veikus* with Him. Almost amazingly, he understands the mishnah as discouraging this behavior as well! אַל תַּעֲשֵׂהָ עֲטָרָה לְהִתְגַּדֵּל בָּהּ — *Do not make it a crown to become **connected** (to Hashem) thereby*. In other words, Torah study must be undertaken completely and wholly for one purpose: only to grant satisfaction to Hashem. One cannot have any self-interest in mind, not even an interest as spiritual and pristine as attaining *d'veikus* to Him!

This notion is truly astounding and truly perplexing. The *sefarim hakedoshim* relate that the ultimate purpose of all 613 mitzvos is to enable a Yid to attain *d'veikus* to Hashem! If only that would be our *kavanah* (intention) when we perform mitzvos! And yet, when it comes specifically to the mitzvah of *talmud Torah*, even this *kavanah* is considered too self-oriented: *why are you concerning yourself with attaching yourself to Hashem; you should be thinking only of pleasing Hashem, and not anything to do with yourself*! How are we to understand what appears to be such excessive restrictiveness when it comes to *kavanah* in Torah study?

The Right Address

Focusing on the nature of a crown and what it represents can help bring us towards a resolution of these issues. Physically, a crown is nothing more than a monarch's ornamental headgear. But in a symbolic sense, it is something far greater. A crown is the personification of monarchy, representing the king, his supremacy and dominion. An affront to the crown is therefore considered with such gravity because the one who causes it has dishonored all aspects of the monarchy.

This is the profundity of Hillel's statement. Torah is a crown — the crown of all of creation. It embodies the reality that the existence of the universe is entirely dependent upon it. A human being is known as an *olam hakatan*, a small world. The Torah serves as the crown of his private universe, as well, reflecting the fact that his existence is entirely contingent upon it.

We can begin to understand, based on this idea, the utter severity with which our mishnah views the prospect of "using" the crown of Torah. Torah is the crown of all creation and of each individual Yid, and these entities derive their continued existence from this crown. One who makes personal use of it, thereby diminishing its honor, has literally usurped the crown, disturbing his very life's source.

This could be what lies behind Rabbi Tzadok's selection of such unique language. Why does he refrain from using the standard expression *mischayeiv b'nafsho* (liable to lose his life), choosing instead to employ the term *notel chayav* (takes his life)? Based on the above, however, we can appreciate his precision. In fact, we could understand that the mishnah is not even delineating a punishment, the retribution that follows from his act of degradation. Rather, it expresses the natural result of dislocating the crown of Torah. As a matter of cause and effect, he is literally removing his life from the world.

Another dimension of the severity of "misusing" the crown of Torah is provided by the *Arvei Nachal*, which explains that there actually a number of "crowns." Every time a person commits an *aveirah*, he presents a crown to the *Sitra Achra*. But the enjoyment the *Sitra Achra* derives from such an offering is somewhat limited; having been fashioned from sin, the crown is sullied and repulsive. Even more to its liking is what occurs when a Yid engages in Torah study but with impure motives. As he was involved with the Holy Torah, the crown of creation, a crown is thus created of the finest gold and studded with the most dazzling jewels. However, since the intentions were impure, the crown is not presented to Hashem but ends up in the clutches of the *Sitra Achra*. In a sense, then, this offense is even more grievous than the weightiest of *aveiros*.

This underscores the egregiousness of misusing the crown of Torah by channeling it for one's own self-glorification. In so doing, he changes the intended destination of this beautiful and sacred crown. This also explains Hillel's unique choice of wording. In expressing this unfortunate phenomenon, Hillel stated, *U'd'ishtameish b'saga chalaf* — "One who exploits the crown will **pass on**." The word *chalaf*, as mentioned previously, also intimates an exchange. For that is what has taken place: the crown of Torah, intended for Hashem, ended up with the *Sitra Achra* instead.

Respect the Connection

There exists yet another facet to the offense of exploiting the crown of Torah. Aside from the actual degradation, itself a grievous travesty, the very fact that it took place is quite revealing about the mindset of this individual. That is, one who allowed himself to exploit the Torah obviously lacks a proper recognition of the august stature of Torah.

A teaching from the Zohar revealed the exact nature of Torah's stature: קב״ה אוֹרַיְיתָא וְיִשְׂרָאֵל כּוּלְהוּ חַד — *Hashem, the Torah, and Yisroel are all one*. As familiar as this statement may be, it is quite important to gain clarity on its meaning. *Chazal* are informing us of the crucial role Torah plays in the forging of the relationship between Hashem and His people. Torah serves as the bridge between the upper and lower spheres, enabling Klal Yisroel to attain *d'veikus* with Hashem.

When a Yid uses the Torah for his own self-aggrandizement, it is not simply an insult; rather, it is a form of profaning the sacred. The mishnah states later in *Avos* (4:6), כָּל הַמְחַלֵּל אֶת הַתּוֹרָה, גּוּפוֹ מְחֻלָּל עַל הַבְּרִיּוֹת — *Whoever profanes the Torah, his body will become profaned among people*. Anyone who can take such an elevated entity — serving, as it does, as the intermediary between Yisroel and the Divine — and "conscript" it for self-serving purposes, has done nothing less than the ultimate act of desecration. Quite obviously, such an individual has no real understanding of the inestimable loftiness of what Torah represents.

Thus we can appreciate the distinction that exists between Torah study and other mitzvos. Any mitzvah is a vital and sacred entity, the fulfillment of which strengthens the bond between a Yid and his Creator. But Torah is of a different league altogether, for it *is* the bond connecting Yisroel to Hashem. The mishnah in *Pe'ah* (1:1), after listing numerous mitzvos, concludes with the statement: וְתַלְמוּד תּוֹרָה כְּנֶגֶד כֻּלָּם — *Torah study is equivalent to them all*. Whereas the purpose of every mitzvah is to bring a Yid closer to Hashem, the Torah encompasses and embodies all of them. It serves as the actual facilitator through which the *Yidden* cleave to Hashem, becoming one with Him.

It is for this reason, as well, that the mishnah states concerning Torah study (*Avos* 1:13): וּדְלָא יָלֵיף, קְטָלָא חַיָּב — *One who does not learn, incurs death*. This certainly seems like a harsh consequence! But in light of the above, it is a clear and logical consequence. One who understands what Torah really is recognizes that it is the very essence of a Yid, whose purpose in life — to cleave to Hashem — can only be realized through the Torah. If he neglects the Torah, then he has, in effect, relinquished his very essence and his right and ability to exist as a Yid. For the same reason, the other teaching of the mishnah similarly depicts a stark fate: כֹּל הַמְחַלֵּל אֶת הַתּוֹרָה, גּוּפוֹ מְחֻלָּל עַל הַבְּרִיּוֹת — *Whoever profanes the Torah, his body will become profaned among people.* Since the very source of a Yid's inherent holiness stems from the Torah, if he desecrates and detracts from that holiness — what, indeed, will become of him? His sacred essence has been relieved of its holiness, and he remains a profaned vessel.

We should now have some inkling as to why Torah study demands such purity of thought — to the extent that even intending to achieve *d'veikus* through learning is discouraged. Something of such elevated and pristine status, serving as the bond between Hashem and Yisroel, requires the most devoted attention in kind. As such, involvement in Torah study calls for only the purest of intentions; any deviation towards the self — even for something as "benign" as striving for *d'veikus* — cannot be allowed. One's thoughts must be concentrated on one single purpose: to please Hashem. Nothing more.

Light Up the Darkness

Rabbi Tzadok had claimed that he derived his own teaching from Hillel's statement of *U'd'ishtameish b'saga chalaf*. We wondered what, exactly, was "derived" from Hillel's teaching, for what followed seemed to be a mere repetition of the identical sentiment. Hillel stated that exploiting Torah's crown leads to death. To all appearances Rabbi Tzadok reiterates this idea, by saying, כָּל הַנֶּהֱנֶה מִדִּבְרֵי תוֹרָה נוֹטֵל חַיָּיו מִן הָעוֹלָם — *Whoever benefits from words of Torah, removes his life from the world.* On the other hand, it could almost be said that Rabbi Tzadok was discussing something else completely; כָּל הַנֶּהֱנֶה מִדִּבְרֵי תוֹרָה sounds like he enjoys his learning. But what is wrong with that, that it should warrant such harsh consequences?

To clarify Rabbi Tzadok's intent, the Nesivos Sholom introduces the novel interpretation of the *Avodas Yisroel*. He explains the phrase נוֹטֵל חַיָּיו מִן הָעוֹלָם in a completely different fashion from how we had understood it until now. In fact, he understands that it may not be such a bad thing after all.

Neheneh midivrei Torah, explains the *Avodas Yisroel*, is, as was intimated above, a praiseworthy practice. This refers to someone who bears a strong and burning love for the Torah, whose sole *hana'ah* (pleasure) is imbibing words of Torah. Such great love is described in *Avos D'Rebbi Nosson* (28:1): אֵין לְךָ אַהֲבָה כְּאַהֲבָה שֶׁל תּוֹרָה — *There is no love like the love for Torah*. The Ohr Hachaim Hakadosh (*Parshas Ki Savo*) provides a classic description of this sentiment. He states that if people would only know and feel the true sweetness and goodness of the Torah, they would literally "go crazy" with excitement in a frenzied attempt to make it into the study hall. All the world's pleasures fade into irrelevancy and oblivion to one who is smitten with such a yearning for Torah's goodness.

Hashem fashioned the world in such a way that it follows the pattern of *zeh l'umas zeh* — "this corresponding to that." What this means is that the world is filled with potential pleasures: there are mundane pleasures and evil tendencies, but also great spiritual ones that serve as their pristine counterparts. Thus there are base desires in which many indulge, but for people of loftiness, there is Shabbos and Torah. And while man's natural inclination is for the lower type, there is no question which kind is ultimately more enjoyable. As the *Mesillas Yesharim* states (ch. 1), all the world's pleasures are as nothing compared to the sanctified pleasure of delighting in Hashem.

And so, when discussing someone who is *neheneh midivrei Torah*, Rabbi Tzadok was describing just such a person: a pristine soul whose sole desire and enjoyment comes from delving into the Torah. And the result of his elevated pleasures and dedicated activities is truly something wonderful: he is נוֹטֵל חַיָּיו מִן הָעוֹלָם.

The key word in this phrase is עוֹלָם — *world*. The great Kabbalah masters teach that the word shares a root with the term הֶעְלֵם, meaning "hidden." This reflects the notion that this is a prime characteristic of the world in which we live: the light of Hashem is largely hidden from view. As such, we perceive a dark and murky world, in which Hashem's light is revealed only through extensive searching and toil. Who is able to access this light, which serves to transform the darkness into brightness and joy? Rabbi Tzadok tells us: It is the one who is *neheneh midivrei Torah* — he can access the light. And so for him, the world is transformed from a place of *helem*, of hiddenness and darkness, to a dazzling arena of light. He is *notel chayav*, he lifts up and transforms his life, out of the *helem/olam*.

From where did Rabbi Tzadok derive this exhilarating message? He saw it in the teaching of Hillel. Although Hillel was delivering a stark admonition, he concurrently revealed the power of Torah as well. Hillel provided a lesson regarding the august stature of Torah; one who exploits it has perpetrated a grave offense, for he has sent his hand against the crown of the entire universe. And so, from the severity of which Hillel spoke, Rabbi Tzadok understood just how lofty and elevated an entity the Torah is, perceived its stature and potency, how it sustains the world and provides life and light. And so he concluded that it is through the power of Torah that one may rise above the *helem*, as the Torah will enliven and enlighten a Yid's life.

This unique property of Torah — to provide a Yid the wherewithal to endure the darkness and hiddenness of This World — was eloquently described by the Divrei Shmuel *ztz"l*. He would relate the following: "When I am beset by worry and consternation, I find that the remedy is to learn one *blatt* (folio) of Gemara. If I am very anxious, I learn two *blatt*. If the anxiety is overwhelming, I learn three *blatt*. Hashem then shines His brightness upon me and the anxiety subsides." One whose pleasure in This World hinges on Torah will find his world lit up, full of light and sweetness, even in the darkest of circumstances.

Mechanics of *D'veikus*

The Nesivos Sholom provides deeper insight into the phenomenon of accessing, through Torah, the light that is "hidden" in the world. He maintains that it occurs through the process of *d'veikus* and supplies some of the details of how this goal is achieved:

Earlier, we mentioned that Torah is the intermediary that binds a Yid to Hashem. The *Me'or Einayim* (*Parshas Bechukosai*) elaborates on this point. Initially, one may wonder how it is even possible for a

Yid to achieve *d'veikus* with Hashem. Man is but a limited, flesh and blood entity, while Hashem is boundless and the source of all purity; how could there be a bond between such polar opposites? This is the role of the Torah. In some sense that we cannot fully grasp, Hashem "placed" Himself within the Torah. By immersing himself in Torah and becoming one with it, a Yid automatically becomes one with Hashem, Who "resides" in the Torah.

This concept is manifest in the teachings of *Chazal*. Commenting on the first word of the *Aseres Hadibros* — אָנֹכִי — the Gemara (*Shabbos* 105a) explains that this term serves as an acrostic, containing the following message uttered by Hashem: אֲנָא נַפְשִׁי כְּתִיבַת יְהָבִית — *I have inscribed "My Soul" (into the Torah), and have given this (to Klal Yisroel).* So to speak, Hashem has placed Himself within the letters and words of the Torah; when He gave the Torah to the Jewish people, He gave of Himself to them. And so, when a Yid becomes attached to the Torah, he thereby becomes attached to Hashem Himself.

Thus, the Torah is an essential tool in resisting the pull of the enemies of the soul. A Yid's purpose in This World is to attain *d'veikus*. At the same time, as the *Mesillas Yesharim* explains, a person is surrounded in This World by numerous forces that constantly seek to counter this ultimate purpose: they try to keep him far from Hashem. And so, to navigate this perilous path, Hashem supplied a Yid with the Torah. It is the object by which one may attain *d'veikus* and derive light from the world of *helem*.

One Urgent Clarification!

Up until this point, the Nesivos Sholom has demonstrated the supreme deficiency of learning Torah without the purest motives. While all definitely true, of course, there is one outstanding issue that needs clarification: How can this notion be reconciled with what *Chazal* state elsewhere about learning *shelo lishmah* (not for its own sake)? While the Gemara certainly concedes that learning *lishmah* is paramount, it does not entirely reject the idea of learning even *shelo lishmah*. In fact, it even counsels this approach, stating, לְעוֹלָם יַעֲסוֹק אָדָם בַּתּוֹרָה וּבַמִּצְוֹת אַף עַל פִּי שֶׁלֹּא לִשְׁמָהּ, שֶׁמִּתּוֹךְ שֶׁלֹּא לִשְׁמָהּ – בָּא לִשְׁמָהּ — *A person should, in any event, occupy himself with Torah and mitzvos even if not for its own sake; for from doing so not for its own sake, he will (eventually) come to do so for its own sake* (*Pesachim* 50b). Which is it, then? Is learning that is non-altruistic something to be avoided at all costs as it constitutes an affront to the crown; or, is it something that one actually *should* do, as apparently advocated by the Gemara in *Pesachim*?

Quoting the *Yesod Ha'avodah*, the Nesivos Sholom contends that, in fact, there is no contradiction. The issue revolves around what type of individual is under discussion. There may be a Yid who is earnest, who wants to learn in the optimal way — *lishmah* — but knows that he's just not holding there yet. In fact, he may even be broken up over the whole ordeal, as he truly desires to learn *lishmah*, but just does not see how it would be possible. The Gemara in *Pesachim* was addressing such an individual. As long as one is learning with the hope and aspiration of eventually attaining the level of *lishmah*, then of course one should begin even on the lower level of *shelo lishmah*. Here, one's ultimate goal is not simply to amass glory for himself, but to eventually reach the highest levels of Torah and *avodah*. As such, he is bidden to engage in learning even *shelo lishmah*; Hashem will bless his efforts and enable him to ultimately reach his *lishmah* goal.

The issue lies only with the individual who doesn't even care to ever come to the level of *lishmah*. For such a person, his ultimate interest is himself and his own self-aggrandizement. As such, he exploits the crown of Torah and profanes his own sanctified essence. Having no higher aspirations, his learning will forever remain deficient.

In Summary

We find a great distinction between Torah and mitzvos, particularly in the area of intent. Even for mitzvos, the ideal is to serve Hashem without ulterior motives. But nowhere is such strong emphasis placed to discourage this conduct as with Torah study. There is something about it that renders pristine intention an absolute necessity.

Perhaps the most extreme manifestation of this idea is with regard to the notion of *d'veikus*. The purpose of all the mitzvos is to lead a Yid to achieve *d'veikus* with Hashem. Nevertheless, the *Avodas Yisroel* interprets our mishnah as discouraging even this intention! It dissuades one from learning *l'hisgadel*, that is, to become connected to Hashem! What is it about Torah that necessitates such single-minded focus to the exclusion of even learning in order to achieve *d'veikus*?

Hillel's teaching, while very succinct, sheds much light on the overall topic. He refers to Torah as a crown, that is, the crown of all creation. It is the life-source of all creation, as well as the private universe that is a person. By affronting the crown through exploitation, a person is disturbing his very source of life. He literally *notel chayav*. Furthermore, as the *Arvei Nachal* teaches, learning Torah with impure motives is worse, in some sense, than committing outright transgressions. When a person sins, he supplies a crown to the *Sitra Achra*, but, coming from sin, it is a repulsive, undesirable crown. When a person learns Torah, he likewise creates a crown — but this one is shining, with dazzling jewels. When impure motives are attached to such learning, however, the crown is handed to the *Sitra Achra*, instead of to Hashem.

Furthermore, it is incumbent on a Yid to be fully aware of the stature and nature of the Torah. The Torah plays the vital role of "intermediary," enabling a Yid to cleave to Hashem through immersion in the Torah. Thus, it is the very bridge that facilitates the realization of קב"ה אוֹרַיְיתָא וְיִשְׂרָאֵל כּוּלְּהוּ חַד. One who has a clear recognition of Torah's august stature and role will likewise understand why his motives in its study must be entirely pristine. Torah is such a lofty entity, serving as the bridge between Klal Yisroel and Hashem, that not even the slightest trace of self-interest is acceptable.

Hillel's teaching highlighted the severity of exploiting the crown of Torah. From this message, however, Rabbi Tzadok derived a powerful and positive lesson, as well. Seeing how Hillel referred to the Torah as the crown of the world, which supplies it with life and light, Rabbi Tzadok understood the potency of Torah and the wonderful effects it can bestow in This World on its adherents. As the masters of Kabbalah explain, the word *olam* is derived from *helem*, meaning "hiddenness," as the light of Hashem is covered up in This World. But for one who delights in the Torah — who is *neheneh midivrei Torah* — he will be able to uncover the hidden light in the world. Such a person will be able to *notel chayav*, derive light and life, *min ha'olam*, from the hiddenness of the world.

It is important to note that the sentiment of our mishnah does not contradict another well-known teaching of *Chazal*. Elsewhere, the Gemara encourages a person to learn Torah even *shelo lishmah*, for learning that is done *shelo lishmah* will eventually lead to *lishmah*. When our mishnah so adamantly insisted on purity of thought in Torah study, it was addressing an individual who had no interest or aspiration of ever learning *lishmah*. Such a person viewed learning Torah purely as an exercise in self-aggrandizement. For this reason, the mishnah outlined the harsh consequences such a person should expect. But an earnest Yid who wants to reach the level of *lishmah*, but is just currently far from that goal, need not be discouraged. As long as his aspirations are to eventually reach *lishmah*, he may and should learn now even *shelo lishmah*. Hashem will recognize his inherently earnest motives and grant him assistance to reach his goal.

פרק ד׳ משנה כ״א

התקן עצמך בפרוזדור כדי שתכנס לטרקלין

Prepare Yourself in the Hallway so That You Enter the Banquet Hall

רַבִּי יַעֲקֹב אוֹמֵר, הָעוֹלָם הַזֶּה דּוֹמֶה לַפְּרוֹזְדוֹר בִּפְנֵי הָעוֹלָם הַבָּא. הַתְקֵן עַצְמְךָ בַּפְּרוֹזְדוֹר, כְּדֵי שֶׁתִּכָּנֵס לַטְּרַקְלִין:

Rabbi Yaakov says: This World is like a hallway before the World to Come; prepare yourself in the hallway so that you may enter the banquet hall.

SOURCES:

הַיּוֹם לַעֲשׂוֹתָם, לְמָחָר לְקַבֵּל שְׂכָרָם. (עירובין כ״ב.)

Today, to do them (the mitzvos); tomorrow (in Gan Eden), to receive their reward. (*Eruvin* 22a)

אָז תִּתְעַנַּג עַל ה׳. (ישעיה נ״ח י״ד)

Then you shall take pleasure in Hashem. (*Yeshayah* 58:14)

לֹא־אַתֶּם שְׁלַחְתֶּם אֹתִי הֵנָּה כִּי הָאֱלֹקִים. (בראשית מ״ה ח׳)

You have not sent me here; rather, it was G-d. (*Bereishis* 45:8)

מִנְחָה הִוא שְׁלוּחָה לַאדֹנִי לְעֵשָׂו. (שם ל״ב י״ט)

It is an offering sent to my master, to Eisav. (*ibid.* 32:19)

התקן עצמך בפרוזדור כדי שתכנס לטרקלין

The Ultimate Worldview

Instant gratification. It may sometimes seem that this is one of the most deeply held values of the world around us.

Despite this challenge, the world of committed Jewry, at least, knows the facts: The principal arena for receiving reward for our actions takes place in *Olam Haba*. As *Chazal* state (*Eruvin 22a*): הַיּוֹם לַעֲשׂוֹתָם, לְמָחָר לְקַבֵּל שְׂכָרָם — *Today, to do them (the mitzvos); tomorrow (in Gan Eden), to receive their reward.*

While Rabbi Yaakov's teaching in this mishnah obviously conforms to this all-important idea, it is more of an elaboration than a reiteration. The *Mesillas Yesharim* (ch. 1) demonstrates the broad ramifications of our mishnah's message: יְסוֹד הַחֲסִידוּת וְשֹׁרֶשׁ הָעֲבוֹדָה הַתְּמִימָה הוּא שֶׁיִּתְבָּרֵר וְיִתְאַמֵּת אֵצֶל הָאָדָם מַה חוֹבָתוֹ בְּעוֹלָמוֹ וּלְמָה צָרִיךְ שֶׁיָּשִׂים מַבָּטוֹ וּמְגַמָּתוֹ בְּכָל אֲשֶׁר הוּא עָמֵל כָּל יְמֵי חַיָּיו. וְהִנֵּה מַה שֶּׁהוֹרוּנוּ חֲכָמֵינוּ זִכְרוֹנָם לִבְרָכָה הוּא, שֶׁהָאָדָם לֹא נִבְרָא אֶלָּא לְהִתְעַנֵּג עַל ה׳ וְלֵהָנוֹת מִזִּיו שְׁכִינָתוֹ שֶׁזֶּהוּ הַתַּעֲנוּג הָאֲמִיתִּי וְהָעִדּוּן הַגָּדוֹל מִכָּל הָעִדּוּנִים שֶׁיְּכוֹלִים לִהְמָּצֵא. וּמְקוֹם הָעִדּוּן הַזֶּה בֶּאֱמֶת הוּא הָעוֹלָם הַבָּא... אַךְ הַדֶּרֶךְ כְּדֵי לְהַגִּיעַ אֶל מְחוֹז חֶפְצֵנוּ זֶה, הוּא זֶה הָעוֹלָם. וְהוּא מַה שֶּׁאָמְרוּ זִכְרוֹנָם לִבְרָכָה: הָעוֹלָם הַזֶּה דּוֹמֶה לַפְּרוֹזְדוֹר בִּפְנֵי הָעוֹלָם הַבָּא. וְהָאֶמְצָעִים הַמַּגִּיעִים אֶת הָאָדָם לְתַכְלִית הַזֶּה, הֵם הַמִּצְוֹת אֲשֶׁר צִוָּנוּ עֲלֵיהֶן הָקֵל יִתְבָּרַךְ שְׁמוֹ. וּמְקוֹם עֲשִׂיַּת הַמִּצְוֹת הוּא רַק הָעוֹלָם הַזֶּה... וְהִנֵּה שְׁמוֹ הַקָּדוֹשׁ בָּרוּךְ הוּא לְאָדָם בְּמָקוֹם שֶׁרַבִּים בּוֹ הַמַּרְחִיקִים אוֹתוֹ מִמֶּנּוּ יִתְבָּרַךְ, וְהֵם הֵם הַתַּאֲווֹת הַחָמְרִיּוֹת אֲשֶׁר אִם יִמָּשֵׁךְ אַחֲרֵיהֶן הִנֵּה הוּא מִתְרַחֵק וְהוֹלֵךְ מִן הַטּוֹב הָאֲמִיתִּי, וְנִמְצָא שֶׁהוּא מוּשָׂם בֶּאֱמֶת בְּתוֹךְ הַמִּלְחָמָה הַחֲזָקָה... וְאִם יִהְיֶה לְבֶן חַיִל וִינַצַּח הַמִּלְחָמָה מִכָּל הַצְּדָדִין, הוּא יִהְיֶה הָאָדָם הַשָּׁלֵם אֲשֶׁר יִזְכֶּה לִידָּבֵק בְּבוֹרְאוֹ וְיֵצֵא מִן הַפְּרוֹזְדוֹר הַזֶּה וְיִכָּנֵס בַּטְּרַקְלִין לָאוֹר בְּאוֹר הַחַיִּים.

The foundation of piety and the root of perfect service of Hashem is that a person should be absolutely clear and know to be true what his obligation in his world is, and to where he should direct his vision and aspirations in all for which he toils all the days of his life. Now, what our Sages of blessed memory have instructed us in this point is the following: **A person was created for the sole purpose of delighting in Hashem and basking in the radiance of His Divine Presence.** *For this is the only true form of delight and the greatest pleasure from all pleasures that can possibly be attained.* **In truth, the arena where this pleasure takes place is in the World to Come...but the pathway whereby one arrives at this coveted destination of ours is through This World.** *It is to this that our Sages of blessed memory were referring when they* said: ***This World resembles a hallway before the World to Come.*** *The means that enable a person to attain this goal are the mitzvos, which G-d, may His Name be blessed, has commanded us.* ***And the place to perform the mitzvos is only in This World...***

Now, Hashem has situated a person in a place where those who seek to distance him from Hashem abound. These come in the form of materialistic desires, for if a person allows himself to be drawn after them, he will become progressively more distant from the true goodness. It thus emerges that, in truth, he is placed in the midst of an intense battle... But if he will be valorous and prevail in this battle from all sides, he will emerge as the complete man who will merit to cleave to his Creator. ***He will leave this hallway and enter into the ballroom to bask in the light of life.***

By way of explanation, the Nesivos Sholom addresses an apparent contradiction regarding a very basic issue. The holy works of our Sages explain what moved Hashem to create the world: for the sake of one who is good, who is drawn to do kindness and show goodness to others. Hashem is the ultimate source of goodness; so He created the world as an act of pure kindness, to act benignly towards His creations. The issue is, however, that This World seems to be punctuated by tribulations and difficulties! How has Hashem been kind by placing us in This World?

The answer is that our general perception of "good" and what is truly "good" are two completely different entities. We presume that an abundant supply of rich and delectable foods is "good," that opulent surroundings are "good." But the One Who created everything knows what is truly "good" and desires that we attain the actual "good." And this true, ultimate, and unmitigated goodness exists only in the World to Come. As the *Mesillas Yesharim* elaborates, any pleasures of This World fade to nothingness in comparison with the goodness of *Olam Haba*.

A person who hopes to attain genuine goodness in This World has a misperception about what This World is all about. True goodness does not exist in This World; there are, of course, pleasures to be had, even in permissible ways, which (when properly utilized) may aid us

התקן עצמך בפרוזדור כדי שתכנס לטרקלין

in our *avodas Hashem*. Ultimately, however, the goal of This World is not about instantaneous gratification, and the true pleasure is yet to come. The crucial factor is to realize with crystal clarity what exactly This World is: the means, the pathway. It is the hallway that leads into the great ballroom of the World to Come, where the ultimate pleasure and goodness resides. As the *navi* states: אָז תִּתְעַנַּג עַל ה' — **Then** shall you delight in Hashem (*Yeshayah* 58:14).

The Right Destination

The mishnah, normally so exacting and economical with its word usage, seems here to have utilized some extraneous language, as the commentaries note. The mishnah states: הַתְקֵן עַצְמְךָ בַפְּרוֹזְדוֹר, כְּדֵי שֶׁתִּכָּנֵס לַטְּרַקְלִין — *Prepare yourself in the hallway* **in order that** *you enter the banquet hall*. Why not simply say: הַתְקֵן עַצְמְךָ בַפְּרוֹזְדוֹר לְהִכָּנֵס לַטְּרַקְלִין — *Prepare yourself in the hallway* **to** *enter the banquet hall*?

The Nesivos Sholom explains that the nuanced language alludes to the true nature of this "hallway." It reminds us that it does not lead exclusively to one destination; it is not a hallway that leads only to *Olam Haba*. There are those who traverse the same walkway, but are led into Gehinnom. Therefore, the mishnah supplies this added warning: prepare yourself, and ensure that you use this hallway *in order* to access the preferred destination — *Olam Haba*.

In fact, there is yet another dimension to the message conveyed by the mishnah's particular wording, as we shall see.

Consider the scenario of spectators at an event. The arena seats a vast audience, with the standard tickets going for $10 each. But there are other options. Sprinkled around the arena are luxury suites, where a well-to-do fellow, for $400 apiece, can seat his friends. Each of his guests was treated to the most luxurious and comfortable seating, along with the best views of the proceedings. This was in contrast to the standard $10 package, complete with partially obstructed views and hard metal seats. Both groups viewed the same event, but what a difference!

The tzaddikim inform us that while many are entitled to enter

Olam Haba, not everyone shares the same experience. The saintly Reb Shlomo of Karlin *ztz"l* related to his students that this lesson had been revealed to him from on High. He was privy to hear a Heavenly voice that discussed the fate of a Yid who was particular in his observance, but neglected to derive spiritual satisfaction from the Shabbos day. Undoubtedly, the voice declared, this Yid would enter into Gan Eden, but he will derive the same pleasure from there as a bench would if it were also placed in Gan Eden. Since he never made an effort to cultivate a "taste" for *ruchniyus* in This World, it will likewise not be forthcoming in the World to Come. As such, he will derive the same enjoyment from the spiritual paradise of Gan Eden as an inanimate object.

This insight demonstrates the significant cause and effect relationship between effort and reward. All activities in This World are the building blocks for the eternal experience of the World to Come. It is said that a professional wine-taster has a very sophisticated palate. He therefore is able to perceive and describe a whole range of flavors, aromas, and nuanced aspects of a given type of wine. But the common folk who never developed such acumen remain with a very primitive sense of taste in this area; to them, all wine tastes basically the same, and bland at that. In a similar fashion, a Yid who didn't revel in the spiritual pleasure of Shabbos cannot experience complete enjoyment in the World to Come. But someone who made the effort to develop sensitivity to and a "taste" for mitzvos will enjoy and distinguish pleasures in Gan Eden that others cannot.

This same principle can work in the converse — to the detriment of a transgressor. There are many people who, unfortunately, stumble in sin. But there are those who have cultivated a real "taste" for *aveiros*, approaching them with great passion. The intensity of the fires of Gehinnom is derived from the fires of lust and relish developed in the pursuit of flaunting Hashem's will.

As noted above, the precise wording of our mishnah alluded to the fact that the *prozdor* (hallway) leads in different directions; a Yid must be careful to utilize it to convey him to the proper destination. From the above we gain an additional understanding of this idea.

התקן עצמך בפרוזדור כדי שתכנס לטרקלין

Not only does the preparation in the hallway determine the ultimate destination, but it also determines the nature and extent of the experience in that destination. Proper "preparation in the hallway" entails ensuring that one's activities in This World supply the necessary means for a full enjoyment of the boundless pleasures of the desired destination.

Which World Do You Live In?

It is important to recognize that as much as this mishnah imparts great truths about the World to Come, it also conveys a crucial lesson about *Olam Hazeh*. The Nesivos Sholom emphasizes that this is also an essential part of the mishnah's message: This World is a hallway to the ballroom — and that's all it is. It is a grave error to view the world as possessing any significance other than as a means to *Olam Haba*.

The *ba'alei mussar* supplied much imagery to illustrate this point. For example, they depict an individual who was an aspiring entrepreneur. He gathered a sizable sum and traveled to a faraway land to acquire merchandise for resale. Of course, he could only stay away from home for so long, but he intended to capitalize on the opportunity by concentrating on items he knew were rare in his locale. In this way, he would be able to resell them and garner some nice profits.

When he arrived, he ended up taking lodgings at a more upscale hotel; after all, he still had plenty with which to make investments. Also, being that it was the first day, he figured that he could afford to indulge a bit. And so he went around town enjoying himself, stopping by some of the finer eateries. He ended up enjoying himself so much that he kept up the practice on the next day. And the next. And for the remainder of his "business" trip.

It was almost time to make the homeward journey. He finally began to feel the urgency to start collecting some promising merchandise. But when he checked his money pouch…alas! His whole stock was virtually used up! Imagine the scorn he would face upon returning home. He could already sense the scolding that awaited: "You went on a business trip, and you used up all of the investment money on fancy hotels and fine dining, with no merchandise to speak of!"

As foolish as this individual appears, it is almost astounding how many people behave in the same fashion! For this is the outcome when one does not inculcate within him the teaching of our mishnah. A person can use up all of his capital — the time and energy he has in This World — just to make his stay in the "hallway" more comfortable! But a wise man realizes that it simply does not pay to expend these precious resources to upgrade his hallway. If one truly recognizes This World for what it is — a means by which to earn life in the World to Come — he will adjust his priorities appropriately, utilizing every moment in the hallway simply as a means to reach the banquet.

This lesson, too, is included in our mishnah's message. A Yid must always remember that This World is merely a means to an end and no more. He must conduct his life in a fashion that reflects his belief that nothing in This World has any intrinsic value, other than as a conduit to the World to Come. Unlike the fool who engages in great efforts to make his stay in the hallway comfortable, the wise man dwells in it only as long as he needs to achieve his sole purpose — to reach the banquet of אָז תִּתְעַנַּג עַל ה׳.

The Birkas Avraham renders a beautiful homiletic interpretation that encapsulates this idea. When Yosef revealed himself to the brothers, he immediately sought to assuage their feelings of guilt. He reassured them that his being sent to Egypt was a very necessary development, all part of the Divine plan. He told them (*Bereishis* 45:8): לֹא־אַתֶּם שְׁלַחְתֶּם אֹתִי הֵנָּה כִּי הָאֱלֹקִים — *You have not sent me here; rather, it was G-d*. But the Birkas Avraham explains this declaration as what a Yid should "say" to the material aspects of This World that vie for his preoccupation and distract him from his true mission in life. "It is not for you that I have been sent here"; that is, it is not on your account that I have been sent by Hashem down to This World. "Rather, it is for Hashem," to serve Him and attain closeness to Him at the eventual banquet. As such, I will not allow you to distract me from this purpose.

התקן עצמך בפרוזדור כדי שתכנס לטרקלין

In keeping with this notion, the mishnah can be used as an excellent barometer for determining every action we may take in This World. "Will this activity bring me closer to the ballroom at the end of the hallway, or lead, G-d forbid, in the opposite direction?" This is a crucial question a Yid must revisit throughout his day, throughout his life. There is yet another homiletic interpretation of the Birkas Avraham that reflects this idea. When Yaakov was preparing to meet his brother and nemesis, Eisav, he dispatched messengers to him, bearing gifts, in an attempt at appeasement. Referring to these gifts, he instructed these messengers to relate to Eisav in his name: מִנְחָה הִוא שְׁלוּחָה לַאדֹנִי לְעֵשָׂו — *It is a gift that is sent to my master, to Eisav* (*ibid.* 32:19). The Birkas Avraham perceives in this an allusion to man's general conduct. In This World, every activity in which a person engages presents a "gift" to one of two entities, either "to my Master," meaning to Hashem, or "to Eisav," the symbol and embodiment of evil. This is how a Yid must consider his actions in This World: is this act a "gift to Hashem" that will lead to the Ballroom, or is it a "gift to Eisav" that leads to the alternative?

This notion is a key element in one's service of Hashem. It is so crucial for a Yid to perpetually drive home the sentiment that This World, essentially, is nothing — nothing more than a means of reaching the ultimate banquet.

There was a common refrain among tzaddikim contrasting the different perspectives through which to view the world: "A simpleton sees This World with his actual eyes, while *Olam Haba* is a matter which is consigned to his belief. A truly righteous man, however, sees the World to Come with his very eyes, while it is This World that is just a matter of belief. What does he even know from worldly matters? Only that which he has heard about from his followers and petitioners."

For someone who is deeply mired in the affairs of This World, the only way out is to fulfill the dictum of our mishnah as characterized by the *Mesillas Yesharim*. It is essential for all to see with the greatest possible clarity the real truth of This World: that it is essentially nothing, save as a means to gain entry into the Great Ballroom. This is the "foundation of piety" upon which rests one's entire *avodas Hashem*.

In Summary

The *Mesillas Yesharim* bases his classic opening in the first chapter on the lesson of this mishnah: The function of This World is as a means to an end — that of achieving the grandeur of the World to Come, the arena where one *misaneig al Hashem* (rejoices in Hashem). Hashem created the world to bestow goodness upon us, and while This World contains many painful tribulations, it is the hallway we traverse to reach the true destination, Gan Eden, where the ultimate goodness resides.

This World is more than just the place where we labor to earn the prize of the World to Come. It is actually the arena in which our deeds forge our own Gan Eden and Gehinnom. Just as one requires a tongue to taste and a nose to smell, our activities in This World create our capacity for the pleasures and tribulations of Gan Eden and Gehinnom, respectively. As Reb Shlomo of Karlin taught: a Yid who did not engage in the pursuit of deriving pleasure from the spiritual aspects of Shabbos will be unable to fully enjoy the spiritual pleasures of Gan Eden. This reflects the fact that our activities in This World are the building blocks for the eternal experience of the World to Come. This carries ramifications for the converse, as well. A Jew who engages in sin with gusto in This World creates the very fires he will endure in Gehinnom.

A Yid must always remember that This World is merely a means to an end and no more. Rather than being a fool whose principal goal is to make his stay in the hallway more comfortable, the wise man views This World for what it really is. He doesn't allow materialistic desires to distract him from the ultimate goal of preparing to enter the banquet of אָז תִּתְעַנַּג עַל ה'.

So fundamental a notion did the *Mesillas Yesharim* consider the message of our mishnah that it was characterized as the very "foundation of piety and pillar of serving Hashem."

פרק ד' משנה כ"ח
הקנאה התאוה והכבוד
Jealousy, Desire, and Honor

רַבִּי אֶלְעָזָר הַקַּפָּר אוֹמֵר, הַקִּנְאָה וְהַתַּאֲוָה וְהַכָּבוֹד מוֹצִיאִין אֶת הָאָדָם מִן הָעוֹלָם:

Rabbi Elazar Hakapar says: Jealousy, desire, and honor remove a person from the world.

GEMS FROM THE *SEFER NESIVOS SHOLOM*

SOURCES:

וּרְקַב עֲצָמוֹת קִנְאָה. (משלי י"ד ל)

Envy causes the bones to rot. (*Mishlei* 14:30)

אֵין אָדָם יוֹצֵא מִן הָעוֹלָם וַחֲצִי תַאֲוָתוֹ בְּיָדוֹ. (קהלת רבה א' כ"ב)

No person – by the time he leaves This World – has fulfilled even half of his heart's desires. (*Koheles Rabbah* 1:22)

כָּל הָרוֹדֵף אַחַר הַכָּבוֹד – הַכָּבוֹד בּוֹרֵחַ מִמֶּנּוּ. (עי' שבט מוסר פרק י"ז)

One who chases after honor – honor flees from him (cf. *Shevet Mussar*, ch. 17)

יַעֲזֹב רָשָׁע דַּרְכּוֹ. (ישעיה נ"ה ז')

Let the wicked abandon his way. (*Yeshayah* 55:7)

וַתֵּרֶא הָאִשָּׁה כִּי טוֹב הָעֵץ לְמַאֲכָל וְכִי תַאֲוָה־הוּא לָעֵינַיִם וְנֶחְמָד הָעֵץ לְהַשְׂכִּיל וַתִּקַּח מִפִּרְיוֹ וַתֹּאכַל. (בראשית ג' ו')

And the woman saw that the tree was good for eating, and that it was pleasing to the eyes, and delightful for discernment, and she took from its fruit, and she ate. (*Bereishis* 3:6)

אִילוּלֵי הַקִּנְאָה אֵין הָעוֹלָם עוֹמֵד. (מדרש שוחר טוב ל"ז א')

If not for *kinah*, the world would not endure. (*Midrash Shocher Tov* 37:1)

קִנְאַת סוֹפְרִים תַּרְבֶּה חָכְמָה. (בבא בתרא כ"א)

Envy amongst scholars increases wisdom. (*Bava Basra* 21a)

עַל שְׁלֹשָׁה דְבָרִים הָעוֹלָם עוֹמֵד, עַל הַתּוֹרָה וְעַל הָעֲבוֹדָה וְעַל גְּמִילוּת חֲסָדִים. (אבות א')

On three things the world stands: on Torah, Divine service, and performing acts of kindness. (*Avos* 1)

פרקי אבות

506

הקנאה התאוה והכבוד

Out of These Worlds

This mishnah presents a concise, bold statement. There is little doubt as to its sentiments regarding the traits of envy, desire, and honor-seeking. Nevertheless, there is something about this crisp statement that does seem unclear — namely, its meaning.

These *middos* "remove a person from the world." What could this possibly mean? A person who indulges in pleasure, or basks in the obsequious honor that others show him, certainly seems to be very much *in* This World, not out of it. Perhaps the mishnah is referring to the World to Come, stating that this type of individual will not merit entry. But mishnayos are quite deliberate in their terminology; had this been the intent, the mishnah could have stated so explicitly. The generic term *olam*, lacking any specification, would intimate that it is all-inclusive — he will be removed from both This World and the Next. Which brings us back to square one. We could understand, perhaps, that subservience to these negative tendencies may lead one down a very sordid path and end up costing him his *Olam Haba*. But what about *Olam Hazeh*? The mishnah implies that he loses this as well; but to all appearances, he sure seems to be having a good time right now and right here.

But looks can be deceiving. In elucidating the mishnah, the Nesivos Sholom highlights the destructive power of these traits. He demonstrates how one who falls prey to them is, indeed, deprived of both worlds.

Not a Life

U'rekav atzamos kinah — "Envy causes the bones to rot" (*Mishlei* 14:30). This *passuk* gives us a fairly good indication of the havoc this attribute can wreak on a person. There is always someone around who has "more" and "better": a nicer house, more popularity, better abilities. As such, there is always something for a jealous person to fret about — a sure recipe for a life of constant bitterness.

The *ba'al ta'avah* does not fare much better. One who is enslaved to his passions will never be at rest; the nature of *ta'avah* is such that

פרק ד'

as much as he fulfills his desires, he will never be content. In fact, *Chazal* inform us (*Sukkah* 52b) that instead of finding satiation, the more one gratifies his desires, the more he will crave. And so, such a person is never at peace, being destined for never-ending pursuit and ultimate frustration. As *Chazal* relate elsewhere (*Koheles Rabbah* 1:22), אֵין אָדָם יוֹצֵא מִן הָעוֹלָם וַחֲצִי תַּאֲוָתוֹ בְּיָדוֹ — *No person, by the time he leaves This World, has fulfilled even half of his heart's desires.*

And someone utterly dependent on the approval of others — what kind of life is he going to have? In the first place, one who constantly seeks honor will not attain it, for "one who chases after honor — honor flees from him" (*cf. Shevet Mussar*, ch. 17). But worse is yet to come. *Chazal* tell us what becomes of a haughty individual who lords it over others, demanding attention and recognition: in the end, even his family members will reject him (*Bava Basra* 98a). Instead of glory, he becomes an object of universal derision.

Thus, someone afflicted by these qualities will literally have no life here in This World. But his woes do not end with his temporary sojourn on earth. One who is caught up in these traits destroys his very soul, rendering it thoroughly wicked. For these three items are not mere shortcomings; they constitute the very essence and root of *ra*. Referring to *middos* such as these, the Rambam (*Hilchos Teshuvah* 7:3) applies the *passuk*, *Ya'azov rasha darko* — "Let the wicked abandon his way" (*Yeshayah* 55:7). It seems that the Rambam perceived the *navi* as speaking not of "**actions**," as he did not state, *Ya'azov rasha* **ma'asav**; rather, the subject was **darko** — "his **way**." Apparently, these *middos* are so severe that one is rendered a *rasha* on their account, even if they have not yet translated into concrete action.

What is it about these particular traits that warrants such intense focus? To clarify this issue, the Nesivos Sholom employs a concept discussed in the *sefarim* that focuses on the internal structure of a human being — in both the physical and the spiritual sense. There are three main elements to a person's anatomical makeup, which are chiefly responsible for his functionality. These are the mind, heart, and liver. Of these organs, the liver is considered the most "physical";

it is the seat of a person's bodily strengths and abilities. It is from here that the force of desire emanates; of the three *middos*, this one is most closely associated with material tendencies. The more spiritual force driving a person is centered within his heart; the sentiments of envy derive from it. The final principal component of a person is his mind, the seat of intellect. A drive for *kavod* — a non-physical entity — is a product of the intellect; it is a state of mind.

These are the main "control centers" of the human being. As such, if they are infested, respectively, with *ta'avah*, *kinah*, and *kavod* — the roots of evil — the result is that *ra* exerts true dominion over the entirety of the person. He becomes wholly given over to, and controlled by, the *yetzer hara*. Obviously, if this state is reached, the effects will be devastating. Such a person becomes removed from "the world(s)."

And such has been the case from the earliest times. This emerges from exploring the arrangement of our mishnah; why were these qualities listed in the specific order of *kinah*, *ta'avah*, and then *kavod*? The Nesivos Sholom explains that this follows the order in which the original examples of man's corruption through these qualities appear in the Torah:

Kinah was manifest in the episode of Kayin and Hevel (*Bereishis*, ch. 4). Seeing that Hevel's offerings to Hashem were accepted while his were not, Kayin grew jealous of his brother. So much so, that it led him to murder. And he was literally removed from the world, forced to wander on the outskirts of civilization.

Ta'avah reached unprecedented levels during the generation of the Flood. As the *passuk* attests (*ibid.* 6:11): כִּי־הִשְׁחִית כָּל־בָּשָׂר אֶת־דַּרְכּוֹ עַל־הָאָרֶץ — *For all flesh had corrupted their way on the earth*. Sunken in the morass of their base desires, the ultimate "removal from the world" was effected through the annihilation of all life by the Flood.

Kavod and self-aggrandizement characterized the building of the Tower of Bavel. This is evidenced by the way they themselves stated their goals (*ibid.* 11:4): הָבָה נִבְנֶה־לָּנוּ עִיר וּמִגְדָּל וְרֹאשׁוֹ בַשָּׁמַיִם וְנַעֲשֶׂה־לָּנוּ שֵׁם — *Come, let us build a city, and a tower whose top reaches the Heavens; **and we shall make for ourselves a name***. But Hashem thwarted their plans by scrambling their languages. Their outcome was precisely what they had sought to circumvent, and they were scattered throughout the land.

Fight Back!

Having expounded upon the nefarious nature and power of these three traits, the Nesivos Sholom now turns to the remedy. These *middos* are perilous to a person's physical and spiritual welfare, but how, indeed, can they be vanquished?

The answer, asserts the Nesivos Sholom, is *emunah*. Through developing and fortifying one's *emunah* in basic fundamentals of *Yiddishkeit*, a person can draw the strength to overpower the force of these nefarious traits. Let us examine just how *emunah* can defeat them.

What lies at the root of envy? Essentially, it is based on a lack of satisfaction with one's portion. Why should a person be interested in what his neighbor has, if he is already content with what is his? Someone who has a deep *emunah* that Hashem has bestowed him with all of his needs is a happy and satisfied person. He clearly recognizes that he was given exactly what is essential for his existence and for the fulfillment of his life's mission. If there was anything else that was necessary for this cause, he rests assured that Hashem would have provided it for him. If he doesn't have it, that is the greatest indication that it's simply not meant for him.

A person with such a mindset is a truly liberated individual. He is secure that he has just what he needs in life, that no one can take it away from him, and that there is nothing he can do to obtain anything more. He knows that if Hashem decreed that he should have a certain object or asset, all the forces in the world would be powerless to remove it from his possession. And if it was decreed that he should not have a certain asset, all of the planning and scheming in the world will not help him to attain it. The end result of such beliefs is a person freed from envy; he is happy with his lot and gives no thought to what "the other guy" has.

In fact, the issue goes a step further. For not only is the *ma'amin* (believer) impartial regarding his neighbor's success and possessions, he is actually thrilled not to have them! We each have our individual task to fulfill on this earth. To complete this mission, Hashem supplies each of us with the exact tools and circumstances necessary to succeed. A wealthy man has his unique mission and was granted wealth in order to accomplish it; a poor man likewise was charged with a task that necessitated a backdrop of poverty. And so the *ma'amin* says to himself, "*Baruch Hashem* that I don't have my neighbor's set of circumstances; if I did, I would not be able to fulfill my life's mission, the very purpose for which I was created!"

Ta'avah can similarly be neutralized by *emunah*. This can be understood on a number of levels. In the beginning of the *Shulchan Aruch* (1:1), the Rama states the following, כְּשֶׁיָּשִׂים הָאָדָם אֶל לִבּוֹ שֶׁהַמֶּלֶךְ הַגָּדוֹל הקב"ה אֲשֶׁר מָלֵא כָּל הָאָרֶץ כְּבוֹדוֹ עוֹמֵד עָלָיו וְרוֹאֶה בְּמַעֲשָׂיו...מִיָּד יַגִּיעַ אֵלָיו הַיִּרְאָה — *When a person focuses his heart on (the fact) that the great King,* Hakadosh Baruch Hu, *Whose glory fills the whole earth, is standing over him and observing his deeds...immediately (these reflections will cause that) he will be infused with awe (of Hashem).* The *yetzer hara* seeks to ensnare a person with powerful temptation. Through solidifying one's faith that the great King is watching, a person can muster the strength necessary to overcome his passions and resist the *yetzer's* lure.

There is another effective aspect, in this regard, on which the *ma'amin* can focus his thoughts. The Beis Avraham provides us with a glimpse into Heavenly workings. He explains that Hashem apportions to each and every person a set amount of experiences with both pleasure and travails. But to some extent, the individual is able to choose where these experiences will be manifest. In other words: Someone may decide to indulge his desires; say, for example, he engages frequently and expansively in gastronomic pleasures. That is his choice; but in so doing, he is depleting his fixed store of enjoyment. Thus, he may end up bringing much harm upon himself, for by "using up" his allotted pleasure on physical indulgences, he will be left with nothing other than a large supply of *tzaros* (difficulties).

Consider, however, how the *ma'amin* can react to this state of affairs. Instead of following this example of pursuing material pleasure, he bears in mind the Beis Avraham's teaching, thus acting with restraint and not simply succumbing to his desires. In effect, he has reversed the arrangement. Resisting desire is no simple matter; by engaging in this worthwhile struggle, he thereby expends from his "painful" account. He is then left with an allotment of abundant pleasure. And as he does not "waste" it on material endeavors, he will derive tremendous delight, instead, from his spiritual pursuits.

Likewise, *emunah* can be enlisted to ward off the craving for *kavod*. What type of person is so drawn after glory? By and large, it is someone with an over-inflated sense of self; he deems himself so important that, in his eyes, it is only fitting that everyone around recognize his greatness and supply him with abundant accolades. A *ma'amin*, however, knows the truth. His thoughts are on the unmitigated greatness of the Creator of the Universe, before Whom he realizes his own insignificance. Negating himself before Hashem and aware of his own limitations, the *ma'amin* will thus feel no need for the world to sing his praises. Furthermore, the believing Yid puts his faith in *Chazal* and their teachings. When they relate how the haughty are so despicable in Hashem's eyes, the *ma'amin* takes it to heart. He won't demand that others puff up his ego by granting him honor.

Thus we see just how potent a tool *emunah* can be in counteracting the three cardinal forces of evil. *Kinah*, *ta'avah*, and *kavod* remove a person from both *Olam Hazeh*, turning his existence into a misery, and *Olam Haba*, by corrupting his character and leading him to all manner of sins. *Emunah* has the completely opposite effect on a person. As we have seen, *emunah* provides a Yid with placidity, even helping him to endure and accept trying circumstances. And, as the great Rebbes have stated, the stronger and clearer a person's *emunah*, the greater a tzaddik he will become, thereby meriting *Olam Haba*.

Beyond the Pale

The Maharal expounds on the notion that these traits "remove a person from the world." He explains the mishnah in a similar fashion, also employing the three-tiered anatomical model. But he also introduces a critical and illuminating factor into the discussion.

The three properties were intended by the Creator to operate within a specific framework. *Ta'avah* is an outgrowth of a person's natural, physical force, which resides within his liver. His vitality, of a more spiritual quality, rests within his heart and is responsible for *kinah*. And, of course, his intellectual prowess resides in the mind. Now, *Hakadosh Baruch Hu* implanted these forces and emotions within a person, having obviously done so for a reason. All three qualities — *when used properly* — actually perform certain functions vital for a person's existence, and for the fulfillment of his life's purpose (as shall be elaborated upon below).

The issue arises when these qualities are used in a manner that goes beyond their mandated boundaries. The Maharal puts forth the profound concept that, in effect, "more is less." When things go beyond the bounds of what is beneficial and necessary, the results are often harmful and debilitating. This, then, is what the three *middos* represent — excesses to the internal forces responsible for a person's functioning. And these excesses lead to deterioration.

The spiritual force of *nefesh*, residing in the heart, is vital to a person's existence. But the *middah* of *kinah* that derives from it is a non-essential entity; why is a person lusting after something that is not his, but instead belongs to someone else? As such, it serves as a superfluous aspect of this overall spiritual force. More is less, and the unnecessary exercise of this force brings loss in its wake. *Ta'avah* is likewise an extraneous manifestation of one's bodily force; so often, a person craves for more than he actually needs. *Kavod*, as well, follows this pattern; deriving from a person's intellectual faculty, one who pursues it often does so in excess. When the three principal forces that propel a person are utilized in a way that pushes beyond the boundaries of "essentiality," the results are severe, indeed. In accordance with the Maharal's principle, all of this excess and abuse leads to the worst sort of waste and devastation, leading to a person's removal from the physical and spiritual worlds.

In fact, explains the Maharal, this phenomenon was manifest at the very beginning of history. The episode of the forbidden fruit clearly demonstrates the destruction wrought by these qualities. Adam and Chavah were told that they could partake of all of the Garden's produce, with one exception: the fruit of the *Eitz Hada'as* (Tree of Knowledge). But the serpentine seducer employed his enticements, inducing the first woman to transgress their sole command. The *passuk* describes the critical moment: וַתֵּרֶא הָאִשָּׁה כִּי טוֹב הָעֵץ לְמַאֲכָל וְכִי תַאֲוָה־הוּא לָעֵינַיִם וְנֶחְמָד הָעֵץ לְהַשְׂכִּיל וַתִּקַּח מִפִּרְיוֹ וַתֹּאכַל — *And the woman saw that the tree was good for eating, and that it was pleasing to the eyes, and delightful for discernment, and she took from its fruit, and she ate* (*Bereishis* 3:6).

The Maharal demonstrates just how this *passuk* reflects the three principal qualities. כִּי טוֹב הָעֵץ לְמַאֲכָל — *That the tree was good for eating*: this phrase corresponds to the *middah* of desire, most closely associated with one's physical needs. וְכִי תַאֲוָה־הוּא לָעֵינַיִם — *And that it was pleasing to the eyes*: this alludes to the attribute of envy, a derivative of the spiritual force that resides in the heart. "The eyes" likewise derive their power from the heart: as *Chazal* state (*Avodah Zarah* 28b), שׁוּרְיָיני דְעֵינָא בְּאוּבְנָתָא דְלִיבָּא תַּלוּ — *The sinews of the eyes are linked with the heart*. And the final phrase, וְנֶחְמָד הָעֵץ לְהַשְׂכִּיל — *And delightful for discernment*, quite clearly reflects the force of **seichel**. And we know the result of succumbing to these traits: the expulsion from the idyllic world and the initiation of mortality.

To Be Used, Not Abused

Continuing with the Maharal's theme, the Nesivos Sholom elucidates this notion of retaining these qualities within their proper boundaries. He begins by addressing a central point: Much has been said already of the potential harm that can be inflicted through these three traits. Why, then, did Hashem implant them within us?

In truth, it is these very qualities that are so very necessary for man to survive and flourish. Had we not been imbued with the force of desire, we would simply starve to death; food and drink would not interest us. And we would certainly never establish a family. Thus, to

הקנאה התאוה והכבוד

a large extent, the *middah* of *ta'avah* is essential for the preservation and continuation of the human race.

Animals share this quality as well, as it is also necessary for their existence. But, as a higher being, only man has a sense of envy, reflective of the fact that it plays a role specific to our advancement. Envy can serve as a significant motivating factor, driving a person to produce and accomplish in competition with his fellows. Who knows how many beneficial innovations and achievements have resulted from the innate push to get ahead and outshine one's peers? *Chazal* go so far as to state, אִילוּלֵי הַקִּנְאָה אֵין הָעוֹלָם עוֹמֵד — *If not for* kinah, *the world would not endure* (*Midrash Shocher Tov* 37:1).

Also unique to man is the preoccupation with *kavod*. If for nothing else, this trait is worthwhile for the crucial role it plays as a benign deterrent. One with a modicum of self-respect, and even concern about how others view him, will likely refrain from improper and harmful behaviors. Without this element to hold him in check, a person would conduct himself like a two-legged beast: succumbing to his every whim and desire, regardless of the negative consequences to himself or others. Thus, the instinct for *kavod* enables human society to function with decency and harmony.

The beneficial aspects of these qualities are not limited to the physical existence and success of a person and his greater community. The Ba'al Shem Tov *ztz"l* demonstrates how these three *middos* can even be utilized for the furtherance of one's spiritual endeavors. A person may be beset by a forbidden temptation, but this can actually be a remarkable spiritual opportunity in disguise! The Ba'al Shem Tov even refers to this situation as a "gift from Heaven." Obviously, if someone has a passion for a forbidden object or act, he must fortify himself and resist the urge. However, he can also utilize the situation as an opportunity to spiritually elevate himself, by channeling this force of passion in the proper direction and converting it to a passion for *avodas Hashem*.

Kinah, as well, can be a source of much goodness. It can serve to spur a person out of spiritual stagnation to achieve ever higher levels. As *Chazal* tell us (*Bava Basra* 21a), קִנְאַת סוֹפְרִים תַּרְבֶּה חָכְמָה — *Envy*

פרק ד'

among scholars increases wisdom. When a genuine Torah scholar exhibits envy towards a colleague, it is not the person of whom he is envious; instead, he covets the pristine *middos* and the Torah that his friend possesses. Rather than hard feelings or strife, this form of envy leads to an emulation of meritorious behavior.

A focus on *kavod* can likewise be channeled to facilitate spiritual growth in the dimensions of refraining from improper behavior and positively engaging in proper practices. When confronted by the *yetzer hara* and tempted by sin, a Yid can muster a sense of self-respect. By focusing on his inherent value as a servant of Hashem, imbued with *kedushah*, he will realize that submitting to the enticement is simply beneath his dignity. With a clear recognition that he is of royal origin — a child of the King of kings — he will be moved to ascend to ever-greater heights of righteousness.

Thus we see that there really is a "good" side to these bad *middos* — if properly employed. When channeled in the right direction and with proper measure, they can have outstanding beneficial effects, both physically and spiritually. But this is true only insofar as one remains within the appropriate boundaries. The slightest deviation or excess could cause irreparable damage.

The Nesivos Sholom compares this situation to that of a very sick patient being treated by an expert physician. There is a cure for his specific illness, but the medicine contains an inherently toxic ingredient, one that is necessary to fight the illness but potentially harmful as well. Given the patient's particular constitution, the doctor knows exactly how much of the medicine to prescribe — enough to be effective but not more than the body can withstand and process. It is absolutely essential that the patient adhere rigidly to the doctor's precise instructions; if he takes even a little more than directed, the results could be fatal. The same holds true for the "ingredients" of *kinah*, *ta'avah*, and *kavod*. When used in the proper proportion, for the correct purposes, they can be of great benefit. If a person goes beyond the mandated parameters, however, he may end up being removed from the world.

In fact, we can see quite clearly how he deserves such a fate. For he has taken the very qualities Hashem imbued in him to serve Him better — and utilized them to transgress His will. This can be understood in light of the important concept put forth in the *mussar* classic, *Tomer Devorah*, which expounds on the attributes of Hashem. It describes the *middah* of *erech apayim* (long-suffering) in the following way: A person exists and functions solely through the power and ability Hashem constantly supplies to him. He can only move his hands or lift his feet if Hashem grants him the ability to do so; the moment it would be withheld, a person would be rendered completely powerless to move or do anything. What happens when a person commits a sin? Consider, for example, one who succumbs to the lure of forbidden sights, turning his eyes to where they should not be. How, at that moment, is he even able to see? Only because Hashem continues to allow his eyes to function properly. In essence, then, this is a betrayal of the highest order on the part of the transgressor. Hashem is gratuitously supplying him with the faculty of vision, and this individual utilizes this gift to violate the will of the Giver! It is only because of Hashem's merciful attribute of *erech apayim* that He does not withhold this person's sight from him.

And so it is with the three qualities. Hashem supplies a person with these forces to enable him to fulfill Hashem's will. How, then, could someone utilize them beyond the intended parameters, in *contradiction* of His will? For example, Hashem imbued within him a sense of *kinah* in order to emulate the good qualities of the righteous. If instead of spiritual properties, a person is envious of his fellow in materialistic matters, he is acting out of bounds, utilizing what Hashem has given him in a way that contravenes His mandate. This constitutes a severe betrayal. It is as if he was granted the King's personal scepter and proceeded to hand it over to the King's enemies.

Retaking the Fortress

In any event, it has been demonstrated how and why these *middos* can prove so detrimental to one who misuses them. These are not simply three random, individual qualities, but the roots of all other nefarious traits. As we have seen, they are associated with the internal makeup of a person, derived from the forces of the three principal elements responsible for one's functioning. These are a person's physical, spiritual, and intellectual forces, residing in the liver, heart, and mind, respectively. But this understanding can also help to enlighten us in how best to reverse their destructive hold on a person.

In war, a prime objective is to gain control of the area strongholds; whoever controls these is in a most commanding position and quite likely to vanquish their opponents. Once these have been captured and secured, the rest of the campaign can be fought with relative ease. The battle with the *yetzer hara* is no different. If we allow it to conquer our three main fortresses — the mind, heart, and liver — then it has effective control over the entire person, dictating his every move. Thus he is removed from the world.

But Hashem has provided another path, one through which a person could take control of these "fortresses" through forces of good. The mishnah near the beginning of *Avos* (1:2) states, עַל שְׁלֹשָׁה דְבָרִים הָעוֹלָם עוֹמֵד, עַל הַתּוֹרָה וְעַל הָעֲבוֹדָה וְעַל גְּמִילוּת חֲסָדִים — *On three things the world stands: on Torah, Divine service, and performing acts of kindness.* These attributes likewise correspond to the three chief forces governing a person's functionality. Torah is studied and absorbed through the faculty of one's intellect. *Avodah* is associated with the heart, as stated in the *passuk* from *Krias Shema*: *U'l'avdo b'chol levavchem* — "and to serve Him with all of your heart" (*Devarim* 11:13). And *gemilus chassadim* is a product of man's physical abilities, performed through his body's limbs.

In our battle against evil, this mishnah provides a strategy for taking control. We don't have to, nor should we, leave our "fortresses" in the hands of the dark forces of *kinah*, *ta'avah*, and *kavod*. Instead, by devoting ourselves to *Torah*, *avodah*, and *gemilus chassadim*, we can infuse these "fortresses" with *kedushah*, thereby forcing the *yetzer hara* to retreat.

In Summary

The Nesivos Sholom begins by clarifying to what the mishnah's bold statement refers. In stating that *kinah*, *ta'avah*, and *kavod* remove a person from the world, the mishnah was apparently referring to *both* worlds — *Olam Hazeh* and *Olam Haba*. These traits are the roots of all bad *middos*; upon them are predicated all manner of sinful conduct. But even in This World, a person wholly given over to these forces will experience a miserable life indeed, full of frustrated ambitions and bitterness.

The severity of these qualities is in large part due to the fact that they are associated so intimately with the three main components of a person's internal makeup. The liver is the center of a person's physical functioning; from here is derived one's passion for material pleasures. Envy infests a person's heart, the seat of a person's more spiritual qualities. And the craving for honor is ultimately a function of his mind's intellect. With these faculties so firmly in the grips of evil tendencies, a person is effectively removed from the world.

Basing himself on the words of the Maharal, the Nesivos Sholom continues with this notion. That Hashem imbued us with these traits indicates that they serve an inherently productive purpose — when properly utilized. In fact, a person's physical survival is based on these qualities, as desire encourages him to seek and attain nourishment, envy propels him to accomplish, etc. They also can be most beneficial for man's spiritual pursuits; as *Chazal* state, for example, that קִנְאַת סוֹפְרִים תַּרְבֶּה חָכְמָה — *Envy among scholars increases wisdom*. But they can only function as a force for good insofar as a person utilizes them within the acceptable boundaries. If one exceeds these bounds, the result will be detraction and destruction, removing him from the world. Just as a medicine containing a toxic substance can cure a person, but only if the directions are adhered to with precision, so any deviation or slight excess can be fatal.

Indeed, history has shown us, from the earliest times, that this is the case. First, Kayin succumbed to jealousy and murdered his brother, Hevel; he was thereby consigned to a life of wandering. Later, the generation of the Flood became steeped in their desire. Their fate was destruction through the waters of the Flood. Following this was the episode of the Tower of Bavel, which was a demonstration of supreme self-aggrandizement. While they wanted to make a name for themselves, their plans came to naught. Instead of the fame they had sought through their ambitious project, they ended up with different languages, scattered throughout the land.

The Nesivos Sholom explains how one may eradicate these evil tendencies: through pure and clear *emunah*. It is crucial to recognize that everything is from Hashem and that He has supplied each of us with exactly what we need to fulfill our mission in life. Such a realization can help to rescue us from being jealous of others, from desiring what is not ours, and from chasing after honor that is not due us.

Additionally, there are elements that directly counteract these forces of evil. One of the most important objectives in any war is obtaining control of key fortifications. One who has command of these is much better positioned to emerge victorious. The "fortresses" of a person are the forces associated with the three elements of his internal makeup: the "physical" force rooted in the liver, the "spiritual" force rooted in the heart, and the intellectual capacity situated in the mind. Control of the human "command centers" determines our status and situation in This World and the Next. If we cede control to the *yetzer hara*, having our essence infested with *kinah*, *ta'avah*, and *kavod*, then we will be removed from the world. On the other hand, we can and should opt for the alternate path. By engaging in Torah, *avodah*, and *gemilus chassadim*, we infuse the "fortresses" with the strength of *kedushah*. Then all will be well in This World and the Next.

Gems From The ספר נתיבות שלום
NESIVOS SHOLOM

פרק ה'

פרק ה' משנה ג'
עד שבא אברהם אבינו וקבל שכר כולם
Until Our Forefather Avraham Arrived, and Received the Reward Due Them All

עֲשָׂרָה דוֹרוֹת מִנֹּחַ וְעַד אַבְרָהָם, לְהוֹדִיעַ כַּמָּה אֶרֶךְ אַפַּיִם לְפָנָיו, שֶׁכָּל הַדּוֹרוֹת הָיוּ מַכְעִיסִין וּבָאִין, עַד שֶׁבָּא אַבְרָהָם אָבִינוּ וְקִבֵּל שְׂכַר כֻּלָּם:

There were ten generations from Noach until Avraham, to make known just how much long-sufferance there is before Hashem; for all these generations were increasingly provoking (of Hashem) – until our forefather Avraham arrived, and received the reward due them all.

GEMS FROM THE *SEFER NESIVOS SHOLOM*

SOURCES:

עֲשָׂרָה נִסְיוֹנוֹת נִתְנַסָּה אַבְרָהָם אָבִינוּ וְעָמַד בְּכֻלָּם, לְהוֹדִיעַ כַּמָּה חִבָּתוֹ שֶׁל אַבְרָהָם אָבִינוּ. (אבות ה׳)

Avraham Avinu was tested with ten trials and withstood them all – to make known the extent of the love of Avraham Avinu. (*Avos* 5)

כָּל מִי שֶׁיֵּשׁ בּוֹ שְׁלֹשָׁה דְבָרִים הַלָּלוּ, מִתַּלְמִידָיו שֶׁל אַבְרָהָם אָבִינוּ...עַיִן טוֹבָה, וְרוּחַ נְמוּכָה, וְנֶפֶשׁ שְׁפָלָה. (שם ה׳)

Whoever possesses the following three traits is from the disciples of Avraham Avinu...a good eye, a humble spirit, and a temperate soul. (*ibid.* 5)

וַיְהִי אַחַר הַדְּבָרִים הָאֵלֶּה וְהָאֱלֹקִים נִסָּה אֶת־אַבְרָהָם. (בראשית כ״ב א׳)

And it was after these things, and G-d tested Avraham. (*Bereishis* 22:1)

אָמַר רַבִּי יוֹסֵי בֶּן קִסְמָא, פַּעַם אַחַת הָיִיתִי מְהַלֵּךְ בַּדֶּרֶךְ וּפָגַע בִּי אָדָם אֶחָד, וְנָתַן לִי שָׁלוֹם, וְהֶחֱזַרְתִּי לוֹ שָׁלוֹם, אָמַר לִי, רַבִּי, מֵאֵיזֶה מָקוֹם אַתָּה, אָמַרְתִּי לוֹ, מֵעִיר גְּדוֹלָה שֶׁל חֲכָמִים וְשֶׁל סוֹפְרִים אָנִי, אָמַר לִי, רַבִּי רְצוֹנְךָ שֶׁתָּדוּר עִמָּנוּ בִּמְקוֹמֵנוּ וַאֲנִי אֶתֵּן לְךָ אֶלֶף אֲלָפִים דִּנְרֵי זָהָב וַאֲבָנִים טוֹבוֹת וּמַרְגָּלִיּוֹת, אָמַרְתִּי לוֹ אִם אַתָּה נוֹתֵן לִי כָּל כֶּסֶף וְזָהָב וַאֲבָנִים טוֹבוֹת וּמַרְגָּלִיּוֹת שֶׁבָּעוֹלָם, אֵינִי דָר אֶלָּא בִּמְקוֹם תּוֹרָה. (אבות ו׳)

Rabbi Yose ben Kisma said: One time, I was walking along the way, and I encountered a certain individual. He greeted me, and I returned the greeting. He said to me: "Rebbi, from which place are you?" I said to him: "I am from a great city of wise men and scholars." He said to me: "Rebbi, would you wish to dwell with us in our location? I will give you millions in gold coins, precious stones, and pearls!" I said to him: "Even if you were to give me all of the silver, gold, precious stones, and pearls that exist in the world, I would still dwell only in a place of Torah!" (*Avos* 6)

עד שבא אברהם אבינו וקבל שכר כולם

High Living — in a Bad Neighborhood

Throughout *Pirkei Avos*, we find numerous references to figures from Tanach — Aharon and Dovid Hamelech, to name a few. However, the individual most frequently featured in this *masechta* may very well be Avraham Avinu. He appears on three different occasions in this *perek* alone.

The first reference is in the mishnah under discussion, proclaiming how Avraham — coming after generations that were increasingly sinful — merited, through his righteousness, to receive all of their reward. The next mishnah (5:3) discusses the ten trials with which Avraham was tested: עֲשָׂרָה נִסְיוֹנוֹת נִתְנַסָּה אַבְרָהָם אָבִינוּ וְעָמַד בְּכֻלָּם, לְהוֹדִיעַ כַּמָּה חִבָּתוֹ שֶׁל אַבְרָהָם אָבִינוּ — *Avraham Avinu was tested with ten trials, to make known the extent of the love of Avraham Avinu*. Later in the *perek*, the mishnah speaks of the attributes of Avraham and his *talmidim*: כָּל מִי שֶׁיֵּשׁ בּוֹ שְׁלֹשָׁה דְבָרִים הַלָּלוּ, מִתַּלְמִידָיו שֶׁל אַבְרָהָם אָבִינוּ...עַיִן טוֹבָה, וְרוּחַ נְמוּכָה, וְנֶפֶשׁ שְׁפָלָה — *Whoever possesses the following three traits is from the disciples of Avraham Avinu...a good eye, a humble spirit, and a temperate soul* (5:19).

But there is more connecting these disparate teachings than that they all feature Avraham Avinu. As we shall see, these statements complement each other, jointly delivering a most important lesson. To uncover this message, however, it is first necessary to address some issues that arise in each of the aforementioned mishnayos:

- The mishnah about the ten generations states that Avraham received *s'char kulam* — "the reward of them all." No doubt that Avraham Avinu was a seminal and righteous figure, who deserves abundant reward for his tremendous accomplishments. But how does that translate into receiving the reward of *others*? And what, in fact, does it even mean that "he received the reward due them all"?

- The mishnah regarding Avraham's *nisyonos* (trials) states that they served to reveal the extent of Avraham Avinu's love. The Ramban (*Sefer Emunah U'bitachon*) remarks that while Avraham is definitely credited for having fulfilled the entire Torah, the

פרק ה׳

principal source of the great favor he found in Hashem's eyes was on account of successfully withstanding the ten trials. Obviously, then, these trials were of inestimable significance. But what, exactly, is the whole notion of a *nisayon*? It seems to be a test of some sort; but what is it that Heaven seeks to "find out"?

- Avraham is principally known for excelling in *chessed*. The Torah elaborates on the extent to which Avraham went in performing acts of kindness, and the *passuk* explicitly links Avraham with this *middah*: תִּתֵּן אֱמֶת לְיַעֲקֹב חֶסֶד לְאַבְרָהָם — *Grant truth to Yaakov,* **kindness to Avraham** (Michah 7:20). He is also noted for his intense love for Hashem, Who refers to him as *Avraham ohavi* — "Avraham who loves Me" (*Yeshayah* 41:8). But when the mishnah later on lists the attributes of Avraham and his disciples, neither of these chief characteristics are mentioned. Rather, the mishnah there speaks only of his good eye, humble spirit, and temperate soul. These are laudable traits, but why bypass the ones for which he is most known? And what is meant by "Avraham's disciples"; who belongs to this enigmatic group?

In the Dark

The Nesivos Sholom begins by getting right to the heart of what a *nisayon* is all about. After all, especially when it comes to someone of Avraham's spiritual stature, the whole idea may seem almost preposterous. *Testing* Avraham to see if he will listen to Hashem? Is there really a question about Avraham's level of devotion? There is a well-known pithy comment of the Rebbe of Kobrin *ztz"l*. Referring to Avraham's fiery love of Hashem, he declared, "Is it really such a *chiddush* that Avraham Avinu was not consumed when cast into the furnace? The real *chiddush* is that Ur Casdim (the city where this episode took place) was not consumed from the flames of intense love for Hashem that burned within Avraham!" What, then, is the point of offering such a trial when the outcome is never really in doubt?

A significant clue comes from the words in the Torah that

עד שבא אברהם אבינו וקבל שכר כולם

introduce the trial of *Akeidas Yitzchak*: וְהָאֱלֹקִים נִסָּה אֶת־אַבְרָהָם — ***And G-d tested Avraham*** (*Bereishis* 22:1). This Name of Hashem — *Elokim* — is associated with Hashem's *middas hadin* (attribute of judgment). Thus, the usage of this term immediately implies that a certain measure of strictness and difficulty is involved in the administering of a *nisayon*. The subject cannot rely on any form of outside support; all indications are that the road ahead will be lonely and anything but easy.

This, then, is the hallmark of a *nisayon*. In order for it to be truly a "test," Hashem employs the *middas hadin* and *temporarily revokes any measure of spiritual attainment that may have otherwise been of assistance in this endeavor*. As such, the individual is left, in a sense, in spiritual darkness. This is what makes the *nisayon* a bona fide challenge.

And this phenomenon is not limited to the trials of Avraham. This we learn from the remarkable statement of the *Me'or Einayim* (*Parshas Va'eira*). He asserts that every single Yid must undergo ten trials, just as his ancestor Avraham did. If a Yid possessed rock-solid faith and perfectly clear spiritual vision at all times, a *nisayon* indeed would be no *nisayon*. And so to offer an actual test, the *Elokim* will significantly conceal His Presence, where the Yid is left to feel somewhat alone, confused, and in the dark. This is the *nisayon*: to test how he will react in the midst of even these trying conditions of darkness.

In this light, we can gain a better understanding of our mishnah regarding the ten generations — an understanding informed by the issue of *nisyonos* dealt with in the succeeding mishnah. For given Avraham's surroundings and the wickedness of the preceding generations, we begin to appreciate just what loneliness and darkness Avraham actually faced.

A certain Yid felt that he was experiencing lapses in the area of *emunah*. He went to the Apter Rav *ztz"l* to lament that, of late, foreign thoughts were intruding upon and diluting his *emunah*. "I will tell you from where these thoughts are coming," the Apter Rav advised him. "They do not originate from within you. Rather, you have a neighbor whose *emunah* is weak, and that has influenced you, as well."

The Apter Rav was uncovering a vital principle that has much bearing on the *avodas Hashem* of each and every one of us. He was referring to the tremendous potency of peer pressure — the strong pull of one's environment and the severe danger it represents.

This same idea is manifest in a later mishnah in *Avos* (6:9). It relates the story of Rabbi Yose ben Kisma, who lived in a city populated by G-d-fearing Torah scholars. One day, he encountered a man from a distant place, who beseeched the sage to move his place of residence to live among the residents of this faraway town. He even offered Rabbi Yose a princely sum to do so. But Rabbi Yose refused, stating: אִם אַתָּה נוֹתֵן לִי כָּל כֶּסֶף וְזָהָב וַאֲבָנִים טוֹבוֹת וּמַרְגָּלִיּוֹת שֶׁבָּעוֹלָם, אֵינִי דָר אֶלָּא בִּמְקוֹם תּוֹרָה — *(Even) if you were to give me all of the silver, gold, precious stones, and pearls in the world, I would only dwell in a Torah environment.* Rabbi Yose's response is quite noteworthy — especially the fact that he turned down such riches. Surely someone of Rabbi Yose's stature would not have used such a fortune just for personal luxuries. Imagine, then, the tremendous good he could have done with such funds — truly meritorious work! But he turned it all down, for one simple reason: He was all too aware of the perils of an environment lacking in Torah values. The spiritual damage that would be wrought from pernicious influences would far outweigh whatever other good he would have been able to accomplish. He thus concluded that it was not at all worth the risk to his spiritual health.

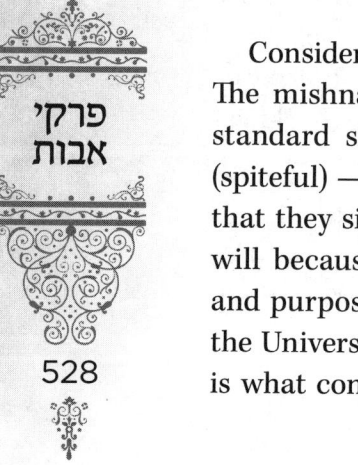

Consider, then, the environment that confronted Avraham. The mishnah mentions that the people were not just committing standard sins, which is bad enough. Rather, they were *machisin* (spiteful) — that is, they were acting *l'hachis* (to provoke). It was not that they simply succumbed to temptation, transgressing Hashem's will because they were overcome by desire. Rather, they willingly and purposefully defied Hashem's word, just to spite the Creator of the Universe. Such behavior is indeed the height of wickedness. This is what constituted Avraham's surroundings and upbringing — not a very supportive, "religious-friendly" environment. For Avraham, it was a situation of real isolation and darkness.

And this is what constituted the real challenge: how would Avraham hold up under these circumstances? And this is why he was entitled to the *s'char kulam*. What did other people's rewards have to do with his righteousness? The answer is: everything. Because it was precisely these other people who contributed to his *nisyonos*; they created the environment of darkness that made his *avodah* that much harder. But amidst all of this spiritual destruction, Avraham Avinu held firm and withstood all of his trials. And so he was granted the reward due them all.

The Secret to Success

As it was with the trials of Avraham, so it is with the tests that every Yid must undergo. In light of the above, we can see that the challenges that confront us are particularly daunting.

What are these "ten trials" that, according to the *Me'or Einayim*, are administered to every Jew? We are woefully below the level of Avraham who had the benefit of receiving instruction from Hashem; in any event, the gift of prophecy was not granted to the later generations. And so, how are we even to *know what these trials are*, let alone to pass them?

The answer, explains the Nesivos Sholom, is that our personal *nisyonos* are connected with our personal mission in This World. The tzaddikim inform us that every Yid is sent to This World from on High, charged with a specific task, to address a matter that requires rectification through his deeds alone. Yet, how are we to know what our task is? It is actually the *yetzer hara* that gives us clarity on this matter. That is, it devotes its principal efforts towards thwarting this mission, seeking to prevent us from successfully carrying it out. As such, it provides clear indication of what the mission entails. The area in which we have the greatest difficulty or find a certain aspect of *avodas Hashem* to be particularly challenging — this is a sign that this is our mission. Perhaps, for example, one person has a difficult time applying himself to Torah study. Someone else may find this easy but struggles instead with a flaring temper, becoming quick to anger. A third person is a diligent student and has an easy temperament; however, he finds himself involved in an almost constant battle to guard his eyes and purify his thoughts. At the very least, such people can know — literally — the work that is cut out for them. In our parlance, the *yetzer hara* has "shown its hand." It is precisely this area of weakness, the item that presents the greatest challenge, that a Yid has been tasked to confront and improve.

Of course, this is no easy task. The *nisayon* is great and is further compounded by the influence of a difficult environment. Such was the case in the time of Avraham. But in our times, this is no insignificant factor, either. In a sense, the environment of modern society mimics Avraham's surroundings rather closely. It almost seems like the culture and behavior of each successive generation stands in opposition to Hashem's values more and more.

So how does a person withstand such daunting challenges? The lure of society, the personal and intense struggles unique to every Yid — is there really a way to successfully pass these *nisyonos*?

The key, explains the Nesivos Sholom, lies in the third teaching regarding Avraham Avinu. We wondered why that mishnah neglects to mention the traits for which Avraham was most well known — his great *chessed* and undying love for Hashem — and instead focused on a trio of internal characteristics. We also were puzzled by the term "*talmidim* of Avraham Avinu"; to whom does this refer? The answer is that this mishnah is relating the strategy for withstanding *nisyonos*. The phrase "disciples of Avraham" refers *to those who duplicate Avraham's feat of successfully enduring the most trying and difficult tests*. They learn from him the secret of how to accomplish this. And this is why the mishnah lists the traits that it does: *these are the specific characteristics necessary to pass a* nisayon. True, Avraham had other qualities for which he may have been better known, but that is not the subject of this teaching. Rather than a recounting of Avraham's most noteworthy traits, this mishnah had a singular focus: what are the traits necessary to confront *nisyonos*?

And so the mishnah lists the attributes of עַיִן טוֹבָה, וְרוּחַ נְמוּכָה, וְנֶפֶשׁ

עד שבא אברהם אבינו וקבל שכר כולם

שְׁפָלָה — *a good eye, a humble spirit, and a restrained soul.* What makes these specific *middos* so critical for dealing with *nisyonos* is the fact that they represent the inner essence of a Yid and relate to his internal makeup. (This idea is further elaborated upon in *ma'amar* תלמידיו של אברהם אבינו.) Notice the specific wording of the mishnah: כָּל מִי שֶׁיֵּשׁ בּוֹ שְׁלֹשָׁה דְבָרִים הַלָּלוּ ... — *Whoever has **within him** these three things...* It is because these *talmidim* of Avraham have so inculcated these traits within themselves — to the point where they have literally become a part of their very essence — that they are able to withstand the most pressing challenges. For although, as mentioned earlier, one's previous spiritual attainments are removed by the *middas hadin* while a *nisayon* is in progress, there is a key exception. The *sefarim hakedoshim* tell us that a spiritual accomplishment that was won through especially strenuous efforts and toil remains with a person even during the darkness of a *sha'as nisayon* (time of trial). One for whom these three traits are so deeply instilled within his soul must have invested much effort to have attained this level. And so, these crucial assets remain with him during his *nisayon*, enabling him to overcome the challenge of the hour.

This, then, is the secret to subduing our *yetzer hara* and successfully passing *nisyonos*. To be a true *talmid* of Avraham Avinu, we must work to implant these very traits within our inner being. They will afford us the strength necessary to overcome the powerful pressures and negative influences of a most unfriendly spiritual environment, and they will aid us in fulfilling the task and challenge for which we were sent to this earth.

This is a particularly pertinent lesson for this time period, as we approach the sacred day of *Kabbalas HaTorah*. Reb Baruch of Mezibuz *ztz"l* stated that Shavuos is similar to — and in a sense, of a more sublime level than — Rosh Hashanah itself. While Rosh Hashanah is a *yom hadin* (day of judgment), this is primarily for our material needs. Shavuos serves as a *yom hadin* for spiritual matters. As such, it is incumbent upon us, as we accept the Torah, to likewise accept upon ourselves to do whatever is necessary towards overcoming those spiritual challenges that we struggle with the most. These challenges represent our unique mission, for which we were brought to This World in the first place; it is only apropos to make a firm decision at this time to redouble our efforts in fulfilling this task. By accepting to devote ourselves to the endeavor of acquiring these foundational traits — a good eye, humble spirit, and temperate soul; the traits that make up a Yid — we will be taking a tremendous step forward towards accomplishing our life's mission.

We live in trying times, indeed, confronted with an environment whose hostility towards *Hakadosh Baruch Hu* rivals that of the times of Avraham Avinu. The challenge of combating such powerful and insidious influence — as well as the epic personal struggles with which we all deal — may seem overwhelming indeed. But Hashem has granted us certain times of illumination, such as the Yom Tov of Shavuos, as opportunities to fortify ourselves in the endeavor of serving Him despite the difficulties that surround us. As we engage in *Kabbalas HaTorah*, we may likewise accept upon ourselves to become "*talmidim* of Avraham Avinu" and inculcate within ourselves the *middos* that characterize this august group. These *middos* will thus afford us the strength necessary to combat evil influences and overcome the most daunting challenges.

In Summary

We find three teachings featuring Avraham Avinu in this *perek*: the ten generations between Noach and Avraham, the ten trials of Avraham, and the three *middos* that characterize the *talmidim* of Avraham. The Nesivos Sholom demonstrates how these seemingly disparate teachings are in fact interconnected, together delivering a vital and powerful message that affects the life of every Jew.

Avraham was tested with ten trials and so, too, states the *Me'or Einayim*, is every Jew. Thus, the nature of Avraham's *nisyonos* shed much light on the *nisyonos* that we, as well, must endure. A key characteristic of Avraham's *nisyonos* was that they were administered by "*Elokim*"; that is, Hashem employed the *middas hadin*. Thus, during a *nisayon*, a Yid is virtually left alone; it is a period of darkness and concealment of the Divine Presence, and spiritual support is

עד שבא אברהם אבינו וקבל שכר כולם

removed. This is the *nisayon*: to remain loyal and devoted despite the darkness and confusion of a *sha'as nisayon*.

A most significant factor contributing to this sense of isolation and to the difficulty of the challenge is the negative influence supplied by a wicked society. Such was the case with Avraham, as he found himself in an environment where the generations were *machisim u'va'im* — increasingly provoking of Hashem through their wanton transgressions. Yet Avraham held firm, and for this reason received the reward that was due them all. For they all made his challenges that much more difficult, yet he emerged victorious.

These are the challenges that confront every Yid. The Nesivos Sholom explains further that we were each sent to This World with a specific mission to fulfill, something that we alone need to rectify. The key to discovering our mission is through identifying the area in which the *yetzer hara* antagonizes us the most. This is its attempt to sabotage our mission. And so it is up to each of us to try to perfect ourselves precisely in this area of greatest challenge. This endeavor is compounded all the more by the powerful and pernicious influence emanating from an environment whose decadence and hostility to righteousness echoes that which confronted Avraham Avinu.

How do we emerge successfully from such daunting *nisyonos*? The answer is supplied by the mishnah, which focuses on the traits of Avraham and his disciples. It is of note that when listing the characteristics of Avraham, the mishnah does not mention his *chessed* or his *ahavas Hashem* — traits for which he was most known. This is because the mishnah was not seeking merely to list Avraham's outstanding traits; rather, it was revealing the key to passing *nisyonos*. This is why it speaks of the "*talmidim* of Avraham," for this is a reference to those who learn from Avraham how to overcome *nisyonos* and challenges.

And the formula is the one listed in the mishnah: to cultivate the traits that constitute the makeup of a Yid: *ayin tovah*, *ruach nemuchah*, and *nefesh shefalah*. By inculcating these *middos* into our essence, we will have the strength and ability to withstand

פרק ה'

the negative environmental influences and to overcome the most daunting challenges, which comprise our mission in life.

פרק ה' משנה ד'
עשרה נסיונות נתנסה אברהם אבינו
With Ten Tests Was Our Forefather Avraham Tested

עֲשָׂרָה נִסְיוֹנוֹת נִתְנַסָּה אַבְרָהָם אָבִינוּ וְעָמַד בְּכֻלָּם, לְהוֹדִיעַ כַּמָּה חִבָּתוֹ שֶׁל אַבְרָהָם אָבִינוּ:

With ten tests was our forefather Avraham tested, and he withstood them all – in order to make known how great was our forefather Avraham's love (for Hashem).

GEMS FROM THE *SEFER NESIVOS SHOLOM*

SOURCES:

וַיְהִי אַחַר הַדְּבָרִים הָאֵלֶּה וְהָאֱלֹקִים נִסָּה אֶת־אַבְרָהָם... וַיֹּאמֶר קַח־נָא אֶת־בִּנְךָ אֶת־יְחִידְךָ אֲשֶׁר־אָהַבְתָּ אֶת־יִצְחָק וְלֶךְ־לְךָ אֶל־אֶרֶץ הַמֹּרִיָּה וְהַעֲלֵהוּ שָׁם לְעֹלָה... וַיַּשְׁכֵּם אַבְרָהָם בַּבֹּקֶר וַיָּקָם וַיֵּלֶךְ... וַיָּבֹאוּ אֶל־הַמָּקוֹם אֲשֶׁר אָמַר־לוֹ הָאֱלֹקִים וַיִּבֶן שָׁם אַבְרָהָם אֶת־הַמִּזְבֵּחַ וַיַּעֲרֹךְ אֶת־הָעֵצִים וַיַּעֲקֹד אֶת־יִצְחָק בְּנוֹ וַיָּשֶׂם אֹתוֹ עַל־הַמִּזְבֵּחַ מִמַּעַל לָעֵצִים. וַיִּשְׁלַח אַבְרָהָם אֶת־יָדוֹ וַיִּקַּח אֶת־הַמַּאֲכֶלֶת לִשְׁחֹט אֶת־בְּנוֹ. וַיִּקְרָא אֵלָיו מַלְאַךְ ה' מִן־הַשָּׁמַיִם... וַיֹּאמֶר אַל־תִּשְׁלַח יָדְךָ אֶל־הַנַּעַר וְאַל־תַּעַשׂ לוֹ מְאוּמָה כִּי עַתָּה יָדַעְתִּי כִּי־יְרֵא אֱלֹקִים אַתָּה... וַיִּשָּׂא אַבְרָהָם אֶת־עֵינָיו וַיַּרְא וְהִנֵּה־אַיִל אַחַר נֶאֱחַז בַּסְּבַךְ בְּקַרְנָיו וַיֵּלֶךְ אַבְרָהָם וַיִּקַּח אֶת־הָאַיִל וַיַּעֲלֵהוּ לְעֹלָה תַּחַת בְּנוֹ... וַיִּקְרָא מַלְאַךְ ה' אֶל־אַבְרָהָם שֵׁנִית מִן־הַשָּׁמָיִם... וַיֹּאמֶר בִּי נִשְׁבַּעְתִּי נְאֻם־ה' כִּי יַעַן אֲשֶׁר עָשִׂיתָ אֶת־הַדָּבָר הַזֶּה וְלֹא חָשַׂכְתָּ אֶת־בִּנְךָ אֶת־יְחִידֶךָ...כִּי־בָרֵךְ אֲבָרֶכְךָ וְהַרְבָּה אַרְבֶּה אֶת־זַרְעֲךָ. (בראשית כ"ב א'-י"ז)

And it was after these things, and G-d tested Avraham... And He said: "Take, please, your only son, that you have loved – Yitzchak, and go for you to the Land of Moriah, and offer him up there as a sacrifice..." And Avraham arose early in the morning, and he got up and went... And they came to the place of which G-d had told him, and Avraham built the altar there, arranged the wood, bound up Yitzchak his son, and placed him on the altar, above the wood. And Avraham sent out his hand, and he took the knife to slaughter his son. And an angel of Hashem called to him from the Heavens...and he said: "Do not send your hand against the lad, nor do anything to him, for now I know that you fear G-d." ... And Avraham lifted his eyes, and he saw that behold – there was another ram, tangled in the thicket by its horns; and Avraham went, took the ram, and offered him as a sacrifice in place of his son... And an angel of Hashem called to Avraham from the Heavens a second time... And he said: "'I have sworn in My Name,' says Hashem, 'that since you have done this thing, and not withheld your son, your only one...that I will bless You, and increase your offspring very much...'" (*Bereishis* 22:1-17)

עשרה נסיונות נתנסה אברהם אבינו

וְאָהַבְתָּ אֵת ה' אֱלֹקֶיךָ בְּכָל־לְבָבְךָ וּבְכָל־נַפְשְׁךָ וּבְכָל־מְאֹדֶךָ. (דברים ו' ה')

You shall love Hashem your G-d, with all of your heart, with all of your soul, and with all of your wealth. (*Devarim* 6:5)

וְאַתָּה יִשְׂרָאֵל עַבְדִּי יַעֲקֹב אֲשֶׁר בְּחַרְתִּיךָ זֶרַע אַבְרָהָם אֹהֲבִי. (ישעיה מ"א ח')

And you are Yisroel My servant, Yaakov whom I have chosen, the offspring of Avraham, who loves Me. (*Yeshayah* 41:8)

וַיַּשְׁכֵּם אַבְרָהָם בַּבֹּקֶר אֶל הַמָּקוֹם אֲשֶׁר־עָמַד שָׁם אֶת־פְּנֵי ה'. (בראשית י"ט כ"ז)

And Avraham arose early in the morning to the place at where he had stood in Hashem's Presence. (*Bereishis* 19:27)

אֵין עֲמִידָה אֶלָּא תְּפִלָּה. (ברכות ו:)

This "standing" refers to none other than praying. (*Berachos* 6b)

אַל תֹּאמַר לִכְשֶׁאֶפָּנֶה אֶשְׁנֶה, שֶׁמָּא לֹא תִפָּנֶה. (אבות ב')

Do not say, "When I become unoccupied, then I shall learn (Torah)," for you may never end up becoming unoccupied. (*Avos* 2)

פרק ה'

The True Test

Often — every day, in fact — we are faced with options from which we must choose. These can sometimes be overwhelming and daunting, as we confront situations that call for agonizing soul-searching and really tough decisions.

At other times, however, the process can be quite easy. Should we stand very close to the edge of a cliff? Not much of a question there. Accept the boss's offer of a paid day-off? A no-brainer.

Thus we approach the august topic of the trials of the *Avos*. These have won the awe and reverence of their progeny throughout the generations, and we often invoke the merit of their successful withstanding of these epic tests. And so our mishnah lauds the efforts of Avraham Avinu, who demonstrated his devotion to Hashem by undergoing the ten trials.

But on second thought — why, exactly, is this considered such an impressive feat? Would any simple Jew have acted differently, given the identical circumstances? Hashem Himself appears to Avraham and issues some instructions. Certainly, as with anyone possessed of even a basic level of *emunah*, Avraham was aware of Hashem's omnipotence and the fact that the life of every creature is completely in His hands. He is the Merciful One, but — if deemed necessary — He could instantaneously visit any manner of retribution on whoever incurs His wrath. Given this, how is listening to His command considered a display of selfless devotion? Isn't the decision to do so an obvious one?

In clarifying this issue, the Nesivos Sholom raises a number of salient points regarding this topic in general and the mishnah in particular:

- The mishnah seems to place an emphasis on the number ten. Is this merely the sum total of Avraham's *nisyonos*, or is there some special significance to this number?

- In stating that Avraham successfully passed all of his trials, the mishnah does not use the language of *avar* (passed) or *hitzliach* (was successful). Instead, the mishnah mentions that he was *amad b'kulam* (withstood — or, literally, "stood" — through them all). What does the mishnah seek to convey with this choice of wording?

- The whole notion of a "test" seems to require some clarification. What, indeed, is the purpose? The mishnah seems to indicate that the trials undergone by Avraham served the function of ascertaining his level of devotion: לְהוֹדִיעַ כַּמָּה חִבָּתוֹ שֶׁל אַבְרָהָם אָבִינוּ — *To uncover how great was Avraham Avinu's love (for Hashem)*. But it seems most unusual — even unnecessary — to orchestrate such trying upheavals and ordeals for this purpose. Didn't Hashem know from the outset that Avraham would pass these tests? Surely, his level of dedication was already known to Him! In truth, the same can be said for the trials that every Jew must undergo. Doesn't Hashem know the outcome already in the beginning? Why, indeed, are they necessary?

- The *sefer Me'or Einayim* teaches that for any Yid to acquire completeness and perfection in his *avodas Hashem*, he must undergo his own version of Avraham Avinu's ten trials. How are we to understand this statement? How, exactly, do the *nisyonos* of Avraham pertain to the everyday lives of ordinary Jews?

- There is one *nisayon* that seems to deviate from the pattern set by the rest. The mishnah states that the *nisyonos* highlighted the aspect of Avraham's love for Hashem — כַּמָּה חִבָּתוֹ שֶׁל אַבְרָהָם אָבִינוּ. Yet, when we examine that trial considered by many to be Avraham's greatest test, we discover something else. At the conclusion of *Akeidas Yitzchak*, when Avraham showed his readiness to sacrifice his beloved son, the angel declares: עַתָּה יָדַעְתִּי כִּי־יְרֵא אֱלֹקִים אָתָּה — *Now I know that you are G-d-fearing* (*Bereishis* 22:12). Were the *nisyonos* a demonstration of *ahavas Hashem*, as implied by the mishnah, or *yiras Hashem*, as stated in the *passuk*?

What Is a *Nisayon*?

The Nesivos Sholom begins his dissertation by quoting the *Chassid Ya'avetz*. His comments enlighten us as to what a *nisayon* really is.

Every person has many "loves": love of family — our spouse and children, love of wealth and possessions, and (sometimes above all) love of self. The nature of a *nisayon* is to demonstrate that our love for Hashem is paramount, more than all the others. Not, of course, that our other loves must be nullified; of course Hashem wills that, for example, we should love our spouse and children dearly. Rather, our love must be dictated by Hashem, as we love that which Hashem desires us to love. And most of all, our love must be directed towards Hashem, stronger than all other sentiments — to the point that, when called upon, we are willing to render all other loves subservient to our love of Hashem.

This, in fact, is derived from the verse in *Krias Shema*. וְאָהַבְתָּ אֵת ה׳ אֱלֹקֶיךָ בְּכָל־לְבָבְךָ וּבְכָל־נַפְשְׁךָ וּבְכָל־מְאֹדֶךָ — *And you shall love Hashem your G-d, with all of your heart, all of your soul, and all of your might* (Devarim 6:5). The *passuk* conveys how all of our loves, emanating from the depths of our heart, must ultimately be subjugated to Hashem. Furthermore, *Chazal* interpret the directive to love Hashem with "all of your soul" to mean "even were He to take your soul"; that is, at the point of death — the ultimate expression of subjugating one's love of self to the Creator. *B'chol me'odecha* refers to our wealth, requiring our love of possessions to likewise be redirected towards Hashem.

And this was the underlying aim of Avraham Avinu's *nisyonos*. Thus we see, for example, that his being cast into the fiery furnace related to his love of self, having to abandon the Land during the time of famine pertained to his love of personal property, and the taking of Sarah to the house of Pharaoh and the trial of the *Akeidah* represented his love of family. Through them all, he demonstrated that his ultimate love was guided by and directed to Hashem, before Whom all else was subservient.

This accomplishment reveals the true greatness of Avraham. The Ramban (*Sefer Emunah U'bitachon*) states that it was not the fact that Avraham fulfilled the entire Torah that reflects his true stature; there have been many worthy Jews who have duplicated this feat. Avraham's uniqueness is chiefly manifested through having successfully undergone these ten *nisyonos*. Through the achievement of *amad b'kulam* — withstanding **all** the trials, transferring all of his love to Hashem, without retaining anything personal for himself — Avraham Avinu displayed the depths of his love and dedication to Him: לְהוֹדִיעַ כַּמָּה חִבָּתוֹ שֶׁל אַבְרָהָם אָבִינוּ.

With this understanding of what Avraham accomplished through the *nisyonos*, we can gain a better understanding of the notion of "ten" trials. Based on the Maharal, the Nesivos Sholom explains that "ten" is more than just the technical tally of Avraham's tests. Rather, the number ten itself possesses a special quality, as it is actually a *mispar kadosh*, a sacred number. We find that a *davar sheb'kedushah* — a holy endeavor, such as the recital of Kaddish or *Kedushah* — requires a quorum of ten men; there were ten commandments presented at Har Sinai; and ten are necessary to effect a *hashra'as haShechinah* (a visitation of the Divine Presence at a particular location). Avraham's experience of the ten trials was the quintessential expression of love for Hashem. As such, he was able to attach himself to the *Shechinah*, attaining the ultimate state of sanctity of *d'veikus baHashem*.

Along similar lines, but on an even deeper level, the ten trials can be understood as corresponding to those elements of especial sanctity — the Kabbalistic notion of the Ten *Sefiros* (spiritual emanations reflecting the Divine attributes). Classified in three main categories, these relate to the components through which a human functions and serves his Creator. *Chachmah-Binah-Da'as* (Wisdom, Discernment, and Knowledge) represent the qualities of the mind; *Chessed-Gevurah-Tiferes* (Kindness, Might, and Splendor) relate to the qualities of the heart/emotions; and *Netzach-Hod-Yesod-Malchus* (Eternity, Glory, Foundation, and Kingship) correspond to the limbs. By undergoing the "ten" trials, Avraham was tapping into the force of the attributes of the *Sefiros*. He thus submitted the love emanating from every fiber of his makeup — mind, heart, and body — in totality to the Almighty.

As such, the mishnah is not merely making a generalized, emphatic statement, לְהוֹדִיעַ כַּמָּה חִבָּתוֹ שֶׁל אַבְרָהָם אָבִינוּ — *To uncover how great was Avraham Avinu's love (for Hashem)*. Rather, it is a quantifiable, measurable entity: to what extent did Avraham love Hashem? He submitted all types of love, from each aspect of his being — intellect, emotions, and actions — to Hashem.

Withstanding — and "Standing" in — a *Nisayon*

We had wondered what, in fact, was the "big deal" about Avraham passing his *nisyonos*; after all, wouldn't anyone so instructed by Hashem likewise make the obvious choice to listen to Him? The Nesivos Sholom adds some insight on this point, further elucidating the makeup of a *nisayon*. For a test to be considered real there is a necessary condition: one's usual level of spiritual fortitude is temporarily suspended. Otherwise, indeed, there would be no challenge to overcome. Thus, at the point of *nisayon*, the individual is bereft of spiritual strength that he otherwise had possessed.

But there is one exception. The only force that the individual under scrutiny retains is that quality over which he had expended extraordinary efforts. If he had attained a certain level through toil, perseverance, and real exertion, he has made an acquisition with a measure of permanence. Thus, this spiritual asset remains with him even in the face of daunting challenges.

And this is the impact of Avraham's undergoing the ten trials. As mentioned, Avraham's quality of unqualified love was on display. This level had been obtained through great self-sacrifice on his part, until he became referred to as *Avraham ohavi* — "Avraham who loves Me" (*Yeshayah* 41:8). That Avraham was able to successfully undergo all of his *nisyonos* was an incredible testament to the work he had already accomplished. For to pass them, it was necessary for him to attain a level of love for Hashem — *l'hodia kamah chibaso* (to uncover how great was his love) — that included and surpassed all other forms of love.

The mishnah alludes to yet another factor through which Avraham Avinu was able to emerge successfully from his trials. As noted, the mishnah uses the phrase *amad b'kulam* — he (literally) "stood" in all of them. According to the Rebbe of Lechovitz *ztz"l*, as seen in the *Toras Avos*, this is actually a reference to the act of *tefillah*.

After having pleaded with Hashem to spare the city of Sodom, the Torah states regarding Avraham: וַיַּשְׁכֵּם אַבְרָהָם בַּבֹּקֶר אֶל־הַמָּקוֹם אֲשֶׁר־עָמַד שָׁם — *And Avraham arose early in the morning to the place at which he had "stood"* (*Bereishis* 19:27). About which the Gemara comments (*Berachos* 6b): "This 'standing' refers to none other than praying."

This was the power Avraham utilized to be **omeid b'nisayon**; that is, he **omeid**, stood, in prayer. And this is the key, as well, for every Jew to withstand the personal *nisyonos* he must undergo throughout his life. Thus, even one who may, as of yet, be lacking the necessary spiritual fortitude, still has recourse to obtain Heavenly assistance. By following in the footsteps of our forefather, he can invoke the power of *tefillah* to successfully navigate whatever challenges confront him in life.

Having gained some clarity of the notion of *nisyonos*, we may now broach the topic of the *Akeidah*, which can be viewed in a new light.

The *Akeidah* — a Loving Fear

At first glance, our original question concerning the *Akeidah* seems to have actually been strengthened based on the above: if the *nisyonos* of Avraham were the ultimate display and expression of love for *Hakadosh Baruch Hu*, then why, regarding the *Akeidah*, does the Torah emphasize Avraham's quality of fear of Hashem — כִּי־יְרֵא אֱלֹקִים אַתָּה?

However, explains the *Yesod Ha'avodah*, this *passuk* about the *Akeidah* actually refers to a *yirah* born out of *ahavah*. In fact, it reflects a spiritual level of great pristine magnitude. Usually, *yiras Hashem* — as vital and great a quality as it is — is considered to be the lesser in comparison to the elevated trait of *ahavas Hashem*. But the *yirah* of which Avraham is characterized here is of a higher level than even that of *ahavah*. For this is a fear regarding the *ahavah* itself; that is, a love so strong between two entities, that one fears lest anything come between them to diminish the love in any way.

The matter can be appreciated even more based on the remarkable comments of the *Derashos HaRan* (sixth discourse). While we usually view the *Akeidah* as one of the most difficult, heart-wrenching commands that Avraham ever received, the Ran depicts the situation somewhat differently. In fact, he asserts, Avraham was *never actually commanded* to sacrifice his son. The *passuk* does not state unequivocally, *Kach es bincha* — "Take your son," but rather *Kach **na** es bincha* — "Take your son, **please**" (*Bereishis* 22:2). In other words, rather than an outright command, Hashem was merely stating a request, revealing that it would please Him if Avraham were to perform this particular act. But Hashem provided Avraham with the option, at the same time, *not* to sacrifice his son. Were Avraham to "opt out," no harm would be done.

This aspect reveals a new dimension to the momentous episode of the *Akeidah*. Not only was Avraham ready to sacrifice his beloved son Yitzchak, in whom rested all of his hopes for the propagation of the Jewish people for future generations — but he was prepared to do so *voluntarily*! What, indeed, would lead him to take such a drastic step without compulsion? Based on the above, the matter can be seen more clearly. This was the *nisayon* of the *Akeidah* and the expression of the highest form of love for Hashem — that is, fear born of love. So great was Avraham's love for Hashem, so concerned was he that not even the slightest blemish or interference manifest itself in this relationship, that he would do anything and everything to preserve it. Upon learning that Hashem's preference was for the sacrifice to take place — albeit with no obligation — Avraham was swift to preserve and demonstrate his undying love for Hashem, and so he took up the task with alacrity.

Why, in fact, is a *nisayon* necessary? Doesn't Hashem already know the outcome? The truth is that the benefit is not to "inform" Hashem, to ascertain on what level the individual stands; that indeed, is known to Hashem. The ultimate purpose is to provide a model, to demonstrate to mankind to what heights the *oveid* can climb. לְהוֹדִיעַ כַּמָּה חִבָּתוֹ שֶׁל אַבְרָהָם אָבִינוּ — the *Akeidah*, like the other *nisyonos*, revealed to the world the greatness Avraham achieved in cultivating such a burning love for Hashem. The tzaddik Reb Leize'la *ztz"l* often shared the sentiment of the Rebbe of Kobrin *ztz"l*, who said, "For his rejection of idolatry and his fealty to the One Hashem,

עשרה נסיונות נתנסה אברהם אבינו

Avraham was cast into a fiery furnace in Ur Casdim, but emerged unscathed. In truth, it is not really such a wonder that the fire of Ur Casdim did not burn him. What is a wonder is that Ur Casdim itself was not scorched by the intense fire of Avraham's burning love for *Hakadosh Baruch Hu*."

And this fiery love was on full display at the *Akeidah*. That even a preference of Hashem's would remain unfulfilled was an unthinkable prospect for Avraham, lest that foster even a tiny chink in the bonds of *ahavah* that connected him with his Creator.

This notion can shed some light on yet another aspect of the *Akeidah*, the "final chapter" in this monumental saga. At the last moment, as Avraham stretched out his hand to slaughter his progeny, the *malach* intervened and ordered Avraham to desist, informing him that he had successfully demonstrated his devotion. In what may seem an afterthought, the Torah records that Avraham discovered a ram and proceeded to offer it as a sacrifice.

But a closer look reveals that this final act is not a mere addendum to the main event. In the most solemn and critical moments, when Klal Yisroel pleads for life and salvation during the Days of Awe, they invoke the memory of the ram sacrificed by Avraham, an aspect incorporated into the *shofar* (ram's horn) itself. The significance of the sacrifice of the ram is further evidenced by the continuation of the Torah's narrative. Avraham was promised that, as a result of the *Akeidah*, he will be blessed and his progeny will increase: בִּי נִשְׁבַּעְתִּי נְאֻם ה' כִּי יַעַן אֲשֶׁר עָשִׂיתָ אֶת־הַדָּבָר הַזֶּה...כִּי־בָרֵךְ אֲבָרֶכְךָ וְהַרְבָּה אַרְבֶּה אֶת־זַרְעֲךָ — *In My Name, I swear, says Hashem, that, since you have done this thing...I will bless you, and increase your offspring...* (Bereishis 22:16-17). What is noteworthy is that this promise was delivered only *after* Avraham sacrificed the ram; an indication that this act, as well, was included in the characterization of "since you have done *this thing*." In some respect, the offering of the ram is considered an inherent part of the *Akeidah* itself.

That is, the bringing of the ram was performed with the same unbridled and burning love with which Avraham carried out the rest of the trial of the *Akeidah*. In fact, it was an extension of the

פרק ה'

Akeidah and a way through which to bring it to fruition. Infused with his unbridled love for *Hakadosh Baruch Hu*, Avraham was prepared to sacrifice his son. He was told by the *malach* to stop, but in a sense, this was a mere "technicality." His passion undiminished, he channeled his act of love into the bringing of the ram, actually fulfilling the original *Akeidah* directive through it. Thus the Torah characterizes his deed as a form of substitution: וַיִּקַּח אֶת־הָאַיִל וַיַּעֲלֵהוּ לְעֹלָה תַּחַת בְּנוֹ — *And he took the ram, and he offered it as a sacrifice* **in place of his son** (ibid. v. 13).

That's Life

There is, however, an important distinction between the *nisayon* of the *Akeidah* and the remainder of Avraham's *nisyonos*. This is underscored by the fact that the *Akeidah* is the only trial that the Torah refers to explicitly as such: וְהָאֱלֹקִים נִסָּה אֶת־אַבְרָהָם — *And G-d tested Avraham* (ibid. v. 1). The term *nisayon* does not appear by the others.

The Nesivos Sholom explains that, in fact, there are two categories of *nisyonos*. The *Akeidah* was an "actual" *nisayon*, thus identified outright as such. It was a directive to perform a particular task, an examination to determine if Avraham would rise to the occasion and actually follow through on the instructions, which, of course, he did.

But there is a different type of *nisayon*, one that doesn't necessary call on the individual to actually "do something." Rather, it is a set of life circumstances with which the individual is presented. Here, the issue is not so much what he will do, but rather, how he will view his circumstances and react to them. For example, when Avraham's wife, Sarah, was taken by Pharaoh and subsequently Avimelech — what, in fact, *could* he do? The situation was as it was: a given set of trying and unfortunate circumstances. Obviously, the prospect of his beloved wife — the quintessential *eishes chayil* (woman of valor), so pure and holy — being abducted by powerful and brutish monarchs must have been an excruciating thought, indeed. The real trial here was a test of acceptance, as this is what the situation called for: developing a real, positive attitude towards what appears as a difficult circumstance.

What is the proper attitude to be cultivated in response to these challenges? This is a crucial question, for it is primarily these types of *nisyonos* — the conditions and situations of life — that confront us on a daily basis. This is our connection to the *nisyonos* of our forefather Avraham.

A person who has a clear understanding of the purpose for which he was created is that much better equipped to cope with, and actually capitalize on, his life challenges. One whose main ambition is self-aggrandizement, and "the pursuit of happiness" in the form of material gain and fulfillment of pleasures, may be in for a rough time, apt to meet with much disappointment. But believing Jews know that they were put on this earth charged with a specific mission. There is something that we have been tasked to rectify — and *there is no one in the entire world, since its inception, more able or qualified to accomplish this mission than we are.*

And it is for this reason we have been bequeathed with our particular life circumstances. Whether it be wealth or poverty, a dynamic personality or a more reserved one, a supportive environment or otherwise, or even a deep struggle with a *yetzer hara* for a particular *aveirah* — it is critical to accept that our situation was not determined randomly, *chas v'shalom*. Rather, it was tailor-made by the All-knowing Hashem for each of us, as He knows exactly which ingredients are necessary for us to fulfill our life's mission. If the circumstances were even one iota different, it would not be possible for us to fulfill the very task for which we were created!

By fully internalizing this fundamental truth, we will not only be better able to accept and tolerate the vicissitudes of life but will be even further empowered, able to actually appreciate and revel in whatever unique circumstances form the contours of our life. Then we will be truly wealthy, as we will have mastered the crucial *middah* of being *samei'ach b'chelko*.

Elsewhere in *Avos* (2:4), the mishnah states: אַל תֹּאמַר לִכְשֶׁאֶפָּנֶה אֶשְׁנֶה, שֶׁמָּא לֹא תִפָּנֶה — *Do not say, "When I become unoccupied, then I shall learn (Torah),"* for you may never end up becoming unoccupied. This is the familiar understanding of *Chazal's* teaching: don't put off learning until you "have time" because it is quite possible that, in fact, you never will "have time." The Saba Kadisha of Slonim *ztz"l* perceives another layer of understanding to this mishnah, relating to the discussion above. It is so very important that a Yid come to peace with, accept, and rise to the occasion presented by his life situation. A person may be burdened and preoccupied, hoping all the while for a respite. "If only my life circumstances will ease," he may muse, "I will be able to learn more Torah and serve Hashem better." But this could be a critical mistake! For Heaven's plan may be specifically for this individual to be preoccupied and serve his Creator amid these trying circumstances. Perhaps it is specifically a situation of *lo sipaneh*, of *not* having the luxury of a leisured, unburdened existence, that is Hashem's desire for him. Were he to be relieved of his circumstances, he would go through life and leave his unique mission unfulfilled. And this would be the greatest tragedy and failure of all.

The truth is, then, that a Jew who cultivates such an attitude not only frees himself from feelings of discouragement over his own situation or from envy of others with circumstances he perceives as more "favorable," but also walks in the footsteps of his forefather Avraham. The Patriarch blazed the path for his offspring by enduring his series of this manner of trials. This is why the term *nisayon* does not appear in connection with the bulk of the "tests" that Avraham had to undergo, for, unlike the *Akeidah*, these were not tests to determine if he would take a certain action. Rather, the challenge was a matter of acceptance, of being able to perceive the true nature of the conditions of his life, and of being happy for the opportunity to carry out the specific life mission Hashem devised for him. And he passed this test in flying colors: *V'amad b'kulam*.

This is the overriding message of the mishnah to each and every one of Avraham's offspring. As was the case for our Patriarch, so it is for us — life is a series of trying circumstances and conditions, not all of them easy or pleasant. And the *nisayon* is for us not to succumb to discouragement but to recognize that each detail of our lives is crucial for the successful completion of the life mission Hashem desires us to fulfill. By recalling the words of the Rebbe of Lechovitz, we can avail ourselves of a wonderful tool to aid us in accomplishing this critical task. He explained that *amidah b'nisayon* — standing with regard to *nisyonos* — refers to none other than *tefillah*. Thus, by pouring out our souls to Hashem and pleading that He grant us the strength and ability to successfully navigate our series of life circumstances, we may be *zocheh*, in the mold of Avraham Avinu, to be *omeid b'kulam*.

In Summary

In elucidating the mishnah of Avraham's ten trials, the Nesivos Sholom goes to the heart of what a *nisayon* is and how it relates to our lives.

The Nesivos Sholom clarifies the ultimate purpose of Avraham's *nisyonos*. It must be more than just a "test" to determine what Avraham would "do" in a certain situation. First, Hashem certainly knew what Avraham would do, and on what level of *avodas Hashem* he stood; was it necessary to orchestrate an elaborate trial just to "clarify" this information? Moreover, regarding the bulk of Avraham's *nisyonos*, there wasn't really any concrete action for Avraham to take; when his wife was taken by powerful monarchs, what exactly was there for him to "do"? Rather, as the mishnah states, the ultimate purpose was to serve as a model for the world, to make known, *l'hodia*, the levels of spiritual grandeur to which a human being can climb.

And it is specifically to the area of *ahavas Hashem* that the *nisyonos* were geared: לְהוֹדִיעַ כַּמָּה חִבָּתוֹ שֶׁל אַבְרָהָם אָבִינוּ. For the essence of the *nisyonos* is to demonstrate that all of one's various loves — for family, wealth, and self — all are subservient to and dedicated to love of Hashem. Through the *nisyonos*, Avraham became known as *Avraham ohavi*.

Even the *Akeidah* shared this component, despite how it seemed initially. After proving his willingness to sacrifice his son to Hashem, the *malach* informed Avraham in Hashem's name, עַתָּה יָדַעְתִּי כִּי־יְרֵא אֱלֹקִים אַתָּה. Thus it would seem that the *Akeidah* related more to the aspect of fear of Hashem. However, explains the Nesivos Sholom, the "fear" referred to here is actually one born out of *ahavah* and is actually the ultimate manifestation of love. The *Derashos HaRan* reveals that, in fact, Avraham was never *obligated* to sacrifice his son; Hashem merely informed him that if he did so, it would be pleasing to Him. But Avraham had the option to decline. Due to his burning love for Hashem, however, Avraham could not even consider this option. So great was his love for Hashem, so much did he cherish his relationship with Him, that he feared lest anything get in the way of this loving relationship, even to the smallest degree. As such, upon learning there was something that would please Hashem, he rushed to fulfill it — even though it entailed sacrificing his precious son and jeopardizing the promise of the future propagation of his offspring.

There is one aspect in which the *Akeidah* differs from the pattern of the remaining trials: only in connection to the *Akeidah* does the Torah explicitly utilize the term *nisayon*. This is because, in fact, there is a fundamental difference in the nature of this trial and that of the others. The *Akeidah* could be characterized explicitly as a *nisayon*, for it was the only one that was a bona fide "test." Avraham was notified of certain instructions; would he, indeed, sacrifice his son? The other trials, however, did not necessarily have this component of testing to determine what action he would take; rather, they were simply a set of circumstances, the life conditions with which he was presented. And the real trial was a question of reaction, which he passed as well. That is, he accepted whatever he was "dealt" and did so with love.

At the root of this acceptance was recognition of what role these circumstances were intended to play, and this is the primary lesson for us, as well. We are each granted our own unique set of circumstances, "custom-tailored" to us for fulfilling our life's mission. This is the reason Hashem put us on this earth in the first place: to fulfill this task which only we — from all of the people of the world, in all the history of the world — are able to accomplish. And were our life conditions altered even minimally, we would be rendered incapable of fulfilling our life's mission. By cultivating this attitude towards our life situation, whatever it is, we can duplicate Avraham's feat and accept it all with love. Such an approach is the hallmark of those who are *samei'ach b'chelko*, happy with their lot. And through it, we are spared from discouragement and envy of the lot of others, and can actually grow and thrive from our own set of circumstances.

In this way we can follow in the footsteps of Avraham, in dealing with the series of trials that comprise our own life situation. A crucial component in being *omeid b'nisayon* is provided by the Rebbe of Lechovitz in his interpretation of this phrase. It is noteworthy that the mishnah utilizes such a term, which literally denotes "standing," as opposed to "passing" or "successfully completing" a test. What the mishnah seeks to convey is a strategy whereby we can elicit crucial assistance in withstanding our trials. For *amidah* is a term used in conjunction with *tefillah*. By pleading to Hashem for help, we can acquire the Divine assistance necessary to be *omeid b'nisayon*.

פרק ה' משנה ז'
עשרה נסים נעשו לאבותינו בבית המקדש
Ten Miracles Were Performed for Our Forefathers in the Holy Temple

עֲשָׂרָה נִסִּים נַעֲשׂוּ לַאֲבוֹתֵינוּ בְּבֵית הַמִּקְדָּשׁ. לֹא הִפִּילָה אִשָּׁה מֵרֵיחַ בְּשַׂר הַקֹּדֶשׁ, וְלֹא הִסְרִיחַ בְּשַׂר הַקֹּדֶשׁ מֵעוֹלָם, וְלֹא נִרְאָה זְבוּב בְּבֵית הַמִּטְבָּחַיִם, וְלֹא אֵרַע קֶרִי לְכֹהֵן גָּדוֹל בְּיוֹם הַכִּפּוּרִים, וְלֹא כִבּוּ גְשָׁמִים אֵשׁ שֶׁל עֲצֵי הַמַּעֲרָכָה, וְלֹא נִצְּחָה הָרוּחַ אֶת עַמּוּד הֶעָשָׁן, וְלֹא נִמְצָא פְסוּל בָּעֹמֶר וּבִשְׁתֵּי הַלֶּחֶם וּבְלֶחֶם הַפָּנִים, עוֹמְדִים צְפוּפִים וּמִשְׁתַּחֲוִים רְוָחִים, וְלֹא הִזִּיק נָחָשׁ וְעַקְרָב בִּירוּשָׁלַיִם מֵעוֹלָם, וְלֹא אָמַר אָדָם לַחֲבֵרוֹ צַר לִי הַמָּקוֹם שֶׁאָלִין בִּירוּשָׁלַיִם:

Ten miracles were performed for our forefathers in the Holy Temple: No woman miscarried from the smell of the sacrificial meat; the sacrificial meat never spoiled; no fly appeared in the slaughterhouse; no emission occurred to the High Priest on Yom Kippur; the rains did not extinguish the fire (burning) upon the arranged wood (on the altar); the wind did not disturb the pillar of smoke; no disqualifying property was found in the offerings of the Omer, the Two Loaves, nor the Showbread; they would stand packed together, but bow with much room; no snake or scorpion ever caused damage in Jerusalem; a man did not say to his fellow: "I am insufficiently provided for in my place of lodging in Jerusalem."

עשרה נסים נעשו לאבותינו בבית המקדש

SOURCES:

וַיַּרְא אֱלֹקִים אֶת־כָּל־אֲשֶׁר עָשָׂה וְהִנֵּה־טוֹב מְאֹד וַיְהִי־עֶרֶב וַיְהִי־בֹקֶר יוֹם הַשִּׁשִּׁי. (בראשית א' ל"א)

And G-d saw all that He had made, and behold, it was very good. And it was evening and it was morning – the sixth day. (*Bereishis* 1:31)

וְגָר זְאֵב עִם־כֶּבֶשׂ וְנָמֵר עִם־גְּדִי יִרְבָּץ. (ישעיה י"א ו')

And the wolf will reside with the lamb, and the leopard will lay next to the kid. (*Yeshayah* 11:6)

בְּשָׁעָה שֶׁהָיוּ יִשְׂרָאֵל עוֹלִין לָרֶגֶל מְגַלְלִין לָהֶם אֶת הַפָּרוֹכֶת, וּמַרְאִין לָהֶם אֶת הַכְּרוּבִים שֶׁהָיוּ מְעוֹרִים זֶה בָּזֶה. (יומא נ"ד:)

When Yisroel would ascend (to the Temple) on their festival pilgrimage, the partition (shielding the Holy Ark) would be rolled back, and they would be shown that the *Keruvim* (Cherubs, normally facing each other at a distance) would be locked in embrace. (*Yuma* 54b)

אֲנִי אָמַרְתִּי אֱלֹקִים אַתֶּם וּבְנֵי עֶלְיוֹן כֻּלְּכֶם אָכֵן כְּאָדָם תְּמוּתוּן. (תהלים פ"ב ו',ז')

I have said that you are G-dly, and children of the Most High. Alas, you shall perish as mortals. (*Tehillim* 82:6, 7)

בְּיוֹם חֲתֻנָּתוֹ וּבְיוֹם שִׂמְחַת לִבּוֹ: בְּיוֹם חֲתֻנָּתוֹ – זֶה מַתַּן תּוֹרָה, וּבְיוֹם שִׂמְחַת לִבּוֹ – זֶה בִּנְיַן בֵּית הַמִּקְדָּשׁ, שֶׁיִּבָּנֶה בִּמְהֵרָה בְּיָמֵינוּ. (תענית כ"ו:)

"In the day of His nuptials, and the day of His heart's rejoicing" (*Shir Hashirim* 3:11). "In the day of His nuptials" – this refers to the giving of the Torah; "and the day of His heart's rejoicing" – this refers to the building of the Holy Temple, may it be rebuilt speedily in our days. (*Ta'anis* 26b)

וְעָשׂוּ לִי מִקְדָּשׁ וְשָׁכַנְתִּי בְּתוֹכָם. (שמות כ"ה ח')

And they shall make for Me a sanctuary, and I shall rest My Presence among them. (*Shemos* 25:8)

פרק ה'

555

GEMS FROM THE *SEFER NESIVOS SHOLOM*

Ten miracles of what *didn't* happen! What about those miracles of an active, positive sort? There were a number of these in the Beis Hamikdash as well. We all know about the one jar of oil that continued to burn for eight days. In a sense, these positive miracles display even more of a "miraculous" quality. Why did the mishnah skip over them, while only including in its miraculous list the somewhat more toned-down phenomena of unpleasantness that was avoided?

For that matter, the whole concept of emphasizing what didn't happen and dubbing that "miraculous" is somewhat of a risky exercise. Why did the mishnah adopt such an approach? If this is the standard, almost anyone can claim miraculous powers. Why, I can make a miracle that there won't be a World War this year. I did the same last year.

The mishnah's intent is clarified by the comments of the *Chassid Ya'avetz*. Aside from just reflecting what didn't occur, the items listed in the mishnah all share a common denominator: they center on the concept of *kilkul* (loss and debasement), or lack thereof — the sacrificial meat never became putrid, there were no flies in the slaughterhouse, etc. He expounds on this idea by describing the state of the world at the very beginning.

The Idyllic State of the World

When Adam first arrived on the scene, he found a world that was utterly pristine. At this time, all of creation was in a state of perfection. וַיַּרְא אֱלֹקִים אֶת־כָּל־אֲשֶׁר עָשָׂה וְהִנֵּה־טוֹב מְאֹד — *And G-d saw all that He had made, and behold, it was very good* (Bereishis 1:31). There was no blemish in Hashem's handiwork, nor any way for it to appear — no injury, no damage, no ruination of any sort. One could bite into an apple, leave it for the next day, and find that it had not turned brown in the slightest. In short, it was a world devoid of *kilkul*.

All of this changed when Adam sinned. The consequences of this act were far-reaching. In a literal sense, *cheit* polluted the *beri'ah*. *Kilkul* was introduced to the world; now, the elements of creation would no longer retain their optimal state. The world and its creatures

עשרה נסים נעשו לאבותינו בבית המקדש

were now susceptible to harm, deterioration, and death. It is only in the future era that the trend will be reversed and rectified. On the day that "the wolf will dwell harmoniously with the lamb" (*Yeshayah* 11:6), the world will once again achieve this state of ultimate perfection.

Actually, there was one place on earth, set aside by Hashem even before the End of Days, that retained this optimal pristine state, one enclave within which the pre-sin environment still functioned. This was the site of the Beis Hamikdash. Within its confines, *kilkul* did not prevail.

This is what the mishnah seeks to impart. It is not merely a list of wondrous acts that occurred in that time and place. Rather, the mishnah is explaining to us what the Beis Hamikdash really was, granting us a taste of its supreme holiness and sublimity. The significance of these ten miracles is that they reflect the pristine nature of the Mikdash, revealing it as a sanctuary for creation at its pinnacle. This is why nothing there can be damaged or ruined, and no one comes to harm. The Mikdash served as a demonstration of life without and before Adam's sin.

This is why the mishnah sticks with "negative" miracles, highlighting what did not occur. By and large, the "active" miracles were a manifestation of reward. For example, *Chazal* relate (*Yuma* 54a) that when Klal Yisroel visited the Beis Hamikdash on their festival pilgrimage, they were treated to a remarkable sight. The *Keruvim* (angelic figures, fashioned from gold), which normally faced each other at wings' length, would be locked in embrace. But this would only occur if the Jewish nation was steadfast in their loyalty to Hashem; if they were not fulfilling His will, the miracle would not occur. Thus, this phenomenon was a matter of reward, accorded to Bnei Yisroel for their observance. The "ten miracles" were of a different sort entirely. Rather than a reward for proper behavior, they reflected a state of being. This was the reality of the Beis Hamikdash environment — the essence of creation. The absence of blemish was an expression of the holy power of the Beis Hamikdash, within which the *beri'ah* was on display in its pristine, natural form.

The Maharal explains this mishnah in a similar fashion. He

פרק ה'

explains that blemish and decay are features of This World, which is a world of troubles and loss. However, this is not a function of the inherent nature of the world but rather a result of the impure powers exercised by the *Sitra Achra*. Sanctity, which rises above This World, is unaffected by loss and decay. As such, the Beis Hamikdash, as well, is a "blemish-free zone." And so shall the whole world be at the End of Days, when creation attains its full rectification.

There was one other time in history when this idyllic state of affairs was once more restored: at *Mattan Torah*. This was considered the pinnacle of creation, which was viewed as having attained complete rectification. All infirmities were healed, and, indeed, death itself was once again banished. The ensuing saga is related in the *passuk* (*Tehillim* 82:6, 7): אֲנִי אָמַרְתִּי אֱלֹקִים אַתֶּם וּבְנֵי עֶלְיוֹן כֻּלְּכֶם אָכֵן כְּאָדָם תְּמוּתוּן — *I have said that you are G-dly and children of the Most High. Alas, you shall perish as mortals*. *Chazal* (*Avodah Zarah* 5a) interpret this *passuk* as reflecting the events at Har Sinai. "I have said that you are G-dly," in that mortality and deterioration were nullified. But, as occurred in Gan Eden at the hands of Adam, the dream was shattered through the perpetration of the sin of the Golden Calf. Death and blemish were summoned back into existence: "Alas, you shall perish as mortals."

These two entities — *Mattan Torah* and the Beis Hamikdash — share a commonality, for which they both merited to host the pristine state of creation. For they represent the fulfillment of the very purpose of creation: that Hashem have a foothold, as it were, in This World. The *passuk* in *Shir Hashirim* (3:11) makes mention of "the day of His nuptials and the day of His heart's rejoicing." According to the Gemara in *Ta'anis* (26b), the reference is to *Mattan Torah* and the completion of the Beis Hamikdash, respectively. These were tremendous causes for Heavenly celebration. *Mattan Torah* and the Beis Hamikdash served as vehicles whereby Hashem could dwell even in the lower realms. As such, they represented the fullness of creation, whose purpose had come to fruition. Through these elements, the pristine state of creation reigned supreme.

The Beis Hamikdash of the Individual

Alas, sin reared its ugly head. The idyllic state at Har Sinai was curtailed because of the Golden Calf, and, eventually, the Beis Hamikdash was lost due to the sins of the nation. That doesn't mean, however, that the pristine existence highlighted in our mishnah has vanished in its entirety. Even now, there exists a way to experience, in some sense, the utopian ideal associated with the Mikdash. In fact, the opportunity is there for each and every Yid — for it exists within the essence of a person.

The *Avodas Yisroel* teaches that the *Churban* — while tragic and broad in its scope — was not a *churban* in total. That is, Klal Yisroel experienced a tremendous loss, but it was confined to the outer, public Beis Hamikdash. The private, inner Mikdash — the sanctuary housed within the heart of every Jew — escaped the *Churban*. In this forum, the Beis Hamikdash continues eternally.

In the commandment to fashion a Mikdash, the precision of the wording is key. The *passuk* states (*Shemos* 25:8), וְעָשׂוּ לִי מִקְדָּשׁ וְשָׁכַנְתִּי בְּתוֹכָם — *And they shall make for Me a sanctuary, and I shall rest My Presence among* **them**. Where shall Hashem rest His Presence? Seemingly, within the confines of the Sanctuary edifice. *Chazal* point out, however, that the verse does not state that Hashem will dwell within *it*; rather, it speaks of Hashem dwelling within *them*. This means that, literally, Hashem will dwell *within them*. Forever, the Jew himself, if he "fashions" himself correctly, serves as the dwelling place for the *Shechinah*.

The obligation to "build" a Mikdash, then, devolves upon each and every Yid. We must cleanse and purify ourselves, making our very self into a vessel suitable for containing the *Shechinah*. By serving as our very own "personal" Beis Hamikdash, we ourselves revert, in some sense, to the idyllic pre-sin state. We experience our own set of Temple miracles. Our very essence can thus become impervious to loss and blemish.

Mattan Torah is likewise an eternal entity, accessible to each and every Jew. *Chazal* refer to Shavuos — the celebration of the Giving of the Torah — as *Zman Mattan Toraseinu* (the time of the Giving of our Torah). A closer look at this title proves most revealing, especially in comparison to the titles by which other festival days are known. For example, Sukkos is called *Zman Simchaseinu*, the time of our joy. The reference is not to past joy, but to the present; it is the day on which — right now — we experience tremendous joy. *Zman Mattan Toraseinu* should be understood in the same way. It is not a mere commemoration of a time long ago, a celebration of some past event. Rather, right now, in the present, it is *our* time of receiving the Torah. The title and the festival reflect the *Mattan Torah* of the present, as on every Shavuos the light of *Mattan Torah* shines forth anew.

Thus we discover that the commandment to build a Mikdash is essentially an eternal commandment, and the gift of *Mattan Torah* is an ongoing one. It is up to each one of us to fashion ourselves into a Mikdash capable of containing the *Shechinah* and to undergo a process of accepting the Torah. In so doing, we can experience within ourselves a semblance of the pristine state that existed at the beginning of time, which shall return in the End of Days.

And as Shavuos approaches, what better way to prepare for *Mattan Torah* than through this form of *avodah*? By cultivating such a level of sanctity as to become capable of housing the *Shechinah*, a Yid attains the ultimate state of purity — from which will be banished all forms of blemish and defilement.

In Summary

The mishnah's list of miracles that took place in the Beis Hamikdash is not an exhaustive one, nor was it intended to be. In fact, the inclusion of these specific items was quite deliberate — as was the fact that they are all "negative" miracles, reflecting unpleasantness that was prevented from happening. For the purpose of the mishnah is to inform us of the true nature of the Beis Hamikdash and what form of existence took place within it.

The Mikdash represents the *beri'ah* at its culmination, as it existed

עשרה נסים נעשו לאבותינו בבית המקדש

in its most pristine state. Before Adam sinned, there was no blemish, deterioration, or death in the world. *Kilkul* was introduced only as a consequence of *cheit*. The Mikdash functioned as an enclave where the pre-sin creation still functioned on earth.

Mattan Torah also shares this aspect. At Har Sinai, the sick were healed and death was banished. So would existence have carried on — if not for, once again, the intervention of the *Sitra Achra*. Through the sin of the Golden Calf, death and *kilkul* returned.

But both these entities continue in some form even today. While the Beis Hamikdash was lost to the *klal*, it still stands for the individual. This is due to the fact that, in truth, each and every Yid can serve as a type of Mikdash, to fulfill the directive *V'shachanti* **b'socham** — "I shall rest My Presence among **them**." It is incumbent upon us to prepare and rectify ourselves to serve as a vessel suitable for housing the *Shechinah*. And we may take part, as well, in *Mattan Torah*. Shavuos is referred to as *Zman Mattan* **Toraseinu**, echoing this basic truth that the Giving of the Torah is an everlasting phenomenon, taking place in the present. And by rising to the occasion and taking part in these acts, a Jew — even today — can attain the idyllic state of the pristine quality of creation.

פרק ה'

פרק ה' משנה י"א
גלות באה לעולם וכו'
Exile Comes to the World...

דֶּבֶר בָּא לָעוֹלָם עַל מִיתוֹת הָאֲמוּרוֹת בַּתּוֹרָה שֶׁלֹּא נִמְסְרוּ לְבֵית דִּין, וְעַל פֵּרוֹת שְׁבִיעִית. חֶרֶב בָּאָה לָעוֹלָם עַל עִנּוּי הַדִּין, וְעַל עִוּוּת הַדִּין, וְעַל הַמּוֹרִים בַּתּוֹרָה שֶׁלֹּא כַהֲלָכָה. חַיָּה רָעָה בָּאָה לָעוֹלָם עַל שְׁבוּעַת שָׁוְא, וְעַל חִלּוּל הַשֵּׁם. גָּלוּת בָּאָה לָעוֹלָם עַל עוֹבְדֵי עֲבוֹדָה זָרָה, וְעַל גִּלּוּי עֲרָיוֹת, וְעַל שְׁפִיכוּת דָּמִים, וְעַל הַשְׁמָטַת הָאָרֶץ:

Pestilence comes to the world on account of capital transgressions which go unpunished by the High Court, and on account of (misuse of) fruits of the Sabbatical year. The sword comes to the world on account of oppression of justice, perversion of justice, and those who issue rulings falsely claiming to accord with the Torah. Wild animals come to the world on account of false oaths and desecration of Hashem's Name. Exile comes to the world on account of idolatry, immorality, murder, and neglect of the commandment to let the land lie fallow (during the Sabbatical year).

SOURCES:

כָּל עֲבֵירוֹת שֶׁבַּתּוֹרָה אִם אוֹמְרִין לְאָדָם עֲבוֹר וְאַל תֵּהָרֵג – יַעֲבוֹר וְאַל יֵהָרֵג, חוּץ מֵעֲבוֹדָה זָרָה וְגִילּוּי עֲרָיוֹת וּשְׁפִיכוּת דָּמִים. (סנהדרין ע״ד.)

(Regarding) all prohibitions of the Torah – if someone is told (by an assailant): "Either violate this transgression, or be killed," one should violate the transgression and avoid death. (This is true in all cases) except for (the following three): idolatry, immorality, and murder. (*Sanhedrin* 74a)

וַיֹּאמֶר ה׳ אֶל־מֹשֶׁה הִנְּךָ שֹׁכֵב עִם־אֲבֹתֶיךָ וְקָם הָעָם הַזֶּה וְזָנָה אַחֲרֵי אֱלֹהֵי נֵכַר־הָאָרֶץ אֲשֶׁר הוּא בָא־שָׁמָּה בְּקִרְבּוֹ וַעֲזָבַנִי וְהֵפֵר אֶת־בְּרִיתִי אֲשֶׁר כָּרַתִּי אִתּוֹ. (דברים ל״א ט״ז)

And Hashem said to Moshe: "Behold, when you pass on to rest among your ancestors, this nation will arise and go astray after the foreign gods of the Land to which they are going within, and they shall abandon Me and violate My covenant which I have forged with them. (*Devarim* 31:16)

לֹא יָדְעוּ אֶת־מִשְׁפַּט אֱלֹקֵי הָאָרֶץ. (מלכים ב׳ י״ז כ״ו)

They did not know the laws of the G-d of the Land. (*Melachim II* 17:26)

כִּי־גֵרְשׁוּנִי הַיּוֹם מֵהִסְתַּפֵּחַ בְּנַחֲלַת ה׳. (שמואל א׳ כ״ו י״ט)

For today they have driven me out from being gathered within Hashem's inheritance. (*Shmuel I* 26:19)

אֶרֶץ אֲשֶׁר ה׳ אֱלֹקֶיךָ דֹּרֵשׁ אֹתָהּ תָּמִיד עֵינֵי ה׳ אֱלֹקֶיךָ בָּהּ מֵרֵשִׁית הַשָּׁנָה וְעַד אַחֲרִית שָׁנָה. (דברים י״א י״ב)

A land that Hashem your G-d seeks out; the eyes of Hashem your G-d are constantly upon it, from the beginning of the year and until the end of the year. (*Devarim* 11:12)

גלות באה לעולם וכו'

כִּי אֶת־כָּל־הַתּוֹעֵבֹת הָאֵל עָשׂוּ אַנְשֵׁי־הָאָרֶץ אֲשֶׁר לִפְנֵיכֶם וַתִּטְמָא הָאָרֶץ, וְלֹא־תָקִיא הָאָרֶץ אֶתְכֶם בְּטַמַּאֲכֶם אֹתָהּ כַּאֲשֶׁר קָאָה אֶת־הַגּוֹי אֲשֶׁר לִפְנֵיכֶם. (ויקרא י"ח כ"ז, כ"ח)

For the people of the Land who preceded you committed all of these abominations and the Land became defiled. Let not the Land vomit you out through your defilement of it, just as it vomited out the nation that preceded you. (*Vayikra* 18:27-28)

כִּי מִזַּרְעוֹ נָתַן לַמֹּלֶךְ לְמַעַן טַמֵּא אֶת־מִקְדָּשִׁי. (שם כ' ג')

For he has given of his offspring to Molech, in order to defile My sanctuary. (*ibid.* 20:3)

כִּי הַדָּם הוּא יַחֲנִיף אֶת־הָאָרֶץ...וְלֹא תְטַמֵּא אֶת־הָאָרֶץ אֲשֶׁר אַתֶּם יֹשְׁבִים בָּהּ אֲשֶׁר אֲנִי שֹׁכֵן בְּתוֹכָהּ. (במדבר ל"ה ל"ג, ל"ד)

For the (spilling of) blood is what brings wickedness to the Land... and do not defile the Land in which you dwell, in whose midst I reside. (*Bamidbar* 35:33-34)

שֶׁתְּרַחֲמֵנִי עוֹד בְּגָלוּתִי לְגָאֳלֵנִי וּלְעוֹרֵר לִבִּי לְאַהֲבָתֶךָ. (תפילת ליל שבת)

To show me mercy even in my exile, to redeem me and awaken my heart to Your love. (Shabbos evening prayer)

Hashem's Domain

Golus — exile. The term is such an intrinsic part of our lives — as has been the case for millennia. Depending on the time and place, its perils are sometimes more apparent, sometimes less. Nevertheless, it still plays such a central role because, after all, we are in it.

Have we ever paused to think, however, about the nature of this particular form of retribution? At the very least, most earnest *Yidden* are aware that we have sinned; otherwise, the Beis Hamikdash would be rebuilt, the *Shechinah* would once again reside in the Land — and so would all of us, under the wings of His protection. But there are many types of punishments that could have been visited upon the Jewish people even within their Land. What, indeed, lies behind this notion of national eviction from Eretz Yisroel?

The mishnah, which focuses on the specific sins that bring about *golus*, offers us some perspective. The immediately noteworthy aspect we see is the composition of the mishnah: the three cardinal sins of idolatry, immorality, and murder, plus the (seemingly unrelated) law of *shemittah* (the Sabbatical year, during which agricultural activity must cease).

There exists an obvious distinction between these two groupings. It's not difficult to understand why exile is an appropriate punishment for the first group. After all, the severity of the cardinal sins is well known, being the only set of prohibitions subject to the requirement of *yehareig v'al ya'avor* ("Let him be killed and not transgress." A Yid may violate all other prohibitions if his life is at stake. These three are the exceptions.). Committing these sins corrupts all three components of man: his mind, heart, and bodily limbs. Idolatry, a deviation from proper faith, corrupts a Yid's mind; immorality, reflecting a slavish indulgence of one's wishes and desires, corrupts his heart; and murder is the quintessential corrupted use of one's limbs. The *Shechinah* can no longer dwell among a people who have wreaked such devastation on their essence. It departs, and exile is the result (see Ramban's introduction to *Sefer Shemos*).

Based on the teaching of the Maharal, we can gain additional insight into the relationship between these three sins and the resultant *golus*. In discussing the quality of *shleimus*, the Maharal identifies three key areas in which a Yid must strive for perfection. He must be at one with Hashem, with his fellow, and with himself. Taken together, the three cardinal sins undermine *shleimus* in each of these areas. Idolatry, quite obviously, constitutes a breach in *shleimus* with Hashem; through the corrupted conduct one displays by engaging in immoral behavior, the perpetrator displays that he lacks *shleimus* with himself; and, of course, murder stands in opposition to *shleimus* with one's fellow. Having so thoroughly distanced himself from achieving *shleimus*, this transgressor has severed his connection with the Almighty, leading to a complete separation from Him in the form of *golus*.

But the other concept listed in our mishnah — *shemittah* — presents something of a puzzle. It doesn't share the same severity as the three cardinal sins, but is relegated to the same category as the remainder of the mitzvos of the Torah. Why, then, is it included among those offenses that result in the penalty of exile?

Egypt — the Exception to the Rule

Let us return to the general notion of *golus* as a form of punishment. As was mentioned, there are no lack of penalties that could have been imposed on the people right where they were. Why was it necessary to have them leave the Land?

There is one prominent exile whose underlying purpose we do know something about: *golus Mitzrayim* (Egyptian exile). This, however, served a specific function — one not even related to punishment and retribution. In fact, the original exiles were not sinful at all; they comprised the righteous Yaakov Avinu and his worthy family. It was only later, well into the duration of the exile, that the descendants had fallen in their spiritual level. By the time of the redemption, the Sages explain, they had reached the forty-ninth level of impurity (out of fifty).

Obviously, this *golus* was not the result of sin. Rather, the Egyptian exile was preordained for a completely different reason; it was a necessary exercise for the ascendancy of Klal Yisroel. Hashem had already informed Avraham Avinu at the *Bris Bein Habesarim* ("covenant between the pieces") that his descendants would need to undergo a protracted purging process. The sojourn in "the House of Bondage" under the harshest of conditions served a very vital function: it was a forging furnace, purifying the nation from the last vestiges of materialism. Painful as it was, the experience gave birth to the Jewish nation, elevating them to the level where they were worthy to be the Chosen People and receive the Torah.

But that was then — the process necessary to forge the nation. What purpose was there to the exiles visited upon Klal Yisroel in their subsequent history, brought about as retribution for their deeds? Why was this form of punishment adopted?

G-d of the Land

We find the Torah employing a curious term to describe the false deities worshipped by the idolators. It refers to them as *elohei neichar ha'aretz* — "the foreign gods of the Land" (*Devarim* 31:16). The Ramban explains that the implication is that the gods themselves are strangers to the Land — which is precisely the case. For in Eretz Yisroel, Hashem reigns supreme; He is the "G-d of the Land." As the *passuk* states: לֹא יָדְעוּ אֶת־מִשְׁפַּט אֱלֹקֵי הָאָרֶץ — *They did not know the laws of the G-d of the Land* (*Melachim II* 17:26).

Of course, Hashem reigns throughout the entirety of the universe that He created. The fundamental difference between Eretz Yisroel and the other lands has to do with their administration. Hashem runs the world but deals with the other lands through designated intermediaries known as *sarim* (celestial officers). The nations of the world were led astray and began worshipping the intermediaries instead of Hashem Himself; in this way, idolatry spread among them (cf. *Rambam*, *Hilchos Avodah Zarah*, ch. 1). In any event, Hashem conducts His world through these "officers" only among the foreign nations. In Eretz Yisroel, everything is conducted directly by His hand alone. He is the G-d of the Land.

גלות באה לעולם וכו'

This is the source of the special relationship we find between Hashem and the Land. Dovid Hamelech refers to Eretz Yisroel as *nachalas Hashem* — "the 'inheritance' of Hashem" (*Shmuel I* 26:19). This is an interesting term to use to refer to Hashem, Who created and owns all, and obviously has no real association with the laws or concept of inheritance. Dovid's intent was that Hashem relates to this Land as one would relate to inherited property that has remained in the family for generations. This land is particularly precious, and thus one devotes more care and scrutiny to its maintenance than he does to other assets that may have come into his possession.

And so we find that Hashem displays especial interest in the affairs of the Land. As the *passuk* describes it (*Devarim* 11:12), אֶרֶץ אֲשֶׁר ה' אֱלֹקֶיךָ דֹּרֵשׁ אֹתָהּ תָּמִיד עֵינֵי ה' אֱלֹקֶיךָ בָּהּ מֵרֵשִׁית הַשָּׁנָה וְעַד אַחֲרִית שָׁנָה — *A land that Hashem your G-d seeks out; the eyes of Hashem your G-d are constantly upon it, from the beginning of the year and until the end of the year.* Eretz Yisroel is Hashem's exclusive domain; there, He does not employ intermediaries. The celestial officers are strangers to the Land, as Hashem Himself maintains constant and direct involvement.

One of the ramifications of this distinction relates to man's access to his needs throughout the year. Generally speaking, issues such as rainfall and sustenance are determined by means of Hashem's judgment on Rosh Hashanah. At that time, man's needs are fixed and allocated for the course of the year. If his judgment was not favorable, his allocation may be paltry; but once the judgment has been set, it would seem that there is not much left for one to do.

Actually, as the Saba Kadisha explains (*Toras Avos, Parshas Vayeitzei*), there is still some recourse. The above represents the normal course of events, the adherence to the system of *din* (judgment) of Rosh Hashanah. There is, however, another "system" in place by which Hashem conducts men's affairs; it is a system that is reliant on special *chassadim* supplied by Hashem. *And it is only in Eretz Yisroel that such a special Providential system is in effect.* Yidden outside of Eretz Yisroel also have an opportunity to tap into this special Divine Providence, but they, too, can only access it by way

פרק ה'

of Eretz Yisroel. As Shlomo Hamelech declares (*Melachim I*, 8:48): וְהִתְפַּלְלוּ אֵלֶיךָ דֶּרֶךְ אַרְצָם — *And they (the Jews outside of the Land) shall pray to You **by way of their Land**.*

The Foundation of *Shemittah*

Based on the above, we have been afforded a fundamental perspective regarding *shemittah*. For the observance of this mitzvah is *the greatest manifestation of the fact that Hashem is the "G-d of the Land."* For a full year, a Yid must effectively relinquish possession of his property. He may not demonstrate ownership through working the land or gathering and selling the fruit of his fields. The lack of our dominion of the land is especially blatant during *yovel* (the jubilee year), when we are required to return purchased fields to the original seller. Thus, the great national work stoppage at these times serves as a resounding, collective declaration: it is a public acknowledgment that we do not own this Land. It is Hashem's sole domain — He is the ultimate Owner.

What happens, then, when the mitzvah of *shemittah* is breached? This is not only a violation of a prohibition; it constitutes *a refusal to concede ownership to the G-d of the Land*. By denying that this Land is under the singular dominance of Hashem, one thereby diminishes the sanctity of the Land. And so, once the *Yidden* abandoned the mitzvah of *shemittah*, they effectively lost their right to continue dwelling in this Land. To dwell in the Land, one must recognize its connection to Hashem, how He endows it with singular oversight. Having thus desecrated the Land and forfeited their merit to remain, *golus* was the natural consequence.

You Shall Not Contaminate the Land

Based on the above, we can gain further insight into the consequence of *golus* as it relates to the three cardinal sins. For the perpetration of these particular transgressions, in addition to the severity of the actual sin, likewise constitute a grave desecration towards the Land itself. The violation of each of these *aveiros* brings with it an element of *tumah*. Warning against immoral acts, the Torah makes clear reference to the impurity it visits upon the Land (*Vayikra* 18:27-28): כִּי אֶת־כָּל־הַתּוֹעֵבֹת הָאֵל עָשׂוּ אַנְשֵׁי־הָאָרֶץ אֲשֶׁר לִפְנֵיכֶם וַתִּטְמָא הָאָרֶץ, וְלֹא־תָקִיא הָאָרֶץ אֶתְכֶם בְּטַמַּאֲכֶם אֹתָהּ כַּאֲשֶׁר קָאָה אֶת־הַגּוֹי אֲשֶׁר לִפְנֵיכֶם — *For the people of the Land who preceded you committed all of these abominations* **and the Land became defiled**. *Let not the Land vomit you out through your defilement of it, just as it vomited out the nation that preceded you.* Similarly, defilement is a symptom of idolatry, as the *passuk* states regarding the worship of Molech (*Vayikra* 20:3): כִּי מִזַּרְעוֹ נָתַן לַמֹּלֶךְ לְמַעַן טַמֵּא אֶת־מִקְדָּשִׁי — *For he has given of his offspring to Molech, in order to* **defile My sanctuary**. Murder, as well, introduces impurity into the Land, as the *passuk* states (*Bamidbar* 35:33-34): כִּי הַדָּם הוּא יַחֲנִיף אֶת־הָאָרֶץ...וְלֹא תְטַמֵּא אֶת־הָאָרֶץ אֲשֶׁר אַתֶּם יֹשְׁבִים בָּהּ אֲשֶׁר אֲנִי שֹׁכֵן בְּתוֹכָהּ — *For the (spilling of) blood is what brings wickedness to the Land...and* **do not defile the Land** *in which you dwell, in whose midst I reside*.

Thus we see that it is not the perpetration alone of these severe sins that incurs *golus*. Retribution for these violations could have occurred within the Land itself. Rather, it was *the contaminating effect* these acts had on the Land that brought about the exile. After wreaking such desecration on the sanctity of the Land, in defiance of the G-d of the Land, the violators forfeited their ability to continue living in the place where Hashem's *Shechinah* dwells.

Personal Exile — and Redemption

One crucial lesson that each and every Yid can glean from this focus on exile is that the same notions apply to one's own personal exile. That is, aside from the removal of a nation from its land, there is also a form of exile that pertains to the individual. And just as the national *golus* affects the physical bodies of the Jews, the personalized form of *golus* relates to the spiritual aspects of one's soul.

In what way does "exile of the soul" manifest itself? The Nesivos Sholom explains that a Jewish heart, in its refined state, should be capable of harboring feelings of *ahavas Hashem*. *Golus* for an individual Yid means that he no longer experiences such feelings, a result of his *nefesh*, *ruach*, and *neshamah* having been "banished"

from their proximity to Hashem. In one of the Shabbos evening *tefillos*, we beseech Hashem, שֶׁתְּרַחֲמֵנִי עוֹד בְּגָלוּתִי לְגָאֲלֵנִי וּלְעוֹרֵר לִבִּי לְאַהֲבָתֶיךָ — *To show me mercy in my exile, to redeem me and awaken my heart to Your love.* This request, referring to the personal *golus* of a Yid's soul, reflects the nature of this exile. This Yid's heart needs to be reawakened to feel genuine love for Hashem.

This personal exile is also caused by the three cardinal sins. Even if one has not violated these actual transgressions, involvement in the subsidiaries (*abizrai'hu*) of these sins can have the same deleterious effects. A Yid may have avoided actual idol worship; however, a weakening in matters of *emunah* is a subsidiary of idolatry and can bring *golus* to one's soul. One who experiences lapses in matters of sanctity has engaged in *abizrai'hu d'arayos* (subsidiaries of immorality). Even though one didn't actually murder his friend, causing him grief or otherwise inflicting physical or emotional harm can be considered, in a sense, a form of murder. And so, any of these or related behaviors can cause *golus* for one's soul.

But just as an individual can experience his own *golus*, he may likewise attain his personal *geulah* (redemption). The causes of *golus* — on both a national and personal scale — have been examined above. This, then, is also the key to redemption. By purifying oneself and rectifying the lapses that gave rise to his exile in the first place, a Yid can thereby merit his personal *geulah*. He can thus come back home to occupy a place close to Hashem and once again express and feel his great love for Him.

In Summary

The mishnah attributes the incidence of *golus* to one of four causes: either one of the three cardinal sins or violation of the *shemittah* laws. The three cardinal sins are known for their severity, and it is not surprising that one incurs *golus* on their account. *Golus* is particularly appropriate in these instances, as the three sins serve to corrupt a man's mind (*avodah zarah*), heart (*arayos*), and limbs (*shefichus damim*, bloodshed). They also thwart the attainment of *shleimus* in the areas of peace with Hashem (through *avodah zarah*), peace with one's self (through *gilui arayos*, immoral acts), and peace with one's fellow (through *shefichus damim*). But what is the connection between *golus* and *shemittah*?

The Nesivos Sholom elucidates the issue by explaining from where *golus* derives. Hashem is referred to as the "G-d of the Land," reflecting the fact that He maintains a special and direct connection with Eretz Yisroel. Whereas the other lands He administers through celestial intermediaries, in Eretz Yisroel Hashem retains full and sole dominion. He regards the affairs of Eretz Yisroel with especial scrutiny and singular Providence. Proper observance of *shemittah* serves as a clear recognition that Hashem is the Master and Owner of the Land, a sentiment that is displayed through the Jews' relinquishment of ownership and dominion during the *shemittah* year. By engaging in the collective work stoppage, the Jewish people demonstrate their acknowledgment that Hashem is the G-d and Owner of the Land. When they violate the laws of *shemittah*, they reveal a denial that this Land is Hashem's domain. In so doing, their connection with and right to live on the Land has been terminated, and the result is *golus*.

This notion can help inform the punishment of *golus* in response to the three cardinal sins, as well. For by each of them, the Torah records that they bring defilement. Thus, by contaminating the Land, they desecrate its sanctity — behaving somewhat similarly to the violators of *shemittah*. Thus they, as well, incur the consequence of *golus*.

Just as exile can pertain to the nation, it can also pertain to the individual. In the same manner that defilement causes a physical separation from the Land, it can lead to a spiritual separation from Hashem. It has the same root causes — if not through the full-blown violation of the three cardinal sins, engaging in the *abizrai'hu* can likewise bring on this *golus*. In the same vein, however, he can effect a personal *geulah* by rectifying those failings that caused the *golus* in the first place.

פרק ה׳ משנה י״ג
ארבע מדות באדם
There Are Four Traits in a Person

אַרְבַּע מִדּוֹת בָּאָדָם. הָאוֹמֵר שֶׁלִּי שֶׁלִּי וְשֶׁלְּךָ שֶׁלָּךְ, זוֹ מִדָּה בֵּינוֹנִית. וְיֵשׁ אוֹמְרִים, זוֹ מִדַּת סְדוֹם. שֶׁלִּי שֶׁלְּךָ וְשֶׁלְּךָ שֶׁלִּי, עַם הָאָרֶץ. שֶׁלִּי שֶׁלָּךְ וְשֶׁלְּךָ שֶׁלָּךְ, חָסִיד. שֶׁלִּי שֶׁלִּי וְשֶׁלְּךָ שֶׁלִּי, רָשָׁע:

There are four traits in a person: One who says, "What's mine is mine, and what's yours is yours" – this is an example of average character; others say this is the character of a Sodomite. (One who says,) "What's mine is yours, and what's yours is mine," is an ignoramus. (One who says,) "What's mine is yours, and what's yours is yours," is pious. (One who says,) "What's mine is mine, and what's yours is mine," is wicked.

GEMS FROM THE *SEFER NESIVOS SHOLOM*

SOURCES:

מָה הַמָּקוֹם...רַחוּם וְחַנּוּן אַף אַתָּה הֱוֵי רַחוּם וְחַנּוּן... מָה הַקָּבָּ"ה...נִקְרָא חָסִיד...אַף אַתָּה הֱוֵי חָסִיד. (ספרי עקב י"ג)

Just as Hashem...is merciful and compassionate, so should you be merciful and compassionate... Just as Hashem...is called, "The Pious One"...so should you be pious. (*Sifri, Eikev* §13)

תֶּן לוֹ מִשֶּׁלּוֹ, שֶׁאַתָּה וְשֶׁלְּךָ שֶׁלּוֹ. (אבות ג׳)

Give Him what is His; for you and yours are essentially His. (*Avos* 3)

אִם־יִתֵּן אִישׁ אֶת־כָּל־הוֹן בֵּיתוֹ בָּאַהֲבָה בּוֹז יָבוּזוּ לוֹ. (שיר השירים ח׳ ז׳)

If one were to give away his estate's entire fortune in exchange for the love, they would scorn him. (*Shir Hashirim* 8:7)

מִנְחָה הוּא שְׁלוּחָה לַאדֹנִי לְעֵשָׂו. (בראשית ל"ב י"ט)

It is an offering sent to my master, to Eisav. (*Bereishis* 32:19)

וַיִּשָּׂא אַבְרָהָם אֶת־עֵינָיו וַיַּרְא וְהִנֵּה־אַיִל אַחַר נֶאֱחַז בַּסְּבַךְ בְּקַרְנָיו וַיֵּלֶךְ אַבְרָהָם וַיִּקַּח אֶת־הָאַיִל וַיַּעֲלֵהוּ לְעֹלָה תַּחַת בְּנוֹ. (בראשית כ"ב י"ג)

And Avraham lifted his eyes, and he saw that behold – there was another ram, tangled in the thicket by its horns; and Avraham went, took the ram, and offered it as a sacrifice in place of his son. (*Bereishis* 22:13)

פרקי אבות

ארבע מדות באדם

Traits, characteristics, *middos*, outlooks, habits: these are terms used to define the qualities of a person. We all want to have traits that will help us succeed in life, perfect our *middos* so that they become stellar, and cultivate positive outlooks on life. One could contemplate, however, whether these are mere aspects of our personality or whether they comprise our very essence, defining who we are.

This distinction is manifest in the mishnayos of this part of the *perek*. This mishnah begins a series of four traits, while each of the next six mishnayos focuses on another set of four characteristics. Notice, however, a significant difference in the wording. The bulk of the mishnayos zero in on a specific area: "Four types of attitudes," "Four types of charity givers," "Four types of *beis medrash* (study hall) attendees," etc. This mishnah, on the other hand, opens with a description of a much more general nature: *Arba middos* **ba'adam** — "There are four traits **in a person**." The implication is that the qualities discussed in this mishnah are not merely isolated, particular details; rather, they signify the inherent nature, the actual makeup of what a man is.

This point requires some clarification. The mishnah seems to be dealing with the concept of generosity versus selfishness. Not in terms of *tzedakah*, as that is the subject of a later mishnah; but, rather, a general tendency to share or withhold. While no doubt an important topic, it is somewhat perplexing that this is considered the most all-encompassing facet of a person, to the extent that it defines his entire self. What, exactly, is the mishnah's intent?

Give and Take

The mishnah puts a premium on this quality: are you a giver or a taker? Apparently, the answer to this query serves to define exactly what type of person one really is.

There is the individual who is neither a giver nor a taker; his attitude towards others is "what's mine is mine and what's yours is yours." Such a person possesses the virtue expressed in the *passuk* (*Mishlei* 15:27): שׂוֹנֵא מַתָּנֹת יִחְיֶה — *One who despises gifts, shall live.* On the other hand, lacking a giving nature, in the eyes of the mishnah, puts him in the category of merely "average" — or much worse. But then there is the quintessential giver, the one whose mantra is "what's mine is yours and what's yours is yours." The greatest joy of such a person is to make others happy and bestow them with benefit. At the same time, this selfless individual himself is loathe to accept gifts from others; being a taker goes against his grain. This is a true chassid, whose very being exudes a desire to give. And then there is the polar opposite, the ultimate taker, who not only aims solely to receive what's best for him but cannot bear to give of himself to others. "What's mine is mine and what's yours is mine" — the mishnah doesn't have a nice word to describe this fellow.

The Nesivos Sholom explains further how it is that these qualities define a person's inherent, overall nature. How is it possible for one to derive true pleasure from bestowing goodness upon others? It must be that such an attitude is derived from a root that is inherently good. A person with such a makeup will thus make giving to others his top priority. On the other hand, one whose nature is inherently wicked and thoroughly self-centered will be interested only in taking; giving to and helping others has no place in the mindset of such a person.

On another level, the trait of giving puts a person, to some extent, on par with Divine attributes. The Torah enjoins us to cleave to Hashem and cultivate those *middos* for which He is known. "Just as He is merciful, so too should you be merciful; just as He is gracious, so too should you be gracious." Of course, Hashem is also characterized as *Hatov V'hameitiv* — "The One Who is good and bestows good upon others." Hashem, of course, is the ultimate embodiment of good, having fashioned an entire world for the purpose of bestowing kindness on His creations. One who constantly desires to benefit others through his self and his possessions has attained the highest degree of emulating his Creator and cleaving to His ways.

In any event, the mishnah's meaning appears much clearer in this light. It speaks not of individualized traits but of the *middos* that comprise the very essence of *adam*. For giving is the ultimate litmus test of what a person's makeup really is. One who derives pleasure from giving to others is obviously in possession of a core of *tov*. For one with an overwhelming preference to be on the receiving end, the matter is different entirely.

In fact, a giving nature reveals yet another dimension about the person: that is, his level of *emunah* and his clarity of vision of his true status. There are poor people and there are rich people — or so we tend to think. A person with a truly developed sense of *emunah* knows that, in reality, the whole notion is ridiculous. Rich, poor — in truth, no human being possesses *anything*. Ultimately, all wealth and all aspects of This World derive solely from Hashem, Who also is the true Owner of heaven, earth, and all that is in it. Elsewhere in *Avos*, *Chazal* relate this sentiment, urging one to utilize his resources in the service of the Almighty. תֵּן לוֹ מִשֶּׁלוֹ, שֶׁאַתָּה וְשֶׁלְּךָ שֶׁלּוֹ — *Give Him what is His; for you and yours are essentially His* (*Avos* 3:7).

Thus, one who truly inculcates this idea — that all that he has is in fact not his at all but Hashem's possessions, temporarily entrusted to his hands — will have no problem giving. On the contrary, he may revel in the prospect of serving faithfully as the *Ribono Shel Olam's* personal trustee, charged with the mission of dispensing His funds as He sees fit.

But someone who lacks this *emunah* will have a much harder time expressing "what's mine is yours." Such an individual is under the illusion that what has been temporarily placed in his hands is actually *his*. This aspect of selfishness causes him to feel that "what is mine, is mine." As such, his lack of giving to others is a sign of a weak sense of *emunah*.

The Slonimer Rebbe *ztz"l* perceived this message manifest in *Shir Hashirim* in a most interesting way. The *passuk* there states (8:7), אִם־יִתֵּן אִישׁ אֶת־כָּל־הוֹן בֵּיתוֹ בָּאַהֲבָה בּוֹז יָבוּזוּ לוֹ. This is usually understood as a reference to the unbreakable bonds of love between Yisroel and *Hakadosh Baruch Hu*. "If one were to give away his estate's entire fortune in exchange for this love" — that is, if he were to attempt to nullify it with an exorbitant bribe — "they would scorn him" for his fruitless efforts.

However, the Slonimer Rebbe interprets this verse homiletically, as a reflection of the ideas mentioned above. Consider a man who makes a substantial donation to a spiritual cause from his vast resources. "Even if one were to give away his entire fortune, if it is *from his estate*," the gift is flawed. Although he seeks to do a good deed, his perception is still skewed, for he perceives himself as actually *giving* away something that was inherently his — *mibeiso*. As such, "they will scorn him" for his gross misperception. It would be much preferred for him to realize that, in truth, he is not "giving" anything but merely returning to Hashem what is already His.

What's Your Angle?

Citing the *Avodas Yisroel*, the Nesivos Sholom presents an entirely different approach to understanding the mishnah. He explains it as dealing with a question of intent, as it relates to one's overall *avodas Hashem*.

Sheli — "What is mine" refers to one's personal affairs, that is, physical needs and activities. *Shelcha* — "What is yours (Yours)" refers to Heavenly matters, such as mitzvah endeavors. The mishnah thus portrays the chassid as one who is entirely given over to Hashem. *Sheli Shelcha* — "What is mine is Yours": Even his engagement in material matters, such as eating or sleeping, is done with a focus on You, Hashem, as an effort to keep healthy to better serve You. As such, even one's mundane activities, undertaken for the sake of Heaven, become a method of serving Hashem. *Shelcha Shelcha* — "What is Yours is Yours": When performing actual mitzvah acts, these are done with pristine intent. There are no ulterior motives to the chassid's *avodah*, he is not trying to impress anyone; rather, all is done for no other reason other than to please "You," the Creator.

For the *rasha's* part, he keeps Hashem much further from his thoughts. *Sheli sheli* — "What's mine is *mine*": When partaking in material pleasures, he thinks only of his own needs. A focus on Hashem's will does not enter into this arena, as that may interfere with his self-serving enjoyment. *Shelcha sheli* — "What's Yours is mine": His focus on self carries over even into the realm of spiritual activities. When engaged in the performance of a mitzvah, his aim is once again for his own benefit, to attain honor or wealth or the like.

This approach likewise sheds light on our mishnah's emphasis on the general *adam* — "Four *middos* in a person" — as opposed to the specific characteristics of the other mishnayos (charity givers, *beis medrash* attendees, etc.). For the mishnah refers to an all-pervasive notion, encompassing basically every activity that one performs — whether physical or spiritual — throughout his day and throughout his life. What is the driving force manifest in all of these facets of his life — is it to serve Hashem or one's self?

The Slonimer Rebbe expresses a thought that captures the pervasive nature of the idea described above. When Yaakov was preparing for the encounter with his brother Eisav — who was also his arch-nemesis — he tried to appease his brother's anger by sending him gifts. He instructed the gift-bearers that when presenting the offering to Eisav, they should proclaim: מִנְחָה הִוא שְׁלוּחָה לַאדֹנִי לְעֵשָׂו — *It is a gift sent to my master, to Eisav* (Bereishis 32:19). The *passuk* does not state "to my master, Eisav," but adds a minor apparent redundancy: "to my master, *to* Eisav." The Slonimer Rebbe understands that the *passuk* can thus be viewed as representing a division and reflecting an overall theme. That is, every single mundane act performed by a Yid can be seen as an "offering" either to "the Master," meaning Hashem, or to Eisav, representing the *Sitra Achra*. If while attending to one's physical needs, a Jew dedicates his action for the sake of Heaven, then his act comprises an offering to Hashem. If, however, Hashem does not figure into his thoughts, then, by default, his act is dedicated to the *Sitra Achra*.

In light of this idea, we see just how far-reaching are the *middos* of our mishnah. A Yid's entire life is comprised of a series of events and moments. Through his focus, he has the power to elevate all of these moments to the level of "holy of holies." If his intent is only for the sake of Heaven, he transforms them all into offerings sent to the Master of the Universe. Conversely, he also has the choice of rendering all of his sacred acts into mundane ones — if they are characterized by selfish motives.

The Heart of the *Akeidah*

We thus discover the potency of intent; how the more our heart underlies our actions, the more we can transform them into the loftiest of entities.

This idea is brought out most dramatically through the episode of *Akeidas Yitzchak*. A particularly noteworthy aspect of this event is the crucial role played by the ram that was sacrificed in place of Yitzchak. At first glance, this occurrence may seem like a postscript to the main part of the *Akeidah*. Avraham demonstrated his utter devotion to Hashem by exhibiting his readiness to sacrifice to Him his beloved son. At the last moment, as he grasped the slaughtering knife in his hand, the angel called out to Avraham to halt, informing him that he had successfully demonstrated his fear of Hashem. Avraham then beheld a ram caught by its horns in a thicket. He proceeded to take this ram and offer it as a sacrifice to Hashem.

A second angel revealed to Avraham that he had merited great blessings as a consequence of the *Akeidah*. Of particular note is the fact that this announcement came only *after* the ram was sacrificed. The implication seems to be that, far from an unrelated detail, the sacrificing of the ram was part and parcel of the actual *Akeidah* itself.

This is underscored by the Torah's emphasis that the ram was slaughtered by Avraham *tachas b'no* — "in place of his son" (*ibid.* 22:13). In other words, Avraham so desired to fulfill Hashem's command that even after he had "passed the test," he yearned to complete Hashem's directive to sacrifice his son. Since this act itself was no longer possible but his heart still strongly desired to do it, Avraham sacrificed the ram with the intent that he was carrying out the original command of offering up his son; the ram was sacrificed, literally, in place of his son — as if he were actually sacrificing Yitzchak. And the deed was credited to him as such. So much did Avraham's heartfelt intent have a bearing on his action, that the bringing of the ram was considered an integral part — and the ultimate completion — of the *Akeidah* itself.

The sheer importance of this deed of Avraham, and the awesome transformative power wrought by the yearnings of his heart, were known to the *Sitra Achra*, which is why he sought to prevent it. The Torah mentions what appears to be an insignificant detail about this particular ram: וַיַּרְא וְהִנֵּה־אַיִל...נֶאֱחַז בַּסְּבַךְ בְּקַרְנָיו — *And he saw, and behold, there was a ram...caught by its horns in the thicket* (ibid.). Why was it necessary for the *passuk* to tell us that it was ensnared in the brush? This is an allusion to the struggle that took place over the ram between the *Sitra Achra* and Avraham. Realizing the significance of sacrificing the ram, serving, as it would, as the fulfillment of the *Akeidah* directive, the *Sitra Achra* attempted to thwart the action, grabbing hold of the ram and trying to keep it from Avraham. Thankfully for him and for his progeny, Avraham prevailed over the Force of Evil and sacrificed the ram in place of his son.

What Avraham revealed to us through this momentous deed is just how critical and powerful it is to invest noble and pristine intent into every facet of our lives. And this is the message of our mishnah, as well. For what lies in man's heart can affect and include everything that he does — reflected in the mishnah's usage of the all-encompassing term of "four qualities *in a man.*" Pure intent can transform the "*Sheli*" — mundane, earthly activities — into spiritual service. Imagine what it can do to spiritual endeavors themselves.

In Summary

We get an inkling of the all-encompassing nature of the message of this mishnah from the wording of its introductory phrase. At this point in the fifth chapter of *Avos*, a series of mishnayos are presented, highlighting various characteristics in groups of four. Most of the mishnayos focus on a specific target: "Four traits of charity givers," "Four traits of *beis medrash* attendees," etc. But our mishnah focuses on a general theme: "Four traits in *a man.*" Apparently, then, the subject of our mishnah is pervasive, reflecting a person's essence and encompassing all areas of his activities and *avodah*. The Nesivos Sholom offers a variety of approaches, elucidating the mishnah along these lines.

The first basic approach interprets the mishnah as referring to the quality of "giving," delineating the difference between those who are inherently "givers" and those who are "takers." This quality really does cut to the root of a person, as it serves as a sort of litmus test of his inherent nature. One whose core is inherently good will be moved to constantly seek ways to benefit others; his greatest pleasure is to do good for others. In this way, he emulates Hashem's attribute, as He is the ultimate *Tov U'meitiv*. The mantra of such an individual will be "What's mine is yours and what's yours is yours." He himself despises gifts and is only concerned with giving to others. But one who lives only to take — "What's mine is mine and what's yours is mine" — is obviously in possession of a coarse and selfish nature.

Another aspect highlighted by the mishnah, beyond our inherent nature, is our level of *emunah*. Being a true giver necessitates a stark realization that, in the final analysis, nothing that we have is our own. Hashem is the ultimate Owner of everything; as such, whatever appears to be in our possession is really Hashem's and has merely been temporarily placed with us for safekeeping — to be used for His service. By internalizing this truth, we cannot and will not be able to state "What's mine is mine," for nothing, in truth, is ours. As such, giving from our self becomes the most natural state of affairs. One who does not give to others is obviously far from recognizing Who is the true Owner.

The mishnah can also be interpreted as referring to our overall *avodas Hashem*, underscoring the notion of intent as it relates to daily activities. Do we perform on behalf of Hashem, or are our activities primarily directed towards ourselves? "*Sheli*" can be understood as referring to our personal, earthly affairs, while "*Shelcha*" refers to what is "Yours" — that is, the spiritual endeavors of Torah and mitzvos. The true chassid dedicates even his mundane activities to Hashem, even eating and sleeping for the sake of Heaven. In effect, he tells the Creator that even *sheli*, "my physical needs," are in essence *Shelcha*, performed "for Your sake." And regarding his performance of actual mitzvos, these are likewise undertaken without selfish, ulterior motives, but purely for the sake of Hashem: *Shelcha Shelcha* — What is Yours is done for You. But the mishnah looks askance at one who takes the opposite approach, where his mundane activities are devoid of any elevated intent and even his spiritual activities are riddled with ulterior motives. Not only is his *sheli, sheli*, but even his *Shelcha* is *sheli*.

Thus the mishnah reflects the great lesson imparted to us by Avraham — that noble intent can so powerfully affect our deeds, transforming them to new levels. At the *Akeidah*, Avraham yearned so deeply in his heart to fulfill Hashem's will that even after being "exempted" from sacrificing his son, he still wished to complete this act. And so he sacrificed the ram with the intent that it should serve as the offering "in place of his son," and the yearnings of his heart successfully transformed this action, which was considered by the Torah as the completion of the actual *Akeidah*. This notion can permeate every facet of our lives; with the proper intent, our mundane activities can be transformed into spirituality, and our spiritual endeavors can truly soar and reach the heights.

פרק ה' משנה י"ט
כל אהבה שהיא תלויה בדבר
Any Love Which Is Conditional on Something

כָּל אַהֲבָה שֶׁהִיא תְלוּיָה בְדָבָר, בָּטֵל דָּבָר, בְּטֵלָה אַהֲבָה. וְשֶׁאֵינָהּ תְּלוּיָה בְדָבָר, אֵינָהּ בְּטֵלָה לְעוֹלָם. אֵיזוֹ הִיא אַהֲבָה הַתְּלוּיָה בְדָבָר, זוֹ אַהֲבַת אַמְנוֹן וְתָמָר. וְשֶׁאֵינָהּ תְּלוּיָה בְדָבָר, זוֹ אַהֲבַת דָּוִד וִיהוֹנָתָן.

Any love which is conditional on something – if that thing becomes nullified, the love will also be nullified. If it is not conditional on anything – it will never become nullified. What is an example of conditional love? This would be the love between Amnon and Tamar. What is an example of unconditional love? This would be the love between Dovid and Yehonasan.

GEMS FROM THE *SEFER NESIVOS SHOLOM*

SOURCES:

וְאָהַבְתָּ אֵת ה' אֱלֹקֶיךָ בְּכָל־לְבָבְךָ וּבְכָל־נַפְשְׁךָ וּבְכָל־מְאֹדֶךָ. (דברים ו' ה')

And you shall love Hashem your G-d, with all of your heart, all of your soul, and all of your resources. (*Devarim* 6:5)

בְּכָל מְאֹדֶךָ, בְּכָל מִדָּה וּמִדָּה שֶׁהוּא מוֹדֵד לְךָ הֱוֵי מוֹדֶה לוֹ בִּמְאֹד מְאֹד.
(משנה ברכות ט' ה')

"With all of your might" – with whatever measure Hashem metes out to you, be excessively grateful to Him. (*Mishnah Berachos* 9:5)

ה' צִלְּךָ עַל יַד יְמִינֶךָ. (תהלים קכ"א ה')

Hashem is your shadow upon your right hand. (*Tehillim* 121:5)

הֵן יִקְטְלֵנִי לוֹ אֲיַחֵל. (איוב י"ג ט"ו)

Even were He to kill me, I would still place my hope in Him. (*Iyov* 13:15)

בָּנִים אַתֶּם לַה' אֱלֹקֵיכֶם. (דברים י"ד א')

You are children of Hashem, your G-d. (*Devarim* 14:1)

קוּדְשָׁא בְּרִיךְ הוּא אוֹרַיְיתָא וְיִשְׂרָאֵל כּוּלְּהוּ חַד. (זהר)

Hashem, the Torah, and Yisroel are all one. (*Zohar*)

וְאָמַרְתָּ אֶל־פַּרְעֹה כֹּה אָמַר ה' בְּנִי בְכֹרִי יִשְׂרָאֵל. (שמות ד' כ"ב)

And you shall say to Pharoah: "So says Hashem: 'Yisroel is My first-born son.'" (*Shemos* 4:22)

אָנֹכִי ה' אֱלֹקֶיךָ אֲשֶׁר הוֹצֵאתִיךָ מֵאֶרֶץ מִצְרַיִם מִבֵּית עֲבָדִים. (שם כ' ב')

I am Hashem Your G-d, Who took you out from the land of Egypt, from the house of bondage. (*ibid.* 20:2)

כל אהבה שהיא תלויה בדבר

עֲשָׂרָה נִסְיוֹנוֹת נִתְנַסָּה אַבְרָהָם אָבִינוּ וְעָמַד בְּכֻלָּם, לְהוֹדִיעַ כַּמָּה חִבָּתוֹ שֶׁל אַבְרָהָם אָבִינוּ. (אבות ה׳)

Avraham Avinu was tested with ten trials and withstood them all – to make known the extent of the love of Avraham Avinu. (*Avos* 5)

כָּל הַכְּתוּבִים קֹדֶשׁ, וְשִׁיר הַשִּׁירִים קֹדֶשׁ קָדָשִׁים. (ידים ג׳ ה׳)

All of the Writings are holy; *Shir Hashirim* is holy of holies. (*Yadayim* 3:5)

מוּסַר ה׳ בְּנִי אַל־תִּמְאָס. (משלי ג׳ י״א)

My son, do not despise Hashem's admonishment. (*Mishlei* 3:11)

פרק ה׳

589

GEMS FROM THE *SEFER NESIVOS SHOLOM*

Unconditional Love

In the world of relationships, there is the concept of a "fair-weather friend." This is someone who displays loyalty and devotion — as long as the chips are up. When there's no longer much to be gained from the friendship in the eyes of this companion, that sense of loyalty suddenly wanes.

Obviously, no one really appreciates a "friend" whose dependability is questionable at best. What is important for us to realize, however, is that it is quite possible that we conduct ourselves in this very fashion when it comes to the most important relationship of all: the love a Yid should bear towards *Hakadosh Baruch Hu*. And so, we must be on the lookout: As it relates to Hashem — do we behave as just a fair-weather friend? The Maggid of Kozhnitz *ztz"l* (*Avodas Yisroel – Avos*) perceives this message in the mishnah from *Avos*.

Reciprocal Relationship

The mishnah states, כָּל אַהֲבָה שֶׁהִיא תְלוּיָה בְדָבָר, בָּטֵל דָּבָר, בְּטֵלָה אַהֲבָה. וְשֶׁאֵינָהּ תְּלוּיָה בְדָבָר, אֵינָהּ בְּטֵלָה לְעוֹלָם — *Whatever love is dependent on a specific cause, if that cause is nullified, the love will likewise be nullified. If, however, it is not dependent on any specific cause, then it will never become nullified.* The mishnah is usually understood to be referring to interpersonal relationships, and it goes on to cite some real-life examples (Amnon and Tamar, Dovid Hamelech and Yehonasan). However, the Maggid of Kozhnitz contends that the mishnah can also be understood on another level, referring to the love a Yid should bear towards Hashem. Such love must be unconditional in nature — as such, it will endure forever.

What the mishnah warns against is playing the role of a fair-weather friend. Someone may be full of gratitude and love for Hashem — for he perceives that, at least for now, things are going well. But one's love for Hashem should not just be predicated on the fact that things are going his way. The wheel of fortune may turn at some point — and then what? One's love for Hashem will dissipate along with the prosperity and success upon which it was predicated. Only one whose love for Hashem is unconditional will be able to maintain it with consistency.

The imperative to love Hashem regardless of circumstances is reflected in the familiar passage from *Krias Shema* (*Devarim* 6:5): וְאָהַבְתָּ אֵת ה' אֱלֹקֶיךָ בְּכָל-לְבָבְךָ וּבְכָל-נַפְשְׁךָ וּבְכָל-מְאֹדֶךָ — *And you shall love Hashem your G-d, with all of your heart, all of your soul, and all of your* **resources** (*your* **me'od**). The mishnah (*Berachos* 9:5) expounds this latter phrase based on its *shoresh*: בְּכָל מְאֹדֶךָ - בְּכָל מִדָּה וּמִדָּה שֶׁהוּא מוֹדֵד לְךָ הֱוֵי מוֹדֶה לוֹ בִּמְאֹד מְאֹד — "*With all of your* **me'od**": *whatever* **measure** *Hashem* **metes out** *to you, be* **excessively grateful** *to Him*. Whatever befalls a person — no matter how apparently difficult — does come from Hashem and is intended solely for one's ultimate benefit. True love for Hashem must transcend whatever particular circumstances one may encounter. This form of love has a permanence that endures forever — אֵינָהּ בְּטֵלָה לְעוֹלָם.

This phrase of the mishnah, אֵינָהּ בְּטֵלָה לְעוֹלָם — *It shall never be nullified*, hints to another aspect of this love. When a Yid loves Hashem unconditionally, it triggers a reciprocal reaction from Above. Hashem in turn showers His enduring love upon the entirety of Klal Yisroel. The *passuk* characterizes a Yid's relationship with Hashem in the following terms: *Hashem tzilcha* — "Hashem is your shadow" (*Tehillim* 121:5). When a person moves his hand, his shadow moves in perfect coordination. Similarly, in large measure, the way the *Yidden* conduct themselves vis-à-vis their Creator determines how Hashem will comport Himself towards us. When a Jew exhibits love for Hashem, he triggers a reciprocal love from Him for the people of Yisroel; when that love is full and unconditional, Hashem loves us unconditionally, as well. In this manner, by loving Hashem in this fashion, it has the effect of bringing love down לְעוֹלָם, to the world.

To What Extent

Of course, there are varying degrees to which a person can love Hashem, of varying levels of greatness. There are people for whom everything seems to go well. Such individuals can and should certainly love Hashem, but, as mentioned, the real test comes when one faces difficulty and challenge. While more daunting, a Yid can still rise to the occasion and exude love for Hashem — unconditional love — despite the rigorous circumstances.

The *Chovos Halevavos* (*Sha'ar Ahavas Hashem* 5:81) provides a portrayal of someone who utilized the most trying circumstances to achieve the pinnacle of *ahavas Hashem*. This righteous Yid was completely destitute; he had no food to eat, clothing to wear, or candles to provide light. He would arise at night and declare, "My G-d, You have starved me and left me naked; You have seated me in the deep darkness of the night; yet, You have shown me Your might and greatness. As such, even if You were to set me on fire, it would only increase my love for You and my joy and contentment with You." In this respect, this pious individual related the same sentiment expressed by Iyov: הֵן יִקְטְלֵנִי לוֹ אֲיַחֵל — *Even were He to kill me, I would still place my hope in Him* (*Iyov* 13:15). Under even slightly easier living conditions, this individual may not have achieved such an extraordinary level of unconditional love of Hashem.

The love in which a Yid is obligated comes in three forms: *ahavas Hashem*, *ahavas Yisroel*, and *ahavas haTorah* (love of Torah). The Nesivos Sholom points out that these three aspects are all interrelated, the latter two being outgrowths of *ahavas Hashem*. When a person develops a complete love for Hashem, he will automatically come to love his fellow Jew, as well. After all, all *Yidden* are Hashem's children, as the Torah attests: בָּנִים אַתֶּם לַה' אֱלֹקֵיכֶם — *You are children of Hashem, your G-d* (*Devarim* 14:1). As children of the same Father, *Yidden* see each other as siblings, loving each other accordingly. Following on the heels of these is *ahavas haTorah*, for it relates to the entity of connection. As the *Zohar* states, קוּדְשָׁא בְּרִיךְ הוּא אוֹרַיְיתָא וְיִשְׂרָאֵל כּוּלְהוּ חַד — *The Holy One Blessed be He, the Torah, and Yisroel are all one*. This remarkable synthesis is achieved by way of the Torah; it serves as the bridge through which a Yid is able to achieve *d'veikus* with Hashem. One who has undying love for Hashem and Yisroel will necessarily bear this love for the object that brings them all together.

כל אהבה שהיא תלויה בדבר

From the Start

When did Klal Yisroel become the Chosen People, Hashem's special and beloved nation? One might assume that this took place with the giving of the Torah on Har Sinai. The *Yidden* had gone through an extended purification process and at that point had achieved extremely elevated levels. And, indeed, their commitment to Hashem was clarified and solidified through this great event.

But the truth is, Hashem's great love for His people was revealed much earlier, even when the *Yidden* occupied the lowest rungs of spirituality. In the thick of the bondage in Egypt, the *Yidden* had descended to the forty-ninth level of impurity — out of fifty levels. Nevertheless, at that very time, Hashem expressed just how dear and special Klal Yisroel were to Him. The very first time Hashem sent Moshe to appear before Pharaoh to demand that he release the slaves, He sent him with the following message: *B'ni bechori Yisroel* — "Yisroel is My first-born son" (*Shemos* 4:22).

The significance of this announcement at such an early date is profound indeed. For it reveals that just as a Yid's love for Hashem should be unconditional, not dependent on favorable circumstances or any other factor, so is Hashem's love for Klal Yisroel. He loves us unconditionally — no matter what our failings may be. To make this point, He purposely declared the Jews to be His special, Chosen People while they were still in Egypt. Specifically when they had sunken to the depths of impurity; specifically when the Attribute of Judgment could rightfully argue that they did not deserve salvation any more than did their Egyptian counterparts, on the grounds that "these and those are both idol-worshippers"; specifically then, He chose to call them *B'ni bechori Yisroel*!

In so doing, Hashem imparted this vital lesson: that He loves Klal Yisroel with an אַהֲבָה שֶׁאֵינָהּ תְּלוּיָה בְדָבָר — a love that is not dependent on any one factor. This is the type of love that אֵינָהּ בְּטֵלָה לְעוֹלָם — *never becomes nullified*. Had Hashem chosen us by *Kabbalas HaTorah*, the time of our greatest heights, our selection might have been viewed as conditional on our deservedness. Hashem chose us much earlier to dispel such a notion.

The above phenomenon is alluded to in the first of the *Aseres Hadibros*: אָנֹכִי ה׳ אֱלֹקֶיךָ אֲשֶׁר הוֹצֵאתִיךָ מֵאֶרֶץ מִצְרַיִם מִבֵּית עֲבָדִים — *I am Hashem your G-d, Who took you out from the land of Egypt, from the house of bondage* (*Shemos* 20:2). This directive for *emunah* actually contains two components: first, we are enjoined to believe and know of Hashem's existence — "I am Hashem"; and second, that Hashem is *Elokecha* — He is "*your* G-d," reflecting the intimate relationship of בָּנִים אַתֶּם לַה׳ אֱלֹקֵיכֶם. The *passuk* continues, making a point of detailing when it was that this special relationship was established: אֲשֶׁר הוֹצֵאתִיךָ מֵאֶרֶץ מִצְרַיִם. It was when Klal Yisroel were in Egypt, the nadir of their spiritual existence, that Hashem revealed His undying and unconditional love for His children.

Love and Trials

The concept of unconditional love — how a Yid should love Hashem in the face of whatever circumstances he encounters — provides much insight into the issue of *nisyonos*. As was mentioned in an earlier mishnah (5:3), Avraham had to undergo ten trials. The basic definition of a *nisayon* is a "test" that determines the devotion of the individual in question. Regarding the trials of Avraham Avinu, we can readily see how some of his trials certainly fall within this categorization. In his first trial, Avraham was presented with a choice: submit to idol worship or be cast into a fiery furnace. He endured this trial, choosing the latter rather than recant his firm belief in the One True Hashem (and, as we know, he was miraculously saved). The final trial of the *Akeidas Yitzchak* likewise tested his level of devotion: would he relinquish his precious son to fulfill Hashem's will? Of course, here he succeeded as well.

But the other *nisyonos* present something of a puzzle; what determination was involved with them? For example, one of the *nisyonos* entailed the incidence of a famine; in another, his wife, Sarah, was abducted and brought to the house of Pharaoh. These are also included in the mishnah's statement that Avraham Avinu underwent and succeeded in ten trials; but how, exactly, are these instances considered tests? There did not seem to be any choice involved in these matters, as they were presented as *faits accomplis*;

a famine came, his wife was taken. Excruciating circumstances, no doubt; but what was the test?

The discussion above clarifies the matter. This itself was the nature of these tests: to determine his level of *ahavah*. Was Avraham's love for Hashem an אַהֲבָה שֶׁאֵינָהּ תְּלוּיָה בְדָבָר, one that remained undiminished despite the excruciating circumstances? Avraham succeeded, demonstrating that his love was not in the least diminished by whatever tribulations he experienced.

The *Me'or Einayim* teaches that every Jew must undergo ten major trials in his lifetime, just like his ancestor, Avraham. These *nisyonos* are patterned after the types of trials that he also had to go through. Some of them may come in the form of challenges regarding specific mitzvos, entailing a difficult decision or the like. Others will be of the variety detailed above: a Yid may have to endure certain troubles or tribulations, which are inevitable parts of *Olam Hazeh*. The real test in these instances is to determine the strength and quality of his *ahavas Hashem*; can he endure these difficulties and still maintain an unbroken love of Hashem? Like his forefather, Avraham, has this Yid cultivated in his heart a sense of unconditional love for Hashem, one that will endure under all circumstances?

"Shir Hashirim Asher L'Shlomo..."

On some level, *Shir Hashirim* is considered the most sacred of all the holy tomes. The mishnah states, כָּל הַכְּתוּבִים קֹדֶשׁ, וְשִׁיר הַשִּׁירִים קֹדֶשׁ קָדָשִׁים — *All of the Writings are holy; Shir Hashirim is holy of holies* (*Yadayim* 3:5). Of obviously elevated status, the contents of this *sefer* are a song offered by Klal Yisroel as they express their burning and undying love for Hashem. As the *passuk* states (*Shir Hashirim* 8:6), כִּי־עַזָּה כַמָּוֶת אַהֲבָה...רְשָׁפֶיהָ רִשְׁפֵּי אֵשׁ שַׁלְהֶבֶתְיָה — *For the love is strong as death... its coals are fiery coals, a G-dly flame.* And when is it, exactly, that Klal Yisroel sings such a song of love to Hashem? In the beginning of his commentary to the *sefer*, Rashi explains the background. This is the song that Klal Yisroel sings, not in the heights of its grandeur, with the *Shechinah* resting in the Beis Hamikdash and Yisroel residing in their Land, but in the depths of their station in *golus*, in the throes of their widowhood. Amid the turmoil of *golus*, throughout the numerous exiles and trials and tribulations they had to endure, the reaction of Klal Yisroel is the song of *Shir Hashirim*. It is no wonder, then, why this *sefer* is considered "holy of holies"; it represents the highest levels of *ahavas Hashem*, an אַהֲבָה שֶׁאֵינָהּ תְּלוּיָה בְדָבָר, which endures throughout the long night of exile.

This undying love, both of Hashem for His people and vice versa, has found expression in numerous ways. For example, the *passuk* states (*Mishlei* 3:11), מוּסַר ה׳ בְּנִי אַל־תִּמְאָס. The standard rendering of this verse has Shlomo Hamelech offering advice to his fellow Yid, encouraging him to accept Hashem's chastisement: "My son, do not be repelled from the chastisement of Hashem." The *Yesod Ha'avodah*, however, offers a homiletic interpretation. *Mussar Hashem*, that is, the *mussar* that Hashem gives, comprises the following: *B'ni!* — "You are My son"; as such, *al timas!* — "Do not allow yourself to become repulsive." Hashem is reminding a Jew that he will always be the son of the King. "You are the son of the King, Who loves you for all time!" This affirmation is the most powerful ethical lecture, as it drives home the lesson that improper behavior is simply unbecoming for someone of such privileged and august stature.

Klal Yisroel expressed their undying love for Hashem at Har Sinai. They proclaimed their unwavering devotion as they signaled their acceptance of the Torah. As one voice, they declared (*Shemos* 24:7), *Na'aseh v'nishma* — "We shall do and we shall listen." What this legendary declaration intimates is that no matter what the circumstances, through thick and thin, we will lovingly follow in Your ways.

Perhaps this relationship of reciprocal love between Hashem and Yisroel is best summed up by none other than Eliyahu Hanavi. The Midrash (*Tanna D'vei Eliyahu Rabbah* 26:5) records this teaching in his name: אֵי זוֹ הִיא אַהֲבָה...שֶׁאֵינָהּ תְּלוּיָה בְדָבָר... כְּגוֹן אַהֲבַת אַבְרָהָם יִצְחָק וְיַעֲקֹב... לָהֶן וְלִבְנֵיהֶן וְלִבְנֵי בְנֵיהֶן עַד סוֹף כָּל הַדּוֹרוֹת — *What is (an example of) unconditional love? For instance, the love of Avraham, Yitzchak, and Yaakov (who love Hashem. Hashem, in turn loves) them, their children and descendants throughout all generations.*

כל אהבה שהיא תלויה בדבר

In Summary

The mishnah, which discusses unconditional love, appears to be talking about interpersonal relationships. Nevertheless, the Maggid of Kozhnitz understands its message as referring, as well, to the love a Yid must bear towards *Hakadosh Baruch Hu*. It is not sufficient to merely love Hashem so long as things are going well; that is *ahavah hateluyah b'davar* (love that depends on a cause). Such *ahavah* does not endure, for as soon as challenges arise, the *ahavah* will be nullified. Rather, a Yid should develop an *ahavah* towards Hashem that is *einah teluyah b'davar* (not dependent on a cause); that is, his love for Hashem continues in strength even in the face of difficult circumstances. There are even such elevated *Yidden* who utilized the most trying situations to increase their unconditional *ahavah* of Hashem. Such *ahavah* endures forever.

In fact, this *ahavah* is what defines a *nisayon*. There are certain *nisyonos* that require the subject to make a decision, such as with Avraham Avinu in Ur Casdim: would he acquiesce to idolatry or remain steadfast and thus be cast into the fiery furnace? He passed, of course, was cast into the flames on account of his belief in Hashem, and emerged unscathed. But there are other *nisyonos* that don't seem to hinge upon making the "right" decision; rather, it is a question of endurance. These are *nisyonos* where difficult challenges and circumstances beset the individual; the test is to determine his level of *ahavah*. One whose *ahavah* is not *talui b'davar* will continue to love Hashem despite the difficulties he must face.

A key facet of this אַהֲבָה שֶׁאֵינָהּ תְּלוּיָה בְדָבָר is that it is reciprocal in nature. Regarding one's relationship with *Hakadosh Baruch Hu*, the *passuk* states: *Hashem tzilcha* — "Hashem is your shadow." When a person moves his hand, his shadow moves in parallel with him. When a Yid loves Hashem with an אַהֲבָה שֶׁאֵינָהּ תְּלוּיָה בְדָבָר, He responds in kind, loving the *Yidden* with an unconditional love.

In fact, Hashem demonstrated from the start that His love for His people was an unconditional love. Rather than waiting until the

פרק ה'

giving of the Torah at Har Sinai to proclaim His special affinity for His children, He did so while they were still in the midst of Egyptian bondage. This is quite remarkable, for at the time, they were on an extremely low spiritual level, having sunk to the forty-ninth level of impurity. Nevertheless, it was specifically then that Hashem declared of Bnei Yisroel, *B'ni bechori Yisroel* — "Yisroel is My first-born son." Hashem purposely did not wait until they had attained an elevated level by Har Sinai to confer on them their status as the Chosen People. He felt that that may impart the wrong message, as if His love for them was conditional upon their maintaining a high spiritual level. By proclaiming His special love for them when they were at the nadir of their spiritual existence in Egypt, Hashem was thereby demonstrating that His love for them was unconditional and hence would last forever.

Eliyahu Hanavi sums up this wonderful state of affairs. In supplying examples of אַהֲבָה שֶׁאֵינָהּ תְּלוּיָה בְדָבָר, he chose the love harbored by Avraham, Yitzchak, and Yaakov for *Hakadosh Baruch Hu* and the reciprocal love *Hakadosh Baruch Hu* harbored for them and their descendants for eternity.

פרק ה' משנה כ'
כל מחלוקת שהיא לשם שמים
Any Dispute Which Is for the Sake of Heaven

בָּל מַחֲלוֹקֶת שֶׁהִיא לְשֵׁם שָׁמַיִם, סוֹפָהּ לְהִתְקַיֵּם. וְשֶׁאֵינָהּ לְשֵׁם שָׁמַיִם, אֵין סוֹפָהּ לְהִתְקַיֵּם. אֵיזוֹ הִיא מַחֲלוֹקֶת שֶׁהִיא לְשֵׁם שָׁמַיִם, זוֹ מַחֲלוֹקֶת הִלֵּל וְשַׁמַּאי. וְשֶׁאֵינָהּ לְשֵׁם שָׁמַיִם, זוֹ מַחֲלוֹקֶת קֹרַח וְכָל עֲדָתוֹ:

Any dispute which is for the sake of Heaven is destined to endure. That which is not for the sake of Heaven, is not destined to endure. What is an example of a "dispute for the sake of Heaven"? This would be the dispute between Hillel and Shamai. And that which is "not for the sake of Heaven"? This would be the dispute of Korach and his whole assembly.

GEMS FROM THE *SEFER NESIVOS SHOLOM*

SOURCES:

הִבָּדְלוּ מִתּוֹךְ הָעֵדָה הַזֹּאת וַאֲכַלֶּה אֹתָם כְּרָגַע. (במדבר ט"ז כ"א)

Separate yourselves from the midst of this assembly, and in a moment I will exterminate them. *(Bamidbar 16:21)*

קוב"ה אורייתא וישראל כולהו חד. (זוהר)

Hashem, the Torah, and Yisroel are all one. *(Zohar)*

עַל־כֵּן יֵאָמַר בְּסֵפֶר מִלְחֲמֹת ה' אֶת־וָהֵב בְּסוּפָה. (במדבר כ"א י"ד)

Therefore it is stated in the Book of the Wars of Hashem: "What was given by the Sea of Reeds." *(Bamidbar 21:14)*

אפי' האב ובנו, הרב ותלמידו, שעוסקין בתורה...נעשים אויבים זה את זה, ואינם זזים משם עד שנעשים אוהבים זה את זה, שנאמר: את והב בסופה. (קידושין ל:)

Even a father and his son, or a *rebbi* and his disciple, who engage in Torah study together...(at first) become as enemies towards each other; but they do not budge from their place before becoming beloved to each other. As it states *(Bamidbar 21:14)*: "Es vaheiv (the love) b'sufah (at its end)." *(Kiddushin 30b)*

וַיְדַבֵּר ה' אֶל־מֹשֶׁה... סָרוּ מַהֵר מִן־הַדֶּרֶךְ אֲשֶׁר צִוִּיתִם עָשׂוּ לָהֶם עֵגֶל מַסֵּכָה וַיִּשְׁתַּחֲווּ־לוֹ... וְעַתָּה הַנִּיחָה לִּי וְיִחַר־אַפִּי בָהֶם וַאֲכַלֵּם. (שמות ל"א ז'-י')

And Hashem spoke to Moshe: "(The people) have turned quickly away from the way in which I commanded them (to follow); they have made for themselves a molten image of a calf, and have bowed to it... And now, leave Me be, and My wrath shall flare against them, and I will exterminate them." *(Shemos 31:7-10)*

וַיֹּצִיאוּ דִּבַּת הָאָרֶץ אֲשֶׁר תָּרוּ אֹתָהּ אֶל־בְּנֵי יִשְׂרָאֵל... וַתִּשָּׂא כָּל־הָעֵדָה וַיִּתְּנוּ אֶת־קוֹלָם וַיִּבְכּוּ הָעָם בַּלַּיְלָה הַהוּא... וַיֹּאמְרוּ אִישׁ אֶל־אָחִיו נִתְּנָה רֹאשׁ

פרקי אבות

600

כל מחלוקת שהיא לשם שמים

וְנָשׁוּבָה מִצְרָיְמָה... וַיֹּאמֶר ה' אֶל־מֹשֶׁה עַד־אָנָה יְנַאֲצֻנִי הָעָם הַזֶּה... אַכֶּנּוּ בַדֶּבֶר וְאוֹרִשֶׁנּוּ. (במדבר י״ג ל״ב-י״ד י״ב)

And they submitted a libelous report to Bnei Yisroel against the Land which they had spied out... And the entire congregation raised and gave forth their voices, and the nation cried on that night... And one man said to another: "Let us appoint a leader, and return to Egypt."... And Hashem said to Moshe: "Until when shall this nation antagonize Me... I shall smite them with pestilence, and destroy them." (Bamidbar 13:32-14:12)

פִּינְחָס בֶּן־אֶלְעָזָר בֶּן־אַהֲרֹן הַכֹּהֵן הֵשִׁיב אֶת־חֲמָתִי מֵעַל בְּנֵי־יִשְׂרָאֵל בְּקַנְאוֹ אֶת־קִנְאָתִי בְּתוֹכָם וְלֹא־כִלִּיתִי אֶת־בְּנֵי־יִשְׂרָאֵל בְּקִנְאָתִי. (שם כ״ה י״א)

Pinchas the son of Elazar the son of Aharon the Kohen has averted My anger from Bnei Yisroel, in avenging My zeal amongst them, and I have not exterminated Bnei Yisroel in My zeal. (ibid. 25:11)

מִבִּרְכָתוֹ שֶׁל אוֹתוֹ רָשָׁע אַתָּה לָמֵד מֶה הָיָה בְּלִבּוֹ. (סנהדרין ק״ה:)

From the blessing of that wicked one, you can derive what had really been in his heart. (Sanhedrin 105b)

לֹא־הִבִּיט אָוֶן בְּיַעֲקֹב וְלֹא־רָאָה עָמָל בְּיִשְׂרָאֵל. (במדבר ל״ג כ״א)

He has not looked upon sin in Yaakov, nor seen iniquity amongst Yisroel. (Bamidbar 23:21)

פרק ה'

The Mechanics of Dispute

There are many items that give the outer appearance of simplicity and straightforwardness. Take a car, for example. On the surface, it may appear sleek and shiny, a streamlined unit perfectly suited for a smooth ride. But when you open up the hood, the picture changes dramatically. Suddenly, you are confronted with a complex network of wires, gadgets, machinery, and instructions. There is a complicated and involved system in operation that provides that smooth ride.

Explosives share this characteristic. After all, a bomb can have the appearance of a simple shell. The classic picture of a round, black ball comes to mind. But the inside is likewise a mass of intertwined wires and electric gadgetry, which all operate in tandem to produce the desired deadly result.

And so it is with that most nefarious form of explosive: *machlokes*. *Chazal* offer stark warnings against its destructive force. Its danger is known and may seem readily apparent, as anyone who has witnessed a cantankerous encounter or widespread dissension can testify. But, as we shall see, there is even more that takes place beneath the surface, as the processes it sets in motion wreak profound and far-reaching devastation.

The mishnah in *Avos* that discusses this matter begins on a positive note. It extols the virtues of a "pristine" dispute, in contrast with the characteristics of the harmful sort. It begins: כָּל מַחֲלוֹקֶת שֶׁהִיא לְשֵׁם שָׁמַיִם, סוֹפָהּ לְהִתְקַיֵּם. וְשֶׁאֵינָהּ לְשֵׁם שָׁמַיִם, אֵין סוֹפָהּ לְהִתְקַיֵּם — *Any dispute which is for the sake of Heaven, is destined (literally: its end will be) to endure, while one that is not for the sake of Heaven is not destined to endure.* While it seems clear that the mishnah is in favor of a dispute that is for the sake of Heaven, the commentators express uncertainty regarding the mishnah's exact meaning: what is this notion of "enduring" of which the mishnah speaks?

The mishnah then provides examples; but the presentation seems somewhat inconsistent. אֵיזוֹ הִיא מַחֲלוֹקֶת שֶׁהִיא לְשֵׁם שָׁמַיִם, זוֹ מַחֲלוֹקֶת הִלֵּל וְשַׁמַּאי. וְשֶׁאֵינָהּ לְשֵׁם שָׁמַיִם, זוֹ מַחֲלוֹקֶת קֹרַח וְכָל עֲדָתוֹ — *What is an example of a "dispute for the sake of Heaven"? This would be the dispute between Hillel and*

כל מחלוקת שהיא לשם שמים

Shamai. And that which is "not for the sake of Heaven"? This would be the dispute of Korach and his whole company. The commentators note that when discussing the positive form of *machlokes*, it mentions the disputants: Hillel vs. Shamai. But when supplying the example for the negative form of *machlokes* — that which is not *l'sheim Shamayim* — the mishnah identifies only the side of the agitators: "the *machlokes* of Korach and his whole assembly." In keeping with the first example, why not state, "the *machlokes* of Korach and Moshe"?

Examining some key aspects of Korach's rebellion will shed much light on these issues.

Letters of Life

The basics of the Korach narrative are well known. Korach publicly challenges the authority of Moshe and Aharon, instigating many others to protest with him against the revered leaders of Klal Yisroel. A test is arranged, whereby both Aharon and Korach's followers will offer incense; the "real" *kohen* will be determined by whose offering is accepted by Hashem.

At one point, things take a dramatic turn. Hashem instructs Moshe and Aharon: הִבָּדְלוּ מִתּוֹךְ הָעֵדָה הַזֹּאת וַאֲכַלֶּה אֹתָם כְּרָגַע — *Separate yourselves from the midst of this assembly, and in a moment I will exterminate them* (*Bamidbar* 16:21). The Ramban points out that "this assembly" does not refer to the limited company comprising Korach's intimate following; rather, it was all of Klal Yisroel who faced the prospect of extermination at that time. While originally it was only Korach who spoke against the leadership, as the events progressed, the entire public became caught up in the contest. Who would "prevail" in the incense test, they wondered. The fact that such thoughts even entered their minds constituted a weakening in their acceptance of their *rebbi's* leadership and his power of prophecy, and was ultimately considered as a lack of reliance on Hashem Himself. Through such unacceptable thoughts they incurred the punishment of death at the hands of Heaven, and it was only through Moshe's intercession that they were spared from complete annihilation.

As unfortunate as this turn of events was, it still appears that the prospective punishment may not have fit the crime. The general populace didn't outright and outwardly rebel against and reject Moshe and Hashem; they merely bided their time to see where the chips would fall. While not a display of stellar loyalty, was it really something for which the entire nation deserved to be wiped out?!

The Nesivos Sholom explains the issue based on the well-known statement of *Chazal*, which so beautifully and succinctly describes the most hallowed and unique relationship in the world: קוּדְשָׁא בְּרִיךְ הוּא אוֹרַיְיתָא וְיִשְׂרָאֵל כּוּלְהוּ חַד — *Hashem, the Torah, and Yisroel are all one* (cf. *Zohar Vayikra*). He cites the sacred source *Me'or Einayim*, which provides a fascinating and revealing exposition of the profundity of this statement. Klal Yisroel is comprised of 600,000 *shorshei neshamos* (roots of souls). This is no random number, for it corresponds to the 600,000 *osiyos* (letters) that comprise the Torah; that is, each *neshamah* is intimately connected with one *os* (letter) from the Torah. In this way the Torah serves as the bridge, so to speak, between a Yid and Hashem. Each *neshamah* derives its sustenance — that is, the spiritual emanation of blessing poured down to it by Hashem above — through its attachment to its *os* of the Torah. While the precise particulars may be above our ability to fully grasp, this notion helps to account in some basic way for the continuum of *Yisroel-Oraisa-v'Kudsha Brich Hu*.

And while the full depth of the matter may be beyond our reach, the *Me'or Einayim* relates another crucial detail we can appreciate. There is a condition for this "mechanism" to work, for a Yid to receive his *hashpa'ah* (emanation of blessing) through his *os* of the Torah. For the effect to be complete, the *osiyos* of the Torah must function as a unit.

And this is the devastation wrought by *machlokes* and *pirud* (division). A Yid involved in divisiveness places himself into a situation of severe danger; for his *os* — which is his lifeline — becomes separated, in some spiritual sense, from the remainder of the *osiyos* of Klal Yisroel's Torah. It is as if this *os* now stands alone, no longer even part of a word, let alone functioning together with the rest of the Torah. With this separation, the *os* no longer functions as a conduit of the Heavenly light of *hashpa'ah* — leaving this Yid cut off from the source of his existence.

A prevalent practice mentioned in the *sefarim hakedoshim* can be understood in light of the above. They state that before engaging in any prayer of mitzvah, a person should accept upon himself to fulfill the mitzvah of *V'ahavta l'rei'acha kamocha* — "You shall love your fellow as yourself" (*Vayikra* 19:18). For a person involved in strife has caused his personal *os* to be separated from the rest of the Torah, no longer able to provide his soul with the necessary sustenance it needs to endure. This unfortunate and perilous state of affairs can be rectified through the unifying act of loving one's fellow *Yidden*; by reconnecting with them, his *os* once again becomes united with the remainder of the *osiyos* of the Torah and can once again provide him with his vital *hashpa'ah*.

In any event, we can now understand how it was that the Yidden during the episode of the rebellion were left open to the harsh prospect of complete eradication. As they skirted such an intense form of *machlokes*, almost the entirety of the *osiyos* of Klal Yisroel's Torah underwent separation en masse. Thus, the multitude was cut off from their vital life source, no longer able to tap into the Divine *hashpa'ah* through their representative *osiyos*. Left in such a state, the terrifying result was expressed in the sentiment: הִבָּדְלוּ מִתּוֹךְ הָעֵדָה הַזֹּאת וַאֲכַלֶּה אֹתָם כְּרָגַע — *Separate yourselves from the midst of this assembly, and in a moment I will exterminate them.*

Love and Strife

Not every form of (what appears to be) strife has this cataclysmic effect. A truly noble *machlokes* — one which is *l'sheim Shamayim* — does not cause a "shake-up" of the *osiyos*, for a simple reason: in effect, it is not a *machlokes* at all.

There is a recurring phrase in Talmudic literature which states: הוֹכִיחַ סוֹפוֹ עַל תְּחִילָּתוֹ — *The end is revealing about the beginning* (*Nedarim* 48a). One of the ways this is manifest is in this very phenomenon of a *machlokes l'sheim Shamayim*. *Chazal* discuss a common instance of combat among companions — something that takes place whenever erstwhile colleagues come together to engage in robust Torah study. To the outside observer, the ensuing debating session may appear fierce and rancorous. The Gemara (*Kiddushin* 30b) describes the scenario: אֲפִי׳ הָאָב וּבְנוֹ, הָרַב וְתַלְמִידוֹ, שֶׁעוֹסְקִין בַּתּוֹרָה...נַעֲשִׂים אוֹיְבִים זֶה אֶת זֶה, וְאֵינָם זָזִים מִשָּׁם עַד שֶׁנַּעֲשִׂים אוֹהֲבִים זֶה אֶת זֶה, שֶׁנֶּאֱמַר: אֶת וָהֵב בְּסוּפָה — *Even a father and son, or a* rebbi *and his disciple, who engage in Torah study together... (at first) become as enemies towards each other; but they do not budge from their place before becoming beloved to each other. As it states (Bamidbar 21:14): "Es vaheiv (the love) b'sufah (at its end)."* While the beginning certainly looked cantankerous, it would be erroneous to conclude that this was anything but an exercise in harmony. The "end" proves the beginning: As they remain, at the conclusion, steadfast friends, their engagement was anything but true discord.

The *passuk* the Gemara cited is quite instructive, shedding much light on the understanding of our mishnah. In fact, the phrase of our mishnah — about which we expressed some perplexity — alludes to the verse and message contained in this teaching of *Chazal*: אֶת וָהֵב בְּסוּפָה — *There is love in* **its end**. This is the "end" to which our mishnah was referring when it stated: כָּל מַחֲלוֹקֶת שֶׁהִיא לְשֵׁם שָׁמַיִם, סוֹפָהּ לְהִתְקַיֵּם — *Any dispute which is for the sake of Heaven,* **in its end** *it shall endure*. When Shamai and Hillel argued to prove a point in Torah, no lasting divisions were created that might have led to the disastrous consequences of "dislodged *osiyos*" from the Torah. On the contrary: love prevailed at the *sof* (end), proving that even the beginning was not divisiveness but vibrant and harmonious engagement. Instead of breaking apart, this type of activity actually brought the *Yidden* together; they and the Torah were strengthened. It was the *machlokes* of the sort waged by Korach that led to separation and destruction.

One point of difficulty remains — the matter of the apparently inconsistent presentation. Why did the mishnah deliver its examples in an asymmetrical manner? Illustrating the positive and productive form of *machlokes*, both parties to the dispute were mentioned: Hillel and Shamai. When discussing the negative type, however, one of the significant sides was deleted; instead of mentioning the "*machlokes* between Korach and Moshe," the mishnah speaks of the "*machlokes* of Korach and his assembly."

כל מחלוקת שהיא לשם שמים

This notion can be clarified in light of an insightful comment of the Noam Elimelech. It appears that not all was rosy on the side of Korach's assembly. The Noam Elimelech explains that, in fact, the members of this group were quarrelling among themselves! In contesting the leadership of Moshe and Aharon, these champions of "equal rights" were all vying among themselves for the position of *kohen gadol* (High Priest). Their sole point of unity was in their rebellion against Moshe Rabbeinu. And in this respect, Moshe was not even considered a disputant, as he had no argument but was confronted by the insubordinate agitators, who were spoiling for a fight. Thus, Moshe is not named in the mishnah as a party to the *machlokes*. Only Korach and his assembly were actual participants in strife.

Be a Part of It

Korach's rebellion was not the only time Klal Yisroel came to the brink of extermination. Altogether, the Torah records four episodes of national sin for which they incurred such a sentence (which was fortunately averted at the last moment): When the Golden Calf was fashioned and worshipped, Hashem initially declared to Moshe: וַיִּחַר אַפִּי...וַאֲכַלֵּם — *My wrath shall flare...and I will exterminate them* (*Shemos* 32:10). A similar reaction occurred when the spies returned from the Land and riled up the people: אַכֶּנּוּ בַדֶּבֶר וְאוֹרִשֶׁנּוּ — *I will smite them with pestilence and destroy them* (*Bamidbar* 14:12). We have already seen what was stated in the case of Korach's revolt: וַאֲכַלֶּה אֹתָם כְּרָגַע — *And I will exterminate them in a moment* (*ibid.* 16:21). Finally, Bnei Yisroel's straying after the daughters of Moav and the idol Ba'al Pe'or likewise brought them to the brink of extinction. Hashem revealed the extent of the danger that had hovered over the nation, averted only as a result of Pinchas's zealous action: וְלֹא כִלִּיתִי אֶת בְּנֵי יִשְׂרָאֵל — *And I have not annihilated Bnei Yisroel* (*ibid.* 25:11).

These sins were noteworthy, obviously, for the magnitude of the punishment they elicited. These were not the only instances where the nation had faltered; but they are the only sins recorded in the Torah that carried such grave consequences. What was it about these particular episodes that so set them apart from all other sinful encounters? As we shall see, they shared a crucial common denominator.

The Noam Elimelech expounds a wondrous concept that sheds much light on the issue. He accentuates the differences between the *prat* and the *klal* — Yidden as individuals as opposed to the collective body — and demonstrates just how powerful the distinction really is. We know well that the ideal state is when the Jewish people unite, functioning as a complete unit. But this is not just a matter of a more preferable mode; rather, the Jewish people as a whole comprise an entirely different entity — a new "world," if you will. This is the world known as *Kol Yisroel* (All Yisroel). This is a pristine world, for individuals may be sullied by sin but this body of *Kol Yisroel* is completely free of blemish. This, then, is a remarkable method for rectifying one's personal failings. By subsuming oneself within the greater collective body of Klal Yisroel, a Yid becomes infused with the pristine sanctity of the *Kol Yisroel* entity, an aura which sin does not penetrate.

A very similar idea is expressed already by the Maharal (*Derech Chaim* 2:4). He also states that sin exists only within the individual; the *tzibbur* is free of sin and hence impervious to the accusations of the Satan. This, explains the Maharal, is the meaning of *Chazal's* teaching (*Berachos* 8a), אֵימָתַי עֵת רָצוֹן – בְּשָׁעָה שֶׁהַצִּבּוּר מִתְפַּלְלִין — *When is considered an auspicious hour? At the time that the* tzibbur *is praying*. As the communal prayers in the synagogue are a function of the *tzibbur*, the Satan cannot interfere. It therefore is an opportunity for especial Divine favor.

One of the most notorious of our enemies, the wicked Bilaam, took aim at this very institution. Klal Yisroel merited a great deliverance from his attempts to bring calamity upon them through his normally effective curses, and his aborted imprecations were transformed into actual blessings. The extensive blessings (listed in *Parshas Balak*) give us a very good sense of what Bilaam's true intentions had been. As *Chazal* relate, מִבִּרְכָתוֹ שֶׁל אוֹתוֹ רָשָׁע אַתָּה לָמֵד מָה הָיָה בְּלִבּוֹ — *From the blessing of that wicked one, you can derive what had really been in his*

heart (*Sanhedrin* 105b); for whatever positive blessing emerged from his mouth was the reverse of what he had intended to say.

One of these blessings relates to the entity of Klal Yisroel directly, a clear indication that this body had been targeted for destruction. This is the blessing contained in the *passuk* (*Bamidbar* 23:21): לֹא־הִבִּיט אָוֶן בְּיַעֲקֹב וְלֹא־רָאָה עָמָל בְּיִשְׂרָאֵל — *He has not looked upon sin in Yaakov, nor seen iniquity among Yisroel*. In this *passuk*, the terms "Yaakov" and "Yisroel" are references to the greater *Kol Yisroel* body. Bilaam had attempted to use his machinations to hit at the very "world" that is *Kol Yisroel*, conjuring those communal sins that could possibly affect even this great entity. Instead, out of his mouth came the very opposite — an affirmation that this body is shielded from sin and its existence is assured. Hashem does *not* see sin when considering *Kol Yisroel*.

What were these unique sins that Bilaam sought to invoke? Apparently, they were of such magnitude that, sans the miraculous thwarting of his plans, they could have toppled the steadfastness of even *Kol Yisroel*, normally impervious to sin. The Nesivos Sholom identifies which sins these are — the four mentioned above, which brought Klal Yisroel to the brink of destruction.

These communal transgressions were able to shake the very foundations of *Kol Yisroel*. Thankfully, Moshe Rabbeinu intervened, and we see from the nature of his petition just what had been at stake. In the episode of Korach's rebellion, for example, Moshe pleaded before Hashem in response to the threat of annihilation: הָאִישׁ אֶחָד יֶחֱטָא וְעַל כָּל־הָעֵדָה תִּקְצֹף — *Could it be that one man would sin, and You would be angered at the entire congregation?* (*ibid.* 16:22). Moshe Rabbeinu sought desperately to defend and preserve the entity of *Kol Yisroel* even from the effects of sins such as these. Thus he insisted that the offense should not be viewed as a communal transgression; rather, it was perpetrated by individuals — *ish echad*. However, he contended, the communal world known as *Kol Yisroel* remained out of reach of the clutches of sin. And his argument prevailed; the entity of *Kol Yisroel* lives on in its unsullied state.

This whole notion delivers a most powerful lesson to every *yachid*

(individual). There are times when a Yid may feel somewhat forlorn; in either material or spiritual matters, he may feel that his situation has undergone a decline. Based on the above, however, we see that he may take heart. A wonderful opportunity awaits: become part of the *klal*. Subsumed within this august entity, this world of spiritual bliss, he will be part of a body over which sin does not reign.

In order to truly be part of the *klal*, however, there is something from which we must steer completely clear — the nefarious exercise of *machlokes*. As we have seen, the vital *hashpa'ah* necessary to sustain and better our life is channeled through our personal *os*. But the *os* can only function in this way if it remains as part of Klal Yisroel's communal Torah; strife will cause it to be separated, and its effectiveness will cease.

The ramifications of this lesson for the entirety of Klal Yisroel are far-reaching indeed. It was *pirud* and *machlokes*, through the medium of *sinas chinam* (baseless hatred), that caused the destruction of the Beis Hamikdash. It will be *ahavas Yisroel* that will reunite and strengthen the entity of Klal Yisroel, and enable the Beis Hamikdash to be rebuilt.

In Summary

From the Torah, from *Chazal*, we know that *machlokes* is a deplorable and destructive trait. Nevertheless, the mishnah in *Pirkei Avos* implies the existence of a positive form of *machlokes* — namely, a *machlokes l'sheim Shamayim*. In describing this entity, the mishnah employs a curious term, *sofah l'hiskayeim* — "it will endure in its end." This is in contrast to a *machlokes she'einah l'sheim Shamayim*, which is not destined to endure.

Based on the *Me'or Einayim*, the Nesivos Sholom provides some fascinating insights into the inner mechanics of *machlokes*, depicting the spiritual ramifications of engaging in this practice. קוב״ה אורייתא וְיִשְׂרָאֵל כּוּלְּהוּ חַד implies the steadfast connection between Yisroel and Hashem, bridged through the Torah. The 600,000 letters of the Torah

כל מחלוקת שהיא לשם שמים

correspond to the 600,000 *shorshei neshamos* of Klal Yisroel. As such, every Yid is connected to his individualized *os*; and through it he can tap into the *hashpa'ah* sent down from Hashem to sustain his life and provide him with blessing. But his *os* only operates in this fashion when it is a part of the unit of the entire Torah. By engaging in strife, his *os* becomes dislodged, in a sense; separated from the rest of the Torah, it can no longer provide him the sustenance he needs.

But a *machlokes l'sheim Shamayim* is of a different sort altogether; one engaged in earnest Torah debate — as were Hillel and Shamai — does not cause disruption to his personal *os*. The reason for this is that, in truth, it is not an act of discord at all but rather one of love. This is borne out by the *sof*, when, as *Chazal* state, the two "combatants" become united in friendship. The mishnah alludes to this phenomenon by borrowing the same terminology: *Sofah l'hiskayeim*.

The other instance of *machlokes* mentioned in our mishnah, that of Korach and his company, had far-reaching effects. At the time, Klal Yisroel had come to the brink of extermination; a feat repeated three other times, as recorded in the Torah. The common denominator among these episodes was the fact that the sin was communal in nature and threatened the collective entity of Klal Yisroel.

The Noam Elimelech reveals that there exists a world of its own known as *Kol Yisroel*. Individual Jews may at times fall prey to sin; but the entity of *Kol Yisroel*, the collective body of the *Yidden* functioning as a unit, is inherently beyond the reach of sin. Thus, it provides the individual with a remarkable opportunity to rectify his decline; for a Yid who has faltered, by becoming subsumed within the body of *Kol Yisroel*, enters a sanctified realm where sin does not prevail.

In these four instances, however, the entity of *Kol Yisroel* was under threat. The magnitude of these four communal sins shook the foundations of this institution, with the result being that Klal Yisroel faced extermination. Moshe Rabbeinu interceded, imploring that the act be viewed as the failings of individuals, whereas the *klal* itself should continue to be viewed as free from blemish. His entreaties were accepted, and the situation of לֹא־רָאָה עָמָל בְּיִשְׂרָאֵל was preserved.

פרק ה׳

611

Thus we discover a vital key to the rectification of the individual and the restoration of Klal Yisroel. Strife is the dividing and destructive force that severs the lifeline of the soul. Through unity and love for our fellow *Yidden*, we may unite in this pristine entity, entering the blissful world of *Kol Yisroel*. It was strife that destroyed the Beis Hamikdash, but it is love and unity that will rebuild it.

פרק ה׳ משנה כ״ב
תלמידיו של אברהם אבינו
Disciples of our Forefather Avraham

כָּל מִי שֶׁיֵּשׁ בְּיָדוֹ שְׁלֹשָׁה דְבָרִים הַלָּלוּ, מִתַּלְמִידָיו שֶׁל אַבְרָהָם אָבִינוּ. וּשְׁלֹשָׁה דְבָרִים אֲחֵרִים, מִתַּלְמִידָיו שֶׁל בִּלְעָם הָרָשָׁע. עַיִן טוֹבָה, וְרוּחַ נְמוּכָה, וְנֶפֶשׁ שְׁפָלָה, מִתַּלְמִידָיו שֶׁל אַבְרָהָם אָבִינוּ. עַיִן רָעָה, וְרוּחַ גְּבוֹהָה, וְנֶפֶשׁ רְחָבָה, מִתַּלְמִידָיו שֶׁל בִּלְעָם הָרָשָׁע. מַה בֵּין תַּלְמִידָיו שֶׁל אַבְרָהָם אָבִינוּ לְתַלְמִידָיו שֶׁל בִּלְעָם הָרָשָׁע. תַּלְמִידָיו שֶׁל אַבְרָהָם אָבִינוּ, אוֹכְלִין בָּעוֹלָם הַזֶּה וְנוֹחֲלִין בָּעוֹלָם הַבָּא, שֶׁנֶּאֱמַר לְהַנְחִיל אֹהֲבַי יֵשׁ, וְאֹצְרֹתֵיהֶם אֲמַלֵּא. אֲבָל תַּלְמִידָיו שֶׁל בִּלְעָם הָרָשָׁע יוֹרְשִׁין גֵּיהִנֹּם וְיוֹרְדִין לִבְאֵר שַׁחַת, שֶׁנֶּאֱמַר וְאַתָּה אֱלֹקִים תּוֹרִידֵם לִבְאֵר שַׁחַת, אַנְשֵׁי דָמִים וּמִרְמָה לֹא יֶחֱצוּ יְמֵיהֶם, וַאֲנִי אֶבְטַח בָּךְ:

All who have these three things are disciples of our forefather Avraham, and three other things are disciples of the wicked Bilaam. A good eye, a humble spirit, and a temperate soul apply to disciples of our forefather Avraham; a bad eye, an arrogant spirit, and an indulgent soul apply to disciples of the wicked Bilaam. What is the difference between the disciples of our forefather Avraham and the disciples of the wicked Bilaam? The disciples of our forefather Avraham eat in This World and inherit the Next World; as it states (*Mishlei* 8:21): "To bequeath those who love Me with plenty, and I will fill their storehouses." While the disciples of the wicked Bilaam inherit Gehinnom and descend to the netherworld; as it states (*Tehillim* 55:24): "And You, O G-d, shall bring them down to the pit of destruction, they are men of blood and deceit – they shall not attain half of their life-span; and I will place my trust in You."

תלמידיו של אברהם אבינו

SOURCES:

הַקִּנְאָה וְהַתַּאֲוָה וְהַכָּבוֹד מוֹצִיאִין אֶת הָאָדָם מִן הָעוֹלָם. (אבות ד')

Envy, desire, and pursuing honor remove a person from the world. (Avos 4)

אֵיזֶהוּ עָשִׁיר הַשָּׂמֵחַ בְּחֶלְקוֹ. (שם ד')

Who is wealthy? One who is happy with his portion. (ibid. 4)

תּוֹעֲבַת ה' כָּל־גְּבַהּ־לֵב. (משלי ט"ז ה')

Anyone proud of heart is an abomination to Hashem. (Mishlei 16:5)

טוֹב־עַיִן הוּא יְבֹרָךְ כִּי־נָתַן מִלַּחְמוֹ לַדָּל. (משלי כ"ב ט')

One who possesses a good eye shall be blessed, for he gives of his bread to the needy. (Mishlei 22:9)

אֵין אָדָם יוֹצֵא מִן הָעוֹלָם וַחֲצִי תַּאֲוָתוֹ בְּיָדוֹ. (קהלת רבה א' כ"ב)

No person leaves This World having fulfilled even half of his desires. (Koheles Rabbah 1:22)

אָנֹכִי עֹמֵד בֵּין־ה' וּבֵינֵיכֶם. (דברים ה' ה')

I was standing between Hashem and you. (Devarim 5:5)

וַיַּעַן אַבְרָהָם וַיֹּאמַר... וְאָנֹכִי עָפָר וָאֵפֶר. (בראשית י"ח כ"ז)

And Avraham answered, and he said... "I am but dust and ashes." (Bereishis 18:27)

מְאֹד מְאֹד הֱוֵי שְׁפַל רוּחַ. (אבות ד')

Be very, very, humble of spirit. (Avos 4)

פרק ה'

615

GEMS FROM THE *SEFER NESIVOS SHOLOM*

כָּל אָדָם שֶׁיֵּשׁ בּוֹ גַסּוּת הָרוּחַ אָמַר הקב"ה: אֵין אֲנִי וָהוּא יְכוֹלִין לָדוּר בָּעוֹלָם. (סוטה ה.)

(Regarding) anyone who has within him a prideful spirit, Hashem declares: "He and I cannot dwell in the world (together)." (*Sotah* 5a)

וַיֹּאמֶר מֹשֶׁה וְאַהֲרֹן... וְנַחְנוּ מָה כִּי תַלִּינוּ עָלֵינוּ. (שמות ט"ז ו', ז')

Moshe and Aharon said... "And what are we, that you should complain against us?" (*Shemos* 16:6, 7)

תלמידיו של אברהם אבינו

Are *middos tovos* important? Or are they just "nice" qualities, the icing on the cake of an observant life?

In a fairly well-known passage in his *sefer Sha'arei Kedushah*, Rav Chaim Vital poses a question. The Torah is replete with laws and commands, yet we find no explicit mitzvah enjoining us to develop proper *middos*. Why is that? He explains that it is essentially impossible for there to be a specific mitzvah concerning *middos*, for a simple reason: they themselves are the foundation of the Torah. There is no commandment to "be a Jew"; rather, it is a Jew who is commanded to fulfill the Torah. If one were not a Jew, the whole prospect of mitzvos doesn't begin in the first place. *Middos* operate on a similar plane, as they form the vessel for Torah. Without a firm basis of *middos tovos*, it is not really possible to properly accept the Torah.

As we shall see, this notion is underscored by the intriguing mishnah that discusses the qualities of Avraham's disciples, and those of Bilaam's. It's a perplexing mishnah, as the overall message seems clear enough, but the manner in which it is conveyed gives rise to a whole host of glaring issues:

- There is a lot of repetition here, particularly with the mention of "disciples of Avraham" and "disciples of Bilaam." The mishnah opens with, "Whoever has the following three traits is of the disciples of Avraham Avinu, and three other traits is of the disciples of Bilaam Harasha." In subsequently listing each set of three traits, the mishnah includes the "disciples" factor once again: "A good eye, a humble spirit, and a temperate soul apply to Avraham Avinu's disciples; a bad eye, an arrogant spirit, and an indulgent soul apply to Bilaam Harasha's disciples." Couldn't the mishnah simply have skipped the introduction entirely? The exact same idea could have been conveyed in a much more succinct form by merely stating from the outset: "Whoever has a good eye, a humble spirit, and a temperate soul is of the disciples of Avraham Avinu; whoever has a bad eye, an arrogant spirit, and an indulgent soul is of the disciples of Bilaam Harasha."

- Three is not such a large number; why was it necessary for the mishnah to point out that the number of listed traits equals three? This is something, presumably, readers could have easily deduced on their own. In fact, elsewhere in *Avos*, a mishnah lists traits without counting them: "Rabbi Elazar Hakapar says: Envy, desire, and the lust for honor remove a person from the world" (4:21). This mishnah there shows no need to do the math for us.

- At one point the mishnah poses a question: "What is the difference between the disciples of Avraham Avinu and the disciples of Bilaam Harasha?" What is the question exactly? The difference certainly seems hard to miss! One group is righteous and destined for *Olam Haba*, and the other group is wicked, on a one-way course straight down. What could possibly have been the mishnah's intent in considering this a topic of contemplation?

- Even the answer the mishnah supplies, which one would think to be straightforward, is puzzling, as it seems to contain an inconsistency. Regarding the disciples of Avraham, the mishnah states that they "eat in This World and inherit the Next." But when outlining the situation of the disciples of Bilaam, the mishnah omits mention of their fate in This World, focusing solely on their experience in the Afterlife: "Bilaam Harasha's disciples inherit Gehinnom and descend to the netherworld."

- The whole structure of the mishnah's statement concerning the fate of the wicked disciples seems strange. As mentioned, it left out the part about their status in This World. Yet it does parallel the treatment of the fate of the righteous disciples; that is, it lists two factors: "They inherit Gehinnom and descend to the netherworld." The only problem is — these appear to be the exact same thing! So instead of duplicating the report on the righteous disciples — spelling out their state in This World and the Next — the mishnah, in dealing with the wicked, deletes mention of their state in This World and relates their fate in the Afterlife twice over.

All of these perplexities indicate that there is much more to this mishnah than meets the eye. It appears that it is not the garden-variety righteous and wicked that are the subject of this mishnah; rather, the discussion centers on something much more subtle and profound, as we shall discover.

The Foundation

Middos: this is the focus of our mishnah. The Nesivos Sholom explains that, in truth, the mishnah throughout — in referring both to the disciples of Avraham and the disciples of Bilaam — is speaking of an observant Jew, who keeps the Torah and fulfills mitzvos. The real divide is manifest in the qualities of the soul, the type of character cultivated by the individual.

In other words, the "disciples of Bilaam" of which the mishnah speaks are not necessarily wanton sinners engaging in all manner of transgression. It could be that they are fulfilling their mitzvah responsibilities. But in the area that forms the basis for mitzvos — the arena of *middos* — they are sorely lacking. Rav Chaim Vital had taught that in order for Torah to be properly and completely absorbed within the essence of a person, he must first refine that essence through the cultivation of proper *middos*. In his *Tzetel Katan*, Reb Elimelech of Lizhensk adds that the very reason a Yid is sent to this earth is to subdue and transform the evil aspects of his nature, such that ultimately goodness permeates his entire being. This is only possible by following the construct of Avraham Avinu, the quintessential *ba'al middos* (master of positive traits). One who allows negative traits to fester and grow within him is adopting, in this respect, the outlook of Bilaam Harasha.

The mishnah purposely selected two examples of opposite extremes. By focusing on Avraham Avinu, the mishnah provided a model of the ultimate in human perfection. In the realm of refining and elevating one's character traits, Avraham demonstrated the highest plateau a living person could attain — if the efforts are invested. And while Avraham serves as the initiator of productive and positive rectification of the world, Bilaam fills the very opposite role. He is the paradigm of corruption, whose unchecked evil tendencies led him down a road of not only personal self-destruction and decadence, but genocidal activities (which thankfully were thwarted). The mishnah, however, speaks to their *talmidim*, asking, "From whom do you wish to learn? Whom would you rather emulate?" It then provides the formula, the necessary background that leads one either in Avraham's direction or in Bilaam's.

This is why the mishnah mentioned the number three. Obviously, it does need to do the counting for us. What the mishnah was emphasizing is that these qualities form a definitive unit; all three together are essential ingredients for duplicating Avraham's approach (or the opposite). When a previous mishnah spelled out those elements that "remove a person from the world" — envy, desire, and lusting for honor — it did not record the tally for the simple reason that they do not necessarily comprise a single unit. Any one of those qualities by itself is sufficient to drive a person from the world; chasing after honor will effectively ruin his life even without the assistance of an envious nature. Such is not the case with our subject. One who possesses a humble spirit and temperate soul has made great strides, but as long as he is missing a good eye, he cannot be deemed a true *talmid* of Avraham. One's inherent nature can only be rectified completely if he has mastered all three qualities. Likewise, someone with an evil eye and haughty spirit, but without an indulgent soul, cannot be categorized as a *talmid* of Bilaam. He has plenty to do if he would like to get back on the proper path, but repentance will be much more accessible than it otherwise would be had he actually been subsumed within Bilaam's program. At that point, he would have crossed a real line, having allowed his nature to degenerate into total wickedness.

The Essentials

Focusing for the moment on the formula for Avraham's *talmidim*, it is interesting to note which items are included on this list — and which aren't. For example, one may have thought that any listing of the pristine qualities of Avraham would have to include *chessed*, as this was an area in which Avraham's excellence is legendary. Alas, this trait received no mention here.

There is good reason for this. The importance of *chessed* is well known and established. But the mishnah is not focusing on specific traits; rather, it outlines those elements that serve as the backdrop for all pristine qualities. The list presented by the mishnah is the formula which, if followed, enables a person to perfect his overall nature; rectifying his character will lead to *chessed* and all manner of worthy traits.

So what is it about these three qualities — *ayin tovah, ruach nemuchah, nefesh sh'falah* — that accounts for their serving as the optimal foundation leading to all good qualities? The Nesivos Sholom explains that a lot has to do with the fact that they are so all-encompassing in nature. They relate to every aspect of a person's makeup — *mo'ach* (mind/intellect), *lev* (heart/emotions), and *eivarim* (limbs).

Ayin tovah, corresponding to the *middos* of the *mo'ach*, is especially far-reaching. The Maharal outlines three major areas of *shleimus* — in relation to one's Creator, his fellow, and his self — all of which are encompassed by this quality:

Shleimus with one's Creator: A person with a positive outlook, identifying and focusing on the good, will readily be *samei'ach b'chelko*, pleased and thankful for all that Hashem does for him and supplies him with. Whatever comes his way, he knows that Hashem's ways are perfect, calculated precisely for his very own maximum benefit. Thus, he sees the good in everything.

Shleimus with one's fellow: One who accustoms himself to perceiving goodness, will likewise see the good in every person — and only the good. He will fulfill the dictum mentioned in the *tefillah* of Reb Elimelech: שֶׁנִּרְאֶה כָּל אֶחָד מַעֲלַת חֲבֵרֵינוּ וְלֹא חֶסְרוֹנָם — *That everyone shall see the positive qualities of their friends, and not their failings.* Imagine what such an outlook can yield. Someone with an *ayin tovah* will have no enemies, as the whole concept of disliking someone is foreign to him. He will not be angered or annoyed by others. If there is something that he does not have that his friend does have, he is not disturbed by this in the least; why should he be, if he sees everything in a positive light, is happy with his share, and takes pleasure in his friend's success?

Shleimus with one's self: Often (if not always), at the root of "crabbiness" or a generally poor disposition is the fact that a person is not happy with himself. As such, he becomes disgruntled and quick to complain, leading to friction and conflict with others. One whose overall outlook is consistently positive, however, is spared from all this unnecessary suffering and drama. Always happy and content, perceiving only good, he will be at peace with himself and with others by extension.

Thus we see that this positive mindset — *ayin tovah* — leads to *shleimus* in all areas.

Ruach nemuchah (a humble spirit) is a function of the heart. This quality counteracts the negative force of *ga'avah*, which is referred to in Scripture as *Gevah lev* — "arrogance of heart" (*Mishlei* 16:5). A haughty spirit is a problem waiting to happen. Someone who is "full of himself" believes himself to be superior to others and thinks he has everything coming to him. Such a sentiment will lead him to fulfill all of his heart's desires, regardless of who gets harmed in the process. Just as arrogance brings one to all manner of poor *middos*, so does a humble spirit reverse the course and lead one to proper *middos* and refined behavior.

Corresponding to the limbs is the quality of *nefesh sh'falah* (a restrained soul). The term *nefesh* reflects one's innate desire. When Avraham was attempting to solicit the assistance of the *bnei Cheis* for the burial of Sarah, he addressed them with the remark, אִם־יֵשׁ אֶת־נַפְשְׁכֶם — *If it be within your* **souls** (*Bereishis* 23:7). Rashi (*ibid.*) interprets this phrase as, אִם־יֵשׁ אֶת־רְצוֹנְכֶם — *If it be your* **will**. The *nefesh* represents the *ratzon*; the limbs are the agents that carry out this *ratzon*. Thus the conduct of a *nefesh sh'falah*, whose *ratzon* is kept in check, will be refined and pristine.

And so — permeating, as they do, every aspect of a person's essence — these foundational qualities serve as the basis for the cultivation of a whole host of desirable traits. By way of illustration, let us stay with the example mentioned above — *chessed*. It is apparent from the words of Shlomo Hamelech that *chessed* is an outgrowth of the quality of *ayin tovah*. As the *passuk* states (*Mishlei* 22:9): טוֹב־עַיִן הוּא יְבֹרָךְ כִּי־נָתַן מִלַּחְמוֹ לַדָּל — *One who possesses a good eye shall be blessed, for he gives of his bread to the needy*. And just as performing kindness is a direct result of the attribute of *ayin tovah*, so it is with the other essential elements mentioned in our mishnah. They perfect a person's nature to the extent that all other admirable qualities will develop as a result.

It bears emphasis, however, that — as mentioned before — these three elements function as a unit. A person must cultivate all three in order for his trajectory to resemble that of Avraham Avinu; it is the amalgamation of them all that fosters overall perfection in *middos*. In a well-known passage, the *Chovos Halevavos* (*Sha'ar Haperishus*, ch. 5) compares good *middos* to a pearl necklace: should one pearl break loose, the others will slide off as well. This notion is certainly applicable to the qualities of our mishnah, as each is an essential and necessary component in character development.

A World of Difference

The mishnah's question is also puzzling. How could it ask what the difference is between the disciples of Avraham and the disciples of Bilaam? Isn't the difference between them as stark as night and day? One is righteous and Heaven-bound, and the other is wicked and headed for eternal retribution. Seemingly, you can't draw a sharper contrast than that.

The Toldos Yaakov Yosef of Polonya *ztz"l* asserts that the mishnah is actually revealing a subtle point. In his *sefer Tzafnas Panei'ach*, he explains that the mishnah's main thrust is not to delineate the difference of their Afterlife experience; that, indeed, should be quite obvious. Less apparent, however, is their experience in the here-and-now. This is what the mishnah seeks to demonstrate here: that the disparity between these two factions in This World is likewise quite substantial.

In other words, one may have made an almost understandable

mistake. We may have thought that the righteous disciples of Avraham will be content in *Olam Haba*, which makes their sacrifices and suffering in This World more bearable. And they shouldn't feel envious of Bilaam's disciples who are having a grand old time here, because after 120, their troubles will begin with a vengeance.

The mishnah clarifies that this is a gross misperception. What, indeed, is the situation of these two groups in *Olam Hazeh*? Just the opposite of the common assumption. The disciples of Avraham literally have the best of both worlds. That they inherit *Olam Haba* should not be too surprising. But even their existence in This World is blissful and harmonious. As the mishnah informs us: תַּלְמִידָיו שֶׁל אַבְרָהָם אָבִינוּ, אוֹכְלִין בָּעוֹלָם הַזֶּה וְנוֹחֲלִין בָּעוֹלָם הַבָּא — *The disciples of Avraham Avinu eat in This World and inherit the World to Come.* Notice that the mishnah does not state that they "reap benefit" in This World, but "eat" in This World. The Toldos Yaakov Yosef explains that the mishnah alludes thereby to the secret of their success in *Olam Hazeh*. As opposed to generalized benefit and pleasure, "eating" refers to the essentials; that is, they take from This World only what is necessary for existence; luxuries and extras are not their concern. And this enables them to enjoy such happiness while still in This World. As their material aspirations are minimal, they are the most content people in the world. As long as they have enough to eat, they feel incredibly blessed. In their eyes, they're not missing out on anything. As such, life in This World is unmitigated contentment.

Contrast this with the disciples of Bilaam. Of course, their eternal end is a horror; but even now, life is far from a party. As a result of their debased character, life for such people is an almost unrelenting series of utter frustration and misery. With their *ayin ra'ah*, they are consistently envious, begrudging others their success. The unchecked desires stemming from their *nefesh rechavah* (haughty soul) leave them constantly pining for more, never satisfied with what they already have. And of course, their *ruach gevohah* (arrogant spirit) convinces them that everything is coming to them, contributing all the more to unbridled ambition and lack of contentment. In short, their *yetzer hara* gives them no rest, stifling their ability to reap enjoyment from life.

תלמידיו של אברהם אבינו

This, then, is the mishnah's intent. We had wondered about its formulation of the fate of Bilaam's disciples. Why didn't the mishnah follow the same pattern of the disciples of Avraham, describing their state in This World and the Next? Instead, when dealing with Bilaam's followers, the mishnah seemed to be speaking exclusively in terms of the Next World: תַּלְמִידָיו שֶׁל בִּלְעָם הָרָשָׁע יוֹרְשִׁין גֵּיהִנָּם וְיוֹרְדִין לִבְאֵר שַׁחַת — *The disciples of Bilaam inherit Gehinnom and descend to the netherworld*. And what is the difference between these two entities anyway? In light of the above, however, the mishnah takes on a new light. The answer is that it did follow the same pattern as by Avraham's followers; that is, even by the disciples of Bilaam, the mishnah is discussing their state both in This World and the Next. The Gehinnom of which the mishnah speaks refers to This World, for such is their experience in life! There is always someone else who has more — a bigger, fancier house; a larger bank account; a more prestigious position. When envy is the master, there is always something of which to be envious! One whose aim is to fulfill every passion has consigned himself to a life of constant disappointment; as *Chazal* tell us (*Koheles Rabbah* 1:34): אֵין אָדָם מֵת וַחֲצִי תַּאֲוָתוֹ בְּיָדוֹ — *No person, by the end of his life, has achieved even half of his desires*. In short, the fate of these individuals is precarious indeed: not only do they descend after death to the netherworld, but their lives in *This World* are a veritable Gehinnom.

The saintly Rebbe of Kobrin *ztz"l* was renowned for his remarkable spiritual attainments. The Slonimer Rebbe *ztz"l* once related how the former even had a Heavenly vision in which he was shown the goings-on in Gehinnom. The Slonimer Rebbe continued, "I, myself, never merited to behold such a spectacle. Nevertheless, I did get a glimpse of this aspect of the Afterlife in a different way. For me, it was enough that I had an audience with a certain individual of unrefined character. I could practically sense the fire of Gehinnom burning above him." It seems the Slonimer Rebbe was expressing the same sentiment as stated in our mishnah. Apparently, the individual he encountered was afflicted with envy and desire; it was plainly recognizable that his life resembled Gehinnom itself.

GEMS FROM THE *SEFER NESIVOS SHOLOM*

There Is and There Isn't

Staying with the same basic theme, the Nesivos Sholom proceeds to introduce another dimension of meaning to the mishnah's message. The idea that these three elements form one unit, and that each is essential towards meeting the overall goal of *middos* perfection, can be better appreciated in light of a simple fact: they all share a common denominator, stemming from the same root.

When Moshe Rabbeinu was recounting the events at Har Sinai, he made mention of the role he played as interlocutor between Hashem and the Jewish people, relating His commands to them. He describes this arrangement as follows (*Devarim* 5:5): אָנֹכִי עֹמֵד בֵּין ה' וּבֵינֵיכֶם — *I (Anochi) am standing between Hashem and you*. The Ba'al Shem Tov perceives here a fundamental aspect of a Yid's overall *avodas Hashem*, upon which everything hinges. He interprets homiletically, "It is *Anochi* — the concept of 'I' — that stands between a Jew and Hashem." In other words, it is the sense of *yeishus* — literally, "something"; a reference to the ego — that interferes with a Jew's relationship with Hashem, preventing him from getting closer. In a sense, *yeishus* resembles *avodah zarah*; that is, the individual gives credence to some entity other than Hashem, be it an idol or his own self. Either way, there is "something" that is separate from the Creator, blocking one's access to Him.

As shall be demonstrated, it is this sense of *yeishus* that is literally the root of all evil, giving rise to bad character within a person. As such, it is the imperative of every Yid who seeks to attain closeness to *Hakadosh Baruch Hu* through character refinement to engage in the opposite endeavor — *bitul hayeishus*, nullifying one's ego and one's "self."

This was an area for which Avraham is particularly well known. His nullification of self was utterly complete, as demonstrated by his immortal pronouncement: אָנֹכִי עָפָר וָאֵפֶר — *I am but dust and ashes* (*Bereishis* 18:27). This was the principal factor responsible for his overall perfection of character; this is the common denominator of the essential items of our mishnah. Conversely, it is a lack of uprooting the ego — the retention and emphasis on *yeishus* — that serves as the basis for the three corruptive qualities of Bilaam's disciples. (We shall see, as well, that these three qualities are intertwined with the attributes that remove a person from This World and the Next. These are envy, desire, and lusting for honor, which likewise spring forth from the evil root of *yeishus*.)

An *ayin ra'ah* — an evil, begrudging eye — corresponds to the attribute of envy. Such an individual experiences little peace, as he is constantly disturbed by the success of others. Approached from a logical standpoint, why should one be bothered by someone else's good fortune? What does it really have to do with him? But someone with an *ayin ra'ah* makes it about himself; because of his overdeveloped sense of *yeishus*, everything centers on his own persona. As such, he reacts to his friend's rise to wealth or prominence as almost a personal affront, as if he is being shunted to the side and out of the limelight.

But one who excels in *bitul hayeishus*, negating his self, is liberated from such destructive sentiments. He develops the *middah* of *ayin tovah*; what does it bother him if his friend is happy? On the contrary, the more, the merrier! As a possessor of an *ayin tovah*, his own expectations and wants for himself are considerably minimized. Thus he is perfectly satisfied with whatever he has, certainly not begrudging others what is theirs. Thus, the *tov ayin*, through the relinquishing of a sense of self, is able to master the trait of being *samei'ach b'chelko*, content with one's lot. In other words, not only is he freed from the negative influence of envy, but he experiences actual, positive emotions as he is happy with whatever portion he receives. This stands in sharp contrast to the *ba'al ayin ra'ah* (possessor of an evil eye), whose sense of entitlement leaves him constantly dissatisfied and craving for more. מִי שֶׁיֵּשׁ לוֹ מָנֶה רוֹצֶה מָאתַיִם — One who has one hundred, wants two hundred.

The attribute of *ruach gevohah*, a haughty spirit, corresponds to the pursuit of honor. This is likewise a product of *yeishus*. One with an inflated sense of self feels a strong need to be the center of attention. To obtain his "due glory," such an individual will be led down a brash and self-destructive path, ultimately "removing himself from the world(s)."

There is something quite noteworthy with regards to the trait of *ruach nemuchah*, reflecting its destructive power. In the first chapter of *Hilchos Dei'os*, the Rambam famously advocates a "middle path." He eschews extreme measures, counseling a person to aim for overall moderation in all traits. This, he asserts, is the *derech yesharah* (straight, proper path). In the very next chapter, however, the Rambam states unequivocally that there are exceptions. When it comes to the subject of our discussion — *gevah lev* (haughtiness of heart) — the Rambam forbids taking the middle ground; here, he exhorts us to go to the extreme! Thus we find the Torah lauding Moshe Rabbeinu not merely for being an *anav*, but specifically emphasizing that he was *anav me'od* — "**extremely** humble." *Chazal* adopt similar phraseology, saying (*Avos* 4:4): מְאֹד מְאֹד הֱוֵי שְׁפַל רוּחַ — *Be very, very, humble*. Apparently, when it comes to *ga'avah*, there is no room for compromise.

There is very good reason for this. The trait of *gevah lev* is the most despicable attribute in the eyes of Hashem. As the *passuk* says (*Mishlei* 16:5): תּוֹעֲבַת ה' כָּל-גְּבַהּ-לֵב — *The haughty of heart is an abomination of Hashem*. Haughtiness is an outgrowth of the pernicious sense of *yeishus*, the inflated ego who believes himself to be Hashem's greatest gift to the world. In fact, by asserting his *yeishus*, he becomes despised by Hashem and has no place in the world. As previously explained, a *yeish* carries an aspect of idolatry — an entity separate from Hashem. As such, Hashem declares about such an individual: אֵין אֲנִי וָהוּא יְכוֹלִין לָדוּר בָּעוֹלָם — *I and he cannot dwell in the world (together)* (*Sotah* 5a). There is not much doubt which of them will have to yield to the Other.

This is why *Chazal* so greatly emphasized and encouraged the cultivation of a *ruach nemuchah*, the polar opposite approach. By following in the footsteps of Avraham Avinu, who considered himself *afar va'eifer*, a Yid negates his *yeishus*. Such a person, having thus refined his character and removed his ego, is ripe for a close relationship with Hashem.

The attribute of desire is represented in our mishnah by the quality of *nefesh rechavah*, an indulgent soul. A person with an overdeveloped sense of *yeishus* is interested in one thing: his personal pleasure. His mentality of entitlement leads him to expend all of his energies on the singular goal of fulfilling every whim and passion. In his view, his will is paramount. It is thus easy to see how the counterpart — the *ba'al nefesh sh'falah* — emanates from the very opposite approach. Such an individual has excelled in the art of *bitul hayeishus*, having relinquished the wanton pursuit of personal desire. The *nefesh sh'falah* is satisfied with his lot, not looking for more. With his inclinations in check, he lives a life of contentment.

Far from a haphazard collection of random qualities, we have learned that the trio of *middos* featured in our mishnah all revolve around the same basic idea: they are all derivatives of the entity of *yeishus*. And this aspect accounts for the essentiality of each and every one of them. For if one were to have eliminated, for example, one's *ayin ra'ah* from within himself, but retained another quality — say, the *nefesh rechavah* — he still possesses a most unhealthy reservoir of *yeishus*. To be a true adherent of the path of Avraham, the *yeishus* within must be completely uprooted through the adoption of all three indispensable *middos*.

This notion can be best understood with an agricultural illustration. A farmer has a number of fruit trees on his property. Even if some of the fruits are blemished, he has not suffered a complete loss; as long as the mainstay of the trees remains healthy, there is always potential for a better crop. But if blight creeps in to the roots, it could spell disaster. In a similar manner, a person must ensure that the root of his soul and character remains unsullied. If he can eradicate *yeishus*, the way is cleared for attaining perfection. But if it remains, this *yeishus* will serve as the root of his overall character, and its corrupt influence will spread throughout.

"What" Is the Difference

The mishnah thus reveals the remarkable reach of the concept of *yeishus* — or its negation. It forms the basis of the person, determining his overall character. And his entire life, in This World and the Next, is all an outgrowth of how he relates to and navigates the concept of "self."

Speaking of one's overall experience in This World, the Rebbe of Kobrin *ztz"l* once made the following remark: *Vus far a zisa velt! Vus far a lichtige velt! Far di vus ligen nisht in ihr* — "What a sweet world it is! What a world filled with light! At least, this is how it is for those who are not immersed in it." The Rebbe's words mirror the mishnah's message, which presented in stark terms the different experiences of the disciples of Avraham and the disciples of Bilaam. The latter assert their *yeishus*; as a result, their life even in This World is a living Gehinnom. They are unsatisfied with their lot, consumed by envy, craving and pursuing, and never obtaining even half of their hearts' desires. What could be a greater Gehinnom than a life of incessant frustration, where the need for more and more gives one's soul no rest? *Chazal* describe what happens to those who constantly indulge their desire: the more they satiate it, the stronger the cravings become (*Sukkah* 52b). And what have they to show after a life of such upheaval? Where has it led them — other than to an eternal Gehinnom? But the disciples of Avraham, who have negated their *yeishus*, have not enslaved themselves to the selfish pursuit of self-gratification. Having refrained from "immersing themselves in This World," it became theirs to enjoy. And after a life of happiness and contentment, they proceed to the eternal bliss of life in the World to Come.

In fact, this very idea is alluded to in the wording of the mishnah. We had wondered about the mishnah's questioning of what the difference was between Avraham's disciples and Bilaam's. Actually, the mishnah can be understood not as asking about the difference, but as stating and explaining what the root of that difference is. **Mah bein talmidav shel Avraham Avinu l'talmidav shel Bilaam** — that itself is the difference: *Mah* — "What"! This term serves as the ultimate statement and demonstration of *bitul hayeishus*. Confronted by Bnei Yisroel in the desert over insufficient food, Moshe and Aharon did not react with arrogance by "pulling rank." Instead, they responded with a statement of their own limitations, saying: *V'nachnu mah* — "What, indeed, are we?" (*Shemos* 16:7). This is considered the paradigm of humility, the ultimate manifestation of *bitul hayeishus*. The Nesivos Sholom explains that the mishnah here is invoking the memory of this legendary model. *Mah* — *bitul hayeishus* — is what best describes the difference between Avraham's path and that of Bilaam, and accounts for all of the far-reaching consequences in This World and the Next. "What" is *the* difference.

And what a difference! Here are the two models, the destinations of the separate paths of negation or exercise of *yeishus*. Avraham was the quintessential practitioner of *bitul hayeishus*; this enabled him to achieve complete character refinement, *ahavas Hashem*, and *d'veikus baHashem*. In short, the highest *madreigos* (levels) a mortal can reach through self-rectification. On the other end of the spectrum is Bilaam, who began with the Divine gift of prophecy. But his preoccupation with *anochi* revealed to all the extent to which it interferes and separates between himself and Hashem. One who could have and should have had such an intimate relationship with *Hakadosh Baruch Hu* ended up, instead, being involved in the most heinous transgressions, including idolatry and immorality. *Chazal* elaborate on the depths of depravity to which he sank, demonstrating to where unchecked self-indulgence can eventually lead.

In a very real sense, this mishnah encapsulates the overarching aim behind Klal Yisroel's practice of learning *Pirkei Avos* at this specific time. Why, indeed, is this time period considered so apropos for this particular course of study? A lot has to do with the teaching of Rav Chaim Vital that opened this discourse. During this lead-up to Shavuos and *Mattan Torah*, our focus is on preparation for this seminal event. Rav Chaim revealed the reason that the Torah does not issue a specific directive to develop proper *middos*; it is not possible to single them out within a particular mitzvah, as they serve as the basis for the entire Torah. There is no mitzvah to "be a Jew," for it is to Jews that the Torah is given. What better way to characterize what a Jew is than the description provided by our mishnah — disciples of the "first Jew," Avraham Avinu.

At this time, we seek to fashion ourselves into vessels worthy to receive and contain the Torah. Our mishnah supplies the formula to accomplish this, outlining what it takes to be considered a *talmid* of Avraham Avinu. Perfection of *middos* is the focal point, as it is character refinement that leads to Torah, mitzvos, and all levels of spiritual attainment.

In Summary

The mishnah outlining the differences between Avraham's disciples and those of Bilaam may appear, at first glance, to contain a relatively simple message. Avraham's disciples are good; Bilaam's are bad. Obviously, the intent is more profound than this superficial glance would convey.

The truth is that the ramifications of this mishnah are truly remarkable. The mishnah is not merely picking a few laudable qualities; rather, it delineates those traits that are most basic to the most important mission of a Yid in This World: character refinement. It is the cultivation of these three traits — *all* three — that enable a person to gain *middos* perfection in all areas; the omission of even one will prevent a Jew from reaching his true potential. This is why the mishnah supplies an entire introductory statement — "Whoever has the following three things is a *talmid* of Avraham Avinu…" — to drive home the crucial point that these elements function as a single, essential unit.

The reason these particular qualities — a good eye, a humble spirit, and a temperate soul — are deemed so foundational is that they encompass every aspect of human functionality. The positive outlook of a *ba'al ayin tovah* is a function of his intellect; the humility embodied in a *ba'al ruach nemuchah* corresponds to the emotions of his heart; and a *ba'al nefesh sh'falah* exercises control over his limbs.

The relationship of these three traits is further cemented by the fact that, essentially, they all derive from the same root. This quality, in fact, is the foundation of a person in his service of Hashem; all aspects of his character emanate from *yeishus*, the ego, or its nullification. One who feels himself to be a *yeish* opens himself up to a whole host of issues, as the mishnah describes. A self-centered person will be plagued with envy, begrudging others their success with his *ayin ra'ah*. His ego convinces himself that he has everything coming to him, contributing to a *ruach gevohah* and spurring him to fulfill all the desires of his *nefesh rechavah*. But *bitul hayeishus*, negating one's "self," will give rise to the essential elements of *ayin tovah*, *ruach nemuchah*, and *nefesh sh'falah*.

The mishnah proceeds to spell out the different fate and experiences of these divergent groups. We may have thought the difference is apparent — one is destined for *Olam Haba*; the other for eternal retribution. But the mishnah has something important to add. The difference is manifest not only in the realm of the Afterlife, but also right here in This World. The *talmidim* of Avraham Avinu, having contained their egos and nullified their *yeishus*, are content and happy people. They are supremely satisfied with whatever they have, feeling no entitlement or craving for more. Freed from envy and spared the frustrations of unfulfilled desire, these elevated individuals are able to enjoy life in This World. Their counterparts, the disciples of Bilaam, have a much tougher time indeed. Although they expend their energies chasing pleasure, their lives are devoid of true enjoyment. Their insatiable appetite gives them no rest. There is always more out there, always someone else who "has it better"; thus, they are beset with incessant envy and unbridled passion that can never be satisfied. For people such as this, life in This World is itself Gehinnom.

As *Pirkei Avos* is studied during the lead-up to *Mattan Torah*, the message this mishnah seeks to inculcate within us comes at an especially auspicious time. The mishnah highlights the central role *middos* must play in the life of a Yid; for this reason, it outlines those elements that are the basic foundation to overall character refinement. This is a critical lesson for our preparation to receive the Torah. Rav Chaim Vital explains why the Torah does not issue a specific command to cultivate *middos tovos*; this is not really possible, since it is the perfection of character that serves as the foundation for all mitzvos. Only a person with pristine qualities can serve as an appropriate vessel for the Torah to rest within. And this, in effect, is the definition of a Yid. Who can receive the Torah? The followers of Avraham Avinu. And being a disciple of Avraham requires the development of pristine character, through the cultivation of the three essential elements propounded by our mishnah.

פרק ה' משנה כ"ג

הוי עז כנמר וכו'
Be as Bold as a Leopard...

יְהוּדָה בֶן תֵּימָא אוֹמֵר, הֱוֵי עַז כַּנָּמֵר, וְקַל כַּנֶּשֶׁר, וְרָץ כַּצְּבִי, וְגִבּוֹר כָּאֲרִי לַעֲשׂוֹת רְצוֹן אָבִיךְ שֶׁבַּשָּׁמָיִם:

Yehudah ben Teima says: Be as bold as a leopard, swift as an eagle, quick as a deer, and mighty as a lion – to do the will of your Father in Heaven.

GEMS FROM THE *SEFER NESIVOS SHOLOM*

SOURCES:

סוּר מֵרָע וַעֲשֵׂה־טוֹב. (תהלים ל״ד ט״ו)

Turn from evil, and do good. (*Tehillim* 34:15)

אֵיזֶהוּ גִבּוֹר, הַכּוֹבֵשׁ אֶת יִצְרוֹ. (אבות ד)

Who is mighty? He who overcomes his inclination. (*Avos* 4)

הוֹצִיאָה מִמַּסְגֵּר נַפְשִׁי. (תהלים קמ״ב ח׳)

Release my soul from captivity! (*Tehillim* 142:8)

אָמַר שִׁמְעוֹן הַצַּדִּיק... פַּעַם אַחַת בָּא אָדָם אֶחָד נָזִיר מִן הַדָּרוֹם, וּרְאִיתִיו שֶׁהוּא יְפֵה עֵינַיִם וְטוֹב רוֹאִי וּקְווּצוֹתָיו סְדוּרוֹת לוֹ תַּלְתַּלִּים. אָמַרְתִּי לוֹ: בְּנִי, מָה רָאִיתָ לְהַשְׁחִית אֶת שְׂעָרְךָ זֶה הַנָּאֶה? אָמַר לִי: רוֹעֶה הָיִיתִי לְאַבָּא בְּעִירִי, הָלַכְתִּי לְמַלְּאוֹת מַיִם מִן הַמַּעְיָן, וְנִסְתַּכַּלְתִּי בִּבְבוּאָה שֶׁלִּי, וּפָחַז עָלַי יִצְרִי וּבִקֵּשׁ לְטוֹרְדֵנִי מִן הָעוֹלָם, אָמַרְתִּי לוֹ: רָשָׁע, לָמָּה אַתָּה מִתְגָּאֶה בָּעוֹלָם שֶׁאֵינוֹ שֶׁלְּךָ, בְּמִי שֶׁהוּא עָתִיד לִהְיוֹת רִמָּה וְתוֹלֵעָה? הָעֲבוֹדָה, שֶׁאֲגַלְּחָךְ לַשָּׁמָיִם. מִיָּד עָמַדְתִּי וּנְשַׁקְתִּיו עַל רֹאשׁוֹ, אָמַרְתִּי לוֹ: בְּנִי, כָּמוֹךָ יִרְבּוּ נוֹזְרֵי נְזִירוֹת בְּיִשְׂרָאֵל. (נדרים ט:)

Shimon Hatzaddik said:... One time there came a certain man, a Nazirite from the South, and I saw of him that he had beautiful eyes, was of pleasing appearance, and had his locks arranged in ringlets. I said to him: "My son, why have you seen fit to destroy this beautiful head of hair of yours (in accordance with the Nazirite procedure)?" He said to me: "I served as a shepherd for my father in my town. I (once) went to draw water from the spring, and as I gazed at my reflection, my evil inclination suddenly surged upon me, and sought to remove me from the world. I said to him: 'Wicked one! Why do you feel pride in a world that is not yours, regarding someone who in the future will be transformed into worms and maggots? I swear – I will shave you away for the sake of Heaven!'" Immediately, I stood up and kissed him on his head. I said to him: "My son, there should be many oath-takers like you in Yisroel, taking the Nazirite vow!" (*Nedarim* 9b)

וַיְצַו אֶת־הָרִאשׁוֹן לֵאמֹר כִּי יִפְגָּשְׁךָ עֵשָׂו אָחִי וּשְׁאֵלְךָ לֵאמֹר לְמִי־אַתָּה וְאָנָה תֵלֵךְ וּלְמִי אֵלֶּה לְפָנֶיךָ. וְאָמַרְתָּ לְעַבְדְּךָ לְיַעֲקֹב מִנְחָה הִוא שְׁלוּחָה לַאדֹנִי לְעֵשָׂו. (בראשית ל"ב י"ח, י"ט)

And he commanded the first one, saying: "When my brother, Eisav, encounters you and asks you, saying: 'With whom are you (associated), where are you going, and whose are these which are before you?' you shall say: 'To your servant, Yaakov; it is a gift sent to my master, to Eisav.'" (*Bereishis* 32:18, 19)

בֶּן אַרְבָּעִים לַבִּינָה. (אבות ה')

At age forty, there is wisdom. (*Avos* 5)

אַל תַּשְׁלִיכֵנוּ לְעֵת זִקְנָה, כִּכְלוֹת כֹּחֵינוּ אַל תַּעַזְבֵנוּ. (סליחות)

Do not cast us away in old age; as our strength ebbs, do not abandon us. (*Selichos*)

Not Just for the Tzaddikim

When we look at the great Rebbes and leaders of Klal Yisroel, we are struck by the sheer enthusiasm and life-force that punctuates their every action. While this observation is often a source of high inspiration, encountering such greatness of spirit can sometimes make us feel small and inadequate. We wonder why we ourselves don't always experience such enthusiasm when performing mitzvos or studying Torah. We may even feel that such levels are relegated only to great tzaddikim; as if they somehow possess special G-d-given powers, perhaps imbued in them from birth through their illustrious ancestry.

We fail to see, however, that these *gedolei Torah* (Torah giants) are, in essence, no different from every other Jew. They have also had their share of ups and downs and days when it is hard to get out of a warm bed to go and lead the community. It appears to us that they have somehow overcome their weaknesses and function in a constant state of *simchah* and *d'veikus*. But we have not observed the many years of hard work they invested in perfecting their *middos*. Their greatness did not emerge overnight; nor were they born with it. They worked on and developed it.

Similarly, this greatness is open to every Yid. Sure, there are barriers, and days when we just feel like we want to curl up under the covers. There are times we feel weak and times we feel strong, times when our souls are filled with deep *emunah* and *bitachon*, and times of struggle against dark thoughts and lingering doubts. No one understood this more than *Chazal*, whose legacy to us is their vast wisdom as recorded in the holy *sefarim*. And it is precisely this issue that Rabbi Yehudah ben Teima addresses in the mishnah above.

Citing this mishnah, the *Tur* asserts that the four attributes listed here are the qualities a Jew requires in order to serve Hashem properly.

"Be as fierce as a leopard" is a fundamental element in *avodas Hashem*. It refers to the unflagging courage we must display in the face of people and obstacles that would prevent us from performing mitzvos. A person may want to do a mitzvah but is reluctant to do so out of fear of ridicule. The mishnah thus warns us not to succumb to the pressure of scoffers but to defy them with fierceness.

"As swift as an eagle," as explained by the Beis Yosef, refers to the faculty of sight. Upon encountering something that is forbidden to look at, a person must act swiftly to close his eyes.

"As quick as a deer" refers to the speed at which we must run to perform good deeds.

"As mighty as a lion" refers to the courage of our heart, which is the root of our strength and power in all areas of *avodas Hashem*.

Turn Away from Evil, and Do Good

You may have noticed some redundancy among these attributes, an issue pointed out by the Beis Yosef. "As fierce as a leopard" and "as mighty as a lion" seem rather similar. Both "as swift as an eagle" and "as quick as a deer" seem to speak of employing alacrity in *avodas Hashem*. Why, then, are they mentioned as four separate attributes? The specific order in which they are listed also requires explanation. Why did the mishnah place the leopard before the lion and the eagle before the deer?

The Nesivos Sholom clarifies the mishnah in light of the familiar *passuk* (*Tehillim* 34:15): סוּר מֵרָע וַעֲשֵׂה־טוֹב — *Turn away from evil, and do good*. This *passuk* encapsulates the two major categories of mitzvah observance: proper performance of the positive commandments and avoidance of the negative prohibitions. There are challenges in both of these areas, from both external and internal factors. This accounts for the apparent redundancy of the mishnah, as well as its order. The four attributes of our mishnah actually comprise two sets of two: the *sur meira* aspect comes with its external and internal pressures, as does the *aseih tov*. Beginning with the external factors, Rabbi Yehudah ben Teima instructs us in how to confront these challenges in both aspects of *avodas Hashem*.

Referring to the pressure presented by scoffers — an external factor — the mishnah tells us to "be as fierce as a leopard" in ignoring their ridicule and fulfilling the positive mitzvos. Turning to negative aspects, the mishnah then addresses a situation where a person is confronted with the temptation to transgress; a luring, forbidden sight appears within his field of view. "Be as swift as an eagle," the mishnah exhorts, to close one's eyes to the external stimuli presented by the *yetzer hara*.

Then there are internal causes, emanating from the person himself. These also affect both aspects — positive and negative — of a person's *avodas Hashem*, which the mishnah proceeds to address. "As quick as a deer" relates to the *middos* that are intrinsically part of a person, such as laziness, indecisiveness, fear, lack of self-belief, or other traits, which prevent him from pursuing good deeds. He must rouse himself to overcome these debilitating emotions and run like a deer to perform mitzvah acts. When it comes to overcoming one's lust and defeating the *yetzer hara*, one must be "strong like a lion" to withstand the temptation and avoid transgression. As the mishnah states elsewhere in *Avos* (4:1): אֵיזֶהוּ גִבּוֹר, הַכּוֹבֵשׁ אֶת יִצְרוֹ — *Who is mighty? He who overcomes his inclination.*

This understanding of the mishnah is summed up in the following table:

	"Turn away from evil…	…and do good"
External aspect	"as swift as an eagle" — to close one's eyes to negative external stimuli	"as fierce as a leopard" — to perform mitzvos despite the pressure exerted by scoffers
Internal aspect	"as mighty as a lion" — to resist inner desires to sin	"as quick as a deer" — to run to do good deeds in opposition of one's natural debilitating tendencies

True Grit

The *Ya'avetz* adds that the elements listed by the mishnah all reflect emotional, rather than physical strength. An ox, for example, exercises great physical strength, but the strength for which a warrior on the battlefield is known has more to do with courage and cool-headedness than actual, physical might. *Chazal* tell us that the mighty person is one who conquers his evil inclination, since that requires more strength and courage than any type of physical ordeal.

The four animals mentioned in the mishnah each excel in their unique characteristic above all the other animals. What Yehudah ben Teima is telling us, explains the Nesivos Sholom, is to learn from these animals about ourselves. If *Hakadosh Baruch Hu* implanted such superior abilities — which transcend mere physical traits — within these animals, they certainly must be present within that elevated, most favored being known as a Jew. A Yid may be currently unaware of them, as he does not sense these latent strengths. Nevertheless, as Yehudah ben Teima exhorts us, he must know that they are there within him, waiting to be accessed and enlisted in the service of Hashem.

A person's inherent, physical nature will often work against him and stifle his spiritual growth. In fact, his natural tendencies can serve as a type of prison, trapping him within the bonds of habit and base desires. Dovid Hamelech refers to just such a situation when he cries out (*Tehillim* 142:8), *Hotziah mimasger nafshi* — "Release my soul from captivity!"

In fact, it would be impossible to break free from these bonds if not for these special *kochos* (abilities), listed in the mishnah, with which Hashem has imbued a Yid. This is the purpose and beneficence of these particular traits; in delineating them, Yehudah ben Teima is demonstrating what tools a Yid possesses and must use to break out of the prison of his base nature. He can tap into his inherent "deer's speed" to overcome his laziness, and his "lion's strength" to overpower his desires. When encountering scoffers, he may utilize the "leopard's brazenness," or be "swift as an eagle" to avoid pernicious temptation. By harnessing these "supernatural" *kochos*, he will succeed in releasing his soul from captivity.

The Four Stages of Life

There is yet another dimension contained within Yehudah ben Teima's teaching. According to the Nesivos Sholom, the four traits of the mishnah also reflect four distinct stages of life.

"Be as fierce as a leopard" refers to one's youth, arguably the stormiest time of a person's life. In relation to the *yetzer hara*, one's blood boils within, blazing like a raging fire. Base desire, fueled by a rampant imagination, can drive one almost to the edge, leading him astray and far away from Hashem. Referring to this period, the Gemara (*Nedarim* 9b) relates the sentiments of a certain youth who was confronted with temptation, but prevailed: פָּחַז עָלַי יִצְרִי וּבִקֵּשׁ לְטוֹרְדֵנִי מִן הָעוֹלָם — *My inclination antagonized me, seeking to drive me from the world.*

The Rebbe, the Zichron Kadosh *ztz"l*, comparing this stage to a crossroads of sorts, interprets the verses regarding the encounter of Eisav and Yaakov in a similar vein (letter 23). The *passuk* states (*Bereishis* 32:18): כִּי יִפְגָּשְׁךָ עֵשָׂו אָחִי וּשְׁאֵלְךָ לֵאמֹר לְמִי־אַתָּה וְאָנָה תֵלֵךְ — *If Eisav my brother will encounter you and ask you, saying, "To whom do you belong, and where are you going...?"* This is an allusion to the *yetzer hara*. He discovers a certain youth striving to walk in the path of Torah and *avodah*, and he seeks to dissuade him. He says to him, "Which path have you chosen in life? Have you not seen This World so full of pleasure?" The proper response to his advances is supplied by the following *passuk* (v. 19). וְאָמַרְתָּ לְעַבְדְּךָ לְיַעֲקֹב — *And you shall say, "I belong to Your servant, Yaakov."* Yaakov personifies the attribute of truth, with which one can perceive the machinations of the *yetzer hara* for what they are: sheer fantasy, built on a foundation of lies. The path of desire may be sweet in its beginning; but its end is misery and bitterness. Whatever pleasure the *yetzer hara* can provide is nothing in comparison to the true joy and delight of Torah and pristine *avodas Hashem*.

As such, Yehudah ben Teima sums up the approach one must

take in navigating this perilous time. A Yid needs to muster the "brazenness of a leopard," referring to a holy brazenness that is crucial in resisting the wiles of the *yetzer hara* that seeks to ensnare him.

"As light as an eagle" corresponds to the next stage in life, which, in some sense, can be even more challenging than the perils of youth. Temptations lurk on one side, while the preoccupation of child-rearing and earning a living assail a person from the other. Oftentimes, even those who emerge successfully from the spiritual rigors of youth find themselves faltering at this stage, fighting this war on two fronts.

Thus, there is only one method of enduring this period, from a spiritual point of view: to soar like an eagle. An eagle's saving grace is its ability to launch into the air, thereby avoiding all of the perils and stumbling blocks that exist on the ground. Likewise, a person at this stage must "lift off," transcending his mundane nature and the attendant earthly temptations. He must utilize his *kochos* to rise above it all.

"As quick as a deer" refers to middle age, concerning which Yehudah ben Teima tells us (in the next mishnah), *Ben arba'im l'binah* — "Age forty is for wisdom" (*Avos* 5:21). Wisdom is necessary in order to begin to rectify one's past, an important undertaking upon reaching these years. This is the significance of the deer model; a deer looks backward as it runs, symbolizing a person who — as he continues to proceed in life — at the same time looks back to determine what aspects of his life need repair.

The Beis Avraham *ztz"l* likens this situation to a soldier on the battlefield. In the thick of battle, a soldier on the front lines has but one recourse: to keep going. Even if he is wounded, he dare not stop to inspect his wounds, for that would signify his end. Rather, he must immediately flee. Once he arrives at some relatively safe location, he can assess the damage and dress his wounds. Life, as well, is a constant battle against a most formidable enemy, the *yetzer hara*. In the throes of youth, the battle is most intense and there is nothing else to do but plough one's way through, fleeing one's *yetzer*, which is in hot pursuit. Only upon reaching the more level-headed years of middle age — *ben arba'im l'binah* — may one begin to look back and address those aspects that need rectification. As *Chazal* state (*Bamidbar Rabbah* 19:8): תָּבֹא אִמּוֹ וּתְקַנַּח אֶת הַצּוֹאָה — *Let the mother come and wipe up the soil (of her child). Eim* (mother) signifies the trait of wisdom. At forty, the age at which one acquires wisdom, one can begin to "wipe up the soil" of the past.

"As mighty as a lion" refers to old age, which is a period marked by paradox. The individual begins to lose his strength and steadily weakens, in both the physical and the spiritual sense. As such, it is especially important to muster one's might to continue to serve Hashem. In another way, though, this period provides some remarkable opportunities for spiritual advancement, such as have never before been available. Now, a person is much more free than he has ever been before, no longer as preoccupied with the pressures of child-rearing and earning a livelihood, and less troubled by his *yetzer*. More able to dedicate themselves to spiritual pursuits and preparation for the final journey, elderly *talmidei chachamim* become even wiser as they age.

But then again, there exists at this time a challenge demanding even greater might than the youth requires to battle his passions. Now, the *yetzer hara* of despair raises its ugly head, attempting to break one's spirit and cause one to submit to defeat. Unfortunately, many succumb at this point to the great temptation of discouragement, and so give up the battle. Regarding this very challenge, we beseech Hashem for Divine assistance, as we recite in the Selichos prayers: אַל תַּשְׁלִיכֵנוּ לְעֵת זִקְנָה, כִּכְלוֹת כֹּחֵנוּ אַל תַּעַזְבֵנוּ — *Do not cast us away in old age; as our strength ebbs, do not abandon us.*

But these four states are not limited to the corresponding stages of life; they all apply within each individual stage as well. Citing the supplication mentioned above, the Ba'al Shem Tov points out that it does not refer to **yemei** *ziknah* — "the **years** of old age," but rather to **eis** *ziknah* — "a **time** of old age." The implication is that a person need not necessarily wait until he actually arrives at his senior years to be in a state of old age; there are those who seem to function in such a state even in their youth. Similarly, the Birkas Avraham *ztz"l* writes (letter 1) that there are young men who have the *yetzer hara* of the elderly, and elderly people who have the *yetzer hara* of young men. As such, we see that the "might of a lion" is not relegated only to old age nor is the "brazenness of a leopard" applicable only to youth. At all times, at each stage of life, a person needs to avail himself of all four sources of strength — ferocity, swiftness, speed, and might — to fight his *yetzer hara*.

As mentioned, these four tools are crucial for a person to break out of the self-prison of his natural tendencies. Even in some high-security penitentiaries, there are courtyards where the inmates may occasionally stroll around outside of their cells. Similarly, a person caught in the confines of his nature and desires may sometimes emerge and improve his standing somewhat. But these respites are usually short-lived and temporary; soon he slips back into the lure of habit. And so, the individual remains entrapped by his nature and *yetzer*. And he is especially bogged down by the overpowering forces of inertia and hopelessness, which perpetuate his failure to reach his potential.

Yehudah ben Teima aims to rectify this state of affairs. He urges the "prisoner" to recognize that there is, in the end, a way out. Everyone possesses tremendous, latent *kochos*. By tapping in to them, one can rise above mediocrity and attain true greatness. This was demonstrated by the *chassidim harishonim* (pious men of antiquity), who would dedicate set times each day to transcend their physicality and reach the apex of a spiritual existence (*cf. Berachos* 30b).

In Summary

In elucidating the mishnah of Yehudah ben Teima, the Nesivos Sholom demonstrates how we can overcome the inner and outer barriers that prevent us from excelling in *avodas Hashem*.

These barriers are experienced by every Jew, from the simplest person to the greatest *talmid chacham*. The timeless advice given by the mishnah is that we can always break through these barriers and fulfill our potential in *avodas Hashem*.

The mishnah discusses the traits of four animals that we must utilize to grow in *ruchniyus*. Quoting the Beis Yosef, the Nesivos Sholom asks two questions: Why does the mishnah list four attributes when it seems, in reality, that there are only two — strength and alacrity? And why are these attributes related in this particular order? He explains that there are indeed two attributes being discussed here, but they each have an inner and outer component, making four altogether.

The listed traits relate to the two main categories of *avodas Hashem*, which emerge from the *passuk* in *Tehillim*: *Sur meira va'aseih tov* — "Turn away from evil (avoid sin) and do good (perform mitzvos)." Thus, the mishnah first addresses the mandated approach to external factors, in both positive and negative aspects. Encountering the external pressure of scoffers, a Yid must be "as fierce as a leopard" to ignore their taunts over his performance of mitzvos. And when confronted with external stimuli luring him to sin, he must be "as swift as an eagle" to close his eyes to evil. He must also counter his internal barriers by being "as mighty as a lion" in order to turn away from the evil of his inner lusts and desires, and be "as quick as a deer" to run to perform mitzvos before becoming overwhelmed by his inner doubts and weaknesses.

These attributes reflect a deep inner strength rather than any physical prowess. The mishnah uses the examples of these four animals, as each one excels in its particular quality. By emulating what these animals represent, we can escape the confines of our base nature and attain great heights in the service of Hashem.

Each attribute also refers to a specific stage of life; the Nesivos Sholom explains how each attribute is particularly suited to each age. The differentiation between the stages of life, however, is not absolute, as each stage contains aspects of all four attributes.

The Nesivos Sholom concludes with the example of the *chassidim harishonim*, who transcended their physical limitations and innate personality traits to become true *ovdei Hashem* (servants of Hashem).

By providing this model, the Nesivos Sholom is exhorting us to emulate their ways and strive to do likewise: rising above our base nature to attain great spiritual heights.

פרק ה׳ משנה כ״ד
עז פנים לגיהנום ובושת פנים לגן עדן
The Brazen-Faced to Gehinnom, and the Shamefaced to Gan Eden

הוּא הָיָה אוֹמֵר, עַז פָּנִים לְגֵיהִנָּם, וּבֹשֶׁת פָּנִים לְגַן עֵדֶן. יְהִי רָצוֹן מִלְּפָנֶיךָ ה' אֱלֹקֵינוּ וֵאלֹקֵי אֲבוֹתֵינוּ, שֶׁיִּבָּנֶה בֵּית הַמִּקְדָּשׁ בִּמְהֵרָה בְיָמֵינוּ, וְתֵן חֶלְקֵנוּ בְּתוֹרָתֶךָ:

(Yehudah ben Teima) would say: The brazen-faced (is destined) for Gehinnom, and the shamefaced for Gan Eden. May it be Your will, Hashem our G-d and the G-d of our fathers, that the Holy Temple be built speedily in our days, and that You grant our portion in Your Torah.

GEMS FROM THE *SEFER NESIVOS SHOLOM*

SOURCES:

יְהוּדָה בֶן תֵּימָא אוֹמֵר: הֱוֵי עַז כַּנָּמֵר, וְקַל כַּנֶּשֶׁר, וְרָץ כַּצְּבִי, וְגִבּוֹר כָּאֲרִי לַעֲשׂוֹת רְצוֹן אָבִיךָ שֶׁבַּשָּׁמָיִם. (אבות ה׳)

Yehudah ben Teima says: Be brazen as a leopard, swift as an eagle, running like a deer, and mighty as a lion to perform the will of your Father in Heaven. (*Avos 5*)

הִזְהִיר שֶׁתָּעִיז מִצְחֲךָ כְּנֶגֶד הַמַּלְעִיגִים וְלֹא תֵבוֹשׁ. (טור אורח חיים א׳)

(Yehudah ben Teima) instructed that one should fortify himself in the face of those who scorn (his service of Hashem), and not be ashamed. (*Tur, Orach Chaim §1*)

תִּתֵּן אֱמֶת לְיַעֲקֹב. (מיכה ז׳ כ׳)

Grant truth to Yaakov. (*Michah 7:20*)

מִפְּנֵי מָה נִתְּנָה תּוֹרָה לְיִשְׂרָאֵל? מִפְּנֵי שֶׁהֵן עַזִּין. (ביצה כ״ה:)

Why was the Torah given to Yisroel? Because they are brazen. (*Beitzah 25b*)

שִׁמְעוֹן בַּר אַבָּא בְּשֵׁם ר׳ יוֹחָנָן אָמַר: אַרְבָּעָה דְבָרִים הֶרְאָה לוֹ – גֵּיהִנָּם, וּמַלְכֻיּוֹת, וּמַתַּן תּוֹרָה, וּבֵית הַמִּקְדָּשׁ. א״ל: כָּל זְמַן שֶׁבָּנֶיךָ עֲסוּקִים בִּשְׁתַּיִם, הֵם נִיצוֹלִים מִשְּׁתַּיִם; פֵּירְשׁוּ מִשְּׁתַּיִם, הֵם נִידוֹנִין בִּשְׁתַּיִם. (בראשית רבה מ״ד כ״א)

Shimon bar Aba said in the name of Rabbi Yochanan: Hashem showed Avraham four things (two sets of two) – Gehinnom and subjugation to gentile dominion, the Giving of the Torah and the Beis Hamikdash. Hashem said to him: "As long as your offspring are engaged with the (second set of) two, they will be spared from the (first set of) two; if they withdraw from the (second set of) two, they will be subjected to the (first set of) two." (*Bereishis Rabbah 44:21*)

עז פנים לגיהנום ובושת פנים לגן עדן

Could it be that *Pirkei Avos* is sending us mixed messages? It certainly appears that way regarding the mishnah's stand on the trait of *azus* (brazenness). At least, this is the initial impression which emerges from a series of statements from the Tanna Yehudah ben Teima towards the end of the fifth *perek*.

Yehudah ben Teima begins with a teaching that is quite familiar, forming, as it does, the opening words of the *Tur*, classic code of Jewish law: יְהוּדָה בֶן תֵּימָא אוֹמֵר, הֱוֵי עַז כַּנָּמֵר, וְקַל כַּנֶּשֶׁר, וְרָץ כַּצְּבִי, וְגִבּוֹר כָּאֲרִי לַעֲשׂוֹת רְצוֹן אָבִיךְ שֶׁבַּשָּׁמַיִם — *Yehudah ben Teima says:* **Be brazen as a leopard**, *swift as an eagle, running like a deer, and mighty as a lion to perform the will of your Father in Heaven* (*Avos* 5:20). Apparently, brazenness is a commendable quality.

But in his very next teaching, he proceeds to state what to all appearances is the complete opposite! הוּא הָיָה אוֹמֵר: עַז פָּנִים לְגֵיהִנָּם — *He would say: The brazen-faced is destined for Gehinnom*. Which one is it? A cornerstone of Judaism, or a one-way ticket to eternal and fiery retribution?

The contradictory implications notwithstanding, this statement of Yehudah ben Teima requires much explanation even if examined in isolation. "The brazen-faced is for Gehinnom" — a rather stark description. What is it about this particular trait — more so than any other negative attribute — for which it was singled out as bearing such grievous consequences?

The final teaching of Yehudah ben Teima is likewise perplexing. In fact, it doesn't appear to be a "teaching" at all, but rather a prayer. יְהִי רָצוֹן מִלְּפָנֶיךָ ה' אֱלֹקֵינוּ שֶׁיִּבָּנֶה בֵּית הַמִּקְדָּשׁ בִּמְהֵרָה בְיָמֵינוּ וְתֵן חֶלְקֵנוּ בְּתוֹרָתֶךָ — *May it be Your will, Hashem our G-d and the G-d of our fathers, that the Beis Hamikdash be built speedily in our times, and that You grant our portion in Your Torah*. A prayer in the middle of the mishnah? What is its place here, and what's the connection to the preceding statement?

Holy Hot-headedness

The Nesivos Sholom elucidates the issue, uncovering the true clarity in Yehudah ben Teima's message. He explains that there are, in fact, two varieties of *azus*, stemming from different sources. Which one a person selects makes all the difference.

Azus need not necessarily be entirely "bad"; in fact, in one form it can be put to great and productive use. This is the *azus* which stems from a sincere desire to fulfill Hashem's will — *La'asos retzon Avicha shebaShamayim*. This type of brazenness (upon which we shall soon elaborate) is the subject of Yehudah ben Teima's first teaching, and certainly deserves its place as the preamble to the code of Torah life. "Be bold as a leopard...to fulfill Hashem's will." This is a selfless *azus*, in which the individual dedicates himself to the Almighty's service.

It is the other form of *azus* which Yehudah ben Teima casts in such harsh terms — and does so with immediacy. This is *azus* which stems from the quality of *yeishus*, a person's overblown sense of self-importance which spurs him to brazenly assert himself in the face of his fellow men. It is this variety that is particularly pernicious in the *Tanna's* eyes.

Rather than a contradiction and a set of mixed messages, Yehudah ben Teima was seeking to provide urgent clarification. He stressed the need for enlisting the trait of *azus* to fulfill Hashem's will. But as necessary as it was to impart this lesson, the mention of this *middah* opens up a proverbial can of worms. Having encouraged the cultivation of this quality — albeit the positive variety — presents a certain danger. Once courting with this *middah*, a person may end up adopting the related form, whose root is essentially evil. To prevent this grievous error, the *Tanna* followed his initial teaching with a strongly-worded warning. Once engaging in the *middah* of *azus*, take care not to embrace its more nefarious aspect; for that leads directly to a most horrifying end.

The same clarification process plays itself out among the statement of the *Tur* and the Beis Yosef's comments to it. After citing Yehudah ben Teima's teaching — *Hevei az kanameir* — the *Tur* continues with some elaboration. "Sometimes," he explains, "a person wishes to perform a mitzvah, but refrains from doing so, having been intimidated by other people who would scoff at him... Therefore, (*Chazal*) exhort him to be brazen-faced against scoffers, *not to be*

ashamed." These concluding words are somewhat curious; why did the *Tur* need to include this additional phrase?

The Beis Yosef elucidates the *Tur's* intent. The *Tur*, it seems, had the identical concern as expressed above. Adopting a path of brazenness in the service of Hashem is a necessary endeavor; but in doing so, one also enters into potentially dangerous territory. It is certainly undesirable that a person acquire an overall brazen bearing. The Beis Yosef explains that the *Tur* was seeking to limit the scope of his encouragement to foster *azus* in the service of Hashem. He was clarifying that — while promoting *azus* to oppose the scoffers — he never intended to sanction actually acting and *speaking* in a brazen manner. In doing so, the potential for damage is too great; if one speaks brazenly even to scoffers, he may cultivate a familiarity with this *middah*, which will carry over into other affairs. Thus, he will end up being brazen in even mundane activities, as it now has become ingrained in his nature.

And so, the *Tur* emphasizes that this is not the way to go; being brazen in Hashem's service is limited to an *internal conviction*. "Do not be ashamed," says the *Tur*; this is the extent to which he "permits" and encourages the exercise of *azus*. It can indeed play an important role in fulfilling His will. But all this positive form of *azus* entails is an inner feeling of confidence; being secure that he walks the right path, the earnest *oveid* will not be intimidated by those who may mock him. But actual *azus* must be avoided.

Azus, explains the Nesivos Sholom, is like medicine. There are medicines which contain poisonous or hazardous ingredients. These ingredients can actually be helpful in fighting certain illnesses — but only if administered by a medical expert. Should someone deviate even minimally from the prescribed amount, ingesting just a bit more of the drug than absolutely necessary — the results can be fatal. Our Sages, the healers of the soul, prescribed a certain measure of *azus* — just the right type and amount to fulfill the will of our Father in Heaven. But a deviation from their exact prescription can lead to Gehinnom.

What role does the concluding "prayer" of the mishnah have in this discussion? We may acquire insight into this issue by examining the two types of *azus* a bit further.

True Jewish Pride — an Outgrowth of Truth

As mentioned, the undesirable form of *azus* stems from a sense of *yeishus*. The mishnah's characterization of *Az panim l'Gehinnom* reveals the extent of just how nefarious this is — apparently, it has its roots in the domain of the *Sitra Achra* itself.

By stark contrast, the *azus* associated with fulfilling Hashem's will is referred to as *azus d'kedushah* — "brazenness of sanctity." This quality is related to another essential entity, as it has its roots in *emes*. This is the nature of the *azus d'kedushah*; the *oveid* is supremely confident in his actions, for he knows that they are rooted in principles of truth. Secure in the righteousness of his ways, he is unintimidated and unfazed in the face of his detractors who advocate a path of falsehood and vice.

This is the full import of the words of the *Tur*, as explained by the Beis Yosef. When confronted by the pressure exerted by the scoffers, there are different ways whereby the earnest *oveid* could respond. Our Sages counseled *azus* in such a situation. One may have thought this entails steeling oneself to do the right thing despite the pangs of shame. But by appending that admonition at the conclusion of his remarks — "Do not be ashamed" — the *Tur* was exhorting one to aim even higher. Real *azus d'kedushah* means not even *feeling* any shame. The *oveid* must know that the truth is on his side; so strong in his convictions should he be that no embarrassment under these circumstances even registers on his being. This is the meaning of true "Jewish pride": a Yid fulfills the will of his Creator, for that is what is right and what is true. Any voices of dissent or scorn simply fade into the background as insignificant noise.

This is where Torah and Mikdash enter the picture. As stated, *azus d'kedushah* is predicated on *emes* — a quality which intensifies through the medium of these two entities. The rebuilding of the Beis Hamikdash will signify the ultimate rectification of the world; it will usher in an era of unprecedented clarity, whereby the entire creation

עז פנים לגיהנום ובושת פנים לגן עדן

will recognize the truth. Torah likewise breeds *emes*, as the *passuk* states (*Michah* 7:20): תִּתֵּן אֱמֶת לְיַעֲקֹב — *Grant truth to Yaakov*. Through the Mikdash and the Torah, which bring *emes* in their wake, a Yid can develop the right kind of *azus* in the most optimal way. This idea is reflected further by *Chazal's* revealing statement (*Beitzah* 25b): מִפְּנֵי מָה נִתְּנָה תּוֹרָה לְיִשְׂרָאֵל? מִפְּנֵי שֶׁהֵן עַזִּין — *Why was the Torah given to Yisroel? Because they are brazen*. To refine their brazen tendencies, and guide them towards the development of its pristine form, the *Yidden* were granted the Torah, to foster *emes* and hence *azus d'kedushah*. As Yehudah ben Teima teaches the importance of proper *azus*, he invokes the entities — Torah and Mikdash — through which one can attain perfection in this essential attribute.

The Maharal provides additional insight as to the inclusion of these two entities in the mishnah. He explains how they relate to the previous statement of Yehudah ben Teima, in which he spoke of the negative aspect of *azus* — *Az panim l'Gehinnom*. This statement is indeed sobering; especially in light of the fact that Yisroel has a certain propensity to this attribute. As *Chazal* remark in *Beitzah* (*ibid.*): *Yisroel azin sheba'umos* — "Yisroel is the most brazen of nations." As such, the danger of this grievous fate may almost seem close at hand, G-d forbid.

To forestall this peril, the Maharal contends, Yehudah ben Teima inserted a prayer, focusing specifically on those entities which can spare Yisroel from Gehinnom: Torah and Mikdash. That they have the power to do so is demonstrated in the Midrash (*Bereishis Rabbah* 44:21) which states: – אַרְבָּעָה דְּבָרִים הֶרְאָה לוֹ שִׁמְעוֹן בַּר אַבָּא בְּשֵׁם ר׳ יוֹחָנָן אָמַר: גֵּיהִנֹּם, וּמַלְכֻיּוֹת, וּמַתַּן תּוֹרָה, וּבֵית הַמִּקְדָּשׁ. א"ל: כָּל זְמַן שֶׁבָּנֶיךָ עֲסוּקִים בִּשְׁתַּיִם, הֵם נִצּוֹלִים מִשְּׁתַּיִם; פֵּרְשׁוּ מִשְּׁתַּיִם, הֵם נִדּוֹנִין בִּשְׁתַּיִם — *Shimon bar Aba said in the name of Rabbi Yochanan: Hashem showed Avraham four things (two sets of two) — Gehinnom and subjugation to gentile dominion, the Giving of the Torah and the Beis Hamikdash. Hashem said to him: "As long as your offspring are engaged with the (second set of) two, they will be spared from the (first set of) two; if they withdraw from the (second set of) two, they will be subjected to the (first set of) two."* Thus we see that Torah and Mikdash have the power to remove Yisroel from the reach of Gehinnom (as well as gentile domination).

How does engagement in Torah and Mikdash accomplish this vital feat? The Maharal explains that they correspond to the principal faculties within man. The centrally located heart is the mainstay of a person, as it pumps life-blood and essential elements to all surrounding portions of the body. In the same vein, Eretz Yisroel is the center of the world, with the Beis Hamikdash as its center. As such, the Beis Hamikdash functions as the "heart" of the world, with the life-force of the universe emanating from within it. A person's mind is responsible for all of his functionality; the Torah plays a similar role, serving as the *seichel* (intellect) of the world. As such, these entities are crucial for deliverance from Gehinnom. Gehinnom is a state which is the quintessential embodiment of *avadon* — degeneration into nothingness. Torah and Mikdash are the perfect counterforce to this *avadon*, serving, as they do, as the world's most premier entities. Forging a connection to them puts the individual on the furthest pole from "nothingness."

The Nesivos Sholom adds to this most profound explanation of the Maharal. Continuing with this theme that they serve as the "mind" and "heart" of the world, he explains their great utility in terms of the positive influence they exert on the *middah* of *azus*. For, as mentioned, Torah and Beis Hamikdash are tremendous assets of *emes*, that quality which so empowers the earnest *oveid* and enables him to cultivate real *azus d'kedushah*. This is why Yehudah ben Teima adds this *tefillah* at the conclusion of his words. He had spoken of the positive form of *azus*, and warned against its more malevolent side. And so he offers this supplication in which he asks for a connection with Torah, and the rebuilding of the Beis Hamikdash. Then, *emes* will be revealed in its full glory, facilitating the rectification of *azus* to the most optimal and far-reaching extent, affecting the minds and hearts of Yisroel.

עז פנים לגיהנום ובושת פנים לגן עדן

In Summary

Yehudah ben Teima addresses the issue of *azus* in a series of what seems to be either contradictory or unrelated statements. He first advocates for this attribute, exhorting a Yid to be "brazen as a leopard." In what appears at first glance to be a 180-degree reversal, he then states in short order that "the brazen-faced is headed for Gehinnom." After which he inserts a prayer about the rebuilding of the Beis Hamikdash, and asking that our portion be in the Torah. What could this all mean?

The Nesivos Sholom demonstrates that, of course, this great *Tanna* is indeed presenting a lucid and urgent teaching. He encourages the cultivation of *azus* in the service of Hashem, but of the specific form referred to as *azus d'kedushah*. This is the *middah* whereby a Yid can serve his Creator, undaunted by the taunts of scoffers. At the same time, however, entering into the territory of *azus* can be fraught with danger, for its other form — stemming from *yeishus* — can be disastrous to one's *ruchniyus*. It is this latter form which leads one to Gehinnom. And so, Yehudah ben Teima's words are not contradictory in the least. Having broached the general topic of *azus*, urging the adoption of its positive form, it was very necessary to issue an immediate warning and clarification. While *azus d'kedushah* is laudable and essential, its counterpart is pernicious. Thus, care must be taken that one not develop the form of *azus* which can have the most horrific consequences.

Yehudah ben Teima then invokes Torah and the Beis Hamikdash. These are entities, as the Maharal explains, which are particularly suited for distancing a person from Gehinnom. The Jewish people, *Chazal* assert, are inherently a brazen nation, thus running the tremendous risk of gravitating towards Gehinnom, G-d forbid. However, as the Midrash states explicitly, the entities of Torah and Mikdash can deliver them from this disastrous fate.

The Nesivos Sholom further explains that Torah and Mikdash are particularly effective for developing the proper form of *azus*.

Essentially, *azus d'kedushah* stems from *emes*, as a Yid becomes secure in his convictions, knowing the truth of his positions. As such, the mockery of the scoffers does not even register on his being. The *Tanna* thus invokes Torah and Mikdash, for both of these entities are renowned for their fostering of *emes* in the world, the essential ingredient for the proper cultivation of *azus d'kedushah*.

פרק ה' משנה כ"ו
הפך בה והפך בה דכלא בה
Delve into It Again and Again, for All Is in It

בֶּן בַּג בַּג אוֹמֵר, הֲפָךְ בָּהּ וַהֲפָךְ בָּהּ, דְּכֹלָּא בָהּ. וּבָהּ תֶּחֱזֵי, וְסִיב וּבְלֵה בָהּ, וּמִנַּהּ לָא תָזוּעַ, שֶׁאֵין לְךָ מִדָּה טוֹבָה הֵימֶנָּה. בֶּן הֵא הֵא אוֹמֵר, לְפוּם צַעֲרָא אַגְרָא:

Ben Bag Bag says: Delve into it again and again, for all is in it; see with it; grow old and worn in it; do not budge from it; for there is no entity greater than it.

Ben Hei Hei says: According to the effort is the reward.

GEMS FROM THE *SEFER NESIVOS SHOLOM*

SOURCES:

אַל תִּהְיוּ כַּעֲבָדִים הַמְשַׁמְּשִׁין אֶת הָרַב עַל מְנָת לְקַבֵּל פְּרָס, אֶלָּא הֱווּ כַּעֲבָדִים הַמְשַׁמְּשִׁין אֶת הָרַב שֶׁלֹּא עַל מְנָת לְקַבֵּל פְּרָס. (אבות א׳)

Do not be as servants who serve their master for the sake of receiving a reward; rather be like servants who serve their master not for the sake of receiving a reward. (*Avos* 1)

בֶּן חָמֵשׁ שָׁנִים לַמִּקְרָא, בֶּן עֶשֶׂר לַמִּשְׁנָה, בֶּן שְׁלֹשׁ עֶשְׂרֵה לַמִּצְוֹת, בֶּן חֲמֵשׁ עֶשְׂרֵה לַגְּמָרָא, בֶּן שְׁמוֹנֶה עֶשְׂרֵה לַחֻפָּה... (שם ה׳)

A five-year old is for Scripture; at ten – for Mishnah; at thirteen – for mitzvos; at fifteen – for Gemara; at eighteen – for marriage... (*ibid.* 5)

יֵצֶר לֵב הָאָדָם רַע מִנְּעֻרָיו. (בראשית ח׳ כ״א)

The inclination of a person's heart is evil from his youth. (*Bereishis* 8:21)

בָּרָאתִי יֵצֶר הָרָע, וּבָרָאתִי לוֹ תּוֹרָה תַּבְלִין. (קידושין ל׳)

I have created the evil inclination; I have created the Torah as its remedy. (*Kiddushin* 30b)

יִצְרוֹ שֶׁל אָדָם מִתְגַּבֵּר עָלָיו בְּכָל יוֹם... יִצְרוֹ שֶׁל אָדָם מִתְחַדֵּשׁ עָלָיו בְּכָל יוֹם. (שם)

A person's evil inclination surges against him every day... A person's *yetzer hara* renews itself against him every day. (*ibid.*)

אָנוּ עֲמֵלִים וְהֵם עֲמֵלִים. אָנוּ עֲמֵלִים וּמְקַבְּלִים שָׂכָר, וְהֵם עֲמֵלִים וְאֵינָם מְקַבְּלִים שָׂכָר. (תפילה על הסיום)

We toil and they toil. We toil and receive a reward, and they toil and do not receive a reward. (Prayer for the completion of a body of Torah study)

פרקי אבות

660

הפך בה והפך בה דכלא בה

אִם אֵין תּוֹרָה, אֵין דֶּרֶךְ אֶרֶץ. אִם אֵין דֶּרֶךְ אֶרֶץ, אֵין תּוֹרָה. (אבות ג׳)

If there is no Torah – there is no propriety. If there is no propriety – there is no Torah. (*Avos* 3)

פרק ה׳

GEMS FROM THE *SEFER NESIVOS SHOLOM*

The End

If you want to get a basic feel for what a particular book is about, there is a simple method that is fairly reliable. Browse the beginning, and take a look at the end. That should supply a general picture of what lies in between. It would be somewhat unusual if the beginning and the end were completely unrelated to the main content of the work.

And yet, this seems to be just the case when it comes to *Pirkei Avos*, the *masechta* devoted to the cultivation of proper *middos*. The fifth chapter is the *actual* final chapter of this *masechta*. (While there is a sixth chapter appended to it in most editions, it is technically not a part of *Maseches Avos*. In fact, it is not even part of the Mishnah, but rather a collection of *Bereisos* [Tannaitic teachings that Rebbi did not incorporate into the main body of Mishnah].) As such, the mishnayos appearing above serve as the final teachings of *Pirkei Avos*. But they do not seem to be discussing the main subject matter of this *masechta*! Instead of *middos*, the main focus seems to be on the topic of Torah study.

This appears to hold true for the beginning of *Avos*, as well. *Pirkei Avos* opens with the statement: מֹשֶׁה קִבֵּל תּוֹרָה מִסִּינַי — *Moshe received the Torah from Sinai*. Torah again! The beginning is Torah, the end is Torah — but, seemingly, that's not the focus of *Pirkei Avos*. How, indeed, are we to understand this apparent incongruity?

The incongruity seems to surface within this very mishnah as well. Ben Bag Bag discusses the importance of Torah study, but right in the middle he mentions the notion of character traits: שֶׁאֵין לְךָ מִדָּה טוֹבָה הֵימֶנָּה — *For there is no greater **trait** than it*; an interesting word selection when speaking of Torah. So, what is this mishnah about: Torah study or development of *middos*?

A perplexing issue is also posed by Ben Hei Hei's teaching: *L'fum tza'ara agra* — "According to the strenuousness is the reward." Why, all of a sudden — at the very conclusion of *Avos*, no less — are we suddenly interested in reward? This seems to contradict the altruistic tone set down at the very beginning of *Avos*, where Antignos Ish

הפך בה והפך בה דכלא בה

Socho stated (1:3): אַל תִּהְיוּ כַעֲבָדִים הַמְשַׁמְּשִׁין אֶת הָרַב עַל מְנָת לְקַבֵּל פְּרָס, אֶלָּא הֱווּ כַּעֲבָדִים הַמְשַׁמְּשִׁין אֶת הָרַב שֶׁלֹּא עַל מְנָת לְקַבֵּל פְּרָס — *Do not be as servants who serve their master for the sake of reward; rather be like servants who serve their master not for the sake of reward.*

What are we to make of these apparent inconsistencies? The Nesivos Sholom provides a way forward. He begins by examining the mishnah immediately preceding these teachings, understanding that they form a continuum of a single theme.

Chosen People

The previous mishnah (5:21) discusses the various stages of a person's life, from early youth through one's advanced years: בֶּן חָמֵשׁ שָׁנִים לַמִּקְרָא, בֶּן עֶשֶׂר לַמִּשְׁנָה, בֶּן שְׁלֹשׁ עֶשְׂרֵה לַמִּצְוֹת, בֶּן חֲמֵשׁ עֶשְׂרֵה לַגְמָרָא, בֶּן שְׁמוֹנֶה עֶשְׂרֵה לַחֻפָּה וכו׳ — *A five-year old is for Scripture; at ten, for Mishnah; at thirteen, for mitzvos; at fifteen, for Gemara; at eighteen, for marriage...* (The mishnah proceeds to outline the various stages, through one hundred years old.) What is somewhat perplexing about this mishnah is that its message is somewhat elusive. At first glance, it seems like just a listing of various ages and stages. What profound lesson does it seek to convey?

The Nesivos Sholom explains that, in fact, the mishnah is imparting some important fundamentals for life. The idea can be brought out by examining the very nature and mission of the Jewish people in This World. The world knows — and essentially acknowledges the fact — that we are the *am hanivchar*, the Chosen People. They may despise and persecute us on this account, but the notion is not unknown to the world, nor has it been throughout the centuries.

But what, indeed, does it mean — "Chosen" for what? Actually, the idea is mentioned quite clearly in the text of the familiar blessing: אֲשֶׁר בָּחַר בָּנוּ מִכָּל הָעַמִּים, וְנָתַן לָנוּ אֶת תּוֹרָתוֹ — *Who has chosen us from all of the nations, and granted us His Torah.* Our survival and purpose as the Chosen Nation is inextricably linked with the Torah Hashem has given us. That is, it is only through the offices of the holy Torah that we are able to accomplish our mission in This World.

GEMS FROM THE *SEFER NESIVOS SHOLOM*

יֵצֶר לֵב הָאָדָם רַע מִנְּעֻרָיו — *The inclination of a person's heart is evil from his youth* (*Bereishis* 8:21). This is the task that faces a Yid in This World: to overcome his inherent tendencies and eradicate the negative qualities from his very essence. In truth, this is a monumental endeavor; not only does it go contrary to his nature, but it is near impossible to accomplish. There is only one avenue, a single antidote Hashem created through which a Yid can emerge victorious. As *Chazal* tell us (*Kiddushin* 30b), Hashem proclaims: בָּרָאתִי יֵצֶר הָרָע, וּבָרָאתִי לוֹ תּוֹרָה תַּבְלִין — *I have created the* yetzer hara; *I have created the Torah as its remedy.*

This, explains the Nesivos Sholom, is the theme of the aforementioned mishnah. Regarding man's mission in the world, the Arizal made a most profound statement. He asserts that every day since the time of Creation carries with it its own unique mission, what needs to be accomplished on that specific day. And the mission is never the same. This is true, as well, with regards to people: No two people — since the inception of the world — are charged with the identical task, and the task of any particular individual can only be fulfilled by him alone. And even regarding individual people, the mission varies based on the times; that is, at each of the different time periods of his life, he has a different mission to fulfill.

But there is only one way to accomplish one's task — and this is the import of the mishnah's teaching. The mishnah seeks to convey that, throughout the various time periods through which a person passes during his lifetime — entailing a new mission with each change — it is only through the *ko'ach haTorah*, the power of Torah, that one can emerge successful. At five it is through Scripture, at ten through Mishnah, etc. At each step along the way, a Yid must enlist the power of Torah and mitzvos in order to accomplish his individualized task.

We can now understand the relevance of the beginning and end of *Avos* to the main content of this *masechta*. What does Torah study have to do with the endeavor to perfect one's *middos*? The answer is: everything. In fact, it's the only way. The overall mission of every Yid on this earth is to uproot the negative traits that infest his essence and transform himself into an elevated individual with pristine

פרקי אבות

664

middos. By beginning and ending the *masechta* with the notion of Torah study, Rebbi — who compiled the Mishnah — is imparting this important fact: it is only through the *ko'ach haTorah* that a person can fulfill the all-important task of refining his *middos*.

The Final Three

Thus we see that this theme runs through the final three mishnayos of the chapter. As previously demonstrated, the mishnah of *Ben chameish l'Mikra* — "A five-year old is for Scripture" contains this important lesson. Ben Bag Bag picks up the thread: הֲפָךְ בָּהּ וַהֲפָךְ בָּהּ...וְסִיב וּבְלֵה בָהּ — *Delve into it again and again...and grow old and become worn away (while still attached) to it.* Referring to the Torah, Ben Bag Bag exhorts us to constantly stay by and utilize the Torah in all situations and throughout all the different time periods of our life. The *yetzer hara* never gives up; it asserts itself throughout our life. As *Chazal* state (*Kiddushin* 30b): יִצְרוֹ שֶׁל אָדָם מִתְגַּבֵּר עָלָיו בְּכָל יוֹם... יִצְרוֹ שֶׁל אָדָם מִתְחַדֵּשׁ עָלָיו בְּכָל יוֹם — *A person's* yetzer hara *surges against him every day... A person's* yetzer hara *renews itself against him every day.* It is only through the Torah that he can resist the *yetzer hara* and weed out his negative tendencies — both in his youth, as well as his old age.

This idea is also the essence of the next phrase: שֶׁאֵין לְךָ מִדָּה טוֹבָה הֵימֶנָּה — *For there is no greater* middah *than it.* Quite purposefully, Ben Bag Bag inserts the term *middah* in the midst of his exhortation to Torah study, for Torah is the factor that enables him to attain proper *middos*. In a sense, this phrase can be understood as saying: "There is nothing that leads to good *middos* like Torah."

Rounding out the chapter is Ben Hei Hei's succinct teaching: *L'fum tza'ara agra* — "In proportion to the strenuousness is the reward." The Nesivos Sholom understands this statement as continuing along the lines of the above. The previous two mishnayos highlighted that Torah is essential for vanquishing the *yetzer hara* and refining one's *middos*. But there is potential for someone hearing this message to become discouraged. Torah study is the most worthwhile and exhilarating experience; but it is also a process, one that requires effort and perseverance. It is not unusual for a person to encounter challenges along the way, and it may appear to him that he is not succeeding in his studies. This can lead to discouragement, as well, in the endeavor to fight one's natural tendencies. "It is only through Torah that I can prevail over my failings," a person may tell himself. "And my success in learning is limited, at best. If that's the case, how will I ever grow spiritually? How can I defeat my *yetzer hara* and perfect my character, if my learning is not up to par?"

And so, Ben Hei Hei aims to forestall these understandable but debilitating thoughts. He encourages a Yid to remember that, as long as he is putting in an earnest effort in his learning, he not only will succeed, he *is* succeeding.

The Chofetz Chaim demonstrates how this is so. He quotes from the prayer (based on *Berachos* 28b) we recite at a *siyum* (celebration upon the completion of a Torah volume): אָנוּ עֲמֵלִים וְהֵם עֲמֵלִים. אָנוּ עֲמֵלִים וּמְקַבְּלִים שָׂכָר, וְהֵם עֲמֵלִים וְאֵינָם מְקַבְּלִים שָׂכָר — *We toil and they toil. We toil and receive a reward, and they toil and do not receive a reward*. This statement differentiates between those who are occupied with Torah and those who are immersed in worldly pursuits. The implication, obviously, is that the former group is much more fortunate, as their toil bears fruit.

But the assertion itself seems puzzling. Others toil for no reward? Is that so? A common refrain of a hard worker is, "I'm not just doing this for my health." Millions of people put in hours upon hours of strenuous activity for the purpose of receiving a paycheck. What does it mean that "they work without receiving compensation"?

The Chofetz Chaim explains that these words reflect a truly breathtaking notion. Of course, people work and receive payment. Otherwise, they wouldn't bother, and rightfully so. What is really being highlighted here is the remarkable opportunity that Torah study affords.

Let us say, for example, that someone was working on an ambitious project — be it in business, the sciences, and the like. After hours and days of painstaking labor, the endeavor, in the end, leads to nothing. The experiment failed, no cure was found, the plan proved unprofitable, etc. Truly a most unfortunate outcome. And what is this worker, who invested so much time and effort, left with? The sad reality is: nothing. This is because, as far as the world at large is concerned, the outcome is paramount. Of course, payment is offered — but for results. The effort may be appreciated but does not translate into actual compensation.

But Torah is different. When it comes to the endeavor of Torah study, just the opposite is true: It is the *effort* that is paramount; the results and success are only secondary. They toil and don't receive reward — when it comes to the raw efforts, the world does not offer rewards. But in the realm of Torah study, this is Hashem's prime interest. The reward is offered *precisely* for the toil — regardless of the actual outcome.

Ben Hei Hei's teaching can be understood in this light. As mentioned, he seeks to give succor to the despondent soul, one who recognizes that he needs Torah to fight his natural tendencies but feels that his learning is unsuccessful. Addressing these concerns, Ben Hei Hei says, "No! This is a grave error! It is not the outcome that matters — it is the effort!" *L'fum tza'ara agra* — "According to the exertion is the 'reward.'" Actually, the "reward" mentioned here is not the "payment" one receives in the World to Come. It is definitely the case that he will receive such reward; but that is not Ben Hei Hei's intent. As Antignos Ish Socho already declared, one should ideally be serving his Master not for the sake of the reward. What Ben Hei Hei is referring to here is actually the aforementioned theme: the power of Torah to elevate a person. This is the "reward" of which Ben Hei Hei speaks: the "fruits" borne by Torah study, which affect a person by refining his essence. Ben Hei Hei exhorts us not to give in to despair. For even if it appears that our learning is not successful, it doesn't mean that it's not productive. On the contrary — as long as we are putting in effort, that is all that really matters. For it is the exertion that ultimately bears fruit, purifies our nature, and helps us to attain exalted levels of spirituality.

Which Came First?

There is one matter that still requires some clarification. Until this point, we have been discussing the essentiality of Torah in the endeavor of rectifying one's character; without the *ko'ach haTorah*, it is not possible to eradicate negative tendencies. On the other hand, however, there appear to be indications that the process is actually reversed.

In his *sefer Sha'arei Kedushah*, Rav Chaim Vital wonders why it is that the Torah does not issue an explicit command concerning proper *middos*. Perfecting one's *middos* is such a vital endeavor; why did the Torah not see fit to ensconce it in the framework of a specific mitzvah? He explains, however, that that is precisely the point. It is *because* it is such a fundamental undertaking that there is no specific mitzvah attached to it. For perfection in *middos* is a prerequisite to Torah and mitzvos; essentially, *middos* serve as the foundation of the entire Torah. Apparently, then, it is *middos* that can serve as the basis for Torah — and not the other way around, as we have been stating until now!

Perhaps even more glaring is the fact that this paradox seems to appear straight out in a mishnah. Elsewhere in *Avos* (3:17), the mishnah states: אִם אֵין תּוֹרָה, אֵין דֶּרֶךְ אֶרֶץ. אִם אֵין דֶּרֶךְ אֶרֶץ, אֵין תּוֹרָה — *If there is no Torah, there is no propriety. If there is no propriety, there is no Torah*. Such a statement raises the obvious question: Which is it? Is it Torah that is necessary for the development of proper attitudes, or is it a decent nature that facilitates Torah?

The Nesivos Sholom clarifies the issue. Based on the commentary of Rabbeinu Yonah, he draws a distinction between the establishment of a base of good *middos*, and attaining perfection of character. In other words, as Rav Chaim Vital asserted, it does all start with a foundation of proper *middos*. The Torah cannot reside within an individual whose character is utterly corrupted; he must first achieve a basic measure of decency and good *middos*. אִם אֵין דֶּרֶךְ אֶרֶץ, אֵין תּוֹרָה.

But to go any further is impossible without harnessing the power of Torah. אִם אֵין תּוֹרָה, אֵין דֶּרֶךְ אֶרֶץ. To perfect one's *middos*, and completely refine one's internal essence — this is the lesson of *Pirkei Avos*. Our task in life is to aim for perfection in the area of *middos*; something that can only be achieved through Torah.

In Summary

On the face of it, the structure of *Pirkei Avos* seems somewhat incongruous. It begins with Torah: מֹשֶׁה קִבֵּל תּוֹרָה מִסִּינַי. It ends with Torah: הֲפָךְ בָּהּ וַהֲפָךְ בָּהּ, דְּכֹלָּא בָהּ. And yet, primarily, this *masechta* is not about the endeavor of Torah study. Rather, it is the treatise for the development of proper *middos*. What, then, is the meaning of this seemingly peculiar arrangement?

The Nesivos Sholom explains that, indeed, the notion of Torah study is not at all incidental to the main subject matter of *Pirkei Avos*, which is good *middos*. The intent of granting Torah such honorable mention in these key places is to convey a vital point: that it is only through the *ko'ach haTorah* that a Yid can even engage in the great process of transforming his *middos*.

This theme runs throughout the final three mishnayos of *Pirkei Avos*. The third-to-last mishnah discusses the various time-periods of a person's life: בֶּן חָמֵשׁ שָׁנִים לַמִּקְרָא, בֶּן עֶשֶׂר לַמִּשְׁנָה וכו׳. The message of the mishnah is that we confront various challenges throughout every stage of our life; in each of these periods, we have a specific mission to fulfill, a task of perfecting our self. And the mission at each phase of existence can only be successfully accomplished by harnessing the *ko'ach haTorah*. Ben Bag Bag continues along these lines, exhorting us to remain immersed in Torah in order to vanquish our *yetzer hara* throughout our life, when both young and old. שֶׁאֵין לְךָ מִדָּה טוֹבָה הֵימֶנָּה — There is nothing that is more beneficial for improving one's *middos* than the Torah; it leads to all good *middos*.

Ben Hei Hei delivers an important message in keeping with this theme. Someone may be experiencing some difficulty with his learning and does not see himself as particularly successful. As such, he may start to worry: Since Torah is essential for self-growth and perfection of character, how will I ever achieve these worthy goals? My learning is flawed! Ben Hei Hei responds to these concerns. He reassures a Yid that as long as he tries earnestly, this itself is the greatest success. *L'fum tza'ara agra.* As the Nesivos Sholom explains, this refers to the effectiveness of Torah to change a person. Success in this regard is not measured by outcome; it is the toil that is paramount. As long as one puts in the effort, this is the greatest success. For through the toil alone, the Yid will become elevated and attain the heights of perfection in *middos.*

And this is what *Pirkei Avos* is all about.

# Gems from the ספר נתיבות שלום NESIVOS SHOLOM

פרק ו'

פרק ו' משנה א'
הָעוֹסֵק בַּתּוֹרָה לִשְׁמָהּ זוֹכֶה לִדְבָרִים הַרְבֵּה
One Who Engages in Torah Study for Its Own Sake Merits Many Things

רַבִּי מֵאִיר אוֹמֵר כָּל הָעוֹסֵק בַּתּוֹרָה לִשְׁמָהּ, זוֹכֶה לִדְבָרִים הַרְבֵּה. וְלֹא עוֹד אֶלָּא שֶׁכָּל הָעוֹלָם כֻּלּוֹ כְּדַאי הוּא לוֹ. נִקְרָא רֵעַ, אָהוּב, אוֹהֵב אֶת הַמָּקוֹם, אוֹהֵב אֶת הַבְּרִיּוֹת, מְשַׂמֵּחַ אֶת הַמָּקוֹם, מְשַׂמֵּחַ אֶת הַבְּרִיּוֹת, וּמַלְבַּשְׁתּוֹ עֲנָוָה וְיִרְאָה, וּמַכְשַׁרְתּוֹ לִהְיוֹת צַדִּיק חָסִיד יָשָׁר וְנֶאֱמָן, וּמְרַחַקְתּוֹ מִן הַחֵטְא, וּמְקָרַבְתּוֹ לִידֵי זְכוּת, וְנֶהֱנִין מִמֶּנּוּ עֵצָה וְתוּשִׁיָּה בִּינָה וּגְבוּרָה. שֶׁנֶּאֱמַר לִי עֵצָה וְתוּשִׁיָּה אֲנִי בִינָה לִי גְבוּרָה, וְנוֹתֶנֶת לוֹ מַלְכוּת וּמֶמְשָׁלָה וְחִקּוּר דִּין, וּמְגַלִּין לוֹ רָזֵי תוֹרָה, וְנַעֲשֶׂה כְּמַעְיָן הַמִּתְגַּבֵּר וּכְנָהָר שֶׁאֵינוֹ פוֹסֵק, וֶהֱוֵי צָנוּעַ וְאֶרֶךְ רוּחַ, וּמוֹחֵל עַל עֶלְבּוֹנוֹ, וּמְגַדַּלְתּוֹ וּמְרוֹמַמְתּוֹ עַל כָּל הַמַּעֲשִׂים:

Rabbi Meir says: Whoever engages in Torah study for its own sake merits many things; furthermore, the (creation of the) entire world is worthwhile for his sake alone. He is called a friend, beloved, one who loves the Omnipresent, one who loves people, one who gladdens the Omnipresent, one who gladdens people. (The Torah) clothes him in humility and fear (of Hashem); it makes him fit to be righteous, pious, upright, and faithful; it keeps him far from sin, and draws him near to merit. From him people enjoy counsel and wisdom, understanding and strength; as it states (*Mishlei* 8:14): "Mine are counsel and wisdom, I am understanding, Mine is strength." (The Torah) grants him kingship, dominion, and analytical judgment; the secrets of the Torah are revealed to him; he becomes like a steadily strengthening fountain and a river that does not cease; he becomes modest, patient, and forgiving of insults to himself. (The Torah) makes him great and uplifts him above all things.

העוסק בתורה לשמה זוכה לדברים הרבה

SOURCES:

מִי־הָאִישׁ הֶחָכָם וְיָבֵן אֶת־זֹאת... עַל־מָה אָבְדָה הָאָרֶץ... וַיֹּאמֶר ה' עַל־עָזְבָם אֶת־תּוֹרָתִי אֲשֶׁר נָתַתִּי לִפְנֵיהֶם וְלֹא־שָׁמְעוּ בְקוֹלִי וְלֹא־הָלְכוּ בָהּ. (ירמיה ט' י"א, י"ב)

Who is the man who is wise to understand this matter... Why has the Land gone lost? ... And Hashem said: "For their forsaking of My Torah which I gave before them, and they did not listen to My voice, nor did they walk in its ways." (Yirmiyahu 9:11, 12)

דָּבָר זֶה נִשְׁאַל לַחֲכָמִים וְלַנְּבִיאִים וְלֹא פֵּירְשׁוּהוּ, עַד שֶׁפֵּירְשׁוֹ הקב"ה בְּעַצְמוֹ, דִּכְתִיב: וַיֹּאמֶר ה' עַל־עָזְבָם אֶת־תּוֹרָתִי... אָמַר רַב יְהוּדָה אָמַר רַב: שֶׁאֵין מְבָרְכִין בַּתּוֹרָה תְּחִלָּה. (נדרים פ"א)

This matter was asked of the Sages and the Prophets, and they were unable to explain it. (It remained unresolved) until Hashem Himself explained it; as it states: "And Hashem said: 'For their forsaking of My Torah which I gave before them...'" ... Rabbi Yehudah said in the name of Rav: (This means) that they did not recite the blessing over Torah beforehand. (Nedarim 81a)

הֵיכַל ה' הֵמָּה. (ירמיה ז' ד')

They (themselves) are Hashem's sanctuary. (Yirmiyahu 7:4)

קוּדְשָׁא בְּרִיךְ הוּא אוֹרַיְיתָא וְיִשְׂרָאֵל כּוּלְּהוּ חַד... קוּדְשָׁא בְּרִיךְ הוּא אוֹרַיְיתָא וְיִשְׂרָאֵל מִתְקַשְּׁרִין דָּא בְּדָא. (זוהר)

The Holy One Blessed be He, the Torah, and Yisroel are all one... The Holy One Blessed be He, the Torah, and Yisroel are bound together, one to the other. (Zohar)

אָנֹכִי ה' אֱלֹקֶיךָ אֲשֶׁר הוֹצֵאתִיךָ מֵאֶרֶץ מִצְרָיִם. (שמות כ' ב')

I am Hashem your G-d Who took you out from the land of Egypt. (Shemos 20:2)

פרק ו'

675

GEMS FROM THE *SEFER NESIVOS SHOLOM*

אָנֹכִי נוֹטְרֵיקוֹן: אֲנָא נַפְשִׁי כְּתִיבַת יְהָבִית. (שבת ק"ה.)

(The word) "*Anochi* (I)" – through (the acrostic device known as) *notreikun* (contains the following message uttered by Hashem): I have inscribed "My Soul" (into the Torah), and have given this (to Klal Yisroel). (*Shabbos* 105a)

הִתְנָה הַקָּדוֹשׁ בָּרוּךְ הוּא עִם מַעֲשֵׂה בְרֵאשִׁית וְאָמַר לָהֶם: אִם יִשְׂרָאֵל מְקַבְּלִים הַתּוֹרָה – אַתֶּם מִתְקַיְּמִין, וְאִם לָאו – אֲנִי מַחֲזִיר אֶתְכֶם לְתוֹהוּ וָבוֹהוּ. (שם פ"ח.)

Hashem made the following stipulation with the works of creation, saying to them: "If Yisroel accepts the Torah, you will endure; but if not, I will return you to emptiness and nothingness." (*ibid.* 88a)

וְעָשׂוּ לִי מִקְדָּשׁ וְשָׁכַנְתִּי בְּתוֹכָם. (שמות כ"ה ח')

And they shall make for Me a sanctuary, and I shall rest My Presence among them. (*Shemos* 25:8)

בְּרֵאשִׁית בָּרָא ...כְּמוֹ שֶׁאָמְרוּ חז"ל: בִּשְׁבִיל הַתּוֹרָה שֶׁנִּקְרֵאת רֵאשִׁית דַּרְכּוֹ וּבִשְׁבִיל יִשְׂרָאֵל שֶׁנִּקְרְאוּ רֵאשִׁית תְּבוּאָתוֹ. (רש"י עה"ת בראשית א' א')

"*Bereishis* Hashem created"... The interpretation (of this term) follows what *Chazal* have expounded: (The world was created) for the sake of the Torah, which is referred to as the "Beginning of His path" (*Mishlei* 8:22), and for the sake of Yisroel which is referred to as "The first of His produce" (*Yirmiyahu* 2:3). (*Rashi*, *Bereishis* 1:1)

בְּכָל יוֹם וָיוֹם בַּת קוֹל יוֹצֵאת מֵהַר חוֹרֵב וּמַכְרֶזֶת וְאוֹמֶרֶת אוֹי לָהֶם לַבְּרִיּוֹת מֵעֶלְבּוֹנָהּ שֶׁל תּוֹרָה. (אבות ו')

Every day, a Heavenly voice resounds from Har Choreiv (Sinai), proclaiming and saying: "Woe to mankind for their insult to the Torah." (*Avos* 6)

העוסק בתורה לשמה זוכה לדברים הרבה

אָמַר רָבָא כַּמָּה טִפְּשָׁאֵי שְׁאַר אִינְשֵׁי דְּקַיְימֵי מִקַּמֵּי סֵפֶר תּוֹרָה וְלֹא קַיְימֵי מִקַּמֵּי גַּבְרָא רַבָּה. (מכות כ"ב:)

Rava said: Some people behave like such imbeciles! For they rise in the presence of a Torah scroll (indicating an awareness of the need to honor the Torah), yet they do not rise in the presence of a great Torah scholar! (*Makkos* 22b)

מָה רַבּוּ מַעֲשֶׂיךָ ה' כֻּלָּם בְּחָכְמָה עָשִׂיתָ, מָלְאָה הָאָרֶץ קִנְיָנֶךָ. (תהלים ק"ד כ"ד)

How numerous are Your works, Hashem! You have fashioned them all with wisdom – the earth is filled with Your possessions. (*Tehillim* 104:24)

גְּדוֹלָה תּוֹרָה יוֹתֵר מִן הַכְּהוּנָה וּמִן הַמַּלְכוּת, שֶׁהַמַּלְכוּת נִקְנֵית בִּשְׁלֹשִׁים מַעֲלוֹת, וְהַכְּהֻנָּה בְּעֶשְׂרִים וְאַרְבַּע, וְהַתּוֹרָה נִקְנֵית בְּאַרְבָּעִים וּשְׁמוֹנָה דְבָרִים. (אבות ו')

Great is Torah, more so than the priesthood and monarchy; for monarchy is acquired with thirty qualities, the priesthood with twenty-four, while Torah is acquired through forty-eight items. (*Avos* 6)

אֵין דִּבְרֵי תּוֹרָה מִתְקַיְימִין אֶלָּא בְּמִי שֶׁמֵּמִית עַצְמוֹ עָלֶיהָ. (ברכות ס"ג:)

Words of Torah only endure by one who "kills himself" over them. (*Berachos* 63b)

תּוֹרָה צִוָּה לָנוּ מֹשֶׁה מוֹרָשָׁה קְהִלַּת יַעֲקֹב – אַל תִּקְרֵי מוֹרָשָׁה אֶלָּא מְאוֹרָשָׂה. (ברכות נ"ז.)

"Moshe instructed us in the Torah; an inheritance of the congregation of Yaakov" (*Devarim* 33:4). Do not read this as stating "*morashah*" (inheritance), rather, read it as "*me'orasah*" (betrothed). (*Berachos* 57a)

בָּרָאתִי יֵצֶר הָרָע, וּבָרָאתִי לוֹ תּוֹרָה תַּבְלִין. (קידושין ל:)

I have created the evil inclination; I have created the Torah as its remedy. (*Kiddushin* 30b)

GEMS FROM THE *SEFER NESIVOS SHOLOM*

אִם יָגַעְתָּ הַרְבֵּה בְּדִבְרֵיהֶם הַקָּבָּ"ה מֵסִיר יצה"ר מִמְּךָ. (במדבר רבה י"ד ד')

If you have exerted much effort to study the Torah teachings of the Sages, Hashem will remove the *yetzer hara* from you. (*Bamidbar Rabbah* 14:4)

בְּג' דְבָרִים נִיתְּנָה הַתּוֹרָה: בְּאֵשׁ, וּבְמַיִם, וּבַמִּדְבָּר. (שם א' ז')

In connection with three elements was the Torah given: with fire, water, and the wilderness. (*ibid.* 1:7)

הַתְקֵן עַצְמְךָ לִלְמוֹד תּוֹרָה, שֶׁאֵינָהּ יְרֻשָּׁה לָךְ. (אבות ב')

Prepare yourself to learn Torah, for it is not given to you as an inheritance. (*Avos* 2)

ה' יִסְפֹּר בִּכְתוֹב עַמִּים. (תהלים פ"ז ו')

Hashem counts with the writing of the nations. (*Tehillim* 87:6)

העוסק בתורה לשמה זוכה לדברים הרבה

The *Churban Beis Hamikdash* — Destruction of the Holy Temple. We know it as one of the greatest tragedies of all time. But more than that, it was also one of the greatest puzzles of all time.

Chazal inform us (*Nedarim* 81a) that the *Churban* caused universal bafflement. The wise Sages didn't understand it, the prophets didn't understand it, even the ministering angels didn't understand it. The great question, עַל־מָה אָבְדָה הָאָרֶץ — *Why was the Land lost?* (*Yirmiyahu* 9:11), was asked, but none could supply an answer.

Then Hashem Himself revealed what it was that brought about the *Churban*: וַיֹּאמֶר ה׳ עַל־עָזְבָם אֶת־תּוֹרָתִי אֲשֶׁר נָתַתִּי לִפְנֵיהֶם וְלֹא־שָׁמְעוּ בְקוֹלִי וְלֹא־הָלְכוּ בָהּ — *And Hashem said: "For their abandonment of My Torah, which I placed before them; and they did not listen to My voice nor walk in (the Torah's ways)"* (ibid. v. 12). *Chazal* identify precisely the offense to which Hashem was referring: שֶׁאֵין מְבָרְכִין בַּתּוֹרָה תְּחִלָּה — *They would neglect to recite the (Torah) blessings before (engaging in) Torah study* (*Nedarim* ibid.).

The issue with this statement of *Chazal* is that, rather than clarifying the mystery, it appears only to add to it. They neglected to recite the proper blessings over engagement in Torah study — this warranted the *Churban Beis Hamikdash*?! This answer somehow cleared away all of the perplexity? And, come to think of it, the deed itself seems kind of strange. The fact that no one could figure out what had resulted in the *Churban* indicates that — to all appearances, at least — Klal Yisroel had seemed to be on admirable standing. Even in the end it was confirmed that, indeed, they had been involved in learning Torah. Their offense was in the fact that they failed to recite the prerequisite blessing. Why, in fact, did they do this? They were upstanding, they were engaging in Torah; why not simply say the right *brachos*? It doesn't seem to be such a particularly hard thing to do, and they could have saved themselves a lot of trouble.

Living Sanctuaries

The Bach enlightens us by showing that a deeper concept is at play here, one that occupies a central place in the teachings of *Chazal*: the idea of *Torah lishmah*. One of the places where it receives much focus is in the sixth *perek* of *Pirkei Avos*, beginning with the first mishnah. This is a most fitting place to begin uncovering the profundity of this all-important topic.

Now, the ideas presented in the mishnah itself require some clarification. The mishnah supplies an impressive list of the numerous qualities and benefits that accrue to someone who learns *Torah lishmah*: he is beloved, he becomes righteous and pious, his counsel is sought and valued, he is granted a measure of dominion, etc. Any time a Yid fulfills any mitzvah, as we know, this is a great achievement, replete with its own rewards. But nowhere do we find such a comprehensive list of benefits, save in connection with learning *Torah lishmah*! What is it about this particular endeavor that warrants such exclusive treatment? After all, shouldn't a Yid fulfill every mitzvah with *kavanah* for no reason other than to fulfill the will of Hashem?

What the mishnah states regarding the "worthiness" of our subject is likewise significant. וְלֹא עוֹד אֶלָּא שֶׁכָּל הָעוֹלָם כֻּלּוֹ כְּדַאי הוּא לוֹ — *Furthermore, the (creation of the) entire world is worthwhile for his sake alone.* Certainly quite a compliment! The entire creation, all it contains, and the world's past and future events are all worthwhile just so that one individual, on one occasion, can learn *Torah lishmah*! What exactly has this individual achieved to be worthy of such accolades?

And what, exactly, *is* this notion of *Torah lishmah*? This needs to be elucidated both in the general sense, clarifying what it entails; but also in the specific sense, as the terminology is somewhat curious. Why does the mishnah refer to it as *Torah lishmah* — "for **its** sake"? Wouldn't it have been more appropriate to state *Torah lishmo* — "for **His** (Hashem's) sake"?

The Nesivos Sholom addresses this last point by drawing a distinction between Torah and other mitzvos. When it comes to fulfilling a "standard" mitzvah, a Yid, ideally, should definitely do so solely for the sake of Hashem, *lishmo*. Engagement in Torah study is unique in that it should be undertaken *lishmah*, for **its** sake, referring to the fact that Hashem gave us the Torah for a specific purpose. One's learning should be conducted with this purpose and intention in mind.

What is this higher purpose for which Hashem gave us the Torah? The Bach (*Orach Chaim*, sec. 47) explains that Hashem's intention was that Klal Yisroel's involvement with Torah would not be limited to merely absorbing information, sacred as it is. Rather, the idea was that *we should become one with the Torah*; that is, our essence should literally become infused with the *kedushas haTorah*. Were Klal Yisroel to study Torah with this aim in mind, they would literally become "chariots" to bear the *Shechinah*, which would reside within them. They would fulfill the exalted description of Yirmiyahu Hanavi, who declared, *Heichal Hashem heimah* — "They (themselves) are Hashem's sanctuary" (*Yirmiyahu* 7:4).

This, the Bach continues, explains the "sin" that caused the *Churban*. It wasn't just that they neglected to make the introductory blessing on the Torah. Rather, it was an issue of attitude; while they did study Torah, their approach to the endeavor was completely wanting. They did not express or feel the gratitude they should have harbored towards Hashem for having bequeathed to them the Torah for the exalted purpose that He had envisioned. By failing to learn Torah for "its" sake — for the sake of the lofty ideal of inculcating Torah within them — they displayed the fact that they were basically uninterested. Having so spurned the *Shechinah*, neglecting to serve as its dwelling place, the *Shechinah* responded in kind and left the Land.

The Nesivos Sholom proceeds to elaborate on the glorious ideal to which the Bach refers. Why and how is it that it's specifically through involvement in Torah study that this monumental purpose is achieved?

D'veikus BaHashem — Forging the Connection

What is the ultimate purpose of Torah and all mitzvos? According to the *sefarim hakedoshim*, the fundamental aim of all *avodas Hashem* is for a Yid to achieve a state of *d'veikus* with Hashem.

But this lofty goal presents a significant problem. How is it even possible? Mortal man is inherently a creature of limitations; how can he attach himself to the infinite and boundless Hashem, an entity Whose nature is completely at odds with that of man! To this problem, Hashem supplied the solution: Torah. Through it, a Yid is able to connect with *Hakadosh Baruch Hu*.

This idea is expressed quite eloquently in the well-known statement of the Zohar: קוּדְשָׁא בְּרִיךְ הוּא אוֹרַיְיתָא וְיִשְׂרָאֵל כּוּלְהוּ חַד — *The Holy One, Blessed be He, the Torah, and Yisroel are all one*. This remarkable synthesis is achieved through the Torah, which serves as the bridge bringing Klal Yisroel together with their Father in Heaven. As the Zohar states further, קוּדְשָׁא בְּרִיךְ הוּא אוֹרַיְיתָא וְיִשְׂרָאֵל מִתְקַשְּׁרִין דָּא בְּדָא — *The Holy One, Blessed be He, the Torah, and Yisroel are bound together, one to the other.*

The *Me'or Einayim* (*Parshas Bechukosai*) provides some insight as to how the Torah serves in this capacity. It refers to an exalted and esoteric concept known as *tzimtzum* (condensation), the parameters of which are well beyond our limited ability to grasp. For our purposes, it intimates the notion that, in some sense, Hashem "condensed" His essence to be "contained" within the Torah. In doing so, Hashem provided an opportunity for the *Yidden* to achieve *d'veikus baHashem*. For when a Yid cleaves to the Torah, he also becomes one with Hashem Himself, Whose Presence resides within the Torah.

This idea is highlighted in *Chazal's* teaching (*Shabbos* 105a). Focusing on the first word of the *Aseres Hadibros*, אָנֹכִי ה' — *I am Hashem*, they apply an interpretive device known as *notreikun*. Essentially similar to an acrostic, they break up the letters of this word to find the following message contained in it: אֲנָא נַפְשִׁי כְּתִיבַת יְהָבִית — *I have inscribed "My Soul" (into the Torah), and have given this (to Klal Yisroel)*. The notion is similar to what the *sefarim hakedoshim* say about a tzaddik. They relate that one may perceive the soul of a tzaddik within his words: נֶפֶשׁ הַצַּדִּיק עָטוּף בְּדִיבּוּרוֹ — *The soul of a tzaddik is enveloped by his words*. On an infinitely higher plane, the same may be said of *Hakadosh Baruch Hu*: Hashem's "soul," as it were, is contained within the words and letters of the holy Torah.

These are the underpinnings of the Bach's monumental teaching. Hashem's intention in giving the Torah, as we have seen, was that a Yid should thereby be able to attain *d'veikus baHashem*. His *Shechinah* is "contained" within the Torah, so that a Jew who immerses himself in Torah will be able to cleave to Hashem Himself. When a Yid learns *lishmah*, with this intention in mind, he literally becomes a chariot and vessel within which Hashem's Presence may reside.

Thus, we have gained much insight into the unique status of Torah study. Whereas mitzvos must be performed *lishmo*, for **His** (Hashem's) sake, Torah study entails the added component of *lishmah*, for **its** sake. That is, the Torah was given for a specific, lofty purpose: to serve as a means of attaining *d'veikus* with Hashem. It is this intention a Yid must have in mind when approaching the supreme task of engaging in Torah study.

We can likewise understand why it is stated specifically about one who undertakes this venture that כָּל הָעוֹלָם כֻּלּוֹ כְּדַאי הוּא לוֹ — *The (creation of the) entire world is worthwhile for his sake alone*. Attaining *d'veikus baHashem* is the ultimate purpose of creation itself; as such, by learning *Torah lishmah*, a Yid fulfills the purpose of creation. He has made it worthwhile.

This last point contains much depth, upon which the Nesivos Sholom elaborates.

Torah and Creation

The Zohar tells us that Hashem gazed into the Torah and created the universe. This appears to be a rather perplexing statement; why did Hashem need to "gaze in the Torah" in order to form the world?

This statement of *Chazal* may be elucidated through a related teaching elsewhere. The Gemara relates (*Shabbos* 88a), הִתְנָה הַקָּדוֹשׁ בָּרוּךְ הוּא עִם מַעֲשֵׂה בְרֵאשִׁית וְאָמַר לָהֶם: אִם יִשְׂרָאֵל מְקַבְּלִים הַתּוֹרָה אַתֶּם מִתְקַיְּימִין, וְאִם לָאו – אֲנִי מַחֲזִיר אֶתְכֶם לְתוֹהוּ וָבוֹהוּ — *Hashem made the following stipulation with the works of creation, saying to them: "If Yisroel accepts the Torah, you will endure; but if not, I will return you to emptiness and nothingness."* A picture of the interrelatedness between the Torah and the *beri'ah* itself begins to emerge.

GEMS FROM THE *SEFER NESIVOS SHOLOM*

This idea is based on what *Chazal* reveal to us about the reason why Hashem created the world in the first place: namely, to acquire for Himself a *dirah batachtonim* — "a dwelling-place in the lower spheres" (*Midrash Tanchuma, Parshas Naso*). That is, Hashem desired to rest His Presence even in This World, the arena of physical desires and base materialism. In the section regarding the building of the Mishkan, the *passuk* states, וְעָשׂוּ לִי מִקְדָּשׁ וְשָׁכַנְתִּי בְּתוֹכָם — *And they shall make for Me a sanctuary, and I will reside therein* (*Shemos* 25:8). The *passuk* did not use the singular, *b'socho* — "in **it**," which would have intimated that the *Shechinah* would reside in the sanctuary. Rather, it utilized the plural form, *b'socham* — "in **them**." This refers to Klal Yisroel; that is, Hashem sought to rest His Presence literally within the body of each and every Yid. They were to serve as His dwelling place in the lower spheres.

Once again, we appear to be faced with a paradoxical — or impossible — objective. How could the lower spheres, the arena of lowly desires and materialism, accommodate the pristine grandeur of the *Shechinah*? In fact, this question is tinged with a certain element of peril; as *Chazal* taught us, this seemingly unattainable goal is the purpose for which the world was created in the first place. If it cannot be achieved, G-d forbid...

A similar query was posed before. We had learned that the purpose of the entirety of Torah and mitzvos is for a Yid to attain *d'veikus* with Hashem; something that likewise seemed impossible to accomplish, for how can a mortal, imperfect, limited being attach itself to the perfect sanctity of the Divine? Yet there is one word that simultaneously solves both issues: Torah. The Torah is that exalted element that binds a Yid to *Hakadosh Baruch Hu*. Thus, the Torah is the facilitating intermediary that makes it possible for the *Shechinah* to actually reside within each member of Klal Yisroel who attaches himself to Torah. It is the vehicle that enables Hashem to have a dwelling place amid the lower spheres, fulfilling thereby the purpose of creation.

With this we may understand the Zohar's intent in revealing that Hashem "gazed in the Torah" to create the world. The Nesivos Sholom explains that Hashem "contemplated" the Torah, which enabled Him to proceed with the process of creating the world. The issue was the one presented before: Hashem wished to have a *dirah batachtonim*, a place to dwell even among the lowliness of This World — but it didn't seem possible. How could base materialism accommodate the holiness of the *Shechinah*? Hashem discerned that there was one way in which this feat could be accomplished: He recognized that the Torah could serve as the intermediary to enable the height of sanctity to have a place amid the lowliness of This World.

The realization is sobering, as well, for without the Torah, the *Shechinah* simply cannot reside in This World, and the purpose of the universe would essentially be for naught. Hashem Himself declared as much, as related earlier, by telling the works of creation: *If* — אִם יִשְׂרָאֵל מְקַבְּלִים הַתּוֹרָה – אַתֶּם מִתְקַיְּימִין, וְאִם לָאו – אֲנִי מַחֲזִיר אֶתְכֶם לְתוֹהוּ וָבוֹהוּ *Yisroel accepts the Torah, you will endure; but if not, I will return you to emptiness and nothingness*. In the awful contingency that Yisroel would not accept the Torah, the universe, indeed, would have no need or reason to continue its existence, as Hashem could no longer dwell in its midst.

What emerges, then, is that the existence of Yisroel — and their acceptance and adherence to the Torah — is vital for the existence of the world. This notion is expressed in the very first word of the Torah. The first *passuk* in the Torah — בְּרֵאשִׁית בָּרָא אֱלֹקִים אֵת הַשָּׁמַיִם וְאֵת הָאָרֶץ — is conventionally translated as, "**In the beginning** G-d created the heavens and the earth." Though a precise rendering of this first term is beyond the scope of this work, *Chazal* do expound on it, breaking it up into two words: בִּשְׁבִיל רֵאשִׁית — (*The world was created*) *for the sake of "Reishis."* Drawing on other Scriptural references, *Chazal* derive that *Reishis* refers alternatively to the Torah or to Yisroel, yielding the following understanding of this *passuk*: "The world was created for the sake of Torah and Yisroel" (*cf. Rashi, Bereishis* 1:1). Thus, right from the start, the Torah lays down this foundational principle that the existence of the universe is indeed predicated on Yisroel's connection to the Torah, for this is what enables the universe to serve the purpose for which it was created.

GEMS FROM THE *SEFER NESIVOS SHOLOM*

When reciting the blessing over the Torah each morning, as we mention that Hashem נָתַן לָנוּ אֶת תּוֹרָתוֹ, we are not merely thanking Him for the fact that "He gave us His Torah." The reference, rather, is to the exalted intention Hashem had in mind for giving us the Torah, as delineated by the Bach. It is the fact that the Torah effectively serves as the *neshamah* of the world, which sustains creation through enabling the *Yidden* to fulfill their ultimate purpose of cleaving to Hashem. When *Chazal* tell us that the *Churban* was caused over the blessing of the Torah, they mean that Hashem's exalted intention in giving the Torah was disregarded, resulting in the spurning of Hashem's desire that the *Shechinah* dwell within Yisroel. Overlooking this lofty *kavanah* constitutes a grave affront to the Torah and the One Who gave it. In fact, this is the meaning of Rabbi Yehoshua ben Levi's message in the next mishnah (6:2), where he states, בְּכָל יוֹם וָיוֹם — בַּת קוֹל יוֹצֵאת מֵהַר חוֹרֵב וּמַכְרֶזֶת וְאוֹמֶרֶת אוֹי לָהֶם לַבְּרִיּוֹת מֵעֶלְבּוֹנָהּ שֶׁל תּוֹרָה — *Every day, a Heavenly voice resounds from Har Choreiv (Sinai), proclaiming and saying: "Woe to mankind for their insult to the Torah."* The "insult" to which Rabbi Yehoshua refers is this lack of awareness of the true value and purpose of the giving of the Torah, for this, indeed, is a dishonor to the Torah.

A Creative Partner

We have already encountered some of the great depth that lies in the beginning of this mishnah, have been apprised of the inherent profundity of Torah *lishmah*, and have gained much insight into the mishnah's assertion that the creation of the world was worthwhile for the sake of one who learns Torah with this intent. The Nesivos Sholom demonstrates how this theme recurs throughout the mishnah.

The mishnah proceeds, referring to one who learns *Torah lishmah* as a *rei'a*. This term implies a level above that of a mere "friend" or "companion"; it refers, rather, to a partner, an equal. Obviously, of course, no person, no matter how worthy, can compare to the perfect Hashem. In this sense, however, he who learns *Torah lishmah* is considered a partner, for he contributes to the maintenance of the world's existence. The world is able to endure as long as it functions as a dwelling place for the *Shechinah*, an objective achieved through the *d'veikus* facilitated by *Torah lishmah*. This, then, is how this "partnership" manifests itself: Hashem created the world for a specific purpose. By helping to fulfill that purpose, this individual is a partner in *ma'aseh bereishis*. And by ensuring that creation fulfills the role Hashem intended for it, one who learns *Torah lishmah* brings great joy to the Creator. As the mishnah states, *mesamei'ach es Hamakom* — "he gladdens Hashem."

The mishnah continues to extol the virtues of one who learns *Torah lishmah*: וְנֶהֱנִין מִמֶּנּוּ עֵצָה וְתוּשִׁיָּה בִּינָה וּגְבוּרָה שֶׁנֶּאֱמַר לִי עֵצָה וְתוּשִׁיָּה אֲנִי בִינָה לִי גְבוּרָה — *From him people enjoy counsel and wisdom, understanding and strength, as it states* (Mishlei 8:14): *"Mine are counsel and wisdom, I am understanding, Mine is strength."* At first glance, this passage seems somewhat puzzling. The *passuk* the mishnah cited for support — לִי עֵצָה וְתוּשִׁיָּה אֲנִי בִינָה לִי גְבוּרָה — sounds as if the Torah is saying of itself that it is the embodiment of wisdom and understanding. How, then, can this be used as proof, not for the Torah itself, but for the one who learns it?

The issue is clarified, however, in light of the above. We have learned that by studying *Torah lishmah*, a Yid attains *d'veikus* with Hashem. He does this by attaching himself to the Torah, within which the *Shechinah* resides. One who learns in this fashion does not merely become proficient in Torah knowledge, itself a notable achievement, but becomes *one with the Torah*. This idea is reflected in the well-known statement of Rava concerning some prevalent conduct that he deplored as completely erroneous: אָמַר רָבָא כַּמָּה טִפְּשָׁאֵי שְׁאָר אִינְשֵׁי דְקָיְימֵי מִקַּמֵּי סֵפֶר תּוֹרָה וְלֹא קָיְימֵי מִקַּמֵּי גַּבְרָא רַבָּה — *Rava said: Some people behave like such imbeciles! For they rise in the presence of a Torah scroll (indicating an awareness of the need to honor the Torah), yet they do not rise in the presence of a great Torah scholar!* (Makkos 22b). What, exactly, was Rava's complaint? Great as he may be, the scholar is a person; why compare him to a Torah scroll? Yet here we discover the great truth that the *talmid chacham is* in fact a *sefer Torah*, in some literal sense! By learning *Torah lishmah*, his essence is infused with the *kedushas haTorah*, and he becomes one with the Torah. Thus, he is actually *part* of the Torah; a walking *sefer Torah*. And so, just as the

Torah itself is inherently wisdom and understanding, the scholar, as part of the Torah, likewise is characterized by these same qualities.

Our mishnah concludes: וּמְגַדַּלְתּוֹ וּמְרוֹמַמְתּוֹ עַל כָּל הַמַּעֲשִׂים — *(The Torah) makes him great and uplifts him above all things.* This statement can be understood in light of the teaching of the Maggid of Kozhnitz *ztz"l*. The phrase in *Tehillim* (104:24), *Malah ha'aretz kinyanecha*, is normally translated as, "The world is filled with Your possessions." The Maggid, however, renders it homiletically as, "The *aretz*" — meaning land-related items (i.e., materialism) — "is filled with opportunities to *koneh* (acquire) You." Accordingly, the *passuk* is informing us that it is possible to utilize even the mundane to acquire closeness to Hashem. How is this accomplished? Through *d'veikus* to Torah, and this is the message of our mishnah. וּמְגַדַּלְתּוֹ וּמְרוֹמַמְתּוֹ עַל כָּל הַמַּעֲשִׂים — *(The Torah) makes him great and uplifts him above all* **ma'asim**. *Ma'asim*, from the *shoresh* עשה — meaning "doing" or "acting" — refers to matters of This World, which is also known as the עוֹלָם הָעֲשִׂיָּיה, the "World of **Action**." What the mishnah is telling us is that *Torah lishmah* has the capacity to uplift one's mundane activities — מְרוֹמַמְתּוֹ עַל כָּל הַמַּעֲשִׂים — which, without Torah, would have remained in their lowly form. Thus, one can now achieve greatness even through whatever engagement he must undertake with the physical world.

This same notion is echoed in the words of the next mishnah: וְכָל מִי שֶׁעוֹסֵק בְּתַלְמוּד תּוֹרָה הֲרֵי זֶה מִתְעַלֶּה, שֶׁנֶּאֱמַר וּמִמַּתָּנָה נַחֲלִיאֵל וּמִנַּחֲלִיאֵל בָּמוֹת — *Anyone who engages in Torah study becomes elevated; as it is said (Bamidbar 21:19): "From Matanah to Nachaliel, and from Nachaliel to Bamos."* (While these names refer to the locations through which Bnei Yisroel journeyed, the Sages interpreted them in a homiletic sense to refer to spiritual ascension: "From *Matanah*," meaning "gift" and referring to the giving of the Torah, "a Yid proceeds to *Nachaliel*," a "Divine heritage," "and from there, *Bamos*," the "heights," referring to the elevated spiritual status he attains [*Rashi*].) Thus we see that proper engagement in Torah study has the power to completely transform a human being, turning him into a new and elevated entity.

The Midrash Shmuel adds that the transformative power of *Torah lishmah* is truly breathtaking. He explains this phrase of our mishnah

העוסק בתורה לשמה זוכה לדברים הרבה

— וּמְגַדַּלְתּוֹ וּמְרוֹמַמְתּוֹ עַל כָּל הַמַּעֲשִׂים — to mean that he is literally uplifted and granted mastery over everything, enabling him to do just about anything, *including being able to summon entirely new creations into existence*. This notion was exhibited by the master Torah scholar of all time, Moshe Rabbeinu, whose Torah study was of the most pristine level imaginable. At the climax of the episode of Korach's rebellion, Moshe Rabbeinu addressed the matter of the rebels' imminent defeat (*Bamidbar* 16:30): אִם־בְּרִיאָה יִבְרָא ה' וּפָצְתָה הָאֲדָמָה אֶת־פִּיהָ — *And if Hashem "creates a creation," and the ground shall open its mouth*. Quoting *Chazal*, Rashi (*ibid.*) accounts for the repetitive terminology ("**creates a creation**"), interpreting the *passuk* as saying, "If Hashem has already **created** a mouth for the earth, brought into existence from the beginning of the world, all is well and good; but if not, He will **create** one anew right here and now."

As remarkable as it may seem, the Midrash Shmuel's rendering of our mishnah fits well with the theme developed above. One who learns *Torah lishmah*, as explained, helps maintain the world. He thus becomes a *rei'a*, a virtual partner in creation. It is no wonder, then, that he should have the ability to engage in new creations.

The Path to Acquisition

The notion of the "exalted intention" behind the giving of the Torah carries with it yet other far-reaching ramifications.

A later mishnah (6:6) compares Torah study with the institutions of the priesthood and monarchy: גְּדוֹלָה תּוֹרָה יוֹתֵר מִן הַכְּהוּנָּה וּמִן הַמַּלְכוּת, שֶׁהַמַּלְכוּת נִקְנֵית בִּשְׁלֹשִׁים מַעֲלוֹת, וְהַכְּהֻנָּה בְּעֶשְׂרִים וְאַרְבַּע, וְהַתּוֹרָה נִקְנֵית בְּאַרְבָּעִים וּשְׁמוֹנָה דְבָרִים — *Great is Torah, more so than the priesthood and monarchy; for monarchy is acquired with thirty qualities, the priesthood with twenty-four, while Torah is acquired through forty-eight items*. The mishnah then proceeds to list what these forty-eight items are.

The commentators note the shift in terminology. In mentioning the acquisition of the priesthood and monarchy, the mishnah states that these are acquired with a certain number of *ma'alos*, virtues. Turning to Torah acquisition, however, the mishnah discusses forty-eight *devarim*, items. Why the switch? The difference is accounted for by the nature of the elements associated with the respective acquisitions. The priesthood and monarchy are acquired with certain *ma'alos*, things that come naturally to the candidate, not necessarily by dint of his own efforts and hard work, but through inheritance. The *devarim* through which one acquires Torah, however, refer to items that necessitate real sweat and toil.

What emerges, then, is the reality that to acquire and master Torah, a Yid must be willing to expend significant *mesiras nefesh*. As *Chazal* state (*Berachos* 63b), אֵין דִּבְרֵי תּוֹרָה מִתְקַיְּימִין אֶלָּא בְּמִי שֶׁמֵּמִית עַצְמוֹ עָלֶיהָ — Words of Torah only endure by one who "kills himself" over them. What is it about Torah — more than any other mitzvah endeavor — that necessitates such intense effort on the part of one who aspires to it?

It is likewise noteworthy that while many of the listed items clearly relate to Torah study — such as *shemi'as ha'ozen* (attentive listening) and *binas halev* (an understanding heart) — there are others that appear to have little or nothing to do with actual study. For example, the mishnah indicates that one must cultivate the quality of *taharah* (purity). What is its connection, exactly, to acquiring Torah?

We may gain some insight from the comments of the *Chassid Ya'avetz* at the beginning of this *perek*. He asserts that the Torah can only reside within someone who has cleared out negative traits from within himself and is filled, instead, with positive qualities. In fact, he explains, this informs the general practice of studying *Pirkei Avos* in the weeks leading up to Shavuos, the Yom Tov of *Kabbalas HaTorah*. The most fitting preparation to receive the Torah is to forge oneself into a receptacle worthy of containing the Torah. Through *Pirkei Avos*, which guides a Yid in the endeavor of character refinement, one may uproot his negative tendencies from within and acquire pristine traits. In this way, he will be fully ready and prepared to receive the Torah and have it reside within him.

This idea takes on added meaning in light of the "exalted intention" of the giving of the Torah, as expounded by the Bach. The purpose of Torah, as stated, is to enable a Yid to achieve *d'veikus* with Hashem

— a feat that is accomplished by becoming attached to the Torah. To become one with the Torah and have the *Shechinah* reside within is not possible so long as one possesses *middos ra'os*; these would prevent the entry of the pristine sanctity of the *Shechinah*. To enable such *d'veikus* to occur, a Yid must transform and elevate his essence.

We may now appreciate what it is about Torah that sets it apart from the other mitzvos, to the extent that one must "acquire" it, enlisting *mesiras nefesh* in order to do so. While any mitzvah enables a Yid to draw nearer to Hashem, it is through Torah that a Yid attains the epitome of *d'veikus*, becoming united with the Torah and hence with Hashem. There is a term used to describe an earnest Torah scholar; he is known as a *ben Torah*, literally a "son of the Torah." This addresses the notion that the approach to Torah goes far beyond the actual mitzvah of studying Torah; rather, it signifies the unbreakable bond that is forged between a Yid and the Torah, and the *Shechinah* that resides within.

We find this concept manifest in a familiar *passuk*: תּוֹרָה צִוָּה־לָנוּ מֹשֶׁה מוֹרָשָׁה קְהִלַּת יַעֲקֹב — *Moshe instructed us in the Torah; it is an inheritance of the congregation of Yaakov* (Devarim 33:4). Focusing on the term מוֹרָשָׁה, *Chazal* employ an expository device: אַל תִּקְרֵי מוֹרָשָׁה אֶלָּא מְאוֹרָשָׂה — *Do not read this phrase as stating "morashah" (inheritance), rather, read it as "me'orasah" (betrothed)* (Berachos 57a). The *passuk* is thus informing us of the nature and magnitude of our relationship with the Torah; it is the "betrothed" of Klal Yisroel. Forging such a close and intensive relationship, becoming bound to Hashem through unification with the Torah, is no simple matter. It requires real *mesiras nefesh*, and forty-eight forms of effort, to make this supreme acquisition. It requires earnest toil to refine one's essence, becoming a fitting vessel to house the *Shechinah*.

Toil, Subservience, and Ease

How does one achieve such an elevated level of learning *Torah lishmah*? The answer can be summed up in one word, which appears prominently in the various teachings of *Chazal*. They mention: עֲמֵלֵי תּוֹרָה (*those who* **toil** *in Torah*); עֲמָלָהּ שֶׁל תּוֹרָה (**toil** *in Torah*); וּבַתּוֹרָה אַתָּה

GEMS FROM THE *SEFER NESIVOS SHOLOM*

עָמֵל (*and you are **toil**ing in Torah* [*Avos* 6:4]); שֶׁתִּהְיוּ עֲמֵלִים בַּתּוֹרָה (*that you should be **toil**ing in Torah* [Rashi, *Vayikra* 26:3]); אָנוּ עֲמֵלִים וּמְקַבְּלִין שָׂכָר (*we **toil** [in Torah] and receive reward* [cf. *Berachos* 28b]); etc. *Amalah shel Torah* can truly aid a Yid in elevating himself. *Chazal* reveal to us how one can overpower his *yetzer hara*. Hashem declares: בָּרָאתִי יֵצֶר הָרָע וּבָרָאתִי לוֹ תוֹרָה תַּבְלִין — *I have created the* yetzer hara, *and I have created the Torah as a remedy for it* (*Kiddushin* 30b). One may have assumed that it is possible to access this power of the Torah to vanquish the *yetzer hara* merely by learning it in any fashion. Elsewhere, however, *Chazal* clarify that this is not the case: אִם יָגַעְתָּ הַרְבֵּה בְּדִבְרֵיהֶם הַקָּבָּ"ה מֵסִיר יצה"ר מִמְּךָ — *If you have exerted much effort to study the Torah teachings of the Sages, Hashem will remove the* yetzer hara *from you* (*Bamidbar Rabbah* 14:4). Thus we see that it is specifically the power of *toil* in Torah that eradicates the evil from a person.

The Nesivos Sholom elaborates on this idea by pointing to the three components that comprise a human being: mind (representing intellectual ability), heart (emotions), and limbs (actions). Before donning *tefillin* each morning on our arm and our head, we recite the following: וְצִוָּנוּ לְהָנִיחַ עַל הַיָּד...נֶגֶד הַלֵּב, לְשַׁעְבֵּד בָּזֶה תַּאֲוֹת וּמַחְשְׁבוֹת לִבֵּנוּ לַעֲבוֹדָתוֹ, יִתְבָּרַךְ שְׁמוֹ, וְעַל הָרֹאשׁ נֶגֶד הַמּוֹחַ, שֶׁהַנְּשָׁמָה שֶׁבְּמוֹחִי, עִם שְׁאָר חוּשַׁי וְכֹחוֹתַי, כֻּלָּם יִהְיוּ מְשֻׁעְבָּדִים לַעֲבוֹדָתוֹ, יִתְבָּרַךְ שְׁמוֹ — *And He commanded us to place them on the arm...opposite the heart, in order to **subjugate** thereby the desires and thoughts of our hearts to the service of Him, may His Name be blessed; and on the head, opposite the intellect, so that the soul residing in my mind — together with my other senses and faculties — will all be **subjugated** to the service of Him, may His Name be blessed.* Through this endeavor, we make our mind and heart subservient to Him. But this still leaves a major component of a person that is not yet fully subservient to Hashem. In fact, the aspect of one's bodily limbs is, in many respects, the most significant component of the person, as it is ultimately responsible for his deeds. This is what *amalah shel Torah* achieves: the completion of man's total subjugation to Hashem by dedicating even one's limbs to the service of the Almighty. A Yid whose entire being is subjugated to Hashem's will is truly ready and able to take on his *yetzer hara*. Thus it is that the power of Torah as a remedy to the *yetzer hara* is realized through the element of *amalah shel Torah*.

The extent of this subservience is further expounded by the Midrash, which states: בְּג׳ דְבָרִים נִיתְּנָה הַתּוֹרָה: בָּאֵשׁ, וּבְמַיִם, וּבַמִדְבַּר — *In connection with three elements was the Torah given: with fire, water, and the wilderness* (*Bamidbar Rabbah* 1:7). These elements, the Nesivos Sholom explains, correspond to certain qualities of a person's makeup. "Fire" relates to the characteristics of anger, as a person can "flare up," and passions, which stem from the "boiling" of the blood. The quality of "water" refers to a person's capacity to love. These must be subjugated to Hashem, as exemplified by the "wilderness," signifying that a person must be willing to give up everything of himself for Hashem's sake, similar to the wilderness, which is ownerless property. In this way a person may truly acquire Torah, as the Midrash informed us: בְּג׳ דְבָרִים נִיתְּנָה הַתּוֹרָה — *Through these three items, the Torah was given.*

Thus we see what it is that *amalah shel Torah* entails: relinquishing and subjugating every aspect of oneself to *Hakadosh Baruch Hu* and His Torah. This point is brought out most dramatically by the *Tanna D'vei Eliyahu* (ch. 22), which records the following dialogue. A certain individual complained that despite his engagement in Torah study, he felt he did not merit true success in the endeavor, to the extent that the Torah was not part of him and one with him. To this claim, the answer came, לֹא זָכָה אוֹתוֹ אָדָם לִדְבַר תּוֹרָה אֶלָּא אִם כֵּן מָסַר עַצְמוֹ לִכְבוֹד שָׁמַיִם לְמִיתָה — *A person cannot truly merit Torah acquisition unless he is willing to offer up his life for the sake of Heaven's honor.*

We learn, therefore, that true success in acquiring Torah comes about only through significant effort and toil, and a willingness to give of oneself totally to Hashem. The mechanics of how this success actually comes about are quite intriguing. The idea emerges from an apparent contradiction. The need to expend effort to acquire Torah is mentioned earlier in *Avos* (2:12): הַתְקֵן עַצְמְךָ לִלְמוֹד תּוֹרָה, שֶׁאֵינָהּ יְרֻשָּׁה לָךְ — *Prepare yourself to learn Torah, for it is not given to you as an inheritance.* The beauty of an inherited item is that one need not perform any work whatsoever in order to acquire it; under the proper circumstances, it simply falls into one's possession. The mishnah exhorts us not to view Torah in this manner; to acquire it, one must be willing to expend great effort. However, this supposition — that Torah is not simply hereditary — seems to be flatly contradicted by an explicit and well-known *passuk* in the Torah: תּוֹרָה צִוָּה־לָנוּ מֹשֶׁה מוֹרָשָׁה קְהִלַּת יַעֲקֹב — *Moshe instructed us in the Torah; it is an **inheritance** of the congregation of Yaakov* (*Devarim* 33:4). Is Torah given as an inheritance, or isn't it?

The answer, asserts the Nesivos Sholom, is that both are true. That is, one acquires an item through inheritance simply by virtue of being the child of the item's owner. When a Yid becomes a *ben Torah*, such that he is inextricably bound to the Torah and is actually part and parcel of the Torah itself, then, of course, the Torah is his inheritance; it gives itself over to him, bestowing all of its power and *kedushah*. But becoming a *ben Torah* requires a tremendous output of toil and effort; to achieve this state, one must first engage in the task of *Haskein atzmecha* — "Prepare yourself," as the mishnah stated. In other words, it is impossible to acquire Torah without genuine *amalah shel Torah*, but one who does give himself over to Torah through *amalah* will eventually "inherit" the Torah in substantial measure. In fact, the acquisition is in proportion to the effort: the more a Yid toils over Torah and engages in self-sacrifice for its sake, the Torah will go to him in even greater measure. And, of course, the more *lishmah* he invests, the more will he achieve *d'veikus* with the Torah and with Hashem — to the extent that the creation of the entire universe will have been worthwhile for his sake alone.

A Bunch of Zeroes

Somewhat uncharacteristically, the Nesivos Sholom turns to address, with some frankness, a contemporary issue. He concludes with a specific and practical solution.

In one sense, what has occurred among the post-Holocaust generations is completely unprecedented in its scope. We have, *baruch Hashem*, witnessed a tremendous resurgence in dedication to Torah study. The numbers of yeshivos and *kollelim*, as well as the students who populate them, are truly astounding; may Hashem help them continue to grow!

The issue that arises — specifically because of the magnitude of this achievement and the monumental importance of the undertaking — is that the *yetzer hara* will not stand for such an outpouring of engagement in Torah study. It is well aware of the significance of Torah study and of Torah's ability and power to subdue it. While it may tolerate other positive endeavors, it devotes most of its energies to battling Torah study, especially when occurring on such a massive scale. And the area where it seems to have found at least a slight opportunity to penetrate is the very issue of our discussion: *Torah lishmah*. While there are many *Yidden* learning great quantities of Torah with great fervor, this particular aspect could be strengthened: learning Torah for no purpose other than solely and completely for the "exalted intention" for which it was given.

But there is a ready solution at hand, a relatively simple way to foster improvement in this area. The idea is based on how the *sefarim hakedoshim* interpret the following *passuk*, which states: ה' יִסְפֹּר בִּכְתוֹב עַמִּים — *Hashem counts with the writing of the nations* (*Tehillim* 87:6). What this refers to, the Nesivos Sholom explains, is that Hashem — in some sense — makes use of the international system for counting and calculations! In the prevalent numeric system (employing "Arabic numerals"), zero is a number with no value. Adding many more zeroes does not add any additional value to the original number. Yet, if a one is placed in front of a string of zeroes, the resulting number represents an astounding sum! What the *passuk* is telling us is that Hashem "uses" this system in relation to the deeds of Klal Yisroel.

For example, a Jew may recite many dozens of prayers with hardly an ounce of dedication and intent. Each of these prayers is essentially a zero. Yet, when he finally decides to give it his all and recite a proper prayer before Hashem, something amazing takes place. This genuine prayer, a real "one," is not treated in isolation. Rather, it is placed before all of the numerous "zero" prayers that were offered in the past. In other words, Hashem raises them all along with this prayer!

The same holds true for Torah study. As we have learned, the ideal in Torah study is learning *lishmah*, with complete dedication, following the intention Hashem had in granting us the Torah: to enable His *Shechinah* to dwell within us. Attaining this level is, of course, no simple matter, with the result that a Yid may have learned much Torah, but much of it has been of a lower caliber.

But what would happen if, even on a somewhat limited basis, a Yid were to exert himself, elevate himself, and learn Torah in a complete and proper manner? This would be a remarkable achievement, which could elevate all of his other learning, as well.

Thus, the Nesivos Sholom submits that we adopt this very practice. He suggest that each Yid — even those fortunate enough to spend many hours each day learning Torah — set aside, every day, a certain amount of time, even of extremely limited duration, just a moment or two, and dedicate this time to learning that is done with complete, pristine intention, with *no ulterior motive and no other thought* than *Torah lishmah*. To ensure that the intention remains pure, this learning should be done *without the knowledge of any other person* and without receiving any other benefit as a result of this learning. Then, through even a short session of Torah study undertaken completely *lishmah*, this Torah will serve as the "one" before all of the "zeroes," elevating together with it *all* of the Torah he has learned. Then, the accumulated potency of all of this "empowered" Torah will serve as the perfect remedy to subdue the *yetzer hara* and to completely refine one's *middos*.

The Divrei Shmuel *ztz"l* would tell of a certain contemporary *rav*, known for his miraculous works. This saintly individual was able to effect many salvations and his predictions would always come true. From where did he derive such extraordinary ability? The Divrei Shmuel revealed the source of his power: "Most probably," he asserted, "it all came from having learned a single mishnah completely *lishmah*." This is one illustration of the power gained from learning even a relatively small amount, as long as it is done *lishmah*. In this way, we discover how it is that *Torah lishmah* is truly within the reach of every single Yid.

העוסק בתורה לשמה זוכה לדברים הרבה

In Summary

The endeavor of Torah study, we find, has a component distinct from any other mitzvah: one who learns *Torah lishmah* merits a whole range of powerful blessings, as outlined in the first mishnah of this *perek*. It is likewise worthy of note that this undertaking is usually referred to — as it is in our mishnah — as *Torah lishmah*, for its sake, and not *Torah lishmo*, for His sake.

The Nesivos Sholom explains what lies behind these issues, based on the Bach's explanation of a well-known *Chazal*. The Gemara tells us that the *Churban Beis Hamikdash* came about, most surprisingly, because of a seemingly minor offense. While the generation was involved in Torah study, they neglected to recite the blessing that precedes such study! The Bach clarifies what warranted such a severe consequence: the issue wasn't so much that they simply omitted the blessing; rather, it was the attitude that characterized their approach to Torah. In giving us the Torah, Hashem had a specific intent: it should serve as the vehicle through which the *Shechinah* could dwell within us. The *Yidden* at the time of the *Churban* disregarded this intent and felt no need to thank Hashem for this opportunity. And so the *Shechinah* departed.

Elaborating on this point, the Nesivos Sholom demonstrates how intrinsic this idea is to the creation of the world itself. The Midrash states that Hashem's desire in creating the world in the first place was to acquire for Himself a *dirah b'tachtonim*, a dwelling place among the lower spheres. This aim is achieved through Klal Yisroel's attachment to Torah, for in some sense, Hashem Himself "resides" in the Torah, having "inscribed His soul" within the words and letters of the Torah. When a Yid becomes one with the Torah, the ultimate bond is achieved between that Yid and Hashem, with the Torah serving as the bridge. This is the manifestation of *Chazal's* statement that *Hakadosh Baruch Hu*, the Torah, and Yisroel are all one.

This was Hashem's objective in granting the Torah to Klal Yisroel, and it is to this objective that the term *Torah lishmah* refers: for the sake of this exalted intention, Klal Yisroel can achieve *d'veikus* with Hashem through attachment to the Torah so that His Presence may dwell within them in the lower spheres. When this objective is achieved, creation has fulfilled its purpose; thus, as the mishnah states, the creation of the entire world is worthwhile for the sake of one who learns *Torah lishmah*. He becomes a *rei'a*, a partner, with Hashem in the maintenance of the world and thereby causes Hashem much gladness: *mesamei'ach es haMakom*.

While the importance of *Torah lishmah* cannot be overstated, achieving this level is not necessarily a simple matter. The Nesivos Sholom asserts that it is only possible through the medium of *amalah shel Torah*, real and earnest toil. *Chazal* exhort us in many places to expend great effort in Torah study. In its fullest sense, *amalah shel Torah* entails an utter and complete subjugation of every facet of our being to Hashem and His Torah. Only when a Yid is willing to sacrifice his life for the sake of Heaven, as the *Tanna D'vei Eliyahu* states, will he truly acquire Torah in all of its fullness.

The Nesivos Sholom also submits a practical suggestion, based on quite a lofty notion related by our Sages, dealing with numbers: "zero," of course, equals nothing; a whole string of zeroes, side by side, also equals nothing. But when a "one" is placed in front of them, the whole number is transformed into a phenomenal sum. And so it is with *avodas Hashem*. A Yid may have recited many "empty" *tefillos*, devoid of feeling or intention. But when he subsequently puts in the effort and recites a complete, heartfelt prayer, he has placed a "one" in front of all the other *tefillos*; then, all of them are elevated to a higher plane.

The same holds true with Torah study. A Yid may have learned much Torah but without the proper *lishmah* intent. The Nesivos Sholom's solution is to set aside time each day, even a very short amount, to learn Torah completely *lishmah*. Such an undertaking should be within everyone's reach. A Yid can elevate all of the Torah he has learned by learning *lishmah* for merely a short time.

פרק ו' משנה א'
זוכה לדברים הרבה
He Merits Many Things

רַבִּי מֵאִיר אוֹמֵר כָּל הָעוֹסֵק בַּתּוֹרָה לִשְׁמָהּ, זוֹכֶה לִדְבָרִים הַרְבֵּה. וְלֹא עוֹד אֶלָּא שֶׁכָּל הָעוֹלָם כֻּלּוֹ כְּדַאי הוּא לוֹ. נִקְרָא רֵעַ, אָהוּב, אוֹהֵב אֶת הַמָּקוֹם, אוֹהֵב אֶת הַבְּרִיּוֹת, מְשַׂמֵּחַ אֶת הַמָּקוֹם, מְשַׂמֵּחַ אֶת הַבְּרִיּוֹת, וּמַלְבַּשְׁתּוֹ עֲנָוָה וְיִרְאָה, וּמַכְשַׁרְתּוֹ לִהְיוֹת צַדִּיק חָסִיד יָשָׁר וְנֶאֱמָן, וּמְרַחַקְתּוֹ מִן הַחֵטְא, וּמְקָרַבְתּוֹ לִידֵי זְכוּת, וְנֶהֱנִין מִמֶּנּוּ עֵצָה וְתוּשִׁיָּה בִּינָה וּגְבוּרָה. שֶׁנֶּאֱמַר לִי עֵצָה וְתוּשִׁיָּה אֲנִי בִינָה לִי גְבוּרָה, וְנוֹתֶנֶת לוֹ מַלְכוּת וּמֶמְשָׁלָה וְחִקּוּר דִּין, וּמְגַלִּין לוֹ רָזֵי תוֹרָה, וְנַעֲשֶׂה כְּמַעְיָן הַמִּתְגַּבֵּר וּכְנָהָר שֶׁאֵינוֹ פוֹסֵק, וֶהֱוֵי צָנוּעַ וְאֶרֶךְ רוּחַ, וּמוֹחֵל עַל עֶלְבּוֹנוֹ, וּמְגַדַּלְתּוֹ וּמְרוֹמַמְתּוֹ עַל כָּל הַמַּעֲשִׂים:

Rabbi Meir says: Whoever engages in Torah study for its own sake merits many things; furthermore, the (creation of the) entire world is worthwhile for his sake alone. He is called a friend, beloved, one who loves the Omnipresent, one who loves people, one who gladdens the Omnipresent, one who gladdens people. (The Torah) clothes him in humility and fear (of Hashem); it makes him fit to be righteous, pious, upright, and faithful; it keeps him far from sin, and draws him near to merit. From him people enjoy counsel and wisdom, understanding and strength; as it states (*Mishlei* 8:14): "Mine are counsel and wisdom, I am understanding, Mine is strength." (The Torah) grants him kingship, dominion, and analytical judgment; the secrets of the Torah are revealed to him; he becomes like a steadily strengthening fountain and a river that does not cease; he becomes modest, patient, and forgiving of insults to himself. (The Torah) makes him great and uplifts him above all things.

זוכה לדברים הרבה

SOURCES:

כִּי נֵר מִצְוָה וְתוֹרָה אוֹר. (משלי ו' כ"ג)

For a mitzvah is a candle, while Torah is light. (*Mishlei* 6:23)

מָשָׁל לְאָדָם שֶׁהָיָה מְהַלֵּךְ בְּאִישׁוֹן לַיְלָה וַאֲפֵלָה, וּמִתְיָרֵא מִן הַקּוֹצִים וּמִן הַפְּחָתִים וּמִן הַבַּרְקָנִים וּמֵחַיָּה רָעָה וּמִן הַלִּסְטִין... נִזְדַּמְּנָה לוֹ אֲבוּקָה... נִצַּל מִן הַקּוֹצִים וּמִן הַפְּחָתִים וּמִן הַבַּרְקָנִים, וַעֲדַיִן מִתְיָרֵא מֵחַיָּה רָעָה וּמִן הַלִּסְטִין... כֵּיוָן שֶׁעָלָה עַמּוּד הַשַּׁחַר נִצַּל מֵחַיָּה רָעָה וּמִן הַלִּסְטִין. (סוטה כ"א.)

A parable: A man was walking in the dark of night, and so feared (coming to harm) from thorns, ditches, thistles, wild beasts, and bandits... He chances upon a torch... He no longer need be concerned from thorns, ditches, and thistles (which can be avoided by the light of the torch), but he is still afraid of wild beasts and bandits (who roam in the night)... Once the dawn breaks, however, he is no longer concerned from beasts and bandits, either. (*Sotah* 21a)

קָדוֹשׁ, קָדוֹשׁ, קָדוֹשׁ, ה' צְבָקוֹת, מְלֹא כָל הָאָרֶץ כְּבוֹדוֹ. (ישעיה ו' ג')

Holy, holy, holy is Hashem of Hosts; His glory fills the whole world. (*Yeshayah* 6:3)

וַיַּרְא אֱלֹקִים אֶת־הָאוֹר כִּי־טוֹב. (בראשית א' ד')

And G-d saw the light that it was good. (*Bereishis* 1:4)

אוֹר שֶׁבָּרָא הקב"ה בְּיוֹם רִאשׁוֹן אָדָם צוֹפֶה וּמַבִּיט בּוֹ מִסּוֹף הָעוֹלָם וְעַד סוֹפוֹ, כֵּיוָן שֶׁהִסְתַּכֵּל הקב"ה בְּאַנְשֵׁי דוֹר הַמַּבּוּל וּבְאַנְשֵׁי דוֹר הַפְלָגָה שֶׁמַּעֲשֵׂיהֶן מְקוּלְקָלִין, עָמַד וּגְנָזוֹ וְהִתְקִינָהּ לַצַּדִּיקִים לֶעָתִיד לָבֹא. (בראשית רבה י"א ב)

With the light Hashem created on the first day, Adam Harishon was able to peer through it and see from one end of the world to the other. However, once Hashem beheld the people of the generation of the Flood and the people of the generation of Enosh whose deeds were corrupted, He stood and stored it (the light) away, setting it aside for the righteous for use in the future. (*Bereishis Rabbah* 11:2)

GEMS FROM THE *SEFER NESIVOS SHOLOM*

הָעָם הַהֹלְכִים בַּחֹשֶׁךְ רָאוּ אוֹר גָּדוֹל. (ישעיה ט׳ א׳)

The nation which walks in darkness has seen a great light. (*Yeshayah* 9:1)

אוֹר גָּדוֹל אוֹר שֶׁנִּבְרָא בְּיוֹם רִאשׁוֹן שֶׁגְּנָזוֹ הַקָּבָּ"ה לְעַמְלֵי תוֹרָה. (מדרש תנחומא נח)

The "great light" is the light which was created on the first day, which Hashem stored away for the (enjoyment of) those who toil in Torah. (*Tanchuma, Parshas Noach*)

וְהָאִישׁ מֹשֶׁה עָנָו מְאֹד מִכֹּל הָאָדָם אֲשֶׁר עַל־פְּנֵי הָאֲדָמָה. (במדבר י"ב ג׳)

And the man, Moshe, was exceedingly humble, more than any man on the face of the earth. (*Bamidbar* 12:3)

פֶּה אֶל־פֶּה אֲדַבֶּר־בּוֹ...וּתְמֻנַת ה׳ יַבִּיט. (שם פסוק ח׳)

Speaker to speaker I converse with him...and he gazes upon the image of Hashem. (*ibid.* v. 8)

לֵב מְלָכִים אֵין חֵקֶר. (משלי כ"ה ג׳)

The (expansiveness of the) heart of kings is beyond discernment. (*Mishlei* 25:3)

וַיֵּרֶד ה׳ עַל־הַר סִינַי. (שמות י"ט כ׳)

And Hashem descended onto Har Sinai. (*Shemos* 19:20)

אַתֶּם רְאִיתֶם כִּי מִן־הַשָּׁמַיִם דִּבַּרְתִּי עִמָּכֶם. (שם כ׳ י"ט)

You have seen that I have spoken to you from the Heavens. (*ibid.* 20:19)

בָּרָאתִי יֵצֶר הָרָע, וּבָרָאתִי לוֹ תוֹרָה תַּבְלִין. (קידושין ל:)

I have created the evil inclination; I have created the Torah as its remedy. (*Kiddushin* 30b)

פרקי אבות

702

The View from Above

"Random" is a term that seems to have become quite prevalent as of late. Whenever a statement is uttered that appears somewhat disjointed, or an item seems out of place, this useful term "random" comes into play.

Torah in general, including the Mishnah in particular, is anything but "random." Every statement and every word is weighed and calculated, employed with the utmost precision.

But then we arrive at this mishnah, delineating the remarkable blessings one merits by learning *Torah lishmah*. A whole list of qualities bestowed on this individual is listed, including the fact that he is considered to be one who loves Hashem and people; he attains humility and fear of Hashem; he acquires a semblance of royalty and dominion; in short, he "merits many things." The issue is that this list of praises and blessings appears to be, at first glance, characterized by randomness!

Surely, however, it cannot be that the mishnah would simply provide a haphazard listing of various positive results. There must be a common thread running through each of these rewards. The question becomes, then, what *is* this common denominator, and what is its relation to the act of learning *Torah lishmah*? Why aren't these same blessings accorded to one who performs other mitzvos, as well?

Torah — Lighting Up the World

כִּי נֵר מִצְוָה וְתוֹרָה אוֹר — *For a mitzvah is a candle, while Torah is light* (*Mishlei* 6:23). This statement of Shlomo Hamelech is one of many instances in which we see Torah associated with the quality of light.

Elaborating on this *passuk*, Chazal (*Sotah* 21a) provide the following parable to illustrate the distinction drawn by Shlomo between Torah and mitzvos: אָדָם שֶׁהָיָה מְהַלֵּךְ בְּאִישׁוֹן לַיְלָה וַאֲפֵילָה, וּמִתְיָרֵא מִן הַקּוֹצִים וּמִן הַפְּחָתִים וּמִן הַבַּרְקָנִים וּמֵחַיָּה רָעָה וּמִן הַלִּסְטִין... נִזְדַּמְּנָה לוֹ אֲבוּקָה... נִצַּל מִן הַקּוֹצִים וּמִן הַפְּחָתִים וּמִן הַבַּרְקָנִים, וַעֲדַיִין מִתְיָרֵא מֵחַיָּה רָעָה וּמִן הַלִּסְטִין... כֵּיוָן שֶׁעָלָה עַמּוּד הַשַּׁחַר נִצַּל מֵחַיָּה רָעָה וּמִן הַלִּסְטִין — *A man was walking in the dark of night and so feared (coming to harm) from thorns, ditches, thistles, wild*

GEMS FROM THE *SEFER NESIVOS SHOLOM*

beasts, and bandits... He chances upon a torch... He no longer need be concerned from thorns, ditches, and thistles (which can be avoided by the light of the torch), but he is still afraid of wild beasts and bandits (who roam in the night)... Once the dawn breaks, however, he is no longer concerned from beasts and bandits, either. In this portrayal, the torch provides assistance — but only to a point. It lights his way enough to enable him to avoid pitfalls. This corresponds to the power of mitzvah performance. Torah, however, is the breaking of the dawn, which entirely dispels the dangers of the night.

What is it, then, about Torah that accounts for its superior light-giving properties, to the extent that only it, above all other mitzvos, is comparable to the brightening day?

The Nesivos Sholom clarifies this issue by discussing the makeup of the universe in general. *Chazal* reveal to us that there are many more worlds in existence than the one we behold with our own eyes. In fact, populating the upper spheres are numerous worlds of exalted and spiritual nature. And all of these worlds are completely bright, illuminated by the dazzling splendor of the G-dly light of the *Shechinah*.

In truth, this G-dly light is present in our world, as well; as the *passuk* states (*Yeshayah* 6:3), מְלֹא כָל־הָאָרֶץ כְּבוֹדוֹ — *The entire world is filled with His glory*. However, the revelation of this light in This World presents an issue: were people to see it freely, they would lose their sense of free choice. Overawed by its radiance, there would be no challenge for mankind in determining the correct path. And so, to retain the notion of free choice, the light in This World had to be obscured from view.

The very name by which our world is known, עוֹלָם, alludes to this phenomenon. *Olam* comes from a related term, *helem*, with which it shares the same *shoresh*, הֶעְלֵם, meaning "hidden." Thus, the very term *olam* refers to the fact that the Divine light in This World is purposely covered up, obscured behind a dense veneer of materialism. The result is that we are essentially looking through eclipsed "lenses" that prevent us from perceiving Hashem's exalted radiance, which fills the world. This is known in the sacred writings as *tzimtzum*;

the inherently infinite Divine light is "contained" within and hidden behind physical, limited entities. While this light serves as the true essence of all physicality and the Force by which it exists, it itself remains unseen.

Even in This World, however, there is one entity through which it is possible to glimpse the hidden light. The Torah removes the dark shades obscuring the brightness. It equips those who engage in it with spiritual, Torah eyes through which to readily perceive the light of Hashem, which is hidden to all others. The Torah thus enables a form of "expansion" from the *tzimtzum*, as the previously constricted light becomes visible and reverts to its quality of boundlessness.

This light, and its interrelationship with Torah, was present from the very beginning of the world. On the first day, the Torah tells us that Hashem created light. The *passuk* states (*Bereishis* 1:4), וַיַּרְא אֱלֹקִים אֶת־הָאוֹר כִּי־טוֹב — *And G-d saw the light that it was good*. This light, according to Rashi, was the *Ohr Haganuz*, the special "archived light." *Chazal* reveal what could be perceived through this light and what eventually became of it: אוֹר שֶׁבָּרָא הקב"ה בְּיוֹם רִאשׁוֹן אָדָם צוֹפֶה וּמַבִּיט בּוֹ מִסּוֹף הָעוֹלָם וְעַד סוֹפוֹ, כֵּיוָן שֶׁהִסְתַּכֵּל הקב"ה בְּאַנְשֵׁי דוֹר הַמַּבּוּל וּבְאַנְשֵׁי דוֹר הַפְּלָגָה שֶׁמַּעֲשֵׂיהֶן מְקוּלְקָלִין, עָמַד וּגְנָזָהּ וְהִתְקִינָהּ לַצַּדִּיקִים לֶעָתִיד לָבֹא — *With the light Hashem created on the first day, Adam Harishon was able to peer through it and see from one end of the world to the other. However, once Hashem beheld the people of the generation of the Flood and the people of the generation of Enosh, whose deeds were corrupted, He stood and stored it (the light) away, setting it aside for the righteous for use in the future* (*Bereishis Rabbah* 11:2).

This is the light that can be accessed, even in This World, by means of the Torah. The *passuk* states (*Yeshayah* 9:1), הָעָם הַהֹלְכִים בַּחֹשֶׁךְ רָאוּ אוֹר גָּדוֹל — *The nation that walks in darkness has seen a great light*. What is this "great light"? The Midrash (*Tanchuma, Parshas Noach*) identifies it with the *Ohr Haganuz*: אוֹר גָּדוֹל אוֹר שֶׁנִּבְרָא בְּיוֹם רִאשׁוֹן שֶׁגְּנָזוֹ הקב"ה לַעֲמֵלֵי תּוֹרָה — *The "great light" is the light that was created on the first day, which Hashem stored away for the (enjoyment of)* **those who toil in Torah**. These individuals, the toilers in Torah, "walk in the darkness," for they chase sleep from their eyes and eat and drink little as they expend their energies plumbing the depths of Hashem's Torah. It is to them that the *Ohr Gadol* (Great Light), the *Ohr Haganuz*, is revealed. They may use its light to see מִסּוֹף הָעוֹלָם וְעַד סוֹפוֹ — *from one end of the world to the other*; in other words, all aspects of the world that are usually hidden and obscured become clarified through the bright light of Torah bringing out the light of Hashem.

It was to this power of Torah to dispel the darkness and obscurity that *Chazal* referred earlier. A mitzvah can save one from pitfalls; but to banish the "bandits," it is necessary to employ the light of Torah, likened to the dawning of the day, when all begins to brighten. These "bandits" refer to the forces of *tumah*, responsible for the *helem* of the world; it is they who prevent a Yid from detecting the G-dly light that fills the world. These bandits of *tumah* are overpowered, however, by the strength of *Torah ohr*, the light of Torah, which illuminates the *helem*.

Just how powerful can this light be? In his commentary to the *Tur*, the Bach remarks that if all of Yisroel would engage in Torah study in the proper way, the entire world would light up with the glory of Hashem! This notion is reminiscent of the Messianic era for which we yearn, as we mention in the *Yedid Nefesh* hymn: *Ta'ir eretz mich'vodecha* — "Illuminate the world with Your glory!" Learning Torah with the proper intent, then, has the power to eliminate the obscuring forces of *tumah* and usher in the light of the era of Mashiach.

Our mishnah takes on new meaning in light of the above. We have discovered that by learning Torah properly, in the manner of *lishmah* to which the Bach referred, a Yid directs the G-dly light into This World, facilitating perception of His radiance. The mishnah stated, כָּל הָעוֹסֵק בַּתּוֹרָה לִשְׁמָהּ...כָּל הָעוֹלָם כֻּלּוֹ כְּדַאי הוּא לוֹ — *Whosoever learns* Torah lishmah...*the (creation of the) entire world is worthwhile for his sake alone*. Indeed, the world should be indebted to such an individual. The world had been a dark and murky place, lacking real value so long as Hashem's Presence was concealed. Then he came along and — through his elevated Torah learning — transformed the world into a place that shines with the radiant, G-dly light!

The Expansive View

With this insight, we may also uncover the common thread that runs through the various items listed in our mishnah as resulting from learning *Torah lishmah*.

One might balk at being asked a question such as, "What is the difference between darkness and light?" The answer is obvious, in fact, as stark as the difference between night and day. But if we were to think deeply about the issue, we may discover that there is another significant factor that captures this difference in precise form. What is the difference between sitting in the darkness and sitting in the light? One who sits in the darkness *sees only one thing*: the darkness. Darkness, by definition, is constricting, a form of *tzimtzum*. In fact, sitting in the dark, one can only really be sure of and concerned with a single entity: himself. By contrast, the light of day is liberating; it provides an expansive view. One can see various objects, can see to great distances. One can focus on others.

Yet, even this view has its limitations. By the physical light of day, one can see only so far and so much. But one who merits seeing by the light of Torah, discerning Hashem's Presence from the midst of the *helem* and accessing His light — his vision is boundless. He can see, as *Chazal* state, מִסּוֹף הָעוֹלָם וְעַד סוֹפוֹ.

Concerning one who learns *Torah lishmah*, the mishnah stated, נִקְרָא רֵעַ, אָהוּב, אוֹהֵב אֶת הַמָּקוֹם אוֹהֵב אֶת הַבְּרִיּוֹת וכו' — *He is called a friend, beloved, one who loves the Omnipresent, one who loves people...* One who walks in darkness and self-centeredness has difficulty viewing anything beyond him; his focus is not on Hashem, nor on others. Conversely, however, one who learns *Torah lishmah*, and merits the Divine light, has a very broad field of view! He perceives and loves Hashem, as well as the people He has created.

Similarly, the other items of the mishnah flow from the same source: וּמַלְבַּשְׁתּוֹ עֲנָוָה וְיִרְאָה — *He is clothed with humility and fear (of Hashem)*, a fairly natural outcome from such clear perception of Him! Overawed by the light of His Presence, so aware of His unmitigated greatness, he clearly discerns his own lowliness in contrast and thus acquires humility and fear before Him. The clearer one's perception of the Almighty, the greater the magnitude of one's resultant humility.

Thus we find in Moshe Rabbeinu a pair of seemingly opposing qualities. On the one hand, he attained prophetic levels greater than did any man before or since: פֶּה אֶל־פֶּה אֲדַבֶּר־בּוֹ...וּתְמֻנַת ה' יַבִּיט — *Speaker to speaker I converse with him...and he gazes on the image of Hashem* (*Bamidbar* 12:8). Having attained such unprecedented achievement, one may have thought that, to some extent, it would affect his perception of self. And yet, almost amazingly, we find the exact opposite: וְהָאִישׁ מֹשֶׁה עָנָו מְאֹד מִכֹּל הָאָדָם אֲשֶׁר עַל־פְּנֵי הָאֲדָמָה — *And the man, Moshe, was exceedingly humble — more so than any man on the face of the earth* (*ibid.* v. 3). How could these two qualities co-exist? The truth is, however, that not only are they compatible, but one is the direct result of the other. It was precisely because Moshe Rabbeinu had the clearest possible perception of Hashem that any mortal could ever attain that he also acquired the most humility. No one had a clearer recognition of Hashem's awesome greatness than Moshe Rabbeinu; consequently, he also saw more clearly how man's lowliness contrasted so sharply with Hashem's majesty.

The mishnah continues: וְנוֹתֶנֶת לוֹ מַלְכוּת וּמֶמְשָׁלָה — *And it grants him royalty and dominion*. There have been many kings in history. Some were outstanding; some were terrible. What is the main characteristic that determines able leadership? Narrow-mindedness renders one poorly suited to lead. How will a potential ruler be able to relate to the needs of his people if he can't see past himself? Only an individual with an expansive view of his surroundings, able to focus on the heart of his nation, can grasp the essentials of leadership. As the *passuk* states (*Mishlei* 25:3), לֵב מְלָכִים אֵין חֵקֶר — *The (expansiveness of the) heart of kings is beyond discernment*. One who learns *Torah lishmah* merits access to the Divine light, receiving thereby a broad view of the entire world. As such, he is particularly suited for leadership. For the same reason, he will be readily able to dispense sound counsel; as the mishnah states, וְנֶהֱנִין מִמֶּנּוּ עֵצָה וְתוּשִׁיָּה — *From him people enjoy counsel and wisdom*. A person could be brilliant but still give lousy advice. To be perceptive, intelligence alone may not be sufficient; one needs to be able to see the broad picture to amply weigh all sides of a given issue. Thus, one who acquires the expansive view provided through *Torah lishmah* will be adept at addressing problems with true wisdom.

Another facet detailed by the mishnah is מְגַלִּין לוֹ רָזֵי תוֹרָה — *the secrets of the Torah are revealed to him*. Of course, treated to the "hidden light," he is able to apply his enhanced view to the Torah itself. His ability to see מִסּוֹף הָעוֹלָם וְעַד סוֹפוֹ enables him to look into the Torah and discover, through it, all the secrets of the universe: from the heavenly realms above to the physical world below. All of these secrets are hidden within the Torah and accessible to the one who possesses such expansive vision.

The rest of the mishnah's qualities follow as well. Through this great light, the student who learns *Torah lishmah* is able to view Hashem's majesty more clearly than most. Privy to such an unobstructed view, his clear recognition of Hashem's greatness enables him to realize his own lowliness and insignificance in comparison, in a manner reminiscent of Moshe Rabbeinu. As such, he attains the all-important achievement of *bitul hayeishus*. And so he becomes, as the mishnah says, *tzanu'a* (modest), for he feels no need to impose his "self" on others. Likewise, with his ego in check, he will be less prone to particularity and anger, cultivating the quality of *erech ruach* (slow to anger).

The common denominator of all of these items is that they result from the broadened view afforded to one who accesses the G-dly light. When one learns *Torah lishmah*, the light of Torah brings out the hidden light from its constricted place within the *helem* of This World. Thus we find that the Sanhedrin (High Court of Torah Law) is referred to by the Torah as *einei ha'eidah* — "the 'eyes' of the congregation" (*Bamidbar* 15:24). This is a reference to the enhanced view afforded to the great Torah leaders; they are the "eyes" of the people, able to see from one end of the world to the other, unencumbered by the forces of *tumah* and *helem* that obscure Hashem's light in the world.

The View from Heaven

Following the giving of the Torah at Har Sinai, the *passuk* makes a somewhat unusual statement. Hashem declares (*Shemos* 20:19), אַתֶּם רְאִיתֶם כִּי מִן־הַשָּׁמַיִם דִּבַּרְתִּי עִמָּכֶם — *You have seen that I have spoken to you from the Heavens.* Why was it necessary to emphasize from where the voice of Hashem emanated? Furthermore, it doesn't even seem to be completely accurate! For the *passuk* states elsewhere (*ibid.* 19:20), וַיֵּרֶד ה' עַל־הַר סִינַי — *And Hashem descended onto Har Sinai,* indicating that Hashem's Presence rested on the mountain and from there He spoke to the people.

The Nesivos Sholom explains that, indeed, it was from the mountain, and not from *Shamayim,* that Hashem delivered His address. When Hashem declared that מִן־הַשָּׁמַיִם דִּבַּרְתִּי עִמָּכֶם, He did not mean that the words emanated from there; rather, the intent was that the words were delivered *from a Heavenly point of view.* If we were to be transported to the Heavenly realms and from there look down at This World, our perspective and perception would be completely different from that of the denizens of the earth. For from *Shamayim,* it is possible to discern This World for what it really is: *Havel havalim* — "Vanity of vanities" (in the words of *Koheles* [1:2]). From that vantage point, we can see that the pursuit of material pleasures is of lowly origin and inherently futile.

This is the message Hashem was seeking to convey. In giving the Torah, Hashem was informing the *Yidden* that, through the Torah, it is possible to view the world from a "Heavenly perspective" and distinguish what is truly of value from that which is ephemeral and nothingness. Through Torah, it is possible to live a Heavenly lifestyle here on earth.

This perspective informs our major struggle in life: the battle with the *yetzer hara.* From a logical standpoint, the *yetzer hara* should not be able to hold any sway over a person. How could one submit to temptation in contradiction of the will of Hashem? The very thought of doing so should be inherently repulsive; not to mention that Hashem Himself stands over a person, observing his every move. One who has a clear perception of *Hakadosh Baruch Hu* should find it simply impossible to sin.

And so the main strategy of the *yetzer hara* is to muddle our vision and perspective. The *yetzer hara* seeks to cover up the G-dly light from our eyes, leaving us under the dominion of the forces of *tumah*. Under such influence, it is possible, indeed, to sin aplenty (Hashem should guard us!).

There is only one antidote to the *yetzer hara's* assault. *Chazal* inform us of Hashem's declaration: בְּרָאתִי יֵצֶר הָרָע וּבָרָאתִי לוֹ תּוֹרָה תַּבְלִין — *I have created the* yetzer hara, *and I have created the Torah as a remedy for it* (*Kiddushin* 30b).

While this is a fairly familiar teaching, it takes on new meaning in light of our discussion. How, exactly, does Torah fend off the *yetzer hara* and cause its defeat? The tzaddikim have a well-known aphorism: מְעַט מִן הָאוֹר דּוֹחֶה הַרְבֵּה מִן הַחוֹשֶׁךְ — *A little light clears away much darkness*. Darkness is the tool of the *yetzer hara*; it knows that with clear vision and straight thinking, a Yid will not come to sin. And so it expends its efforts plunging the world into darkness so that the G-dly light is hidden behind a murky veneer. But as we have seen, the Torah has the power to ignite the light, to bring out that G-dly light from the recesses of the world of *helem*. With the *Torah ohr*, a Yid can see past the delusions fostered by the *yetzer hara*. One does not physically remove darkness; when the light goes on, the darkness flees of its own accord. Learning Torah in the proper manner can illuminate the world of a Yid. In its dazzling, clear light, he will abandon the enticements of the *yetzer hara*.

In Summary

The comparison of Torah to light goes a long way in explaining our universe and illuminating our mishnah, as well.

The *sefarim hakedoshim* tell us that the word *olam* derives from *helem*, meaning "hidden." For such is the nature of This World: The dazzling radiance of Hashem's G-dly light shines forth on all of the worlds of the upper spheres and is inherently present in our world, too. But since its presence would impede the exercise of free will, it is covered up. Through *tzimtzum*, the Divine light is contained behind a veneer of dense and dark physicality.

There is only one way to access this light, a branch of the *Ohr Haganuz* through which one may see from one end of the world to the other. By learning *Torah lishmah*, a Yid can retrieve the G-dly light from within its "containment" and see past the cloak of darkness set up by the forces of *tumah*. Then his view and perspective on the world will be expansive and clear: מִסּוֹף הָעוֹלָם וְעַד סוֹפוֹ.

Now able to perceive Hashem's light even in This World, this individual's field of view has increased exponentially. He can see and understand in ways that no one else is able. Thus, he is able to help his fellow man in greater capacity. With his new-found broad vision, he has the suitable qualities for leadership and dispensing counsel. Furthermore, he has a clear perception of *Hakadosh Baruch Hu*, such that he realizes his own insignificance. As such, he will be modest, humble, and patient. His love for Hashem and His creatures will be supreme.

And through the light of Torah, he will be empowered to vanquish the *yetzer hara*. No clear-headed individual would entertain thoughts of sin; how could one violate Hashem's will as He stands watching, let alone that the notion of sin itself is inherently repulsive! It is only by imposing on people the darkness of confusion that the *yetzer hara* is able to muddle their vision and entice them to sin. But one who learns Torah properly has access to the light of Torah, which brings out the G-dly light from the shadows. With this great light, he can recognize Hashem clearly. The restoration of his clear vision will thus enable him to abandon the *yetzer hara*.

פרק ו' משנה א'
ענין העוסק בתורה לשמה
(Discourse on) the Topic of Engaging in Torah Study for Its Own Sake

רַבִּי מֵאִיר אוֹמֵר כָּל הָעוֹסֵק בַּתּוֹרָה לִשְׁמָהּ, זוֹכֶה לִדְבָרִים הַרְבֵּה. וְלֹא עוֹד אֶלָּא שֶׁכָּל הָעוֹלָם כֻּלּוֹ כְּדַאי הוּא לוֹ. נִקְרָא רֵעַ, אָהוּב, אוֹהֵב אֶת הַמָּקוֹם, אוֹהֵב אֶת הַבְּרִיּוֹת, מְשַׂמֵּחַ אֶת הַמָּקוֹם, מְשַׂמֵּחַ אֶת הַבְּרִיּוֹת, וּמַלְבַּשְׁתּוֹ עֲנָוָה וְיִרְאָה, וּמַכְשַׁרְתּוֹ לִהְיוֹת צַדִּיק חָסִיד יָשָׁר וְנֶאֱמָן, וּמְרַחַקְתּוֹ מִן הַחֵטְא, וּמְקָרַבְתּוֹ לִידֵי זְכוּת, וְנֶהֱנִין מִמֶּנּוּ עֵצָה וְתוּשִׁיָּה בִּינָה וּגְבוּרָה. שֶׁנֶּאֱמַר לִי עֵצָה וְתוּשִׁיָּה אֲנִי בִינָה לִי גְבוּרָה, וְנוֹתֶנֶת לוֹ מַלְכוּת וּמֶמְשָׁלָה וְחִקּוּר דִּין, וּמְגַלִּין לוֹ רָזֵי תוֹרָה, וְנַעֲשֶׂה כְּמַעְיָן הַמִּתְגַּבֵּר וּכְנָהָר שֶׁאֵינוֹ פּוֹסֵק, וֶהֱוֵי צָנוּעַ וְאֶרֶךְ רוּחַ, וּמוֹחֵל עַל עֶלְבּוֹנוֹ, וּמְגַדַּלְתּוֹ וּמְרוֹמַמְתּוֹ עַל כָּל הַמַּעֲשִׂים:

Rabbi Meir says: Whoever engages in Torah study for its own sake merits many things; furthermore, the (creation of the) entire world is worthwhile for his sake alone. He is called a friend, beloved, one who loves the Omnipresent, one who loves people, one who gladdens the Omnipresent, one who gladdens people. (The Torah) clothes him in humility and fear (of Hashem); it makes him fit to be righteous, pious, upright, and faithful; it keeps him far from sin, and draws him near to merit. From him people enjoy counsel and wisdom, understanding and strength; as it states (*Mishlei* 8:14): "Mine are counsel and wisdom, I am understanding, Mine is strength." (The Torah) grants him kingship, dominion, and analytical judgment; the secrets of the Torah are revealed to him; he becomes like a steadily strengthening fountain and a river that does not cease; he becomes modest, patient, and forgiving of insults to himself. (The Torah) makes him great and uplifts him above all things.

ענין העוסק בתורה לשמה

SOURCES:

הַלּוֹמֵד תּוֹרָה עַל מְנָת לְלַמֵּד, מַסְפִּיקִין בְּיָדוֹ לִלְמוֹד וּלְלַמֵּד. וְהַלּוֹמֵד עַל מְנָת לַעֲשׂוֹת, מַסְפִּיקִין בְּיָדוֹ לִלְמוֹד וּלְלַמֵּד לִשְׁמוֹר וְלַעֲשׂוֹת. (אבות ד')

One who learns Torah in order to teach it, is granted the ability to learn and to teach. One who learns in order to do, is granted the ability to learn and to teach, to observe and to do. (*Avos 4*)

כָּל הַנּוֹתֵן ד"ת עַל לִבּוֹ מְבַטְּלִין מִמֶּנּוּ הִרְהוּרֵי חֶרֶב הִרְהוּרֵי רָעָב הִרְהוּרֵי שְׁטוּת הִרְהוּרֵי זְנוּת הִרְהוּרֵי יֵצֶר הָרָע הִרְהוּרֵי אֵשֶׁת אִישׁ... וְכָל שֶׁאֵינוֹ נוֹתֵן ד"ת עַל לִבּוֹ נוֹתְנִין לוֹ הִרְהוּרֵי חֶרֶב הִרְהוּרֵי רָעָב הִרְהוּרֵי שְׁטוּת הִרְהוּרֵי זְנוּת הִרְהוּרֵי יֵצֶר הָרָע הִרְהוּרֵי אֵשֶׁת אִישׁ... (אבות דר' נתן כ' א')

Whoever sets words of Torah upon his heart, (will merit that the following) will be removed from (his heart): Thoughts of: the sword, famine, foolishness, promiscuity, the evil inclination, another man's wife... But whoever does not set words of Torah upon his heart, will have (the following) imposed on (his heart): Thoughts of: the sword, famine, foolishness, promiscuity, the evil inclination, another man's wife... (*Avos D'Rebbi Nosson 20:1*)

וְתַלְמוּד תּוֹרָה כְּנֶגֶד כֻּלָּם. (פאה א' א')

Torah study is equivalent to them all. (*Pe'ah 1:1*)

הַשַּׁבָּת שְׁקוּלָה כְּנֶגֶד כָּל הַמִצְוֹת. (שמות רבה כ"ה י"ב)

Shabbos is equal to all of the mitzvos. (*Shemos Rabbah 25:12*)

נָכְרִי שֶׁשָּׁבַת חַיָּב מִיתָה, שֶׁנֶּאֱמַר וְיוֹם וָלַיְלָה לֹא יִשְׁבֹּתוּ. (סנהדרין נ"ח:)

A gentile who observes Shabbos is liable for death, as it states (*Bereishis* 8:22): "Day and night, they shall not cease." (*Sanhedrin 58b*)

פרק ו'

715

תָּנוּ רַבָּנָן: בְּשִׁשִּׁי בַּחֹדֶשׁ נִיתְּנוּ עֲשֶׂרֶת הַדִּבְּרוֹת לְיִשְׂרָאֵל. רַבִּי יוֹסֵי אוֹמֵר: בְּשִׁבְעָה בּוֹ... דְּכוּלֵּי עָלְמָא – בְּשַׁבַּת נִיתְּנָה תּוֹרָה לְיִשְׂרָאֵל. (שבת פ"ו.)

The Rabbis taught: The Ten Commandments were given to Yisroel on the sixth of the month (of Sivan). Rabbi Yosi says: It was the seventh (of the month)... All are in agreement that it was on the day of Shabbos that the Torah was given to Yisroel. (Shabbos 86b)

קוּדְשָׁא בְּרִיךְ הוּא אוֹרַיְיתָא וְיִשְׂרָאֵל כּוּלְּהוּ חַד. (זוהר)

The Holy One Blessed be He, the Torah, and Yisroel are all one. (Zohar)

הִתְנָה הַקָּדוֹשׁ בָּרוּךְ הוּא עִם מַעֲשֵׂה בְרֵאשִׁית וְאָמַר לָהֶם: אִם יִשְׂרָאֵל מְקַבְּלִים הַתּוֹרָה – אַתֶּם מִתְקַיְּימִין, וְאִם לָאו – אֲנִי מַחֲזִיר אֶתְכֶם לְתֹהוּ וָבֹהוּ. (שבת פ"ח.)

Hashem made the following stipulation with the works of creation, saying to them: "If Yisroel accepts the Torah, you will endure; but if not, I will return you to emptiness and nothingness." (Shabbos 88a)

כָּךְ הִיא דַּרְכָּהּ שֶׁל תּוֹרָה, פַּת בַּמֶּלַח תֹּאכַל וּמַיִם בִּמְשׂוּרָה תִּשְׁתֶּה וְעַל הָאָרֶץ תִּישַׁן וְחַיֵּי צַעַר תִּחְיֶה וּבַתּוֹרָה אַתָּה עָמֵל, אִם אַתָּה עֹשֶׂה כֵּן, אַשְׁרֶיךָ וְטוֹב לָךְ. אַשְׁרֶיךָ בָּעוֹלָם הַזֶּה וְטוֹב לָךְ לָעוֹלָם הַבָּא. (אבות ו׳)

Such is the path to Torah: Eat bread with salt, drink water in measure, sleep on the ground, live a life of deprivation – while you toil in the Torah. If you do so – "You will be happy and it shall be good for you" (Tehillim 128:2). "You will be happy" – in This World; "and it shall be good for you" – in the World to Come. (Avos 6)

וְהָיָה אִם־שָׁמֹעַ תִּשְׁמְעוּ אֶל־מִצְוֹתַי אֲשֶׁר אָנֹכִי מְצַוֶּה אֶתְכֶם הַיּוֹם לְאַהֲבָה אֶת־ה' אֱלֹקֵיכֶם. (דברים י"א י"ג)

עניין העוסק בתורה לשמה

And it shall be, if you listen to My mitzvos that I command you today, to love Hashem your G-d. *(Devarim 11:13)*

שֶׁמָּא תֹּאמַר הֲרֵי לָמַדְתִּי תּוֹרָה בִּשְׁבִיל שֶׁאֶהְיֶה עָשִׁיר וּבִשְׁבִיל שֶׁאִקָּרֵא רַבִּי וּבִשְׁבִיל שֶׁאֲקַבֵּל שָׂכָר ת"ל לְאַהֲבָה אֶת־ה' אֱלֹקֵיכֶם כָּל מַה שֶּׁאַתֶּם עוֹשִׂים לֹא תַעֲשׂוּ אֶלָּא מֵאַהֲבָה. *(ספרי)*

One might say: "I learn Torah to enable me to become wealthy, or that the title *Rebbi* be conferred upon me, or in order that I receive reward." (To negate these sentiments,) the verse states: "To love Hashem your G-d." (The message of the *passuk* is:) Whatever you do (to serve Hashem), do it without any other impetus save for love (of Hashem). *(Sifri)*

וְאָהַבְתָּ אֵת ה' אֱלֹקֶיךָ בְּכָל־לְבָבְךָ וּבְכָל־נַפְשְׁךָ וּבְכָל־מְאֹדֶךָ. *(דברים ו' ה')*

You shall love Hashem your G-d, with all of your heart, with all of your soul, and with all of your wealth. *(Devarim 6:5)*

וְאָהַבְתָּ אֵת ה' אֱלֹקֶיךָ בְּכָל־לְבָבְךָ אֵינִי יוֹדֵעַ בְּאֵיזֶה צַד אוֹהֲבִים אֶת הַקָּבָ"ה ת"ל וְהָיוּ הַדְּבָרִים הָאֵלֶּה אֲשֶׁר אָנֹכִי מְצַוְּךָ הַיּוֹם עַל־לְבָבֶךָ תֵּן הַדְּבָרִים הָאֵלֶּה עַל־לְבָבְךָ שֶׁמִּתּוֹךְ כָּךְ אַתָּה מַכִּיר אֶת הַקָּבָ"ה וּמְדַבֵּק בִּדְרָכָיו. *(ספרי)*

"And you shall love Hashem your G-d with all of your heart." Yet, I do not know through which means one should love Hashem. Therefore, the (next) *passuk* comes to teach us: "And these matters about which I am commanding you today should be on your heart" *(ibid. v. 6)*. (This verse conveys:) Set these matters upon your heart; through doing so, you will come to recognize Hashem and thus cling to His ways. *(Sifri)*

אָמְרוּ חֲכָמִים הָרִאשׁוֹנִים שֶׁמָּא תֹּאמַר הֲרֵינִי לָמֵד תּוֹרָה בִּשְׁבִיל שֶׁאֶהְיֶה עָשִׁיר... תַּלְמוּד לוֹמַר לְאַהֲבָה אֶת־ה' כָּל מַה שֶּׁאַתֶּם עוֹשִׂים לֹא תַעֲשׂוּ אֶלָּא מֵאַהֲבָה. *(יד החזקה פ"י מהל' תשובה הל"ד)*

The early Sages expounded: One might say: "I learn Torah to enable me to become wealthy..." (To negate such sentiment,) the

פרק ו'

verse states: "To love Hashem." Whatever you do, do it without any other impetus save for love (of Hashem). (*Yad Hachazakah, Hilchos Teshuvah* 10:4)

עֲשֵׂה דְבָרִים לְשֵׁם פָּעוּלָתָם וְדַבֵּר בָּהֶם לִשְׁמָן. (ספרי)

Discharge duties for the sake of their activity, and speak of them for their own sake. (*Sifri*)

וְעָשׂוּ לִי מִקְדָּשׁ וְשָׁכַנְתִּי בְּתוֹכָם. (שמות כ"ה ח')

And they shall make for Me a sanctuary, and I shall rest My Presence among them. (*Shemos* 25:8)

מִי שֶׁנְּשָׂאוֹ לִבּוֹ לְקַיֵּם מִצְוָה זוֹ כָּרָאוּי וְלִהְיוֹת מֻכְתָּר בְּכֶתֶר תּוֹרָה, לֹא יַסִּיחַ דַּעְתּוֹ לִדְבָרִים אֲחֵרִים, וְלֹא יָשִׂים עַל לִבּוֹ שֶׁיִּקְנֶה תּוֹרָה עִם הָעוֹשֶׁר וְהַכָּבוֹד כְּאַחַת... מִי שֶׁרָצָה לִזְכּוֹת בְּכֶתֶר הַתּוֹרָה יִזָּהֵר בְּכָל לֵילוֹתָיו וְלֹא יְאַבֵּד אֲפִלּוּ אֶחָד מֵהֶן בְּשֵׁנָה וַאֲכִילָה וּשְׁתִיָּה וְשִׂיחָה וְכַיּוֹצֵא בָּהֶן אֶלָּא בְּתַלְמוּד תּוֹרָה. (יד החזקה פ"ג מהל' תלמוד תורה הל' ו', י"ג)

One whose heart uplifts him to fulfill this mitzvah properly, and to be crowned with the crown of Torah, should not allow his mind to be distracted to other matters, nor should he set his heart to acquire Torah together with wealth and honor... One who desires to merit the crown of Torah must be careful regarding all of his nights, not to allow even one of them to go to waste through sleeping, eating, drinking, prattle, and the like – (engaging) only in Torah study. (*Yad Hachazakah, Hilchos Talmud Torah* 3:6, 13)

וַיָּבֹאוּ כָּל־אִישׁ אֲשֶׁר־נְשָׂאוֹ לִבּוֹ וְכֹל אֲשֶׁר נָדְבָה רוּחוֹ אֹתוֹ הֵבִיאוּ אֶת־תְּרוּמַת ה' לִמְלֶאכֶת אֹהֶל מוֹעֵד. (שמות ל"ה כ"א)

And they came – any man whose heart uplifted him, and whose spirit moved him to donate – and they brought the gift for Hashem, for the work of the Tent of Meeting. (*Shemos* 35:21)

עניין העוסק בתורה לשמה

The Hidden and Revealed Worlds of Torah

Torah lishmah. Obviously, this is the major theme of the first mishnah of this *perek*, which begins, רַבִּי מֵאִיר אוֹמֵר כָּל הָעוֹסֵק בַּתּוֹרָה לִשְׁמָהּ, זוֹכֶה לִדְבָרִים הַרְבֵּה — *Rabbi Meir says: Whosoever learns Torah lishmah merits many things*. (The mishnah then supplies a comprehensive list of the benefits accrued to one who studies *Torah lishmah*.) Beyond that, the idea appears in numerous other teachings of *Chazal*. Yet, are we sure about what it means? It would seem worthwhile to have a solid grasp of this notion we hear so much about. What, exactly, does the lofty ideal of *Torah lishmah* entail?

As we shall see later, elucidation of this idea may come from a somewhat unexpected source: through a close examination of the nature of *Shabbos Kodesh* (the holy Shabbos), we may gain a clearer understanding of the concept of *Torah lishmah*, as well.

First, however, the Nesivos Sholom raises a number of points regarding *Torah lishmah* in particular and the subject of Torah study in general:

- There is a mishnah appearing earlier in *Pirkei Avos* that also discusses the notion of learning with specific intent: הַלּוֹמֵד תּוֹרָה עַל מְנָת לְלַמֵּד, מַסְפִּיקִין בְּיָדוֹ לִלְמוֹד וּלְלַמֵּד. וְהַלּוֹמֵד עַל מְנָת לַעֲשׂוֹת, מַסְפִּיקִין בְּיָדוֹ לִלְמוֹד וּלְלַמֵּד לִשְׁמוֹר וְלַעֲשׂוֹת — *One who learns Torah in order to teach it, is granted the ability to learn and to teach. One who learns in order to do, is granted the ability to learn and to teach, to observe and to do*. The tone of this mishnah seems laudatory; that is, it appears that learning Torah in order to teach it is considered meritorious, and one who does so will receive Heavenly assistance. Perhaps learning in order to do is an even higher level. Either way, both efforts seem to be manifestations of fulfilling the mitzvah of *talmud Torah* in an enhanced and praiseworthy fashion.

  Where does *Torah lishmah* fit in on this scale? It seems to be yet an additional level. In what way does it differ from the above? Is it a superior way to fulfill the mitzvah of *talmud Torah*? Or is it a separate entity, an endeavor in a league by itself?

- For that matter, from where do we even derive this whole notion of *Torah lishmah*? Does it have its own Scriptural source? From where did the mishnah learn that it comes with such an array of happy results? And why are these specific rewards relegated specifically to the endeavor of learning *Torah lishmah*, more so than for any other mitzvah?

- We find another list of benefits accrued specifically to one who learns Torah. *Chazal* inform us (*Avos D'Rebbi Nosson* 20:1) that proper Torah study can purge a Yid from unwanted and impure thoughts: כָּל הַנּוֹתֵן ד"ת עַל לִבּוֹ מְבַטְלִין מִמֶּנּוּ הִרְהוּרֵי חֶרֶב הִרְהוּרֵי רָעָב הִרְהוּרֵי שְׁטוּת הִרְהוּרֵי זְנוּת הִרְהוּרֵי יֵצֶר הָרָע הִרְהוּרֵי אֵשֶׁת אִישׁ... וְכֹל שֶׁאֵינוֹ נוֹתֵן ד"ת עַל לִבּוֹ נוֹתְנִין לוֹ הִרְהוּרֵי חֶרֶב הִרְהוּרֵי רָעָב הִרְהוּרֵי שְׁטוּת הִרְהוּרֵי זְנוּת הִרְהוּרֵי יֵצֶר הָרָע הִרְהוּרֵי אֵשֶׁת אִישׁ... — Whoever sets words of Torah upon his heart (will merit that the following) will be removed from (his heart): Thoughts of the sword, famine, foolishness, promiscuity, the evil inclination, another man's wife... But whoever does not set words of Torah upon his heart, will have (the following) imposed on (his heart): Thoughts of the sword, famine, foolishness, promiscuity, the evil inclination, another man's wife... Once again, we find a whole range of consequences that are unique to *talmud Torah* particularly. Why are these items not equally applicable to all instances of mitzvah fulfillment? Don't they also have the capacity to confer *kedushah* on a person?

- Another facet that seems limited to the area of Torah study appears in a later mishnah (6:6). The mishnah lists forty-eight items *shehaTorah nikneis bahem* — "through which the Torah is 'acquired.'" This is found only in connection with Torah study; why don't we encounter any notion of making a *kinyan* on any other type of mitzvah?

There is yet another area where we find the mitzvah of *talmud Torah* standing out from all other mitzvos. The Rambam (*Hilchos Talmud Torah* 3:3) states that *talmud Torah* is indeed the most outstanding mitzvah, equivalent to all of the mitzvos put together. This notion also demands explanation: What is it about *talmud Torah* that accounts for its supremely unique status? In this regard, however, *talmud Torah* does have a companion of sorts. For the same holds true for Shabbos, which *Chazal* state is also equivalent to all of the mitzvos (*Shemos Rabbah* 25:12). Why is Shabbos considered to be so grand, equal to all the mitzvos? And is it mere coincidence that both *talmud Torah* and Shabbos are characterized as such? Or, as would appear more likely, is there some common thread between them?

To discover this common denominator, we must delve into the essence of Shabbos, in an attempt to find the source of its uniqueness.

The Shabbos Connection

The Nesivos Sholom explains that every mitzvah is actually comprised of two components: the *nigleh*, the revealed part that we see with our eyes, and the *nistar*, the hidden, sublime aspect of the mitzvah. The Torah itself, we find, is divided in this fashion: Its *nigleh* aspect is readily apparent, while the mystical secrets that comprise the *Toras Hanistar* (the Hidden Torah) were not written explicitly in the Torah, quite purposely so. The *nigleh* aspect of Shabbos, of course, is Shabbos observance. With our eyes we behold *Yidden* refraining from *melachah* (labor) on Shabbos. But only *Chazal*, imbued with G-dly wisdom, are able to uncover the *nistar* aspect of a given mitzvah and particularly the sublime and hidden component of Shabbos. Its esoteric nature is alluded to in the Zohar, which asserts that Shabbos is actually comprised entirely of the Name of Hashem.

The *nistar* quality of Shabbos is characterized by the exclusive relationship between *Hakadosh Baruch Hu* and Klal Yisroel, hinted to by the Torah's description of Shabbos as being בֵּינִי וּבֵין בְּנֵי יִשְׂרָאֵל — *between Me and Bnei Yisroel* (*Shemos* 31:17). Shabbos reveals Hashem's singular focus on Yisroel, to the extent that it is considered a capital offense for a gentile to observe Shabbos (*Sanhedrin* 58b). This reflects the intensity of the relationship between Hashem and the *Yidden*, compared by *Chazal* (*Shemos Rabbah* 25:11) to a king involved in a private nuptial celebration. At such a time, an outsider dare not enter.

In this sense, explains the Nesivos Sholom, Shabbos fulfills the very purpose for which the world was created: namely, Hashem sought to acquire a dwelling place among the lower spheres. Shabbos embodies this ideal; through it, a Yid — a material being, denizen of the lower world — sheds his physicality, attaining *d'veikus* to Hashem. As the Zohar states, Shabbos is in no way a *yoma d'gufa*, day of the physical body; rather, it is referred to as the *yoma d'nishmasa*, day of the soul. The most treasured tribute one can offer the king is one that comes from far away, and nothing is "further" from the pristine, infinite sanctity of *Hakadosh Baruch Hu* than the lowliness of This World. Yet this was Hashem's desire, that there be a linkage between Him and the lower creatures. Thus, when a Yid shakes off his material tendencies, tapping instead into the sublime spirituality of the Shabbos day, he becomes attached to Hashem, the Most High. This is the most precious form of tribute and a fulfillment of just what Hashem envisioned in creating the world in the first place.

This idea is reflected in the enlightening comments of the Ohr Hachaim Hakadosh (*Parshas Bereishis*). One may have assumed that the world was created to endure, following a seven-day-a-week pattern. That is, the world continues along its intended course; as it does, the *Yidden* observe Shabbos every seventh day. The Ohr Hachaim informs us that this is not the case. In fact, the world actually has a surprisingly short "shelf life"; it was created to endure for only a single week! What happens, though, is that when the *Yidden* keep Shabbos, this triggers a renewal of the *beri'ah* for yet one week more. And so, the world may endure — as long as there are *Yidden* in the world who keep Shabbos. That the world exists in the merit of Shabbos is quite an understandable prospect, in light of what we have learned that, through Shabbos, the purpose of creation is fulfilled.

And so it emerges that Shabbos is comprised of these two components: the *nigleh* aspect is the actual observance of Shabbos, the stoppage of labor, and the *nistar* aspect is the *d'veikus baHashem* one achieves on this sublime day. A human being is likewise composed of two aspects: the *guf*, which is perceived, is the *nigleh* aspect; however, the life-force of a person is provided by the *neshamah* within, which is the *nistar* aspect. In this sense, the tangible *guf* of Shabbos is the act of refraining from work, but the *neshamah* that keeps it "alive" is the *d'veikus* component.

This notion is reflected in the teachings of the great chassidic masters. The prayers recited on Shabbos night (according to those who follow the rite of *Nusach Sefard*) include a selection from the Zohar known by its beginning word, *Kegavna*. In this passage, the following phrase appears, רָזָא דְשַׁבָּת אִיהִי שַׁבָּת — *The secret of Shabbos, this is Shabbos*. The Rebbe of Lechovitz *ztz"l* explained this enigmatic phrase based on its *gematria* (numerical value). The *gematria* of the word רז (secret) — 207 — is equal to that of the word אור (light). Thus, the phrase can be understood as stating, "What is Shabbos? The 'light' of Shabbos." In other words, the principal aspect of Shabbos is its spiritual aspect, the light of Shabbos, which is its soul. A Shabbos that one goes through without detecting and feeling this light is like a body without a soul.

Along similar lines, the saintly Reb Shlomo of Karlin emphasized the need *to derive serene pleasure* from the spiritual nature of Shabbos. He reported hearing a proclamation from a Heavenly voice on the subject. The voice announced the fate of one who observes the Shabbos but derives no spiritual pleasure from its sublime nature; the rendering was that, certainly, such a Yid would merit to enter Gan Eden, but, having neglected to develop the propensity to detect and delight in spirituality, this lack of feeling would carry over into the Afterlife, as well. Thus, he will have a portion there but will derive as much satisfaction from it as would a wooden stool that had been placed in the Garden.

The upshot of these teachings reflects the aforementioned thought. It is the pleasure of *d'veikus* that is the *neshamah*, the principal aspect of Shabbos. *And it is for this reason that* Chazal *considered Shabbos as equal to all of the mitzvos.* As the *sefarim hakedoshim* teach us, the aim and purpose of all 613 mitzvos is to enable a Yid to come close to Hashem; essentially, they are 613 different ways to reach the ultimate goal of *d'veikus baHashem*. As Shabbos is principally characterized by *d'veikus*, the "soul" of Shabbos, and it is through Shabbos that this critical goal can be reached, it is deemed equal to all of the mitzvos.

GEMS FROM THE *SEFER NESIVOS SHOLOM*

Shabbos, Torah, and the World

It is for this reason, as well, that Torah is equal to all of the mitzvos; for Torah shares this essential component. The Gemara (*Shabbos* 86b) records a dispute as to the exact date on which the Torah was given on Har Sinai. On one count, however, all are in agreement: which day of the week it was. According to all opinions, the Torah was given on Shabbos. This is no mere coincidence. Shabbos is characterized by pristine spirituality; its principal aspect, its *nistar* component, is *d'veikus baHashem*. The *nistar* aspect of the mitzvah of *talmud Torah*, as well, is *d'veikus*; for Torah is the quintessential vehicle for *d'veikus*. The Zohar tells us of a remarkable bond: קוּדְשָׁא בְּרִיךְ הוּא אוֹרַיְיתָא וְיִשְׂרָאֵל כּוּלְהוּ חַד — *The Holy One Blessed be He, the Torah, and Yisroel are all one*. The Nesivos Sholom explains how it is that Yisroel, as mere mortals, can attain such closeness with Hashem, the infinite Source of purity and sanctity. This synthesis is achieved through the Torah, which serves as the bridge between Yisroel and *Hakadosh Baruch Hu*. By attaching themselves to the Torah — in which resides Hashem's *Shechinah* — Yisroel becomes attached to Hashem Himself. The purpose of all of the mitzvos, *d'veikus baHashem*, is attained through Torah; as such, Torah is considered equal to them all.

Just like Shabbos, Torah also serves as the foundation for the world's continued existence. *Chazal* tell us (*Shabbos* 88a): הִתְנָה הַקָּדוֹשׁ בָּרוּךְ הוּא עִם מַעֲשֵׂה בְרֵאשִׁית וְאָמַר לָהֶם: אִם יִשְׂרָאֵל מְקַבְּלִים הַתּוֹרָה – אַתֶּם מִתְקַיְּימִין, וְאִם לָאו – אֲנִי מַחֲזִיר אֶתְכֶם לְתוֹהוּ וָבוֹהוּ — *Hashem made the following stipulation with the works of creation, saying to them: "If Yisroel accepts the Torah, you will endure; but if not, I will return you to emptiness and nothingness."* As previously explained, Hashem's purpose in creating the world was to connect with even the lower creatures; therefore, for the world to be worthwhile, mortals must shake off their physicality to cleave to Hashem. It is through the Torah that people may attain *d'veikus* with Hashem; without it, G-d forbid, the world has no purpose and could just as well revert to emptiness and nothingness.

It is for this reason as well that, later in this *perek*, *Chazal* call for seemingly harsh measures to attain Torah. As the mishnah states (6:4), כָּךְ הִיא דַּרְכָּהּ שֶׁל תּוֹרָה, פַּת בַּמֶּלַח תֹּאכֵל וּמַיִם בִּמְשׂוּרָה תִּשְׁתֶּה וְעַל הָאָרֶץ תִּישָׁן וְחַיֵּי

עניין העוסק בתורה לשמה

צַעַר תִּחְיֶה וּבַתּוֹרָה אַתָּה עָמֵל — *Such is the path to Torah: Eat (only) bread with salt, drink water in measure, sleep on the ground, live a life of deprivation, and toil in the Torah.* For this is actually the purpose of creation: that a Yid *should* shake off his materialistic tendencies in order to attain *d'veikus baHashem*. And fortunate for the world — and for him — if he does so. As the mishnah concludes, אִם אַתָּה עֹשֶׂה כֵּן...אַשְׁרֶיךָ בָּעוֹלָם הַזֶּה וְטוֹב לָךְ לָעוֹלָם הַבָּא — *If you do so...you will be happy in This World, and all will be good for you in the World to Come.*

Attachment to Hashem, Love of Hashem

Earlier, we had asked where, in comparison to learning in order to teach and learning in order to do, did the concept of learning *lishmah* fit in. We wondered, as well, what the Scriptural basis was for the whole notion of *Torah lishmah*.

To address these issues, the Nesivos Sholom advances a tremendous *chiddush* (novel Torah thought) regarding *Torah lishmah*. He asserts that, in fact, it *is not a subsidiary* of the actual mitzvah of *talmud Torah*. This may be the province of learning to teach/to do, which are superior ways of fulfilling this mitzvah. *Torah lishmah*, however, is in a category all of its own, separate even from the actual mitzvah of *talmud Torah*. (This is not to say, of course, that one who learns *Torah lishmah* does not fulfill the mitzvah of *talmud Torah*; of course he does. The Nesivos Sholom's intent is that it is not the mitzvah of *talmud Torah* that necessitates that the Torah be learned *lishmah*; rather, the imperative comes from elsewhere, as we shall see.)

The Nesivos Sholom cites two passages from the *Sifri*, each commenting on separate but related *pesukim* from *Krias Shema*. As we shall see, these citations not only serve to identify the source for the whole notion of *Torah lishmah*, but also shed light on its proper characterization.

The first selection is based on the *passuk* (Devarim 11:13): וְהָיָה אִם־שָׁמֹעַ תִּשְׁמְעוּ אֶל־מִצְוֹתַי אֲשֶׁר אָנֹכִי מְצַוֶּה אֶתְכֶם הַיּוֹם לְאַהֲבָה אֶת־ה' אֱלֹקֵיכֶם — *And it shall be, if you listen to My mitzvos that I am commanding you today, to love Hashem your G-d.* The *Sifri* expounds: שֶׁמָּא תֹּאמַר הֲרֵי לָמַדְתִּי תּוֹרָה

GEMS FROM THE SEFER NESIVOS SHOLOM

בִּשְׁבִיל שֶׁאֶהְיֶה עָשִׁיר וּבִשְׁבִיל שֶׁיִּקָּרֵא רַבִּי וּבִשְׁבִיל שֶׁאֲקַבֵּל שָׂכָר ת"ל לְאַהֲבָה אֶת־ה' אֱלֹקֵיכֶם — כָּל מַה שֶׁאַתֶּם עוֹשִׂים לֹא תַעֲשׂוּ אֶלָּא מֵאַהֲבָה — One might say: "I learn Torah to enable me to become wealthy, or that the title Rebbi be conferred upon me, or in order that I receive reward." (To negate these sentiments,) the passuk states: "**To love Hashem your G-d.**" (The message of the passuk is:) Whatever you do (to serve Hashem), do it without any other impetus save for love (of Hashem).

In the other passage from the *Sifri*, *Chazal* comment on some earlier verses: וְאָהַבְתָּ אֵת ה' אֱלֹקֶיךָ בְּכָל־לְבָבְךָ אֵינִי יוֹדֵעַ בְּאֵיזֶה צַד אוֹהֲבִים אֶת הקב"ה ת"ל וְהָיוּ הַדְּבָרִים הָאֵלֶּה אֲשֶׁר אָנֹכִי מְצַוְּךָ הַיּוֹם עַל־לְבָבֶךָ תֵּן הַדְּבָרִים הָאֵלֶּה עַל־לְבָבְךָ שֶׁמִּתּוֹךְ כָּךְ אַתָּה מַכִּיר אֶת הקב"ה וּמִדַּבֵּק בִּדְרָכָיו — "And you shall love Hashem your G-d with all of your heart" (Devarim 6:5). Yet, I do not know through which means one should love Hashem. Therefore, the (next) passuk comes to teach us: "And these matters about which I am commanding you today should be on your heart" (ibid. v. 6). (This passuk conveys:) Set these matters upon your heart; through doing so, you will come to recognize Hashem and thus cling to His ways.

Through the interpretations of the *Sifri*, we discover something monumental. It appears that *Torah lishmah* is an outgrowth of the mitzvah to love Hashem. In other words, as the Nesivos Sholom had claimed, there is a separate directive regarding Torah study, one of the 613 mitzvos. Purely from the standpoint of this specific mitzvah, perhaps we may not have known of any particular preference for *Torah lishmah*. What the *Sifri* reveals is that *Torah lishmah* is actually a subsidiary of a different idea — the mitzvah to love Hashem. We have already encountered the relation of *Torah lishmah* to the achievement of *d'veikus*, a notion solidified by this *Sifri*: *U'misdabeik b'derachav* (cling to His ways). Apparently, it is likewise associated with the related quality of *ahavas Hashem*. The cycle of attaining closeness with the Almighty is centered on Torah study: by "setting these matters upon your heart," a Yid will come to *v'ahavta es Hashem*; having enhanced his love of Hashem, he will be able to study Torah from this impetus alone.

In his *halachic* code, the Rambam cites this teaching of the *Sifri* that exhorts us to learn Torah for no other reason than love of

ענין העוסק בתורה לשמה

Hashem (שֶׁמָּא תֹּאמַר...לֹא תַעֲשׂוּ אֶלָּא מֵאַהֲבָה). It is quite noteworthy *where* the Rambam, renowned both for his sagacity and precision, placed this particular teaching. Although he does devote a section of his code to the laws of learning Torah (*Hilchos Talmud Torah*), he did *not* place this teaching in that section. Rather, it was included in the final *perek* of *Hilchos Teshuvah*, a chapter that elaborates on the mitzvah of *ahavas Hashem*. Thus, from the Rambam as well, we see that *Torah lishmah* is more aptly classified as an aspect of *ahavas Hashem* than simply a particular of the mitzvah of *talmud Torah*.

A Different Person

Further insight into *Torah lishmah* can be gleaned from yet another teaching of the *Sifri*, which states, עֲשֵׂה דְבָרִים לְשֵׁם פָּעֳלָתָם וְדַבֵּר בָּהֶם לִשְׁמָן — *Discharge duties for the sake of their "activity," and speak of them for their own sake.* "Speak of them for their own sake" indicates that *Torah lishmah* is the subject of this teaching. The Nesivos Sholom understands the initial phrase — "Discharge duties for the sake of their 'activity'" — as referring to the *purpose* of the activity. That is, Torah should be studied for the sake of the original intent for which the Torah had been given. As stated previously, Hashem's purpose in granting the Torah to Yisroel was to elevate the *beri'ah*; that is, through the Torah, a person can transform his nature from one that is base and animalistic to one that is pristine and sanctified. In this way, he will be able to achieve *d'veikus* with Hashem.

Taking this notion one step further, we can discern in what way the endeavor of Torah study actually differs from that of Shabbos. We have seen that both are endowed with an elevated, unique status and share many qualities in this regard. The existence of the world depends on these entities; they are equivalent to all mitzvos, and they are both, in essence, characterized by *d'veikus baHashem*. And both are intensive manifestations of spirituality, able to uplift a person from the bonds and limitation of his physicality.

But it is in this latter aspect that there exists a difference. Shabbos, as previously mentioned, is referred to as the *yoma d'nishmasa*. That is, Shabbos has the power to purify and elevate the soul of a Yid and all of its components. Torah provides an added degree of refinement. When a Yid learns Torah in the proper and most elevated fashion, doing so *l'sheim pe'ulasam* (for the sake of its exalted intent), even the *physical aspects* of his *guf* become purified and uplifted. His flesh becomes a different type of flesh, of an elevated, spiritual quality. The Maharal on *Avos* (2:5) explains that this is the derivation of the term by which an ignoramus is known: *Am ha'aretz*. *Aretz* refers to the earth, the flesh's place of origin. By nature, a person is inherently "earthly," connected to the earth through his base instinct and tendencies. So he remains if he does not fill himself with the *kedushas haTorah*. Conversely, one who does immerse himself in Torah is able to elevate his essence and his very flesh.

This idea is in keeping with the ultimate intent of the giving of the Torah, reflecting the purpose of creation. Hashem desired to have a dwelling place among the lower spheres. He granted the Torah so that a Yid can transform all aspects of himself, transforming the material into spiritual, thereby providing the *Shechinah* a suitable resting place in which to dwell. As *Chazal* derive from the *passuk* regarding the building of the Sanctuary (*Shemos* 25:8): וְעָשׂוּ לִי מִקְדָּשׁ וְשָׁכַנְתִּי בְּתוֹכָם — *And they shall make for Me a sanctuary, and I will reside therein*. The *passuk* did not use the singular *b'socho* — "in **it**," but rather the plural *b'socham* — "in **them**." The implication, *Chazal* understand, is that Hashem sought to rest His Presence literally within the body of every Yid. When a Yid learns Torah with this aim in mind, he achieves thereby the essence of *d'veikus baHashem*.

We can now better appreciate the statement of *Avos D'Rebbi Nosson*, that by "placing words of Torah upon one's heart," a person is spared from unwanted, impure thoughts. For through the proper approach to and engagement in Torah, a Yid becomes completely transformed, as he fashions himself into a suitable dwelling place for the *Shechinah*. His soul, his very flesh, represents the epitome of spirituality. By so connecting to the sanctity of the Most High, a Yid is uplifted, transcending his base nature and elevating himself beyond the realm of such earthly musings.

Levels of Aspiration

It is worthwhile to peer at some of the Rambam's comments regarding the proper method of studying and acquiring Torah, as this may shed further light on the subject of *Torah lishmah*.

In the *Hilchos Talmud Torah* section of his code, the Rambam writes extensively of the numerous laws and aspects that govern the all-important endeavor of Torah study. After having provided many of these details, the Rambam then writes the following (3:6), מִי שֶׁנְּשָׂאוֹ לִבּוֹ לְקַיֵּים מִצְוָה זוֹ כָּרָאוּי וְלִהְיוֹת מוּכְתָּר בְּכֶתֶר תּוֹרָה, לֹא יַסִּיחַ דַּעְתּוֹ לִדְבָרִים אֲחֵרִים, וְלֹא יָשִׂים עַל לִבּוֹ שֶׁיִּקְנֶה תּוֹרָה עִם הָעוֹשֶׁר וְהַכָּבוֹד כְּאַחַת... — *One whose heart uplifts him to fulfill this mitzvah properly and to be crowned with the crown of Torah, should not allow his mind to be distracted to other matters, nor should he set his heart to acquire Torah together with wealth and honor...* The Rambam continues along these lines further on (3:13), מִי שֶׁרָצָה לִזְכּוֹת בְּכֶתֶר הַתּוֹרָה יִזָּהֵר בְּכָל לֵילוֹתָיו וְלֹא יְאַבֵּד אֲפִילוּ אֶחָד מֵהֶן בְּשֵׁינָה וַאֲכִילָה וּשְׁתִיָּה וְשִׂיחָה וְכַיּוֹצֵא בָּהֶן אֶלָּא בְּתַלְמוּד תּוֹרָה — *One who desires to merit the crown of Torah must be careful regarding each one of his nights, not allowing even one of them to go to waste through sleeping, eating, drinking, prattle, and the like — (engaging) only in* talmud Torah.

As always, the words of the Rambam are very enlightening. He began this dissertation with the phrase: מִי שֶׁנְּשָׂאוֹ לִבּוֹ לְקַיֵּים מִצְוָה זוֹ כָּרָאוּי... — *One whose heart uplifts him to fulfill this mitzvah properly...* This phrase actually appears in the Torah, in the section detailing Klal Yisroel's donations towards the building of the Mishkan: וַיָּבֹאוּ כָּל־אִישׁ אֲשֶׁר־נְשָׂאוֹ לִבּוֹ — *And all whose heart uplifted them came (to deliver their donations to the building)* (*Shemos* 35:21). The Ohr Hachaim Hakadosh there addresses the significance of the terminology. Regarding donations, he explains that there are actually two classes of donors, corresponding to two different appellations that appear in that section. There are those who donate according to their means, a fair and laudable proposition. Such people are referred to by the term *nadvah rucho* — "his spirit moved him to donate." But then there is the individual who yearns to go above and beyond, whose heart moves him to give of himself even beyond his present ability; he feels he simply must give more and more. This type of donor is a *nesa'o libo* — "his heart has lifted him up."

GEMS FROM THE *SEFER NESIVOS SHOLOM*

This is the intent of the Rambam as well; in his *Hilchos Talmud Torah* section, he likewise referred to the different gradations. Initially, he spoke of the praiseworthy fellow who wants to "fulfill the mitzvah"; once again, a laudable goal, but basically sticking to what needs to be done. By introducing (in the third *perek*) the idea of *keser Torah* (crown of Torah) — מִי שֶׁנְשָׂאוֹ לִבּוֹ... לִהְיוֹת מוּכְתָּר בְּכֶתֶר תּוֹרָה — the Rambam shifted the discussion to one who desires to go above and beyond. Rather than being satisfied with simply discharging his practical obligation to fulfill the mitzvah, this individual is *nesa'o libo*, of a different class altogether. He desires to be crowned with the crown of Torah, a reference to the endeavor of becoming one with the Torah to attain *d'veikus* with Hashem.

And so the Rambam warns: One who desires to do so must take care to avoid *hesech hada'as*, an interruption of one's focus. His mind must be constantly attuned to the Torah. The Toldos Yaakov Yosef (*Parshas Beshalach*) issues the same warning regarding the "sister" activity of *talmud Torah* — namely, Shabbos. He proclaims that on the Shabbos day, one must not break his focus from the sanctity of Shabbos even for a moment. He has an interesting derivation for this idea, drawing on the *tzitz*, one of the sacred items worn by the *kohen gadol*. The *tzitz* was a golden plate that rested on the *kohen gadol's* forehead, on which was engraved the Name of Hashem. The prohibition against *hesech hada'as* applied to this item; as long as it was carried by the *kohen gadol*, he could not divert his mind from its sanctity. The Toldos applies here the exegetical device known as *kal vachomer* (characterized by employment of the phrase: "How much more so..."): The *tzitz* contained only one appearance of Hashem's Name; nevertheless, it was forbidden to divert one's mind from it. *Kal vachomer*, how much more so, then, with regards to Shabbos. We had learned earlier that, as the Zohar states, Shabbos is entirely comprised of the Names of Hashem; certainly, then, one may not divert his mind from the sanctity of Shabbos, even for a moment!

The Torah, as well, is considered a manifestation of the Names of Hashem and contains His *Shechinah* within. As such, the *kal vachomer* of the Toldos would certainly also apply to Torah, hence the Rambam's admonition that one must take care not to have any *hesech hada'as* from Torah. Through proper engagement in Torah, especially by someone in the category of *nesa'o libo*, a Yid attains *d'veikus* with Hashem. *Hesech hada'as* would amount to a pause in and contradiction to this *d'veikus*. He must remain attached to Hashem through his Torah, avoiding any unnecessary interruption. As such, he must value every moment, taking care not to lose out on even a single evening devoted to Torah.

The above informs, as well, the idea of "acquiring" Torah, necessitating the forty-eight items to solidify this acquisition. We had wondered why it is that of all the mitzvos, we only find such a phrase regarding the mitzvah of *talmud Torah*. Based on the above, it emerges that, in fact, the technical mitzvah of *talmud Torah* may be no different. When the mishnah later on discusses the notion of making an "acquisition" of Torah, it was not referring to the individual who is satisfied with simply fulfilling the mitzvah of *talmud Torah*, praiseworthy as it is. Rather, the reference is to someone who is *nesa'o libo*, someone who is striving for *d'veikus* through Torah. The forty-eight items are intended for one who aspires to the more elevated level, one who wishes to truly "acquire" Torah, be crowned with its crown, and through it attain *d'veikus* with Hashem.

In Summary

Though he has addressed this topic before, the Nesivos Sholom edifies us in the notion of *Torah lishmah*.

We find an interesting correlation between the entities of Torah and Shabbos. *Chazal* tell us that they are each equivalent to the entirety of all other mitzvos put together. The existence of the universe depends upon each individually, and both Shabbos and Torah are in some sense manifestations of the Names of Hashem. Understanding the nature of Shabbos will enlighten our understanding of Torah as well.

Every mitzvah, the Nesivos Sholom explains, has two components: the *nigleh* and the *nistar*. Regarding Shabbos, which we perceive, the *nigleh* aspect is the work stoppage that is observed on this day. The *nistar* aspect, largely hidden from view, is the sublime spiritual experience of Shabbos, known as the *yoma d'nishmasa*, the day of the soul. The spiritual pleasure to be felt on Shabbos is its primary component, and it is manifest largely through the attainment of *d'veikus* with Hashem. It is for this reason that the maintained existence of the world is so inextricably linked with Shabbos; after all, the attainment of *d'veikus* is the purpose for which the world was created, as Hashem desired to acquire a dwelling place even among the beings of the lower world. As such, the primary aspect of Shabbos is for a Yid to shed his physicality and connect with Hashem in utmost *d'veikus*.

The Torah was given on Shabbos, for it shares this component as well. *Chazal* tell us that *Hakadosh Baruch Hu*, the Torah, and Yisroel are all one, for it is through cleaving to the Torah that a Yid is able to attain *d'veikus* with Him. *Torah lishmah* entails learning Torah for the purpose of Hashem's intent in granting it in the first place; *Chazal* stress that one should learn Torah *l'sheim pe'ulasam*, for the purpose of this lofty intent. Hashem gave Yisroel the Torah so that they could transform their earthly selves into pristine vessels capable of serving as a resting place for the *Shechinah*. And in this respect, Torah's power exceeds that of Shabbos; for while Shabbos refines the soul, Torah is able to elevate every aspect of a person, including his very flesh. As such, one who learns Torah properly fulfills the purpose of creation and Hashem's intent in granting the Torah — that man be able to connect with Hashem in utter *d'veikus*.

The Nesivos Sholom points out that the intimation of *Chazal* is that *Torah lishmah*, in fact, is not necessarily a subsidiary of the mitzvah of *talmud Torah* itself. This we see from the *derashos* (expositions) of *Chazal*, who derive the notion of *Torah lishmah* from the directive to love Hashem. As such, it would appear to be an aspect of the mitzvah of *ahavas Hashem*, with which it is so closely associated. *Chazal* tell us that one should not learn Torah for any purpose other than pure love for *Hakadosh Baruch Hu*. They inform us further that it is through "setting the words of Torah on one's heart" that one engenders *ahavas Hashem*. The *nistar* of Torah, its inner essence,

ענין העוסק בתורה לִשְׁמה

is one of *ahavas Hashem* and *d'veikus* to Him. What emerges is a glorious cycle of attaining closeness to Hashem: Torah leads one to *ahavas Hashem*, which in turn enables a Yid to learn *Torah lishmah*, a manifestation of *d'veikus baHashem*, in accordance with the exalted intent for which Torah was granted.

Another component necessary to attain the level of *Torah lishmah* emerges from the Rambam. In discussing the individual who desires to be crowned with the *keser Torah*, the Rambam refers to such an individual as *mi shenesa'o libo*, one whose heart uplifts him. As the Ohr Hachaim explains, this refers to an individual who yearns to go above and beyond what is merely obligatory. As it relates to Torah study, this term refers to someone who wants to do more than simply fulfill the mitzvah of Torah study, who wants to become one with the Torah and thereby achieve *d'veikus* with Hashem. To achieve this, the Rambam instructs that one may not engage in *hesech hada'as* from the Torah. This is a very understandable charge, as one who wishes to maintain this sublime state cannot afford to divert his attention even for a moment, for by so doing, he would be interrupting his *d'veikus* with Hashem.

פרק ו׳

פרק ו' משנה ב'
אוי להם לבריות מעלבונה של תורה
Woe Is to People for Their Insult to Torah

אָמַר רַבִּי יְהוֹשֻׁעַ בֶּן לֵוִי, בְּכָל יוֹם וָיוֹם בַּת קוֹל יוֹצֵאת מֵהַר חוֹרֵב וּמַכְרֶזֶת וְאוֹמֶרֶת אוֹי לָהֶם לַבְּרִיּוֹת מֵעֶלְבּוֹנָהּ שֶׁל תּוֹרָה. שֶׁכָּל מִי שֶׁאֵינוֹ עוֹסֵק בַּתּוֹרָה נִקְרָא נָזוּף, שֶׁנֶּאֱמַר נֶזֶם זָהָב בְּאַף חֲזִיר אִשָּׁה יָפָה וְסָרַת טָעַם. וְאוֹמֵר וְהַלֻּחֹת מַעֲשֵׂה אֱלֹקִים הֵמָּה וְהַמִּכְתָּב מִכְתַּב אֱלֹקִים הוּא חָרוּת עַל הַלֻּחֹת, אַל תִּקְרָא חָרוּת אֶלָּא חֵרוּת, שֶׁאֵין לְךָ בֶּן חוֹרִין אֶלָּא מִי שֶׁעוֹסֵק בְּתַלְמוּד תּוֹרָה. וְכָל מִי שֶׁעוֹסֵק בְּתַלְמוּד תּוֹרָה הֲרֵי זֶה מִתְעַלֶּה, שֶׁנֶּאֱמַר וּמִמַּתָּנָה נַחֲלִיאֵל וּמִנַּחֲלִיאֵל בָּמוֹת:

Rabbi Yehoshua ben Levi said: Every single day, a Heavenly voice resounds from Mount Choreiv (Sinai), proclaiming and saying: "Woe is to the people for their insult to Torah." For whoever does not engage in Torah study is considered to be censured; as it states (*Mishlei* 11:22), "A golden nose ring in the snout of a swine, is a beautiful woman who turns away from reason." And it states (*Shemos* 32:16): "And the tablets are the work of G-d, and the writing is G-d's writing, engraved on the tablets";

read not, "engraved" (*charus*) but, "liberty" (*cheirus*) – for there is no free individual, save for one who engages in the study of Torah. And whoever engages in the study of Torah becomes elevated, as it states (*Bamidbar* 21:19): "And from Matanah to Nachaliel, and from Nachaliel to Bamos."

אוי להם לבריות מעלבונה של תורה

SOURCES:

וּדְלָא יָלֵיף, קְטָלָא חַיָּב. (אבות א׳)

One who does not learn – incurs death. (*Avos* 1)

אָנֹכִי ה׳ אֱלֹקֶיךָ אֲשֶׁר הוֹצֵאתִיךָ מֵאֶרֶץ מִצְרָיִם. (שמות כ׳ ב׳)

I am Hashem your G-d Who took you out from the land of Egypt. (*Shemos* 20:2)

אָנֹכִי נוֹטְרֵיקוּן: אֲנָא נַפְשִׁי כְּתִיבַת יְהָבִית. (שבת ק״ה.)

(The word) "Anochi (I)" – through (the acrostic device known as) *notreikun* (contains the following message uttered by Hashem): I have inscribed "My Soul" (into the Torah), and have given this (to Klal Yisroel). (*Shabbos* 105a)

גְּדוֹלָה תּוֹרָה יוֹתֵר מִן הַכְּהוּנָה וּמִן הַמַּלְכוּת. (אבות ו׳)

Torah is greater than the priesthood and the monarchy. (*Avos* 6)

כָּל הָעוֹסֵק בַּתּוֹרָה לִשְׁמָהּ תּוֹרָתוֹ נַעֲשֵׂית לוֹ סַם חַיִּים... הָעוֹסֵק בַּתּוֹרָה שֶׁלֹּא לִשְׁמָהּ נַעֲשֵׂית לוֹ סַם הַמָּוֶת. (תענית ז.)

Whoever engages in Torah study for its own sake, the Torah (he has learned) becomes for him like a salve for life... One who engages in Torah study not for its own sake, it becomes for him like fatal poison. (*Ta'anis* 7a)

לְעוֹלָם יַעֲסוֹק אָדָם בַּתּוֹרָה וּבַמִּצְוֹת אַף עַל פִּי שֶׁלֹּא לִשְׁמָהּ, שֶׁמִּתּוֹךְ שֶׁלֹּא לִשְׁמָהּ – בָּא לִשְׁמָהּ. (פסחים נ:)

A person should, in any event, occupy himself with Torah and mitzvos even if not for its own sake; for from doing so not for its own sake, he will (eventually) come to do so for its own sake. (*Pesachim* 50b)

פרק ו׳

GEMS FROM THE *SEFER NESIVOS SHOLOM*

Rabbi Yehoshua ben Levi said: Every day, a Heavenly voice resounds from Mount Choreiv (Sinai), proclaiming and saying: "Woe is to the creatures who insult the Torah." For one who does not occupy himself in Torah is considered to be censured; as is stated (*Mishlei* 11:22), "A golden nose ring in the snout of a swine, a beautiful woman bereft of reason." And it is stated (*Shemos* 32:16): "And the tablets are the work of G-d, and the writing is G-d's writing, engraved on the tablets"; read not "engraved" (*charus*) but "liberty" (*cheirus*) — for there is no free individual, except for one who occupies himself with the study of Torah.

Many of us have had the good fortune to have enjoyed an extended yeshivah experience — *beis medrash* for young men, seminary for young women. While a number of important lessons are conveyed, there is one area that is promoted above all others: the supremacy of Torah study. Graduates are often encouraged to seek a spouse who shares the common goal of continuing intensive Torah study even after marriage, by settling in Yerushalayim or some other Torah community to pursue full-time *kollel* careers.

It is interesting to note that, in the Torah itself, the endeavor of Torah study is listed as a mitzvah, just like any of the 613 mitzvos. Why, then, have our sacred institutions placed such added and enthusiastic emphasis on this particular mitzvah? They have taken their cue from *Chazal*, who likewise go to great lengths to stress the importance and supremacy of Torah study and its centrality to our lives and to the existence of Klal Yisroel.

Take, for example, this very *perek* of *Pirkei Avos*. The sixth chapter devotes so much attention to the notion of Torah study, speaking in such glorious and lofty terms, that it is known by the appellation *Kinyan Torah* ("Torah Acquisition"). It covers such topics as the greatness of Torah in contrast to the monarchy and priesthood (6:6); the pursuit of Torah study for its own sake and the many wonderful blessings this brings (6:1); the fact that the creation of the entire universe is considered worthwhile just for one who learns Torah properly (*ibid.*); and others.

We also find, in this *perek* and elsewhere, that *Chazal* describe the magnitude of the offense of *bitul Torah* in no uncertain terms. Rabbi Yehoshua ben Levi's teaching (6:2) is a perfect example, as he states, כָּל מִי שֶׁאֵינוֹ עוֹסֵק בַּתּוֹרָה נִקְרָא נָזוּף — *Whosoever does not occupy himself with Torah study is considered "censured."* *Nazuf* (censured) refers to a form of excommunication, indicating the extent to which one who neglects Torah becomes distanced from Hashem. In an assessment that is no less stark, the mishnah states earlier (1:13), וּדְלָא יָלֵיף, קְטָלָא חַיָּב — *One who does not learn incurs death.* Other shortcomings are not commonly described in such terms; the intensity seems to be reserved for this area alone.

What is it, then, about Torah study in particular that elicits such all-out focus on the part of *Chazal*, as they so eloquently and elaborately encourage its study and so vociferously warn against its neglect?

The Gift of Torah

To begin to appreciate the true value of the venture of Torah study, it is important to note how *Chazal* characterize Klal Yisroel's reception of the Torah. As the Gemara states (*Berachos* 5a), it is a *matanah tovah*, a precious gift. Consider the following scenario: A loyal subject performed a special service on behalf of the king. As a token of appreciation, the king issues him a pass with the following handwritten instruction: "Whenever you want to see your king, show this pass at the palace gates. You will gain immediate entry." What a gift! The recipient is set apart from all other subjects by his ability to access the king. This is the gift of Torah.

Further revelations about the unique nature of this gift are uncovered by *Chazal* (*Shabbos* 105a). Commenting on the first word of the *Aseres Hadibros* — אָנֹכִי (*I*) — they explain that this term serves as an acrostic, containing the following message uttered by Hashem: אֲנָא נַפְשִׁי כְּתִיבַת יְהָבִית — *I have inscribed "My Soul" (into the Torah), and have given this (to Klal Yisroel).* Thus we see that the Torah is far more than merely a collection of rules and instructions detailing how to live our lives in fulfillment of the mitzvos. An embodiment of Hashem's very essence, it is a vehicle to become one with Hashem — enabling each Yid to connect with Him in a state of utmost *d'veikus*! And the way this lofty goal is accomplished is through intensive Torah study. In this way, through connecting to the Torah, a Yid's soul becomes bound up with the very "Soul" of Hashem.

Not a Punishment

Knowledge of this idea can affect one's Torah study in a number of ways. One who views Torah as merely a record of commandments may very well end up limiting the scope of and time spent on his learning. Why review the *halachos* of Chanukah or Pesach again when you know them so well from the year before? Why learn the laws associated with the Temple service today when we lack the Beis Hamikdash? Such will be the attitude of a person who views Torah in purely practical terms, as a mere instruction manual to mitzvah performance. And what a regrettable mistake this is; this individual is completely oblivious to Torah's prime function as a bridge to Hashem!

A person with this mistaken mindset does a lot more than simply engage in *bitul Torah*, in violation of the exhortation of the *navi*: וְהָגִיתָ בּוֹ יוֹמָם וָלַיְלָה — *And you shall meditate therein by day and by night* (*Yehoshua* 1:8). This in itself is severe enough, but the offense goes even deeper. Through his lack of appreciation for the true nature and value of Torah as described above, such an individual slights the Torah in a most grave fashion. And — as the Torah is a manifestation of the *Anochi* of Hashem (אֲנָא נַפְשִׁי כְּתִיבַת יְהָבִית) — it constitutes, in effect, a grievous insult to Hashem Himself. This is the full import of Rabbi Yehoshua ben Levi's teaching, as he describes the cry that emanates from Sinai: אוֹי לָהֶם לַבְּרִיּוֹת מֵעֶלְבּוֹנָהּ שֶׁל תּוֹרָה — *Woe is to people, for their insult of the Torah!* By neglecting Torah study and refusing to recognize the remarkable opportunity of reaching the *d'veikus* it provides, one spurns the King's very gift.

The continuation of Rabbi Yehoshua ben Levi's teaching can likewise be understood in light of the above. כָּל מִי שֶׁאֵינוֹ עוֹסֵק בַּתּוֹרָה נִקְרָא נָזוּף — *Whosoever does not occupy himself with Torah study is considered "censured" (excommunicated).* As noted previously, this reflects the tremendous distance from Hashem at which one who insults the Torah finds himself. But it is not necessarily a punishment, retribution for his poor attitude. Rather, this is a simple and unfortunate state of being, a cause-and-effect result of having devalued the Torah. For Torah is the vehicle through which a Yid is able to cleave to Hashem. By neglecting to partake in this all-important endeavor, one naturally remains distant and detached from Hashem.

But one who capitalizes on the King's gift, drawing closer to Him through the Torah, is not only meritorious but most fortunate as well. In so doing, a person becomes truly liberated; attached to the Divine, he is freed from the powerful forces of the material world that draw him away from Hashem and His Torah. Rabbi Yehoshua further mentions this aspect in stating: אֵין לְךָ בֶּן חוֹרִין אֶלָּא מִי שֶׁעוֹסֵק בְּתַלְמוּד תּוֹרָה — *The only one considered truly free is someone who involves himself with Torah study.*

We may understand the statement of the later mishnah in a similar same vein: גְּדוֹלָה תּוֹרָה יוֹתֵר מִן הַכְּהוּנָּה וּמִן הַמַּלְכוּת — *Torah is greater than the priesthood and the monarchy* (6:6). A person fortunate enough to be qualified for these institutions — and use them properly — can attain a great measure of closeness with the Almighty. The *kohen* is constantly involved in Hashem's special service in the most sacred of places, and many righteous kings of Yisroel utilized their office to serve a higher purpose, thereby elevating their spiritual level. But Torah outdoes them, as its capacity for drawing a Yid closer to Hashem far exceeds that of any other endeavor.

A Double-Edged Sword

Precisely *because* it plays such a crucial role in our lives, presenting the most remarkable of spiritual opportunities, there is a danger, as well, that lurks in Torah's "vicinity." The *ba'alei mussar* teach us that the *yetzer hara* functions as any crafty enemy would. Engaged in battle, the enemy devotes the bulk of its energy and resources to neutralizing its opponent's primary weapon. In the battle to distance a Yid from Hashem, the *yetzer hara* employs the same strategy. It is well aware of the unequaled opportunity the Torah provides to enable a Yid to connect with Hashem, and so it does everything in its power to prevent him from partaking of this opportunity. Its first line of offense is to entice one to neglect Torah study altogether; there are no lack of distractions and obstacles it places in one's path.

If unsuccessful in this outright effort and unable to bring about a cessation in one's studies, the *yetzer hara* has another tactic in its arsenal. It may allow a Yid to continue learning but will poison his motivations and intentions, such that his learning will be undertaken *shelo lishmah*, with ulterior and impure motives. As such, although the actual learning progresses, its power to connect a Yid to his Creator becomes severely limited. This is the meaning of *Chazal's* assertion (*Ta'anis* 7a) that for some, Torah is the elixir of life, while for others it is fatal poison. Learning *Torah lishmah* entails a complete immersion of one's mind and heart in the words of Torah. By becoming one with the Torah in such a fashion, a person enters the spiritual gates of love and fear of Hashem, connecting to Him at the highest levels. This is the greatest accomplishment and happiness in life; it is life itself. But if the *yetzer hara* is able to contaminate one's intentions, his activity can be a potion for death. For not only does learning Torah *shelo lishmah* fail to create a connection, it has the capacity to increase the distance between the individual and Hashem.

Here, some important clarifications are in order. Based on the frightening picture painted above, it would appear that Torah learning that is not *lishmah* is something to be avoided at all costs; after all, it is fatal poison. How can this be reconciled with another teaching of *Chazal*, which — while acknowledging that *lishmah* is the ideal — still encourages any type of learning, even if the motives are not completely altruistic? As the Gemara states (*Pesachim* 50b), לְעוֹלָם יַעֲסוֹק אָדָם בַּתּוֹרָה וּבְמִצְוֹת אַף עַל פִּי שֶׁלֹּא לִשְׁמָהּ, שֶׁמִּתּוֹךְ שֶׁלֹּא לִשְׁמָהּ – בָּא לִשְׁמָהּ — *A person should in any event involve himself in Torah and mitzvos, even though he does so* shelo lishmah; *for by starting out* shelo lishmah, *he will (eventually) come to do so* lishmah. So which is it? Is learning undertaken *shelo lishmah* considered toying with death, or is it a recommended activity that can lead to the highest levels? And how can we even begin to fathom that learning *shelo lishmah* will lead to *lishmah*? As we have seen above, a lack of pristine intentions causes one to become distanced from *Hakadosh Baruch Hu*. How, then, will such an endeavor bring a person to the apex of *d'veikus baHashem*, which is the result of learning *lishmah*?

A Little *Lishmah* Goes a Long Way

The matter is clarified by the *Yesod Ha'avodah*, who, in fact, establishes the strictest requirements when defining *Torah lishmah*. Nevertheless, he recognizes that there must be a workable and accessible path for even the average person. As *Chazal* state (*Avodah Zarah* 3a), אֵין הַקָּדוֹשׁ בָּרוּךְ הוּא בָּא בִּטְרוּנְיָא עִם בְּרִיּוֹתָיו — *Hashem does not impose impossible demands upon people*.

Thus, the *Yesod Ha'avodah* explains: Of course, as *Chazal* state in *Pesachim*, even Torah study that is *shelo lishmah* sometimes can and should be undertaken. The key element is one's *long-term goal and aspiration*. Obviously, the ideal is to learn entirely *lishmah*. But the average person may not yet be holding there and so must consider learning *shelo lishmah* if he is going to learn at all. The question becomes: Do you even *want* to learn *lishmah*? Are you hoping and trying to get there? If a person becomes complacent with his current state — coming to terms, in effect, with a mode of learning that is inherently deficient — then, indeed, he is in for trouble. It is to such a situation that *Chazal* were referring when they characterized non-altruistic learning as fatal poison. This type of activity will render him more distant from Hashem.

But if one aspires for improvement, actively seeking to one day achieve the *madreigah* of *lishmah* — that is a different story altogether. In fact, this, too, is considered somewhat *lishmah*. Although one's motives might not yet be completely altruistic, since that is his long-term goal, even his current efforts are characterized by a semblance of *lishmah*. Even today, then, such learning has some power to draw him closer to Hashem.

Furthermore, by fulfilling *Chazal's* dictum that learning *shelo lishmah* leads to *lishmah*, the earnest student is bound to encounter some completely pure learning even now. Notice that *Chazal*

prefaced their teaching with the term *l'olam*, intimating constancy: "One should always learn, even if *shelo lishmah*..." The implication, of course, is to learn *a lot*. As such, by engaging in intense and extended learning, even if initially undertaken *shelo lishmah*, one will most likely end up learning at least a small portion of this session with completely pure intentions.

The total percentage of such learning that was actually done *lishmah* may be quite minimal. Nevertheless, its value should not be underestimated. Even these few moments of *lishmah* are extremely dear to Hashem — and very potent. The Divrei Shmuel *ztz"l* would tell of a certain contemporary *rav* who was known to effect miraculous salvations. Of a saintly and elevated stature, his predictions and affirmations would all come true. When asked about the source of his astounding abilities, the pious man replied simply, "These achievements are all the result of having learned a single mishnah entirely *lishmah*."

Yom Tov Preparations

By sacred custom, wide segments of Klal Yisroel learn *Pirkei Avos* on the *Shabbosos* between Pesach and Shavuos, one *perek* each week. As such, the learning of the sixth *perek* — Kinyan Torah — falls on the Shabbos immediately preceding the Yom Tov of Shavuos.

This is no coincidence. The Nesivos Sholom points out that whereas Shavuos is called *Zman Mattan Toraseinu*, this does not mean that we are merely commemorating the long-ago event of the giving of the Torah on Har Sinai. The Yom Tov of Sukkos is called *Zman Simchaseinu*, an appellation referring to the present. Today, we rejoice on the Sukkos festival. Similarly, the title *Zman Mattan Toraseinu* of Shavuos is likewise a reference to the present. Just as Sukkos is a time of joy in the here and now, so, too, Shavuos is a time of receiving the Torah in the here and now. This notion speaks to the fact that every year, *Hakadosh Baruch Hu* grants us the Torah anew. And so, how do we ready ourselves for this year's *Kabbalas HaTorah*? By studying the section of *Pirkei Avos* that is dedicated to the topic of Torah study. This is the prime preparation to reach the grandest levels of proper *Kabbalas HaTorah*, whereby a Yid achieves *d'veikus* with Hashem.

And, as we see in this mishnah in particular, the primary focus is on *eisek haTorah*, involvement in Torah study: אֵין לְךָ בֶּן חוֹרִין אֶלָּא מִי שֶׁעוֹסֵק בְּתַלְמוּד תּוֹרָה. It is noteworthy that the mishnah does not speak of someone who **lomeid** Torah (**learns** Torah), but is **oseik baTorah** (**involved** in Torah study). The difference is significant, as being *oseik baTorah* entails a *preoccupation* with Torah, in that the individual is completely immersed in its sacred words. Even if this is done in a manner of *shelo lishmah*, as long as the aspiration is to eventually attain the level of *lishmah*, the *eisek* will be most effective. By adhering to the message of this *perek* and becoming wholly absorbed in one's learning, one is firmly on the path towards *Kabbalas HaTorah*. As we have seen, Torah — which contains Hashem's "essence" — is the vehicle through which a Yid can connect to Hashem. And so, through a most supreme *Kabbalas HaTorah*, a Yid will be able to attain all of the lofty *madreigos* of *avodas Hashem*: *yiras Hashem*, *ahavas Hashem*, and *d'veikus baHashem*. The Rebbe of Kobrin *ztz"l* notes that these primary qualities are all alluded to through the spelling of the word, "Yid." While pronounced "Yid," the actual (Yiddish) spelling is איד, which stands for אַהֲבָה, יִרְאָה, דְּבֵיקוּת. Thus we see that *eisek haTorah*, especially at this crucial time, is the gateway through which one enters to reach the loftiest heights of what it means to be a Yid.

A Torah Life

The Nesivos Sholom uncovers additional layers of meaning in many of the teachings and terms discussed above.

Rabbi Yehoshua ben Levi stated that the Heavenly voice that bemoans the insult to the Torah rings out *b'chol yom vayom*, every single day. The implication is that this lament has been constant throughout the generations: *b'chol yom vayom*. What is puzzling about this, however, is that there were generations where devotion to Torah study was *de rigueur*. During the reign of King Chizkiyahu, for example, every man, woman, and child in the length and breadth of Eretz Yisroel were experts in even the most complex Torah subjects and laws (*Sanhedrin* 94b). What was there to bemoan in a time such as that? Far from degrading the Torah, the dedication to Torah of that generation was universally supreme!

The issue, explains the Nesivos Sholom, is that our learning must translate into and be apparent in our *daily actions*. The word "Torah" stems from the term *hora'ah*, instruction. This is precisely what Torah is — our instruction guide for living life in a most elevated fashion. Torah is likewise referred to as *Toras Hashem*, pointing to its utility as an assessment tool for us to determine whether we are conducting all aspects of our life in accordance with Hashem's will.

This, then, is the intent of the Heavenly voice's lament. Learning itself is a vital and lofty undertaking, but if not reflected in one's actions, there is an inherent flaw in one's approach to and estimation of the Torah. That is, it is not sufficient to merely be *lomeid* Torah; rather, as the mishnah asserts, one must be *oseik* in Torah. *Eisek haTorah* implies an *involvement* in Torah; that is, one is constantly involved in fulfilling the purpose of Torah, such that it permeates all of his activities. But if one restricts his relationship to Torah just to his study sessions, this reveals an inherent flaw. One who fails to ensure that all actions are aligned with Hashem's will as expressed in the Torah, demonstrates that he doesn't value Torah's supreme sanctity. And this constitutes a severe insult to Torah: אוֹי לָהֶם לַבְּרִיּוֹת מֵעֶלְבּוֹנָהּ שֶׁל תּוֹרָה!

The definition of *eisek haTorah* as allowing Torah to permeate one's entire existence is manifest in the entirety of Rabbi Yehoshua ben Levi's teaching. Rabbi Yehoshua cited the *passuk* (*Mishlei* 11:22) from which he derived his assertion that one who is not *oseik* in Torah is considered *nazuf*: נֶזֶם זָהָב בְּאַף חֲזִיר — *A golden nose ring in the snout of a swine* (the emphasized letters spell out **nazuf**). As we explained, even if one does study Torah but is not *oseik* in it — having it permeate his entire life — this constitutes a devaluation of the Torah. Just like a piece of jewelry on a pig that cannot appreciate its adornment.

Rabbi Yehoshua ben Levi brings a Scriptural proof for the next part of his teaching, as well: וְאוֹמֵר, וְהַלֻּחֹת מַעֲשֵׂה אֱלֹקִים הֵמָּה וְהַמִּכְתָּב מִכְתַּב אֱלֹקִים הוּא חָרוּת עַל הַלֻּחֹת, אַל תִּקְרָא חָרוּת אֶלָּא חֵרוּת, שֶׁאֵין לְךָ בֶּן חוֹרִין אֶלָּא מִי שֶׁעוֹסֵק

אוי להם לבריות מעלבונה של תורה

בְּתַלְמוּד תּוֹרָה — *And it is stated* (*Shemos* 32:16): *"And the tablets are the work of G-d, and the writing is G-d's writing, engraved on the tablets"; read not "engraved"* (charus) *but "liberty"* (cheirus), *for there is no free individual, except for one who occupies himself with the study of Torah.* What is somewhat perplexing about this citation is that the *passuk* discusses the makeup of the *Luchos* but doesn't seem to make any mention about Torah study. Why, then, did Rabbi Yehoshua seek to use this as his proof? How does he derive from here the idea that Torah study makes a person free?

The Nesivos Sholom explains Rabbi Yehoshua's intent here based on a previously mentioned teaching of *Chazal*. As stated earlier, the *Luchos* — on which was engraved the word *Anochi* — contained that singular message about the true nature of Torah: אֲנָא נַפְשִׁי כְּתִיבַת יְהָבִית — *I have inscribed "My Soul"* (into the Torah), *and have given this* (to Klal Yisroel). This notion is also alluded to in the *passuk* cited by Rabbi Yehoshua: וְהַלֻּחֹת מַעֲשֵׂה אֱלֹקִים הֵמָּה וְהַמִּכְתָּב מִכְתַּב אֱלֹקִים — *And the tablets were the work of G-d, and the writing was the writing of G-d.* Hashem, as it were, resided within the *Luchos* and the Torah they represent.

Someone who recognizes this fact and appreciates Torah's sanctity will be moved to infuse Torah-awareness into every facet of his life. After all, it is *Toras Hashem*, a guide to align all of our deeds with His will. This is the definition of *eisek haTorah*. As such, one who fails to do so reveals his disdain for Torah and for the Divine aspect that resides within. And this constitutes a grave *elbon* (insult) to the Torah and to Hashem.

Furthermore, one who is not *oseik* in Torah — that is, he does not allow it to affect and elevate his life — is, in effect, a slave to his base passions and materialistic tendencies. But of one who is *oseik baTorah*, Rabbi Yehoshua declares that he is the true *ben chorin* (free man). His appreciation for the true sanctity of Torah enables him to be truly liberated from the endless pursuit of the pleasures of This World.

The Nesivos Sholom offers an additional meaning to the phrase *elbonah shel Torah*. Until now, this phrase has been understood to refer to the *elbon*, the insult to the Torah perpetrated by those who do not give it appropriate regard. But it could alternatively refer to disdain directed at these very people. That is, the Torah disdains those who neglect to immerse themselves in its great beauty and ignore its lofty message. "Woe to those people," laments the Heavenly voice, "who are disdained by the Torah." For such unfortunates are distanced from Hashem and considered *nazuf*. But one who properly values the Torah, heeds its teachings, and involves himself completely in it — such a person is truly free and intimately close with Hashem.

In Summary

We find a phenomenon of sorts when it comes to the mitzvah of Torah study. More so, perhaps, than with any other particular precept, *Chazal* go to great lengths extolling the virtue of this endeavor — throughout the sixth *perek* of *Avos*, as well as throughout the length and breadth of *Shas* and *Midrashim*. To understand what prompted such unprecedented and enthusiastic exhortation, it is necessary to get a clear picture of the nature and purpose of the Torah.

This can be uncovered by examining *Chazal's* interpretation of the word *Anochi* (heading the *Aseres Hadibros*). They understand this word to be serving as an acrostic delivering a most important message about the sanctity of Torah: אֲנָא נַפְשִׁי כְּתִיבַת יְהָבִית — *I have inscribed "My Soul"* (into the Torah), and have given this (to Klal Yisroel). Thus we discover that, as it were, an aspect of Hashem Himself resides within the Torah. This reflects, as well, the primary purpose of Torah: to enable a Yid to attain *d'veikus* with Hashem. As Hashem's "essence" is contained in the Torah, by attaching oneself to Torah, one becomes attached to *Hakadosh Baruch Hu*.

Thus we can better understand why it is that *Chazal* were so unstinting in their encouragement to involve oneself with Torah. More than a mere collection of information — albeit sacred wisdom — the Torah is a vessel whose words envelop the Divine. As such, it serves as the vehicle through which we can fulfill the very purpose of creation — *d'veikus* with Hashem.

אוי להם לבריות מעלבונה של תורה

This noble idea informs the teaching of Rabbi Yehoshua ben Levi. He reveals to us the existence of a Heavenly voice that laments the *elbon* of the Torah. This refers to an individual who does not recognize and appreciate what Torah really is: a vessel containing Hashem's "Soul." Failing to appreciate this vital aspect of Torah constitutes a grave insult to the Torah, and, as it were, to Hashem Himself. Furthermore, through such an attitude, this unfortunate will not seize the opportunity to utilize Torah to achieve *d'veikus*. Instead, he will remain distant from Hashem. As Rabbi Yehoshua ben Levi characterizes it, he will be *nazuf*.

A further message inherent in Rabbi Yehoshua ben Levi's teaching relates to the need to make Torah a part of one's life. That is, one who truly appreciates what Torah is — a guide to living all aspects of one's life in accordance with Hashem's will — will always ensure that all of his deeds, both spiritual and mundane, align with Hashem's desire. But there are those who may enjoy studying Torah yet prefer that it not "interfere" with their daily activities. They would rather continue to pursue their materialistic desires, unconcerned with reconciling their actions with Hashem's will. The very fact that they could conduct themselves in such a manner demonstrates a fundamental lack of understanding and appreciation for what the Torah is. They perceive it merely as some intellectual pursuit, not as an entity that should influence their lives. This constitutes a grave insult to the Torah. Their lack of appreciation for the true value of Torah mimics the scenario of a pig that remains unimpressed with the gold ring festooning its snout.

And furthermore, such an individual cannot be called truly free, as he remains entrapped by and enslaved to his materialistic desires. For this reason, Rabbi Yehoshua ben Levi declares that there is only one type of person who is really a *ben chorin*. This is someone who not only "learns" Torah but is actually *oseik* in Torah. That is, his involvement in Torah permeates throughout all aspects of his life, as all of his actions reflect a concern with fulfilling the will of Hashem. Such a person is truly liberated from the base tendencies that keep a person tethered to materialism. This *oseik baTorah* will be the one

פרק ו'

who is able to achieve the ultimate state available to a Yid — that of *d'veikus baHashem*.

פרק ו' משנה ו'
התורה נקנית בארבעים ושמונה דברים
The Torah Is Acquired Through Forty-Eight Items

גְּדוֹלָה תוֹרָה יוֹתֵר מִן הַכְּהֻנָּה וּמִן הַמַּלְכוּת, שֶׁהַמַּלְכוּת נִקְנֵית בִּשְׁלֹשִׁים מַעֲלוֹת, וְהַכְּהֻנָּה בְּעֶשְׂרִים וְאַרְבַּע, וְהַתּוֹרָה נִקְנֵית בְּאַרְבָּעִים וּשְׁמוֹנָה דְבָרִים. וְאֵלּוּ הֵן, בְּתַלְמוּד, בִּשְׁמִיעַת הָאֹזֶן, בַּעֲרִיכַת שְׂפָתַיִם, בְּבִינַת הַלֵּב, בְּאֵימָה, בְּיִרְאָה, בַּעֲנָוָה, בְּשִׂמְחָה, בְּטָהֳרָה, בְּשִׁמּוּשׁ חֲכָמִים, בְּדִקְדּוּק חֲבֵרִים, בְּפִלְפּוּל הַתַּלְמִידִים, בְּיִשּׁוּב, בְּמִקְרָא, בְּמִשְׁנָה, בְּמִעוּט סְחוֹרָה, בְּמִעוּט דֶּרֶךְ אֶרֶץ, בְּמִעוּט תַּעֲנוּג, בְּמִעוּט שֵׁנָה, בְּמִעוּט שִׂיחָה, בְּמִעוּט שְׂחוֹק, בְּאֶרֶךְ אַפַּיִם, בְּלֵב טוֹב, בֶּאֱמוּנַת חֲכָמִים, בְּקַבָּלַת הַיִּסּוּרִין, הַמַּכִּיר אֶת מְקוֹמוֹ, וְהַשָּׂמֵחַ בְּחֶלְקוֹ, וְהָעוֹשֶׂה סְיָג לִדְבָרָיו, וְאֵינוֹ מַחֲזִיק טוֹבָה לְעַצְמוֹ, אָהוּב, אוֹהֵב אֶת הַמָּקוֹם, אוֹהֵב אֶת הַבְּרִיּוֹת, אוֹהֵב אֶת הַצְּדָקוֹת, אוֹהֵב אֶת הַמֵּישָׁרִים, אוֹהֵב אֶת הַתּוֹכָחוֹת, וּמִתְרַחֵק מִן הַכָּבוֹד, וְלֹא מֵגִיס לִבּוֹ בְּתַלְמוּדוֹ, וְאֵינוֹ שָׂמֵחַ בְּהוֹרָאָה, נוֹשֵׂא בְעֹל עִם חֲבֵרוֹ, וּמַכְרִיעוֹ לְכַף זְכוּת, וּמַעֲמִידוֹ עַל הָאֱמֶת, וּמַעֲמִידוֹ עַל הַשָּׁלוֹם, וּמִתְיַשֵּׁב לִבּוֹ בְּתַלְמוּדוֹ, שׁוֹאֵל וּמֵשִׁיב שׁוֹמֵעַ וּמוֹסִיף, הַלּוֹמֵד עַל מְנָת לְלַמֵּד וְהַלּוֹמֵד עַל מְנָת לַעֲשׂוֹת, הַמַּחְכִּים אֶת רַבּוֹ, וְהַמְכַוֵּן אֶת שְׁמוּעָתוֹ, וְהָאוֹמֵר דָּבָר בְּשֵׁם אוֹמְרוֹ,

GEMS FROM THE *SEFER NESIVOS SHOLOM*

הָא לָמַדְתָּ כָּל הָאוֹמֵר דָּבָר בְּשֵׁם אוֹמְרוֹ מֵבִיא גְאֻלָּה לָעוֹלָם, שֶׁנֶּאֱמַר, וַתֹּאמֶר אֶסְתֵּר לַמֶּלֶךְ בְּשֵׁם מָרְדֳּכָי:

Great is Torah, more so than the priesthood and the monarchy; for the monarchy is acquired with thirty benefits, the priesthood with twenty-four, while Torah is acquired through forty-eight items. They are the following: with diligent study, attentive listening, arranged speech, understanding of the heart, awe, fear, humility, joy, purity, attending Sages, precision with colleagues, debate with disciples, composure, Scripture, Mishnah, limitation in: commerce, worldly matters, pleasure, sleep, conversation, and laughter; with patience, a good heart, faith in the Sages, acceptance of suffering; by one who recognizes his place, is happy with his portion, makes a fence for his words, does not accord undue credit to himself, is beloved, loves: Hashem, people, righteousness, uprightness, and reproof; by one who distances himself from honor, is not prideful in his learning, is not joyful to render rulings, bears the burden with his fellow, gives him the benefit of the doubt, sets him on the true path, sets him on the peaceful path, settles his heart in his learning, asks and answers, listens and adds, learns in order to teach, learns in order to do, increases the wisdom of his *rebbi*, reconciles his lessons, and repeats a matter in the name of its author. Thus you learn that whoever repeats something in the name of its author brings redemption to the world; as it states (*Esther* 2:22): "And Esther said to the king in the name of Mordechai."

התורה נקנית בארבעים ושמונה דברים

SOURCES:

אֵין דִּבְרֵי תּוֹרָה מִתְקַיְּמִין אֶלָּא בְּמִי שֶׁמֵּמִית עַצְמוֹ עָלֶיהָ. (ברכות ס"ג:)

Words of Torah only endure by one who "kills himself" over them. (*Berachos* 63b)

מִי שֶׁנְּשָׂאוֹ לִבּוֹ לְקַיֵּם מִצְוָה זוֹ כָּרָאוּי וְלִהְיוֹת מוּכְתָּר בְּכֶתֶר תּוֹרָה, לֹא יַסִּיחַ דַּעְתּוֹ לִדְבָרִים אֲחֵרִים, וְלֹא יָשִׂים עַל לִבּוֹ שֶׁיִּקְנֶה תּוֹרָה עִם הָעֹשֶׁר וְהַכָּבוֹד כְּאַחַת. (יד החזקה פ"ג מהל' תלמוד תורה הל' ו')

One whose heart uplifts him to fulfill this mitzvah properly, and to be crowned with the crown of Torah, should not allow his mind to be distracted to other matters, nor should he set his heart to acquire Torah together with wealth and honor. (*Yad Hachazakah, Hilchos Talmud Torah* 3:6)

אִם יֹאמַר לְךָ אָדָם יֵשׁ חָכְמָה בַּגּוֹיִם, תַּאֲמֵן... יֵשׁ תּוֹרָה בַּגּוֹיִם, אַל תַּאֲמֵן. (איכה רבה ב' י"ג)

If a person will say to you, "Wisdom is to be found among the gentiles" – believe him. (But if he says,) "Torah is to be found among the gentiles" – do not believe him. (*Eichah Rabbah* 2:13)

הַלּוֹמֵד תּוֹרָה בְּיַלְדוּתוֹ, דִּבְרֵי תוֹרָה נִבְלָעִין בְּדָמָיו. (אבות דר' נתן כ"ד ד')

When one learns Torah in his youth, the words of Torah are absorbed into his bloodstream. (*Avos D'Rebbi Nosson* 24:4)

הָאִשָּׁה נִקְנֵית בְּשָׁלֹשׁ דְּרָכִים... (משנה קידושין א' א')

There are three methods through which a woman is betrothed... (*Mishnah Kiddushin* 1:1)

תּוֹרָה צִוָּה-לָנוּ מֹשֶׁה מוֹרָשָׁה קְהִלַּת יַעֲקֹב - אַל תִּקְרֵי מוֹרָשָׁה אֶלָּא מְאֹרָשָׂה. (ברכות נ"ז.)

פרק ו'

753

"Moshe instructed us in the Torah; an inheritance of the congregation of Yaakov" (Devarim 33:4). Do not read this as stating "morashah" (inheritance), rather, read it as "me'orasah" (betrothed). (Berachos 57a)

בְּיוֹם חֲתֻנָּתוֹ וּבְיוֹם שִׂמְחַת לִבּוֹ: בְּיוֹם חֲתֻנָּתוֹ – זֶה מַתַּן תּוֹרָה. (תענית כ"ו:)

"In the day of His nuptials, and the day of His heart's rejoicing" (Shir Hashirim 3:11). "In the day of His nuptials" – this refers to the giving of the Torah. (Ta'anis 26b)

כָּךְ הִיא דַּרְכָּהּ שֶׁל תּוֹרָה, פַּת בַּמֶּלַח תֹּאכַל וּמַיִם בַּמְּשׂוּרָה תִּשְׁתֶּה וְעַל הָאָרֶץ תִּישַׁן וְחַיֵּי צַעַר תִּחְיֶה וּבַתּוֹרָה אַתָּה עָמֵל, אִם אַתָּה עוֹשֶׂה כֵּן, אַשְׁרֶיךָ וְטוֹב לָךְ. אַשְׁרֶיךָ בָּעוֹלָם הַזֶּה וְטוֹב לָךְ לָעוֹלָם הַבָּא. (אבות ו')

Such is the path to Torah: Eat bread with salt, drink water in measure, sleep on the ground, live a life of deprivation, and toil in the Torah. If you do so, "You will be happy and it shall be good for you" (Tehillim 128:2). "You will be happy" in This World; "and it shall be good for you" in the World to Come. (Avos 6)

יֶאֱהַב אֶת ה' אַהֲבָה גְּדוֹלָה יְתֵירָה עַזָּה מְאֹד עַד שֶׁתְּהֵא נַפְשׁוֹ קְשׁוּרָה בְּאַהֲבַת ה' וְנִמְצָא שׁוֹגֶה בָּהּ תָּמִיד כְּאִלּוּ חוֹלֵי הָאַהֲבָה שֶׁאֵין דַּעְתּוֹ פְּנוּיָה... וְהוּא שׁוֹגֶה בָּהּ תָּמִיד בֵּין בְּשִׁבְתּוֹ בֵּין בְּקוּמוֹ בֵּין בְּשָׁעָה שֶׁהוּא אוֹכֵל וְשׁוֹתֶה... (יד החזקה פ"י מהל' תשובה הל' ג')

He should love Hashem with a love which is great, immense, and extremely strong, to the point where his soul is bound up in love with Hashem. It shall thus emerge that he will be constantly preoccupied with (this love), as one who is lovesick, whose mind is never free... He is constantly preoccupied with it, when he sits, when he stands, when he eats and drinks... (Yad Hachazakah, Hilchos Teshuvah 10:3)

Prized Possession

Do you know anybody who has a close and personal relationship with mathematics?

Obviously, the whole notion is preposterous. Someone may be good at and know a lot of math; perhaps even knowing how to put it to good use, such as in business or the like; maybe he's a math whiz; maybe he even loves the subject. But to suggest that he is the "owner" of math or "married" to it is at best a form of hyperbole.

Yet, as we shall see, this is exactly what *Chazal* have to say about a Jew's relation to the Torah. This emerges from the enigmatic mishnah that lists the many qualities associated with the mastery of Torah.

As is his practice, the Nesivos Sholom begins his elucidation of the issue by putting forth a number of pointed questions concerning the mishnah and its subject matter:

- It is noteworthy that the mishnah uses different terminology, depending on the matter under discussion. When speaking of *kehunah* (priesthood) and *malchus*, the mishnah employs the term *ma'alos*. Addressing Torah, however, the mishnah states that it is acquired through forty-eight *devarim*. What accounts for the shift?

- The mishnah goes on to list the conditions necessary to acquire Torah: Many of the items are clearly related to amassing Torah knowledge: *shemi'as ha'ozen*, *binas halev*, and *dikduk chaveirim* (dialogue with colleagues), to name a few. But some apparently unrelated qualities are included as well, such as *anavah*, *oheiv es haMakom* (loving Hashem), *oheiv es haberi'os* (loving people), and others. Undoubtedly, these are virtuous traits, but what place do they have in a list of ways to attain Torah wisdom?

- A careful scrutinizing of the mishnah reveals another mystifying aspect. The mishnah presents a list of forty-eight items. But there seems to be a divide of sorts among them, separating the list into two sets of twenty-four each. (In fact, in some printed editions, the mishnah is actually broken up at the midpoint into two separate mishnayos.) The first set has its own style, distinct from that of the second half. The first twenty-four items each begin with the *beis* prefix, denoting "with": בְּאֵימָה, בְּיִרְאָה, בַּעֲנָוָה, בְּשִׂמְחָה, בְּטָהֳרָה, וכו׳ — *With awe, with fear, with humility, with joy, with purity, etc.* Suddenly, after the halfway mark, the *beis* is dropped and the listing of the items takes on a different tone: הַמַּכִּיר אֶת מְקוֹמוֹ, וְהַשָּׂמֵחַ בְּחֶלְקוֹ, וְהָעוֹשֶׂה סְיָג לִדְבָרָיו, וכו׳ — *One who recognizes his place, one who is happy with his portion, one who makes a safeguard for his words, etc.* To what can we attribute this somewhat curious arrangement?

- The whole notion of *kinyan*, as it relates to Torah, requires clarification. It is a term that is used in conjunction with excelling in Torah. This is apparent from our mishnah, הַתּוֹרָה נִקְנֵית בְּאַרְבָּעִים וּשְׁמוֹנָה דְבָרִים — *The Torah is acquired through forty-eight items*, and from other places as well. *Chazal* tell us (*Bamidbar Rabbah* 1:7): כָּל מִי שֶׁאֵינוֹ עוֹשֶׂה עַצְמוֹ כַּמִּדְבָּר הֶפְקֵר, אֵינוֹ יָכוֹל לִקְנוֹת אֶת הַחָכְמָה וְהַתּוֹרָה — *Whosoever does not conduct himself as "unclaimed property" (in the manner of) a wilderness, will be unable to* **acquire** *Torah wisdom.* But what, exactly, does this mean? How does one "take possession" of Torah? Seemingly, Torah is a body of sacred information that a person must know and master. Studying this material is a mitzvah to be fulfilled, as with any of the 613 mitzvos. As such, we make a blessing before this endeavor, using the same formulation as any other mitzvah: בָּרוּךְ אַתָּה...אֲשֶׁר קִדְּשָׁנוּ בְּמִצְוֹתָיו, וְצִוָּנוּ לַעֲסוֹק בְּדִבְרֵי תוֹרָה — *Blessed are You...Who has sanctified us with His commandments and commanded us to engage in words of Torah.* Thus, it would seem more appropriate to state that the Torah is something to "know," a mitzvah to be "fulfilled." How does "acquisition" come into the picture? Why, of all mitzvos, was this one singled out to be referred to in this way?

- We find another aspect uniquely associated with Torah study, more so than any other mitzvah. In general, there is a certain overarching principle that applies to performance of the mitzvos: *Vachai bahem* — "and you shall live by them," the *passuk* states (*Vayikra* 18:5), implying that *V'lo sheyamus bahem* — "you should not perish through them" (*Yuma* 85b). And yet, when it comes to Torah itself, we find just the opposite. As *Chazal* state (*Berachos* 63b), אֵין דִּבְרֵי תוֹרָה מִתְקַיְּמִין אֶלָּא בְּמִי שֶׁמֵּמִית עַצְמוֹ עָלֶיהָ — *Words of Torah only endure by one who "kills himself" over them.* Again, to what can this "special treatment" be attributed?

- Elsewhere in *Avos* (4:13), there is another mishnah reminiscent of ours. It also speaks of the three entities of our mishnah: שְׁלֹשָׁה כְתָרִים הֵם: כֶּתֶר תּוֹרָה וְכֶתֶר כְּהֻנָּה וְכֶתֶר מַלְכוּת — *There are three crowns: the crown of Torah, the crown of priesthood, and the crown of the monarchy.* The Rambam (*Hilchos Talmud Torah* 3:6) discusses how one may merit to be crowned with Torah's crown: מִי שֶׁנְּשָׂאוֹ לִבּוֹ...לִהְיוֹת מוּכְתָּר בְּכֶתֶר תּוֹרָה, לֹא יַסִּיחַ דַּעְתּוֹ לִדְבָרִים אֲחֵרִים, וְלֹא יָשִׂים עַל לִבּוֹ שֶׁיִּקְנֶה תּוֹרָה עִם הָעוֹשֶׁר וְהַכָּבוֹד — *One whose heart has moved him...to be crowned with the crown of Torah, cannot allow his thoughts to be distracted by other matters; he cannot set his heart to acquire Torah together with wealth and glory.* Once again, we encounter conditions regarding the acquisition of Torah that do not apply to the other arenas. There is no restriction upon an aspiring monarch, for example, to foreswear an interest in acquiring wealth in addition to his position. Why is it that when it comes specifically to Torah, the aspirant must banish all other ambitions from his heart?

Be Prepared

The Nesivos Sholom perceives that a number of these issues point in the same direction. Apparently, there is a lot more to the mastery of Torah than merely learning and retaining a body of knowledge. Torah is indeed a completely different "field" from other branches of knowledge. In fact, Torah is not merely just another subject, even a revered and important one; rather, it is an actual sacred entity. It is not sufficient just to learn it and absorb the knowledge. Torah is something that needs to be *acquired*.

And this is no simple endeavor. The Maharal stresses that Torah is a manifestation of "Divine intellect," a product of Heavenly wisdom. This presents a real challenge: how could something so elevated and pristine, a part of the Divine, reside within the confines of the materialistic body of a mortal human, with its frailties and inherent coarseness? There is only one possible answer: anyone desiring to truly acquire Torah and have it be absorbed within his essence has ahead of him the task of purging and rectifying his essence in order to ready it to serve as a resting place for the holy Torah. It is true that the Crown of Torah differs from the other two, in that the Crown of Kingship and the Crown of Priesthood depend on certain uncontrollable factors such as lineage, whereas the Crown of Torah can be lifted and donned by anyone who so desires. But that doesn't mean that it doesn't first require great efforts to be deemed worthy.

How does a person reach such a stage? What must one do to become a fitting receptacle for this wondrous, sacred entity? Our mishnah is the answer; it supplies the forty-eight guidelines to be followed to facilitate the actual acquisition of Torah.

Thus we can account for the two "halves" of the mishnah's list, as there are two different components to the mastery and acquisition of Torah. Of course, there is the academic component; the need to study, understand, and retain the actual sacred knowledge. This is the basic purview of the first part of the mishnah's list, which details the qualities necessary to master the Torah's wisdom. It therefore includes items whose connection to Torah learning are apparent: attentive listening, studying Scripture and Mishnah, etc.

The second half of the mishnah shifts the focus to the acquisition of the Torah itself; that is, how one "prepares" his body and his self to absorb the Torah and effectively serve as its residence. This section outlines the preconditions and necessary elements for transforming one's essence and elevating one's entire self and personality into an entity capable of bonding with the Torah. And so we find among the items of this list certain things we would not have ordinarily associated with Torah acquisition, such as loving Hashem and loving people. For the thrust of this stage of the mishnah is not so much on amassing knowledge but on purifying one's character and elevating one's personality to the heights of pristine spirituality.

We can gain more insight into the notion of the singularity of Torah through a curious statement in the Midrash. *Chazal* tell us (*Eichah Rabbah* 2:13), אִם יֹאמַר לְךָ אָדָם יֵשׁ חָכְמָה בַּגּוֹיִם, תַּאֲמֵן... יֵשׁ תּוֹרָה בַּגּוֹיִם, אַל תַּאֲמֵן — *If a person will say to you, "Wisdom is to be found among the gentiles," believe him. (But if he says,) "Torah is to be found among the gentiles," do not believe him.* What message is the Midrash seeking to convey? That gentiles are capable of certain academic achievements? Is that a surprise? We see every day that there are advances in science, technology, and countless other areas. Even the statement concerning Torah seems difficult. Especially today, with the proliferation of translations in so many languages, what is to stop any person, anywhere in the world, from partaking in and amassing Torah knowledge?

The Nesivos Sholom explains that Torah, not secular knowledge, is the subject of the entirety of this statement of *Chazal*. *Chachmah* refers here to the body of Torah wisdom. If someone claims that this can be found among the gentiles, it is certainly believable. Whoever makes the endeavor to learn and understand can amass the subject matter that comprises Torah knowledge. What is beyond their reach, however, is the aspect previously discussed: if someone claims that "Torah" is to be found among the gentiles, he is not to be believed. This refers to the *kedushah* of Torah; that aspect of Torah that sets it apart so dramatically from all other disciplines. Only a Yid has the ability — after concerted effort — of inculcating the *kedushas haTorah* within his very essence. While a gentile may be able to learn and understand Torah, he cannot make it part of him.

This underscores the power of Torah and its effect on the individual who properly prepares himself to receive it. The Maharal elaborates on this point, explaining that the difference between a *talmid chacham* and an *am ha'aretz* is not merely a matter of intellect; the physical makeup of a *talmid chacham* is likewise different from that of an *am ha'aretz*, just as a human being is clothed in different flesh from that of an animal. That is, a *talmid chacham's* preparations and dedication to Torah facilitates the fusion of Torah with his essence, transforming him into a new, more elevated entity. As *Chazal* state (*Avos D'Rebbi Nosson*, ch. 24), הַלּוֹמֵד תּוֹרָה בְּיַלְדוּתוֹ, דִּבְרֵי תוֹרָה נִבְלָעִין בְּדָמָיו — *When one learns Torah in his youth, the words of Torah are absorbed into his bloodstream.* It is hard to imagine a closer association to

Torah than this — where the Torah becomes a part of one's very self, spreading its pristine quality throughout.

It is worthwhile to note that the concept known as *da'as Torah* is related to this notion in a most significant way. The attitudes and opinions of a bona fide *talmid chacham* are so utterly reliable because they are an expression of *da'as Torah*, the opinion and rendering of the Torah itself. The *talmid chacham* has excelled in inculcating the Torah within him to the point that it is fused with his very essence. Torah literally runs through his veins. As such, it is no wonder that his thoughts constitute the pristine thoughts of the Torah itself.

A Special Mazel Tov

This idea informs the mishnah's usage of unique terminology in describing Torah mastery: *kinyan*. Nor is the implication for a standard form of "possession." The *kinyan* referred to here reflects an intimate connection, reminiscent of its usage by *Chazal* in describing the bond of marriage at the beginning of *Maseches Kiddushin*: הָאִשָּׁה נִקְנֵית בְּשָׁלֹשׁ דְּרָכִים... — *There are three methods through which a woman is betrothed...*

This is a recurrent theme in *Chazal*. Not only is Klal Yisroel's relationship with the Torah framed in terms of a betrothal (*eirusin*), but it is further characterized as having progressed to the stage of a complete marriage bond (*nisu'in*). The Gemara in *Berachos* (57a) cites the well-known *passuk*, תּוֹרָה צִוָּה־לָנוּ מֹשֶׁה מוֹרָשָׁה קְהִלַּת יַעֲקֹב — *Moshe instructed us in Torah; it is the inheritance of the congregation of Yaakov* (*Devarim* 33:4). The Gemara then proceeds with an exposition on this verse: אַל תִּקְרֵי מוֹרָשָׁה אֶלָּא מְאוֹרָשָׂה — *Do not read (the word as stating) "morashah"; rather (read it as if it stated) "me'orasah."* That is, the Gemara understands this familiar *passuk* as conveying this very message: the Torah is the "betrothed" of Klal Yisroel. *Chazal* (*Ta'anis* 26b) then take it to the next step. Citing a phrase from *Shir Hashirim* (3:11), they refer to *Mattan Torah* as *yom chasunaso* — "the day of His wedding." For this is essentially what took place at that grand assembly: the Jewish people entered into a sacred marriage-bond with the holy Torah.

התורה נקנית בארבעים ושמונה דברים

There are, however, certain key differences between these two processes. The three methods whereby one acquires a wife are options; he need only select one. If he opts to go with the monetary method, for example, he need not devise a *shtar* (document), and vice-versa. Acquiring Torah entails a much more thorough endeavor. The forty-eight items listed by our mishnah are not simply options from which one need choose only one or another. Rather, all forty-eight ways must be employed to make an actual *kinyan* of Torah. The process of acquiring Torah and inculcating it within one's very self is a process of self-transformation. In order to convert one's entire being into a vessel suitable to contain the *kedushas haTorah*, one must fulfill all the forty-eight preconditions to purge one's being of its material tendencies.

There is another significant way in which the *kinyan* of Torah differs from all other types of *kinyanim*. Whatever it is that a person seeks to acquire, once he performs the *ma'aseh kinyan* (act of acquisition), his task, in this regard, is done. Having assumed ownership, he is now the owner forever, until such time as he decides to sell or otherwise actively relinquish his power of ownership. But it is another matter entirely when it comes to the "possession" of Torah. One who has successfully completed the "program" of the forty-eight items has certainly achieved elevated levels of spirituality. He has acquired the Torah and wears its glorious and sacred crown. But there is no guarantee that he will always retain it; the Torah does not just "automatically" remain with him once he has performed the *ma'aseh kinyan*. The elevated levels he has attained — the necessary preconditions for housing the Torah within him — must be maintained. Any deviation from these conditions or reduction of his spiritual state will result in a loss of "his" Torah.

We now have a better understanding of yet more of the issues identified at the outset. Why, we wondered, is the "crown of Torah" treated differently from the crowns of royalty or priesthood? These latter two can be acquired along with other benefits; when it comes to the crown of Torah, however, the Rambam warned that it cannot be attained together with wealth or honor. Beyond this, we see that even once the Torah is acquired, and one has merited its crown, it is still

פרק ו

no small matter to retain it. Any deviation from the levels necessary for its retention can result in the Torah's departure. For the Torah to remain with him, a person must dedicate his undivided attention to it. Were he to be distracted for even a moment — were any other "value" such as wealth or honor to occupy a place of prominence in his eyes — he would be at risk of losing the *kedushas haTorah* he worked so hard to attain.

We can likewise now appreciate the variant terminology employed by the mishnah. When speaking of the monarchy and the priesthood, the mishnah refers to *ma'alos*, connoting "benefits" or "exalted qualities." The word literally is related to "ascension," and this usage is indeed apropos. In these areas, once a person "goes up" and accedes to the monarchy, it is there that he remains. Once a king, always a king. The same is true for a *kohen*. Regarding the acquisition of Torah, however, the mishnah speaks of the *devarim* through which one attains it. The implication here is that these are the things upon which one's connection to Torah rests; if even one is suspended, the connection is severed. As such, one must retain these *devarim* at all times, in order to remain attached to the Torah.

The Big Day Is at Hand

The notion that Yisroel's *kinyan* of Torah is likened to the marriage bond highlights another aspect that is unique to Torah. We are familiar with the important concept of *ahavas Hashem* and a desire to fulfill His mitzvos out of this love. Rarely, however, do we encounter such a description referring to a specific mitzvah, such as *ahavas lulav* or *ahavas matzah*. There is one notable exception: there is ample reference to the idea of *ahavas haTorah*.

Now why should this be the case? After all, studying Torah is a mitzvah like all of the other mitzvos. We speak of *ahavas Hashem*, but why do we likewise refer to *ahavas haTorah*?

The Nesivos Sholom explains that, in truth, this concept is in keeping with the ideas discussed above. Torah is not just an assemblage of important bits of information. It is a sacred entity, an emanation from the Divine. That the relationship of the Jewish people to Torah is that of a groom to his beloved bride accentuates this key point. As a part of Hashem, the Torah, in effect, is the vehicle through which a Yid becomes attached to *Hakadosh Baruch Hu* Himself. In essence, *ahavas haTorah* is a manifestation of *ahavas Hashem*. By clinging to the Torah, a Yid can attain the ultimate level of *d'veikus* to *Hakadosh Baruch Hu*.

This understanding provides us with fresh insight into another of the issues mentioned at the outset. *Chazal* imposed another unique requirement through which to excel in Torah study, one not found by other mitzvos. They proclaimed, אֵין דִּבְרֵי תוֹרָה מִתְקַיְּימִין אֶלָּא בְּמִי שֶׁמֵּמִית עַצְמוֹ עָלֶיהָ — *Words of Torah only endure by one who "kills himself" over them.* This expression refers to a complete withdrawal from materialistic pursuits. Why the demand for such seemingly harsh measures for dedication to Torah study? The truth is, however, that the adoption of such a path is also an outgrowth of a burning love for Hashem and His Torah. And, as we shall see, it is anything but harsh for those who are truly worthy of this level. For those who truly bear the crown of Torah on their heads, this state of affairs is the most joyous imaginable experience, one they would not exchange for anything.

One of the forty-eight listed items of our mishnah is *mi'ut ta'anug*, limiting (physical) pleasure. According to the Ba'al Shem Tov, this reflects a particular mindset. That is, the mishnah refers to an individual whose love and passion for Torah is so great that, in comparison, material pleasures hold no value for him. *Mi'ut ta'anug*, then, is the devaluation of earthly pleasures.

A person may enjoy food; eating and drinking affords him much pleasure. Imagine, however, that such a person receives some wondrous tidings while he is dining. In the midst of a delicious roast, he is suddenly informed that his investments have prospered; he has become an instant multimillionaire! Most likely — for the moment, at least — he will no longer be thinking of his succulent roast. Suddenly, such pleasures fade into insignificance.

This illustration provides a glimpse into the world of a truly elevated Yid, one who bears such yearning and undying love for the sacred Torah. All other pleasures and pursuits simply pale in significance; his appreciation for Torah is such that the affairs of the world don't even register on his radar screen.

There is another mishnah in this *perek* that, at first glance, seems quite perplexing. The mishnah states (*Avos* 5:4), כָּךְ הִיא דַּרְכָּהּ שֶׁל תּוֹרָה, פַּת בְּמֶלַח תֹּאכֵל וּמַיִם בִּמְשׂוּרָה תִּשְׁתֶּה וְעַל הָאָרֶץ תִּישָׁן וְחַיֵּי צַעַר תִּחְיֶה וּבַתּוֹרָה אַתָּה עָמֵל, אִם אַתָּה עֹשֶׂה כֵּן, אַשְׁרֶיךָ וְטוֹב לָךְ. אַשְׁרֶיךָ בָּעוֹלָם הַזֶּה וְטוֹב לָךְ לָעוֹלָם הַבָּא — Such is the way of Torah: Eat bread (only) with salt, drink water in measure, sleep on the ground, live a life of deprivation, and (at the same time) toil in the Torah. If you do this, "You are fortunate, and it is good for you" (Tehillim 128:2). "You are fortunate" in This World. "And it is good for you" in the World to Come.

The mishnah is obviously advocating an approach whereby one's paramount concern is for growth in Torah; one pushes forward through even the most strenuous conditions for Torah's sake. It is the mishnah's concluding statement that requires especial clarification. We can definitely appreciate that things will be "good for you" in the World to Come; all the suffering and exertion is worth it for the immeasurable bliss that awaits in the Future World. But how does the mishnah assert that he is fortunate yet in *This World*? Wasn't the mishnah describing a scenario of abject indigence, stating explicitly that one should be willing to subject himself to a life of anguish and deprivation? This is called "You are fortunate in This World"?!

The Nesivos Sholom explains that the answer is unequivocally "yes." For the mishnah is speaking of the individual, previously described, who bears an unquenchable love and thirst for the Torah. For such a person, all worldly matters are as if they do not exist. The pleasures of This World hold no meaning in his eyes; likewise, he does not even feel the deprivation. So consumed is he by love for Torah, deriving boundless pleasure from its sacred words, that no material pleasure holds any place of importance in his eyes.

Could there be a more blissful existence than this — existence in This World? Such a person is fortunate indeed! Who is happier, and who enjoys life in This World more than he? Is it someone who constantly pursues material gain and earthly pleasures? *Chazal*

inform us that those who lust after earthly attainments are doomed to frustration. They are caught in a race that never ends and cannot be won. "Whoever attains one hundred, wants two hundred" (*cf. Koheles Rabbah* 1:13). Such people have no peace, as they constantly pine for more and more. By contrast, the Torah devotee lives in constant bliss; his pleasure is not only boundless, but it is attainable. And he craves not anything else. In fact, the great tzaddikim who achieved this ideal state of being made a most poignant observation. They observed about people who run after worldly pleasures, "If the greatest *ba'alei ta'avah* in the world would ever experience a taste of this pristine holiness, they would instantly cast aside all of their pursuits and immerse themselves solely in the Torah."

We study *Pirkei Avos* as a lead-up to the Yom Tov of Shavuos. Specifically, on the Shabbos preceding this great festival, we focus on this very *perek* — the chapter known as *Kinyan Torah* (reflecting the principal subject matter it contains). In light of the above, this period can become a truly transformative experience.

After all, what is *Kabbalas HaTorah*, the focus of this Yom Tov? As described earlier, it is the *yom chasunaso*, the great wedding day. On this day, at Har Sinai, Klal Yisroel attained the most elevated levels, experiencing an unprecedented manifestation of a "retreat" from the materialism of This World. As *Chazal* relate (*Shabbos* 88b), they were drawn so intensely to the sacred beauty of the words of Torah emanating from Hashem, that their souls became detached from their very bodies, thereby attaining a semblance of an angelic existence.

And this spiritual ecstasy is manifest every year at this time, as we once again experience *Kabbalas HaTorah*. And so, to be fully and properly prepared, we undergo a purification process with an especial focus on the forty-eight items through which one acquires Torah. This is the ultimate preparation for the upcoming *yom chasunaso*, when we may forge the ultimate bond with the holy Torah.

It is no coincidence that the study of this particular topic — *Kinyan Torah* — falls on the Shabbos immediately preceding Shavuos. The *sefarim hakedoshim* inform us that the spiritual essence and emanations associated with a given Yom Tov already become manifest in the world on the Shabbos preceding the festival. Thus we find, for example, that Shabbos Shuvah, the Shabbos before Yom Kippur, is an especially auspicious time for *teshuvah* and attaining closeness to the Almighty. In the same vein, then, the essence of the *yom chasunaso* begins on this Shabbos. How appropriate, then, to engage in study that serves as the singular preparation for this august experience! It is a most fitting time to utilize the forty-eight *devarim* to purify our essence and fashion ourselves into a vessel worthy of housing the *kedushas haTorah*.

The *Ahavah-Yirah* Continuum

While the main focus until this point has been on *ahavah*, there is another component that is no less essential and in fact serves as a prerequisite to attaining true *ahavah*. This is the quality of *yirah*.

A phrase that recurs throughout our *tefillos* is *b'dechilu u'rechimu* — "with awe and with love." The Ba'al Shem Tov explains that the order is quite deliberate; if not preceded by true fear of Hashem, even the *ahavah* one experiences will be of a mere outer, superficial quality.

This idea can be understood in light of the profound teaching of the Saba Kadisha of Slonim *ztz"l*. He explains that, in order for a person to excise the power of *ra* that resides within him, he must harness the proper forces. The issue is that intellect alone is insufficient in this endeavor, since *ra* permeates one's essence. In a sense, then, one must "fight fire with fire" and likewise utilize a force that stems from his internal being.

Now, when considering the qualities of both *yirah* and *ahavah*, one may assume that it is *yirah* that is a product of the intellect, while *ahavah* is more closely associated with one's inner emotions and essence. Were that to be the case, the primary weapon with which to fight the *ko'ach hara* (force of evil) would be through *ahavas Hashem*.

Somewhat surprisingly, however, it appears that the opposite is true. We find that it is *yirah* that influences one's essence, as its effects permeate even one's blood. *Chazal* tell us (*Niddah* 9a), "Trembling causes the blood flow to retreat." And it is *ahavah* that is a product of the intellect, as is apparent from the following passage in the Rambam (*Hilchos Yesodei HaTorah* 2:2): וְהֵיאַךְ הִיא הַדֶּרֶךְ לְאַהֲבָתוֹ וְיִרְאָתוֹ, בְּשָׁעָה שֶׁיִּתְבּוֹנֵן הָאָדָם בְּמַעֲשָׂיו וּבְרוּאָיו הַנִּפְלָאִים הַגְּדוֹלִים וְיִרְאֶה מֵהֶן חָכְמָתוֹ שֶׁאֵין לָהּ עֵרֶךְ וְלֹא קֵץ מִיָּד הוּא אוֹהֵב וְכוּ׳ — *What is the way to (attaining) love of Him and awe of Him? When a person contemplates His works and His great and wondrous creations, and perceives therein His boundless and limitless wisdom, immediately he (begins to) love (Hashem)...* Thus we see that it is intellectual contemplation that breeds *ahavas Hashem*.

The Rambam continues, וּכְשֶׁמְּחַשֵּׁב בִּדְבָרִים הָאֵלּוּ עַצְמָן מִיָּד הוּא נִרְתָּע לְאַחוֹרָיו וְיִפְחַד וְכוּ׳ — *When he sets his mind to these very matters, immediately he* **retreats backwards,** *experiencing awe...* This constitutes a display of awe that apparently has affected his very being.

Complementing each other, the teachings of the Ba'al Shem Tov and the Saba Kadisha reveal the full cycle in which the qualities of *ahavah* and *yirah* interact to enable a Yid to attain the highest levels. It all begins with an *ahavah sichlis*, a love based on intellect. In and of itself, such *ahavah* is of superficial quality and hence insufficient to eradicate the inner evil. However, it does lead to a *yirah* that permeates the bloodstream and excises the evil from within. Then — *b'dechilu u'rechimu* — this internal *yirah* sets the stage for the onset of a real, inner *ahavah*, through which a Yid comes to truly delight in Hashem and His Torah.

This form of *ahavah* is described elsewhere in the Rambam (*Hilchos Teshuvah* 10:3), echoing the unparalleled bliss experienced by those who have donned the crown of Torah, having truly acquired and attached themselves to it. The Rambam's depiction of those who love Hashem and His Torah with such a burning love is simply a wonder to behold: יֶאֱהַב אֶת ה׳ אַהֲבָה גְדוֹלָה יְתֵירָה עַזָּה מְאֹד עַד שֶׁתְּהֵא נַפְשׁוֹ קְשׁוּרָה בְּאַהֲבַת ה׳ וְנִמְצָא שׁוֹגֶה בָּהּ תָּמִיד כְּאִלּוּ חוֹלֶה חוֹלִי הָאַהֲבָה שֶׁאֵין דַּעְתּוֹ פְּנוּיָה... וְהוּא שׁוֹגֶה בָּהּ תָּמִיד בֵּין בְּשִׁבְתּוֹ בֵּין בְּקוּמוֹ בֵּין בְּשָׁעָה שֶׁהוּא אוֹכֵל וְשׁוֹתֶה — *He should love Hashem with a love that is great, immense, and extremely strong, to the point where his soul is bound up in love with Hashem. It shall thus emerge that he will be constantly preoccupied with (the object of his love), as one who is lovesick, whose mind is never free... He is constantly preoccupied with (the object of his love): when he sits, when he stands, when he eats and drinks.*

One who attains this powerful, genuine form of *ahavah* will surely be uninterested in worldly pleasures, for what greater pleasure is there in the world than true love of Hashem and attachment to Him?

In Summary

Torah is not just a collection of intellectual and academic material; it is a sacred entity, a portion of the Divine. This distinction is brought out most dramatically in the mishnah listing the forty-eight items through which one "acquires" Torah.

The very notion of "acquiring" Torah underscores this idea. There is no other field or discipline where the student takes "possession" of the object of his study. He may know it, remember it, and understand it, but it does not become a part of his essence. When it comes to Torah, however, the task at hand goes well beyond merely mastering the material. In addition, a Yid can inculcate the Torah within his very essence. This is the primary role of the forty-eight items. By applying them all, a person refines his very self, fashioning his being into a fitting receptacle to hold the *kedushas haTorah*.

When the mishnah speaks of a *kinyan* of Torah, it is not referring to just an ordinary *kinyan*. Rather, it reflects a *kinyan* of the most intimate type, on the model of the one by which a groom forms a bond with his bride. *Chazal* ascribe to the relationship between Yisroel and the Torah elements of both *eirusin* and *nisu'in*. The day of *Kabbalas HaTorah* itself is referred to as *yom chasunaso* and reflects the intense love for the Torah felt by a Yid who bears the crown of Torah. This love is so great that it essentially negates all interest in worldly activities, leaving its bearer completely infatuated, blissfully preoccupied with Torah thoughts. The Torah serves as the vehicle through which a Yid attaches himself to *Hakadosh Baruch Hu*; by cleaving to the Torah, a portion of the Divine, he achieves *d'veikus*

with Hashem Himself. Ultimately, then, his undying love for the Torah is an undying love for Hashem.

The whole program of the forty-eight items thus serves as the perfect backdrop to the Yom Tov of Shavuos. For once again, *Kabbalas HaTorah* — the *yom chasunaso* — is set to take place. What better way to prepare for this seminal event than by engaging in the forty-eight items! Through them, a Yid refines his character and his essence and readies himself to make the ultimate *kinyan*, when he shall acquire his "bride." Then he will become one with the Torah and revel in it in happiness and spiritual bliss. Thus he can achieve the ultimate fortune, delighting in the love of Hashem and His Torah — the greatest delight one could possibly achieve.

פרק ו' משנה ז'
גדולה תורה שהיא נותנת חיים לעושיה
Great Is Torah for It Grants Life to Those Who Adhere to It

גְּדוֹלָה תוֹרָה שֶׁהִיא נוֹתֶנֶת חַיִּים לְעוֹשֶׂיהָ בָּעוֹלָם הַזֶּה וּבָעוֹלָם הַבָּא, שֶׁנֶּאֱמַר כִּי חַיִּים הֵם לְמוֹצְאֵיהֶם וּלְכָל בְּשָׂרוֹ מַרְפֵּא, וְאוֹמֵר רִפְאוּת תְּהִי לְשָׁרֶּךָ וְשִׁקּוּי לְעַצְמוֹתֶיךָ. וְאוֹמֵר עֵץ חַיִּים הִיא לַמַּחֲזִיקִים בָּהּ וְתֹמְכֶיהָ מְאֻשָּׁר. וְאוֹמֵר כִּי לִוְיַת חֵן הֵם לְרֹאשֶׁךָ וַעֲנָקִים לְגַרְגְּרוֹתֶיךָ. וְאוֹמֵר תִּתֵּן לְרֹאשְׁךָ לִוְיַת חֵן עֲטֶרֶת תִּפְאֶרֶת תְּמַגְּנֶךָּ. וְאוֹמֵר כִּי בִי יִרְבּוּ יָמֶיךָ וְיוֹסִיפוּ לְּךָ שְׁנוֹת חַיִּים. וְאוֹמֵר אֹרֶךְ יָמִים בִּימִינָהּ בִּשְׂמֹאולָהּ עֹשֶׁר וְכָבוֹד, וְאוֹמֵר כִּי אֹרֶךְ יָמִים וּשְׁנוֹת חַיִּים וְשָׁלוֹם יוֹסִיפוּ לָךְ וְאוֹמֵר דְּרָכֶיהָ דַרְכֵי נֹעַם וְכָל נְתִיבוֹתֶיהָ שָׁלוֹם:

Great is Torah, for it grants life to those who adhere to it – in This World and the World to Come. As it states (*Mishlei* 4:22): "For they are life to those who find them, and a healing to all of his flesh." And it states (*Mishlei* 3:8): "A healing it shall be for your sinews, and marrow for your bones." And it states (*Mishlei* 3:18): "It is a tree of life for those who hold on to it, and those who support it are fortunate." And it states (*Mishlei* 1:9): "For they are a garland of grace for your head, and a necklace for your neck." And it states (*Mishlei* 4:9): "It shall place upon your head a garland of grace, and provide you with a crown of glory." And it states (*Mishlei* 9:11): "For through me, your days will increase, and years of life will be added on for you." And it states (*Mishlei* 3:16): "Long life is in its right hand, in its left hand are wealth and honor." And it states (*Mishlei* 3:2): "For length of days, years of life, and peace shall be added on for you." And it states (*Mishlei* 16:31): "Its ways are ways of pleasantness, and all of its paths are peace."

גדולה תורה שהיא נותנת חיים לעושיה

SOURCES:

שְׂכַר מִצְוָה בְּהַאי עַלְמָא לֵיכָּא. (קידושין ל"ט:)

The reward for mitzvos is not given in This World. (*Kiddushin* 39b)

כִּי־עִמְּךָ מְקוֹר חַיִּים. (תהלים ל"ו י')

For with You is the source of life. (*Tehillim* 36:10)

וְאַתֶּם הַדְּבֵקִים בַּה' אֱלֹקֵיכֶם חַיִּים כֻּלְּכֶם הַיּוֹם. (דברים ד' ד')

And you, who cleave today to Hashem your G-d – you are all alive, as of this day. (*Devarim* 4:4)

צַדִּיקִים...בְּמִיתָתָם קְרוּיִים חַיִּים... רְשָׁעִים...בְּחַיֵּיהֶן קְרוּיִין מֵתִים. (ברכות י"ח.)

The righteous...even after their passing are called "alive"; ... The wicked...even during their lifetimes are called "deceased." (*Berachos* 18b)

כִּי לֹא עַל־הַלֶּחֶם לְבַדּוֹ יִחְיֶה הָאָדָם כִּי עַל־כָּל־מוֹצָא פִי ה' יִחְיֶה הָאָדָם. (דברים ח' ג')

For it is not through bread alone that a man shall live; rather, a man lives by whatever is uttered from the mouth of Hashem. (*Devarim* 8:3)

ה' אֱלֹקֶיךָ עִמָּךְ לֹא חָסַרְתָּ דָּבָר. (שם ב' ז')

Hashem your G-d is with you; you are not in want of anything. (*ibid*. 2:7)

פרק י'

773

The Meaning of Life

Who is really living? It may seem to us, perhaps, that someone who is outwardly "successful" is really living life to the fullest. A stately mansion, beautiful grounds, expensive vacations, rubbing shoulders with leaders and elite members of society — that's what "life" is all about.

That is how things may appear on the surface. In the light of Torah truth, however, there is another stark reality: it is quite possible that such a person is actually counted among the living dead. Just as someone who barely makes (or doesn't make) ends meet, seeming to suffer deprivation and want, may be the one who is truly alive — both in the Next World and *right now*.

This mishnah is devoted to clarifying what "life" really is. The Nesivos Sholom elucidates this monumental teaching of *Chazal*, shedding much light on the meaning of life.

Attached to the Source

From where does life emanate? What is its source? The mishnah is unequivocal on this point: It is the Torah that grants us life, in This World and the Next.

Here it is possible to develop a misconception. One may have understood that there is a simple equation: if one learns and fulfills the Torah, he is rewarded with life. If not, then…not.

In fact, this is not the mishnah's intent at all. There are plenty of people who are walking around, living long, healthy lives, despite their most unfortunate non-compliance with and disassociation from the Torah.

Furthermore, the very idea runs counter to some basic principles of *s'char va'onesh* (Divine reward and punishment). *Chazal* inform us that שְׂכַר מִצְוָה בְּהַאי עָלְמָא לֵיכָּא — *Reward for a mitzvah is not granted in This World* (*Kiddushin* 39b). The principal arena in which one receives his reward is in the World to Come. Thus, the mishnah's message

גדולה תורה שהיא נותנת חיים לעושיה

cannot be that in return for fidelity to Torah, a person is "rewarded" with life (in This World).

Based on the Maharal's commentary, the Nesivos Sholom explains what the mishnah sought to convey. It is not a question of reward and payment, but of reality: Torah is simply the key to life. A tree branch can flourish; it can be festooned with much foliage, blossom, and produce luscious and abundant fruit. What happens, however, if that same branch breaks off from the trunk? It will soon wither and die. Is that a "punishment"? Not really. It is simply an effect of being detached from its life source. No longer attached to the trunk, it has lost its link to the vital network of roots and tubes and veins that conduct nourishment to all parts of the tree. The mishnah informs us that the same is true of a Jew: to continue to "live," he must be connected to Torah, the life-giving source. Otherwise, he cannot survive.

To be sure, it is the *Ribono Shel Olam* that is the Source of all life. As the *passuk* states (*Tehillim* 36:10), כִּי־עִמְּךָ מְקוֹר חַיִּים — *For with You is the source of life*. Therefore, it is only through cleaving to Hashem that one can truly access life, as the Torah attests (*Devarim* 4:4), וְאַתֶּם הַדְּבֵקִים בַּה׳ אֱלֹקֵיכֶם חַיִּים כֻּלְּכֶם הַיּוֹם — *And you, who cleave today to Hashem your G-d, you are all alive, as of this day*. Yet, our mishnah states that it is the Torah that gives one life. Of course, there is no contradiction; the mishnah is merely identifying the vehicle through which we attach ourselves to *Hakadosh Baruch Hu*. The Torah is this vehicle; it is an entity that derives from Hashem Himself. And so, when a Yid immerses himself in the Torah and attaches himself to it, he becomes attached thereby to Hashem. And so he is connected to the Source of Life.

So, what *does* it mean that Torah grants "life"? And how exactly do we reconcile the dichotomy of those who are far removed from Torah but certainly seem to be quite alive? The answer is that it depends on what we are talking about. Physically, yes, such people are alive. But when it comes to the primary mode of existence — the life of the soul — this is where attachment to the Torah is the crucial factor.

For living beings to survive, they require maintenance in the form

פרק ו׳

of nourishment. A body deprived of food for too long will expire. The truth is that the soul's existence works in the same way; without its nourishment, the soul and its components — *nefesh*, *ruach*, and *neshamah* — cannot exist. A person requires a specific diet, certain nutrients and ingredients, in order to continue to function and to live. The soul, as well, has its own specific needs. As the mishnah tells us, the nourishment of the soul is the Torah. A soul imbued with the sanctity of Torah is a healthy soul; through Torah's life-giving power, the soul thrives in This World and continues its eternal existence in the blissful radiance of the World to Come.

When you see a living person in This World, it doesn't necessarily mean that the person is truly "alive." That is, the physical body is alive. But the true essence — the soul — depends on its connection to the Source, based on how attached that individual is to Torah. In other words, a Jew who, R"l, is far removed from Torah, may be physically alive. But the Jewish soul within, other than the spark of the little spark — a *pintele Yid* — sadly, is dead.

In some instances, the Torah mandates a severe punishment for the violation of certain grave transgressions: הִכָּרֵת תִּכָּרֵת הַנֶּפֶשׁ הַהִוא עֲוֹנָה בָהּ — *That soul shall be cut off; its iniquity is within it* (*Bamidbar* 15:31). The essence of this form of penalty can be understood along the same lines of our discussion. There are many sinners in This World, unfortunately. Ostensibly, a number of them have incurred this punishment known as *kareis*, excommunication. Yet, despite the fact that their souls have been "cut off," they continue to walk the streets. But as we discovered, there is nothing necessarily surprising about this. Their bodies may be in great shape, but their Jewish soul has been severed from the Source of Life, having shriveled up and withered within them.

This is the profundity of *Chazal's* statement (*Berachos* 18b): רְשָׁעִים בְּחַיֵּיהֶן קְרוּיִין מֵתִים — *The wicked, even during their lifetimes, are called "deceased."* While to all appearances they cavort and continue their daily activities, the reality is otherwise. Their actual "selves" — their *nefesh*, *ruach*, and *neshamah* — have perished deep within.

The converse is true as well. צַדִּיקִים בְּמִיתָתָם קְרוּיִים חַיִּים — *The righteous,*

גדולה תורה שהיא נותנת חיים לעושיה

even after their passing are called "alive." They are a branch firmly joined to the Tree of Life. As such, they continue to draw sustenance, garnering life and strength for their eternal souls, which thrive in both worlds. Their physical bodies may be undergoing a respite, but they, themselves, are as alive as ever. Forever.

This notion is beautifully captured in the familiar *passuk* that discusses the phenomenon of the *mann*, the wondrous bread sent from Heaven, which nourished Yisroel on their journeys: כִּי לֹא עַל־הַלֶּחֶם לְבַדּוֹ יִחְיֶה הָאָדָם כִּי עַל־כָּל־מוֹצָא פִי ה' יִחְיֶה הָאָדָם — *For it is not through bread alone that a man shall live; rather, a man lives by whatever is uttered from the mouth of Hashem* (Devarim 8:3). The verse can be seen as alluding to the subject of our discussion. Bread only fortifies a person's physical being; his soul, on the other hand, is nourished through *kol motza pi Hashem* — the sacred words of the Torah.

The repercussions of this concept are quite astounding. The mishnah has sharpened our outlook on life, highlighting what is real living and what is not. And of course, it has supplied us with an edifying lesson on the centrality of Torah to our lives and how inextricably connected it is to our very existence. Who would dream of willingly going a day without eating? This is universally viewed — rightly so — as a form of affliction. But a day without learning is no different, or, even more profoundly, it is a day on which the soul is deprived of its vital spiritual sustenance.

The Good Life

The mishnah provides further insight into the secrets of living a joyous and productive life. *Chaim* can refer not only to the actual living process, but to a state of being. How does one cultivate vitality for life, the ability to remain upbeat and vigorous even in the face of life's vicissitudes? It is the Torah that grants this form of *chaim* as well, endowing one's soul with strength and fortitude.

While it may not be readily apparent, it is often the case that a spiritual malady lays at the root of one's suffering. A person may find himself in a state of dejection; he is often morose, deriving little satisfaction from life. The Nesivos Sholom asserts that this state of mind can actually be an outgrowth of his spiritual situation. That is, it is really his soul that lacks vitality, as his connection with the true life source is somewhat tenuous. Wanting for spiritual nourishment, it is actually the soul that suffers deprivation. A general lack of fulfillment and satisfaction sets in, which then permeates his entire being.

The remedy, then, is to reconnect to the source. "Great is Torah; for it grants *chaim* in This World…" A connection to Torah infuses the soul with a new sense of life and exuberance. Without it, even one's mundane existence will be devoid of meaning. It is also one's experience in the World to Come that is greatly affected in this way. The tzaddikim explain that the delight of Gan Eden is largely derived from the enjoyment a Yid has from his spiritual endeavors in This World. Thus, the measure of delight one takes in Shabbos and Torah will serve as the basis for the *chaim* he attains in the World to Come.

A significant aspect of Torah's ability to grant *chaim* even in This World relates to one's ability to face the challenges that periodically surface in life. Such a sentiment is echoed by Dovid Hamelech, when he states (*Tehillim* 119:92), לוּלֵי תוֹרָתְךָ שַׁעֲשֻׁעָי אָז אָבַדְתִּי בְעָנְיִי — *Were it not for Your Torah as my delight, then I would have been lost through my afflictions.*

The Rav of Zhitomir related what he was told by the Divrei Shmuel *ztz"l*. The latter revealed his strategy in dealing with difficult situations that would arise: "When I am confronted by a most distressing circumstance, I sit down to learn a *blatt* of Gemara. Then, I am able to bear the pain. If, however, the situation is even more intense, I learn two *blatt* of Gemara. And in an extraordinarily challenging time, I learn three *blatt*. Then I have the strength to withstand almost anything."

The reason such a strategy is most effective is that it puts a Yid in close contact with Hashem Himself. Recall that Torah is the conduit through which one can cleave to *Hakadosh Baruch Hu*; by becoming one with the Torah, a Jew achieves *d'veikus* with Hashem. "And you who are attached to Hashem, you are alive as of this day." Once reaching such a state, there is virtually nothing that a Yid

גדולה תורה שהיא נותנת חיים לעושיה

cannot face. A Jew who has attained this closeness with his Creator is imbued with life and succor in the face of even the most daunting, debilitating afflictions. As the *passuk* states (*Devarim* 2:7), ה׳ אֱלֹקֶיךָ עִמָּךְ לֹא חָסַרְתָּ דָּבָר — *(When) Hashem your G-d is with you, (then) you are not in want of anything.*

In Summary

In telling us that Torah grants a person life, the mishnah does not appear to be referring to mere physical existence. There are numerous people, unfortunately, who are far from Torah, but who are very much alive in This World. Rather, as the Maharal explains, the implication is the life of the *soul*. Thus, a person may be walking around on earth, seemingly alive; yet, in another respect — the infinitely more important respect — he is not alive at all. This is not a question of reward and punishment, but of reality. A branch that is severed from a tree will wither and die, for it is cut off from its source of sustenance. For the sacred soul of a Yid, the source of sustenance is the Torah. A Jew whose soul is removed from this life source is a soul that is no longer alive. His body may be alive, but his true essence has perished.

However, a Yid who is attached to the Torah has access to the greatest source of true life. Through the Torah, a Yid becomes attached to Hashem Himself, the ultimate life-giver. And so his soul will be fortified, both for the duration of his sojourn in This World and for the eternity of *Olam Haba*.

There is yet another sense in which Torah grants life to a Jew — that is, it gives him vitality, a reason and imperative to live. Through the life-giving source of the Torah, a Yid can experience true enjoyment and excitement in life, for the essence of his soul obtains real nourishment. The satiated soul gives him exuberance. Conversely, when one has little connection with the Torah, his soul remains unfulfilled, a condition that often permeates his whole self, leading to a general feeling of moroseness and dissatisfaction with life.

GEMS FROM THE *SEFER NESIVOS SHOLOM*

A person who is "fortified" with Torah gains not only a zest for living, but also the strength to withstand the numerous obstacles and challenges that inevitably surface along the way. Imbued with Torah, we have the fortitude and courage to face whatever confronts us. Being immersed in Torah causes us to be attached to Hashem. With *Hakadosh Baruch Hu* at our side, we will be truly alive, not wanting a thing.